Publications of the

National Bureau of Economic Research, Inc.

Number 45

Income from Independent Professional Practice

Income from

Independent Professional

Practice

by Milton Friedman
and
Simon Kuznets

National Bureau of

Economic Research

NEW YORK · 1954

Relation of the Directors
to the Work and Publications
of the National Bureau of Economic Research

1. The object of the National Bureau of Economic Research is to ascertain and to present to the public important economic facts and their interpretation in a scientific and impartial manner. The Board of Directors is charged with the responsibility of ensuring that the work of the National Bureau is carried on in strict conformity with this object.

2. To this end the Board of Directors shall appoint one or more Directors of Research.

3. The Director or Directors of Research shall submit to the members of the Board, or to its Executive Committee, for their formal adoption, all specific proposals concerning researches to be instituted.

4. No report shall be published until the Director or Directors of Research shall have submitted to the Board a summary drawing attention to the character of the data and their utilization in the report, the nature and treatment of the problems involved, the main conclusions and such other information as in their opinion would serve to determine the suitability of the report for publication in accordance with the principles of the National Bureau.

5. A copy of any manuscript proposed for publication shall also be submitted to each member of the Board. For each manuscript to be so submitted a special committee shall be appointed by the President, or at his designation by the Executive Director, consisting of three Directors selected as nearly as may be one from each general division of the Board. The names of the special manuscript committee shall be stated to each Director when the summary and report described in paragraph (4) are sent to him. It shall be the duty of each member of the committee to read the manuscript. If each member of the special committee signifies his approval within thirty days, the manuscript may be published. If each member of the special committee has not signified his approval within thirty days of the transmittal of the report and manuscript, the Director of Research shall then notify each member of the Board, requesting approval or disapproval of publication, and thirty additional days shall be granted for this purpose. The manuscript shall then not be published unless at least a majority of the entire Board and a two-thirds majority of those members of the Board who shall have voted on the proposal within the time fixed for the receipt of votes on the publication proposed shall have approved.

6. No manuscript may be published, though approved by each member of the special committee, until forty-five days have elapsed from the transmittal of the summary and report. The interval is allowed for the receipt of any memorandum of dissent or reservation, together with a brief statement of his reasons, that any member may wish to express; and such memorandum of dissent or reservation shall be published with the manuscript if he so desires. Publication does not, however, imply that each member of the Board has read the manuscript, or that either members of the Board in general, or of the special committee, have passed upon its validity in every detail.

7. A copy of this resolution shall, unless otherwise determined by the Board, be printed in each copy of every National Bureau book.

(Resolution adopted October 25, 1926 and revised February 6, 1933 and February 24, 1941)

Preface

THIS STUDY OF INCOMES from independent professional practice can be viewed as a detailed description of the income structure of five professions, as an empirical case study of the factors
determining the incomes individuals receive for their work,
and as an attempt to arrive at conclusions relevant to public
policy. From the first point of view, the substantive results for
the individual professions are of major interest. These are
presented in detail in the separate chapters and are summarized in Chapter 9; they call for no further comment here.

The comments that follow are addressed to readers interested in the broader implications of the study and the general
approach adopted. This approach treats professional activity
as taking place in an economy best described as a free enterprise
system in which the production of goods and distribution of
incomes are regulated primarily by the impersonal mechanism
of the market. The efficient functioning of such a system depends greatly on the freedom with which resources flow from
one use to another in response to changes in economic conditions. The incentive to the flow of resources is provided by
changes in the prices paid for them and hence in the incomes
individuals receive.

The incomes that individuals receive thus play a dual role:
they help to regulate the allocation of resources among different uses and they are the means whereby the social product
is distributed. To evaluate their effectiveness in regulating the
allocation of resources, it is essential to separate differences in
income that are consistent with the free flow of resources from
those that are not. If every individual were entirely free to
choose his occupation, the "whole of the advantages and disadvantages" of different occupations would continually tend
toward equality for persons with similar ability. Persistent
differences in pecuniary returns would compensate for differ-

ences in training, the attractiveness of the work, the risks involved, and the like. Actual differences in income are a combination of such 'equalizing' differences, temporary differences that arise from imperfect adjustment to changing economic conditions, and differences that reflect persistent hindrances to the free choice of occupation. These hindrances may arise from the requirement of relatively rare abilities, or they may be implicit in the institutional setting, or they may be introduced by society at large or groups within it.

Average earnings of professional workers are substantially higher than average earnings of nonprofessional workers. Part of this difference compensates for the longer period of training needed by professional workers and is therefore an 'equalizing' difference. The analysis presented in Chapter 3 suggests that the entire difference cannot be thus explained; at least in part, it reflects a hindrance to the free choice of occupation. Individuals are not equally free to choose a professional or nonprofessional career. The professions require a relatively high level of ability, and for many persons entry into the professions is hindered by the social and economic stratification of the population. The economic stratification of the population is important because capital invested in professional training, unlike capital invested in factories and machines, can rarely be obtained on the open market; it must be provided by the prospective practitioner himself, his parents, or a benefactor. The many young men who do not have and cannot get the money needed to finance their training are barred from the professions. In consequence, the amount invested is controlled only in part by expected returns.

Public investment in professional training by government and by philanthropists has supplemented private investment. Few if any professional workers pay the entire cost of their training. This public investment in professional training raises two important questions of social policy. First, how much public investment is needed? Second, should the returns from public investment accrue to the individuals in whose training the investment is made? An answer to the first question requires not only data on current public investment but also clarification of the meaning of 'proper' amount of public investment. Neither is provided by our analysis which takes account only of private investment. From one point of view, investment in professional training would be adjusted to investment in other fields if average earnings in the professions exceeded average earnings in comparable pursuits by an amount sufficient to replace public plus private investment and to pay the market rate of interest on that investment. But if public investment were so adjusted, the second question would arise, since, under present institutional arrangements, the return on the public investment would accrue to the professional workers. Whether this is socially desirable and if not what policies should be adopted to distribute the costs and gains in a socially advantageous way are problems that may force themselves upon public attention before long.

The hindrances to the free choice of occupation that hamper adjustments between the professions and other occupations do not seriously hamper adjustments within the professions. In the absence of purposeful interference, there appears to be sufficient mobility among the different areas of professional practice to make the differences in pecuniary returns reflect differences in age, costs of training, the nonpecuniary advantages of the type or location of practice, and the like. In other words, these differences tend to be of the 'equalizing' type. True, adjustment is not perfect, and at times may be slow and halting; but adjustment there is. This conclusion is supported by our analysis of income differences among professions, regions, and communities of varying size, and by the evidence we have collected on the influence of type and organization of practice, and number of years in practice.

Purposeful interference is often present. In a large and apparently increasing segment of the field, governmental bodies or professional associations are in a position to hinder adjustments that would otherwise occur. It is not part of our task to judge the desirability of these interferences. Our task is merely to evaluate their effects on the incomes of professional workers. This we have attempted to do in one special case, limitation of entry into medicine. The analysis has both methodological and substantive interest. Presented in detail in Chapter 4, it is a by-product of an attempt to explain the observed difference between average income in medicine and average income in dentistry, a similar profession in which there is little or no difficulty of entry other than that arising from scarcity of ability and cost of training. The available evidence on the conditions of entry in the two professions demonstrates that average income in medicine exceeds average income in dentistry by more than it would if entry into the two professions were equally easy. To determine how much larger the difference is, we resorted to the device of estimating what the difference would be if entry were equally easy. The analysis is necessarily conjectural and our quantitative results are only a rough approximation. But the problem is real, and a rough approximation seems better than none.

It is not easy to evaluate the importance of the factors that give rise to 'equalizing' differences. These factors are numerous and varied, many are vague and subjective, and their quantitative effects are merged. The attempt in Chapter 4 to explain the observed difference between average incomes in medicine and dentistry is an experiment in estimating the separate influence of these factors by interweaving empirical observation, personal judgment, and theoretical analysis. The conclusions reached are obviously restricted to medicine and dentistry, but the methods used are of fairly general applicability.

Analysis of the factors determining the incomes individuals receive contributes to an understanding not only of how incomes regulate the allocation of resources but also of how they distribute the social product, and the conclusions reached may have an important bearing on the desirability of measures designed to change the distribution of income. For example, the desirability of relating federal grants to the per capita income of particular states depends in part on the factors explaining income differences among states. As already noted, the

analysis presented in Chapter 5 suggests that community differences in professional incomes are primarily 'equalizing'.
The differences are small among communities of the same size
but in different geographic regions of the country. Though
decidedly larger, the differences among communities of varying size in the same region do not appear attributable to
immobility. We do not know whether a similar conclusion is
valid for other occupations or the public at large; but its apparent validity for the professions warns against the acceptance
of the opposite conclusion for other groups without investigation.

Most of the questions that arise when incomes are viewed
as the means whereby the social product is distributed differ
from those so far considered. How much do incomes vary from
individual to individual? Is the inequality of income greater
or smaller in years of prosperity than in years of depression?
Are the income differences among individuals fairly stable, or
does the relative income status of individuals shift considerably from year to year? What are the factors responsible for
the inequality of income among individuals pursuing the same
occupation in the same community?

We have attempted to answer these questions for professional workers in Chapters 4, 5, 6, and 7. Few of our substantive
results are of general interest. Perhaps the most novel part of
the analysis is our attempt, particularly in Chapter 7, to investigate changes in the relative income status of individual
professional workers. Paucity of data has prevented most
previous studies of the distribution of income from tackling
this problem, though it is clearly an important one. A wide
variability of annual income has a very different meaning if
the disparities it reflects are persistent than if they are temporary in the sense that individuals who rank high in the
income scale one year may rank low the next. We found a surprising degree of stability in the relative income status of
professional workers. The variability of income for a two- or
three-year period is not much smaller than the variability of
annual income (Chapters 4 and 7). Without further investiga-

tion, this conclusion cannot be assumed valid for other groups. But the methods by which it was reached are applicable to the extensive data that are now becoming available on the incomes of the same individuals in successive years.

A recurrent question about the distribution of income is whether there is a consistent relation between inequality of income and general economic conditions. Other studies have suggested that such a relationship does exist, though the evidence is far from conclusive. The data have never been adequate, nor has the relation between inequality and general economic conditions been clear-cut. We found no consistent relation for the professions. The changes in inequality from year to year, though sizable, are irregular; and we are inclined to attribute them to that convenient catchall—chance variation.

The analysis presented in this book was completed in 1941; and the data utilized cover primarily the years from the late 'twenties through 1936. No attempt has been made since the completion of the analysis to bring it up to date, either by a search for more recent data or by a thorough treatment of them. However, as questions arose concerning the validity of some conclusions in the original draft of the report, we used such of the data for more recent years as were easily available to see whether they confirmed or disproved the conclusions drawn from the data for earlier years.

To the extent that our detailed analysis is confined to data for a few years, our conclusions may be limited by the peculiarities of that segment of historical reality. We have tried to reduce these limitations by making the conclusions independent of year-to-year fluctuations in the data; by supplementing statistical data with qualitative evidence on the institutional background of the professions over a longer period than can be covered by statistical series; and by pressing the analysis to a level at which some of the important factors that account for the observed income similarities and differences can be approximated. We present the detailed evidence in order to permit readers to judge the extent to which our attempt to overcome the limitations of a brief historical period is successful.

One aim of our analysis is to reduce a segment of changing reality to factors whose persistence over time can be more easily appraised. Yet judgments may naturally differ as to the likelihood that the observed similarities and differences in income among the professions and between professions and other pursuits, as well as the factors that account for these similarities and differences, will persist. Such judgments must rest upon one's view of the persistence or transitoriness of a variety of institutional peculiarities of our economic society; and they will naturally differ so long as our knowledge of the factors that make for social development is incomplete. We have tried to add to such knowledge and thus narrow the area within which judgments can honestly diverge. The absolute and relative quantitative differences shown by our data will naturally change, and have already changed, as life went on and people were born, worked, fought, and died. In that sense our report is a still-life picture of a segment of the past. But some of the factors suggested and their consequences are likely to persist. And it is particularly hoped that the methods used in the analysis have validity beyond the limits of the historical data used; and will stand the test of further use for some time to come.

The present investigation began in 1933, as a by-product of the study of national income of the United States for 1929–32 conducted by the U. S. Department of Commerce in collaboration with the National Bureau. In connection with this study, which was under the general direction of Simon Kuznets, a special questionnaire survey of the more important professional groups was undertaken to remedy the lack of reliable data on income originating from independent professional practice. Usable data for 1929–32 were obtained for four groups: physicians, dentists, certified public accountants, and consulting engineers. The obvious significance of these data for purposes other than that for which they were collected led Kuznets to undertake a detailed analysis of them. Early in 1936, he completed a tentative manuscript summarizing the findings for the four professions and four years for which data were then available. This first draft was incomplete and needed much further work, but the pressure of other tasks made it impossible for him to devote the time needed.

Milton Friedman took up the work in 1937, and from then on both the statistical analysis and the preparation of the manuscript were in his charge, though plans for further work were developed jointly by the two authors, and Kuznets critically reviewed the manuscript and participated in its revision. Friedman expanded the study to include additional samples collected by the Department of Commerce, providing data for years after 1932 for lawyers, as well as for three of the four professions previously covered. This expansion involved testing the samples for bias, devising methods for correcting biases (see Appendix A), summarizing the statistical evidence, and integrating it with earlier results. The wider range of years and professions permitted new inferences to be drawn, and provided a check on the inferences previously drawn by Kuznets. Friedman also added new material. The result of Friedman's work was a completely rewritten version of the earlier manuscript. Chapter 3, Section 2 of Chapter 4, Chapter 7, Appendix A, the appendices to Chapters 4, 5, and 7, and most of Chapter 2 are entirely new, and the remainder has been altered very substantially in both form and content.

In a preface written by two individuals jointly, it is naturally difficult for either properly to indicate his feeling of indebtedness to the other. Perhaps it will suffice to say that each of us feels that whatever defects the present work may have would have been multiplied many-fold but for his collaborator.

No study can pass through the hands of the research staff and directors of the National Bureau without being improved in the process. Thanks are due the staff members and the directors for the elimination of many deficiencies of the original manuscript, and apologies for those that still remain.

Careful scrutiny of the manuscript by Wesley C. Mitchell removed errors, changed the emphasis at several important points, and made many a page more readable. In addition, his steady and unflagging support greatly eased our task. The organization of the book was improved as a result of extensive discussions with Arthur F. Burns, who read several drafts of the entire manuscript and made many valuable suggestions. Chapters 3 and 4, parts of which were published in *Bulletin* *72–73*, owe much to the stimulating criticism of Frederick C. Mills. W. Allen Wallis and Moses Abramovitz read the entire manuscript in draft form and made many helpful suggestions, the former, particularly on Chapters 5 and 7, the latter, particularly on Chapters 3 and 4.

The manuscript was commented upon by several directors of the Bureau. We are indebted to each of them, especially C. Reinold Noyes, William L. Crum, Theodore O. Yntema, and Winfield W. Riefler, for their criticisms and constructive suggestions.

Edna E. Deutsch assisted Friedman from the time he took over the direction of the study in 1937. She organized and carried out most of the computations, prepared Appendix B, assisted in the gathering of source material, compiled the indexes, and checked the proof. In addition, she carried most of the load of seeing the manuscript through its several versions. We are deeply indebted to her for faithful and exact work. Thanks are also due Lucille Kean, Arthur Stein, and Richard Machol, who assisted in the early stages of the work. We are grateful to Martha Anderson for editing the manuscript with her usual care, and to H. Irving Forman for the excellence of the charts.

We are indebted to the Department of Commerce for making the original questionnaire returns available to us, for permission to use them, and for generous cooperation in other ways. Officials of various professional societies and firms publishing professional directories have always provided needed information. Specific acknowledgment for detailed information is made at the appropriate points in the text.

MILTON FRIEDMAN
SIMON KUZNETS

Contents

Preface   v

CHAPTER 1   The Five Professions Studied   3
1   Medicine   8
2   Dentistry   21
3   Law   30
4   Certified Public Accountancy   39
5   Consulting Engineering   43

CHAPTER 2   The Data on Income from Independent Professional Practice   46
1   The Original Data   47
2   Correction for Bias   50
   a   Biases affecting all samples   51
   b   Biases affecting specific samples   53
     Medicine   53
     Dentistry   54
     Law   55
     Certified public accountancy   56
     Consulting engineering   57
3   Tests of the Reliability of the Corrected Data   57

CHAPTER 3   Incomes in the Professions and in Other Pursuits   62
1   The Plan of the Study   62
2   Statistical Evidence on Differences in Income   67
   a   Level of income   67
   b   Variability of annual income   71
3   Factors Making for Differences of Income   81

CHAPTER 4   Incomes in the Five Professions   95
  1 Statistical Evidence on Differences in Income   99
     a Level of income   99
     b Variability of annual income   105
     c Variability of income for a longer period   115
  2 Factors Making for Differences in Level of Income,
     with Special Reference to Physicians and Dentists   118
     a Effect of differences in length of training   125
     b Effect of variability of income   127
     c Nonpecuniary factors affecting the choice of a
        profession   130
     d Influence of demand   132
     e Barriers to rapid adjustment   134
     f Difficulty of entry   135
  3 Factors Making for Differences in the Variability of
     Income   137

Appendix to Chapter 4   142
  1 How the Effect of Difference in Length of Training is
     Estimated   142
     a Physicians and dentists   142
     b Professional and nonprofessional workers   148
  2 The Statistical Validity of the Estimated Difference
     between Average Incomes in Medicine and Dentistry   151
     a Sampling fluctuations   152
     b The correction applied to dental incomes   153
     c Differences in age distribution and geographic
        location   153
     d Combined influence of the possible deficiencies   153
  3 Demand and Supply Curves for Professional Services   155
     a Theoretical   155
        i   The supply curve   155
        ii The demand curve   157
        iii The 'equilibrium' difference   159
     b Statistical   161

CHAPTER 5   Income and the Location of Practice   173
  1 Level of income   181
     a Size of community differences   181
     b Regional differences   189

2 Variability of Income 199
3 Summary 219

Appendix to Chapter 5 220
1 Tests of the Existence of Regional and Size of Community Differences in Average Income 220
2 Regional Differences in the Average Income of Physicians and Dentists 229

CHAPTER 6 Other Determinants of Professional Income 235
1 Training and Ability 235
2 Number of Years in Practice 237
3 Type and Organization of Practice 260
   a Type of practice 262
   b Organization of independent practice 279
   c Salaried and independent practice 295

CHAPTER 7 The Stability of Relative Income Status 300
1 The Incomes of the Same Individuals in Different Years 301
2 An Interpretation of the Linear Regressions 325

Appendix to Chapter 7 338
1 Statistical Tests of the Linearity of Regression between Income in Two Years 338
   a Effect of unequal variances 341
   b Effect of nonnormality 346
   c An alternative test of linearity 349
2 The Analysis of Changes in Relative Income Status for Periods Longer than Two Years 352
   a The mean assumption 355
      i The procedure 355
      ii Illustrative computations of percentage contributions 359
   b The variability assumption 363
      i The procedure 363
      ii Illustrative computations of percentage contributions 364

CHAPTER 8 Temporal Changes in Income 365
1 Changes in Average Income 365
2 Changes in Variability of Income 369

3   Changes in Income by Size of Community   373
4   Changes in Income by Geographic Region   379
5   Changes in Income by Type and Organization of
    Practice   384

CHAPTER 9   Summary   390
1   Professional Workers and Others—Numbers and Earn-
    ings (Ch. 3)   390
2   Earnings from Independent Practice and from Salaried
    Employment (Ch. 6)   392
3   Average Level of Income in the Five Professions
    (Ch. 4)   393
4   Variability of Income in the Five Professions (Ch. 4)   395
5   Stability of Relative Income Status (Ch. 4 and 7)   396
6   Factors Determining Size of Earnings within the Pro-
    fessions   397
    a   Location of practice (Ch. 5)   398
    b   Specialization (Ch. 6)   400
    c   Organization of practice (Ch. 6)   401
    d   Years in practice (Ch. 6)   402
7   Changes in Income from 1929 to 1936 (Ch. 8)   403
8   Income from Independent Professional Practice and
    Total Income   404

DIRECTOR'S COMMENT   405

APPENDIX A   The Reliability of the Department of Com-
             merce Samples   411
1   The Sampling Method   411
    a   The lists employed   412
        i   The incompleteness of the lists for the earlier
             years   412
        ii   The inclusion of persons not in independent
             practice   414
        iii The medical, legal, and accountancy lists   415
        iv   The dental list   415
        v   The engineering list   419

b The selection of the persons to whom questionnaires were sent   419
  i The nonrandomness of the 1937 medical and
    legal samples by states   419
  ii The size of community bias in the medical and
    legal samples   421
  iii The overrepresentation of certain types of
    physicians and lawyers   429
  iv The firm member bias in the legal and ac-
    countancy samples   430
c The return of questionnaires by the respondents   438
d The editing of the questionnaires   446
2 Tests of the Reliability of the Data   448
a Comparison with geographic distribution of all
  practitioners   448
b Comparison of different samples for the same profession   455
c Comparison of our samples with other studies   461
  i Incomes of physicians in 1929   461
  ii Incomes of dentists in 1929   467
  iii Incomes of physicians and dentists in Cali-
    fornia   472
  iv Other studies of the incomes of physicians   477
  v Incomes of dentists in Minnesota   481
  vi Incomes of lawyers   483
  vii Incomes of consulting engineers   486

APPENDIX B Supplementary Material   489
  Explanatory Note   489

APPENDIX C Samples of Questionnaires Sent Out by Department of Commerce   571

Tabular Index   581

Author Index   585

Subject Index   587

Publications   595

List of Tables

1 Number of Persons in Five Professions and Number and Percentage in Independent Practice   5

2 Admissions to Approved Medical Schools in the United States, 1926–1929 and 1932–1941   14

3 Admissions to the Bar, 1927–1940   38

4 Methods of Selecting Samples and Coverage of Samples   48

5 Arithmetic Mean Income in Years Covered by More than One Sample for the Same Profession   52

6 Summary of Comparisons between the Department of Commerce and Other Samples
Physicians, Dentists, Lawyers, and Consulting Engineers   60

7 Average Earnings
Certified Public Accountants, Physicians, Dentists, and All Gainfully Occupied Persons   68

8 Average Income of Nonrelief Families in Seven Occupational Groups
National Resources Committee Estimates, 1935–1936   69

9 Comparison between Discounted and Cost Values of Special Training
J. R. Walsh's Estimates   85

10 Arithmetic Mean and Median Incomes, and Number of Persons Covered   101

11 Final Estimates of Arithmetic Mean Income
Physicians and Certified Public Accountants, 1929–1936; Dentists, 1929–1934   104

12 Median and Quartile Incomes   106

13 Measures of Variability of Income   108

14 Rough Estimates of Coefficient of Variation for One-, Two-, and Three-year Income Periods   117

15 Alternative Estimates of the Percentage Difference between the Arithmetic Mean Incomes of Physicians and Dentists   154

16 Arithmetic Mean Income, Relatives of Arithmetic Mean Income, and Number of Persons Covered, by Size of Community   180

17 Arithmetic Mean Income and Relatives of Arithmetic Mean Income, by Size of Community
Professions and All Nonrelief Families   184

18 Arithmetic Mean Income, Relatives of Arithmetic Mean Income, and Number of Persons Covered, by Region
Professions and All Persons   190

19 Difference between Highest and Lowest Size of Community and Regional Relatives of Arithmetic Mean Income   193

20 Rank Difference Correlation Coefficients between Per Capita Income and Average Professional Income, and between Average Incomes in Different Professions, 1934 and 1936
48 States and the District of Columbia   195

21 Coefficient of Variation and Relative Interquartile Difference, and Relatives of Coefficient of Variation and Relative Interquartile Difference, by Size of Community
Professions and All Nonrelief Families   204

22 Coefficient of Variation and Relative Interquartile Difference, and Relatives of Coefficient of Variation and Relative Interquartile Difference, by Region
Professions and All Nonrelief Families   206

23 Ranking of Regions by Coefficient of Variation and by Relative Interquartile Difference   216

24 Difference between Highest and Lowest Size of Community and Regional Relatives of Coefficient of Variation and Relative Interquartile Difference   217

25 Arithmetic Mean Income and Number of Persons Covered, by Region and Size of Community
Physicians, 1934: 1935 Sample   221

26 Ranking of Regions by Arithmetic Mean Income, by
    Size of Community
    Physicians, 1934: 1935 Sample   222
27 Ranking of Size of Community Classes by Arithmetic
    Mean Income, by Region
    Physicians, 1934: 1935 Sample   223
28 Tests of the Significance of Size of Community and
    Regional Differences in Arithmetic Mean Income   226
29 Arithmetic Mean Income Standardized with Respect
    to Size of Community, and Relatives of Actual and
    Standardized Arithmetic Mean Income, by Region
    Physicians and Dentists   230
30 Median Income, by Prelegal Training and by Type
    of Law School Attended
    New York County Lawyers, 1933 and 1928–1932   236
31 1932 Professional Income, by Grade in Law School
    Graduates of University of Wisconsin Law School   237
32 Average Income, by Years in Practice
    Physicians, Dentists, and Lawyers: Selected Studies 240
33 Percentage Distribution by Years in Practice; Arith-
    metic Mean Income and Number of Persons Covered,
    by Years in Practice and Type of Practice
    Physicians, 1936   244
34 Arithmetic Mean Income and Number of Persons Cov-
    ered, by Years in Practice and Size of Community
    a   All Physicians, 1936   252
    b   General Practitioners, 1936   252
    c   Partial Specialists, 1936   253
    d   Complete Specialists, 1936   254
35 Age Distribution, by Size of Community
    All Physicians, General Practitioners and Partial Spe-
    cialists, and Complete Specialists, 1931: 16 States and
    the District of Columbia   257
36 Arithmetic Mean Income and Percentage Distribu-
    tion, by Type of Practice
    Physicians and Dentists: Selected Studies   265
37 Arithmetic Mean Income, by Type of Practice
    Physicians, 1929–1936   266
38 Median and Quartile Incomes, by Type of Practice
    Physicians, 1934–1936   267

39   Measures of Variability of Income, by Type of Practice
     tice
     Physicians, 1934–1936   268

40   Median and Quartile Incomes, and Measures of Variability, by Type of Practice
     ability, by Type of Practice
     Dentists in 20 States, 1929: Committee on Costs of
     Medical Care Study   269

41   Distribution by Type of Practice, by Size of Community and by Region
     munity and by Region
     Physicians, 1936   270

42   Distribution by Type of Practice, by Size of Community
     munity
     Physicians Listed in 1931 Directory of American Medical Association
     cal Association   270

43   Arithmetic Mean Income, Relatives of Arithmetic
     Mean Income, and Number of Persons Covered, by
     Size of Community and by Region
     All Physicians, General Practitioners, Partial Specialists, and Complete Specialists
     ists, and Complete Specialists   272

44   Arithmetic Mean Income Standardized with Respect
     to Size of Community, by Type of Practice
     Physicians, 1929–1936   275

45   Distribution by Type of Practice, by Years in Practice
     Physicians, 1936   277

46   Percentage of Persons in Independent Practice Who
     are Members of Firms and Number of Persons Covered
     Certified Public Accountants, Lawyers, and Consulting Engineers
     ing Engineers   280

47   Arithmetic Mean Income, by Organization of Practice
     Certified Public Accountants, Lawyers, and Consulting Engineers
     ing Engineers   283

48   Median and Quartile Incomes, by Organization of
     Practice
     Certified Public Accountants, Lawyers, and Consulting Engineers
     ing Engineers   284

49   Measures of Variability of Income, by Organization
     of Practice
     Certified Public Accountants, Lawyers, and Consulting Engineers
     ing Engineers   286

50 Percentage of Persons in Independent Practice Who
    are Members of Firms, by Size of Community and by
    Region
    Certified Public Accountants, Lawyers, and Consult-
    ing Engineers   289
51 Difference between Arithmetic Mean Incomes of Firm
    Members and of Individual Practitioners
    Certified Public Accountants, Lawyers, and Consult-
    ing Engineers   292
52 Difference between Arithmetic Mean Incomes of Firm
    Members and of Individual Practitioners, Based on
    Averages Standardized with Respect to Size of Com-
    munity
    Certified Public Accountants, Lawyers, and Consult-
    ing Engineers   293
53 Distribution by Organization of Practice and Year of
    Admission to Bar
    New York County Lawyers, 1933   294
54 Arithmetic Mean and Median Incomes of Salaried
    Employees and Independent Practitioners
    Physicians and Lawyers: Selected Studies   299
55 Relation between 1932 and 1934 Incomes
    Dentists, 1935 Sample   302
56 Correlation Coefficients between Incomes in Different
    Years, and Number of Returns Correlated   305
57 Computation of Transitory Component in Deviation
    of Average 1932 Income for 1932 Income Classes from
    Average Income for Profession
    Dentists, 1935 Sample   331
58 Percentage Contribution of Transitory Component
    to Deviation of Average Income for Each Income
    Class from Average Income for Profession   337
59 Tests of Linearity of Regression between Incomes in
    Different Years
    Physicians, Dentists, Lawyers, and Certified Public Ac-
    countants   340
60 Constants of Original and Weighted Regression Equa-
    tions   344

61 Test of Consistency of Deviation of Points from Regressions
Physicians 350

62 Percentage of Total Variance Attributable to Permanent, Quasi-permanent, and Transitory Components Computed under Mean Assumption 360

63 Percentage of Total Variance Attributable to Permanent, Quasi-permanent, and Transitory Components Computed under Variability Assumption 364

64 Indices of Arithmetic Mean Income
Professions and All Gainfully Occupied Persons 366

65 Change in Arithmetic Mean Income, by Size of Community
Average for Period Covered = 100 375

66 Change in Arithmetic Mean Income, by Region
Average for Period Covered = 100 381

67 Indices of Arithmetic Mean Income, by Type of Practice
Physicians, 1929–1936 384

68 Indices of Arithmetic Mean Income, by Organization of Practice
Certified Public Accountants, Lawyers, and Consulting Engineers 387

A 1 Average Number of Names per Column of the Directory of the American Medical Association, by Size of Community 422

A 2 Effect of Size of Community Bias on Arithmetic Mean Income
Physicians, 1932: 1933 and 1935 Samples 424

A 3 Average Number of Names per Page of the *Martindale-Hubbell Law Directory,* by Size of Community 425

A 4 Test of the Existence of Firm Member Bias
Lawyers, 1935 and 1937 Samples 434

A 5 Test of the Existence of Firm Member Bias
Certified Public Accountants 437

A 6 Number of Questionnaires Returned
Number Usable, and Number not Usable, by Reasons 447

A 7 Comparison between Distributions of Samples by Geographic Units and Estimated Distributions of All Practitioners

Physicians, Dentists, Lawyers, and Certified Public Accountants 449

A 8 Rank Difference Correlation Coefficients between Sample Average Income and Ratio of Sample to Universe
Physicians, Dentists, Lawyers, and Certified Public Accountants 453

A 9 Comparisons between Distributions of Successive Samples for Overlapping Years
Physicians, Dentists, and Certified Public Accountants 456

A 10 Rank Difference Correlation Coefficients between the Ratio of the Number of Persons in One Sample to the Number in Another Sample for the Same Profession and the Differences in Average Income, by States
Physicians, Dentists, and Certified Public Accountants 458

A 11 Arithmetic Mean and Median Gross and Net Incomes
Physicians: Department of Commerce, Committee on Costs of Medical Care, and American Medical Association Samples 463

A 12 Arithmetic Mean Gross and Net Incomes
Dentists in 20 States: Department of Commerce and Committee on Costs of Medical Care Samples, 1929 469

A 13 Arithmetic Mean Gross and Net Incomes, and Number of Persons Covered
California Physicians: Department of Commerce Samples and California Medical-Economic Survey, 1929–1934 474

A 14 Arithmetic Mean Gross and Net Incomes, and Number of Persons Covered
California Dentists: Department of Commerce Samples and California Medical-Economic Survey, 1929–1934 476

A 15 Arithmetic Mean Gross and Net Incomes, and Number of Persons Covered
Wisconsin Physicians: Department of Commerce Samples and Study of Wisconsin State Medical Society, 1930 479

A 16 Arithmetic Mean Gross and Net Incomes, and Number of Persons Covered
Michigan Physicians: Department of Commerce Sam-

List of Charts

1   Frequency Histogram of Net Incomes of Dentists, 1934   63

2   National Resources Committee Distributions of Income, 1935–1936
Nonrelief Families in Five Occupational Groups   72

3   National Resources Committee Distributions of Income, 1935–1936
Nonrelief Business and Professional Families   73

4   National Resources Committee Distributions of Income, 1935–1936
All Nonrelief Families, All Families, and All Families and Single Individuals   74

5   National Resources Committee Distribution of Income for Nonrelief Independent Professional Families, 1935–1936, and Distribution of Income from Independent Practice for Four Professions Combined, 1933   77

6   Distribution of Income for All Individuals in the United States, 1918, and Distribution of Income from Independent Practice for Four Professions Combined, 1933   79

7   Arithmetic Mean and Median Income   100

8   Absolute Variability of Income Measured by Interquartile Difference   110

9   Two Measures of Relative Variability of Income   113

10   Distribution of Income, 1929 and 1933   114

11   Relation among Arithmetic Mean Income of Dentists in 1934, Dentists per 10,000 Population in 1936, and per Capita Income in 1934
Based on Data for 48 States and the District of Columbia   165

12 Relation among Arithmetic Mean Income of Dentists
    in 1936, Dentists per 10,000 Population in 1936, and
    per Capita Income in 1936
    Based on Data for 48 States and the District of Co-
    lumbia   166
13 Relation between the Ratio of Income of Physicians
    to Income of Dentists and the Ratio of Number of
    Physicians to Number of Dentists
    Based on Data for 48 States and the District of Co-
    lumbia, 1934 and 1936   170
14 Relatives of Arithmetic Mean Income by Size of Com-
    munity
    Professions and All Nonrelief Families   185
15 Relatives of Arithmetic Mean Income by Region
    Professions and All Persons   192
16 Relation between Standard Deviation and Arithmetic
    Mean; and between Interquartile Difference and Me-
    dian, by Size of Community   200
17 Relation between Standard Deviation and Arithmetic
    Mean; and between Interquartile Difference and Me-
    dian, by Region   201
18 Relatives of Coefficient of Variation and Relative In-
    terquartile Difference by Size of Community
    Professions and All Nonrelief Families   208
19 Relatives of Coefficient of Variation and Relative In-
    terquartile Difference by Region
    Professions and All Nonrelief Families   210
20 Arithmetic Mean Income of Physicians and Dentists
    by Years in Practice   239
21 Average Income of Lawyers by Years in Practice   242
22 Arithmetic Mean Income of Physicians by Type of
    Practice and Years in Practice, 1936   245
23 Arithmetic Mean Income of Physicians by Type of
    Practice, Size of Community, and Years in Practice   248
24 Distribution of Physicians by Type of Practice, by
    Years in Practice   279
25 Relation between Incomes of Same Individuals in
    Different Years   310
26 Relation between Absolute Variability and Size of In-
    come in Base Year   320

27 Relation between Relative Variability and Size of Income in Base Year   323
28 Illustration of Transitory Component   333
29 Illustration of Different Types of Regression   334
30 Indices of Arithmetic Mean Income for Five Professions and Indices of Employee Compensation plus Entrepreneurial Withdrawals per Gainfully Occupied Worker   367
31 Two Measures of Absolute Variability of Income   370
32 Two Measures of Relative Variability of Income   371
33 Arithmetic Mean Income by Size of Community   374
34 Relatives of Arithmetic Mean Income by Size of Community   377
35 Arithmetic Mean Income by Region   380
36 Relation between Relatives of Regional Changes from One Year to the Next in Professional Income and in per Capita Income
    Regional Change for U. S. = 100   383
37 Indices of Arithmetic Mean Income by Type of Practice
    Physicians, 1937 Sample   385
38 Indices of Arithmetic Mean Income by Organization of Practice
    Certified Public Accountants, Consulting Engineers, and Lawyers   388
A 1 Difference between Arithmetic Mean Incomes from Successive Samples   459
A 2 Distribution of Gross Income by Size
     Physicians, 1929: Committee on Costs of Medical Care and Department of Commerce Samples   464
A 3 Difference between Arithmetic Mean Gross Incomes from Committee on Costs of Medical Care and Department of Commerce Samples
     Physicians, 1929   465
A 4 Distributions of Gross and Net Income by Size
     Dentists in 20 States, 1929: Committee on Costs of Medical Care and Department of Commerce Samples   471

Income from

Independent Professional

Practice

CHAPTER 1

The Five Professions Studied

THE OCCUPATIONAL HIERARCHY progresses by slow steps from the completely unskilled laborer to the specialist who has spent a considerable part of his life preparing for his work. Each step merges into the next and overlaps it. Somewhere toward the upper end of this hierarchy is a group of occupations that we designate 'professional'. Its boundaries are neither precise nor stable. A century ago the 'learned professions' meant medicine, law, and theology; today they include a host of other occupations; and a century hence they will include still others. These occupations are alike in that all require prolonged and specialized training and involve work that has something of an academic and intellectual flavor—no purely mechanical or commercial pursuit can qualify. They differ in almost all other respects. By common consent, the professions include pursuits as diverse as journalism and medicine, architecture and law.

At present there are some three million persons in the United States in the professions.[1] The majority are salaried employees of other professional men or of business enterprises and governmental organizations. Some 600,000 are in independent practice, selling their services on a fee basis.[2] This is the group with which we shall be primarily, though not exclusively, concerned. In professions like medicine and dentistry that render services directly to ultimate consumers, independent practice is likely to be the rule, salaried employment partaking of an apprenticeship. In professions like teaching and the ministry that render services to groups of consumers, or like accountancy and engineering that serve the

[1] A. M. Edwards, *Social-Economic Grouping of the Gainful Workers of the United States, 1930* (U. S. Bureau of the Census, 1938), p. 3.
[2] The estimates of the total number of independent professional workers are those prepared by Simon Kuznets for use in his study of national income.

3

consumer indirectly through the medium of business enterprises or governmental organizations, salaried employment is
usual. The few persons in these professions who practise independently form auxiliary groups rendering highly specialized services.

While all professions require specialized training, there are
sizable differences in the amount of training required and in
the extent to which the requirements are formalized. Practically all professions require at least the equivalent of a
college education; some require no more than that; others require the completion of professional school after college. A
growing number of professions are restricted to persons 'licensed' by the state; and candidates for licensure must ordinarily satisfy minimum educational requirements and
demonstrate an acceptable level of competence. In other professions not under state licensure, educational requirements
are a matter of custom.

The five professions that we study intensively—medicine,
dentistry, law, certified public accountancy, and consulting
engineering—exemplify these differences. Most persons entering engineering have had only a college education; most persons entering medicine, a college education plus four years of
medical school plus one year of internship in a hospital. Four
of the five professions are under state licensure; the fifth, engineering, is not. The rest of this chapter presents a more
detailed description of these five professions; a description that lays special emphasis on educational and training requirements and other factors governing entry into the
professions. What these have been in the past few decades has
greatly influenced the present supply of professional men and
hence the level of their income; what they are at present is one
of the principal determinants of the future supply of professional men and hence of the changes that will occur in the
level of their income.

As Table 1 shows, these five professions include over 300,000
persons in independent practice, or more than half of all
professional men in independent practice. Estimates of the

TABLE 1

Number of Persons in Five Professions and
Number and Percentage in Independent Practice

		TOTAL IN PROFESSION	IN INDEPENDENT PRACTICE	
			Number	Percentage
		(thousands)		
Physicians	1930	154	121	78
	1936	165	133	80
Dentists	1930	71	58	82
	1936	75	62	
Lawyers	1930	161	110	68
	1935	188	130	69
Certified public accountants	1930	14.8	9.9	67
	1937	16.5	11.1	
Engineers	1930	226	10	4.4
Total	1930	627	309	
Total (excl. engineers)	1930	401	299	
	1936	444	336	

SOURCES OF AND NOTES ON ESTIMATES:

PHYSICIANS

1930

Total: *Census of Population*, Vol. 5.

Percentage in independent practice: Maurice Leven, *Incomes of Physicians* (University of Chicago Press, 1932), p. 103.

1936

Total: 1936 Directory of the American Medical Association.

Percentage in independent practice: computed by straight line interpolation between 78.2, percentage for 1930, and 81.2, percentage for 1938 from data in *Number of Physicians in the United States by County, July 1, 1938* (American Medical Association, 1938), pp. v-vi.

DENTISTS

1930

Total: *Census of Population*, Vol. 5.

Number in independent practice: "furnished from the register of the American Dental Association"; see *National Income in the United States, 1929–35* (U. S. Department of Commerce, 1936), pp. 213, 290.

TABLE 1, NOTES (cont.)

1936

Total: dentists in practice on July 1, 1936 as reported by State Boards of Dental Examiners; see R. P. Thomas, 'Dental Survey', *Journal of American Dental Association and the Dental Cosmos*, Jan. 1938, pp. 153-60. Thomas gives 80,495 as the total number of dentists in all states except New Mexico. We added 100 for New Mexico and subtracted 5,370 to allow for an apparent overestimate for Illinois. Thomas gives 11,370 for Illinois, whereas the 1930 Census gives 5,873. Our correction assumes that 6,000 is the correct figure for Illinois.

Percentage in independent practice: assumed same as in 1930. Probably an underestimate since the count by the examining boards presumably excluded a larger proportion of dentists who were retired or not in practice than the Census.

LAWYERS

1930

Total: *Census of Population*, Vol. 5.

Number in independent practice: *Census of Population* gives 139,059 as engaged in 'professional service'. This checks closely with the 141,501 listed in the *Martindale-Hubbell Law Directory* for 1930, which presumably excludes lawyers employed by business enterprises or governmental agencies. (Figures supplied by Martindale-Hubbell. The directory is issued early in the year and hence gives number of lawyers in 1929.) Both totals include lawyers who are salaried employees of other lawyers. A New York County study indicated that these constitute 21.14 per cent of all lawyers in practice. This percentage checks closely with that for the country from the Department of Commerce sample, but the latter is probably high (see Ch. 6). Nonetheless, the estimate in the table is 78.86 per cent of the total given by the Census as in 'professional service' (139,059). See *Survey of the Legal Profession in New York County* (N. Y. County Lawyers Association, 1936), p. 12; *National Income in the United States, 1929–35*, pp. 214, 292.

1935

Total: number in *Martindale-Hubbell Law Directory* for 1936 (as furnished by Martindale-Hubbell) multiplied by the ratio of the total number listed in the 1930 Census to the number in the *Martindale-Hubbell Law Directory* for 1930.

Number in independent practice: 78.86 per cent of the total number listed in the *Martindale-Hubbell Law Directory* for 1936.

CERTIFIED PUBLIC ACCOUNTANTS

1930

Total: *Census of Population*, Vol. 5; number of accountants and auditors in professional service. This excludes certified public accountants employed by nonaccounting firms, but it includes noncertified accountants in public practice or employed by accounting firms.

Number in independent practice: a sample count of the 1938 Directory of the New York State Society of Certified Public Accountants gave 32.91 per cent as

TABLE 1, NOTES (concl.)

salaried employees of accounting or nonaccounting firms. A sample count of
the 1933 Directory of the American Institute of Accountants gave an almost
identical percentage, 33.03. The membership of each society or even of both
societies includes a minority of all certified public accountants and is a highly
biased sample of all certified public accountants. The similarity of these two
figures suggests that the bias does not affect the proportions employed on salary
since the membership of the Institute is a much more biased sample than the
membership of the New York State Society. Hence, 67 per cent was used.

1936

Total: estimated by the American Institute of Accountants.

Percentage in independent practice: assumed same as in 1930.

ENGINEERS

1930

Total: *Census of Population*, Vol. 5.

Percentage in independent practice: a study of engineers by the BLS indicates
that 4.45 per cent of all engineers professionally active and in engineering work
in 1929 were independent consultants. The number in independent practice
computed by multiplying this percentage by the total number of engineers
checks closely with an estimate of 9,818 computed by multiplying the percentage
from the Department of Commerce sample by the total number of engineers
listed by the *Census of Population* in professional service. See 'Employment in
the Engineering Profession', *Monthly Labor Review*, April 1937, p. 868; *National
Income in the United States, 1929–35*, pp. 215, 293.

total number of persons in the profession and of the number
practising independently are given for each profession for
1930, a year near the beginning of the period our primary data
cover (principally, 1929-36) and for each except engineering
for a year near the end of the period. These estimates vary in
accuracy. Moreover, since the estimates for the earlier and
later years are not derived from the same source, the difference
between the two is subject to an especially large margin of
error.

The table illustrates the difficulty of drawing a sharp line
between a profession and neighboring pursuits, let alone between professions as a whole and all other pursuits. Certified
public accountants, to cite the most extreme example, are but
formally differentiated from the entire group of accountants

and auditors, which numbered 192 thousand in 1930.[3] Accountants who are not certified are almost everywhere permitted to practise independently, but a much smaller proportion of noncertified than of certified accountants do so. Had the table included all accountants and auditors along with certified public accountants, less than a tenth would have been listed as in independent practice instead of two-thirds. The dividing line is less nebulous for most of the other professions; but for none is it unmistakably clear.

1 MEDICINE

During the last few decades, both technical and economic factors have contributed to a very rapid extension of specialization in medicine. The advance of medical science has made specialization both desirable and possible; the financial gains promised by specialization have furnished an economic incentive. A count of the 1931 Directory of the American Medical Association indicates that only 68 per cent of all physicians considered themselves general practitioners, the other 32 per cent being almost equally divided between partial and complete specialists.[4] Sample studies indicate an even larger proportion of specialists. Moreover, specialization seems to be still increasing.[5]

This increase in specialization has been stimulated and accompanied by a rapid advance in training requirements. The first state board of medical examiners was created in 1873 in Texas, and "by 1895 practically every state had created some kind of administrative organization to examine and license physicians".[6] Yet as late as 1904 only 20 states had requirements about premedical education and of these only 10 required as much as a standard four-year high school education. Only 36 states required that all applicants for licenses be graduates of

3 *Census of Population*, Vol. 5.
4 R. G. Leland, *Distribution of Physicians in the United States* (American Medical Association, 1936), pp. 31, 39.
5 See Ch. 6.
6 *Final Report of the Commission on Medical Education* (New York, 1932), p. 156.

a medical school.[7] The standards of the medical schools themselves were no higher. "In 1900 less than 25 per cent of the number of medical schools exacted graduation from a high school for admission",[8] and the quality of professional training was so poor that, in Flexner's opinion, of the 131 medical schools in the United States in 1910, fewer than 40 supplied "the distinctly better quality of medical training".[9] In the inferior schools the actual period of training was short and the standards low.

The creation by the American Medical Association in 1904 of a permanent Council on Medical Education and the publication in 1910 of Flexner's monumental study ushered in a period of rapid rise in premedical requirements and standards of professional training and of rapid decline in the number of medical schools and medical students. By 1915, 85 of the 96 schools in existence required either one or two years of college as a minimum preparation [10] and the medical course was almost universally four years. The number of medical students declined from a high point of approximately 28 thousand in 1904 to under 15 thousand in 1915, and under 14 thousand in 1920.

In 1940 there were 77 approved [11] medical schools in the United States, of which 5 required a college degree for entrance; one, four years of college; 60, three years; and 11, two years. The Council on Medical Education recently recommended that the minimum requirement for premedical education be raised from two to three years of college.[12] All approved schools give a medical course lasting four years of approximately thirty-two weeks each (or an equivalent amount

7 *Ibid.*, Appendix Table 88.
8 W. J. Gies, *Dental Education in the United States and Canada* (Carnegie Foundation for the Advancement of Teaching, 1926), p. 125.
9 Abraham Flexner, *Medical Education in the United States and Canada* (Carnegie Foundation for the Advancement of Teaching, 1910), p. 12.
10 *Final Report of the Commission on Medical Education*, p. 11.
11 'Approved' means approved by the Council on Medical Education and Hospitals of the American Medical Association.
12 R. L. Wilbur, 'Report of the Council on Medical Education and Hospitals', *Journal of the American Medical Association*, April 23, 1938, pp. 1327-8.

of time concentrated in fewer years). In addition, thirteen medical schools in the United States require a one-year internship in a hospital for the M.D. degree.

The legal requirements for premedical education generally match the requirements that medical schools must impose in order to be approved by the Council on Medical Education. Forty-three states and the District of Columbia require a minimum of two years of college; of the other five states, two require one year of college and three a high school education or its equivalent. Moreover, most of these five states do not license graduates of unapproved American schools.[13] Since unapproved schools are few and supply at most 5 to 7 per cent of all applicants for medical licenses, they are of minor importance.[14] Twenty-one states and the District of Columbia require a one-year hospital internship of applicants for licensure.

The training legally required of medical practitioners has thus been extended since the beginning of the century from three or four years of professional education preceded by one or two years of high school to six or seven years preceded by graduation from high school.

The actual level of premedical and medical training is higher than is required by medical schools or by law. In 1936-37, 56 per cent of the freshmen enrolled in medical schools

[13] 'Medical Licensure Statistics for 1937', *ibid.*, April 23, 1938.
[14] According to the *Final Report of the Commission on Medical Education*, p. 90, there were in 1932 six unapproved schools. There appear to be no other data on the number of unapproved schools or the enrollment in them.

The percentage of all persons taking the licensure examination who were graduates of unapproved schools has varied between 4.7 and 7.5 per cent from 1930 to 1941, and the percentage of these who failed the examination, between 32 and 59 per cent. The percentage of failures among graduates of approved medical schools, on the other hand, has exceeded 5 per cent only once, in 1940, when it was 5.1 per cent. Because of the relatively high percentage of failures among graduates of unapproved schools, the percentage of all persons passing the licensure examination who were graduates of unapproved schools has been considerably lower than the percentage of all persons taking the examination—between 2.2 and 4.9 per cent from 1930 to 1941. See the annual articles on 'Medical Licensure Statistics' in the *Journal of the American Medical Association*.

received a college degree before they began medical training, an additional 5 per cent had four years of college, 27 per cent, between three and four years, and only 12 per cent the minimum, two years of college. Less than 4 per cent of the freshmen enrolled in 1938-39 had only the minimum two years. Of the 5,183 graduates of medical schools in the United States in 1936, 77 per cent held baccalaureate degrees.[15] Of the graduates in 1935 of approved medical schools *not* requiring internship for the degree, 98 per cent were interning in 1935-36.[16] Most of those entering the medical profession at present have had between eight and ten years' training after high school.

As already noted, the rapid increase in training requirements was accompanied by a marked decline in the number of medical schools and, until about 1920, in the number of students. In consequence, the number of physicians increased far less rapidly than total population during the last 30 or 40 years, whereas the reverse occurred in most other professional pursuits. Indeed, the absolute number of physicians declined from 1910 until about 1920, and in 1930 was not much higher than in 1910. The number of physicians per 100,000 persons declined from approximately 157 in 1900 to 145 in 1914 and 125 in 1929, a low point from which it rose to 130 in 1938.[17] Initially, this decline in the number of physicians relative to

15 'Medical Education in the United States and Canada', *ibid.*, Aug. 29, 1936, Aug. 28, 1937, Aug. 26, 1939.

The possession of a baccalaureate degree at graduation from medical college does not necessarily represent the completion of four years of college; the degree is frequently granted *in absentia* at the end of the first year in medicine. In addition, thirty-one schools offer a B.S. degree in medicine at some stage of the medical course. (*Ibid.*, Aug. 29, 1936, p. 671.)

16 *Ibid.*, Aug. 29, 1936, pp. 668-9.

17 Leland, *Distribution of Physicians*, p. 7; *Number of Physicians in the United States by County, July 1, 1938* (American Medical Association, 1938); *Statistical Abstract of the United States, 1939* (U. S. Department of Commerce, 1940), p. 10. The number of physicians used in the calculations cited is taken from *Polk's Directory* for 1900, and from the Directory of the American Medical Association for the other years. It includes not only physicians in active practice but also some who are retired or out of practice for other reasons. The population estimates are the annual midyear estimates of the Bureau of the Census for

total population was an unplanned by-product of the intensive drive for higher standards of medical education. During recent years, however, the limitation in the number admitted to medical schools has come to be interpreted by many leaders of the profession as representing more than a relative decline in the number of applicants willing and able to meet the higher professional standards. "Too many are still unaware," said Harold Rypins, then Secretary of the New York State Board of Medical Examiners, "that American medical schools are definitely committed to a policy of restricting the number of their students. In all the professions there has developed in the last few years, an aristocratic, or at least a restrictive movement which, in a sense, is reminiscent of the medieval guilds. The trend is still in an early stage, but in law, medicine, dentistry and other professions under control of state licensure, the signs are apparent. . . . Without intention or design, the far-reaching steps taken by the physicians to raise educational standards during the past twenty-five years has resulted in limiting the number of students. Now, realizing the advantages of this unplanned restriction, leaders . . . are taking definite steps to cut down the professional class." [18]

---

continental United States. In interpreting the figures given above, physicians frequently emphasize that the rapid growth of transportation and hospital facilities has increased the number of patients a physician can care for effectively. On the other hand, the advances in medical science have probably increased the attention that must be devoted to the treatment of each patient as well as the number of cases recognized as requiring medical attention.

18 'Toward Professional Guilds', *Federation Bulletin*, Sept. 1933, pp. 277–84.

A careful search of the literature by the writers shows this statement to be representative of the opinion of medical leaders. See, for example, A. D. Bevan, 'The Over-Crowding of the Medical Profession', *Journal of the Association of American Medical Colleges*, Nov. 1936, pp. 377–84; J. A. Miller, 'Some Problems in Medical Ethics and Economics', *ibid.*, July 1937, pp. 218–26; W. L. Bierring, 'Social Dangers of an Oversupply of Physicians', *Federation Bulletin*, April 1934, pp. 117–24; C. B. Pinkham, 'Foreign Medical Students', *ibid.*, May 1938, pp. 132–43; E. P. Lyon, 'Swans Sing Before They Die', *Proceedings of the Annual Congress on Medical Education, Medical Licensure, and Hospitals, 1936;* Raymond Walters, 'Should the Number of Professional Students be Restricted?', *Journal of the American Medical Association*, March 30, 1935, pp. 1051–6; Wilbur, 'Report of the Council on Medical Education and Hospitals'.

The organization of medical education in the United States permits close control over the admission practices and standards of the individual medical schools. In all but three states, either legal requirements or the rules of the Board of Examiners specify that among individuals studying in this country or Canada only graduates of medical schools approved by the Council on Medical Education and Hospitals of the American Medical Association may take the examination for admission to practice.[19] The Council on Medical Education thus has almost complete control over the number of medical schools, a control that seems to have been exercised on the basis of quality of training offered and to have had a salutary influence on the standards of medical education.[20] In addition, the Council has direct contact with and influence over each school through its accrediting activities.

Late in 1934 or early in 1935 the Council on Medical Education issued a warning "against the admission of larger classes than can properly be accommodated or than can reasonably be expected to satisfy approved scholastic standards" with the comment: "seven schools have definitely stated that their enrollment will be decreased and others have indicated adherence to the Council's principles".[21] The warning seems to have had a decided effect on the number of students admitted to medical schools (Table 2). Each of the five years prior to 1934 for which data are available, with the possible exception of

[19] The three exceptions are Illinois, Ohio, and Massachusetts. In Massachusetts the law has been amended so that since 1940 the Board has had the authority to limit examinations to graduates of approved schools. 'Medical Licensure Statistics for 1936', *Journal of the American Medical Association*, April 24, 1937. Several other states occasionally admit graduates of unapproved schools, mainly through certification, but sometimes through examination. The three states mentioned seem to be the only ones where this practice is either regular or of any importance.

[20] See, however, S. P. Capen, 'Results of the Work of the Commission on Medical Education', *Proceedings of the Annual Congress on Medical Education and Licensure* (American Medical Association, 1933).

[21] 'Medical Education in the United States and Canada', *Journal of the American Medical Association*, Aug. 31, 1935, p. 686.

1929, showed an increase in the number of applicants accepted while each of the six years from 1934 to 1939 showed a decrease. Especially large decreases occurred in the two years immediately following the publication of the warning, 1935 and 1936. In recent years, the number of applicants accepted has been 700 to 1300 less than in the peak year, 1933, and

TABLE 2

Admissions to Approved Medical Schools in the United States, 1926–1929 and 1932–1941

| | | NUMBER OF APPLICANTS | | |
	Total	Accepted	Rejected	% ACCEPTED
1926	10,006	6,420	3,586	64.2
1927	11,019	6,496	4,523	59.0
1928	12,420	6,974	5,446	56.2
1929	13,655	7,035*	6,620	51.5
1932	12,280	7,357	4,923	59.9
1933	12,128	7,543	4,585	62.2
1934	12,779	7,419	5,360	58.1
1935	12,740	6,900	5,840	54.2
1936	12,192	6,465	5,727	53.0
1937	12,207	6,410	5,797	52.5
1938	12,131	6,223	5,908	51.3
1939	11,800	6,219	5,581	52.7
1940	11,854	6,328	5,526	53.4
1941	11,940	6,822	5,118	57.2

From articles by F. C. Zappfe, *Journal of the Association of American Medical Colleges,* March 1933; July 1937; May 1938; July 1939; July 1940; Sept. 1941; May 1942. Annual study on which these data are based was not made for 1930–31.

* Includes 405 accepted by Canadian medical schools.

about the same as in 1926, the earliest year for which we have comparable data. The *percentage* of applicants accepted declined not only from 1933 to 1938 but also from 1926 to 1929.

In recent years almost half of those applying for admission to approved United States schools have been refused. Of course, many who are refused in one year apply again. Of 3,586 individuals refused in 1926, 29 per cent had been accepted by 1929, 17 per cent had been repeatedly refused, and

54 per cent had not applied again.[22] If these figures give a true picture of the situation in recent years, approximately 67 per cent of all who attempt to enter approved United States medical schools eventually succeed. Interestingly enough, the percentage of applicants previously refused who are accepted is only slightly lower than the percentage of first applicants who are accepted.[23]

Not all of the 67 per cent who succeed in entering approved United States medical schools graduate from them and gain permission to practise. Some drop out of school of their own accord, some cannot meet scholastic standards and fail to graduate, some graduate but then fail the examination for a license to practise. The net result of failures at these stages can be estimated for recent years. These estimates, combined with the estimate of 67 per cent based on data for 1926–29, indicate that not more than 55 per cent of all persons who attempt to enter approved United States medical schools gain entry, graduate from an approved school, and pass the licensure examination. This estimate allows for repeated attempts at all stages.[23a]

[22] B. D. Myers, 'Report on Applications for Matriculation in Schools of Medicine of the United States and Canada, 1929–1930', *Journal of the Association of American Medical Colleges,* March 1930, pp. 65–89. These percentages as well as those in the next footnote include Canadian as well as United States schools. However, the Canadian schools accounted for only 3 to 5 per cent of all applications filed.

[23] According to Myers (*ibid.*):

	NEW APPLICANTS			APPLICANTS PREVIOUSLY REFUSED		
	1927	*1928*	*1929*	*1927*	*1928*	*1929*
Total	9,680	10,631	11,092	1,339	1,789	2,563
Accepted	5,746	6,000	5,802	750	971	1,233
Percentage accepted	59.4	56.4	52.3	56.0	54.4	48.1

[23a] The figure of 55 per cent is the product of (1) the estimated proportion of persons attempting to enter approved U. S. schools who ultimately succeed, (2) the estimated proportion of persons matriculating in approved schools who ultimately succeed in graduating from approved schools, and (3) the estimated proportion of persons graduating from approved schools who succeed in passing the licensure examination.

Item (1) is the 67 per cent explained in the text. The basis for the other items is as follows:

(2) For each year from 1936 to 1942, the number of persons graduated from approved U. S. schools in that year was divided by the number of persons

Of course, there are channels other than approved United States schools by which entry into medical practice could be secured. Some of the persons who fail to enter practice through approved United States schools may be able to go to one of the few unapproved schools or to a foreign school, and then pass the examination for licensure. New entrants to the medical profession may also include some who never tried to enter

---

matriculated in approved U. S. schools four years earlier. The average of these ratios is .806 for the period 1936 to 1940, .828 for the period 1936 to 1942. The number of graduates and the ratio were abnormally high in 1941 because two schools discontinued internship requirements and hence each graduated two classes. The 1942 ratio was also much higher than for any preceding year. Consequently, we use a range from .806 to .828. Graduates in each year were not all necessarily in the freshman class four years earlier. In some schools, students graduate only after internship, so that a five-year period elapses between matriculation and graduation, and in one or two schools, students may graduate after three years. In addition, some persons drop out of school for a year or more and then return, some spend more than one year in the same class, and some may enter as advanced students (e.g., persons who received some training abroad or in unapproved schools). The changing body of students represented means that the ratios cited may be interpreted as taking full account of persons who enter as advanced students and of repeated attempts by persons who fail courses.

(3) For each year we have data on the number of graduates of approved U. S. medical schools who take state licensure examinations and the number who pass. The average percentage passing for 1935 to 1941 is 96.1. These figures are unsatisfactory because some persons may take the examination in more than one state and be counted twice and because some persons who take the examination have previously been admitted to practice in other states. Further, the percentage passing in any one year clearly understates the percentage who ultimately pass, since a person who fails the examination in one year or in one state can take it in another year or in another state. Probably very few fail to pass the examination eventually. In addition, some graduates may get licenses on the basis of the examinations of the National Board of Medical Examiners without taking the licensure examination though the number who do so is relatively small. Because of these difficulties, we use here a range of .961 to 1.0.

Multiplying together items (1) and (2) gives a range of 54.0 to 55.4 for the percentage of persons who attempt to enter approved U. S. medical schools who ultimately graduate from them; multiplying together items (1), (2), and (3) gives a range of 51.9 to 55.4 for the percentage who succeed also in passing the licensure examination.

It should be noted that about six per cent of the persons who in any year apply to approved medical schools and are accepted never enroll. We have ignored this source of loss since presumably such persons either did not seriously intend to enter medical schools when they applied or changed their

approved United States medical schools: residents of this country who initially went to unapproved United States schools or to foreign schools, and foreigners who emigrated to this country after being trained abroad. But these other channels of entry account for only a minor share of all new entrants. It is clear from the available data that the bulk of all new entrants are graduates of approved United States medical schools, although these data are inadequate to provide an exact quantitative estimate.[23b]

Possibly in response to the increased difficulty of being admitted to American medical schools, the number of Americans studying abroad rose from 710 in 1930 to 2,054 in 1932. In 1933 the Federation of State Medical Boards adopted a resolution urging the strengthening of the requirements for admission to the examinations for licensure.[24] The number studying

---

minds later. In either case they cannot properly be included as persons attempting to enter medical schools. In ignoring this group, while using the figure of 67 per cent based on *all* persons who file applications, we implicitly assume that if the persons refused entry had been accepted, the same percentage would not have enrolled as of the persons actually accepted.

The sources for the basic data are annual compilations of educational and licensure data in *Journal of the American Medical Association* and *Journal of the Association of American Medical Colleges.*

23b From 1932 to 1941 between 78.4 and 93.2 per cent of all persons passing the examination for licensure were from approved schools. But (1) these figures include some persons more than once since a person who takes and passes the examination for licensure in more than one state in the same year will be counted once in each state; (2) persons passing the licensure examination include some persons who are already in practice in other states and hence are not new entrants; (3) some persons are admitted to practice without taking state licensure examinations on the basis of the certificate of the National Board of Medical Examiners, the government service, Canadian and foreign credentials. We know that the number in the third group accounts in general for less than 10 per cent of the total net addition to the profession; we do not, however, know how many of these are graduates of approved schools, though we suspect that most of them are since, as is noted below, securing a license on foreign credentials without examination is extremely difficult.

24 This resolution was to the effect "that no American student matriculating in a European medical school subsequent to the academic year of 1932–33 will be admitted to any state licensing examination who does not present satisfactory evidence of premedical education equivalent to the requirements of the Association of American Medical Colleges, and the Council on Medical Education

abroad thereupon declined to less than 1,500, or 7 per cent of the total enrollment of 22,000 to 23,000 in the United States in the years from 1934 to 1937.

Similarly, the prospect of an influx of foreign physicians after Hitler's rise to power in Germany led to more rigorous requirements for immigrants. It is no longer possible in any state for physicians to be licensed by indorsement without examination. Moreover, 16 states refuse to recognize under any circumstances credentials of schools not in the United States; 21 states and the District of Columbia recognize such credentials only after additional work in the United States— usually a year of internship in an approved hospital or a senior year in an approved medical school, or in some instances, both. Only 11 states recognize such credentials without additional work. The imposition of citizenship requirements in many states and the universal requirement that applicants take the medical examination in English have placed further obstacles in the path of foreigners seeking permission to practise. Of the 32 states and the District of Columbia recognizing credentials of foreign schools, 20 require full citizenship, and 10, the declaration of intention to become citizens ('first papers'). The requirements about both additional training and citizenship seem to apply to all individuals, no matter how long they may have practised abroad.[25]

The concern over the influx of foreign physicians and the

---

and Hospitals . . . , and graduation from a European medical school after a medical course of at least four academic years, and further submit evidence of having satisfactorily passed the examination to obtain a license to practice medicine in the country in which the medical school from which he is graduated is located. This policy of the Federation has been made effective by individual action on the part of some of the State licensing boards and the National Board of Medical Examiners." ('Medical Education in the United States and Canada', *Journal of the American Medical Association*, Aug. 26, 1933, p. 685.)

25 'Medical Licensure Statistics for 1940', *ibid.*, May 3, 1941, p. 2045; Harold Rypins, 'The Increase in the Number of Practitioners in the Country', *Proceedings of the Annual Congress on Medical Education and Licensure, 1937.*

According to Rypins, the average number of foreign-born graduates licensed annually throughout the country during the five years 1932–36 was less than 300: 200 by examination and 100 by certification. About 6,000 new physicians are licensed annually. See also Pinkham, 'Foreign Medical Students'.

number of Americans studying abroad found expression also in a series of resolutions by the House of Delegates of the American Medical Association. In 1936 a resolution was adopted urging that graduates of medical schools of other countries be expected to prove their fitness for medical practice by being in possession of a license to practise in the country of their graduation and a certificate of internship in a hospital approved for such training or complete the fourth year in an American Class A medical school.[26] In 1938 a resolution was adopted stating: "it is highly desirable that an additional requirement of full citizenship in the United States of America be demanded" of "foreigners, graduates of foreign institutions, . . . before being admitted to practice." [27] The Council on Medical Education of the American Medical Association, which approves hospitals for internship, passed a resolution "that, when suitable graduates of Class A schools in the United States and Canada are not available, hospitals approved for intern training may accept graduates of European universities who have passed parts I and II of the examinations of the National Board of Medical Examiners." [28]

The increasing number of graduates of foreign schools seeking entry to practice in this country is reflected in the percentage of candidates failing the medical examination for licensure. After declining uninterruptedly from 14.8 in 1923 to 5.7 in 1930, the percentage failing rose in every year thereafter through 1940 except 1933 and 1937, when it remained unchanged from the preceding year. In 1941, the percentage

26 'Medical Education in the United States and Canada', *Journal of the American Medical Association*, Aug. 27, 1938, p. 801.

27 One implication of the two resolutions deserves mention. Since many foreign countries grant licenses to practise only to their citizens, an American studying in one of these countries would have to become a citizen of that country in order to qualify under the first resolution. When he returned to the United States, he would have to regain his citizenship in order to qualify under the second.

28 'Medical Licensure Statistics for 1938', *ibid.*, April 29, 1939, p. 1720. While on the surface this resolution may seem a relaxation of restrictions, it is really the reverse, since a corollary of the resolution is that graduates of European universities may not be accepted if graduates of American schools are available.

failing declined to 19.7 from the peak of 20.7 reached the preceding year. This ten-year rise in the percentage failing was due primarily to the increasing number of graduates of foreign schools who took the examination, a group that has a very high percentage of failures. The number of graduates of foreign schools taking the medical examination for licensure rose from under 200 prior to 1934 to a peak of over 2,000 in 1940. The percentage of these failing varied from a minimum of 31 per cent in 1935 and 1937 to a peak of 60 per cent in 1941. Among graduates of approved United States medical schools, the percentage failing has been in the neighborhood of only 3 to 5 per cent.[29]

The formal premedical and medical training requirements are thus not the only, and may not even be the most important, factor governing entry into medicine. The attitudes and actions of the American Medical Association and its Council on Medical Education, of individual medical schools and their national association, and of the state boards of medical examiners and their national federation also play an important role, a role that in recent years has been to make entry more difficult.

For our purpose, it is sufficient to describe this role in terms of its overt expression and its effect on the supply of physicians, since it is in this way that it bears on our primary problem—the analysis of factors determining the incomes physicians receive for their work. But such a description is entirely inadequate as a basis for judging the social implications of the control of entry. From this point of view, the description we have given is incomplete, since it is concerned with quantity rather than quality, results rather than causes, and actions

[29] The figures for graduates of foreign schools do not include graduates of approved Canadian schools.

The percentage of all persons taking the examination (graduates of U. S. approved, unapproved, and extinct schools, Canadian schools, and foreign schools) who failed is as follows for each year since 1930: 1930, 5.7; 1931, 6.2; 1932, 7.6; 1933, 7.6; 1934, 8.4; 1935, 9.1; 1936, 10.0; 1937, 10.0; 1938, 11.7; 1939, 16.3; 1940, 20.7; 1941, 19.7. See the annual articles on 'Medical Licensure Statistics', *Journal of the American Medical Association*.

rather than motives. The social desirability or undesirability of the changes here described has been much debated, but that large issue lies outside the scope of this investigation.[30]

2 DENTISTRY

Dentistry resembles medicine in function, organization, kind of training, and clientele. Specialization is far less wide-spread in dentistry than in medicine, though in both it has increased markedly during the last few decades. According to the study of the Committee on the Costs of Medical Care, in 1929, 3 per cent of the dentists regarded themselves as complete specialists and 8 per cent as partial specialists, but many of the 89 per cent who engaged in general practice excluded certain fields.[31] Similarly, dentistry has experienced much the same changes in training requirements as medicine, but with a lag of about a decade and with the general level of requirements still appreciably lower than in medicine even in recent years.

The apprentice system of training, originally dominant in both medicine and dentistry, lasted much longer in dentistry. In 1870 less than 15 per cent of the dentists were graduates of professional schools, the first of which in this country had been established in 1840. The adoption by all states between 1870 and 1900 of laws providing for licensing dental school graduates without the examination required of nongraduates gradually led to the termination of the apprentice system. By 1901, 60 per cent of all dentists were graduates of dental schools; by 1925, 97 per cent.[32]

[30] Control of entry by professional organizations deserves study in its own right and not merely as an incident in a study of incomes. Medicine offers an opportunity to observe a form of politico-economic control that promises to become increasingly important and that offers one type of pattern for the future organization of our society. Leaders of medicine are pretty generally convinced that it is a form of control that has been in the social interest and deserves imitation. There are others who think the opposite. The need for a thorough investigation and evaluation of these opposing viewpoints is clearly indicated. Source materials for such an investigation are plentiful.

[31] Maurice Leven, *Practice of Dentistry and the Incomes of Dentists in Twenty States: 1929* (University of Chicago Press, 1932).

[32] Gies, *Dental Education*, pp. 43, 45.

The relatively late rise of the dental schools, the lowly status accorded dentistry until recently, and the important role played in the early years of dental education by privately owned schools conducted for profit combined to keep the requirements for admission to professional training low and the training itself unsatisfactory. As late as 1879 the majority of dental schools required for admission to professional training only the 'rudiments of an English education'. By 1902 two years of high school were required; by 1910, graduation from a high school; by 1917, graduation from a four-year high school.

In 1921, five years after a university dental school began to exact two years of work in an academic college for admission, and a year after one of the schools had inaugurated the one-year requirement, fourteen other schools began to enforce the one-year requirement which by 1925 became a minimum in twenty-eight of the forty-four schools in the United States.[33]

The Dental Educational Council, recently replaced by the Council on Dental Education, was established in 1909, five years after the formation of the Council on Medical Education. It did not issue a public classification of the dental schools until 1918. Of the forty-nine dental schools in the United States in 1918, the Council rated sixteen Class A, twenty-seven Class B, and four Class C. Two were not officially mentioned. Of these 49 schools, 16 were proprietary, that is, privately owned and conducted for profit. By 1925, 24 of the 43 schools in existence were rated Class A, and only 3 were proprietary. Not until 1926, however, was an entrance prerequisite of one year of college work included among the minimum requirements for the Council's Class A or B rating.

The dental course itself increased in length and comprehensiveness. With the exception of a short-lived extension to four years by some schools in 1903-04, the dental course was almost universally three years until 1917 when it was extended to four. Throughout the period, the standard academic year

---

[33] *Ibid.*, pp. 55, 125. It will be recalled that in 1915, 85 of the 96 medical schools in existence required either one or two years of college work as a minimum preparation.

was being lengthened and a larger proportion of the schools were conforming to the standard.[34]

Legal requirements, like those of the schools, were raised materially during this period but nonetheless lagged considerably behind the rising requirements in medicine. In 1925 only one state required two years of college of prospective dentists; 4 states, one year; 32 states and the District of Columbia, graduation from high school; and 11 had no preprofessional requirements. In the same year 38 states and the District of Columbia required two years of college of prospective physicians; 4 states, one year; and the other 6 states, graduation from high school.

By 1941 all 39 dental schools in the United States gave a four-year course. One school required 3 years of college for admission, the other 38, two years. However, 44 per cent of the 2,074 freshmen enrolled in 1938-39 had more than 2 years of predental training: 16 per cent had 3 predental years, and 28 per cent, 4 or more predental years. Of the 1,794 graduates of dental schools in 1939, 22 per cent held baccalaureate degrees.[35]

The legal requirements have not changed much since 1925. Only 9 states appear to require college training and of these, 6 specify only one year. However, nearly all states require graduation from a 'reputable', 'recognized', or 'approved' school, and the list of American schools the state boards will recognize is ordinarily identical with that of the Council on Dental Education. In consequence, the explicit legal requirements are of little practical importance. Five states specify that the applicant be a citizen, and four that he have his 'first papers'.[36]

[34] Ibid., pp. 55, 117, 124.

[35] Dental Students' Register (Council on Dental Education, 1940), Tables 3 and 5.

[36] This summary of legal requirements is based on information generously furnished by S. R. Lewis, Secretary of the Committee on Legislation of the American Dental Association. At its first meeting in May 1938 the Council on Dental Education passed a resolution asking all dental schools to cease using the rating given them by the Dental Educational Council, the former accrediting body. The Council on Dental Education is now engaged in rating the dental schools anew. (We are indebted to G. D. Timmons, Secretary-Treasurer of the American Association of Dental Schools, for this information.)

In dentistry as in medicine, the rise in entrance requirements was accompanied by a sharp drop in students and graduates. Total enrollment decreased from 13,000 in 1922-23 to under 7,500 in recent years; and the number of graduates, from a high point of 3,400 in 1924 to slightly more than half that number.[37] The number of dentists per 100,000 persons has declined during the last decade, and possibly during an even longer period. This relative decline in the number of dentists seems attributable entirely to a decline in the number of students willing and able to meet the higher standards. Neither dental literature nor the meagre data on admissions to dental schools or to practice furnish any evidence of concern about the number of entrants as such.[38] Indeed, perhaps the most important article we have found on the subject was concerned with the possibility that the increase in training requirements might curtail too greatly the number of prospective dentists.[39]

Data on the number of persons applying for entry to dental schools are not available prior to the academic year 1941–42. For that year, the following figures have been compiled by the Council on Dental Education for all schools in the United States: [40]

	NUMBER	PERCENTAGE OF TOTAL
Applicants (academic year 1941–42)		
Accepted and in attendance	2,476	73.9
Accepted and not in attendance	321	9.6
Total accepted	2,797	83.5
Refused admittance	553	16.5
Total applicants	3,350	100.0

37 W. J. Gies, 'Is the Influx of New Graduates Commensurate with the Demand for Dental Service, or Should the Educational Requirements be Altered?', *Journal of the American Dental Association*, April 1931, pp. 589–99; *Dental Students' Register*, Tables 1 and 3.

The more rapid decline in graduates than in enrollment reflects, of course, the lengthening of the dental course.

38 The paucity of data on admissions is itself circumstantial evidence of the absence of any concern as to numbers, since such data would be one of its first by-products.

39 Gies, 'Is the Influx of New Graduates Commensurate with the Demand for Dental Services?'.

40 *Journal of the American Dental Association*, Dec. 1942, p. 2257.

While precisely comparable data are not available for earlier years, enough data are available to suggest that the same percentage can safely be used at least for 1939, and probably for a somewhat longer period.[40a] The percentage of persons applying for entry to dental schools who were refused admittance may therefore reasonably be assumed to have been about 16.5 per cent in recent years. The corresponding figure for medicine is between two and three times as large—43 per cent in 1941, between 45 and 50 per cent in every year from 1935–40, and above 35 per cent in every year from 1926–34 for which data are available (1926–29, 1932–34, see Table 2). These figures are directly comparable: for both medicine and dentistry they are based on the total number of persons applying for entry, including persons who were accepted but did not enroll. Moreover, the percentage of persons accepted who did not enroll is very similar in the two professions.

The percentages for dentistry just cited do not take account of repeated attempts to enter schools; so that we cannot obtain for dentistry a figure comparable to the 67 per cent of applicants to approved United States medical schools who succeed in entering after one or several attempts. But even if we assume that none of the 16.5 per cent of applicants to United States dental schools who are each year refused tries again or that none succeeds in later attempts, the resulting percentage who fail to gain entry is still only one-half of that estimated for

[40a] The data available for 1939 give the total number of *applications* received. This figure clearly overstates the number of *persons* applying for entry since many persons apply to more than one school. There is a parallel distinction between the number of applications accepted and the number of persons accepted, since a person may be accepted by more than one school and hence counted more than once in the number of applications accepted. In 1941, the total number of *applications* received by dental schools, before correction for multiple applications, was 5,479. The number of applications accepted was 59 per cent of the total number of applications received; the number of freshmen enrolled, 45 per cent of the total number of applications received. In 1939, the number of applications accepted was 56 per cent of the total number of applications accepted or rejected (4,479, excluding 345 for which no information on acceptance or rejection is given); the number of freshmen enrolled, 45 per cent. See *Dental Students' Register for 1939*, Table 5.

applicants to medical schools after allowing for repeated attempts.

Candidates for a dental license, on the other hand, have on the average had somewhat more difficulty in passing the licensure examination than candidates for a medical license. The percentage failing the dental examination has been fairly stable at about 18 to 20 per cent.[40b] In medicine, as noted above, the percentage failing the licensure examination has been rising. For the years 1935–41 it averaged about 14 per cent. The figures cited for both medicine and dentistry are for all persons taking the examination, whether graduates of United States schools or not.[40c]

The present data do not permit us to combine consistently the experience of would-be entrants into both the medical and dental professions in the long process from application for admission to the professional school through the licensure examination. One cannot start with a cohort of such would-be entrants for each of the two professions, and cumulate the percentages of failures at successive stages into final percentages showing what proportions of the initial cohorts succeed in passing the full series of tests. But it is fair to state that the partial data available on proportions of persons accepted by approved schools who graduate, and of persons taking licensure examinations who pass, fail to show differences that would significantly reduce the initial excess of the rate of

40b R. P. Thomas estimates for 41 states the number of dentists taking the examination for licenses annually and the percentage of failures for the five years 1932–36. His figures suggest that 18 per cent of all who took the examination failed—16 per cent of recent graduates and 29 per cent of the dentists out of school one year or longer ('Dental Survey', *Journal of the American Dental Association and the Dental Cosmos,* Jan. 1938, p. 157). Figures for more recent years are given annually in the *Journal of the American Dental Association.* In 1939, 20 per cent, and in 1940, 17 per cent failed.

40c The figures for both medicine and dentistry overstate, of course, the percentage who are never admitted, since individuals who fail once may take the examination again. Both sets of figures contain duplications since individuals may take the examination for licensure in more than one state; and both include individuals previously admitted to practice in other states.

failures among applicants to medical schools over that among applicants to dental schools.

However comprehensive and consistent percentages of the type discussed above may be, they measure relative difficulty of entry in a sense different from that of a comparison of requirements for pre-professional and professional training. The well-established fact, already discussed, that medicine has higher requirements for such training than dentistry means, in and of itself, greater difficulty of entry in the sense of requiring greater persistence in study, possibly higher mental ability, and certainly greater economic sacrifice prior to beginning of practice. We have also noted that among the leaders of the medical profession, in contrast to the leaders of the dental profession, there has been explicit concern about rapid increase in the number and possible deterioration in the quality of students and practitioners—a concern that may well have led to raising the hurdles which prospective entrants to the medical profession must clear. By the very facts of higher educational requirements and of the tendency toward restriction of numbers, the greater difficulty of entry into the medical profession is demonstrated; and would remain so even if the percentage of failures among would-be entrants into medicine were equal to or lower than among would-be entrants into dentistry.

Differences are present in the percentage of such failures in spite of the well-known higher requirements for entry into and pursuit of the medical profession, in spite of presumptive pre-selection in the sense that only those try who consider themselves possessed of the ability and training to satisfy these higher requirements. This may mean either that medicine appeals to proportionately larger groups of those who, by objective standards, cannot satisfy the requirements of the medical profession than dentistry does to those who, by equally objective standards, cannot satisfy the requirements of the dental profession; or that greater restriction of numbers in medicine bars otherwise fit candidates. The relative weight of these two and other possible explanations, is not and cannot be adequately measured by mere percentages of failures and success among experimentally uncontrolled groups of applicants, students, and examinees.[40d]

It should also be noted that the percentages of failures at entry or on licensure examinations are based on data for the last 5 to 10 years, whereas the data on income analyzed in this study are for persons who were graduated during a considerably earlier period. The difference between ease of entry into medicine and dentistry, as measured by training requirements, was probably even greater then than it is now. The intensive drive for higher standards of medical education which resulted in a rapid and sharp decline in number of schools and students began in 1910; the corresponding drive in dentistry, not until the early 1920's. During the intervening period, requirements for entry to dental practice were extremely low and proprietary schools—privately owned and conducted for profit—were common. As late as 1925, requirements of dental schools were considerably lower than those imposed in medicine by 1915 or earlier.

Despite the greater difficulty of entry into medicine, the number of persons who each year succeed in entering the profession has been in recent years a larger percentage of the total number already in practice than in dentistry. The reason for this is, of course, that there is an even larger difference between medicine and dentistry in the percentage that persons applying for entry are of all persons in the profession. Expressing the estimated number of persons applying for entry annually during 1935–41 as a percentage of the estimated number of persons in the profession in 1936, we get 7.3 per cent for medicine and 3.9 per cent for dentistry. Expressing the average number of graduates in 1935–41 as a percentage of the same total, we get 3.1 per cent for medicine and 2.3 per cent for dentistry.[40e]

40d See, however, discussion in Ch. 4, Sec. 2f.

40e The reason for using figures on graduates is that there are no reliable figures for both professions on actual new entrants. The figures on persons granted licenses are unreliable as indicators of actual entrants because (1) some new entrants get licenses in more than one state, (2) some persons who get licenses are not new entrants, having previously practised in other states. Figures cor-

Stated differently, there were each year more than four times as many persons applying for entry into medical schools as into dental schools, if we include both persons applying for the first time and persons applying again after an earlier refusal; between three and a half and four times as many applying for the first time; three times as many graduates from medical schools as from dental schools; and more than twice as many physicians as dentists.[40f]

rected for these items are available for medicine but not for dentistry. Further, in both medicine and dentistry, and particularly during the last few years in medicine, new entrants include a sizable number of persons other than graduates of American schools, primarily recent immigrants who formerly practised abroad. While these persons are properly included in the total number of new entrants, such a total is not comparable with our figures on persons trying to enter the professions, which are solely for persons applying for entry to American schools. In view of these difficulties, the number of graduates is probably the index of new entrants most nearly comparable with the available data on persons trying to enter the professions.

[40f] The detailed figures underlying these ratios and the percentages given above are as follows:

	YEARS AVERAGED	NUMBER IN Medicine	NUMBER IN Dentistry	RATIO OF NUMBER IN MEDICINE TO NUMBER IN DENTISTRY
Persons applying for entry	1935–41	12,123	2,929	4.1
Persons applying for entry for first time				3.5 to 4.1
Graduates	1935–41	5,188	1,734	3.0
Persons				
In independent practice	1936	133,000	62,000	2.1
In profession (including salaried and some persons retired or out of practice)	1936	165,000	75,000	2.2

The figure for dentistry on number of persons applying for entry was obtained by raising the average freshman enrollment for 1935–41 by the ratio of the number of persons applying for entry in 1941 to the number of persons enrolled in 1941. The figures on number of persons in independent practice and in the profession are taken from Table 1. The figures for persons applying for the first time are explained below. The rest of the figures are arithmetic averages of the corresponding annual figures.

The figures on the number of persons annually applying for entry include some persons who have been refused in earlier years but are applying again. They therefore overstate the number applying for the first time. This overstatement is probably larger in medicine than in dentistry because the percentage of persons refused admission is larger. The only evidence on the importance of

Unless the age distributions of physicians and dentists, the retirement rates in various age classes, and the like, are appreciably different, a continuation of this much greater rate of additions to medicine would serve to increase the ratio of the number of physicians to the number of dentists. The most comprehensive data available, those of the Census of Occupations, show, however, that between 1910 and 1930, the ratio of the number of physicians to the number of dentists *declined* from 3.78 to 2.19 (the number of physicians, including osteopaths, being 151 and 154 thousand in 1910 and 1930 respectively; and of dentists, 40 and 71 thousand); and that only from 1930 to 1940 did the ratio rise from 2.19 to 2.35. Apparently, the greater rate of additions to the medical profession is a relatively recent and mild trend.

It should be noted that these figures reflect the different dates at which educational standards were raised and, as a consequence, the number of students declined, in the two professions. The decline in the number of medical students began before 1910; in the number of dental students, almost twenty years later. The period from 1910 to 1930 naturally reflects most of the decline in medicine and hardly any in dentistry; the latter began to have a significant effect only about 1930.

3 LAW

The increasing complexity and scope of industry, finance, and government, the enormous growth of administrative tribunals, and the multiplication of laws affecting business have greatly

---

this factor is the special study of medical applicants cited in footnote 22 above. Calculations based on this study give as a minimum estimate of the ratio of persons applying for the first time in medicine to persons applying for the first time in dentistry a figure in the neighborhood of 3.5. The ratio of applicants in the two professions is therefore somewhere between 3.5 and the figure of 4.1 given above.

It should be noted that the figures on persons applying for entry during 1935–41 are not strictly comparable with the figures on graduates during 1935–41, since the latter applied for entry during an earlier period. It is for this reason that ratios for the same calendar period, such as those in this footnote, give only rough indications of the relative ease of entry into the two professions.

extended legal functions. As a result, individuals in their private capacity are becoming relatively less important as purchasers of legal services, and government and business more important; the proportion of all lawyers who are salaried employees is increasing; and 'office activities' now exceed in importance the trial work which originally constituted the lawyer's major function and with which law is still primarily associated in the lay mind.[41]

Partnerships or firms, almost entirely absent in the curative professions, play an important role in law. Approximately 25 per cent of all lawyers practising independently are members of firms.[42] To some extent, organization into firms serves the same function in law as specialization does in the curative professions since the larger legal units are in a position to assign firm members or salaried employees to specific segments of legal practice. In addition, there is some specialization by individual lawyers and by firms, but it is neither so widespread nor so formalized as in medicine.

Marked increases in the requirements for admission to practice began later in law than in either medicine or dentistry. Not until after the promulgation by the American Bar Association in 1921 of proposed standards for admission to the bar did really effective increases in training requirements occur. The recommended standards included two years of college education prior to law study and three years of full-time or a longer course of part-time study in schools approved by the Council on Legal Education.[43]

When this recommendation was made, not a single state required any college education and only 27 states and the District of Columbia as much as 3 years of legal training before admission to the bar. Eighteen states and the District of Columbia had no requirement about general education, and 10 states did

41 L. K. Garrison, 'Survey of the Wisconsin Bar', *Wisconsin Law Review,* Feb. 1935, pp. 136, 149; A. Z. Reed, *Annual Review of Legal Education for 1930,* p. 6.
42 See Ch. 6.
43 Reed, *Present-Day Law Schools in the United States and Canada* (Carnegie Foundation for the Advancement of Teaching, 1928), pp. 58–60.

not specify a definite period of legal training. As late as 1925 only one state, Kansas, required 2 years of college or its equivalent prior to the study of law. By 1937, on the other hand, 29 states required a minimum of 2 years of college prior to the study of law,[44] and 7 states, 2 years of college education before admission to the bar but not necessarily before law study. Forty states and the District of Columbia required three or more years of legal training, 4 states, no more than 2 years, and 4 had no requirement. In addition, 22 states did not admit graduates of other than 'approved' law schools.[45]

Unlike medical or dental training, the prescribed legal training need not be taken in school. All but seven states permit the entire period of training to be spent in a law office. However, "the number availing themselves of the privilege of study by clerkship is almost negligible as, except in rare cases, the bar examination cannot be successfully passed without formal school training." [46] Moreover, five states require that some part of the professional training be acquired in a law office [47]—four states, 6 months, one, 12 months.

A much more important difference between the legal and curative professions is that in the former it is possible to get professional training by attending school in the afternoon or evening on a part-time basis. This increases the possibility of individuals' 'working their way' through professional schools and thus lessens the dependence on others for the funds needed to finance training.

Of 190 law schools in existence in 1936, 73 offered solely part-time instruction, 34 both full- and part-time, and 83, exclusively full-time. Almost 19,000 students were classified as

---

44 Two of these required a college degree or passage of a general educational examination and one, again Kansas, had passed a law requiring that, effective July 1, 1940, all students have a college degree.

45 *Progress of Legal Education* (Carnegie Foundation for the Advancement of Teaching, 1922); *Annual Review of Legal Education for 1937*.

46 J. G. Rogers, 'The Standard American Law School', *Annual Review of Legal Education for 1936*, p. 15.

47 An additional state, New York, requires clerkship of candidates who are not college graduates (*ibid.*, p. 37).

attending afternoon and evening classes and only slightly more as attending morning classes.[48] The proportion of all law graduates receiving their education on a part-time basis is somewhat smaller than the proportion of students, since part-time students typically attend law school during more years than full-time students. The trend in the proportion of students taking part-time work cannot be determined with any exactitude from available data. It is clear, however, that the proportion of schools offering part-time work increased very rapidly from 1870, when the first important part-time schools were established, until about 1920, and at a somewhat slower pace thereafter. The proportion of students taking part-time work has probably undergone similar changes.[49]

Part-time schools cater to the less affluent, are less often affiliated with a university, and are more frequently conducted for profit than full-time schools. As a result their standards have been lower and their requirements less rigid, as the accompanying tabulation indicates.

	1922		1937	
	FULL-TIME	PART-TIME AND MIXED	FULL-TIME	PART-TIME AND MIXED
Total number of schools	70	77	84	101
Number of schools requiring for admission:				
No college education	18	67	2	36
1 year of college	14	4	0	3
2 years of college	30	6	45	58
More than 2 years but no degree	5	0	30	2
College degree	3	0	7	2

Progress of Legal Education, p. 29; *Annual Review of Legal Education for 1937,* pp. 34–63.

With one exception, all the full-time schools in existence in 1937 gave a 3-year law course. A directly comparable figure

[48] *Ibid.,* p. 72. These figures exclude approximately 2,000 graduate and unclassified students.

[49] Reed, *Annual Review of Legal Education for 1930,* p. 25, and *Training for the Public Profession of the Law* (Carnegie Foundation for the Advancement of Teaching, 1921), pp. 397–8.

cannot be cited for part-time schools because of the difficulty
of comparing time spent in part-time work and time spent in
full-time work.[50] But we have Reed's authority for the statement that despite the "general movement for lengthening the
course in part-time law schools, such schools are far from catch-
ing up with their full-time rivals, as regards the amount of
time that is measured by their law degree. On the contrary,
they are being more and more outdistanced in this respect." [51]

The increase in training requirements for admission to the
bar from two or three years in 1920 to a minimum of five years
at present was accompanied by a rapid increase in lawyers, law
schools, and law students. The number of lawyers per 100,000
persons declined steadily from 144 in 1900 to 116 in 1920 but
then rose to 131 in 1930 and seems to have continued to increase thereafter, despite a moderate decrease in the number of
law students. Although, as we shall show in Chapter 4, the decline in the incomes of lawyers from 1929 to 1933 roughly
paralleled the decline in the incomes of physicians, the prior
rapid increase in the number of lawyers seemed to give greater
support to the contention of 'overcrowding' and to make the
problem more prominent. In any event, during recent years
discussion and advocacy of limitation of entry have probably
been even greater among lawyers than among physicians—a
phenomenon perhaps not unrelated to the smaller degree of
actual restriction in law.[52]

[50] Hours of classroom instruction are not a valid basis for comparison because
they take no account of outside study required of or done by the student.
[51] *Annual Review of Legal Education for 1930*, pp. 26–8.
[52] See 'The Overcrowding of the Bar', *Notes on Legal Education,* June 1932;
' "Life" in Bar Admission Standards', *ibid.,* Dec. 1936; 'Modern Bar Admission
Standards and the List of Approved Law Schools', *ibid.,* July 1937; 'Admissions
to the Professions of Medicine and Law: A Comparison', *ibid.,* July 1933;
'Pennsylvania Considers Adoption of a Quota System', *Bar Examiner,* July 1933;
C. E. Clark, 'The Selective Process of Choosing Law Students and Lawyers', *ibid.,*
Sept. 1933; C. E. Dunbar, Jr., 'The Bar Association Standards and Part-Time
Legal Education', *ibid.,* Jan. 1940; A. J. Harno, 'Lights and Shadows in Qualifi-
cations for the Bar', *ibid.,* Nov. 1932; C. E. Clark and W. O. Douglas, 'Trends
in Legal Education and Bar Admission Requirements', *Recent Social Trends*
(McGraw-Hill, 1933), II, 1480–8; H. C. Horack, 'Supply and Demand in Legal

The legal profession has sought with some success to have admission to bar examinations limited to graduates of 'approved' law schools.[53] As noted above, in 1937, 22 states admitted only graduates of schools approved by the Section on Legal Education and Admissions to the Bar of the American Bar Association. These ratings seem to have no direct influence in the remaining jurisdictions.[54] As a result, in 1936, there were 96 unapproved law schools with an enrollment of 18 thousand or 45 per cent of all law students.[55] The most important of the law school associations, the Association of American Law Schools, had only 84 members, all on the approved list. In all there were 94 approved law schools.[56]

Because the legal profession has had so little direct control over the number of law schools or their policies, the pressure for limiting the number of lawyers has been directed mainly toward more severe educational requirements and greater

Profession', *American Bar Association Journal*, Nov. 1928; C. H. Kinnane, 'The Threatened Inundation of the Bar', *ibid.*, July 1931; Sidney Teiser, 'A Proposal for a Limited Bar', *ibid.*, Jan. 1935; I. M. Wormser, 'Fewer Lawyers and Better Ones', *ibid.*, April 1929; M. R. Kirkwood, 'Some Problems in Admission to the Bar that Affect the Law Schools', *American Law School Review*, April 1930; O. J. Phillips, 'Building a Better Bar', *ibid.*, Dec. 1934; symposium on 'The Overcrowding of the Bar and What can be Done about It', papers by Y. B. Smith and J. G. Rogers, *ibid.*, Dec. 1932; S. T. Wallbank, 'The Function of Bar Examiners', *ibid.*, Dec. 1931; P. J. Wickser, 'Ideals and Problems for a National Conference of Bar Examiners', *ibid.*, Dec. 1931, and 'Law Schools, Bar Examiners, and Bar Associations—Co-operation versus Insulation', *ibid.*, April 1933; Garrison, 'Survey of the Wisconsin Bar'.

53 "Generally the feeling in this country is that the adoption of a quota is unnecessary and would result in vociferous protest from the public. If our lawyers act intelligently they will forestall it by adopting those methods which have been so successful in the medical profession. First, they will require the two-year college standard before the beginning of law study, and second, they will, through their Boards of Bar Examiners, require graduation from law schools which competent agencies declare give an adequate legal education." 'Admissions to the Professions of Medicine and Law: A Comparison'.

54 *Annual Review of Legal Education for 1937.*

55 In interpreting these figures, the cautions given above should be borne in mind, since the unapproved law schools are predominantly part-time or mixed schools.

56 *Annual Review of Legal Education for 1936.*

stringency by bar examiners and the courts.[57] Explicit action by examining boards has taken several forms. The most extreme is probably the establishment in several counties in Pennsylvania of a quota system whereby only a certain number of lawyers are admitted each year.[58] Very similar is a recent ruling of the Delaware Supreme Court that permits the bar examiners to limit the number of registrations for law study.[59] Some states have limited the number of times candidates may take the bar examination.[60] One state, New Mexico, has established a 'probationary' bar, providing for a temporary license after the bar examination has been passed, and a permanent license, a year later. The numerous other proposals for limited or graded bars seem not to have been enacted in any jurisdiction.[61]

As noted above, the control of entry by professional associations is considerably weaker in law than in medicine. To some extent, this smaller degree of control may reflect the opposition within the legal profession to the adoption of policies designed to solve the problem of overcrowding through limitation of entry. Three other factors, however, help to explain why this opposition has been more successful than the corresponding opposition within the medical profession. In the first place, the drive for higher training requirements began at a later date

[57] H. W. Arant, President of the Association of American Law Schools, states: "If the profession really is overcrowded, they [the bar examinations] must be thought of as . . . devices for regulating the size of the legal profession." 'The Relationship Between Legal Education and Bar Examinations', *Annual Review of Legal Education for 1937*, p. 4.

[58] See *Bar Examiner*, July 1933.

[59] *Annual Review of Legal Education for 1937*, p. 21.

[60] Approximately 7 states have an absolute limitation on the number of reexaminations. In addition, 8 require special permission after a specified number of examinations. See B. L. Adams, 'Restrictions on Reexaminations', *Bar Examiner*, Aug. 1932; and the *Annual Review of Legal Education* for more recent years.

[61] Reed, *Annual Review of Legal Education for 1934*, p. 35. See also *Annual Review of Legal Education for 1929*, pp. 26–31.

In New Jersey, there are two classes of lawyers—attorneys and counsellors. But this distinction seems largely a relic of earlier regulations and to have little practical importance.

in law than in medicine. In medicine, this drive arose from a pressing need for better standards of training, and limitation of entry was an entirely unintended by-product. The success of the drive left the medical profession in a position to control entry for other purposes. In law, too, the initial drive for higher training requirements had little or no connection with any desire to limit entry. But starting later, it had proceeded less far when the problem of overcrowding seemed to become urgent. In the second place, the harm done to the public by low educational standards and requirements is more immediate and more easily recognized in medicine than in law. Finally, and probably most important, the political leadership of the country has been so largely recruited from the bar as to give rise to a general belief that it would be undesirable in a democracy to restrict entry into the bar to any limited social or economic class. It so happens that few part-time schools are on the list of 'approved' schools. In 1936, 75 of the 83 full-time schools were on the approved list, 18 of the 34 mixed schools, and only one of the 73 part-time schools. Restricting admission to the bar to graduates of approved schools in effect means denying admission to graduates of part-time schools. Yet the part-time schools are likely to be the only recourse of young men from poor families who must support themselves while getting their training.[62]

Table 3 suggests that the agitation for restriction led to an initial sharp increase in stringency by bar examiners, but that this increase has not been cumulative. The percentage passing the bar examination fell from 59 in 1927 to 45 in 1932 and 1934, and then rose to 51 in 1940. These figures understate the percentage finally admitted to the bar even more than the percentage of applicants annually accepted by medical schools understates the percentage of all applicants who are eventually accepted. The bar examination is taken at a much later stage

[62] For a profound and penetrating analysis of this problem, see F. M. Shea, 'Overcrowded?—the Price of Certain Remedies', *Columbia Law Review*, Feb. 1939, pp. 191–217.

TABLE 3

Admissions to the Bar, 1927–1940

| | APPLICANTS TAKING EXAMINATION | | | NUMBER ADMITTED ON | | | APPLICANTS TAKING EXAMINATION FOR FIRST TIME | | APPLICANTS REPEATING EXAMINATION | |
	Total	No. passing	% passing	Diploma[1]	Examination & diploma[2]	Motion[3]	Total	% passing	Total	% passing
	(1)	(2)	(3)	(4)	(5)	(6)	(7)	(8)	(9)	(10)
1927		8,825	59	553	9,378	876				
1928[4]	17,288	9,276	54	617	9,893	731				
1929[4]	18,305	9,387	51	630	10,017	765				
1930[2]	19,830	9,445	48	567	10,012					
1931[4]		9,129	48							
1932	19,470[5]	8,774	45[5]	566	9,340	634				
1933	18,314[5]	8,494	46[5]	764	9,258	678	7,253[6]	50[6]	7,210[6]	36[6]
1934	17,958[5]	8,245	45[5]	854	9,099	775	9,054[7]	51[7]	7,816[7]	38[7]
1935	16,812[5]	8,149	48[5]	822	8,971	601	8,476[8]	55[8]	7,027[8]	38[8]
1936	16,435	7,651	47	976	8,627	502	8,507[9]	54[9]	6,303[9]	38[9]
1937	16,629	7,989	48	945	8,994	618	7,944[10]	57[10]	6,554[10]	38[10]
1938	16,789	8,105	48	692	8,797	591	8,305[9]	58[9]	6,350[9]	39[9]
1939	15,985	8,102	51	429	8,531	471	8,170[9]	60[9]	5,882[9]	41[9]
1940	14,581	7,414	51	528	7,942	431	7,556[9]	60[9]	5,208[9]	41[9]

1927; col. 4: L. K. Garrison, 'A Survey of the Wisconsin Bar', *Wisconsin Law Review*, Feb. 1935, p. 134.

1928, 1929, 1930; col. 2, 3, 4, 5, and 6: Will Shafroth, *Bar Examiners and Examinees* (Council of the American Bar Association on Legal Education and Admission to the Bar). Figures in the table embody revisions furnished by Mr. Shafroth.

All other data: Bar Examiner, Aug. and Sept. 1932; April and May, 1934 to 1938; April 1939, 1940, and 1941.

[1] Several states admit graduates of specified law schools to the bar without examination.

[2] Represents total new admissions.

[3] Represents admission of lawyers previously admitted in another state.

[4] Year ending July 1.

[5] Excludes Arkansas.

[6] Excludes Arizona, Arkansas, District of Columbia, Michigan, New Jersey, Ohio, Texas.

[7] Excludes Arizona, Arkansas, District of Columbia.

[8] Excludes Arkansas, District of Columbia, Louisiana.

[9] Excludes District of Columbia, Georgia.

[10] Excludes District of Columbia, Georgia, Iowa.

in the candidate's training than that at which application is made for admission to medical school; hence, a much larger percentage of those who fail the bar examination try again. A study conducted some years ago indicated that 92 per cent of those who took the bar examination eventually passed.[63] The subsequent increase in the number of states limiting re-examinations and decrease in the percentage passing the bar examination has presumably led to a diminution in the percentage who eventually pass. Individuals who take the bar examination after having previously failed have considerably less success than those taking the examination for the first time. Approximately 55 per cent of first-timers have passed in recent years as compared with 38 per cent of repeaters, a difference much larger than that between the percentage of first applicants who are accepted by medical schools and the percentage of applicants previously refused who are accepted.

New entrants into the legal profession declined from approximately 10,000 annually during 1928–30 to fewer than 9,000 annually during 1935–37. The number taking the examination declined from approximately 20,000 in 1930 to fewer than 17,000 in 1937 (Table 3).

4 CERTIFIED PUBLIC ACCOUNTANCY

Certified public accountants render services to business enterprises and governmental agencies almost exclusively. As in law, salaried employment is common, and partnerships and firms play an important role. Approximately a third of all certified public accountants are salaried employees, and a third of those practising independently are members of firms.[64]

The functions of certified public accountants practising independently are of two distinct types: auditing, supervising,

[63] 'Admissions to the Professions of Medicine and Law: A Comparison'.

The figure of 92 cited in the text represents the percentage of all candidates examined in California, Colorado, Illinois, New York, and Pennsylvania during 1922–24, and in Ohio during 1926–28 who had been admitted to the bar by January 1932.

[64] See Ch. 6.

and analyzing the results of operations of business enterprises; and providing specialized counsel in bookkeeping and other control activities.[65] The need for an agency outside the business enterprise to perform the first function arises from a desire to have a check that is not affected by the interests of the business enterprise itself and that will therefore be accepted by others as impartial.

The first statute dealing with certified public accountants was enacted in 1896 by the New York State legislature. Within the next twenty-five years all states enacted similar statutes. The laws provided for the restriction of the title 'Certified Public Accountant' to individuals who meet certain preliminary requirements. The profession of public accountancy was not restricted to those certified, and, until recently, noncertified public accountants were not appreciably fewer than certified.

In all states candidates for the title of Certified Public Accountant are now required to pass an examination. In the past, usually when the original statute was enacted, large groups of individuals in practice were accorded the title without examination. The educational and experience requirements that must be complied with before a candidate for the Certified Public Accountant title is admitted to the professional examination vary widely.

Three states, Iowa, New York, and New Jersey (since Jan. 1, 1941), require graduation from a college or school of accountancy; one state, Kansas, 2 years of college; 42 states and the District of Columbia, a high school education (four of these states will permit the substitution of lengthy experience with an accountant for a high school education); and 2 states, Florida and Louisiana, have no educational requirements. All states except Delaware and Montana require some accountancy experience, the minimum amount accepted varying from one to five years. Four states require one year; 12 states, 2 years;

65 See Marvin Isaacs, *Professional Accountancy and Training in Collegiate Schools of Business* (Far Rockaway, 1933), pp. 6–7.

26 states and the District of Columbia, 3 years; 2 states, 4 years; and 2 states, 5 years. This summary understates somewhat the experience requirements, since in several states the amount of experience required depends on the kind of experience, the amount required ordinarily being least if the experience is with a certified public accountant. Eighteen states and the District of Columbia will permit a candidate to substitute higher education for experience; in 5 states, for the entire experience requirement; in 7 states, for one year of experience; in one state, for a year and a half of experience; and in 5 states and the District of Columbia, for 2 years of experience.[66]

Except in Iowa, New York, and New Jersey,[67] the educational and training requirements in certified public accountancy are lower than in the other professions considered. On the other hand, the examination that candidates for certification must take seems to be a much more important selective factor than the licensure examinations in the other professions—80 to 90 per cent of all candidates have failed in recent years, as compared to 40 to 60 per cent in law, 15 to 20 per cent in dentistry, and less than 10 per cent in medicine. Not only the percentage of individuals passing each examination but also the percentage who eventually pass is materially lower than in the other professions. A study for 1932-37 showed that 33 per cent of those permitted to take the examination eventually pass.[68] Of course, the consequences of failure are less serious in accountancy than in the other professions since the accountant who is not certified can still practise his profession, while the lawyer, physician, or dentist who fails to get his license cannot.

[66] T. W. Byrnes and K. L. Baker, *Do You Want to Become an Accountant?* (F. A. Stokes, 1940), pp. 32–42.
[67] This exception is, however, exceedingly important. New York alone contains almost one-third of all certified public accountants as compared with about 13 per cent of physicians and dentists and 17 per cent of lawyers.
[68] 'Certified Public Accountant Examination Certificates', *Journal of Accountancy*, April 1938, pp. 277–8. The 33 per cent is based on figures for 1932–37 submitted by 20 state accountancy boards and one territorial board. Figures for 9 states show that 41 per cent of college graduates eventually pass compared with 32 per cent of nongraduates.

As in the other professions, legal regulation lags behind
actual practice. Of some 700 new members admitted to the
American Institute of Accountants between January 1, 1927,
and September 1, 1934, 34 per cent were college graduates;
of the 1,406 new members admitted to the New York Society
of Certified Public Accountants during approximately the
same period, 54 per cent were college graduates. At the time
they received their certificates, the average age of the new
members of the New York Society who were educated in the
United States (1,343 out of 1,406) was 31.6 years for the 588
high school graduates and 28.4 years for the 755 college graduates. The latter average is almost two years higher than the
average age, 26.5 years, of the 1937 graduates of medical
schools.[69]

An interesting feature of the training requirements, in comparison with those of the other professions considered, is the
extent to which apprenticeship is still the principal legally
recognized method for obtaining professional training. Even
the four states requiring formal training in a professional
school specify that a candidate have some experience before he
is granted the certificate—in two states, one year; in the other
two, three years. As in law, however, it is difficult to pass the
examination without some formal training, and consequently
most of the candidates take courses in professional schools,
many in part-time and evening schools.

In striking contrast to the medical and legal journals, the
accounting journals seldom contain articles or editorials on
'overcrowding'. Occasionally, current problems of unemploy-
ment and reduced income are mentioned, but they are almost
universally attributed to the general business situation, not
to any 'overcrowding' in the profession itself. Presumably this
reflects both the apparently rising secular trend in the demand
for certified public accountants and the intimate connection

[69] W. W. Nissley, 'Education for Professional Accountants', *Journal of Accountancy*, Jan. 1935, pp. 18–20; 'Medical Education in the United States and Canada',
Journal of the American Medical Association, Aug. 28, 1937.

between accountants and business enterprises which leads to a general recognition of the close integration of the economic fortunes of the accounting profession with the business cycle.

The absence of concerted effort to restrict entry on grounds of 'overcrowding' might conceivably be combined with, and explained by, the presence of highly successful restrictive measures. In fact, however, there seems to have been no deliberate restriction of entry. The very low proportion passing examinations for the certificate—about 15 per cent—is rather to be explained by the absence of high educational or training requirements for admission to the examination.

Interestingly enough, while there seems to be no deliberate restriction of entry, the institutional arrangements governing the certification of public accountants are so developing as to be peculiarly well adapted to restriction. In all except nine states—these nine states include, however, over half of all certified public accountants—the state examining boards use examinations prepared by a professional association, the American Institute of Accountants.[70] Moreover, in almost all states using the Institute examinations, the grading is done by Institute examiners who send to the state examining board class grades—A, B, C, and D—rather than numerical grades, thus making it difficult for the state boards to vary the passing grade. In the nine states not using the Institute examinations, the state board prepares and grades the examinations.

5 CONSULTING ENGINEERING

The demand for consulting engineers, like that for certified public accountants, arises in the main from the need for independent and impartial advice and review. The functions of this group have been described as follows:

70 The 9 states are Kentucky, Maryland, Michigan, New Jersey, New York, Ohio, Pennsylvania, Virginia, and Wisconsin. This information about the examination mechanism was furnished by the American Institute of Accountants, as were the estimates of the number of certified public accountants by states.

"The consulting engineers who can fairly and honestly use the term comprise those engineers in private practice who may confidently count upon retainers from public and private enterprises. . . . Their clients are the larger corporations who desire to consult an engineer upon some project in which their own engineering staff needs advice and guidance from an engineer probably more open-minded upon the subject under consideration than is the chief engineer of such enterprise.

Public authorities of municipalities and of state and federal governments seek professional advice in a similar manner. Oftentimes the consulting engineer with his own large staff is retained by public authorities for the complete design, execution and direction of large engineering enterprises. . . .

Another and important employment of consulting engineers by various clients is that of reporting upon existing properties, especially as to operating conditions, with recommendations in respect to new financial structures and more economical methods of operation." [71]

Other functions of consulting engineers include minor forms of expert service, such as serving on boards investigating or controlling existing or proposed projects and furnishing expert testimony in litigation.[72] As in law and certified public accountancy, firms are of considerable importance. Almost half of all consulting engineers are members of firms.[73]

Consulting engineering is the only one of the five professions that is not under state licensure. Presumably anybody, whether or not he has had formal training, can function as an engineer, if business or public enterprises entrust him with a job. In practice, however, the great majority of all engineers are graduates of engineering schools, involving a professional training period of four years and a general prerequisite of graduation from high school. Of 52,589 engineers supplying usable information to the U. S. Bureau of Labor Statistics in

[71] F. A. Molitor, 'Consulting Engineering', *Vocational Guidance in Engineering Lines* (American Association of Engineers, 1933), pp. 126–7.
[72] *Ibid.*, pp. 121–9.
[73] See Ch. 6.

reply to a questionnaire mailed in 1935, 79.6 per cent had received an engineering degree from a college or university, 2.5 per cent had a nonengineering degree, 10.8 per cent had some engineering training in college but had not completed the course, 5.1 per cent had received training in noncollegiate technical schools, and 1.8 per cent had only a secondary school education. Moreover, an analysis of the returns by year of graduation for graduates and by age for nongraduates indicated that the proportion of all engineers who are engineering graduates has increased considerably. "Of the engineers classified as 'recent' since they entered the profession after the 1930 census, 18,451, or 98.48 per cent, reported as being graduated between 1930 and 1934. Contrasted to this group, there are only 286 or 1.52 per cent 'other engineers', i.e., those who did not report graduation but were born within the period of 1910–15." [74]

The relatively few engineers who have attained a place in their profession that allows them to practise as private consultants presumably differ in many respects from their fellow engineers. Unfortunately, data are available only on age and experience. A study of the 1930 earnings of mechanical engineers yielded a median age of 35 years for the entire sample, but a median age of about 44 years for independent consultants.[75] In the Bureau of Labor Statistics study men-

---

[74] Andrew Fraser, Jr., 'Educational Qualifications in the Engineering Profession', *Monthly Labor Review*, June 1936, pp. 1528–42. The 52,589 usable returns represent 30.4 per cent of the 173,151 questionnaires sent out. In a later article on this survey ('Employment in the Engineering Profession, 1929 to 1934', *ibid.*, April 1937, p. 861) it is indicated that a larger proportion of recent graduates reported than of the older engineers. In view of the declining importance of nongraduates, the figures in the text above are presumably biased in favor of engineering graduates. We have made no attempt to adjust for the bias in the sample, since the broad conclusion would remain unchanged. The Bureau of Labor Statistics figures presented in the later articles on the survey, dealing with other aspects of the results, have been adjusted for this bias.

[75] *Mechanical Engineering*, Nov. 1931, p. 817, and Dec. 1931, p. 880. About 8,000 were included in the sample of whom approximately 300 were independent consultants.

tioned above, 4 per cent of the engineers professionally active prior to 1930, but only 0.3 per cent of those entering the profession in 1930–32, were independent consultants in 1934.[76]

CHAPTER 2

The Data on Income from Independent Professional Practice

THE FIVE PROFESSIONAL GROUPS we study include over 300,000 persons in independent practice; the primary data on which the analysis is based are for 13,000 persons in all and considerably fewer for any single year. What is true of the 13,000 need not be true of the 300,000. Whether we can pass with confidence from our samples to the universes they purport to represent depends on how the samples were selected, what biases they have, what corrections can be made for these biases, the internal consistency of the samples, their consilience with

[76] *Monthly Labor Review*, April 1937, p. 868. The sample on which these percentages are based included 31,252 'older engineers' and 9,469 engineers entering the profession between 1930 and 1932. Among the 7,403 in the sample who entered the profession in 1933 and 1934, 0.2 per cent were independent consultants in 1934.

An earlier study of engineering graduates, which covered every fifth class from 1889 to 1919, showed that in 1924, 2.7 per cent of the sample for the class of 1919, and 18.8 per cent of the combined classes of 1884 and 1889 were engaged in the consulting branch of the profession. The total sample included 2,336 graduates, of whom approximately 445 were in the class of 1919 and 95 in the classes of 1884 and 1889. *Study of Engineering Graduates and Non-Graduate Former Students* (Society for the Promotion of Engineering Education, 1926), p. 34.

other comparable studies, and the like. These questions are investigated in detail in Appendix A; the results are summarized in this chapter.

1 THE ORIGINAL DATA

The original data analyzed were collected by questionnaires sent to professional men by the U. S. Department of Commerce as part of a broad study of the size of the national income. In conformity with the needs of the larger study, data were collected only for professional men practising independently, and their analysis by the Department of Commerce was restricted in the main to the derivation of the countrywide average income of each profession.[1]

Table 4 lists the samples that we have used and summarizes the salient features of each. Four of the 11 samples were collected in 1933, 4 in 1935, and 3 in 1937. They provide data for physicians and certified public accountants for the entire period 1929–36; for dentists, for 1929–34; for lawyers, for 1929 and 1932–36; and for consulting engineers, for 1929–32. (The basic data from these samples are given in some detail in Appendix B.) As the last column of Table 4 indicates, the usable returns in each sample are a small fraction of the universe they purport to represent. For physicians, dentists, and lawyers the coverage is between 1 and 3 per cent; for consulting engineers, about 5.5 per cent; and for accountants, between 9 and 15 per cent.

The information obtained varies from profession to profession and from sample to sample for the same profession.[2] All

---

[1] This investigation was initiated in 1933 in cooperation with the National Bureau of Economic Research. The original study covered 1929–32 and was summarized in *National Income in the United States, 1929–32*, Senate Doc. 124 (Washington, 1934), pp. 148–50, 206–9, 245–58. Results for later years appeared in *National Income in the United States, 1929–35* (U. S. Department of Commerce, 1936), pp. 213–6, 226–7, 290–3, 300–1; and in Walter Slifer, 'Income of Independent Professional Practitioners', *Survey of Current Business*, April 1938, pp. 12–6. In addition to national averages, the first reference presents average incomes for each profession by states; the third, a brief summary analysis of the distribution of income by size.

[2] The questionnaire forms are shown in Appendix C.

TABLE 4

Methods of Selecting Samples and Coverage of Samples

SAMPLE & YEAR SENT (1)	YEARS FOR WHICH INCOME WAS OBTAINED (2)	LIST USED FOR SAMPLING (3)	METHOD OF SELECTING NAMES (4)	QUESTIONNAIRES SENT (5)	QUESTIONNAIRES RETURNED[1] Total (6)	Usable[2] (7)	Not usable (8)	% USABLE QUESTIONNAIRES ARE OF Total sent (9)	% USABLE QUESTIONNAIRES ARE OF Total Universe[3] (10)
Physicians									
1 (1933)	1929-32	Latest issue of annual Directory of the American Medical Association	Specified no. of names taken from each page by laying straight edge marked off at equally spaced intervals against a column. For samples 1 & 2 the no. taken from each page was the same for all pages; for sample 3 it varied from state to state.	8,893	2,882	2,438	444	27.4	2.0
2 (1935)	1932-34			8,000[4]	1,686	1,588	98	19.8	1.3
3 (1937)	1929-36			9,472	1,647	1,577	70	16.6	1.2
Dentists									
1 (1933)	1929-32	Membership list of the American Dental Association for year in which questionnaires were sent out	Details of method uncertain. Presumably every n-th addressograph plate. Same proportion of names for all states.	5,000[4]	1,609	1,499	110	30.0	2.5
2 (1935)	1932-34			5,000[4]	1,171	1,122	49	22.4	1.9
Lawyers[5]									
1 (1935)	1932-34	Latest issue of annual *Martindale-Hubbell Law Directory*	Same as for physicians. For sample 1 the no. taken from each page was the same for all pages; for sample 2 it varied from state to state.	6,000[4]	1,161	1,050	111	17.5[6]	1.1[7]
2 (1937)	1929, 1932-36			10,182	1,260	1,068	197	10.4[6]	0.9[7]

Certified public accountants [5]

1 (1933)	1929-32	5,000[4]	977	679	298	13.6[6] 11.3[7]
2 (1935)	1932-34	7,000[4]	1,255	1,062	193	15.2[6] 18.7[7]
3 (1937)	1929, 1934-36	7,809	853	752	101	9.6[6] 9.4[7]

Mailing list of the American Society of Certified Public Accountants for year in which questionnaires were sent out. List included both members & nonmembers.

Every 2d or 3d name. Proportion varied from sample to sample.

Consulting engineers [5]

1 (1933)	1929-32	3,286	804	415	389	12.6[6] 5.5[7]

Directories of American Institute of Electrical Engineers, American Institute of Mining & Metallurgical Engineers, American Society of Mechanical Engineers, American Society of Civil Engineers

American Engineering Council checked the names of individuals recognized as consultants. Every name checked was used.

[1] Excludes questionnaires returned by post offices as undeliverable.

[2] Includes all returns containing any usable information. The numbers in this column are therefore somewhat greater than the numbers on which most of the results in later chapters are based.

[3] The numbers in the universe on which these percentages are based were computed from estimates in Table 1 by straight line interpolation or extrapolation.

[4] Approximate; exact figure not known.

[5] Number of returns equals the number of persons practising individually plus the number of firms. The number of practitioners covered by the returns would be considerably larger, since firm members were requested to report for the entire firm.

[6] Questionnaires were sent to individuals, whereas replies were requested for firms, as units. More than one member of a firm may have been included among the individuals to whom questionnaires were sent, although only one return from the firm is presumably included among the usable returns. This would tend to lower these percentages artificially.

[7] For reasons mentioned in notes 5 and 6 it would be meaningless to express the number of usable returns as a percentage of the number of persons in the professions. Hence, these percentages were computed by expressing the number of persons covered by usable returns as a percentage of the total number of persons in the professions. This should give approximately the same result as expressing the number of usable returns as a percentage of the total number of professional units (i.e., firms plus individual practitioners).

questionnaires asked gross and net income for a period of years; most of them, the number and salaries of employees; those for the business professions—law, accountancy, and engineering—the number of partners in the firm; the questionnaire sent to physicians in 1937, the type of practice (general, specialized, special interest with general practice), and the number of years in practice; and the questionnaire sent to lawyers in 1937, detailed information on training and experience. Only the questionnaires sent in 1937 explicitly asked the name of the community in which the individual or firm practises; in the other samples the location of the practice was inferred from the postmark on the envelope in which the questionnaire was returned.

Almost no use is made in this study of the data on gross income. Net income, to which the analysis is mainly restricted, was defined on the questionnaires to include net income from independent practice alone; income from salaried employment, nonprofessional activities, property, or other sources was excluded. Net income from independent practice was defined as gross income less professional expenses, but no explicit instructions were given about the items to be included in professional expenses.

2 CORRECTION FOR BIAS

The process of obtaining a sample involves first, the designation of a list of names to serve as the basis for sampling; second, the choice of the persons on the list to whom questionnaires are to be sent; third, the return of the questionnaires by the respondents; and fourth, the editing of the returned questionnaires before final use. Biases may enter at each stage: the list may be defective, the method of choosing names may not yield a truly 'random' sample, those who reply may differ from those who fail to reply, the answers of those who reply may have a systematic bias, and the questionnaires rejected in the process of editing may differ systematically from those retained.

Examination of the methods used to obtain our samples and of the final samples themselves discloses that biases have entered at all stages. Some affect all samples, others do not; some can be eliminated by adjusting the data, others cannot.

a Biases affecting all samples

None of the biases affecting all samples seem substantial. The most important is probably the upward bias in the trend of income over time. The questionnaires requested information for a period of years from a sample of professional men chosen from a list presumed to be comprehensive for the end of the period. Such a sample might be entirely random for the end of the period, yet it would be biased for the earlier years since it would exclude those who had meanwhile left the profession. Moreover, a list that purports to be comprehensive for a given year seldom is: it tends to cover new entrants to the profession incompletely. The effect of these deficiencies in the lists depends on the income characteristics of the persons excluded. For the professions, the persons excluded in the earlier years appear to have an average income higher than the average for all persons, and new entrants excluded in the terminal year clearly have an average income lower than the average for all persons. Consequently, the incompleteness of the lists tends to impart a downward bias to the average incomes for the earlier years and an upward bias to both the average income for the latest year and the trend of income over the period. The earlier of two samples for the same profession would therefore tend to yield a higher average for an overlapping year— a tendency that is reflected in our data after correction is made for the specific biases discussed below. Of the ten differences summarized in Table 5, seven are in the expected direction. The only sizable differences in the opposite direction are for lawyers, for whom the 1937 sample, as we shall show below, is suspect on other grounds. Except for one of the comparisons for accountants, the positive differences are moderate, the largest being 13 per cent. And even the 35 per cent difference between the 1929 averages from the 1933 and 1937 accountancy samples is not disturbing since the bias in question should be larger the longer the time elapsing between the selection of the two samples, and between these dates and the date for which the comparison is made. We have not adjusted the data for this bias.

The inclusion of salaried employees in the lists from which the samples were chosen is a minor source of bias since it may mean that our final samples are not restricted exclusively to

TABLE 5

Arithmetic Mean Income in Years Covered by More than One Sample for the Same Profession

SAMPLES COMPARED	YEAR OF COMPARISON	ARITH. MEAN INCOME* FROM		DIFFERENCE	% BY WHICH AVG. FROM EARLIER SAMPLE EXCEEDS AVG. FROM LATER SAMPLE
		EARLIER SAMPLE	LATER SAMPLE		
		(dollars)			
Physicians					
1933 & 1935	1932	3,434	3,107	+327	+10.5
1933 & 1937	1932	3,434	3,165	+269	+8.5
1935 & 1937	1932	3,107	3,165	—58	—1.8
1935 & 1937	1934	3,296	3,276	+20	+0.6
Dentists					
1933 & 1935	1932	2,943	2,704	+239	+8.8
Lawyers					
1935 & 1937	1932	3,508	5,303	—1,795	—33.8
1935 & 1937	1934	3,248	4,567	—1,319	—28.9
Certified Public Accountants					
1933 & 1935	1932	4,777	4,218	+559	+13.3
1933 & 1937	1929	7,926	5,858	+2,068	+35.3
1935 & 1937	1934	4,274	3,984	+290	+7.3

* Arithmetic means are adjusted for specific biases, as described in Section 2b of this chapter.

professional men in independent practice. It is unlikely, however, that many salaried employees are included in the final samples. The questionnaires emphasized that information was desired solely from persons in independent practice; in addition, the many items on the questionnaires not applicable to salaried employees facilitated the identification of questionnaires inadvertently returned by them.

A third bias affecting all samples is more conjectural than the other two. Examination of the returns suggests that erroneous interpretations of the questions by the respondents may have resulted in a tendency to understate net income: some respondents seem to have interpreted 'net income' as 'net taxable income'; others seem to have deducted personal as well as professional expenses from gross income in arriving at net income. In general, the instructions on this point were more detailed and explicit in the later samples. The higher averages for the overlapping years yielded by the earlier samples thus suggest that this bias is considerably less important than the first bias discussed.

b Biases affecting specific samples
The biases in the samples and the devices used to correct them are listed below, profession by profession.

Medicine
1) Physicians in small communities are underrepresented in all samples. The samples were obtained by taking a specified number of names from each page of the Directory of the American Medical Association. Unfortunately, the total number of names on a directory page is somewhat greater for small communities than for large. Such variation obviously tends to introduce a bias into a sample obtained by taking the same number of names from each page: communities for which the total number of names per page is relatively large tend to be underrepresented. Tests indicate that the bias, while present, is small and its effect on the national averages slight. Consequently, no correction was made.

2) The 1937 sample is intentionally nonrandom among states: the number of names taken from each page of the directory was varied from state to state. To correct for the non-randomness of the sample, all averages and frequency distributions were computed for each state separately and combined by weighting by the estimated number of physicians in active practice in each state in 1936. (More exactly, each return has

been weighted by the ratio of the estimated total number of physicians in the state to the number in the sample for that state.) In the two earlier medical samples (1933 and 1935 samples), the same number of names was taken from each page for all states.

3) Specialists may be slightly overrepresented in all samples. The samples were chosen by laying a straight edge marked at equally spaced intervals along a column of names. More lines tend to be devoted to a specialist than to a general practitioner since the directory indicates his specialty and the professional societies to which he belongs. The chance that a mark on a straight edge will fall opposite an individual's name is clearly greater the more space devoted to him; hence a specialist is more likely to be included in the sample than a general practitioner. However, comparison of the proportion of specialists in the 1937 sample—the only sample for which this information is available—with the proportion indicated by other studies does not confirm the existence of this suspected bias. No correction was made.

Dentistry

1) Dentists with low incomes are underrepresented in both samples because the samples were restricted to members of the American Dental Association. Previous studies—one of incomes in 1929 and another of incomes in 1933—suggest that the average net income of American Dental Association members is approximately 30 per cent larger than that of nonmembers. Since approximately 46 per cent of all dentists were American Dental Association members when our samples were selected, a difference of 30 per cent between the incomes of members and nonmembers would imply that the average income of all dentists is 87.6 per cent of the average of members alone. In deriving the final estimates of the average incomes of dentists (Table 11) we use this percentage to correct for the bias arising from the exclusion of nonmembers. The average incomes obtained in this way are almost identical with the averages from a more recent and more comprehensive study

by the Department of Commerce. (Comparison is possible for two years; the difference is a trifle greater than 2 per cent in one year and 0.5 per cent in the other.) Except for the averages in Table 11, none of the data presented for dentists have been corrected for this bias. Consequently, the data for dentists in all other tables should be interpreted as referring solely to members of the American Dental Association.

Law

1) Lawyers in large communities are underrepresented in both samples because of variation in the number of names on a directory page. This bias is similar to the one described under point 1 for physicians but larger and in the opposite direction. In the legal directory the number of names per page varies from approximately 148 for cities over 1,500,000 in population to about 86 for cities under 100,000. The samples were corrected for the bias by computing averages and frequency distributions for each size of community class separately. The number of lawyers in the sample in each size of community class was then adjusted on the basis of the estimated number of names per page for communities of that size. These adjusted numbers were used as weights in combining the results for different size of community classes.

2) The 1937 sample, like the corresponding sample for physicians (see point 2 under physicians), is intentionally nonrandom among states. The averages and frequency distributions were therefore computed for each state separately and combined by weighting by the number of lawyers in each state listed in the *Martindale Hubbell Law Directory* for 1936. In the 1935 sample the same number of names was taken from each page for all states.

3) There is *a priori* reason to expect an overrepresentation of firm members in both samples. The list used for sampling was a list of lawyers, not of firms plus individual practitioners, but each lawyer to whom a questionnaire was sent was requested, if a member of a firm, to reply for the firm as a whole. By the procedure followed, a firm had a greater chance of

being included in the sample than an individual practising alone, since it was included if *any one* of its members was included. Tests indicated the presence of the firm member bias in the 1935 sample but not in the 1937 sample. The 1935 sample was adjusted to eliminate the firm member bias by computing averages and frequency distributions for firms of each size separately. The results for firms of different size were combined by weighting inversely to the expected overrepresentation. The 1937 sample was not adjusted. The failure of this sample to confirm expectation renders its results suspect.

4) Older and prominent lawyers may be overrepresented in both samples because the samples were selected by laying a straight edge marked at equally spaced intervals along a column of names. More space tends to be devoted to established and prominent lawyers (see point 3 for physicians). However, comparisons with studies of lawyers in Wisconsin and in New York County suggest that the bias is not very important since our samples yielded lower average incomes than the other studies. No correction was made for the suspected bias.

Certified public accountancy
1) An overrepresentation of firm members is to be expected for reasons discussed under point 3 for lawyers. All three samples seem to fulfill this expectation. Consequently, the type of adjustment used to correct the 1935 legal sample was applied to the three accountancy samples.

2) The more affluent accountants may be overrepresented in the 1937 accountancy sample. The questionnaire requested a recipient who was a salaried employee of an accounting firm to hand the questionnaire to his employer. Consequently, an accountant with salaried professional employees would be more likely to be included in the final sample than an accountant without such employees since the former might receive a questionnaire either directly or from one of his employees. However, the two bits of evidence that we have on this bias suggest that it is unimportant.

Consulting engineering
1) Consulting engineers with low incomes are probably greatly underrepresented because of deficiencies in the list used for sampling. The American Engineering Council selected the names of consulting engineers from the directories of four national engineering societies. The names selected totaled fewer than 3,500, yet apparently there were approximately 10,000 independent consulting engineers in 1930 (Table 1). The list clearly excludes consultants not members of engineering societies. In addition, it excludes engineers who may have been consultants but whose status was not known by the American Engineering Council. Both deficiencies operate in the same direction: that is, to exclude the less prominent and less well-known engineers, who might be expected to have relatively low incomes. No correction for this bias was possible.

3 TESTS OF THE RELIABILITY OF THE CORRECTED DATA
Examination of the methods used to obtain a sample is an indispensable step in evaluating the reliability of the sample. Alone, however, it cannot be conclusive. Even though no biases are discovered, or correction is made for any biases that are discovered, the sample may still yield inaccurate or biased results. Examination of the methods must be supplemented by objective tests of the reliability of the data. We have applied three types of objective tests to our data: (1) comparison of the distribution of each sample by geographic units with the estimated distribution of all practitioners, (2) comparison of the different samples for the same profession with one another, (3) comparison of our samples with other studies.

The major general conclusion that emerges from these tests is the great difference in the presumptive reliability of our data on the *number* and *proportion* of practitioners in various geographic units and our data on *income*: we have good reason to suspect the former, but we also have good reason for confidence in the latter.

Every test of the geographic distributions of our samples impugns their reliability: the proportion of the questionnaires sent out that were returned differs significantly from state to state; the distributions of our samples by states or by regions and size of community classes differ significantly from the estimated distributions of all practitioners; successive samples for the same profession differ significantly from one another though less than each differs from the universe it is supposed to represent. There are several possible explanations of these discrepancies other than the unreliability of our data: inadequacies in the lists from which the samples were chosen that affect the tests but not the samples themselves; errors in the estimated distributions of all practitioners; differences among the universes the successive samples are supposed to represent; etc. But it is not possible to establish satisfactorily that these explanations tell the whole story. Whatever their causes, the discrepancies revealed by the tests mean that no great confidence can be placed in our data on the number and proportion of professional men in various states, regions, or size of community classes.

The presumptive unreliability of the geographic distributions of our samples is in itself not serious, since we have little interest in using our samples to study the geographic distribution of professional men. But it inevitably arouses suspicion about the reliability of the income data, since biases in the geographic distributions of the samples might be expected to be associated with income. None of our tests confirm this expectation: the ratio between the number of practitioners in a state who replied and the number to whom the questionnaires were sent is uncorrelated with the average income of those who replied; the ratio between the number of practitioners who replied and the estimated total number of practitioners is uncorrelated with the average income of those who replied whether the correlation is computed from data for states or for regions and size of community classes; the ratio for a state between the number of returns in one sample and the number in another for the same profession is un-correlated with the difference between the average incomes for the same year from the two samples.

The apparent absence of any relation between average income and the biases in the geographic distribution of our samples leads to two inferences about the reliability of our data on income. First, it suggests that income figures for groups of states will not be contaminated by the nonrandomness of the geographic distributions; such figures will of course be subject to random errors but not, on this score at least, to bias. Second, it suggests that an individual's willingness to reply is not closely related to his income. If such a relationship existed, the considerable geographic differences in income would tend to give rise to biases in geographic distributions that would be correlated with income. We cannot, of course, regard it as conclusively established that the incomes of those who reply do not differ widely from the incomes of those who fail to reply, since differences that were not the same for all parts of the country might not be revealed by our tests, and since the differences might affect aspects of the frequency distribution of income other than the average. Unfortunately, other studies add little to our knowledge. The results of the few relevant studies are inconsistent, and each is tinged with special circumstances that make generalization hazardous. If they reveal any tendency, it is toward somewhat greater reluctance to reply on the part of the lower income groups; but this tendency is exceedingly uncertain.

Further evidence on the reliability of the income data is furnished by the average incomes from different samples for the same profession. As noted above, most of the differences between the national averages for the overlapping years are moderate in size and in the expected direction (see Table 5). The differences between the state averages for the overlapping years that do not reflect the general bias arising from the time elapsing between the selection of the samples seem entirely attributable to random factors.

TABLE 6

Summary of Comparisons between the Department of Commerce and Other Samples

Physicians, Dentists, Lawyers, and Consulting Engineers

SAMPLES WITH WHICH COMPARISON IS MADE	D. OF C. SAMPLES	GEOGRAPHIC UNIT	YEARS OF COMPARISON	BRIEF SUMMARY OF RESULTS
Physicians				
Committee on the Costs of Medical Care and American Medical Association	1933, 1937	Primarily country as a whole, also regional and size of community groups	1929	Checked rather closely in practically all respects. If anything, avg. from 1933 D. of C. sample trifle higher.
California Medical-Economic Survey	1933, 1935, 1937	California	1929-34	Avg. net incomes from 1935 sample significantly below C.M.E.S. avg. Other comparisons very satisfactory.
Wisconsin State Medical Association	1933, 1937	Wisconsin	1930	Close agreement.
Michigan State Medical Society	1933, 1937	Michigan	1929, 1931	Close agreement.
Utah State Medical Association	1933, 1935, 1937	Utah	1929-31, 1933	Avg. incomes from 1933 sample significantly below Utah avg. Other samples agree closely.
Dentists				
Committee on Costs of Medical Care	1933	20 states	1929	Differences among results are of kind to be expected from restriction of D. of C. sample to members. Corrected avg. reasonably close, with D. of C. avg. lower.
California Medical-Economic Survey	1933, 1935	California	1929-34	Close agreement after correction for restriction of D. of C. sample to members.
University Relations Committee	1935	Minnesota	1933-34	Close agreement after correction for restriction of D. of C. sample to members.
Lawyers				
L. K. Garrison	1935, 1937	Wisconsin	1932	1935 sample agrees closely; 1937 sample yields very much lower avg. than Garrison's though difference is within range of sampling variation.

TABLE 6 (cont.)

SAMPLES WITH WHICH COMPARISON IS MADE	D. OF C. SAMPLES	GEOGRAPHIC UNIT	YEARS OF COMPARISON	BRIEF SUMMARY OF RESULTS
		Lawyers (cont.)		
New York County Lawyers Association	1935, 1937	New York City	1933	1937 sample agrees very well; 1935 sample yields much lower avg. than Association's though difference is within range of sampling variation.
		Consulting Engineers		
BLS	1933	United States	1929, 1932	Poor agreement; BLS measures lower for 1929, as might be expected from known bias in D. of C. sample, but higher for 1932.

The comparisons, summarized in Table 6, between our samples and other studies suggest that our failure to find substantial biases in the income figures is attributable to their absence. On the whole, our samples, after allowance is made for specific biases, agree very well with the other studies. This agreement extends not only to average incomes but also to quartile measures, standard deviations, and the distribution of income by size. The few differences do not indicate persistent or uniform biases. For example, our 1933 medical sample yields average incomes for 1929 that seem a trifle high compared with the 1929 study of the Committee on Costs of Medical Care; yet the same sample yields average incomes for Utah that are decidedly too low compared with the special Utah study. Compared with the results of the California Medical-Economic Survey, the averages for California from the 1933 medical sample seem entirely satisfactory, but the averages from the 1935 medical sample seem too low. Comparison with the Utah sample seems to warrant exactly the opposite conclusion: the 1935 sample is satisfactory, but the averages from the 1933 sample are low.

Admittedly, these comparisons are fragmentary and, alone, inconclusive. While most of the other studies are based on much larger samples, they are subject to error and bias; in addition, sampling fluctuations are so great, especially when comparisons are made for individual states, that they may have concealed real differences. At the same time, in conjunction with other parts of our analysis, the comparisons give important confirmatory evidence of the general reliability of our data on income.

CHAPTER 3

Incomes in the Professions and in Other Pursuits

THE INCOMES that individuals receive from professional practice fluctuate widely from year to year, and the differences among individuals in any one year are even more striking. Of the 1,500 physicians in our 1935 sample, 3 had incomes above $40,000 in 1934, and 261 had incomes below $500—25 of them suffering losses. Of the 1,100 dentists, 4 had incomes above $16,000 in 1934, and 6 suffered losses. This wide variability of income characterizes not only professions but also other pursuits. Frequency distributions of income by size are very similar for the different professions, and are well illustrated by the sample distribution in Chart 1. Considerable skewness, wide variability, and great peakedness—these are the hallmarks of distributions of income from independent professional practice.

1 THE PLAN OF THE STUDY

General observation and previous studies suggest numerous factors responsible for variability of income. We know that the income a professional man receives in a year depends on the state of the nation's business, the profession and type of practice he engages in, the organization and location of his practice, the number of years he has been in practice, his

CHART 1

Frequency Histogram of Net Incomes of Dentists, 1934

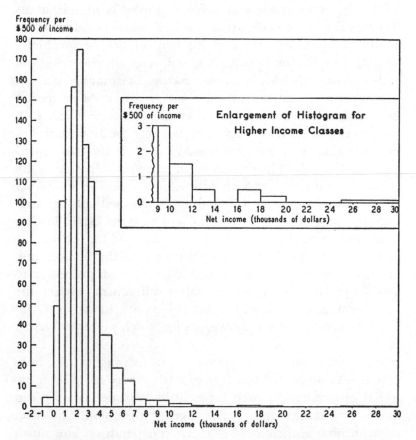

training, ability, personality, reputation, character, and general good fortune. But it is not enough merely to name factors making for variability of income. To be useful, the catalog must be quantitative as well as qualitative; the importance of the different factors and the direction and magnitude of their influence must be measured. For many of the factors listed, even measurement is little more than taxonomy. If we find that a New York physician tends to earn more than a lawyer in Tulsa, Oklahoma, we have progressed only a short way. Why does this difference exist? Why has the ceaseless attempt of countless individuals to better their economic status not eradicated it?

The first step in the search for improved economic status is the choice of an occupation. An individual decides—or his family or conditions beyond his control decide for him— whether to train for a profession, and, if so, which profession. This choice, in which economic factors presumably play an important role, is not irrevocable but to give up a profession for which one has been trained entails heavy sacrifice. As a rule, the original choice more or less sets the boundaries of the individual's future strivings. What effect the choice will have on the income he can count on receiving depends on the character of the market for his chosen profession—the number of competitors and the circumstances that will induce new ones to enter the profession and old ones to leave, institutional factors governing entry, and the demand for the services of men in the profession. The character of the market and, in consequence, the incomes received, vary from profession to profession. In this chapter we analyze differences between the professions as a whole and all other pursuits; in the next, differences among the five professions for which we have detailed data.

The second step is to decide where to practise. An individual may be completely free to settle where he will, or external circumstances may leave little latitude. But he can move more easily than he can change his profession. The effect upon income of the choice of location depends on how much mobility there is, the nonpecuniary advantages and disadvantages attached to the location chosen, the economic fortunes of the selected community, and the like. The relation of location to income is considered in Chapter 5.

Having completed his training and decided where to practise, an individual is embarked on his professional career. In its course, he may become a salaried employee or practise independently, specialize or engage in general practice, become a member of a firm or practise alone. He will surely accumulate experience and acquire a reputation—good, bad, or indifferent. His training, innate skill and ability, personality, social connections, and the like will all contribute to shaping his career and determining his income. Some of these determinants of professional status are considered in Chapter 6, but the paucity of data severely limits the number of which account can be taken.

A professional man's income seldom remains the same from one year to the next. His relative status in the profession changes as his professional career gradually unfolds and as random events impinge upon him. In addition, the ups and downs in the economic fortunes of the economy leave their mark on the incomes of professional men. The stability of professional status over time is considered in Chapter 7; changes in the economic fortunes of the professional groups, in Chapter 8. This, in general, is the plan of the present study.

Throughout, we shall be interested in the income distribution as a whole. For want, however, of any simple method of describing it compactly yet completely, we concentrate on the two most important aspects of the distribution—the level of income, and the variability of income about the level.

As a measure of the level of income we use principally the arithmetic mean and occasionally the median—the value that divides into two equal groups an array of persons by size of income. Some of the reasons for our choice of the arithmetic mean, other than its statistical convenience, center about its peculiar relevance to one aspect of the choice of profession by prospective practitioners (see Ch. 4). In addition, the arithmetic mean is, by definition, the income each person would receive if the total income of the professional group were divided equally; it is therefore a convenient base for studying inequality in the distribution of income. It should be borne in mind that the same arithmetic mean can be obtained from different distributions of income. But this is true of any summary measure and is, of course, the reason an analysis of other characteristics of the frequency distribution is essential.

As measures of absolute variability, i.e., variability measured in dollars, we use the interquartile difference and the standard deviation. As measures of relative variability, i.e., variability measured in percentages of the level of income, we use the interquartile difference divided by the median, the ratio of the third quartile to the first quartile, the coefficient of variation, and the Lorenz curve.[1] We use several measures because of the difficulty of attaching a precise and exact meaning to the concepts 'variability' and 'inequality'.[2] Reliance on a single measure might well lead to erroneous conclusions.

[1] The interquartile difference is the absolute difference between the third and the first quartile. The third quartile is the lowest income of the 25 per cent having the highest incomes; the first quartile, the lowest income of the 75 per cent having the highest incomes; the median is the lowest income of the 50 per cent having the highest incomes. In obtaining the standard deviation, each observation is expressed as a deviation from the arithmetic mean; these deviations are then squared and their sum divided by the number of observations; the square root of the resultant quotient is the standard deviation. The coefficient of variation is the ratio of the standard deviation to the mean. The Lorenz curve is explained below. The other measures are self-explanatory.

[2] See especially D. B. Yntema, 'Measures of the Inequality in the Personal Distribution of Wealth or Income', *Journal of the American Statistical Association*, Dec. 1933, pp. 423–33. This article summarizes material included in an unpublished University of Michigan doctoral thesis entitled *Measurement of Inequality in the Personal Distribution of Wealth or Income*.

The previously noted similarity in the general shape of income distributions suggests that a single simple mathematical formula might adequately represent all. The availability of such a formula would make it unnecessary to limit analysis to selected aspects of the distributions since the computed formulae would describe them compactly and completely. This procedure is not, however, practicable. Despite the great similarity among income distributions, none of the many attempts to discover a formula that describes them adequately has yet met with success.

The most celebrated is the attempt by Vilfredo Pareto, who suggested the curve that bears his name and less widely known variations of it. The Pareto curve gives a reasonably good fit solely for the higher income groups, and its adequacy even for these has been seriously disputed. Moreover, it cannot cope with negative incomes. F. R. Macaulay, who has made an exhaustive investigation of its validity, concludes not only that "Pareto's Law is quite inadequate as a mathematical generalization" but also that "it seems unlikely that any

2 STATISTICAL EVIDENCE ON DIFFERENCES IN INCOME

a Level of income
The data on the level of income in the professions and in other pursuits summarized in Tables 7 and 8, though not entirely satisfactory for our purposes, leave no doubt that incomes are considerably higher in the professions than in other pursuits as a whole, whether the comparison is made for independent professional men alone or for independent and salaried professional men. Table 7 presents estimates of the average income from employment of all gainfully occupied workers and of the average income in three of the five professions covered by our detailed data. The average income of dentists, though less than that of any of the other four professional groups, is more than three times the average for all pursuits. The average income from independent practice in the five professions

---

useful mathematical law describing the entire distribution can ever be formulated". See Wesley C. Mitchell, W. I. King, F. R. Macaulay, O. W. Knauth, *Income in the United States* (National Bureau of Economic Research, 1922), II, 393. H. T. Davis has recently suggested a formula that may be considered a generalization of Pareto's; but it seems no more applicable to distributions including negative incomes and so far as we know, no exhaustive test of its empirical validity has been made. See 'The Significance of the Curve of Income', *Report of the Fourth Annual Research Conference on Economics and Statistics* (Cowles Commission for Research in Economics, 1938), pp. 119–22.

The logarithmic normal curve is perhaps the closest approximation to the desired formula yet discovered, since it often fits the data rather well. However, it occasionally gives a poor fit; the small deviations from it when it does fit reasonably well do not seem randomly distributed; and it also is unable to represent negative incomes. A slight modification of the logarithmic normal curve suggested by R. Gibrat, *Les Inégalités Economiques* (Paris, 1931), makes it possible to include negative incomes, but only at the expense of obtaining poorer fits to the data. Gibrat suggests that the logarithm of the differences between the actual observations and an origin not necessarily zero will be normally distributed. The use of a negative origin would make it possible to include negative incomes. In actually fitting the curve, however, Gibrat ordinarily obtains the best fit by using a positive origin, thus increasing the difficulty. An additional weakness of Gibrat's formula is that there is as yet no analytical method for fitting it—Gibrat himself uses a graphical method—and hence no accurate technique for testing statistically the adequacy of the fit.

combined is probably four times the average earnings in all other pursuits.

Table 8 presents estimates for salaried professional workers as well as for independent practitioners, and for subgroups of the other pursuits. The professional groups are comprehensive; they include not only the five professions our sample data cover but also all other professions.[3] These estimates confirm the conclusion inferred from Table 7 about the difference be-

TABLE 7

Average Earnings

Certified Public Accountants, Physicians, Dentists, and All Gainfully Occupied Persons

	ARITHMETIC MEAN	
	1929–34	*1929–36*
	(dollars)	
Income from independent professional practice		
Certified public accountants	5,311	5,180
Physicians	4,081	4,031
Dentists	3,081	
Employee compensation plus entrepreneurial withdrawals per gainfully occupied person	991	976

Professions, Table 11; estimates of employee compensation plus entrepreneurial withdrawals by Simon Kuznets, *National Income and Its Composition, 1919–1938* (National Bureau of Economic Research, 1941), Table 68; number of gainfully occupied persons in the United States by Daniel Carson, *Labor Supply and Employment* (National Research Project, mimeo., Nov. 1939).

tween the incomes of independent professional men and all other workers: the arithmetic mean income of independent professional families is approximately four times that of all other families combined. Salaried professional families had a decidedly smaller mean income than independent professional families but a larger one than any other group except salaried business families. The professional group as a whole

[3] The estimates are for the 12 months from July 1935 through June 1936, were prepared by the National Resources Committee, and are based on data obtained from approximately 300,000 families through personal interviews and from federal income tax returns. *Consumer Incomes in the United States* (National Resources Committee, 1938).

had an average income some 30 per cent larger than that of the closest comparable group, business families, and 140 per cent larger than that of all other families combined. The medians, though somewhat closer together, tell essentially the same story as the arithmetic means.

TABLE 8

Average Income of Nonrelief Families in Seven Occupational Groups

National Resources Committee Estimates, 1935–1936

| OCCUPATIONAL GROUP [1] | NO. OF FAMILIES | INCOME PER FAMILY | |
		Arith. mean	Median
		(dollars)	
Farming [2]	6,166,600	1,259	965
Wage earning	9,459,300	1,289	1,175
Clerical	3,626,200	1,901	1,710
Business			
All	3,485,300	3,079	
Salaried	1,112,600	4,212	2,485
Independent	2,372,700	2,547	1,515
Professional			
All	1,330,100	4,022	
Salaried	989,200	3,087	2,100
Independent	340,900	6,734	3,540
Total, excl. professional	22,737,400	1,653	
Total	24,067,500	1,784	

Consumer Incomes in the United States (National Resources Committee, 1938), Table 9. Excludes all families receiving direct or work relief (however little) at any time during the year. Estimates relate approximately to the 12 months, July 1935 through June 1936.

[1] Families are classified according to the major source of family earnings.
[2] Includes all families living on farms in rural areas. Excludes village and city families with major earnings from farming.

Strictly speaking, these differences in family income bear only indirectly on the differences in individual earnings with which we are primarily concerned. (1) Family income, as defined by the National Resources Committee, includes not only earnings but also income from property and other sources; it includes the income not only of the principal earner but also of all other persons in the family. The omission of income from sources other than earnings would probably narrow the differential between professional and other families since income from property is likely to constitute a larger proportion of the total income of professional than of other families. Omission of the earnings of supplementary earners would probably have the opposite effect, since supplementary earners are likely to be more common among nonprofessional families (except salaried business families). It seems unlikely, however, that the omission of these types of income would substantially alter the differentials between professional and other families.[4] (2) The estimates in Table 8 are for families who did not receive relief at any time during the year covered. The exclusion of relief families has the advantage from our point of view of diminishing the importance of sources of income other than earnings. On the other hand, many of the excluded families received only a small part of their total income from relief; and a sizable part of relief payments were in the form of work relief, which it might be desirable to include. The inclusion of families receiving relief would affect the professional group less than most of the other groups and hence would widen the differentials. (3) The estimates are for families of two or more; single individuals are excluded. The effect that the inclusion of single individuals would have on the income differentials depends in large part on how the professional group is defined. If trained nurses were considered professional workers, the differentials might well be narrowed since private nurses, predominantly single individuals, would constitute about a sixth of all independent professional workers and probably receive considerably smaller incomes than

4 This statement is based on an examination of the figures from the Study of Consumer Purchases—the major source on which the National Resources Committee estimates are based—for separate communities. Although data on individual earnings were obtained in the Study of Consumer Purchases, national estimates similar to those in Table 8 have not been prepared. See bulletins of U. S. Bureau of Labor·Statistics and U. S. Bureau of Home Economics summarizing the results of the Study of Consumer Purchases.

most other professional workers. On the other hand, if trained nurses were not considered professional workers, the inclusion of single individuals would almost certainly widen the differentials, since professional workers so defined tend to be older than other workers and hence are more likely to be married; and single individuals probably receive lower average incomes than older married persons. (4) Since the family is the income unit, the family as a whole must be classified by occupation. This was done by assigning each family to the occupational group from which the largest amount of family earnings was derived. Consequently, some professional workers are included in families classified in other occupational groups because other family members (or the same individual) received larger earnings from the other occupation. Conversely, professional families include some gainfully occupied workers who are not professional workers. It is doubtful, however, that much heterogeneity arises from this source.

This listing of the deficiencies of the National Resources Committee estimates for our purpose does not tell us their combined effect on income differentials: some tend to narrow the differentials, others to widen them. However, the differentials are sufficiently large to lead us to believe that removal of the deficiencies would not seriously alter our conclusion that independent professional men receive average earnings 250 to 350 per cent larger than the average earnings of all other workers, and that the professional group as a whole—including both independent and salaried professional men—receives average earnings 100 to 200 per cent larger than the average earnings of all other workers.

b Variability of annual income
Data on variability of income in the professions and other pursuits are even less adequate than data on income level. Major reliance must be placed on one of the sources used in the preceding section—the distributions of income for 1935–36 prepared by the National Resources Committee and presented

CHART 2

National Resources Committee Distributions of Income, 1935–1936 Nonrelief Families in Five Occupational Groups

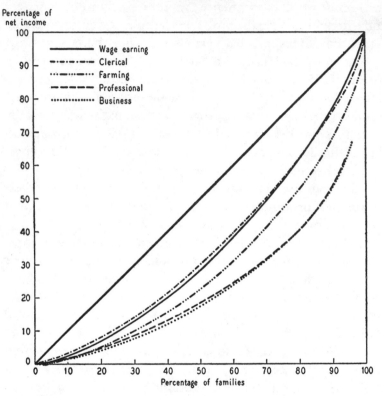

in the form of Lorenz curves in Charts 2 and 3.[5] According to Chart 2, professional families display about the same relative variability of income as business families but greater variabil-

[5] The Lorenz curve is a useful device for depicting graphically the degree of relative variability or inequality of income. Along the horizontal axis is measured the percentage of individuals, arrayed in order of the size of their incomes (from small to large). Along the vertical axis is measured the percentage of the total income received. The various points on a Lorenz curve indicate the proportion of the total income received by the 1 per cent, 2 per cent, etc., of individuals with the lowest incomes. If each individual received the same income, the percentage of income would be the same as the percentage of individuals, and the Lorenz curve would be a straight line. The straight diago-

CHART 3

National Resources Committee Distributions of Income, 1935–1936
Nonrelief Business and Professional Families

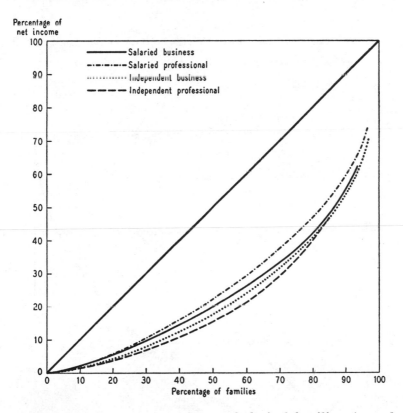

ity than farming, wage earning, and clerical families. According to Chart 3, which presents incomplete Lorenz curves for

nal lines in these charts are therefore designated the line of equal distribution.
The greater the divergence between the observed Lorenz curve and the line
of equal distribution the greater the inequality of income. M. O. Lorenz,
'Methods of Measuring the Concentration of Wealth', *Quarterly Publications
of the American Statistical Association*, June 1905, pp. 209–19. The Lorenz
curves were computed from the distributions in *Consumer Incomes in the
United States*, pp. 26 and 97, supplemented by unpublished subdivisions of
the highest class intervals made available by Hildegarde Kneeland, supervisor
of the study.

subdivisions of the business and professional groups, relative
variability of income is greater for the independent than for
the salaried groups. For the income classes for which data are
available, independent professional families display greater

CHART 4

National Resources Committee Distributions of Income, 1935–1936

All Nonrelief Families, All Families, and All Families and

Single Individuals

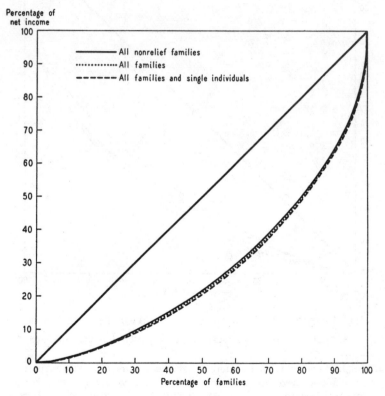

variability than families of independent businessmen. However, it appears from the chart that, for the income classes for
which data are not available, independent professional families may display less variability than the independent and
salaried business families and possibly even the salaried pro-

fessional families, i.e., it appears that the missing segment of the Lorenz curve may intersect the Lorenz curves for the other groups.

These differences in the variability of family income cannot be interpreted as necessarily reflecting corresponding differences in the variability of individual earnings. From this point of view, the National Resources Committee distributions of income are subject to the deficiencies listed in the preceding section in discussing the estimates of average income: they are for nonrelief families of two or more, for family income from all sources, and for groups classified by 'family occupation'.

Some indication of the effect of excluding relief families and single individuals is given by Chart 4 which presents Lorenz curves based on the National Resources Committee distributions for (1) all nonrelief families of two or more, (2) all families of two or more, relief and nonrelief, (3) all families and single individuals. The curve for nonrelief families shows somewhat less variability than the curve for all families, and the latter than the curve for families and single individuals. However, the differences are exceedingly small. The negligible effect that the inclusion of single individuals and families receiving relief would have on the Lorenz curve for all occupational groups combined does not, by itself, justify the assumption that their inclusion would alter equally little the Lorenz curves for the separate occupational groups. But, together with several other considerations, it does establish a presumption that the relation among the Lorenz curves would not be significantly altered.[6]

The fact that the National Resources Committee distribu-

[6] These considerations are: (1) The differences among the five Lorenz curves in Chart 2, or even among the four in Chart 3, are very much greater than among the three curves in Chart 4. To alter significantly the relations among the occupational groups, inclusion of relief families and single individuals would have to change the Lorenz curve for a specific occupational group by many times the amount it changes the curve for all occupational groups combined— an unlikely result. (2) Both single individuals and relief families probably constitute a greater proportion of the wage earning and clerical groups than of the business and professional groups, since earners in the latter not only

tions are for family income from all sources is more trouble-some than the exclusion of relief families and single individuals. Some indication of the possible difference between a distribution of total family income and a distribution of earnings is given by the two Lorenz curves in Chart 5. The one for 1935–36 incomes of nonrelief independent professional families has already been presented in Chart 3. The other is based on a distribution of 1933 income from independent professional practice obtained by combining the distributions for physicians, dentists, lawyers, and certified public accountants from our 1935 samples. (These are plotted separately in Lorenz curve form in Chart 10.) [7]

The difference between the two Lorenz curves, though fairly large, is not unreasonable. The Lorenz curve for families is at first above but thereafter considerably below the Lorenz curve for individuals, i.e., the families who fare worst tend to have incomes closer to the average for the group as a whole than the individuals who fare worst, but the families who fare best

receive higher incomes but also tend to be older. (As noted in the preceding section, this statement would have to be qualified if private nurses were considered independent professional workers.) And these are the groups whose Lorenz curves differ most from the Lorenz curve for the professional families. (3) Finally, since all Lorenz curves would presumably be altered in the same direction, only differential effects could change their relative position.

[7] The sample distributions of income were expressed in percentage form, multiplied by the total number of independent practitioners in each profession in 1930 as estimated in Table 1, and summed, income class by income class. The total income in each income class was estimated separately for each profession and then summed, income class by income class.

The National Resources Committee distribution includes all professions; that based on our data includes only physicians, dentists, lawyers, and certified public accountants. According to Table 1, there were approximately 300,000 independent practitioners in these four professions in 1930. The total number of independent professional practitioners in 1930 may be estimated as slightly less than 600,000, of whom over 100,000 were private nurses (based on figures used in Simon Kuznets' estimates of national income). The National Resources Committee sets the total number of nonrelief independent professional families of two or more in 1935–36 at 340,900 (*Consumer Incomes in the United States*, p. 26). These four professions therefore include at least half of all independent professional practitioners, and probably an even larger proportion of the independent professional practitioners who are members of families of two or more.

CHART 5

National Resources Committee Distribution of Income for Nonrelief Independent Professional Families, 1935 – 1936, and Distribution of Income from Independent Practice for Four Professions Combined, 1933

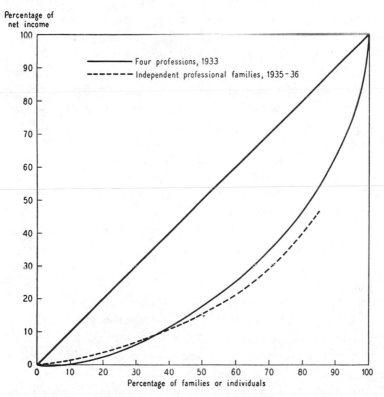

tend to have incomes further above the average for the group than the individuals who fare best. Presumably, both the lowest and the highest professional incomes tend to be received by individuals who are members of families with other sources of income. At one extreme, a low professional income may represent returns from an independent practice that is merely a part-time activity or that is conducted by a supplementary earner; at the other extreme, a high professional income may have made possible additional income from property, or conversely, the status implied by large income from other sources may have made possible the high professional income.[8]

A distribution of individual earnings might be expected to differ from a distribution of family income in the same way, but not necessarily to the same extent, for other occupational groups as for independent professional workers. The difference would probably be less for wage earning and clerical workers than for business and professional workers since the former presumably receive less of their income from sources other than earnings. If this presumption is correct, converting the distributions of family income in Chart 2 into distributions of individual earnings would lessen the divergence between (a) the wage earning and clerical groups, and (b) the business and professional groups; however, the divergence between the distributions of family income for the two sets of occupations is so large compared to the divergence between the two curves in Chart 5 that it would almost certainly not be eliminated entirely. What effect the conversion would have on the relations among the Lorenz curves in Chart 3 for the four business and professional groups is much less clear. We have little basis for judging which groups are most dependent on income from sources other than the earnings of the principal earner, and the differences among the Lorenz curves for the four groups are of about the same order of magnitude as the differences between the two curves in Chart 5, so that the possibility that the conversion would alter the relations among them cannot be ruled out.

One final bit of evidence on the difference between the variability of income from independent professional practice

[8] An analogous result was obtained in the Australian Census of Wealth and Income for 1915. The average wealth of individuals was found to be higher for the two lowest income classes than for the intermediate income classes. Thereafter the average wealth increased steadily with income. The explanation given was that the intermediate income classes derived their income predominantly from earnings. See G. H. Knibbs, *Private Wealth of Australia and its Growth* (Commonwealth of Australia, Commonwealth Bureau of Census and Statistics, 1918), pp. 30, 31, 49.

CHART 6

Distribution of Income for All Individuals in the United States, 1918, and Distribution of Income from Independent Practice for Four Professions Combined, 1933

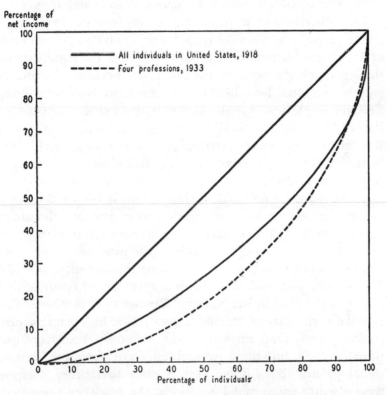

and from other pursuits is presented in Chart 6 which compares the 1933 distribution of professional income of physicians, dentists, lawyers, and certified public accountants (repeated from Chart 5) with the 1918 distribution of total income of all individual income recipients prepared by the National Bureau of Economic Research.[9] For our purpose, the National Bureau distribution has one advantage over the National Resources Committee distribution for families and

[9] Mitchell, King, Macaulay, and Knauth, *Income in the United States,* I, 134.

single individuals: it is based on individual rather than family income. This advantage is, however, more than counterbalanced by the fact that it is for 1918. The Lorenz curves for our professions change little from year to year; but this hardly justifies the assumption that the distribution of the income of all individuals changed little between 1918 and 1933.

The distribution of professional income displays much greater variability than the 1918 distribution throughout most of the range. Indeed, the difference between the two distributions is much greater than the difference between the former and the National Resources Committee distribution for families and single individuals. Whether the explanation is that the National Bureau distribution is for 1918 and the National Resources Committee distribution for 1935–36, or that the National Bureau distribution is for individual income, it is impossible to say.

The evidence presented in this section is both too meagre and subject to too many qualifications to justify a definitive conclusion about the relative variability of earnings from professional practice and from other pursuits. We have been forced to work with concepts of income that are inappropriate for this purpose, and with the extremely broad occupational classification used by the National Resources Committee. The relative variability of income is greater for independent professional men than for any of the other six broad occupational groups, but there undoubtedly are narrower occupational groups that display even greater variability. Despite these qualifications and limitations, the evidence presented, while certainly insufficient to demonstrate that the incomes of independent professional men are more variable than those of any other occupational group, does seem to warrant the conclusion that earnings from independent professional practice display greater relative variability than earnings from all pursuits combined and probably than earnings from most other pursuits taken separately. A similar but more equivocal conclusion is probably justified about the earnings of all professional workers, salaried and independent.

3 FACTORS MAKING FOR DIFFERENCES IN INCOME

It is clear from the evidence of the preceding section that the 3 million persons engaged in professional work are on the whole a fortunate group. Their earnings, though less equally distributed than those of nonprofessional workers, are between two and three times as large.

In small part this difference between the countrywide averages is illusory, reflecting differences in the location and age of the two groups of workers. Professional workers tend to be concentrated in the larger communities in which average incomes are relatively high. According to the National Resources Committee estimates for nonrelief families, over 40 per cent of professional families, but less than 30 per cent of other families, live in cities with populations over 100,000. Nonrelief families living in cities of this size received an average income in 1935–36 that was 56 per cent larger than that of nonrelief families living in small communities.[10] A rough estimate suggests that if other workers were distributed by size of community as professional workers are, their average income would be raised slightly less than 7 per cent.[11] Hence, professional workers apparently receive an average income be-

---

10 *Consumer Incomes in the United States,* pp. 23, 103.

11 This estimate is based on the National Resources Committee estimates of the average incomes of nonrelief families in six types of communities—communities with populations of 1,500,000 and over, 100,000–1,500,000, 25,000–100,000, 2,500–25,000, rural nonfarm communities, and farms. For the present purpose we combined the last two groups. The average incomes for the five groups were then weighted, first, by the percentage distribution of nonprofessional families, second, by the percentage distribution of professional families. The first set of weights yielded an average of $1,774; the second, of $1,891, or 6.6 per cent larger. The procedure is rough because the averages used relate solely to nonrelief families, to families rather than individuals, to total income from all sources rather than earnings alone, and to all families rather than nonprofessional families alone. The last defect is not, however, serious because professional families are few relatively to nonprofessional. In addition, we show in Chapter 5 that size of community differences in the average income of independent professional workers are roughly similar to the corresponding differences in the average income of all nonrelief families. Hence, the exclusion of the professional families would have little effect on the size of community differences in average income.

tween 85 and 180 per cent larger than that of nonprofessional workers living in communities of the same size.

It is more difficult to correct for the apparent concentration of professional workers in the younger age groups, which has presumably resulted from the rapid growth of professional activity in recent decades.[12] The corresponding period of the professional career includes both the early years of low earnings and the intermediate years of average or better than average earnings. It is therefore not clear whether correction for the concentration of professional workers in the younger age groups would raise or lower the differential between the earnings of professional and nonprofessional workers. The net effect would probably be small.

These purely statistical factors therefore explain only a small part of the observed difference between the average incomes of professional and nonprofessional workers. There remains a difference of some 85 to 180 per cent between the average incomes of professional and nonprofessional workers in the same community and in the labor market the same number of years. What factors account for this large difference? Why does it not lead young men to flock into the professions, thereby driving incomes in the professions down relatively to incomes in other pursuits?

One reason why this does not occur is that young men choosing their lifework take account of many factors other than expected earnings. They compare not monetary returns alone but, in Adam Smith's phrase, "the whole of the advantages and disadvantages" of different occupations. The larger average earnings in the professions are balanced against the costs of the additional training that must be acquired. And purely pecuniary considerations are supplemented by many others—the character of the work in different occupations, the responsibilities involved, the possibilities of rendering service, their social standing, the hardships and pleasures attached to the work, and so on.

12 Edwards, *Social-Economic Grouping of the Gainful Workers of the United States, 1930*, p. 26.

The most objective of these additional factors is the longer period of training required of a professional man and the attendant extra investment. In most other fields, a man is ready to pursue his occupation at an early age. The professional man, as we saw in Chapter 1, must undergo four to nine years of specialized training, at considerable expense and at the sacrifice of income that might otherwise have been earned. The professional man who goes into independent practice must in addition purchase capital equipment and in many cases provide for his maintenance during the initial years of practice.

In order that the "whole of the advantages and disadvantages" may be the same as in other pursuits, pecuniary returns in the professions would have to be sufficiently high—relatively to the level that would be considered adequate on other grounds—to hold out reasonable prospects of recouping this extra investment. "When any expensive machine is erected, the extraordinary work to be performed by it before it is worn out, it must be expected, will replace the capital laid out upon it, with at least the ordinary profits. A man educated at the expense of much labor and time to any of those employments which require extraordinary dexterity and skill, may be compared to one of those expensive machines. The work which he learns to perform, it must be expected, over and above the usual wages of common labor, will replace to him the whole expense of his education, with at least the ordinary profits of an equally valuable capital. It must do this, too, in a reasonable time, regard being had to the very uncertain duration of human life, in the same manner as to the more certain duration of the machine." [13]

The data available are so meagre and unsatisfactory that it is impossible to do more than make the roughest kind of guess about the percentage by which the average earnings of the professional worker would have to exceed the average earnings of the nonprofessional worker to compensate for the

[13] Adam Smith, *Wealth of Nations* (Everyman's Library; E. P. Dutton, 1910), I, 88–9.

extra capital investment required. Our guess is that the difference would not have to be more than 70 per cent and might
be a good deal lower. Interestingly enough, almost half of the
70 per cent is accounted for by the postponement of income
involved in the choice of a professional career. The assumptions leading to the upper estimate of 70 per cent are presented in detail in the Appendix to the next chapter (Sec.
1b). The more important are that the average period of training in the professions is 7 years, the specific costs of professional training (tuition fees, books, special equipment, etc.)
are $500 per year, the life expectancy of professional workers
is three years longer than that of nonprofessional workers, and
the average income of nonprofessional workers is equal to that
of unskilled laborers, or approximately $750 per year. If the
average income of nonprofessional workers is assumed equal
to that of skilled laborers, or $1,430 a year, the differential
needed to make professional and nonprofessional pursuits
equally attractive financially is reduced to 55 per cent.

On the basis of these figures, the actual difference between
the incomes of professional and nonprofessional workers seems
decidedly larger than the difference that would compensate
for the extra capital investment required. The only other empirical study of this question of which we know, a study by
J. R. Walsh, reaches essentially the same conclusion.[14] Walsh
compares the present value of the life earnings of individuals with the cost of the special training they have had.
The principal results are summarized in Table 9. The estimates of the present value of life earnings in columns 2, 4,
and 6 are based on scattered studies for years between 1926
and 1929, and are admittedly subject to wide margins of error.
They were computed by determining the median earnings for
different numbers of years of experience, adjusting these figures to allow for deaths and for the percentage of persons
employed at each age so as to get the total amounts actually
earned by the survivors, discounting the individual amounts

14 'Capital Concept Applied to Man', *Quarterly Journal of Economics*, Feb. 1935.

at 4 per cent, and summing to obtain the present value of life earnings as of the middle of the first year of employment. The difference between the returns at a later and at an earlier stage of training were then compared with the corresponding difference in costs.

Columns 4 and 5, which compare the returns of training

TABLE 9

Comparison between Discounted and
Cost Values of Special Training

J. R. Walsh's Estimates

RANK OF EDUCATION (1)	DISC. VALUE OVER ELEM. EDUC. (2)	COST VALUE OF SAME (3)	DISC. VALUE OVER H. S. EDUC. (4)	COST VALUE OF SAME (5)	DISC. VALUE OVER B.A. (6)	COST VALUE OF SAME (7)
			(dollars)			
			Men			
High school	7,142	5,000				
B.A.			35,009	6,398		
M.A.			36,041	9,848	1,032	3,450
Ph.D.			43,226	21,413	8,217	15,015
B.B.A. or B.C.S.			57,631	12,963	22,622	6,565
M.D.			37,690	22,143	2,681	15,745
LL.B.*			67,784	16,447	32,775	10,049
LL.B.*			83,386	16,447	48,377	10,049
Engineers *			42,101	13,000	7,092	6,602
Engineers *			49,003	13,000	13,994	6,602
			Women			
B.A.			9,030	6,398		
M.A.					4,631	2,950

Reproduced from 'Capital Concept Applied to Man', *Quarterly Journal of Economics*, Feb. 1935, Table V, with a few minor corrections.
* Two estimates based on different sources.

beyond high school with the corresponding costs, are of primary interest for an analysis of the professions as a whole. For every group the returns are considerably higher than the costs. Columns 6 and 7, which compare the returns of training beyond college with the corresponding costs, offer additional evidence on the adjustment among different levels of training. Even these comparisons show returns that exceed costs for 6 out of 9 groups. And for 1 of the 3 groups for which the reverse is true, medicine (M.D.), the return computed by Walsh seems unduly low.[15]

Walsh's procedure is superior to ours in two important respects: first, it makes explicit allowance for differences among individuals in length of life; second, the income data purportedly are for individuals grouped by training rather than by the occupation they engage in.[16] Counterbalancing these advantages are a number of defects that make correct interpretation of the results difficult.[17] On balance, it appears that

[15] Walsh estimates the discounted value of median life earnings of M.D.'s as $70,327 (ibid., p. 267). H. F. Clark, on the other hand, estimates the discounted value of median life earnings of physicians for 1920–29 as $106,000 on the basis of one body of data, and as $116,000 on the basis of a second. He also gives an estimate for 1920–36 of $98,000. See Life Earnings in Selected Occupations in the United States (Harper, 1937), p. 70. Both investigators use an interest rate of 4 per cent in discounting returns. Although the methods differ in other respects, the estimates for the other two occupations for which comparison is possible, law and engineering, give no reason to suppose that Clark's method has an upward bias relatively to Walsh's.

[16] The reason that this is an advantage is that individuals planning to become lawyers, for example, must take account of the possibility that after completion of training they will be unable to practise or that their training will stand them in better stead in other pursuits. Unfortunately, reliable data for groups classified by character of training are exceedingly rare. All the data in the preceding section on incomes in the professions and in other pursuits are for groups classified by present occupational attachment. It is difficult to judge the magnitude of the error introduced in this way. Some individuals engage in occupations other than those they prepare for because the other occupations offer greater returns (e.g., many with legal training); others because they find themselves unsuited to the occupation they initially chose. The former may well receive larger incomes than their fellow students; the latter probably receive smaller incomes, since training for a profession is ordinarily less valuable in other pursuits. Probably most people practise the professions they prepare for. If so, the net difference between classifying individuals by present occupation and by character of training cannot be large.

[17] There are four defects in Walsh's procedure. (1) Walsh's cost figures include not only special expenditures for education but also living expenses and foregone income, income that would have been earned during the time devoted to additional training. These two items clearly duplicate each other; moreover, neither should be included for the present purpose. The foregone income included in the costs, say, of a college education is automatically counted in the returns to those with only a high school education. When the latter is subtracted from the returns to those with a college education, allowance is implicitly made for foregone income. Hence, including it in the cost figure involves

correction of Walsh's figures for their defects would probably strengthen rather than weaken the conclusion suggested by Table 9; namely, that returns in the professions exceed returns in other pursuits by an amount considerably in excess of the extra costs involved, a conclusion independently supported by our earlier analysis.[18]

---

duplication. (See point (1) in Sec. 1a of the Appendix to the next chapter.) (2) The use of median earnings makes the estimates of returns too low. The actuarial nature of the problem clearly requires arithmetic mean earnings, which are usually considerably higher than median earnings. (3) The present value of returns and the accumulated costs refer to an age that differs from one level of training to the next since they are computed as of the middle of the first year of employment. To make the comparison valid they should refer to the same age for the different levels of training. The net effect of this defect is to inflate the difference between excess returns and excess costs at the later stages by accumulated interest on the difference between returns and costs at the earlier stage. The reason for this is that the difference between the present value of returns at the later and earlier stages is larger than it would be if the present values at both stages referred to the same age. The excess is equal to interest on the present value at the earlier stage for the intervening period. The difference between the costs at the later and earlier stages is affected in similar fashion. If the present value of returns equaled costs at the earlier stage, both sets of figures would be affected equally and the comparison between the excess returns and excess costs would be entirely valid. In fact, however, returns uniformly exceed costs at the earlier stages. (4) No allowance is made for differences among the groups in their distribution by location.

18 The first two defects listed in the preceding footnote tend to make the estimated costs too high and the estimated returns too low and thus tend to lessen the spread between returns and costs. The third and fourth defects have the opposite effect. Rough estimates of the influence of the third defect suggest that it does not affect the results seriously; correction for it would make the cost value in column 7 of Table 9 for the first group of engineers exceed the discount value in column 6, but would not alter the direction of the difference between returns and costs for any of the other comparisons. The second defect is considerably more important. Use of mean instead of median earnings would probably add between $5,000 and $20,000 to the figures in columns 4 and 6 and might well make the estimated returns of training beyond college greater than the corresponding costs for all groups. This estimate of the effect of using mean instead of median earnings is based on measures of the present value of both mean and median earnings given by Clark (op. cit.) for several occupations. According to these estimates, the present value of mean earnings exceeds that of median earnings by 10 to 20 per cent. Walsh's estimates of the present value of median earnings for groups with college training vary from $32,000 for women with a B.A. degree to $208,000 for one of the groups with an LL.B. degree.

Taking account of the extra costs as well as the extra returns of professional work weakens the pecuniary incentive to enter the professions, but apparently does not remove it. Extra costs can at most explain part of the difference between incomes of professional and nonprofessional workers. There must be other reasons why individuals do not flock into the professions in sufficient numbers to erase the rest of the difference.

It is hard to believe that one of these reasons is that a profession is considered a less desirable vocation than a nonprofessional pursuit. Professional men are everywhere held in high esteem and are ordinarily among the leaders of their communities. In addition, professional work is ordinarily regarded as more interesting than nonprofessional work, as socially more valuable, as giving greater play to individual aptitudes and initiative. These are necessarily qualitative judgments, and we could not easily test or prove them. Yet the balance seems so clear that we have no hesitation in discarding this possible explanation of the excess of pecuniary returns over pecuniary costs.

If this judgment is correct, the difference between incomes in the professions and in other pursuits is larger than can be explained by the free choice of occupations by young men. There is nothing surprising about this finding. It is clear that young men are, in fact, not equally free to choose a professional or nonprofessional career. There are two major reasons why this is so. First, the professions require a different level of ability than other pursuits; second, the economic and social stratification of the population leaves only limited segments really free to enter the professions.

In some professions, such as medicine, dentistry, law, and certified public accountancy, the need for special ability has been explicitly recognized by society. The practice of these professions is open solely to persons licensed by the state, and a license is granted only after the demonstration of a certain level of competence. Persons who cannot meet these standards are excluded from the professions. Some, recognizing their lack of aptitude or having it pointed out to them by their parents or teachers or friends, make no attempt to enter the professions; others are weeded out by the colleges and professional schools; still others, though as we saw in Chapter 1 relatively few, by the licensure examinations. In professions not under state licensure the first two tendencies alone are operative, but these are enough to assure that on the whole persons who enter the professions have the special aptitudes required in higher degree than those who either decide not to enter the professions or are weeded out in the earlier stages. Persons who enter the professions might therefore earn more in other pursuits than persons who do not, though this would clearly not be universal, since special aptitude for one pursuit may not qualify a man for another. More important, earnings in the professions depend not on the total number of persons who would like to enter the professions, but on the number who have sufficient ability to do so.

The second factor that limits the number who are free to choose a professional career is the economic and social stratification of the population. It is not enough that a young man who wishes to enter the professions have sufficient ability; he must also be able to command funds to pay the expenses of training and to support himself during the training period. Because of the peculiar character of the capital investment in training, these funds cannot be obtained on the open market as a purely 'business loan', and hence are not freely available to all. "The worker sells his work, but he himself remains his own property: those who bear the expenses of rearing and educating him receive but very little of the price that is paid for his services in later years." [19] Consequently investment in training is not governed by the usual profit incentives. The noneconomic values attached to a professional training might well lead an individual to invest in himself, his children, or his protégés even though he did not expect the added income to repay the cost; on the other hand, no investor in search of profit would invest in the education of strangers even though

19 Alfred Marshall, *Principles of Economics* (8th ed; London: Macmillan, 1930), pp. 560–1.

he expected that the return to the latter would greatly exceed the cost. The fact that the returns from capital investment in training and education seldom accrue to the person making it means that there is no reason to expect such investment to be pushed to the 'margin', i.e., to the point at which the accumulated cost, including interest, would equal the present value of expected future returns.[20] If, relatively to the demand for professional services, there are few young men interested in entering the professions who can get the necessary funds, one would expect underinvestment; in the contrary case, overinvestment.

No hard and fast line divides occupations requiring a long period of specialized education from occupations requiring a short period. In Marshall's day the considerations set forth above may well have applied to all occupations requiring

---

[20] See Walsh, 'Capital Concept Applied to Man', pp. 276–7.

The argument may be put in a somewhat different fashion by using an analogy that at first blush may seem fantastic. Investment in professional training will not necessarily be pushed to the margin because earning power is seldom explicitly treated as an asset to be capitalized and sold to others by the issuance of 'stock'. An individual will rarely sell a fixed proportion of his future income to an investor (i.e., he will rarely sell 'stock' in himself), though he may borrow money, obligating himself to repay the principal and to pay interest at a rate that ordinarily cannot exceed a legally stipulated maximum (i.e., he may sell 'bonds'). Under such conditions, an investor who loaned money to a prospective professional man could at most get back his capital and the interest on it; he could never realize a 'capital gain'. But he could, and frequently would, suffer a 'capital loss', since, despite the average profitability of professional training, professional incomes differ greatly so that many individuals fare poorly and would be unable even to repay the principal. For this reason, it would be profitable for an investor to finance the professional training of individuals with no resources other than their expected future incomes only at a rate of interest that would be sufficiently high to provide for capital losses as well as for the usual interest charges. Such a rate of interest would probably exceed the expected return from investment in training even though the latter were well above the market rate of interest. On the other hand, if individuals sold 'stock' in themselves, i.e., obligated themselves to pay a fixed proportion of future earnings, investors could 'diversify' their holdings and balance capital appreciations against capital losses. The purchase of such 'stock' would be profitable so long as the expected return on investment in training exceeded the market rate of interest. Such investments would be similar to others involving a large element of risk, a type of investment usually financed by stocks rather than bonds.

special training; and in no small degree they do even to-day.[21] But the widespread extension of free secondary education and the raising of the minimum age at which children may leave school mean that no considerable voluntary investment is likely to be required prior to entrance to college. The need for capital investment thus seriously impedes entry only into occupations requiring a college education.[22]

[21] See A. G. B. Fisher, 'Education and Relative Wage Rates', *International Labour Review*, June 1932, pp. 742–64. A report by the Educational Policies Commission presents an impressive summary of evidence from a variety of studies on the role that the lack of funds plays in barring youths from high school and college. According to this report "large numbers of youths are prevented from continuing their education through high school and into college, because of lack of ability to meet expenditures required. Many of these youths have superior ability. Where these superior youths are given financial aid permitting them to continue their education, they make superior records." *Education and Economic Well-Being in American Democracy* (Educational Policies Commission, National Education Association of United States and American Association of School Administrators, 1940), p. 152.

[22] Walsh, in the article cited above, presents some estimates of the cost of special training, which include:

"(1) Tuition, fees, and the like, paid to the school
(2) Board and room
(3) Equipment, such as books, and the like
(4) Personal expenses: clothes, recreation, travel
(5) Loss of that income which would, on the average, have been earned if the individual had not continued in school. From this amount was deducted the estimated average earnings of students during the school year and vacation periods.
(6) Annual cumulative interest at 4 per cent on the sum of the above" (pp. 268–9).

On this basis the cost of a high school education is estimated as $5,000, while the additional costs of special training are estimated at amounts that range from about $6,400 for a bachelor's degree, $10,000 for a master's degree, and $13,000 for engineers to $22,000 for physicians.

As measures of the funds individuals would need in order to finance special training these estimates, especially the cost of a high school education, are obviously too large, since from this point of view foregone income, income that could have been earned, should be excluded. In addition, even personal costs incurred in connection with the part of the high school education that is had at an age below the minimum legal age for leaving school should be excluded; only those special costs incurred for a better education than would normally be provided should be counted, except so far as legal minima may not be strictly enforced.

Adjustment for these defects would considerably reduce the cost estimates

The professions bulk large in this group, though they do not exhaust it.

Entry into a profession is likely to depend not only on deliberate comparison of alternative occupations and the possession of adequate financial resources, but also on educational facilities, the connections that a young man can exploit when he begins his career, his awareness of available opportunities, and the like. These aspects of occupational determination are, in turn, likely to be related to a young man's social and national background, his geographic location, cultural environment, etc. These factors are far less important in the United States than in most countries, and far less important today than prior to the enormous development of higher educational opportunities supported by the state. The choice of occupation has probably never been so much restricted by social stratification in the United States, and it certainly is not today, as it was in England when, in 1848, John Stuart Mill was able to write: "So complete, indeed, has hitherto been the separation, so strongly marked the line of demarcation, between the different grades of labourers, as to be almost equivalent to an hereditary distinction of caste; each employment being chiefly recruited from the children of those already employed in it, or in employments of the same rank with it in social estimation, or from the

---

presented by Walsh—for a high school education, probably to a relatively small figure. For advanced degrees, however, formidable sums would be needed, even if a large allowance were made for costs that should not be included from this point of view. (The validity of Walsh's estimates for comparing extra returns in different occupations with the extra costs involved is considered above in footnote 17.)

The force of this argument is somewhat lessened by the growing possibility and tendency for students to 'work their way' through school and to receive aid in the form of scholarships. But it may be doubted that this tendency is as yet sufficiently important, at least for the professions, to negate the statements in the text. Moreover, children of poor parents are prevented from getting training not only by lack of funds but frequently also by the necessity of going to work as soon as possible to supplement the family income. The availability of scholarships or of opportunities for earning the expenses of education would not remove hindrances of the latter type, the importance of which is often underestimated.

children of persons who, if originally of a lower rank, have succeeded in raising themselves by their exertions. The liberal professions are mostly supplied by the sons of either the professional, or the idle classes: the more highly skilled manual employments are filled up from the sons of skilled artizans, or the class of tradesmen who rank with them: the lower classes of skilled employments are in a similar case; and unskilled labourers, with occasional exceptions, remain from father to son in their pristine condition." [23]

Despite the enormous decline in the importance of these factors, it is still true that they affect in no small measure the occupational opportunities open to a young man. For example, the child of a professional man is more likely to be cognizant of opportunities in the professions and better able to seize them than the child of an unskilled laborer, even though the professional man and the unskilled laborer have the same income and capital. The child of the professional man will have a background and associations that facilitate entry into the professions and make it seem natural; he will have contacts after he finishes his professional training that will ease his path.

The inference from this analysis is that professional workers constitute a 'noncompeting' group. The number and hence the incomes of professional workers are determined less by the relative attractiveness of professional and nonprofessional work than by the number of young men in the community who can finance their training, are cognizant of opportunities, and have the necessary ability, background, and connections. Our data suggest that this group is sufficiently small to lead to underinvestment in professional training, i.e., that in the absence of financial and social limitations on entry, incomes in the professions would exceed incomes in other pursuits by less than they do now. The limitations of the data and the speculative character of our analysis necessarily make this conclusion tentative. Moreover, the conclusion relates solely to

[23] *Principles of Political Economy* (Ashley ed; Longmans, Green, 1909), p. 393.

voluntary investment by prospective practitioners themselves, their parents, or their direct benefactors. No allowance has been made for the investment by society in institutions of higher education and in professional schools. From the broad social standpoint of the efficient utilization of resources, investment of the latter type should also be taken into account.

At present, the limitations on the number of persons in a position to enter the professions must be considered the basic reason for the difference between extra returns and extra costs; more basic even than the difference in ability needed. A sizable number, perhaps a majority, of all young men are unable to enter the professions because they cannot make the necessary capital investment or for other reasons. If these hindrances were removed, the reservoir of persons unable to enter the professions could surely furnish many persons as able as those who now embark on professional careers. A higher level of ability among those who enter the professions may help to explain the current levels of remuneration; it could not maintain them if the other hindrances to entry were removed. At the same time, the higher level of specialized abilities among those who enter the professions and the insistence upon high qualifications for prospective professional men might well mean that, even if all other hindrances to entry were removed, earnings in the professions would still exceed earnings in other pursuits by more than enough to cover the extra pecuniary costs.

CHAPTER 4

Incomes in the Five Professions

THE FACTORS that make the professions as a whole a' 'noncompeting group' affect individual professions as well. The capital investment needed varies from profession to profession and young men who have enough funds to enter one profession may not have enough funds to enter another. Similarly other social and economic factors that hinder passage between professional and nonprofessional pursuits also restrict movement among professions.

These hindrances to free choice of occupation are of course matters of degree. And it seems clear that they are far less potent among professions than between professions and other pursuits. The undoubted heterogeneity within the professional group pales into insignificance relative to the difference between the professions as a whole and pursuits not requiring a college education. It is doubtful, therefore, that differences among the professions in capital investment needed constitute a barrier to entry at all approaching in importance that set by the minimum capital investment needed to enter any profession. The proportion of young men able to enter the professions whose choice among them is restricted by lack of funds is almost certainly much smaller than the proportion of all young men entirely barred from the professional fold.

Differences in capital investment may seldom bar a person from going into one profession rather than another but they frequently affect his choice. Parents and candidates will be influenced by the returns a profession is expected to yield and the costs that must be incurred. A profession must have compensating advantages if it is to be selected in preference to another requiring a smaller capital outlay. Of course, pecuniary returns and pecuniary costs are not the only items considered in deciding on a profession; "the whole of the advantages and disadvantages" of the different professions will be compared. A profession is a 'way of life' as well as an income-yielding occupation. Personal aptitudes and preferences, the desire to render service, and the like doubtless play an important role, often completely outweighing pecuniary considerations. Adjustment of differences in income to differences in capital investment does not require that every prospective entrant choose his profession on the basis of economic considerations or even be influenced in his choice by them. Adjustments take place on the 'margin' and there are many different 'margins'. It is sufficient that *some* prospective entrants be influenced by economic considerations and that the larger the differences in pecuniary returns the larger is the number who are influenced. The adjustments will take place more rapidly, the larger the number who are influenced by any given difference in pecuniary returns.

Even this restricted emphasis on pecuniary considerations may strike many readers as unrealistic; recalling the factors that determined the occupations chosen by themselves and their friends, they may view pecuniary considerations as least important. One reason that pecuniary considerations seem so unimportant is that the balance brought about by free choices of individuals within the broad noncompeting professional group is ordinarily maintained so well that it need hardly be taken into consideration. Precisely in the measure that pecuniary considerations are effective and operative, they recede from the level of consciousness. The operator of a smoothly working machine is seldom conscious of the nice balance of its many parts; only when the machine stops working smoothly does he become conscious of its complexity. So it is with price and income adjustments. Let incomes in two fields, open to the same group of persons, become markedly out of line, and the importance of pecuniary considerations will assert itself.

Several factors hinder or retard adjustments among different professional groups. "Not much less than a generation elapses between the choice by parents of a skilled trade [profession] for one of their children, and his reaping the full results of their choice. And meanwhile the character of the trade [profession] may have been almost revolutionized by changes, of which some probably threw long shadows before them, but others were such as could not have been foreseen even by the shrewdest persons and those best acquainted with the circumstances of the trade [profession]." [1] The difficulty of forecasting the demand for a service would be of minor importance if the number of professional persons could be adjusted quickly to changes in demand. This is not the case. The abilities acquired by training are highly specialized and can seldom be profitably turned to other pursuits. Even large decreases in relative return will not lead to an appreciable shift of those already in the field into other pursuits, nor can many individuals pursuing other callings readily enter the field in response to large increases in relative return. Adjustment must take place in the main through a slowing down or speeding up in the number newly entering the profession. And even this adjustment, which would in any event be relatively slow, is retarded by the long period that elapses between the choice of a profession and the completion of preparation for it. A change in demand today that is broadly recognized will be reflected not in the number of new entrants this year, but in the number who this year start their professional training.[2] Moreover, most people have but hazy notions of the state of the market for professional services. Secular changes in demand may not be immediately recognized and short time cyclical rises or declines may be interpreted as secular changes. These difficulties still further impede the tendency to adjustment.

The influence of these factors affecting the choice of a profession by individuals is limited by the fact, noted in Chapter 1, that a person who desires to enter a profession and has the funds to prepare himself may not be free to do so. In the first

1 Marshall, *Principles of Economics*, p. 571.
2 To some degree, of course, a decrease in demand will doubtless lead to an increase in the number discontinuing training at an intermediate stage or shifting from one type of training to another before their invested capital is either very great or very specialized. These effects are probably of secondary importance.

place, practice of some professions is restricted to those licensed by the state. Licensing is of little importance from the present point of view when it is automatic, constituting essentially a device for the registration of practitioners. Licensing is important when the demonstration of some degree of competence is required, and more especially when the level of competence demanded—or what is the same thing, the number of applicants refused licenses—is influenced by an explicit or implicit desire to limit the number of practitioners. Such limitation obviously nullifies to some extent whatever 'automatic' adjustment from the side of individual choice might otherwise occur. In the second place, limitation of entry takes place in some professions at an earlier stage, namely, before admission to professional training. The effect is the same as limitation at the time of application for licensure.[3]

The degree to which the factors enumerated prevent the number of practitioners from responding to changes in demand varies greatly from profession to profession and from period to period. The tendency toward adjustment is clearly greatest in those professions in which entry is easiest, training least expensive and time-consuming, and demand most stable. Similarly, adjustment is likely to be most rapid when general economic conditions are least subject to violent and erratic fluctuations.

The extent to which incomes in various professions are adjusted to the conditions of demand and supply cannot be judged solely in terms of actual incomes received. Equal incomes in two professions are no test of a close adjustment of supply to demand. Incomes in one profession may have to be

[3] These limitations not only affect the extent to which 'automatic' adjustments take place; they also affect the criteria on the basis of which individuals decide whether to try to enter a profession. To the degree that the training is of little value in other occupations, the capital investment of those who prepare for a profession but are never given an opportunity to practise must be included along with the costs of those who are able to practise in computing the 'average' cost of becoming a professional practitioner. The two types of limitation differ in this connection, since limitations before admission to professional school involve much smaller costs without any return than limitations at the stage of licensure.

considerably higher than in another to compensate for other disadvantages; or to induce enough persons to enter that profession to satisfy a strong demand for its services. At the same time, an examination of actual incomes received is a prerequisite to a more detailed and quantitative analysis of the factors making for differences in income. We turn therefore to a description of the income structure in five professions—medicine, dentistry, law, certified public accountancy, and consulting engineering—as revealed by our primary data. We shall then return to the theme of the preceding few pages, attempting to fill in the details and sketch the quantitative importance of the factors responsible for the observed income differences among the professions.

1 STATISTICAL EVIDENCE ON DIFFERENCES IN INCOME

a Level of income

Table 10 and Chart 7 give the arithmetic mean and median net incomes computed from our samples.[4] The different samples for the same profession are not designated on the chart but can be easily distinguished by the period each line covers. For three professions the evidence is quite clear: certified public accountants have a distinctly larger arithmetic mean income than physicians, and physicians than dentists.[5] Similarly, certi-

---

[4] For reasons indicated in more detail in footnote 8 below, frequency distributions were computed for the 1937 medical and accountancy samples only for 1934–36; none were computed for the 1937 legal sample. Hence, medians are available for fewer years than arithmetic means.

[5] The results for 1929–32 from the 1933 samples are sufficient to establish the statistical significance of the observed differences between the arithmetic means. The average difference for the four years between physicians and dentists is $656, between certified public accountants and dentists, $2,380, and between certified public accountants and physicians, $1,725. To determine exactly the standard errors of these differences is difficult, since they depend on the correlation between the incomes of the respondents in different years. However, the standard error of the average difference cannot be larger than the largest of the standard errors of the differences for each year separately. For each pair of professions, the standard error of the difference is largest for 1929. We may, therefore, take these as maximum estimates of the standard error of the average difference. They are approximately $180, $270, and $290 for the differences between physicians and dentists, certified public accountants and

CHART 7

Arithmetic Mean and Median Income

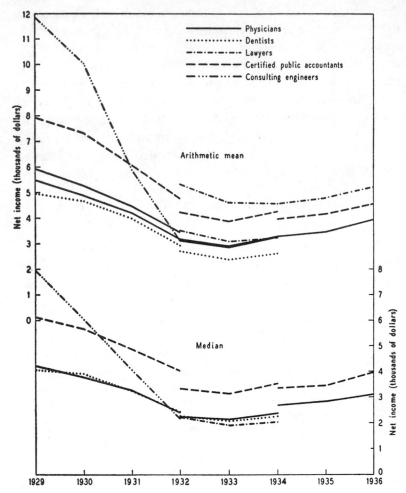

fied public accountants have a larger median income than either physicians or dentists, and, while the latter two groups have almost identical medians, physicians would almost cer-

dentists, and certified public accountants and physicians respectively. Each average difference is considerably more than three times the maximum estimate of its standard error.

TABLE 10

Arithmetic Mean and Median Incomes, and Number of Persons Covered

PROFESSION & SAMPLE	1929	1930	1931	1932	1933	1934	1935	1936
				Arithmetic Mean (dollars)				
Physicians								
1933	5,916	5,270	4,564	3,434				
1935				3,107	2,867	3,296		
1937	5,493	4,878	4,199	3,165	2,903	3,276	3,470	3,944
Dentists								
1933	4,969	4,664	3,986	2,943				
1935				2,704	2,381	2,609		
Lawyers								
1935				3,508	3,096	3,248		
1937	8,118			5,303	4,604	4,567	4,795	5,202
Certified public accountants								
1933	7,926	7,314	6,072	4,777				
1935				4,218	3,886	4,274		
1937	5,858					3,984	4,177	4,556
Consulting engineers								
1933	11,840	10,037	5,887	3,116				
				Median (dollars)				
Physicians								
1933	4,223	3,798	3,275	2,400				
1935				2,247	2,137	2,378		
1937						2,690	2,824	3,100
Dentists								
1933	4,080	3,911	3,238	2,414				
1935				2,260	2,080	2,266		
Lawyers								
1935				2,218	1,906	2,028		
Certified public accountants								
1933	6,116	5,647	4,780	4,017				
1935				3,336	3,129	3,515		
1937						3,358	3,460	3,963
Consulting engineers								
1933	7,943	6,016	4,041	2,178				
				Number of Persons Covered*				
Physicians								
1933	2,139	2,220	2,281	2,288				
1935				1,392	1,452	1,497		
1937	912	867	906	972	1,043	1,238	1,294	1,408
Dentists								
1933	1,335	1,383	1,418	1,452				
1935				1,026	1,061	1,107		
Lawyers								
1935				1,269	1,332	1,377		
1937	724			805	945	929	1,016	1,168
Certified public accountants								
1933	963	1,002	1,020	1,063				
1935				1,415	1,489	1,518		
1937	689					901	971	1,043
Consulting engineers								
1933	471	481	476	474				

* Actual number of *persons covered* by the returns used, before any weighting or adjustment. Table 4 gives total number of *returns received*.

tainly have the higher median income if that of dentists were corrected for the restriction of our samples to American Dental Association members.

The standing of the other two professions is less clear. The arithmetic mean income of consulting engineers for 1929–32 is almost $1,200 higher than the corresponding mean income of certified public accountants; the median income of consulting engineers is about as far below the median income of accountants in the last two years as it is above in the first two. Much of the difference between the arithmetic means may be due to the upward bias in the data for consulting engineers (see Ch. 2). Even if the data are accepted as correct, the fall in the mean income of consulting engineers from 1929 to 1932 was so sharp that it is difficult to infer what the results would be were data available for the entire period 1929–36. Would the fall have continued until 1933, as in other professions, and if so, would it have carried the income of consulting engineers below that of dentists? And would the income of engineers have risen, as in the other professions, from 1933 to 1936? If so, would the rise have been as sharp as the fall, relatively to the other professions? Affirmative answers would probably mean that over the period as a whole consulting engineers received a somewhat larger average income than certified public accountants, and hence a considerably larger average income than physicians and dentists. However, the lateness and mildness of the recovery in private construction and producers' goods industries in general may well have made the rise in the income of consulting engineers considerably less sharp than the fall, relatively to the other professions. In view of these doubts, little can be said about the standing of consulting engineers, except for the few years specifically covered by our data.

The difficulty of judging the standing of lawyers arises from a different source: the wide divergence between the results of the two samples. Both the means and the medians from the 1935 sample place lawyers on about the same income level as physicians; the means from the 1937 sample, on the other hand, place lawyers above even certified public accountants.[6] For reasons given in Chapter 2, the later legal sample is suspect. In addition, over half of the difference between the means from the two samples is attributable to a single extreme return included in the 1937 sample. It seems reasonable to conclude that the average net income of lawyers is about the same as, or larger than, that of physicians.

On the basis of our data alone, the order of the five professions by size of net income (from large to small) is apparently: consulting engineering, certified public accountancy, law, medicine, and dentistry. The positions assigned consulting engineering and law are the most doubtful.

We may go somewhat further in assessing the differences in the income levels of physicians, certified public accountants, and dentists—the three professions for which data are available for the longest continuous periods and for which different samples give the most nearly identical results. The estimates in Table 11 were obtained by combining the different samples for each profession into a single series [7] and correcting the arithmetic mean incomes of dentists for the restriction of the samples to American Dental Association members.

Average net income during 1929–34 was about $5,300 for certified public accountants, $4,100 for physicians, and $3,100 for dentists. The averages for certified public accountants and physicians during 1929–36 are slightly lower, about $5,200 and $4,000 respectively. On the average, certified public ac-

---

6 Since no frequency distributions were computed for the 1937 legal sample, medians are not available.

7 In combining the samples we resorted to averaging the averages for 1932 from the different samples. We do not attribute any inherent logical merit to this procedure. For reasons given in Chapter 2 we suspect that the 1932 averages from the earlier samples have an upward bias and from the later samples a downward bias, and hence that the best estimate of the correct figure is between the two. Averaging seemed the simplest objective procedure for selecting such a figure. Moreover, the differences between the several samples are so small, except possibly between the first and the two later accountancy samples, that alternative procedures applied consistently to all professions would have yielded results differing but slightly from those in Table 11.

TABLE 11

Final Estimates of Arithmetic Mean Income

Physicians and Certified Public Accountants, 1929–1936; Dentists, 1929–1934

	1929	1930	1931	1932	1933	1934	1935	1936	Average	
									1929–34	1929–36
Arithmetic mean income (dollars)										
Certified public accountants [1]	7,149	6,597	5,477	4,309	3,970	4,366	4,578	4,993	5,311	5,180
Physicians [2]	5,573	4,965	4,300	3,235	2,985	3,431	3,633	4,129	4,081	4,031
Dentists [3]	4,176	3,920	3,350	2,473	2,178	2,387			3,081	
Absolute difference (dollars) between arithmetic mean incomes of										
Certified public accountants & physicians	1,576	1,632	1,177	1,074	985	935	945	864	1,230	1,149
Certified public accountants & dentists	2,973	2,677	2,127	1,886	1,792	1,979			2,230	
Physicians & dentists	1,397	1,045	950	762	807	1,044			1,000	
% excess of										
Certified public accountants over physicians	28.3	32.9	27.4	33.2	33.0	27.3	26.0	20.9	30.1 [4]	28.5 [4]
Certified public accountants over dentists	71.2	68.3	63.5	74.2	82.3	82.9			72.4 [4]	
Physicians over dentists	33.5	26.7	28.4	30.8	37.1	43.7			32.5 [4]	

[1] See Table B 10 for method of computing these averages.

[2] See Table B 3 for method of computing these averages.

[3] The averages in Table B 5 were multiplied by .876 to adjust for restriction of samples to American Dental Association members. This adjustment factor assumes that average income of members exceeds the average income of nonmembers by 30 per cent and that 46.2 per cent of the dentists are members.

[4] Since these percentages are based on average incomes for the entire period, they represent weighted averages of the annual percentages, the weights being the average income for the profession on which the percentages are based.

countants received about 30 per cent more than physicians and physicians about 32 per cent more than dentists.

These differences among the professions are evidently not temporary aberrations. They have persisted over the entire period and the percentage differences have shown no consistent tendency to diminish. The percentage difference between certified public accountants and physicians increased somewhat during the downswing from 1929 to 1933 and then decreased from 1933 to 1936; i.e., the average income of physicians fell relatively more than that of certified public accountants during the downswing but rose more during the upswing. The average income of dentists seems to have declined relatively to incomes in the other two professions from 1929 to 1934; i.e., the percentage differences between dentists and the other two professions increased somewhat.

b Variability of annual income

In any one year, few persons in a profession receive the 'average' income; most receive incomes that vary more or less from the average, some receiving incomes far larger than the average, others receiving incomes far smaller. The extent to which individual incomes deviate from the average is not the same for all professions in all years.

Quartile and median incomes are given in Table 12 and measures of variability in Table 13.[8] The measures for den-

---

[8] Quartiles, medians, and measures of variability were computed from the 1933 and 1935 samples for all the years they cover—1929–32 and 1932–34; but from the 1937 medical and accountancy samples only for 1934–36. None have been computed from the 1937 legal sample. The earlier years were omitted in analyzing the 1937 medical and accountancy samples for reasons of economy. That little information is lost thereby is suggested by the consistent results about average income yielded by the various samples. The omission of the 1937 legal sample seemed desirable not only because of the labor entailed by its analysis, but also because, as previously noted, its reliability is peculiarly suspect. Since the 1937 legal sample was not random among states and, in addition, has a size of community bias, it would have been necessary to compute frequency distributions for each size of community class within each state separately, combining them by weighting by the estimated number of lawyers in the corresponding class. In view of the presumptive unreliability of the data, it scarcely seemed worth while to perform these arduous computations.

TABLE 12

Median and Quartile Incomes

	1933 SAMPLES				1935 SAMPLES			1937 SAMPLES		
	1929	1930	1931	1932	1932	1933	1934	1934	1935	1936
					(dollars)					
Third Quartile										
Physicians	7,374	6,560	5,828	4,268	3,791	3,462	4,073	4,290	4,473	5,056
Dentists	6,003	5,794	4,885	3,512	3,352	2,996	3,304			
Lawyers					4,339	3,620	3,936	4,967	5,073	5,687
Certified public accountants	9,308	8,560	7,326	5,993	5,029	4,724	5,232			
Consulting engineers	14,805	11,721	8,631	4,785						
Median										
Physicians	4,223	3,798	3,275	2,400	2,247	2,187	2,378	2,690	2,824	3,100
Dentists	4,080	3,911	3,238	2,414	2,260	2,080	2,266			
Lawyers					2,218	1,906	2,028	3,358	3,460	3,963
Certified public accountants	6,116	5,647	4,780	4,017	3,336	3,129	3,515			
Consulting engineers	7,943	6,016	4,041	2,178						
First Quartile										
Physicians	2,253	1,982	1,600	1,163	1,158	1,068	1,216	1,554	1,588	1,824
Dentists	2,802	2,599	2,111	1,558	1,420	1,260	1,408			
Lawyers					1,140	982	967	2,296	2,479	2,684
Certified public accountants	4,099	3,883	3,217	2,541	2,235	2,127	2,356			
Consulting engineers	3,570	2,719	1,456	33						

tistry in Tables 12 and 13 have not been corrected for the restriction of the samples to American Dental Association members, which tends to make the quartiles and medians too high. Its effect on the measures of variability is less clear; although there is some reason to suppose that it makes them too low. The measures of variability for law, certified public accountancy, and consulting engineering—the three professions in which firms are common—are too low. The questionnaires for these professions requested the recipient, if a firm member, to reply for the firm as a whole. The reporting of income in this way does not affect our estimates of average income, but it does affect our estimates of the frequency distributions of income.[9] In computing frequency distributions we must perforce divide the total income of the firm by the number of members and attribute this average amount to each member. In fact, firm members do not invariably 'share and share alike'. The actual frequency distributions of income for firm members would therefore display greater absolute and relative variability than those we have computed by attributing to each member an equal share of the total firm income. The frequency distribution for the profession as a whole is affected considerably less than the distribution for firm members alone. Nonetheless, there is an error of uncertain magnitude in our frequency distributions of the incomes of lawyers, accountants, and consulting engineers that tends to make them more concentrated than the 'true' distributions.[10]

[9] The overrepresentation of firm members that resulted from requesting data for firms from a sample selected from a list of professional men (rather than of professional units) does of course affect both average incomes and frequency distributions, and both have been adjusted for this firm member bias (see Ch. 2).

[10] To estimate the size of this error requires knowledge of the relationship among the incomes of members of the same firm. If total income were always divided equally among the members there would be no error. If the correlation among the incomes of members of the same firm were zero the variance of the 'true' frequency distribution for members of firms of size n would tend to be n times the variance of the distribution we compute. In fact, of course, the correlation is greater than zero and the error is between the two limits noted. Rough estimates of measures of variability corrected for this error are presented in the footnote to Table 13.

TABLE 13

Measures of Variability of Income

	1933 SAMPLES				1935 SAMPLES		1937 SAMPLES		
	1929	*1930*	*1931*	*1932*	*1933*	*1934*	*1934*	*1935*	*1936*
Interquartile Difference (dollars)									
Physicians	5,121	4,578	4,227	3,104	2,394	2,857	2,736	2,885	3,232
Dentists	3,201	3,195	2,774	1,954	1,736	1,896			
Lawyers				3,199	2,648	2,069			
Certified public accountants	5,209	4,677	4,109	3,452	2,597	2,876	2,671	2,594	3,003
Consulting engineers	11,235	9,002	7,175	4,752					
Standard Deviation (dollars)									
Physicians	6,855	6,448	5,473	4,270	3,675	4,250	2,965	3,057	3,631
Dentists	3,706	3,653	3,294	2,687	2,025	2,066			
Lawyers				4,369	4,368	4,164			
Certified public accountants	6,723	6,410	5,152	3,708	3,360	3,483	3,072	3,334	3,240
Consulting engineers	14,580	16,669	9,010	6,462					
Relative Interquartile Difference									
Physicians	1.213	1.205	1.291	1.293	1.120	1.201	1.017	1.022	1.043
Dentists	.785	.817	.857	.809	.835	.837			
Lawyers				1.442	1.384	1.464			
Certified public accountants	.853	.828	.860	.859	.890	.818	.795	.750	.758
Consulting engineers	1.414	1.496	1.776	2.182					
Ratio of Quartiles									
Physicians	3.273	3.311	3.642	3.669	3.242	3.350	2.761	2.817	2.772
Dentists	2.142	2.229	2.814	2.254	2.378	2.347			
Lawyers				3.806	3.686	4.070			
Certified public accountants	2.271	2.204	2.279	2.357	2.221	2.221	2.163	2.046	2.119
Consulting engineers	4.147	4.311	5.928	145.000					
Coefficient of Variation									
Physicians	1.159	1.224	1.199	1.243	1.265	1.276	.886	.862	.902
Dentists	.746	.783	.826	.896	.843	.787			

	1933 SAMPLES				1935 SAMPLES			1937 SAMPLES		
Lawyers	.843	.865	.843	.768	1.236	1.390	1.266	.761	.784	.700
Certified public accountants					.840	.854	.803			
Consulting engineers	1.231	1.647	1.548	2.124						

All measures are computed from frequency distributions rather than from original data. For consistency, the arithmetic mean computed from the frequency distribution, rather than from the original data, was used in computing the coefficient of variation. Since corrections for grouping would not have affected the results appreciably they were not made.

All measures of variability for lawyers, certified public accountants, and consulting engineers are too low because the frequency distributions were computed by dividing the total income of a firm equally among its members. Two sets of rough estimates of the resultant error in the standard deviations (and consequently the coefficients of variation) for lawyers and accountants were prepared by assuming that (1) the correlation coefficient between the incomes of members of the same firm is .5; (2) the correlation is zero.

For simplicity, all firms were assumed to be two-member firms. This minimizes the upward adjustment. However, two-member firms are considerably more common than firms of any other size and include somewhat more than half of all firm members. Aside from the neglect of the larger firms, the assumption of zero correlation should give an upper limit to the possible error. That the intermediate assumption of a .5 correlation is not entirely unreasonable is suggested by the meagre evidence on the degree of correlation furnished by the 1937 legal sample. The questionnaire sent to lawyers in 1937 requested them to report their individual incomes from legal practice as well as the firm income. The intraclass correlation computed from data for both members of 25 two-member firms was .44; the corresponding value computed from data for all three members of 6 three-member firms was .32. (The fiducial limits, or confidence belts, corresponding to a .05 level of significance, are .07 to .71 for the first correlation and −.24 to .95 for the second.) The estimates of the standard deviations and coefficients of variation on the basis of these assumptions are:

ASSUMED CORRELATION	1933 SAMPLES				1935 SAMPLES			1937 SAMPLES		
	1929	1930	1931	1932	1932	1933	1934	1934	1935	1936
STANDARD DEVIATION (dollars)										
Accountants										
.5	7,369	7,085	5,647	4,045	3,788	3,581	3,710	3,253	3,580	3,488
0	8,514	8,273	6,526	4,647	4,192	3,985	4,126	3,589	4,026	3,822
Lawyers										
.5					4,597	4,609	4,380			
0					5,025	5,056	4,781			
COEFFICIENT OF VARIATION										
Accountants										
.5	.930	.969	.930	.847	.898	.922	.868	.816	.857	.755
0	1.074	1.131	1.075	.973	.994	1.025	.965	.901	.964	.889
Lawyers										
.5					1.310	1.489	1.349			
0					1.432	1.683	1.472			

CHART 8

Absolute Variability of Income Measured by Interquartile Difference

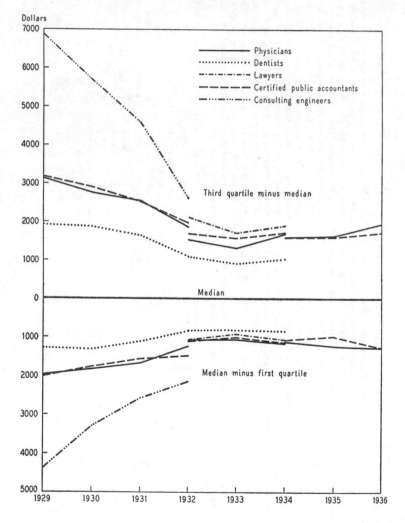

Dollars

Physicians
Dentists
Lawyers
Certified public accountants
Consulting engineers

Third quartile minus median

Median

Median minus first quartile

1929   1930   1931   1932   1933   1934   1935   1936

Chart 8 summarizes the information from the quartile measures of absolute variability. For each profession and sample there are two lines in the chart: the upper line shows the difference between the third quartile and the median; the lower, the difference between the median and the first quartile. The vertical distance between the two lines is the interquartile difference. Judged by both the interquartile differences and the standard deviations in Table 13, absolute variability seems greatest for consulting engineers and least for dentists. The three intermediate professions—law, medicine, and accountancy—differ little; though incomes are perhaps a bit more widely dispersed in law than in the other two professions. Adjustment of the measures of variability for the downward bias arising from attributing equal shares of the total income of a firm to its members would probably place law definitely above medicine; the effect it would have on the position of accountancy relative to medicine is less clear.[11]

The quartiles and medians in Table 12 are helpful in interpreting the meaning of the differences in absolute variability. They tell an especially interesting story for medicine and dentistry. The third quartile in medicine is considerably higher than in dentistry; but the first quartile is considerably lower. The difference between these professions means that a larger percentage of physicians than of dentists receive relatively

[11] The original standard deviations for lawyers (Table 13) exceed those for physicians in two out of three years. Both sets of adjusted standard deviations for lawyers (footnote to Table 13) exceed the original standard deviations for physicians in all three years. Two of the ten original standard deviations for accountants exceed those for physicians; five of the ten adjusted standard deviations do so if the correlation is taken as .5, and nine of the ten, if the correlation is taken as zero. The standard deviations alone thus suggest that medical incomes display smaller absolute variability than legal incomes, but about the same variability as accountancy incomes.

It is not feasible to correct the interquartile differences for their downward bias. It seems reasonable, however, that such a correction would place accountancy as well as law above medicine. Six of the ten original interquartile differences for accountants exceed those for physicians, and even more would if the interquartile differences for accountants were corrected for their downward bias.

high incomes; at the same time, a larger percentage of physicians than of dentists receive relatively low incomes.

Except for the interchanged positions of accountancy and law, the order of the professions by absolute variability is the same as their order by income level. Do the differences among

ORDER (FROM LARGE TO SMALL) BY

ABSOLUTE VARIABILITY	INCOME LEVEL
Consulting engineering	Consulting engineering
Law	Certified public accountancy
Certified public accountancy and medicine	Law
	Medicine
Dentistry	Dentistry

the professions in absolute variability merely reflect differences in the levels around which incomes vary? In other words, if variability were measured in percentages rather than in dollars might not the professions display approximately equal variability?

A negative answer is given by the two measures of relative variability—the relative interquartile difference and the coefficient of variation—depicted in Chart 9. Both tell much the same story. Relative variability is about the same for accountancy and dentistry, smaller for both than for any of the other professions, and largest for engineering. The relative interquartile difference is larger for lawyers than for physicians; the coefficient of variation, about the same. This discrepancy in the conclusions suggested by the interquartile difference and the coefficient of variation reflects a relatively larger number of extremely high incomes in our samples for physicians than in our samples for lawyers.[12] If we take account of the downward bias in the measures of variability for lawyers, accountants, and engineers, it seems reasonable to conclude that the order of the professions by relative variability of in-

12 As shown in Table 13, the coefficient of variation is larger for law than for medicine in 1933, but smaller in 1932 and 1934. However, if, for both the legal and medical samples, the highest income is excluded, the coefficient of variation for law exceeds that for medicine in 1932 and 1934 as well.

CHART 9

Two Measures of Relative Variability of Income

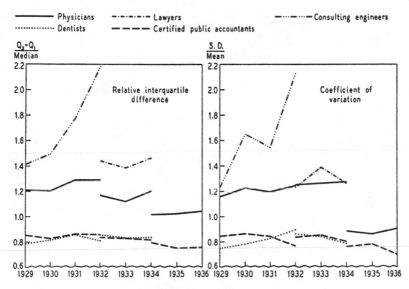

come (from large to small) is : engineering, law, medicine, accountancy, and dentistry.[13] The largest differences between successive members of this sequence seem to be from engineering to law and from medicine to accountancy. This order is confirmed by the other measures of relative variability in Table 13 and by Chart 10, which presents Lorenz curves for 1929 and 1933—the initial peak and the trough of the business cycle covered by our data.[14]

The similar order of the five professions by income level, absolute variability, and relative variability, while interesting

[13] Only one of the three original coefficients of variation for lawyers, but all the adjusted coefficients, exceed the corresponding coefficients for physicians (Table 13). Similarly, five out of seven of the original coefficients for accountants, but all except one of the adjusted coefficients, exceed those for dentists. Correction for the downward bias in the coefficient of variation thus seems to place law definitely above medicine, and accountancy above dentistry. However, the figures for dentists are solely for American Dental Association members and might be expected to be somewhat larger if they covered all dentists.

[14] See Ch. 3, footnote 5, for a description of the Lorenz curve.

CHART 10

Distribution of Income, 1929 and 1933

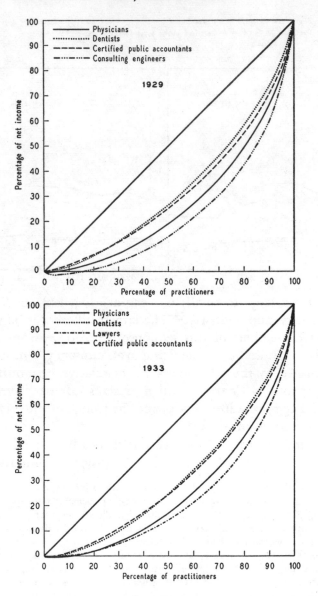

and suggestive, cannot be regarded as conclusively established. The number of professions is so small that chance alone might give rise to a considerable degree of similarity though it would be unlikely to give rise to so marked a degree of similarity as that observed; [15] in addition, considerable doubt attaches to the exact position assigned the professions by each criterion. The apparent association between relative variability and income level for the professions other than accountancy may well be accidental; the differences among them in relative variability may be the product of very different factors that happen in this instance to vary with income level. This possibility deserves special emphasis since the factors adduced in Section 3 of this chapter to explain the observed differences in relative variability seem to bear no necessary relation to income level.

c Variability of income for a longer period

A profession includes substantially the same individuals in successive years. Measures of the variability of annual income such as those used in the preceding section can be misleading because they take no account of this simple fact but are computed for each year as a self-contained unit. For example, suppose that two professions have identical frequency distributions of income in each year; that in one profession each individual maintains the same position in the income distribution from year to year, while in the other the positions of individuals change markedly, many of those at the top of the distribution in one year being at the bottom in another, and con

15 The probability that a degree of agreement in excess of that observed would arise from chance alone can be determined by computing the statistic χ_r^2 for the 5x3 table of ranks. χ_r^2 is 10.67 and would be exceeded by chance less than once in a hundred times. For a description of this test and for the tables used in determining the probability of exceeding the observed value of χ_r^2, see Milton Friedman, 'The Use of Ranks to Avoid the Assumption of Normality Implicit in the Analysis of Variance', *Journal of the American Statistical Association*, Dec. 1937, pp. 675–81, and 'A Comparison of Alternative Tests of Significance for the Problem of m Rankings', *Annals of Mathematical Statistics*, March 1940, p. 88.

versely. Clearly, there would be a real difference in the income structure of the two professions that could never be discerned from measures of the variability of annual income. In the first profession, income for a period longer than a year would vary exactly as much among the members of the profession as annual income; in the second, it would vary much less than annual income.

Fortunately, our data enable us to investigate the variability of income for periods longer than a year since each sample gives information on the incomes of the same individuals in three or four successive years. For this purpose, the data do have one shortcoming: they probably overstate the stability of individuals' incomes. The request that a respondent report his income for several years probably led some to report the same figure for each year, even though their incomes had varied. However, the resulting bias is probably not important, since the same income was reported for all years on relatively few returns.

Measures of the variability of income for a period longer than a year could be derived directly by computing the income of each individual for a two-, three-, or four-year period, and constructing the corresponding frequency distributions. We have not used this arduous method. Instead we have estimated the coefficient of variation for two- and three-year periods indirectly from the coefficients of variation of annual income and the correlation coefficients between the incomes of the same individual in different years. These correlation coefficients had to be computed for another purpose (see Ch. 7). None of the other measures of the relative variability of annual income can be easily converted into measures for a longer income period. The estimates of the coefficients of variation, as well as of the correlation coefficients used in deriving them, are given in Table 14.

Comparison of the coefficients of variation for two- and three-year income periods with those for a one-year period reveals a lessening of the differences among the professions, and some shift in their positions. For a one-year period, the

TABLE 14

Rough Estimates of Coefficient of Variation for
One-, Two-, and Three-year Income Periods

| | CORRELATION COEFFICIENT | | COEFFICIENT OF VARIATION FOR INCOME INTERVAL OF | | |
	Consecutive pair of years [1]	Nonconsecutive pair of years, 1 year intervening [2]	1 year [3]	2 years [5]	3 years [5]
Consulting engineers [4]	.672	.628	1.64	1.50	1.44
Lawyers [4]	.844	.795	1.30	1.24	1.22
Physicians	.933	.914	1.23	1.21	1.20
Certified public accountants [4]	.869	.758	.83	.80	.78
Dentists	.921	.875	.82	.80	.80
% by which largest figure in column exceeds smallest			100	88	80

[1] For physicians, dentists, lawyers, and engineers, arithmetic average of all consecutive-year correlation coefficients in Table 56. For accountants, arithmetic average of 1929–30, 1932–33, 1933–34 correlation coefficients.

[2] For physicians, dentists, lawyers, and engineers, arithmetic average of all correlation coefficients in Table 56 for nonconsecutive years, one year intervening. For accountants, arithmetic average of 1929–31, 1932–34 correlation coefficients.

[3] For dentists, lawyers, and engineers, arithmetic average of all coefficients of variation in Table 13. For physicians and accountants, arithmetic average of coefficients of variation from 1933 and 1935 samples only.

[4] Data for lawyers, accountants, and engineers are for individual practitioners only.

[5] The formulae used in computing the coefficients of variation for two- and three-year income periods are:

$$V_2 = V_1 \sqrt{\frac{1 + r_{12}}{2}};$$

$$V_3 = V_1 \sqrt{\frac{1}{3} + \frac{4 r_{12} + 2 r_{13}}{9}},$$

where V_1, V_2, and V_3 are the coefficients of variation for income periods of one, two, and three years respectively; r_{12} is the correlation coefficient between incomes in two successive years; r_{13} is the correlation coefficient between incomes in two nonconsecutive years with one year intervening. These formulae assume that the average annual income is the same in all three years and the standard deviation of annual income is the same in all three years. In addition, the second formula assumes that r_{12} is equal to r_{23}, i.e., that the correlation coefficient between incomes in the first and second years of the three-year period is the same as the correlation coefficient between incomes in the second and third years.

If we make a less restricted assumption, namely, that the coefficients of varia-

TABLE 14, NOTES (cont.)

tion in the different years are equal but the means and standard deviations separately need not be equal, and retain the assumption about the correlation coefficients we obtain the formulae

$$V_2 = V_1 \sqrt{1 - \frac{G^2_{12}}{2A^2_{12}}(1 - r_{12})};$$

$$V_3 = V_1 \sqrt{1 - \frac{2}{9A^2_{123}}\left[(G^2_{12} + G^2_{23})(1 - r_{12}) + G^2_{13}(1 - r_{13})\right]},$$

where G is the geometric mean of the arithmetic means of annual incomes, A, their arithmetic mean, and the subscripts to G and A, the years averaged. Since the geometric mean is equal to the arithmetic mean when the items averaged are equal, but less than the arithmetic mean otherwise, the coefficient of variation is reduced less by using a longer income period when the average income differs from year to year than when it is the same. Under the assumptions on which the last two formulae are based, the figures in the table overestimate somewhat the reduction in the coefficient of variation effected by using a longer income period.

largest coefficient of variation exceeds the smallest by 100 per cent; for a two-year period, by 88 per cent; and for a three-year period, by 80 per cent. The coefficient of variation is larger in accountancy than in dentistry for a one-year period, equal for a two-year period, and smaller for a three-year period. Despite these changes, the major conclusion of the earlier analysis is unaffected. Even for a three-year period, incomes vary decidedly more in engineering than in law and medicine, and more in these than in accountancy and dentistry. Except for engineering, not even the degree of variability is altered much. Apparently, in the other professions the income differences among individuals summarized by the measures of relative variability persist with extension of the period for which income is measured.

2   FACTORS MAKING FOR DIFFERENCES IN LEVEL OF INCOME, WITH SPECIAL REFERENCE TO PHYSICIANS AND DENTISTS

We can analyze in detail the factors making for interprofessional differences in average income for only two of the five professions covered by our primary data—medicine and dentistry. Lawyers are excluded because of the inadequacy of our data; we were able to determine their position relative to the other professions but not to assess the difference between average income in law and in the other professions.[15a] Consulting engineers and independent certified public accountants are excluded because the high income of these groups requires no detailed analysis.

The high income of these groups simply reflects the fact that they are small and select segments of broader professional groups, comprised of persons who perform the more difficult tasks and who have become independent in the main because they could thereby make more effective use of their training and skill. Independent certified public accountants numbered in 1930 about 10,000, all certified public accountants, 15,000, and all accountants and auditors, 192,000. Similarly, consulting engineers numbered in 1930 approximately 10,000, whereas all engineers numbered 226,000. The average income of these specialized groups might be expected to exceed the average income of other accountants and engineers.[16] Nor is it surprising that it exceeds the average income of independent practitioners in law, medicine, and dentistry, professions in which independent practice predominates.

A detailed comparison of the incomes of accountants and engineers with the incomes of the other professional groups would be justified only if our data were for all accountants and all engineers. The income differences among, let us say, all accountants and all lawyers or physicians could not be attributed to the mere technical fact that a narrow segment of one occupational group is being compared with another

15a The margin of uncertainty in our data for lawyers is exemplified by the fact that, according to the 1935 legal sample, the average income of lawyers in 1932–34 was about 2 per cent higher than the average income of physicians in the same years, while, according to the 1937 legal sample, it was about 50 per cent higher.

16 See Ch. 6, Sec. 3c for a discussion of the difference between the incomes of salaried and independent professional men.

broad occupational group, but would reflect basic economic factors such as the number of persons interested in entering various professions and able to do so, the number of persons already in the various professions, and the demand for their services. An analysis of the considerations that lead men to choose one profession rather than another must run in terms of the alternatives as they view them—not, of course, in terms of the particular niches, high or low, that they later attain. In selecting a profession, a person will usually contrast accountancy as a whole with other pursuits. Even if he does set the top grade of the profession, certified public accountancy, as his goal, he will probably realize that it will be some years after he has begun the practice of accountancy before he will become certified. In addition, he can seldom be sure in advance whether he will practise independently or as a salaried employee. The opportunities that arise after completion of training are likely to determine this issue. Similar considerations apply to men considering engineering, or one of its specific branches, as a profession. A man may 'decide' to be a civil, mechanical, or electrical engineer; he can hope but he cannot very well decide to practise at the 'top level' of his chosen profession—that is, practically speaking, to become a consulting engineer.

Our data for medicine and dentistry, however, permit fuller analysis. Although these data are also limited to persons in independent practice, in both professions independent practice predominates. The proportion of all practitioners in salaried employment is small, probably well under one-fifth, and is about the same for both professions (see Table 1). Their inclusion would not affect the average income of either group considerably; the difference between the averages would be affected even less. Moreover, our data yield estimates of differences in income level between medicine and dentistry that are sufficiently reliable to justify intensive analysis.

The comparison we propose to make in this section is between the level of income of all physicians and of all dentists.

A question might be raised whether the much greater importance of specialization in medicine than in dentistry does not make this comparison inappropriate. May not young men really choose between general practice in medicine and general practice in dentistry, or between specialized practice in medicine and specialized practice in dentistry, rather than simply between medicine and dentistry? The answer to this question seems to us to be clearly in the negative. During the period when the physicians and dentists covered by our data were trained, and in the main even today, few prospective physicians or dentists could be sure in advance of the type of practice they were going to follow. Specialization was a hope for some, a possibility for most, and an undesirable outcome for only a few. And upon graduation from professional school few men immediately became specialists and then remained specialists for their entire career. Young men ordinarily started as general practitioners. In the course of time, some developed special interests and acquired a reputation and clientele that permitted them to concentrate on those special interests and made it worth while for them to do so. Others developed special interests too, but were unable to concentrate on them because they could not attract sufficient clientele. Still others remained general practitioners from inclination. Probably the bulk of the men who became specialists had little or no extra training and incurred little extra cost (a condition that has changed somewhat during recent years with the establishment of separate boards and requirements for the specialties). Since most persons thinking of becoming physicians or dentists consider specialization a possibility, the earnings of specialists are no less relevant to their choice of occupation than the earnings of general practitioners. The relevant occupational groups for a comparative analysis are therefore physicians as a whole and dentists as a whole, just as we saw above that the relevant groups are accountants as a whole and engineers as a whole.[17]

[17] The fact that physicians as a whole and dentists as a whole are the relevant occupational groups for our present purpose does not, of course, mean that the greater specialization in medicine has no influence on the levels of income in

The average income of all physicians, according to the estimates in Table 11, is approximately 32 per cent larger than
that of all dentists.[18] Moreover, this difference between the
countrywide averages understates the difference between the
average incomes of physicians and dentists in the same community and in practice the same number of years; i.e., according to the data summarized in the next two paragraphs,
adjusting the average incomes for the difference between physicians and dentists in their distribution by number of years
in practice or by location would widen rather than narrow the
gap between the averages.

Estimates for 1929 of the average net income of dentists in
general practice by year of graduation from dental school, and
the percentage distribution of physicians by number of years
in practice, are given by Maurice Leven.[19] The average income
of the dentists is $4,790. Assuming dentists distributed by
years in practice as physicians are, i.e., weighting the average
income of the dentists in each 'years-in-practice' group by the
percentage of physicians in that group, gives an average of
$4,764, which is slightly *lower* than the original average. Data
for 1933 from the *California Medical-Economic Survey* con-

---

the two professions, or that the differences between the incomes of specialists
and general practitioners are not of interest in their own right. Perhaps the
major effect of the greater specialization in medicine on levels of income is
through the greater variability of income in medicine than in dentistry for
which it is partly responsible. This effect is discussed below in Sec. 2b. The
income differences among physicians and dentists classified by type of practice
(general practitioners, partial specialists, and complete specialists) are discussed
in Ch. 6, Sec. 3a.

18 See the Appendix to this chapter (Sec. 2), for a detailed examination of the
statistical validity of the observed difference of 32 per cent.

19 *Practice of Dentistry*, p. 125, and *Incomes of Physicians* (University of Chicago
Press, 1932), p. 114. Leven's dental sample of 4,189 dentists in 20 states includes
311 dentists whose incomes he used only in obtaining the average for the
sample as a whole because the year of graduation was either unknown or before
1890. The average we use excludes these 311 dentists. The distribution of
physicians by number of years in practice is based on a random sample of
11,766 physicians in the 1929 Directory of the American Medical Association
taken proportionately from cities of different size.

firm these results.[20] The average income of the physicians covered by this survey is $3,567, of the dentists, $2,769. The average income of physicians, weighted by the years-in-practice distribution of dentists, is $3,705. The average income of dentists, weighted by the years-in-practice distribution of physicians, is $2,635. Both methods of adjusting for the difference in distribution by years in practice widen the spread between the averages for the two professions.

Evidence on the influence of geographic location and size of community is provided by our own data. If we omit from our 1935 samples the 29 returns for physicians and the 12 returns for dentists for which size of community or region is unknown, the average 1934 income of physicians is $3,324, and of dentists, $2,616. Weighting the averages for each profession in each size of community class in each region by the number of returns for the other profession in the corresponding class gives averages of $3,482 for physicians and $2,595 for dentists. Both comparisons suggest that correcting for differences in location would widen the spread between the average incomes.

What factors explain the large and seemingly persistent difference between the average incomes of physicians and dentists living in the same community and in practice the same number of years? Medicine and dentistry are related professions requiring somewhat similar abilities and training. Many of the persons choosing one of the professions might be expected to have considered the other as an alternative. Moreover, since the preliminary training required for the two professions is virtually identical,[21] the final choice between them can be post-

[20] *Formal Report on Factual Data* (California Medical Association, 1937), pp. 80, 88. This survey provides data for 2,686 physicians and 1,595 dentists on average net income in 1933 by the number of years since completion of training as well as the corresponding frequency distributions of the samples. These figures, as well as those cited in the text, exclude 51 physicians and 20 dentists whose period of practice was unknown.

[21] The period of training after high school required before admittance to professional school is ordinarily shorter for dentistry. However, the predental curriculum, as far as it goes, is almost identical with the corresponding portion of the premedical curriculum.

poned longer than between most other professions. If entry into the two professions were equally easy or difficult, one might expect an adjustment of the levels of return in them that would equalize their net attractiveness in the eyes of a considerable fraction of those in a position to choose between them. Any difference in income would then be explained by the type of adjustment discussed in the introduction to this chapter, i.e., the levels of return would be 'equilibrium' levels, in the sense that they would be relative returns resulting from the free and moderately rational choice of profession by prospective entrants.[22]

It is clear from the discussion in Chapter 1 and from the data on entrants there presented that the actual levels of return are not 'equilibrium' levels in this sense. During recent years, more than four times as many persons applied annually for admission to American medical schools as for admission to American dental schools. If we correct for persons who were applying again after having previously been refused, between three and a half and four times as many persons were seeking to become physicians as dentists, although there were only slightly over twice as many physicians as dentists in practice.[23] The number seeking to enter medicine would doubtless have been even greater, were not potential entrants aware of the greater difficulty of entry into medicine; and the number seeking to enter dentistry is doubtless swelled by persons who think they may be or actually are unsuccessful in gaining entry into medicine.

Apparently, at existing levels of remuneration, prospective practitioners consider medicine more attractive than dentistry: were entry into the two professions equally easy, there would be a tendency for the number of physicians to increase relatively to the number of dentists and for the gap between average incomes to narrow. The observed difference in in-

22 See Sec. 2d below for a more rigorous definition of 'equilibrium' levels of return.
23 See Ch. 1, Sec. 2, especially footnote 40f.

comes is therefore apparently greater than the 'equilibrium' difference.

The figures on entry are *alone* sufficient to establish this qualitative conclusion. But we must go beyond them and tread on much less firm ground to determine how much of the more than 32 per cent difference between the average incomes of physicians and dentists living in the same community and in practice the same number of years is attributable to factors connected with the free and moderately rational choice of profession by prospective entrants and how much to the greater difficulty of entry into medicine. In analyzing income differences between the professions and other pursuits in the preceding chapter, we made no attempt to answer the parallel question in precise quantitative terms. It seems worth attempting to arrive at such an answer for medicine and dentistry, if only to illustrate more comprehensively and exactly the considerations on which the answer depends. These fairly clearly defined and relatively homogeneous professions, for which data are reasonably plentiful, lend themselves to such an analysis far better than such vague and heterogeneous groups as the professions, on the one hand, and all other pursuits, on the other. Though phrased in terms of medicine and dentistry, the analysis is of fairly general applicability. The factors considered are important not only for these professions but for others, and for many nonprofessional pursuits.

a Effect of differences in length of training

One of the major factors making for a difference in average income is the difference in the period of training. Typically, physicians beginning practice have had from eight to ten years of training after high school; dentists, from five to seven.[24] The physician's three additional years of training entail special costs for tuition fees, professional equipment, books, and the like. Moreover, if we may assume an equally long expected active life for physicians and dentists, the addi-

[24] The periods of training cited represent current experience rather than legal requirements; the latter are usually somewhat lower (see Ch. 1).

tional years of training shorten the period during which the physician earns an income. More important than either, however, is the cost arising from the postponement of income. The prospective physician or dentist must consider that if he chooses medicine each annual installment of income will be received three years later than if he chooses dentistry. At an annual interest rate of 4 per cent each installment of income from medicine would have to be approximately 12.5 per cent larger than the corresponding installment from dentistry in order that the 'present value' of the two installments, at the time of making the decision, may be equal.[25] The influence of the first two items, the additional special costs and the shorter working life of physicians, is more difficult to estimate. However, the exceedingly rough data we have assembled suggest that the figure of 12.5 per cent just cited would have to be raised to about 17 per cent to take these into account; i.e., that the expected annual return from medicine would have to be 17 per cent more than from dentistry to make the two professions equally attractive financially (or actuarially).[26] It should be noted that this figure of 17 per cent is valid only for the expected (arithmetic mean) annual return. Because of the difference between the frequency distributions of income in the two professions, a different (and lower) figure would be valid for median incomes, and still another for modal incomes. We have not attempted to estimate corresponding figures for such other measures of the level of income, since they would add nothing to the substance of the analysis but would merely permit its restatement in different terms.

The relevance of this figure of 17 per cent for an analysis of actual income differences may be questioned. Young men choosing a profession have neither the knowledge of costs

25 By 'corresponding' installments we mean installments received the same number of years after *beginning practice*. There will obviously be a difference of three years in the dates at which these installments would be received. The figure 12.5 is equal to 100 $[(1.04)^3 - 1]$, assuming annual compounding.

26 A detailed explanation of the way the figure of 17 per cent was derived and of the assumptions underlying it is given in the Appendix to this chapter (Sec. 1a).

and returns nor the mathematical training needed to arrive at such an estimate; moreover, even if they had this knowledge, few would take the trouble to make an exact numerical calculation. And, of course, many men have so definite a liking for one profession or another that pecuniary calculations play a minor role in their choice. The computation and presentation of a figure with the aura of exactness possessed by '17 per cent' may seem an attempt to force into a rigid and precise mold a process that is essentially vague and unprecise. But if few or no individuals go through the reasoning or calculation underlying our estimate, many do try to take account in some way of the differential costs attached to the choice of one profession rather than another. Implicitly or explicitly, they do attempt to estimate the difference in incomes that will compensate for these costs. It seems reasonable to suppose that they are as likely to overestimate as to underestimate; and, on the whole, we may expect the estimates to cluster about the correct value. And 17 per cent is our best (though admittedly rough) *estimate* of this correct value. It summarizes the objective facts that impinge more or less strongly and more or less accurately on individual evaluations of costs and returns. It is of little use in explaining the behavior of any one individual; it may be significant in explaining the behavior of the group of prospective entrants as a whole.

b Effect of variability of income

So far we have considered only what might be called the 'actuarial' aspect of the choice of a profession. Consequently, we have been concerned solely with the arithmetic mean incomes of physicians and dentists, since these are the figures required for an analysis of 'expected' returns. Presumably individuals' decisions are affected not only by the expected arithmetic mean income but also by the variability of income within the profession, i.e., by the likelihood of receiving incomes that deviate more or less from the average.

As we saw in the preceding section of this chapter, physicians' incomes display greater absolute and relative variability than dentists'. The wider variety of services rendered by physicians gives wider scope for diversity of talent and for specialization of activity (see Sec. 3 below). In consequence, a larger percentage of physicians than of dentists receive exceedingly low incomes and at the same time, a larger percentage of physicians than of dentists receive exceedingly high incomes. Median incomes in medicine and in dentistry are closer than mean incomes. Indeed, the median incomes computed from our original samples are about equal for the two professions: the median income of physicians ranges from $4,223 in 1929 to $2,400 in 1933; the median income of dentists, from $4,080 in 1929 to $2,414 in 1933 (Table 10). However, if the medians for dentists were corrected for the restriction of our samples to American Dental Association members they would be below those for physicians—though how much below we are not in a position to say.[27] Similarly, the modal incomes in the two professions—the most frequent incomes—are closer than the mean incomes and indeed may be lower in medicine than in dentistry, though again the bias in our dental samples makes a definite statement impossible.

Whether wide variability of income acts as an attraction or a deterrent is not clear. Does the gambling instinct outweigh the urge for security and lead more young men to choose medicine than would do so if the variability of income were the same? Or is the reverse true? There is no empirical basis for either conclusion; and on subjects such as these, *a priori* speculation is peculiarly subject to error. Nevertheless, we may hazard the guess that the greater variability of income acts as an attraction. The urge for security among the parents of prospective entrants is likely to be more than counterbalanced by a natural overvaluation of their progeny's ability and

27 It should be recalled that we lowered the *arithmetic mean* income of dentists 12.4 per cent to correct for the restriction of the samples to American Dental Association members. We do not know whether a larger or smaller correction should be applied to the medians.

chance of success; and among the prospective entrants themselves the gambling instinct is likely to be the stronger.[28] If
these observations are correct, then, if *all other things were the
same,* a difference in expected average income just sufficient

[28] "Two different causes contribute to recommend them [the liberal and honor-
able professions]. First, the desire of the reputation which attends upon superior
excellence in any of them; and, secondly, the natural confidence which every
man has more or less, not only in his own abilities, but in his own good
fortune. . . .

The overweening conceit which the greater part of men have of their own
abilities is an ancient evil remarked by the philosophers and moralists of all
ages. Their absurd presumption in their own good fortune has been less taken
notice of. It is, however, if possible, still more universal. There is no man
living who, when in tolerable health and spirits, has not some share of it. The
chance of gain is by every man more or less over-valued, and the chance of
loss is by most men under-valued, and by scarce any man, who is in tolerable
health and spirits, valued more than it is worth. . . .

The contempt of risk and the presumptuous hope of success are in no period
of life more active than at the age at which young people choose their professions. How little the fear of misfortune is then capable of balancing the
hope of good luck appears still more evidently in the readiness of the common
people to enlist as soldiers, or to go to sea, than in the eagerness of those of
better fashion to enter into what are called the liberal professions." Smith,
Wealth of Nations, pp. 95–7.

"There are many people of a sober steady-going temper, who like to know
what is before them, and who would far rather have an appointment which
offered a certain income of say £400 a year than one which was not unlikely to
yield £600, but had an equal chance of affording only £200. Uncertainty, therefore, which does not appeal to great ambitions and lofty aspirations, has
special attractions for very few; while it acts as a deterrent to many of those
who are making their choice of a career. And as a rule the certainty of moderate
success attracts more than an expectation of an uncertain success that has an
equal actuarial value.

But on the other hand, if an occupation offers a few extremely high prizes,
its attractiveness is increased out of all proportion to their aggregate value.
For this there are two reasons. The first is that young men of an adventurous
disposition are more attracted by the prospects of a great success than they
are deterred by the fear of failure; and the second is that the social rank of
an occupation depends more on the highest dignity and the best position which
can be attained through it than on the average good fortune of those engaged
in it." Marshall, *Principles of Economics,* pp. 554–5.

That the present instance is of the second rather than the first of the types
considered by Marshall is fairly clear, both from the wide dispersion and the
extreme skewness of the frequency distribution of incomes in medicine and
from the existence even in our samples of a few incomes in medicine much
larger than any reported in dentistry.

to compensate for the extra financial costs incident to the choice of medicine, combined with a greater variability of income in medicine, would mean that more individuals would choose medicine than dentistry as a career.

c Nonpecuniary factors affecting the choice of a profession
But what are these 'other things' assumed the same in the preceding sentence? And what is their effect on the rates of return that would be considered 'equivalent' by prospective entrants? In the main, they include those nonpecuniary advantages and disadvantages that must be valued and added to or subtracted from expected earnings in order to obtain what Marshall has designated an occupation's "net advantages".[29] The decisions of prospective entrants to a profession are affected not only by expected pecuniary returns but also by such subjective and intangible factors as the prestige value attached to the profession, the opportunity it offers for rendering service and making 'social contacts', the conditions under which professional work is performed, and personal predilections for one type of work rather than another. Here again, empirical analysis is difficult. But there would probably be little disagreement with the conclusion that, if pecuniary returns were equal, the "net advantages" would very definitely be on the side of medicine. Medicine, indeed, involves less regular and longer hours, less personal freedom, the inconvenience of 'home' calls at any hour of the day or night, and consequently, greater physical and mental strain. Another factor that may be important is that the individual choosing medicine must ordinarily reckon on postponing both marriage and the attainment of financial independence longer than if he entered almost any other profession. On the other hand, medicine is held in higher general esteem than dentistry, offers greater opportunity to render service, partakes more of a 'professional' and 'scientific' character as opposed to a 'commercial' one, and involves work that most people would probably consider more 'interesting'.

It seems clear that although a 17 per cent excess of the aver-

29 *Ibid.*, pp. 73, 557.

age income of physicians over that of dentists might make the two professions equally attractive financially, medicine would be the more attractive if nonpecuniary factors were considered as well; i.e., if incomes differed by 17 per cent, more persons would choose medicine than would choose dentistry—and we suspect, very many more.[30]

As this analysis implies, individuals differ in their evaluation of the advantages and disadvantages of a particular profession. Some would prefer dentistry to medicine even if medicine promised a much larger income, although presumably fewer would do so the larger the expected excess of the income from medicine. Conversely, some would prefer medicine to dentistry even if dentistry promised a much larger income, although again presumably fewer would do so the larger the expected financial advantage of dentistry. Not only may individuals regard other advantages as more than compensating for a financial sacrifice, but also they may not consider themselves equally suited for the two professions. An individual who has a relatively greater aptitude for dentistry may well feel that *he* will be able to earn more in dentistry even though average income is larger in medicine, and conversely. The difference in aptitude may be so great for some individuals as to rule out one or the other profession completely; these will be little affected by relative returns in the two professions. Our analysis assumes that there are many whose aptitudes are not so specialized—clearly a valid assumption for two professions

[30] An interesting check on the validity of our conclusion that the nonpecuniary advantages are on the side of medicine is provided by the replies of a group of college freshmen and sophomores to the questions whether they would expect higher incomes from medicine or dentistry and which profession they would prefer. Of the 73 replying, 40 thought medicine would yield the larger income, and 35 of these preferred medicine. Of the 33 who thought dentistry would yield the larger income, 26 preferred medicine. Thus most students preferred medicine whether or not they expected it to yield the larger income; a slightly larger proportion of those who thought medicine would yield the larger income preferred medicine than of those who thought dentistry would yield the larger income. The students to whom the questions were put were in the main not premedical or predental students, although a few may have been. We are indebted to C. L. Harriss for having conducted this experiment for us.

as similar as medicine and dentistry; for these, differences in aptitude will enter into the choice of a profession but will not determine it.

If all individuals evaluated identically the pecuniary and nonpecuniary factors, the 'equilibrium' difference in income, as we use that term, would necessarily be the difference that would make the two professions equally attractive to *all* prospective entrants, and hence would depend solely on conditions of supply. Since individual evaluations are not the same, the actual difference between the 'equilibrium' levels of return depends also on the relative demand for the services of the two professions.

d Influence of demand

The larger the demand for medical services relatively to the demand for dental services, the larger the ratio of physicians to dentists that is consistent with any specific ratio between their incomes; or, alternatively, the larger the ratio between their incomes that is consistent with a specific ratio between their numbers. Under given conditions of demand, the 'equilibrium' difference is the difference that induces prospective entrants to choose medicine and dentistry in just the proportion required to maintain the existing ratio of physicians to dentists, i.e., to maintain the existing ratio between their incomes. In other words, to any given difference in average income, say 17 per cent, corresponds a definite ratio of (1) physicians to dentists, and (2) persons seeking to enter medicine to persons seeking to enter dentistry. The assumed difference of 17 per cent is the 'equilibrium' difference if the second of these ratios is just large enough to maintain the first, i.e., roughly speaking, if the second ratio is about equal to the first.[31] The 'equilibrium' difference is more than 17 per cent

31 The qualification 'roughly speaking' is necessary because differences in age distribution, ability required, etc., may mean that the ratio of applicants would have to differ somewhat from the ratio of practitioners to keep the latter constant.

if the second ratio is smaller than the first, and less than 17 per cent if the second is larger than the first.[32]

At present, average incomes differ by over 32 per cent, there are slightly over twice as many physicians as dentists, and from three and a half to four times as many persons seeking to become physicians as dentists. To reduce the difference in average income to 17 per cent, the number of physicians would have to increase relatively to the number of dentists. It is, of course, impossible to say exactly how much, but it may be hazarded that, at most, there would have to be about three times as many physicians as dentists.[33] If so, about 75 per cent of all entrants to the two professions would have to choose a medical career promising a difference of 17 per cent in average income in order that such a difference, once achieved, might be maintained, i.e., in order that 17 per cent might be the 'equilibrium' difference. On the basis of our preceding analysis and of the number of persons currently seeking to enter the two professions, the choice of medicine by an even greater proportion of new entrants seems not unreasonable. We are led to the highly tentative conclusion, based on many questionable figures and uncertain assumptions, that the equilibrium rate

[32] This theoretical statement is in some degree inexact, since, under given conditions of demand, it is entirely possible for more than one ratio of the number of practitioners to be consistent with a fixed ratio of incomes, if the number of practitioners in the two professions combined varies. Exactness would have required phrasing the discussion in terms of absolute incomes and of the absolute number of practitioners and of new entrants in each profession. The conclusions would in no wise have been altered, but the exposition would have been more complicated. The theoretical nature of the concepts used is discussed in greater detail in Sec. 3a of the Appendix to this chapter

[33] The ratio of 3 to 1 as a maximum estimate is suggested by the following considerations:

1) If the ratio of the total sum spent on medicine to the total spent on dentistry were to remain constant, a rise in the ratio of the number of physicians to the number of dentists from the present figure of 2.1 to 2.4 would suffice to reduce the ratio of average incomes from 1.32 to 1.17.

2) The reduction of the ratio of incomes from 1.32 to 1.17 as a result of a rise in the ratio of the number of practitioners from 2.1 to 3.0 would imply a 27 per cent increase in the ratio of the total amount spent on medicine to the total spent on dentistry.

See also the Appendix to this chapter (Sec. 3b, footnote 23).

of return in medicine would not exceed that in dentistry by more than about 17 per cent; i.e., that 17 per cent can be accepted not only as the difference in income that would make the two professions equally attractive financially, but also as an upper estimate of the equilibrium difference.

e Barriers to rapid adjustment

The observed difference between the average incomes of physicians and dentists in the same community and in practice the same number of years is over 32 per cent; about twice as large as our upper estimate of the 'equilibrium' difference. Before attaching any great importance to this divergence, we must investigate the possibility that it is merely a transitional phenomenon.

The long training required for both professions necessarily makes for slow adjustment of the number of practitioners to changes in cost or in conditions of demand. The great majority of the men now practising medicine and dentistry were affected in their choice of profession by conditions prevailing a decade or more ago. Consequently the excess of the observed over the 'equilibrium' difference might be interpreted as reflecting a rise in the demand for medical services relative to the demand for dental services, or a decline in the extra costs attached to the choice of medicine and, hence, in the 'equilibrium' difference. And, according to this interpretation, sufficient time has not yet elapsed for complete adjustment to the new conditions.

This interpretation is of doubtful validity. There is no evidence to suggest that demand for medical services has risen relatively to demand for dental services; indeed, a rising level of education and living could more plausibly be expected to favor greater attention to dental care than to the more obvious and longer recognized need for medical care. Other things the same, this would have resulted in an observed difference less than the 'equilibrium' difference. The possibility that the observed difference has as yet failed to catch up with a decline in the extra costs attached to the choice of medicine, and, hence, in the 'equilibrium' difference, seems equally unlikely. The data underlying our estimate of the 'equilibrium' difference relate not solely to the last year or two, but to a longer period, dating back at least to 1929. The major part of the equilibrium difference as approximated would have been little affected had the approximation been made for, say, the middle or late 'twenties. Hence the change in the excess costs attached to becoming a physician, required by this interpretation, would have had to take place at the very latest about ten years prior to the end of the period covered by our income data. Sufficient time would thus have elapsed for the process of adjustment to have started, although not necessarily to have been completed. But, if the adjustment had started, the gap between incomes in medicine and dentistry would have narrowed during the period for which we have income data, whereas it has, if anything, widened.

The period covered by our data is perhaps too short to justify a definitive judgment whether the income differential is transitory. And the possibility is not barred that the recent trends in relative demand were in favor of medicine rather than dentistry. At the same time, such evidence as is available runs counter to an interpretation that would assign differential trends in demand or costs a significant part in explaining the divergence between the observed and 'equilibrium' differences in medical and dental incomes.

f Difficulty of entry

It seems reasonable to conclude that this divergence between the observed and 'equilibrium' difference is primarily attributable to the greater difficulty of entry into medicine than into dentistry noted in Chapter 1.[34]

There are three possible explanations of this difference between medicine and dentistry in ease of entry. One is that it reflects a factor omitted from the analysis underlying our estimate of the 'equilibrium' difference, namely, the relative sup-

[34] See particularly the discussion in Ch. 1, Sec. 1 and 2.

ply of 'innate abilities' needed in the two professions. According to this explanation, the greater difficulty of entry into medicine is a result of a greater scarcity of the 'innate abilities' needed in medicine than of those needed in dentistry. This may be part of the explanation; two considerations—one *a priori,* the other empirical—give reason to doubt that it is the entire explanation. In the first place, much the same type of ability seems to be needed for both professions. In the second place, the particular applicants admitted are presumably those whom the medical schools deem ablest; yet, only a slightly smaller proportion of applicants who have previously been refused are accepted than of new applicants—that is, those applying for the first time. The percentage of new applicants accepted in 1927, 1928, and 1929 can be estimated as 59.4, 56.4, and 52.3, respectively, and the percentage of applicants previously refused who were accepted as 56.0, 54.4, and 48.1.[35] The time elapsing between the first refusal and subsequent application may, indeed, have been spent in additional training and a larger proportion of the applicants previously refused than of new applicants may apply to medical schools with relatively low percentages of refusals. Nevertheless, it seems probable that the supply of innate ability is sufficient to furnish each year more medical students than are admitted to medical schools. Certainly the opposite view has not been established.

A second possible explanation is that the difference in ease of entry reflects a scarcity of training facilities, so that the admission of more students would crowd the existing facilities and impair standards. The persistence of the difference does not of itself undermine this explanation. Facilities may have been expanded in response to the demand for medical training, but standards of education and the quantity of equipment required for each student may have risen equally rapidly. An adequate judgment of this explanation would require a far more intimate and detailed knowledge than we possess of

[35] See Ch. 1, footnote 23.

physical and human facilities, the possibilities of expanding them, the equipment needed to provide adequate training, changes in the nature of training deemed adequate by qualified judges, etc.

A third possible explanation is that the difference in ease of entry reflects a deliberate policy of limiting the total number of physicians to prevent so-called 'overcrowding' of the profession. An adequate judgment of this explanation would be exceedingly difficult and is well outside the scope of this study. It would require an analysis of the motives, acts, and influence of each group involved in controlling entry into medicine—the American Medical Association and its Council on Medical Education, the individual medical schools and their national association, the state boards of medical examiners and their national federation.[36]

As already suggested, we are in no position to judge the relative importance of these possible explanations of the greater difficulty of entry into medicine. But the effect of this greater difficulty of entry seems clear: it has made possible or has maintained a level of income in medicine exceeding that in dentistry by more than can be attributed to the free working of the much-abused law of supply and demand. If we accept our highly tentative figure of 17 per cent as an upper estimate of the excess of mean income in medicine consistent with completely free and moderately rational choice of profession, then about half of the observed difference between the mean incomes of physicians and dentists is attributable to the greater difficulty of entry into medicine.

3 FACTORS MAKING FOR DIFFERENCES IN THE VARIABILITY OF
   INCOME

In our analysis of levels of income, we treat each profession as a unit and emphasize its homogeneity. From the standpoint of a young man balancing the advantages of one profession against another, differences among professions are more im-

36 See in this connection Ch. 1, Sec. 1.

portant than differences within professions. Not knowing what
position he will ultimately attain in the profession he chooses,
he must contrast one profession as a whole with another. In an
analysis of variability of income, we must emphasize the
heterogeneity of each profession. From this standpoint, the important aspect of a profession is the variety of services rendered
and prices charged.

The personal nature of professional services limits the
quantity that any practitioner can render. Expansion through
the employment of assistants is possible but cannot go far because the professional man himself must take prime responsibility. Differences among professional men in the quantity of
services they sell can therefore lead to differences in income
only at the lower end of the income scale; the major part of
the variability of income must reflect primarily differences in
the prices charged.

If professional services were standardized and competition
pervaded the market for them, price differences could not arise
within a profession. The professional man who charged a high
price would lose his customers; the professional man who
charged a low price would have more customers than he could
handle. But professional services are not standardized and
competition is far from perfect. The professional man renders
services whose quality cannot easily be judged by a layman
objectively; the 'customer' often does not even know what he
wants to buy; he buys what the professional man tells him he
needs. Since he can seldom judge directly the quality of the
highly specialized services, he must discriminate among professional men on the basis of reputation, personal integrity,
personality, and the like. Hence, the market for professional
services is dominated by differentiation of product and imper-
fection of competition. Different practitioners can charge different prices for services that seem similar, though they may
not be so; and each can charge different prices to different customers, as the widespread use of the 'sliding scale' testifies.[37]

37 See Leven, *Incomes of Physicians*, pp. 61–4, and *Practice of Dentistry*, pp. 65,
205.

Each has customers he will not lose by charging higher prices than his rivals, and each knows that he cannot attract large numbers of new customers by charging lower prices.

Though differentiation of product characterizes all professions it is not equally important and does not lead to the same variety of prices in all. How widely prices will vary depends on (1) the 'real' quality variation in the services rendered by professional men, (2) the role played by subjective criteria of quality, and (3) the importance consumers attach to purchasing services that they think are 'better'. Medicine and dentistry exemplify how differences in these factors can lead to differences in the variability of income. (1) Medical services are probably intrinsically more variable in quality and less standardized—note the much greater specialization in medicine than in dentistry. (2) Subjective criteria have greater scope in medicine both because medical services are less easily judged and because consumers more often purchase—and know that they are purchasing—the same type of dental service from time to time than the same type of medical service. (3) Medical services are ordinarily deemed more essential than dental, i.e., an individual's demand for medical services is more inelastic; a smaller incentive is required to induce an individual to patronize a dentist he considers inferior to another than to patronize a physician he considers inferior. All three factors work in the same direction and help to account for the greater variability of medical than of dental incomes. The only factor that might work in the opposite direction would be a greater possibility in dentistry than in medicine of expanding the quantity of service rendered by a professional unit; but if there is such a difference, it can scarcely be large.

The very much greater variability of income in engineering than in accountancy can be accounted for by the same factors. Much of the accountant's work is routine and recurs regularly—the books must be audited periodically and each audit is similar to the preceding. Consulting engineers, on the other hand, are usually required only in connection with a new undertaking, different from preceding ones. Their services are seldom required periodically. Hence, (1) there is greater intrinsic variability in the kind of work consulting engineers perform; (2) the purchasers of their services rarely have an opportunity to 'shop around', to experiment under similar conditions now with one engineer, now with another, or even to specify very exactly the kind of work required; (3) more importance is attached to the proper choice of a consulting engineer, since the costs incident to a bad choice are larger.

The degree to which the factors so far discussed can produce variability of professional income is conditioned by the variability among consumers in the resources they have or can command. Variability of income is pervasive: present in one sector of the economy, it is likely to lead to variability elsewhere. If all consumers had the same resources, professional men whose services were generally considered superior would still receive higher prices; but price differences would be far smaller than at present when differences in quality judgments are reinforced by differences in resources. Price differences are now so great as to lead to extensive stratification of practitioners in terms of the economic status of their clientele.[38] The role played by the variability of resources among purchasers is responsible for our limitation of the comparisons made above to professions serving essentially the same market: physicians and dentists serve ultimate consumers almost exclusively, engineers and accountants serve business enterprises and governmental bod-

[38] In a study of dentists' incomes in 1929, the respondents were requested to specify the percentage of their patients whose annual family income was less than $1,500, between $1,500 and $3,000, between $3,000 and $6,000, and over $6,000. Of 3,600 replying, 2,133 reported that 60 per cent of their clients were included in one of these classes; only 27 had a clientele so scattered that 60 per cent were not included within two classes. Among the 2,133 dentists, a much larger percentage of complete and partial specialists than of general practitioners had a clientele concentrated in the upper income groups. That is, of course, what would be expected from and would be expected to lead to the higher incomes of specialists. An analysis of charges for specified dental services likewise reveals, with few exceptions, that the higher the income class from which most of the practitioners' clients come, the higher the average charge. See Leven, *Practice of Dentistry*, pp. 39–42, 62–3, 217. (The figure of 3,600 for the number of dentists replying to the question on the economic status of their clientele is derived from other figures given by Leven.)

ies. We have not compared law with any other profession, because law serves both ultimate consumers and business enterprises.

Business enterprises almost certainly vary more in the resources they have or can command than ultimate consumers, and we suspect that this is true also of the business enterprises that are prospective purchasers of accounting and engineering services. This difference in the variability of resources would tend to make for greater variability of income in engineering and accountancy than in medicine and dentistry. Another factor that would work in the same direction is the greater possibility in the business than in the curative professions of expanding the quantity of service rendered by means of the employment of assistants. There is one important factor, however, that would tend to work in the opposite direction. An ultimate consumer tends to buy smaller quantities of services than a business enterprise, he buys the same type of service less frequently, and he is less addicted to economic calculation.[39] In consequence, he is much less able or likely to get objective evidence on quality or to let pecuniary considerations guide his purchases. Here, as elsewhere, differentiation of product is likely to be more widespread on the market for consumers' goods than on the market for producers' goods.

We have no basis for judging the quantitative importance of these counterbalancing tendencies. We know only their joint effect on variability of income: the order of the professions by relative variability of income (from large to small) is engineering, law, medicine, accountancy, and dentistry.

[39] See Wesley C. Mitchell, *Backward Art of Spending Money* (McGraw-Hill, 1937), pp. 3-19.

APPENDIX TO CHAPTER 4

1 HOW THE EFFECT OF DIFFERENCE IN LENGTH OF TRAINING IS ES-
TIMATED [1]

a Physicians and dentists

As stated in Section 2a of the text, medical training is approximately three years longer than dental. How can we estimate the difference in average incomes that would compensate for the extra costs entailed by this three-year difference? Let

u = number of years by which working life in dentistry exceeds working life in medicine;

t = number of years of extra training in medicine;

V = present value of the returns in dentistry for all except the last u years of the dentist's working life;

v = present value of the returns in dentistry for these last u years;

c = present value of the extra costs incident to acquiring a medical education;

i = interest rate at which future returns and costs are discounted; this is the rate implicit in the three present values just defined.

V, v, and c may be computed as of any date. For convenience, we take them to refer to the date of beginning the practice of *dentistry*.

For the two professions to be financially equivalent, each installment of income from medicine should bear to the 'corresponding' installment of income from dentistry, i.e., to the installment received the same number of years after beginning practice, a ratio

$$(1) \qquad k = \frac{V + v + c}{V} (1 + i)^t.$$

[1] A friend suggests that a not unimportant by-product of this section is that it demonstrates the difficulties involved in a serious attempt to choose between professions on strictly financial grounds, and the uncertain applicability of the most careful calculations to the fortunes of a given individual in the uncertain future. An appreciation of these difficulties and uncertainties goes far toward explaining and perhaps justifying the loose methods by which young men seem to form their expectations and choose their occupations.

The numerator of the fraction is the present value of the income sacrificed by an individual choosing medicine plus the present value of the extra costs of a medical education. It therefore indicates what the present value of the physician's series of returns would have to be, if they were received at the same dates as the dentist's returns, in order to equal the total financial sacrifice made in choosing medicine. The denominator of the fraction is the present value that would be sacrificed by the physician if there were no difference in working life or in educational costs. The fraction gives the figure by which each installment of income entering into V would have to be multiplied in order that the present value of the installments should equal the numerator of the fraction.[2] The second part of the formula, $(1 + i)^t$, allows for the fact, so far neglected, that each installment of income from medicine is received t years later than the 'corresponding' installment from dentistry.

Since k is the ratio between 'corresponding' installments of income, it can be interpreted as the ratio of the average annual income from medicine to the average annual income from all but the last u years of dentistry. In order to compute the ratio of average incomes, where for both professions the averages are for the entire working life, we need to know the ratio of the average income from dentistry during the last u years to the average income for the rest of the period. Call this ratio p, and let y equal the length of the dentist's working life in years. Then R, the ratio of the average income in medicine to that in dentistry, where both averages are for the entire working life, is given by

$$(2) \qquad R = \frac{yk}{(y - u) + up}.$$

The numerical values used in the computations are:

$u = 3$	$c = \$722$
$t = 3$	$i = .04$
$V = \$93,084$	$p = 0.9$
$v = \$2,316$	$y = 45$

[2] The installments of income entering into V are not assumed to be equal, but may be taken to vary in any desired fashion with the number of years in practice. It is assumed, however, that the income of physicians varies with the number of years in practice in the same way as the income of dentists, since the ratio between 'corresponding' instalments of income is treated as a constant. Section 1 of Chapter 6 indicates that this assumption accords reasonably well with the facts (see especially Chart 20).

From these, k is found to be 1.162, and R, 1.169. The facts and assumptions underlying these figures are:

1) The relevant costs during training are taken to include solely special expenditures for education. They do not include living costs, i.e., board, lodging, clothing, etc. This restriction of costs to tuition fees, professional equipment, and the like, is the only procedure consistent with our treatment of future returns. If living expenses were included as costs during training, it would logically be necessary to include them also in whole or in part as costs during the years when income is received, and to make some assumption about the part of the living costs in each profession to be considered in some sense an 'occupational expense' rather than expenditure for ultimate consumption. Such a procedure is neither feasible nor logically desirable. Similarly, the income that might have been earned during the training period is not to be considered a cost. For a comparison restricted to medicine and dentistry the only relevant alternative income is what the medical student might have earned as a dentist during his last three years of training. But this is already taken into account in the present value of the dentist's expected returns; to include it as a cost for the medical student would allow for it twice.

2) The costs of the six years of training in dentistry are assumed equal to those of the first six years of medical training. This assumption is clearly valid for the two or three overlapping years of preprofessional training. That it is not far wrong for the two overlapping years in professional school is suggested by data on costs of medical and dental education from two surveys of students' expenditures: one, by R. G. Leland, covering medical students throughout the country, the other, dental students in Minnesota.[3] During the rest of the period, either one or two years, the dental student receives professional, the medical student preprofessional, training. The costs are doubtless higher for the dental student, but the difference cannot be large.

3) The costs of the three extra years of medical training are assumed to total $750: $400 for the first year, $350 for the second, and zero for the third. They have been assumed to be incurred at

[3] 'The Costs of Medical Education', *Journal of the American Medical Association*, Feb. 28, 1931, pp. 682–90; 'Report of the University Relations Committee', *North-West Dentistry*, April 1936, pp. 79–89.

the middle of the year. The cost figures for the first two years are approximately those given by Leland [4] for 'Tuition and Fees' and 'Medical Books, Instruments, etc.' for the third and fourth year of medical school respectively. The last of the three extra years is usually the year of internship. Ordinarily an intern receives at least his room and board and occasionally a modest stipend. The monetary value of these returns certainly more than covers any extra professional costs. Logically, the excess should be regarded as a positive income item, counterbalancing the extra costs. In the absence of any data on its amount we have disregarded it. Similarly, we have disregarded any earnings during the other two years, although according to Leland's figures, they averaged almost $125 per student per year.

4) Training costs, other than those incurred during the first nine years by physicians and the first six years by dentists, are not allowed for. In both professions, persons desiring to become specialists frequently receive additional formal training, either before beginning practice or later. Since a much larger proportion of physicians than of dentists are specialists, the neglect of the costs of special training tends to make too small our estimate of R, i.e., our estimate of the difference in incomes that would make the two professions equally attractive financially.

5) The capital investment necessary to equip an office to begin dental practice is assumed equal to that necessary to begin medical practice and hence does not enter our formula. The 'Report of the University Relations Committee' [5] gives $1,782 as the average cost of equipment to 34 dentists who began to practise in 1934 and 1935. This is probably more than the average amount spent by beginning physicians.

6) For the present value of returns from dentistry over the entire working life, as of the date of beginning practice, we use $95,400, the figure given by Clark.[6] It is for 1920–36, is based on an interest rate of 4 per cent and an assumed working life of 45 years, and makes no allowance for differences among individuals in the age of retirement. Clark gives also a figure of $108,000 for 1920–29. The use of the smaller figure yields a slightly higher estimate of R.

4 'The Costs of Medical Education', Table 5.
5 P. 84. The figure cited does not include the cost of equipment purchased while in dental school, which averaged approximately $500.
6 *Life Earnings in Selected Occupations*, p. 43.

7) All members of each profession are assumed to have the same working life: 42 years for physicians and 45 years for dentists. These are the figures given by Clark [7] and are the only ones that would be consistent with assumption 6. Since Clark's estimates of average working life assume retirement only through death,[8] they are probably somewhat too large. In addition, the use of average expected working life instead of maximum working life is the only allowance that is made for the possibility that the actual working life is longer or shorter than that assumed. It is doubtful that this method makes sufficient allowance for the influence of differences in length of life. These deficiencies affect our results in three ways. Our estimate of R tends to be too small, first, because the assumed period over which the training costs of physicians can be recovered is too long; second, because insufficient allowance is made for the lower certainty to physicians than to dentists of 'corresponding' installments of income. Our estimate tends to be too large because we assume that the dentist is certain to receive his three extra installments of income. It is difficult to see how the corresponding adjustments would balance out, but we suspect that, on the whole, these deficiencies tend to make our estimate of R too small. However, rough computations suggest that the maximum error from this source is probably about 2 percentage points, i.e., that making accurate allowance for the probability of living to each age would be unlikely to raise our estimate by more than from 17 to about 19 per cent.

8) The average income of dentists during the last three years of their working life has been taken as $4,333, the figure given by Leven for the average income in 1929 of dentists in general practice who graduated from dental school between 1890 and 1894, i.e., in practice between 35 and 39 years.[9] The restriction to general practitioners probably tends to make this figure too low, although 89 per cent of Leven's sample were general practitioners. Moreover, this tendency is probably more than counterbalanced by two other factors: first, the figure is for dentists in practice 35 to 39 years, whereas we use it for dentists in practice 43 to 45 years, and the average income of the latter group is known to be lower than the average income of the former; second, it is for 1929, whereas

[7] *Ibid.*, pp. 43, 79.
[8] *Ibid.*, pp. 46, 79, 150.
[9] *Practice of Dentistry*, p. 125.

we use it in connection with figures for 1920–36 (see point 6 above).

9) The ratio of the average income of dentists during the last three years of their working life to their average income for the rest of their professional career is taken as 0.9. This figure is based on Leven's data and is consistent with assumption 8.

10) An interest rate of 4 per cent is used in discounting future returns and costs.

Deficiencies in assumptions 2, 3, 5, and 8 make for an overestimate of R; in 4 and possibly 7 for an underestimate. Our estimate of R (17 per cent) would therefore seem unlikely to be much of an underestimate for an interest rate of 4 per cent, and may well be an overestimate of the percentage by which the expected income of physicians would have to exceed that of dentists to make the two professions equally attractive financially.[10]

Changes in the interest rate used would affect the result considerably. The absence of data on the present value of life earnings based on any other rate makes it difficult to derive any estimates of R even as rough as the one made for a 4 per cent rate. However, some indication how changing the interest rate would affect R is given by computing the allowance necessary for the postponement of the income stream for three years. This allowance is 12.5 per cent for an interest rate of 4 per cent; 6.1 per cent for an interest rate of 2 per cent; and 19.1 per cent for an interest rate of 6 per cent. R would probably be about 11 or 12 per cent for an interest rate of 2 per cent, and 22 or 23 per cent for an interest rate of 6 per cent.

Just what interest rate should be used depends on the function it is to perform. If the interest rate is to include an allowance for 'uncertainty' of one sort or another, we ordinarily, though not always, would use a higher rate than if it is to serve solely the function of allowing for the postponement of income considered certain.[11]

10 The conclusion reached in Section 2 would be strengthened if the correct figure were smaller than the one we use; weakened if the correct figure were larger.

11 It is by no means clear that 'uncertainty' necessarily raises the rate at which future returns are discounted, or, what is the same thing, lowers the capital value attached to an expected income stream. Capitalizing the 'expected' income stream already takes account of one aspect of uncertainty: the 'uncertainty' implies the possibility of receiving an income stream larger or smaller than the 'expected' stream. An additional allowance needs to be made only so far

We have attempted to allow for uncertainty directly rather than through the medium of the interest rate. The uncertainty arising from variability of income we consider in Section 2b of the text: the uncertainty of success is but another aspect of variability of income. The uncertainty arising from differences in length of life we consider in assumption 7 above. The uncertainty arising from changes in income over time is relevant only so far as medicine and dentistry differ in this respect. It is doubtful that there is such a difference, but even if there is, it can hardly be large. Consequently the relevant interest rate for our purpose is one that makes no allowance for uncertainty. In view of the alternative opportunities for investment open to prospective entrants, there would probably be little disagreement that 4 per cent is not too low a figure to use as the 'riskless' interest rate but rather, if anything, too high.

b Professional and nonprofessional workers

Formulae (1) and (2) developed at the beginning of the preceding section are as applicable to a comparison between the professions and all other pursuits as to a comparison between medicine and dentistry. It is only necessary to substitute 'nonprofessional pursuits' for 'dentistry', and 'professions' for 'medicine' in the definitions of the symbols and the discussion of the formulae.

Two estimates of the ratio of incomes that would make the professions and all other pursuits equally attractive financially have been prepared. The estimates, used in the analysis in Chapter 3, Section 3, are designated R_1 and R_2, and differ solely in the values assigned V and v. Corresponding subscripts distinguish the alterna-

---

as the existence of uncertainty is itself a deterring or attracting factor; the interest rate should be raised if it is a deterring factor, lowered if it is an attracting factor. Moreover, the allowance that should be made cannot be determined solely from a single expected income stream taken by itself, even if we know the items underlying the expected income stream, namely, the different income streams conceived of as possible and the probability of each. The allowance to be made will depend also on the number of investments an individual—or other economic unit—contemplates making and the degree of independence among the various investments with respect to the probabilities attached to the possible returns from each. The larger the number of independent investments, the larger the diversification of risk, and the smaller the allowance needed for uncertainty, i.e., the smaller the degree of uncertainty attached to the investments viewed as a whole.

tive values. The absence of a subscript means that the same figure is used for both estimates. We consider R_1 an upper estimate of the ratio of incomes that would compensate for the extra investment in professional training.

The numerical values used in the computations are:

$$u = 4 \qquad V_2 = \$28,100 \qquad i = .04$$
$$t = 7 \qquad v_2 = \$500 \qquad p = 0.5$$
$$V_1 = \$14,939 \qquad c = \$3,060 \qquad y = 46$$
$$v_1 = \$261$$

From these k_1 is found to be 1.608; k_2, 1.482; R_1, 1.682; R_2, 1.550. The facts and assumptions underlying these figures are:

1) The nonprofessional worker is assumed to begin work, and the professional worker to begin his extra training, at the age of 18.

2) Training in the professions (t) is assumed to last 7 years, which is probably longer than the actual average period of training in all professions combined. The 9-year training period for physicians is probably longer than in any other profession. To cite a few more nearly typical examples: lawyers spend 5 to 7 years; dentists, 6 years; engineers, 4 years.

3) The annual costs of professional training are assumed to be $500 and to be incurred at the middle of the year. This figure is intended to include solely special expenditures for education (see point 1 in the preceding section), and is probably an overestimate. Costs are probably as high in medicine as in any profession, yet the available data suggest that average costs during the last two years of medical school do not exceed $400 (see point 3 in the preceding section). Earnings during years of professional training have been disregarded.

4) No allowance is made for costs incurred after the initial 7 years of training. Such costs, either for additional training or for equipment, though important for some professions, are probably negligible for the professional group as a whole, most of whom are salaried employees.

5) All members of each occupational group are assumed to have the same working life: 46 years for the nonprofessional worker and 42 years for the professional worker; i.e., u is assumed to be 4. These figures assume retirement only through death and therefore imply that the average age at death is 64 for the nonprofessional worker and 67 for the professional. Clark sets the expected average

age at death of males who were 20 in 1930 at 69 years for agricultural, professional, clerical, mercantile, and commercial workers, and at 62 years for workers in manufacturing, mining, transportation, and mechanical pursuits.[12] The nonprofessional occupations include mainly though not exclusively workers in the second group. We have set the average age at death at 64 years to allow for the admixture of workers in the first group. We have set the average age at death in professional pursuits at 67 years instead of 69 years to allow for some professional activities that may not strictly belong in the first group. The estimate of R is larger the higher the figure used for the age at death of nonprofessional workers and the lower the figure used for the age at death of professional workers. Not allowing for differences in the length of life affects the comparison between professional and nonprofessional workers in the same fashion as that between medicine and dentistry (see point 7 in the preceding section). We there concluded that this deficiency probably tends to make the estimate of R too low. However, in the comparison between professional and nonprofessional workers this tendency may be more than offset by a factor not relevant to the comparison between medicine and dentistry. It seems reasonable that 'occupational obsolescence' in general occurs at a considerably earlier age in nonprofessional than in professional pursuits, and hence that forced retirement prior to death is more common. This difference in forced retirement is probably more important than differences between the two groups in voluntary retirement. The average working life of nonprofessional workers may therefore be shorter relatively to that of professional workers than is implied by the figures we use. This deficiency would tend to make the estimate of R too high.

6) For the present value of life earnings in nonprofessional pursuits we use Clark's figure [13] for unskilled labor, $15,200, in estimating R_1, and his figure for skilled labor, $28,600 in estimating R_2. These figures are for 1920–36, and are based on an interest rate of 4 per cent and a working life of 44 years. The assumed working life is inconsistent with assumption 5. However the difference in the assumed working life is slight, and correction for it would tend to raise the present value of life earnings and hence to lower the estimate of R, since R is larger the smaller the value assigned to

12 *Life Earnings in Selected Occupations*, p. 150.
13 *Ibid.*, pp. 110, 131.

the present value of life earnings. We use these figures solely as rough approximations to the present value of life earnings in non-professional pursuits as a whole. The present value of the earnings of unskilled labor is almost certainly below and the present value of the earnings of skilled labor almost certainly above, the present value of the earnings of all nonprofessional workers. The average annual earnings corresponding to the present values cited, computed by dividing Clark's figures on 'total amount of mean life earnings' by the length of the working life, are approximately $750 and $1,430. In Chapter 3 we set the average earnings of all gainfully occupied workers at slightly under $1,000 for 1929–36 (see Table 7).

7) The average annual income during the last four years of the nonprofessional person's working life is arbitrarily taken as one-half the average annual income during his entire working life, i.e., $375 in estimating R_1, and $715 in estimating R_2. The value of p is consequently taken as 0.5. No adequate data are available for determining p. If anything, the value we use is probably below the correct value, which would tend to make R too high.

8) An interest rate of 4 per cent is used in discounting future returns and costs. The reasons for using this interest rate are discussed in the preceding section.

The value of R_1 computed on the basis of these assumptions is almost certainly an overestimate, since in general the assumptions err in a direction that would tend to make it too high. R_2, on the other hand, may well be an underestimate, though it is not impossible that it too is an overestimate.

2 THE STATISTICAL VALIDITY OF THE ESTIMATED DIFFERENCE BETWEEN AVERAGE INCOMES IN MEDICINE AND DENTISTRY

The figure we cite as the difference between the average incomes of physicians and dentists, 32 per cent, plays an important role in the analysis in Section 2 of the text. It is the basis of our conclusion that "if we accept our highly tentative figure of 17 per cent as an upper estimate of the excess of mean income in medicine consistent with completely free and moderately rational choice of profession, then about half of the observed difference between the mean incomes of physicians and dentists is attributable to the greater difficulty of entry into medicine." It is also important, if only as confirmatory evidence, for our qualitative conclusion that

the greater difficulty of entry into medicine "has made possible
or has maintained a level of income in medicine exceeding that in
dentistry by more than can be attributed to the free working of
the . . . law of supply and demand", although this qualitative
conclusion is independently validated by data on the number of
persons seeking admission to medicine and dentistry, the number
admitted, and the number of persons in the two professions.

The importance of our figure of 32 per cent suggests the desirability of considering, in more detail than heretofore, its statistical
validity. Of particular importance are deficiencies that might make
the figure too large: for only if 32 per cent is considerably too large
would our conclusions be seriously affected.

The possible magnitude of three types of error can be estimated:
errors due to sampling fluctuations, the correction applied to dental
incomes, and differences in age distribution and geographic location.

a   Sampling fluctuations
The information available is not sufficient to enable us to estimate
accurately the sampling errors of the average difference between
the means. However we have noted above that $180 is the
maximum estimate of the standard error of the difference between
the 1929–32 averages for physicians and dentists from the 1933
samples (footnote 5 of the text). The corresponding maximum estimate for the 1935 samples is $132. Consequently, $111 is the
maximum estimate of the standard error of the difference between
the averages for physicians and dentists from the two samples combined. These are maxima in the sense that accurately computed
standard errors would necessarily be smaller. Moreover, they take
no account of the use of the 1937 sample in deriving the final
average for physicians. Thus, the correct *maximum* estimate of the
standard error is definitely below $111.

Assume, now, that the difference between the average incomes of
physicians and dentists is too *large* because of a sampling error
twice the maximum estimate of the standard error. Under this
highly unfavorable assumption, the difference between the average
incomes is reduced from $1,001 to $779, and if half of the error is
allocated to dentists and half to physicians, the percentage excess
of physicians' incomes is reduced from 32.5 to 24.4.

b   The correction applied to dental incomes
To correct our dental averages for the restriction of our samples
to American Dental Association members, we multiplied the
sample averages by .876. The basis for this correction factor is discussed in detail in Appendix A, where it is indicated that the extreme values justified by the available evidence are .829 and .933.
Had the latter been used, the average for dentists would have been
raised from $3,081 to $3,281 and the percentage difference would
have been lowered from 32.5 to 24.4. As is noted in Appendix A,
the validity of the correction factor that we used is independently
confirmed by the results of a more recent study by the Department
of Commerce covering both members and nonmembers. Comparison is possible for two years. The difference between our adjusted
average and theirs is a trifle greater than 2 per cent in one year, and
one-half of one per cent in the other.

c   Differences in age distribution and geographic location
The income differential directly comparable to our estimate of
the equilibrium difference would be the differential between
physicians and dentists in the same community and in practice the
same number of years. In fact, physicians and dentists are distributed differently by both number of years in practice and geographic location. We make no correction in the text for this difference because we are able to show that such correction would raise
rather than lower the actual differential. In the present connection, it may be of interest to indicate the magnitude of the correction involved.

   The different figures cited in the text lead to different numerical
corrections. The figures leading to the smallest upward correction
would raise the percentage differential from 32.5 to 34.2; those
leading to the largest upward correction, from 32.5 to 45.9 (see
line *a* of Table 15).

d   Combined influence of the possible deficiencies
In the preceding paragraphs, we have considered the possible deficiencies one by one and have indicated that the maximum possible
correction for each deficiency separately would still leave the percentage excess of physicians' incomes considerably larger than the
estimated equilibrium difference. Table 15 summarizes these re-

sults and indicates the effect of various possible combinations of
the deficiencies.

The assumption that would affect our conclusion most seriously
is that the figures are subject to an error from sampling as large
as is at all reasonable, that the correction applied to dental incomes
resulted in as large an underestimate of the average income as

TABLE 15

Alternative Estimates of the Percentage Difference between the
Arithmetic Mean Incomes of Physicians and Dentists

ADJUSTMENTS FOR POSSIBLE ERROR IN DENTAL CORRECTION FACTOR & FOR SAMPLING ERROR	CORRECTION [1] APPLIED FOR DIFFERENCE IN DISTRIBUTION BY YEARS IN PRACTICE AND BY LOCATION						
	None	#1	#2	#3	#4	#5	#6
	Estimated Percentage Difference						
a) None [2]	32.5	34.2	38.8	39.5	40.4	44.3	45.9
b) Maximum error in dental correction [3]	24.4	26.1	30.3	31.0	31.8	35.5	36.9
c) Maximum sampling error [4]	24.4	26.0	30.3	31.0	31.8	35.5	37.0
d) Both (b) and (c) [5]	17.1	18.6	22.6	23.3	24.0	27.5	28.9

[1] Corrections 1–6 are alternative corrections obtained by combining the averages
in Section 1 of the text in all possible ways. They are numbered in the order of
magnitude: #1 involves the smallest upward correction, #6, the largest.
[2] Based on the averages actually used in Section 1 of the text, they reflect the
effect of correcting solely for differences in age and geographic distribution.
[3] Based on what the averages would have been if we had used .933 as the correction factor for dentists instead of .876. Our best estimate of the maximum
possible correction factor, .933, assumes that the differential between the average
incomes of members and nonmembers of the American Dental Association is
20 per cent, and that 60 per cent of the independent practitioners are members.
[4] Assuming a difference between medical and dental averages less than that
shown by averages used in Section 1 of the text by twice our estimate of the
maximum standard error of the difference.
[5] Based on what the averages would have been had both the adjustment in line
(b) and that in line (c) been made.

seems at all likely, and that the minimum upward correction
should be applied for differences in distribution by years in practice and location. The net effect of these assumed deficiencies
would be to lower the estimated percentage excess of the average
income of physicians from 32.5 to 18.6, which is still above our
estimated equilibrium difference of 17 per cent. The point to observe is that even the cumulative effect of such a series of unreal and
extreme assumptions is not sufficient to reverse our conclusion.

3   DEMAND AND SUPPLY CURVES FOR PROFESSIONAL SERVICES

a Theoretical

Since the analysis in Section 2 of the text implicitly uses concepts of demand and supply that differ somewhat from those ordinarily used, we describe them explicitly.

The quantities demanded and supplied are ordinarily treated as functions of a 'price' that is taken to refer to each individual item supplied and demanded; i.e., it is assumed that the supply and demand curves relate to commodities or services that sell in the same market for the same price. In an analysis of medical and dental services, however, it is not obvious even what the relevant unit of service supplied or demanded is. And no matter how this 'unit' is defined, there is clearly no single price at which it sells; rather, there is a frequency distribution of prices.

i *The supply curve.* On the side of supply, the relevant 'unit' seems to be the individual practitioner. The quantity of service any practitioner stands ready to offer depends but little on the 'price' he can get, although, of course, the quantity he actually renders doubtless does depend on the 'price' the consumer must pay. The total amount of service the profession stands ready to offer depends primarily on the number of practitioners. Over short periods the number is little if at all affected by the current economic fortunes of the profession. Individuals rarely leave the medical or dental profession to take up other pursuits; death and voluntary retirement are the principal reasons why individuals leave either profession. Similarly, the number entering the profession is determined largely by the number currently graduating from professional schools and passing the licensing examinations. Over longer periods, the number of withdrawals from the profession, but not the number seeking to enter, is still almost completely determined by noneconomic factors. The brighter the economic prospects of one profession relatively to others the larger the number who may be expected to try to enter it. Over these longer periods, economic factors affect the supply of service offered, i.e., the total number of practitioners, primarily through their effect on the number who try to enter the profession.[14]

14 This statement assumes, of course, relatively free entry. If the number permitted to enter is fixed, the supply of practitioners will be almost completely

The 'price' that determines the 'supply' of entrants is clearly the income or returns that individuals count on receiving. But this 'price' is not a single figure. Incomes received differ greatly among communities and types of practice. Moreover, for any particular community and type of practice, individuals recognize that the return they will receive may vary within exceedingly wide limits, and, indeed, the degree of variation considered likely is one of the factors affecting their decisions. Under these conditions, what meaning can be attached to a supply curve of the sort we have implicitly used; namely, one in which the number deciding to enter a profession is treated as a function of expected arithmetic mean income?

Fundamentally, the situation is not so unusual as might appear at first glance. In order to draw any supply (or demand) curve it is necessary to make assumptions—explicitly or implicitly—about 'other things'; the supply curve would be different if these 'other things' were different. In the present instance the nature of the expected probability distribution of returns—both between and within communities and types of practice—must be treated as one of these 'other things'. We need not assume this distribution to have a particular structure identical for all values of expected mean income; we may assume instead that each value of the expected mean income corresponds to a particular structure of a probability distribution.

Drawing the supply curve under definite assumptions concerning the nature of factors other than those explicitly included in the curve does not mean that these other factors are neglected or treated as of no importance. Rather, it means that changes in them are treated as producing 'shifts' of the curve rather than movements along it. Accordingly in our analysis we first consider the nature of the supply curves under the assumption that all factors other than expected mean returns are 'neutral' as between medicine and dentistry; we then attempt to evaluate the 'shift' of these curves that results from the existing differences in these factors, including the expected probability distribution of returns.

---

independent of the economic fortunes of the profession. We abstract from limitation of entry because a major purpose of determining the 'equilibrium' difference is to estimate the part of the observed difference attributable to limitation of entry, and to do this we need to know what the actual difference would be were entry free.

So far the analysis has indicated no reason for selecting expected mean income as *the* variable to be used in drawing the supply curve. Indeed, it suggests that, formally at least, any summary figure can be used as the ordinate of the curve. The median, mode, or any other characteristic of the probability distribution of returns would do as well. Any point of the supply curve is determinate solely because definite assumptions are made concerning the nature of the probability distribution of returns that corresponds to it. But this means that we can, in theory, determine the value of the median, mode, etc., that corresponds to that point. From a supply curve using one summary figure as the ordinate we can therefore easily pass to a supply curve using any other summary figure.

In practice, however, there is a very good reason for using the arithmetic mean rather than any other summary figure. If we abstract from all factors affecting the choice of a profession other than actuarial ones, the supply of new entrants depends solely on the relative arithmetic mean returns and costs.[15] The nature of the probability distribution of returns is of little or no importance. The most convenient procedure is to begin by analyzing the influence of the actuarial factors, and then modify the results by analyzing the influence of the nonactuarial factors. Since in dealing with the latter it makes little difference what summary figure is used, it is simplest to retain the arithmetic mean throughout. Moreover, as we indicate below, the arithmetic mean income seems the relevant figure for an analysis of demand.

ii *The demand curve.* On the side of demand as well as supply there is no easily specified 'unit' or single 'price'. Individuals demand 'medical service' or 'dental service'. But not only does 'medical service' cover a wide variety of services differing in quality and 'quantity'; also different prices are paid for supposedly the same quality and quantity of medical service by different 'customers' of the same physician (the 'sliding scale') and by customers of different physicians. Moreover, the character of the items composing the complex bundle 'medical service' is to a minor extent at the choice of or determined by the purchaser. The 'purchaser'

15 This is probably most easily seen by analogy with the way insurance companies determine premiums. For example, if fire insurance premiums were based on median loss, they would be zero.

selects the physician; the physician selects the items the 'purchaser' buys. The only thing that seems relevant is the total sum that consumers as a whole are willing to spend for medical services.

The total sum that consumers are willing to spend depends, in part at least, on the total number of practitioners, both because of the reduction (increase) in monetary and nonmonetary costs—fees, cost of travel, time lost, etc.—to consumers produced by the greater (smaller) availability of practitioners and because of the habituation fostered by their presence. The importance of the number of practitioners as a determinant of the sum consumers are willing to spend is enhanced by the customary character of medical and dental scales of fees, and the almost complete absence of direct price competition. We may, therefore, conceive of a demand curve for 'physicians' in which the 'price' is the average gross income per physician and the 'quantity', the number of physicians. But we cannot use this demand curve for our purposes. It is the average *net* rather than *gross* income that is the relevant figure to the prospective practitioner. However, to each possible value of total gross income corresponds a fairly determinate value of total net income. We can therefore pass from a demand curve in which the 'price' is the average gross income to one in which the 'price' is the average net income. This demand curve can be taken as negatively inclined: although an increase in the number of physicians (or dentists) might cause an increase in the total sum spent, it seems exceedingly doubtful that it would cause a proportionate or more than proportionate increase in total expenditures on medical (or dental) service. It is this type of demand curve that is used in our analysis and that underlies our rough estimate of the increase in the ratio of physicians to dentists that would be necessary to reduce the ratio of their incomes from 1.32 to 1.17 (see Sec. 2d of the text and footnote 33).

A demand curve of this type is, of course, not theoretically determinate unless assumptions are made about the behavior of 'other things'. In the present instance the most important is how additional practitioners would be distributed among regions, size of community classes, and types of practice. The effect on average net income of any given addition to the total number of practitioners would clearly be very different if they all settled in the same community than if they were more widely distributed. To each point on a demand curve corresponds some assumption about the distribution of the relevant number of practitioners. Clearly, the realistic assumption is that the choice of location is made by the new practitioners themselves. This, in turn, would presumably mean distributions of practitioners similar to the existing distribution.

iii *The 'equilibrium' difference.* The preceding discussion of the nature of the supply and demand curves on which our analysis is based runs in terms of each profession separately. Couched in terms of absolute average income and absolute number of practitioners, the rough scheme presented is designed to determine the equilibrium level of average income in each profession. Since we were concerned solely with a comparison between medicine and dentistry, we did not actually construct such curves. Rather, for convenience, we used a supply curve and a demand curve that applied to the two professions combined. This we did by the device of using as the ordinate (see figure), the ratio of the average income of physicians to that of dentists, and as the abscissa, the ratio of the number of physicians to that of dentists. For the

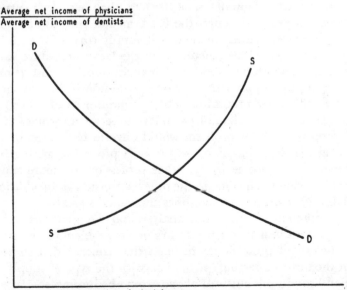

demand curve (DD) the latter ratio is for persons in practice. For the supply curve (SS) it is for persons seeking to enter the professions. The illustrative figure that presents these curves conceals a not unimportant detail. In order to make the two curves comparable, the scale used along the horizontal axis for the supply curve must be related in a special way to that used for the demand curve. The distance from the origin to any point on the horizontal axis must measure (1) the ratio of all physicians to all dentists, (2) the ratio of medical applicants to dental applicants that is needed in order to maintain ratio (1). For example, suppose that two and a half times as many medical as dental applicants are needed to maintain a ratio of 2:1 between all physicians and all dentists because of differences between medicine and dentistry in age distribution or other factors. Then, the same abscissa should represent 2:1 for the demand curve and 2.5:1 for the supply curve.

If the curves are drawn in this fashion the ordinate of the point of intersection is the 'equilibrium' ratio of incomes. Our upper estimate of this ordinate is 1.17; our upper estimate of the corresponding abscissa is 3:1.

As indicated in footnote 32 of the text, the use of such curves is somewhat inexact, although the fundamental conclusions would not be altered by using demand and supply curves for each profession separately. The difficulty with the latter procedure is that one of the 'other things' about which an assumption must be made in drawing the supply curve for one profession is the average income in the other profession. This assumption is of crucial importance for the problem of the relation between incomes in the two professions. This problem would have to be treated by considering the shifts in the curve for each profession arising from changes in the income in the other profession, or, more simply, by introducing the income in the other profession as an additional variable. Our procedure simplifies the analysis greatly.

The difference between our analysis and the usual analysis has an important bearing on the nature of the problem to be studied. An analysis of professional incomes that concerned itself solely with the factors affecting 'price', i.e., with the type of supply and demand conditions outlined above, would be incomplete. In addition, an analysis is needed of the factors making for intraprofessional differences in 'prices' or returns; i.e., of the factors making for variability of income within each profession.

b Statistical

No data are available that could be used to derive a supply curve of all professional persons. Applications to medical and dental schools give one empirical point on the type of joint supply curve used in our analysis: they indicate that at a ratio of incomes of 1.32, the ratio of prospective entrants is between 3.5 and 4.1. Our investigation of the relative pecuniary advantages of medicine and dentistry and our qualitative discussion of other aspects of the choice of a profession suggest that at a ratio of incomes of 1.17 the ratio of prospective entrants would be considerably larger than 1, and we hazarded the opinion that it would be sufficiently large to lead to a ratio of physicians to dentists that would enable a ratio of incomes as low as 1.17 to be maintained. But aside from these two points—the second of which can hardly be called an empirical observation—the supply curve cannot be estimated from available data.

The prospect of deriving statistical demand curves is somewhat more promising. Data are available on the number of practitioners by states, on their average incomes, and on the per capita income of the public at large. The last variable is needed to allow for the relation between the income of the public and the number of professional men whose services they will wish to purchase. If it were not introduced into the analysis, a positive relation between number of professional men and their average income might well emerge: professional men tend both to be numerous and to receive relatively large incomes in prosperous communities.

The number of practitioners in one state can be compared with the number in another only if some adjustment is made for the size of the 'market' served by each group. The total population would seem to provide an excellent index of the size of the market for medical and dental services. Consequently, we may take the number of physicians and dentists per capita, or per 10,000 people, as measures of what might be called the 'density' of physicians and dentists.

The use of the state as the unit is somewhat arbitrary and our results might be altered if other units were used, for example, individual cities or groups of cities cross-classified by size and regional location. The analysis is restricted to states for two reasons. First, satisfactory data on the income of the public at large are not available for any other relatively small units. Second, for most other units that might be used, the size of the market could not be considered proportional to the number of residents in the unit. For example, physicians in a large city tend to serve not only the residents of that city but also the residents of neighboring communities. The market for the services of physicians in the neighboring communities is correspondingly reduced. This difficulty seems far less serious for states, though it is doubtless present to some extent. The contribution of New Jersey to the market for New York physicians and of New Jersey and Delaware to the market for Philadelphia physicians are obvious examples.

To isolate the influence of the number of physicians per 10,000 people on average medical income, we computed a multiple regression equation for 1934 (using the 1935 medical sample) between average medical income in a state as the dependent variable and physicians per 10,000 people and per capita income as the independent variables.[16] Surprisingly enough, the number of physicians per 10,000 people seems to be uncorrelated with average income of physicians for a fixed per capita income—the partial correlation coefficient is .033.[17] Study of the interrelations among

[16] The equation fitted was of the form
$$\log y = a + b_1 \log x_1 + b_2 \log x_2,$$
where $y =$ income per physician in 1934, $x_1 =$ number of physicians in active practice per 10,000 people in 1934, and $x_2 =$ per capita income in 1934. In fitting the equation we weighted the observations by the number of physicians in each state reporting their 1934 income in the 1935 sample. The number of physicians in active practice in each state in 1934 was obtained by multiplying the number of physicians listed for each state in the 1934 Directory of the American Medical Association by the 1931 ratio of physicians in active practice to total physicians in that state obtained from figures given by Leland, *Distribution of Physicians*. The 1934 population in each state used to obtain physicians per 10,000 people was taken from the official Census estimates in the *Statistical Abstract*. Per capita income in each state in 1934 was obtained from R. R. Nathan and J. L. Martin, *State Income Payments, 1929–37* (U. S. Department of Commerce, 1939), p. 6.

[17] The computed equation is:
$$\log y = 2.68 + .021 \log x_1 + .304 \log x_2.$$
$$\quad\quad\quad\quad (.296) \quad\quad (.190)$$
The figures in parentheses are the standard errors of the corresponding coefficients. The multiple correlation coefficient, R, is .438 and is significant; the partial correlation coefficients among the variables indicated by the subscripts and defined in footnote 16 are:
$$r_{y x_1 . x_2} = .033; \; r_{y x_2 . x_1} = .213; \; r_{x_1 x_2 . y} = .836.$$

the variables, however, suggests an entirely reasonable explanation of what at first seems an extremely unreasonable result. The number of physicians per 10,000 persons is highly correlated with per capita income: the simple correlation coefficient between the logarithms of the variables is approximately .86, the partial correlation for fixed average medical income, .84.[18] We have in effect but one variable: the number of physicians per 10,000 people is much the same for states that have the same per capita income. Consequently, we have few data from which to estimate the separate influence of number of physicians.

Despite the apparent absence of any relation between the income of physicians and their number, the results, on closer examination, are reasonable. We should expect that, for states with the same per capita income, physicians' incomes would be smaller the larger the number of physicians; for states with the same number of physicians, physicians' incomes would be larger the larger per capita income; and, for states with the same income per physician, the number of physicians would be larger the larger per capita income. What we find is that when per capita income is larger, so are both the number of physicians and the income per physician, but not in the same proportion. For example, if the income of the population increases by, say, 10 per cent, total *net* receipts by physicians for medical services increase by approximately 9 per cent, one-third of which is absorbed by a 3 per cent increase in the income per physician, the other two-thirds, by a 6 per cent increase in the number of physicians.[19]

18 These are approximate because they are computed from the weighted data used in computing the multiple regression equation. The correct weights for the latter are not the correct weights for the correlation coefficients cited.

19 Expressed in somewhat different terms, the elasticity of physicians' income with respect to per capita income is approximately 0.3; the elasticity of the number of physicians with respect to per capita income, approximately 0.6. Because of the low partial correlation between the income of physicians and their number for fixed per capita income, simple and multiple regressions yield approximately the same values for the elasticities. Consequently, the elasticities are to be interpreted as total, rather than partial; i.e., they indicate the percentage change in each variable that is associated with a one per cent change in per capita income when the remaining variable changes in the way it actually does. For this reason, the elasticity of total net receipts is equal to the sum of the other two elasticities.

It is tempting to compare these elasticities with the elasticity of expenditures on medical care shown by family budget studies. The validity of such a com-

We have data on the number of dentists by states only for 1936.[20] However, it is doubtful that the number in each state in 1936 and 1934 differed significantly. Consequently we may safely use these figures in conjunction with our data on dental incomes in 1934. More troublesome is the restriction of our income data to American Dental Association members only, while it is obviously the total number of dentists per 10,000 people that must be used. Fortunately, a more recent survey by the Department of Commerce gives data on the 1936 incomes of all dentists by states. As we shall see, these data give essentially the same results as our 1934 data.

Two differences between the data for physicians and for dentists combine to make it possible to isolate the separate influence of the number of dentists. In the first place, the correlation between dentists per 10,000 people and per capita income is somewhat lower than the corresponding correlation for physicians—the simple cor-

---

parison is, however, dubious. In the first place, expenditures by families on the services of physicians represent 'gross' rather than 'net' receipts. Second, our data indicate the effect on total receipts of an increase in per capita income associated with an increase in the number of physicians, while family budget data give the expenditures by families at different income levels but living in the same community and hence with the same availability of physicians. The elasticity of family expenditures might be expected to be between the partial elasticity of physicians' receipts when the number of physicians remains unchanged, and the total elasticities we derive. Finally, most budget studies give data solely on total expenditures on medical care, including in that category not only expenditures on the services of physicians but also payments to dentists, osteopaths, oculists, etc., and for hospital service, drugs, and medical supplies. However, various studies suggest that something over a third of total expenditures on medical care represents payments to physicians. See P. A. Dodd and E. F. Penrose, *Economic Aspects of Medical Services* (Graphic Arts Press, 1939), pp. 116–20.

In view of these limitations, about all we can say is that family budget data are not inconsistent with our findings. The estimates of average expenditures on medical care at different income levels for the country as a whole suggest that the percentage of total family income spent on medical care declines very slowly as family income increases, i.e., that the elasticity is slightly less than unity. See *Consumer Expenditures in the United States* (National Resources Committee, 1939), pp. 38–40, 77–8. A California study of family expenditures on medical care yields a similar result. See *California Medical-Economic Survey*, p. 48.

20 Thomas, 'Dental Survey'. We adjusted the figures given by Thomas, which relate to July 1, 1936, in two ways: we substituted 6,000 for the 11,320 listed for Illinois; and we used a figure of 100 for New Mexico, the one state for which Thomas gives no estimate.

CHART 11

Relation among Arithmetic Mean Income of Dentists in 1934, Dentists per 10,000 Population in 1936, and per Capita Income in 1934 Based on Data for 48 States and the District of Columbia

Average income based on reports of
■ fewer than 5 dentists, ● 5–50 dentists, ▲ more than 50 dentists

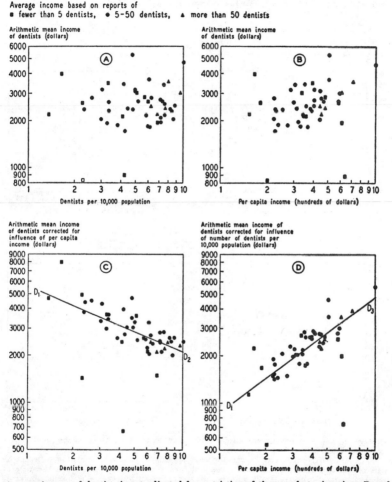

Average income of dentists is not adjusted for restriction of the sample to American Dental Association members. All scales are logarithmic. Each point relates to an individual state.

$D_1 D_2$ and $D_1 D_3$ are partial regression equations. $D_1 D_2$ shows the relation between the part of average dental income not accounted for by per capita income and the part of number of dentists per 10,000 population not accounted for by per capita income. Similarly, $D_1 D_3$ shows the relation between the part of average dental income not accounted for by number of dentists per 10,000 population and the part of per capita income not accounted for by number of dentists per 10,000 population.

CHART 12

Relation among Arithmetic Mean Income of Dentists in 1936, Dentists
per 10,000 Population in 1936, and per Capita Income in 1936
Based on Data for 48 States and the District of Columbia

Average income based on reports of
■ fewer than 20 dentists, ● 20-300 dentists, ▲ more than 300 dentists

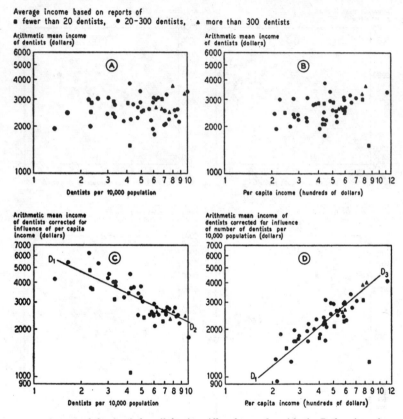

Average income of dentists is for *all* dentists. All scales are logarithmic. Each point relates
to an individual state.

$D_1 D_2$ and $D_1 D_3$ are partial regression equations. $D_1 D_2$ shows the relation between the
part of average dental income not accounted for by per capita income and the part of
number of dentists per 10,000 population not accounted for by per capita income. Similarly,
$D_1 D_3$ shows the relation between the part of average dental income not accounted for by
number of dentists per 10,000 population and the part of per capita income not accounted
for by number of dentists per 10,000 population.

relations are .75 for 1934 income, and .81 for 1936 income. In the second place, and more important, the number of dentists per 10,000 people varies considerably more from state to state than the number of physicians per 10,000 people. Consequently, the variation in the number of dentists per 10,000 people that remains after eliminating the influence of per capita income is not only a slightly larger part of the total; it is also larger absolutely, and hence gives more information on the influence of the number of dentists than the corresponding data for physicians give on the influence of the number of physicians.

As shown by panel A on Charts 11 and 12, the original figures on average income of dentists and number of dentists per 10,000 people show a slight positive correlation. However, eliminating the influence of per capita income produces a decided negative relation (Charts 11 and 12, panel C). The solid lines D_1D_2, representing the partial regression between average income per dentist and number of dentists per 10,000 people,[21] summarize this re-

[21] The multiple regression equations and the correlation coefficients are:

1934

$$\log y = 1.794 - .421 \log x_1 + .742 \log x_2.$$
$$(.099) \qquad (.110)$$

$R = .713$

$r_{yx_1} = .134$ $\qquad\qquad$ $r_{yx_1.x_2} = -.531$

$r_{yx_2} = .561$ $\qquad\qquad$ $r_{yx_2.x_1} = .706$

$r_{x_1x_2} = .754$ $\qquad\qquad$ $r_{x_1x_2.y} = .828$

1936

$$\log y' = 1.545 - .463 \log x_1 + .826 \log x'_2.$$
$$(.082) \qquad (.091)$$

$R = .814$

$r_{y'x_1} = .237$ $\qquad\qquad$ $r_{y'x_1.x_2} = -.644$

$r_{y'x_2} = .653$ $\qquad\qquad$ $r_{y'x_2.x_1} = .802$

$r_{x_1x_2} = .805$ $\qquad\qquad$ $r_{x_1x_2.y'} = .883$

where y = average income in 1934 of dentists in each state who were American Dental Association members;

y' = average income in 1936 of all dentists in each state;

x_1 = dentists per 10,000 people in each state in 1936;

x_2 = per capita income in each state in 1934;

x'_2 = per capita income in each state in 1936;

R = multiple correlation coefficient;

lation. The 1934 and 1936 data yield almost identical partial regression equations. For fixed per capita income, a one per cent increase in dentists per 10,000 people would mean a decline in the average income per dentist of .42 per cent according to the 1934 data, and of .46 per cent according to the 1936 data. Similarly both sets of data yield essentially identical estimates of the influence of per capita income (Charts 11 and 12, panels B and D). For a fixed number of dentists, a one per cent increase in per capita income would mean an increase in dental income of .74 or .83 per cent, according to the 1934 or 1936 data respectively.

The partial regression equations in Charts 11 and 12 are analogous to demand curves of economic theory. They depict the relation between the 'price' of dentists (their average income) and the 'quantity' of dentists whose services are purchased (number of dentists per 10,000 people). Both curves indicate an elasticity of demand with respect to price slightly greater than 2, suggesting that an increase in the number of dentists would mean a rise in their total net receipts. The formal similarity of the regression curves and elasticity coefficients to their theoretical counterparts is, however, somewhat misleading. The latter are assumed to indicate not only the effect on price of a change in quantity but also the effect on quantity of a change in price. The computed 'demand curves' in Charts 11 and 12 and their elasticity coefficients indicate only the former: they can safely be used to estimate the effect of a change in the number of dentists on average income; they may give entirely erroneous results if used to estimate the effect of a change

---

$r =$ simple or partial correlation coefficient among the logarithms of the variables indicated by subscripts.

The figures in parentheses are the standard errors of the corresponding coefficients. All the regression coefficients are very much larger than their standard errors.

In fitting the equations and computing the correlation coefficients, we weighted the observations by the number of dentists reporting their income. Figures on the average income of all dentists in 1936 by states were kindly furnished by the U. S. Department of Commerce and were obtained from the survey described by Herman Lasken, 'Incomes of Dentists and Osteopathic Physicians', *Survey of Current Business*, April 1939. Number of dentists per 10,000 people in each state was obtained from Thomas' figures on dentists previously cited and the official Census estimates of population. The figures on per capita income were obtained from *State Income Payments, 1929–37*.

in the 'price' of dental services on the quantity that would be purchased. The computed curves relevant to this problem have an elasticity of demand less than unity.[22]

We can summarize these results in terms of the total net receipts of dentists. When per capita income increases by, say, 10 per cent, total net receipts of all dentists increases by 12 or 13 per cent, about one-third of which is absorbed by a 4 per cent increase in the average income of dentists and the other two-thirds by an 8 to 9 per cent increase in the number of dentists. Interestingly enough, the proportions absorbed by increases in dental income and in the number of dentists are almost identical with those we previously found for physicians. We can go further in interpreting these results for dentists than we could for physicians. If, as per capita income rose 10 per cent, the number of dentists remained the same, their average income, and hence their total net receipts, would rise about 8 per cent. In fact, the number of dentists does not remain the same, but rises about 9 per cent. Since the elasticity of demand is slightly over two, a 9 per cent rise in the number of dentists, if per capita income were constant, would mean a 4 per cent drop in average dental income. The increase in the number of dentists that accompanies a rise in per capita income thus reduces the percentage rise in dental income from 8 to 4, the rise we observe. These results make possible a different breakdown of the rise of 12 to 13 per cent in total net receipts of dentists: if the

[22] To estimate the influence of a change in average dental income on the number of dentists we need the regression of number of dentists on average income. In the same symbols as in footnote 21 the multiple regression equations with number of dentists as the dependent variable are:

1934

$$\log x_1 = .207 - .670 \log y + 1.096 \log x_2.$$
$$\qquad\qquad (.158) \qquad\quad (.110)$$
$$R = .831.$$

1936

$$\log x_1 = -1.049 - .889 \log y' + 1.262 \log x'_2.$$
$$\qquad\qquad (.157) \qquad\quad (.099)$$
$$R = .890.$$

To maintain comparability, the same weights were used in computing the regressions as in footnote 21. Logically, these are not the proper weights: the correct weights are inversely proportional to the variances of x_1, not to the variances of y.

Once again the two regressions are similar.

CHART 13

Relation between the Ratio of Income of Physicians to Income of Dentists
and the Ratio of Number of Physicians to Number of Dentists
Based on Data for 48 States and the District of Columbia, 1934 and 1936

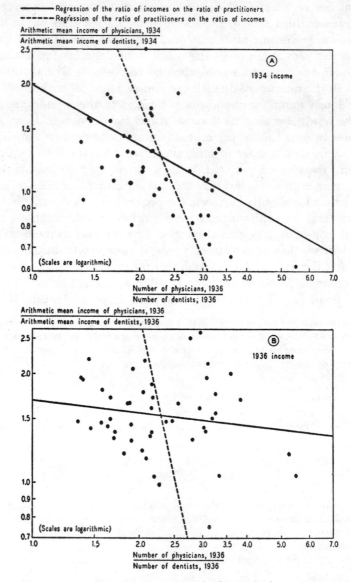

In panel A the extreme observation (1.577, 6.415) has been omitted.

number of dentists remained the same, their total net receipts would rise only about 8 per cent. The concomitant increase in number of dentists and resulting moderation of the rise in average dental income account for the other 4 or 5 per cent of the increase in total net receipts.

In the theoretical discussion in Section 2 of the text we use a demand curve in which the 'price' is the ratio of the average income in medicine to the average income in dentistry; the 'quantity', the ratio of physicians to dentists. The data so far used in our separate analyses of medicine and dentistry may also be used to obtain an empirical estimate of such a demand curve. Once again taking the state as a unit, we need simply correlate the ratio of incomes and the ratio of practitioners. Since the 'market' for medical and dental services may be assumed to vary in the same way from state to state, ratios of practitioners are directly comparable from state to state and are not affected by differences in the size of the states. Similarly, the ratio of incomes for different states may be assumed comparable and not affected by differences in the per capita income of the population as a whole.

The two panels of Chart 13 present scatter diagrams relating the ratio of incomes to the ratio of practitioners. In both panels the ratios of practitioners are for 1936, since data on the number of dentists are available for that year alone. In panel A the income ratios are for 1934; the income of dentists—the denominator of the ratio—is for dentists who are American Dental Association members. In panel B the income ratios are for 1936; dentists' incomes were obtained from the Department of Commerce survey previously referred to and are for all dentists.

The two lines in each panel are the simple regression equations between the logarithms of the variables: one is the regression of the ratio of incomes on the ratio of practitioners; the other, the regression of the ratio of practitioners on the ratio of incomes. Both panels show negative correlation, but the correlation coefficient computed from the 1936 data (−.16) is very small and is not statistically significant. The 1934 data show a considerably more pronounced but still far from perfect correlation (−.47).[23] About

23 Because of the extreme complexity of the weights that should theoretically have been used, none were used in computing the correlation coefficients. The regression equations are:

all we can infer from these results is the existence of the negative relation theoretically to be expected. The correlation is too low to enable us to say much about the character of the relation between the two variables that, if all other things were the same, might be presumed to exist.

Analyses similar to those presented for physicians and dentists cannot be made for lawyers and accountants. The basic obstacle is the absence of any index of the size of the 'market' and the consequent impossibility of rendering comparable the figures on the number of practitioners in different states. The total population will obviously not serve for these professions: e.g., there are about five times as many accountants per capita in New York State as in Nevada, but although per capita income in the two states is fairly similar, there is no reason to expect accountants in New York State to have a decidedly lower income than accountants in Nevada. The difference in the 'density' of accountants reflects the inadequacy of population as an index of the size of the 'market' and cannot be expected to manifest itself in income differences.

The absence of an index of the size of the market makes impossible an analysis for each profession separately. There still re-

---

1934	1936
$\log y = .299 - .552 \log x;$	$\log y' = .227 - .116 \log x;$
$\log x = .401 - .407 \log y.$	$\log x = .400 - .215 \log y',$

where $y =$ ratio of incomes in 1934; $y' =$ ratio of incomes in 1936; $x =$ ratio of practitioners in 1936.

These regression equations give us some, though by no means an adequate, basis for checking the statement in Section 2d of the text concerning the rise in the ratio of physicians to dentists that would be needed to reduce the ratios of their incomes from 1.32 to 1.17 (see footnote 33 in text). It was there hazarded that it would have to rise at most from 2.1 to 3.0. According to the first regression for 1934 (the y on x regression) a ratio of practitioners of 2.1 would be associated with an income ratio of 1.32; a ratio of practitioners of 3.0, with an income ratio of 1.09. Since the other regression for 1934 would show an even more marked drop in the ratio of incomes corresponding to the same difference in the ratios of practitioners, the 1934 data substantiate our earlier conclusion. However, the 1936 data do not. According to the first regression for 1936 a rise in the ratio of practitioners from 2.1 to 3.0 would mean a decline in the ratio of income from 1.55 to only 1.49, considerably smaller than from 1.32 to 1.17. According to the second 1936 regression, ratios of practitioners of 2.1 and 3.0 would be associated with income ratios of 2.30 and 0.44 respectively. However, strictly speaking, it is the regression of ratio of incomes on ratio of practitioners—the first regression— that is relevant.

mains the possibility of an analysis for the two professions combined. We have previously indicated that in large part accountants and lawyers serve the same clientele. This suggests that the ratio of lawyers to accountants might be comparable from state to state and might be correlated with the income ratio in the two professions. For both 1934 and 1936 the correlation is negative, but so small that the data are best described as showing zero correlation.[24] Several factors may be assumed to contribute to this low correlation. Accountants and lawyers serve essentially the same business clientele, but accountants serve business enterprises almost exclusively, whereas lawyers render services to ultimate consumers as well. The market for legal services partakes of the characteristics of the market for medical and dental services as well as of that for accounting services. In addition to this theoretical difficulty, the data used are defective. The chief defect is that the available figures on number of practitioners include both salaried employees and independent practitioners while our income data are for the latter alone.

CHAPTER 5

Income and the Location of Practice

A WISE CHOICE of a profession may improve an individual's chance of earning a good livelihood; it cannot guarantee him success. The attempts of numerous individuals to choose wisely limit the opportunities for profiting by a wise choice and tend to equalize, not incomes, but the "whole of the advantages and disadvantages" of different professions. In addition, as we have

24 The rank difference correlation is —.078 for 1934, and —.076 for 1936.

seen, the incomes of men who practise the same profession differ widely. Some attain a professional status that enables them to sell at attractive prices all the services they care to render; others find it difficult to sell their services even at low prices.

The factors that determine a professional man's income are numerous and varied. Some, like profession, give rise to differences that the forces of competition continually tend to obliterate. Others, either by their very nature or for institutional reasons, give rise to differences competition alone cannot touch. Few are susceptible of quantitative or objective evaluation. How can we measure 'personality', the influence of family and personal connections, and the like? Finally, there are the many factors of which we are ignorant; these we usually combine with the ever-present element of 'pure luck', under the convenient heading of 'chance'.

In this and the next chapter, we consider a few of the many factors that account for differences among incomes received by men in the same profession. In this chapter we consider the effect of the location of practice, so far as this effect is revealed by a classification of communities by geographic location and size. In the next chapter, we consider a variety of factors, some having to do with the 'quality' of the practitioner—training and ability, and number of years in practice; the rest, with the type of practice he engages in and the way that practice is organized—general vs. specialized practice, practice as an individual vs. practice as a firm member, independent vs. salaried practice.

Though almost all of the factors analyzed in this and the next chapter definitely play a part in determining the income a man receives, even taken all together they account for only a small part of the total variability of income among men in the same profession. Individuals alike with respect to all still receive incomes that differ widely. To some extent, the variability we are unable to account for reflects the effect of factors that limitations of our data make it impossible for us to study. To a not inconsiderable extent, however, it also reflects the influence of chance occurrences that make a man's income relatively high this year and relatively low next year. Some light is thrown on the importance of such chance occurrences by Chapter 7, in which we investigate the fluctuations from year to year in the relative positions men occupy in an array of practitioners by size of income.

Experimental computations contained in the Appendix to Chapter 7 (Sec. 2a ii) illustrate the possible importance of the groups of factors just discussed. Of the total variability of physicians' incomes in 1933, some 22 per cent can be attributed to size of community, number of years in practice, and type of practice—factors studied in this and the next chapter. Another 13 per cent can be attributed to factors present in 1933 but not in both 1932 and 1934—to factors that can perhaps be identified with 'chance occurrences'. The remaining 65 per cent of the variability is accounted for either by factors that we have been unable to study or by chance occurrences whose effects were present over the whole of a three-year period. This 65 per cent that remains is both a measure of our failure and a challenge to future investigators.

Changes in the relative economic advantages of different professions are reflected primarily in the number of young people who each year start to train for them. Changes in the relative advantages of different localities, on the other hand, are reflected in the geographic distribution of both young people just beginning practice or training and persons already in active practice. However, the difference between professional and geographical mobility is probably not great. The uncertainties attached to beginning anew elsewhere, the capital needed to cover living expenses during the period of adjustment, and the direct costs of moving combine with inertia and habit to keep professional men from moving to new and possibly more advantageous locations. These obstacles are especially serious for men in independent practice because of the capital value represented by an established practice, and the inevitably low level of earnings during the initial period in a new location. The individuals who have fared poorly in their present location have the greatest incentive to move; but they are least likely to have the necessary capital. Those who have done well will probably have less difficulty in procuring capital, but they have less to gain and more to lose by moving. Consequently, new entrants probably play almost as large a role in adjustments among localities as in adjustments among professions.[1]

The place where a man practises, like the profession of which he becomes a member, is determined by a wide variety of considerations, differing from person to person. Most individuals like to live near their families and friends in surroundings to which they are habituated. For some, this desire is reinforced by professional advantages from family and personal connections, greater possibility of getting income from nonprofessional activities, and ignorance of opportunities elsewhere. For others, it may be offset by greater earning possibilities in other communities and a desire for change. Whenever the relative pecuniary attractiveness of alternative locations affects the

[1] New admissions to the bar averaged approximately 7,500 annually for the decade of the 'twenties and 9,000 for 1932–39, while the number of lawyers admitted to the bar who had previously been admitted in other states averaged 900 and 600 respectively. Some of them may not have changed the location of their practice but merely made arrangements to practise in more than one state at the same time. New admissions to medical practice averaged less than 6,000 for 1933–38, while new licenses issued averaged about 8,500. The difference between these two figures overstates the number of physicians shifting from one state to another, since some new entrants simultaneously take out licenses in more than one state. The total number of lawyers in independent practice was about 110,000 in 1930, the total number of physicians, about 120,000. See Tables 1–3; 'Admissions to the Bar by States, 1920 to 1930', *Bar Examiner*, Aug. 1932, p. 273; 'Medical Licensure Statistics for 1936'; 'Medical Licensure Statistics for 1938'.

It is clear from these figures that the number who actually change location is small relatively to both new entrants and all practitioners. However, they describe actual rather than potential mobility. The greater movement in law during the 'twenties than later suggests but of course does not establish that mobility is greater in good times than in bad.

decision, it will be balanced against other advantages or disadvantages. Differences in cost of living, climate, physical and cultural characteristics, and the professional facilities available may all play a part. In short, individuals compare the "whole of the advantages and disadvantages" of alternative locations.

Even if all professional men were in a position to settle where they would, or to move from one place to another, and even if many took economic considerations into account in deciding where to practise, incomes in different communities, like incomes in different professions, would not necessarily be equal. Rather they would tend to be 'equivalent': income differences would reflect and compensate for generally recognized differences in nonpecuniary advantages. As already pointed out, not all professional men are in a position to settle where they will, or move from one place to another. The actual degree of mobility may or may not be sufficient to bring about a close adjustment among incomes in different localities; if it is not, differences in income attributable to immobility will be superimposed on 'equalizing' differences.

A direct approach to measuring how much of the existing differences in income is attributable to differences in nonpecuniary advantages and how much to immobility offers little promise. Most of the considerations governing the choice of a place to live are not subject to even rough quantitative evaluation. One important factor that may compensate for differences in pecuniary returns—differences among communities in cost of living—is susceptible to measurement but has not yet been gauged with sufficient accuracy to justify intensive analysis.

An indirect approach to the problem that seems somewhat more promising is to compare differences in professional income with differences in the income of other persons. Most of the nonpecuniary advantages or disadvantages of a particular locality are evaluated similarly by nonprofessional and professional persons. Though the latter are not a 'representative' sample of the population, and their tastes probably differ in many respects from the tastes of the rest of the population, it seems likely that, at least for comparisons among localities, the similarities are far more important than the differences.[2] In the absence of immobility, differences among communities in professional income might therefore be expected to parallel corresponding differences in income from other pursuits. Departures from parallelism might be interpreted as reflecting a different degree of mobility in the professions than in other pursuits, though obviously any conclusions reached in this indirect manner would be subject to numerous qualifications.

The existence of parallelism, however, cannot be interpreted as reflecting mobility in both professional and nonprofessional pursuits or as any indication of a close adjustment of incomes in different communities. Immobility as well as mobility might give rise to similar locational differences. Prosperity (or the reverse) is likely to be diffused among all classes of the population. The professional men selling services to the ultimate consumer—physicians, dentists, in lesser degree lawyers, etc.—are affected directly. Their incomes are likely to be large if their clients' incomes are; and in the absence of mobility large incomes will not lead to an influx of practitioners that would prevent the large incomes from being maintained. Professional men serving business enterprises—accountants, engineers, etc.—are also affected, though less directly. The fortunes of many enterprises are closely related to, or immediately affect, the fortunes of the communities in which they are located, and their prosperity may well be reflected in the prosperity of the professional workers whose services they purchase and who, in the absence of mobility, are secure from competition.

In this chapter we attempt to determine the character and magnitude of the existing differentials among communities in the level and variability of professional income and to compare

2 For example, cost of living differentials may well be one of the important factors affecting the relative desirability of different localities, and these are similar for professional and other persons at the same income level.

these differentials with those in the income of the public. We group communities by size and by region. The smallness of our samples necessitates fairly coarse groupings. We use from six to eight size of community groups, the exact number varying from profession to profession, and the nine Census regions.[3]

Only the questionnaires sent to lawyers and physicians in 1937 asked the respondent to designate the community in which he practised. In the other samples, location was inferred from the postmark on the returned envelope, an obviously inexact procedure. Some persons living in one community but practising in another may have posted the questionnaire from their homes rather than their offices. However, since the addresses to which the questionnaires were sent were taken from professional directories, most of them must have been business addresses. The information needed to fill out the questionnaire would ordinarily be on records at the place of business. Consequently, probably few were erroneously classified on the basis

[3] The size of community classes, in terms of the population of the communities in each class, are:

Physicians and dentists: under 2,500; 2,500–10,000; 10,000–25,000; 25,000–50,000; 50,000–100,000; 100,000–500,000; 500,000 and over.

Lawyers: under 2,500; 2,500–10,000; 10,000–25,000; 25,000–100,000; 100,000–250,000; 250,000–500,000; 500,000–1,500,000; 1,500,000 and over.

Certified public accountants: under 25,000; 25,000–100,000; 100,000–250,000; 250,000–500,000; 500,000–1,500,000; 1,500,000 and over.

Consulting engineers: under 5,000; 5,000–25,000; 25,000–100,000; 100,000–250,000; 250,000–500,000; 500,000–1,500,000; 1,500,000 and over.

The Census regions and the states in each are:

New England: Maine, New Hampshire, Vermont, Massachusetts, Rhode Island, Connecticut.

Middle Atlantic: New York, New Jersey, Pennsylvania.

East North Central: Ohio, Indiana, Illinois, Michigan, Wisconsin.

West North Central: Minnesota, Iowa, Missouri, North Dakota, South Dakota, Nebraska, Kansas.

South Atlantic: Delaware, Maryland, District of Columbia, Virginia, West Virginia, North Carolina, South Carolina, Georgia, Florida.

East South Central: Kentucky, Tennessee, Alabama, Mississippi.

West South Central: Arkansas, Louisiana, Oklahoma, Texas.

Mountain: Montana, Idaho, Wyoming, Colorado, New Mexico, Arizona, Utah, Nevada.

Pacific: Washington, Oregon, California.

TABLE 16

Arithmetic Mean Income, Relatives of Arithmetic Mean Income, and Number of Persons Covered, by Size of Community

SIZE OF COMMUNITY	PHYSICIANS 1929–36	DENTISTS 1929–34	LAWYERS 1932–36	CERTIFIED PUBLIC AC- COUNTANTS 1929–36	CON- SULTING ENGINEERS 1929–32
Arithmetic Mean Income [1] *(dollars)*					
1,500,000 & over	} 4,310	} 4,227	6,709	6,031	12,600
500,000–1,500,000			3,756	4,747	6,401
250,000– 500,000	} 4,812	} 3,838	4,286	5,435	5,678
100,000– 250,000			3,827	4,945	5,394
50,000– 100,000	4,913	3,721	} 3,791	} 4,475	} 4,574
25,000– 50,000	4,608	3,748			
10,000– 25,000	4,373	3,518	4,052	} 3,507	} 3,130
5,000– 10,000	} 3,600	} 2,982	} 2,538		
2,500– 5,000					} 4,933
Under 2,500	2,414	2,247	1,880		
U. S.	4,031	3,517	4,082	5,180	7,720
Relatives of Arithmetic Mean Income (U.S. = 100)					
1,500,000 & over	} 106.9	} 120.2	164.4	116.4	163.2
500,000–1,500,000			92.0	91.6	82.9
250,000– 500,000	} 119.4	} 109.1	105.0	104.9	73.5
100,000– 250,000			93.8	95.5	69.9
50,000– 100,000	121.9	105.8	} 92.9	} 86.4	} 59.2
25,000– 50,000	114.3	106.6			
10,000– 25,000	108.5	100.0	99.3	} 67.7	} 40.5
5,000– 10,000	} 89.3	} 84.8	} 62.2		
2,500– 5,000					} 63.9
Under 2,500	59.9	63.9	46.1		
U. S.	100.0	100.0	100.0	100.0	100.0
Number of Persons Covered [2]					
1,500,000 & over	} 1,168	} 581	230	1,283	149
500,000–1,500,000			154	556	121
250,000– 500,000	} 1,020	} 426	322	551	78
100,000– 250,000			270	421	37
50,000– 100,000	389	220	} 404	} 531	} 46
25,000– 50,000	397	242			
10,000– 25,000	568	333	321	} 257	} 22
5,000– 10,000	} 570	} 386	} 428		
2,500– 5,000					} 21
Under 2,500	1,022	337	400		
U. S.	5,193	2,559	2,545	3,624	474

[1] Computed by averaging averages for individual years in Tables B 3, B 5, B 8, B 10, and B 11.

[2] Actual number of persons covered by the returns used before any weighting or adjusting, i.e., the sum of the numbers of persons covered by the samples. We

of the postmark. Whatever ambiguity there is doubtless affects the groupings by size of community more than the groupings by region.[4]

1 LEVEL OF INCOME

a Size of community differences

The outstanding feature of Table 16 is the low average income of professional men in very small communities. If we may judge from the three professions (medicine, dentistry, law) for which we have segregated communities under 2,500 in population, average incomes in these communities are only one-half to two-thirds as large as in communities over 10,000 in population; and average incomes in communities of 2,500–10,000, about two-thirds as large. Engineering is the only profession in which the smallest communities segregated do not have the lowest average income: the income of engineers is apparently decidedly lower in communities of 5,000 25,000 and slightly lower in communities of 25,000–100,000 than in communities under 5,000. However, the averages for consulting engineers in these three community size groups are based on so few returns that the apparent exception may well be fortuitous.[5]

[4] A comparison of the number of lawyers listed in the *Martindale-Hubbell Law Directory* for some of the larger cities with the number listed in the 1930 *Census of Population* suggests that the difference between a classification of professional persons by residence and by location of practice may be sizable. According to the 1930 Census, 1,898 lawyers lived in Boston, while according to the 1936 legal directory, 4,374 lawyers practised there. Yet the totals for Massachusetts agree very well: the Census total is 6,940; the directory total, 7,150. (The figures on the names listed in the directory were kindly furnished to us by Martindale-Hubbell.)

[5] The difference between the averages for the two smallest size of community classes is less than twice its standard error.

Another possible explanation suggested to us by C. Reinold Noyes is that the high incomes in small communities may reflect the incomes of engineers specializing in mining.

FOOTNOTES TO TABLE 16 (cont.)

used the number reporting their incomes for the last year covered by each sample, i.e., for the 1933 samples, the number reporting 1932 incomes; for the 1935 samples, the number reporting 1934 incomes; for the 1937 samples, the number reporting 1936 incomes.

In the three business professions—law, accountancy, and engineering—average incomes are highest in the largest communities—those with populations over 1,500,000. The very high average in Table 16 for lawyers in the largest communities is for the most part attributable to extraordinarily high averages for that size of community from the second legal sample.[6] The corresponding averages from the first legal sample are larger than for any other size of community, but by a much smaller amount. The real excess in the average income of lawyers in the largest communities is probably nearer the 16 per cent excess suggested by Table 16 for accountants than the 64 per cent for lawyers. In dentistry also, average income is highest in the largest communities—this time those with populations over 500,000. In medicine, average income in communities of this size appears to be somewhat lower than in communities of intermediate size.

The intermediate size of community classes show little regularity. There is some tendency for average income to decrease with size of community, but this tendency is not clear-cut.

The averages in Table 16 on which these statements are based are for groups of communities that not only differ in size but also are concentrated in different parts of the United States. In consequence, what seems to be a size of community difference might really be a regional difference in disguise. We show in the Appendix to this chapter that this is not the case. For communities of the same size, regional differences in average income are not statistically significant for lawyers, accountants, or engineers and seem to be much less marked than size of community differences for physicians and dentists. Other computations we have made lead to the same general conclusion and indicate that averages corrected for differences in the regional composition of the size of community classes would differ merely in detail from those presented in Table 16 and the later tables of this section.

[6] These extraordinarily high values are due to the one firm commented on in Ch. 4, Sec. 1a.

The size of community differences in professional income are compared with corresponding differences in the income of the public in Table 17, the first column of which gives the National Resources Committee estimates of the 1935–36 average income of nonrelief families. So far as we know, these are the only available countrywide data on size of community differences in the income of the public. They are for size of community classes even broader than ours. To make the averages for the professions as nearly comparable as possible to those for nonrelief families, we have grouped the original size of community classes for the professions into those indicated in Table 17. In addition to the actual averages, the table gives relatives obtained by expressing the average income in each size of community class as a percentage of a national average.[7] The relatives are depicted in Chart 14.

The conclusion suggested by Table 17 is that both the general character and the magnitude of the size of community

[7] The national average used as the base of the relatives is a weighted arithmetic mean of the size of community averages. The weights are the same for all professions and for nonrelief families, and are the percentage of all nonrelief families in each size of community. The use of these 'standardized' averages yields relatives that are not affected by differences among the professions or between the professions and other occupations in size of community distributions.

The weights used are based on the percentage distribution of families by size of community in *Consumer Incomes in the United States*, Table 4B. The weight for communities with populations of 100,000–1,500,000 was apportioned among the relevant subclasses on the basis of the number of families of two or more persons recorded in the 1930 Census; and for communities with populations of 2,500–25,000, on the basis of population in 1930. The final weights used were the proper combinations of the accompanying estimated percentage distribution of nonrelief families. The 'under 2,500' class includes nonrelief families living on farms.

SIZE OF COMMUNITY	ESTIMATED % OF NONRELIEF FAMILIES
1,500,000 and over	11.3
500,000–1,500,000	5.4
100,000– 500,000	13.3
25,000– 100,000	10.4
5,000– 25,000	12.5
2,500– 5,000	3.9
Under 2,500	43.2

TABLE 17

Arithmetic Mean Income and Relatives of Arithmetic Mean Income, by Size of Community

Professions and All Nonrelief Families

SIZE OF COMMUNITY	NONRELIEF FAMILIES [1] 1935–36	PHYSICIANS 1929–36	DENTISTS 1929–34	LAWYERS 1932–36	CERTIFIED PUBLIC ACCOUNTANTS 1929–36	CONSULTING ENGINEERS 1929–32
Arithmetic Mean Income (dollars)						
1,500,000 & over	2,704			6,709	6,031	12,600
500,000 & over		4,310	4,227			
100,000–1,500,000	2,177			4,004	5,038	5,996
100,000– 500,000		4,812	3,838			
25,000– 100,000	1,813	4,764	3,734	3,791	4,475	4,574
5,000– 25,000						3,130
2,500– 25,000	1,653	4,416	3,231	3,163		
Under 25,000					3,507	
Under 5,000						4,933
Under 2,500	1,408 [2]	2,414	2,247	1,880		
U. S. actual avg.	1,781	4,031	3,517	4,082	5,180	7,720
U. S. standardized avg. [3]		3,622	3,105	3,232	4,179	5,735
Relatives of Arithmetic Mean Income (U. S. standardized avg. = 100)						
1,500,000 & over	151.8			207.6	144.3	219.7
500,000 & over		119.0	136.1			
100,000–1,500,000	122.2			123.9	120.6	104.6
100,000– 500,000		132.9	123.6			
25,000– 100,000	101.8	131.5	120.3	117.3	107.1	79.8
5,000– 25,000						54.6
2,500– 25,000	92.8	121.9	104.1	97.9		
Under 25,000					83.9	
Under 5,000						86.0
Under 2,500	79.1	66.6	72.4	58.2		
U. S. standardized avg.	100.0	100.0	100.0	100.0	100.0	100.0

[1] Averages for nonrelief families are for the 12 months, July 1935 through June 1936; see *Consumer Incomes in the United States* (National Resources Committee, 1938), pp. 1, 23.

[2] National Resources Committee estimate for all rural communities.

[3] The standardized averages are weighted averages of the averages for each size of community, the weights being the estimated percentage of nonrelief families in each.

CHART 14

Relatives of Arithmetic Mean Income by Size of Community
Professions and All Nonrelief Families

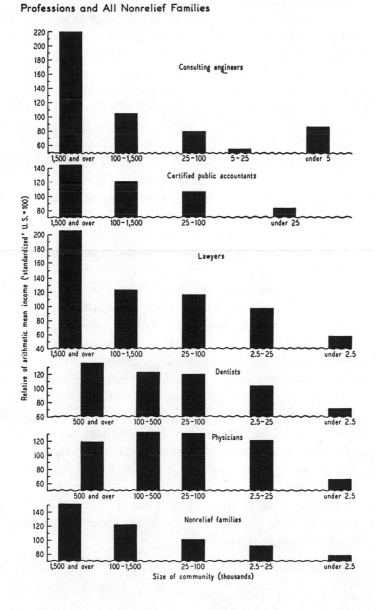

differences in average income from independent professional practice in large part reflect similar differences in the average income of the public. The average income of nonrelief families decreases consistently with size of community from 150 per cent of the national average in communities over 1,500,000 in population to 80 per cent in communities under 2,500. Dentists, lawyers, and accountants follow exactly the same pattern, and physicians and consulting engineers deviate from it only slightly: physicians receive a lower average income in the largest communities than in any except the smallest; engineers receive a higher average income in the smallest communities than in the two preceding size of community classes. Though the dispersion of the relatives is about the same for the professional groups as for the public—for three professions it is somewhat smaller, for two, somewhat larger—size of community differences in professional income diverge more in magnitude than in pattern from those in the income of nonrelief families. Errors in our data apparently account for several of the more striking discrepancies, notably the relatively high income of lawyers in the largest communities, which is entirely attributable to the peculiarities of our second legal sample,[8] and the lack of agreement between the relatives for consulting engineers and nonrelief families, which probably reflects the smallness of our engineering sample. Chief among the discrepancies that cannot be so accounted for are the relatively low average income of physicians in communities over 500,000, revealed by each of the three medical samples separately as well as by the combined samples and independently confirmed for 1929 by the survey of the Committee on the Costs of Medical Care;[9] the relatively low income of physicians, dentists, and lawyers in very small communities; and the relatively high income of physicians and dentists in intermediate size communities.

8 The first legal sample alone yields a relative of 144.7 as compared to a relative of 151.8 for nonrelief families.
9 Leven, *Incomes of Physicians*, p. 35.

These discrepancies between the size of community differences in professional income and in the income of the public might be accounted for by many factors: certain nonpecuniary advantages of communities of varying size may apply to one' profession but not to others or may be evaluated differently by members of one profession than by members of another or by the general public and this may be reflected in the relative supply of practitioners; size of community differences in the ease of entering practice or getting training that affect only certain professions may render mobility less in those professions than in others; size of community differences in the variability of income may not be the same for all professions or for the professions and the public and hence may lead to different relations among average incomes; there may be differences among the professions in the location or prosperity of clients that for one reason or another have not been fully offset by adjustments in the number of practitioners; size of community differences in the distribution of practitioners by number of years in practice may not be uniform for all professions, or if they are, the relation between income and experience may not be; and so on. Unfortunately, statistical data by size of community that would enable us to evaluate the importance of these factors are exceedingly scarce.

Data are available on the number of physicians practising in communities of different size; but alone, they are entirely inadequate. First, a high average income of the public at large would presumably mean both relatively many physicians per capita, and a relatively high income per physician. Second, a comparison of physicians per capita in communities of different size is misleading since physicians in cities are likely to draw their clientele from neighboring communities as well. The relatively large number of physicians per capita in communities with populations over 500,000 cannot be considered a satisfactory explanation of their relatively low incomes any more than the relatively small number of physicians per capita in communities with populations under 2,500 can be considered inconsistent with their relatively low incomes. Neither comparison is meaningful without further evidence on the relation between number of physicians and the average income of the public for a fixed income per physician, and on the population that is in some sense 'served' by the physicians in communities of each size.

In part, the relatively low income of physicians in large communities is attributable to a concentration of young men in those communities. But the data cited in the next chapter demonstrate that this is not the entire explanation: age class by age class physicians receive a lower average income in the largest communities than in communities of an intermediate size. Another possible explanation is that better medical facilities in very large cities constitute an attraction to physicians that has no counterpart in the other professions.

Interesting as these discrepancies are, they are overshadowed by the similarity among the professions and between the professions and the public at large in the general character and magnitude of size of community differences in income. As noted in the introduction to this chapter, this similarity is consistent with either mobility among communities of different size or immobility: with mobility, since differences in nonpecuniary advantages that would lead to differences in monetary returns might be expected to be much the same for men in different professions and for professional and nonprofessional men; with immobility, since differences in the prosperity of communities of different size might be expected to leave their impress on the incomes of professional men practising in them, an impress that in the absence of mobility would not be erased by an influx of new professional men, or by a departure of professional men in the community to better locations.

Alone, the data on size of community differences in income give no basis for choosing between these alternatives. But combined with data on regional differences in income, they may. Mobility among regions is probably less than among communities of different size. Individuals are likely to know more about economic and other conditions in communities of different size but in the same region than about conditions in widely separated communities. In addition, their background and associations, the desire to live near their families and friends, and their fears of the unknown are likely to set narrower limits on the region than on the size of the communities in which they feel free to practise. Consequently, if immobility is the explanation for the size of community differences, we should expect the even greater immobility among regions to lead to wide regional differences in professional incomes.

If, on the other hand, mobility is the explanation we might expect to find narrower regional than size of community differences. Cost of living almost certainly differs more between urban and rural communities in the same region than among urban communities in different regions, or rural communities in different regions. (Note that the most striking size of community differences are between very small communities and the rest.) While somewhat more dubious, it seems reasonable that nonpecuniary advantages also differ more among communities of different size than among regions. A resident of New York City could probably more easily change places with a resident of San Francisco than either could with a resident of a small village in the same state. Living in a large city implies an entirely different 'way of life' from living in a small community; living in one region rather than another rarely does.

We turn now to data on regional differences in professional income to see which interpretation of the size of community differences they support.

b *Regional differences*
Regional differences in the average income of professional men and the public at large are summarized in Table 18 [10]

[10] As in Table 17, the base of the relatives is a weighted average of the regional averages. The weights are the same for all professions and for the public at large and are the percentage of the total population in each region during 1929–36 (*Statistical Abstract for 1936*, Table 11).

TABLE 18

Arithmetic Mean Income, Relatives of Arithmetic Mean Income, and Number of Persons Covered, by Region

Professions and All Persons

	ALL PERSONS (per capita)[1] 1929–36	PHYSI-CIANS[2] 1929–36	DENTISTS[2] 1929–34	LAWYERS[2] 1932–36	CERTIFIED PUBLIC ACCOUN-TANTS[2] 1929–36	CON-SULTING ENGI-NEERS[2] 1929–32
	Arithmetic Mean Income (dollars)					
New England	623	4,860	3,778	4,253	4,961	6,327
Middle Atlantic	691	4,239	4,423	4,423	6,188	11,527
E. N. Central	517	4,075	3,225	5,427	4,905	5,854
W. N. Central	402	3,886	2,843	2,976	4,812	4,818
S. Atlantic	339	4,046	3,657	3,510	4,638	} 5,388
E. S. Central	220	3,174	2,640	3,690	4,727	
W. S. Central	295	3,294	3,269	2,866	4,609	4,176
Mountain	440	4,057	3,367	2,786	4,114	2,815
Pacific	653	4,282	3,762	4,141	4,118	4,450
U. S. actual avg.	486	4,031	3,517	4,082	5,180	7,720
U. S. standardized avg.[4]		4,000	3,530	4,057	5,018	6,537
	Relatives of Arithmetic Mean Income *(U. S. standardized avg. = 100)*					
New England	128.2	121.5	107.0	104.8	98.9	96.8
Middle Atlantic	142.2	106.0	125.3	109.0	123.3	176.4
E. N. Central	106.4	101.9	91.4	133.8	97.7	89.6
W. N. Central	82.7	97.2	80.5	73.4	95.9	73.7
S. Atlantic	69.8	101.2	103.6	86.5	92.4	} 82.4
E. S. Central	45.3	79.4	74.8	91.0	94.2	
W. S. Central	60.7	82.4	92.6	70.6	91.8	63.9
Mountain	90.5	101.4	95.4	68.7	82.0	43.1
Pacific	134.4	107.0	106.6	102.1	82.1	68.1
U. S. standardized avg.	100.0	100.0	100.0	100.0	100.0	100.0
	Number of Persons Covered[3]					
New England		405	188	179	249	43
Middle Atlantic		1,027	489	407	1,276	196
E. N. Central		1,017	606	443	691	58
W. N. Central		593	403	437	190	30
S. Atlantic		514	207	254	356	} 36
E. S. Central		289	81	151	150	
W. S. Central		380	122	215	204	15
Mountain		323	118	217	132	10
Pacific		595	312	231	350	86
U. S.		5,193	2,559	2,545	3,624	474

and Chart 15. The estimates of the average income of the public during 1929–36 are computed from the Department of Commerce estimates of income by states, and purport to cover all income recipients. They are therefore somewhat more satisfactory for our purposes than the National Resources Committee estimates for nonrelief families we were forced to use in the size of community analysis.

There is a fair degree of similarity, both among the professions and between the professions and the public, in the direction of the regional differences.[11] Average incomes are relatively high in the Middle Atlantic, New England, and East North Central regions—all highly urbanized—and relatively low in the West North Central, Mountain, East South Central, and West South Central regions—the least urbanized. The Pacific region ranks near the top for the population as a whole, physicians, dentists, and lawyers, but is near the bottom for accountants and consulting engineers. The relation between regional differences in professional income and in the income of the public is closer for physicians and dentists than for the other professions. But even for these two professions the income differences, though similar in direction, are not very similar in magnitude to those for the population as a whole. In general, there is far less similarity between regional differences in professional income and in the income of the public than between size of community differences (cf. Tables 17 and 18).

[11] If the averages for all persons and each profession in Table 18 are ranked, the resulting table of ranks yields a χ_r^2 of 30.8, indicating a degree of consilience that would be exceeded by chance less than once in a thousand times.

FOOTNOTES TO TABLE 18

[1] Averages are based on state averages; see R. R. Nathan and J. L. Martin, *State Income Payments, 1929–37* (U. S. Department of Commerce, 1939).
[2] Computed by averaging averages for individual years in Tables B 3, B 5, B 8, B 10, and B 11.
[3] Actual number of persons covered by returns used before any weighting or adjusting; see footnote 2 to Table 16.
[4] The standardized averages are weighted averages of the regional averages, the weights being the average percentage of the total population residing in each region, 1929–36.

CHART 15

Relatives of Arithmetic Mean Income by Region
Professions and All Persons

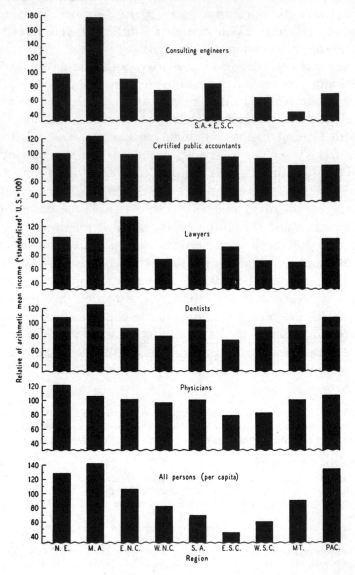

The regional averages for the professions are considerably less dispersed than the size of community averages, as Table 19 indicates. Despite the larger number of regional than of size of community classes and hence the greater opportunity for variation, the difference between the highest and lowest regional relatives is less than the difference between the highest and lowest size of community relatives for each profession. Moreover, these differences between the regional relatives

TABLE 19

Difference between Highest and Lowest Size of Community and Regional Relatives of Arithmetic Mean Income

	DIFFERENCE BETWEEN HIGHEST AND LOWEST RELATIVES FOR	
	SIZE OF COMMUNITY CLASSES [1]	REGIONS [2]
Public [3]	72.7	96.9
Physicians	66.3	42.1
Dentists	63.7	50.5
Lawyers	149.4	65.1
Certified public accountants	60.4	41.3
Consulting engineers	165.1	133.3

[1] Size of community classes used in Table 17.
[2] Regions used in Table 18.
[3] Size of community relatives based on data for all nonrelief families; regional relatives based on data for all persons.

overstate the differences attributable to region proper since the averages from which they have been computed represent geographic units that differ widely in degree of urbanization. While almost half of the residents of the Middle Atlantic region live in cities with populations over 100,000, fewer than one-eighth of the residents of the Mountain region live in cities of that size. And what is true of the population at large is no less true of professional groups. Almost two-thirds of the physicians in the Middle Atlantic region but only a quarter of the physicians in the Mountain region practise in cities over 100,000 in population. Hence, differences among the regional averages so far presented must reflect the wide income differences among communities of different size described in the preceding section as well as income differences among communities of the same size but in different regions. Our finding that incomes are relatively high in the most urbanized regions and relatively low in the least urbanized suggests that the differences in the size of community composition of the regions may be responsible for much of the observed regional differences in income.

Tests of the existence of regional differences for communities of the same size and of size of community differences for communities in the same region are presented in Section 1 of the Appendix to this chapter. These tests give no evidence of any 'pure' regional differences in the incomes of lawyers, accountants, or engineers. For these professions the differences among the averages in Table 18 must be interpreted as reflecting differences in the size of community composition of the regions plus random error. Since the regional differences reflect the size of community differences only in 'diluted' form, it is clear why the former should be smaller (see Table 19). For physicians and dentists, 'pure' regional differences apparently exist. In Section 2 of the Appendix to this chapter we attempt to measure them by eliminating the influence of differences in the size of community composition of the regions. The results confirm the impression given by Table 19: the 'pure' regional differences are smaller than the differences among the crude regional averages in Table 18, and hence considerably smaller than the size of community differences.

A somewhat more detailed analysis of the relations among geographical differences in income, made possible by data on per capita income in each state, confirms and extends some of our findings. Rough measures of the relation between average professional income and per capita income in a state and between average income in different professions are presented in Table 20.

These rank difference correlation coefficients support our

earlier finding that the relation between per capita income and average income in medicine and dentistry is significant and closer than the relation between per capita income and average income in law and accountancy. The latter, on a state by state

TABLE 20

Rank Difference Correlation Coefficients between per Capita Income and Average Professional Income, and between Average Incomes in Different Professions, 1934 and 1936

48 States and the District of Columbia

SERIES COMPARED	RANK DIFFERENCE CORRELATION COEFFICIENTS FOR	
	1934	*1936*
Per capita income & income of		
Physicians	.382*	.427*
Dentists	.325*	
Lawyers [1]	.262	.112
Certified public accountants [2]	.036	—.081
Incomes of		
Physicians & dentists	.390*	
Lawyers [1] & certified public accountants [2]	.160	.340*
Physicians & lawyers [1]	.241	.060
Physicians & certified public accountants [2]	—.201	—.307*
Dentists & lawyers [1]	—.045	
Dentists & certified public accountants [2]	.069	

* Indicates that the coefficient is 'significant', i.e., greater than the value that would be exceeded by chance once in twenty times. Standard error of the correlation coefficient is between .14 and .15 for all coefficients in the table.
[1] The 1934 averages are for lawyers practising alone (i.e., exclude firm members); the 1936 averages are for all lawyers.
[2] Both the 1934 and 1936 averages are for accountants practising alone (i.e., exclude firm members).

basis, are not even statistically significant. Somewhat more novel are the results suggested by the correlations among professions. The four professions included in the table may be divided into the curative professions—medicine and dentistry—and the business professions—law and accountancy. Average incomes in the professions in each pair are significantly correlated; but there is little, or inverse correlation, between average incomes in a curative profession and a business profession. The explanation presumably lies in the clientele served by the various professions. Physicians and dentists serve the population at large; in the short run, at least, their incomes depend primarily upon the incomes of the people in the communities in which they practise; consequently medical and dental incomes are correlated and both are correlated with per capita income. Accountants and lawyers, on the other hand, serve primarily business enterprises —accountants almost exclusively, and lawyers in large part. Moreover their services are not used in equal measure by all business enterprises; incorporated businesses and especially the relatively large ones, are their best customers. The demand of business enterprises for the services of accountants and lawyers may be none too closely related to the incomes of the business enterprises, and the incomes of business enterprises using the services of accountants and lawyers practising in an area are, in turn, only indirectly related to the average income of the residents of that area. It is not surprising, therefore, that the incomes of lawyers and of accountants in different states should be correlated and that both should be more tenuously related to per capita income than are the incomes of physicians and dentists.

All correlation coefficients between per capita income and average professional income are fairly low: diversity of per capita incomes accounts for a minor part of the diversity of professional incomes. Much of the residual diversity doubtless represents simply chance error arising from the smallness of our samples. But it seems reasonable that at least part is attributable to other factors.

Our data on regional differences in professional income leave little doubt that they are considerably smaller than size of community differences. According to the analysis presented at the end of the preceding section, this finding means that both sets of differences are to be interpreted as arising from mobility rather than immobility. The large size of community differences in professional income must reflect either differences in the net advantages attached to practising in communities of varying size or a general tendency for the abler men to be concentrated in the larger communities. Either interpretation implies that incomes in communities of varying size are adjusted to one another rather than maladjusted. Of course, this statement is intended only as a broad generalization and does not rule out the possibility that at least some part of the existing differentials is attributable to immobility (see Ch. 6, Sec. 2). The small regional differences are to be interpreted as reflecting the absence of wide differences in nonpecuniary advantages among communities of the same size but in different regions. Conceivably these small regional differences could also be consistent with large differences in nonpecuniary advantages rendered ineffective because mobility is absent. However, this alternative interpretation is hardly tenable, since it assumes the remarkable coincidence that immobility has prevented incomes from being as low as they otherwise would be in just those regions that have the greatest nonpecuniary advantages.

The neatness of the picture that can be pieced together from the data on differences in professional income is somewhat marred if we try to add to it the relationship between professional income and the income of the public at large. We saw earlier that size of community differences in professional income parallel those in the income of the public. If the former are consistent with mobility it seems reasonable that the latter are as well, since there is no reason to suppose that mobility in the professions would give rise to income differences similar to those that would arise in other pursuits in the absence of mobility. This interpretation would lead us to expect regional differences in the income of the public that not only parallel but also are of about the same magnitude as the regional differences in professional income. Professional and other workers would be unlikely to place the same evaluation on the nonpecuniary advantages of communities of varying size but different evaluations on the nonpecuniary advantages of regions.

In fact, however, the regional averages for the public are more widely dispersed than the averages for the professional groups (Tables 18 and 19). Only the sample for consulting engineers, the inconsistent behavior of which we have previously had occasion to note, does not conform to this generalization. Moreover, the greater dispersion is not attributable to a single high or low value of per capita income; if we exclude the highest and lowest, or the two highest and two lowest, or even the three highest and three lowest from all sets of relatives, per capita incomes consistently show the widest dispersion, not even consulting engineers being an exception. Regional averages for the public not only diverge more widely than regional averages for the professions; they also diverge more widely than size of community averages for the public. However, this relation would be reversed if the estimates of regional differences in the income of the public were based on the same data as the estimates of size of community differences, i.e., on the National Resources Committee estimates.[12]

Two possible explanations can be suggested of the apparent inconsistency among (1) the similarity of the size of community differences for the public and the professions, (2) the dissimilarity of the regional differences, (3) our interpretation of the differences in professional income as consistent with mobility. First, for reasons outlined at the end of the preceding section, there may be greater mobility among communities of varying size than among regions; the difference may exist in both professional and nonprofessional pursuits but be greater in the latter; hence, while it may not prevent adjustments in the professions, it may prevent them in other pursuits. Second, our data on professional incomes are for homogeneous occupa-

12 The National Resources Committee estimates of the average income of nonrelief families are available for only five regions, broader than the Census ones (*Consumer Incomes in the United States*, p. 22). The difference between the highest and the lowest relatives computed from these figures is 32.6 as compared with the difference of 72.7 between the highest and lowest size of community relatives. The range of the regional relatives for all nonrelief families is about the same as the range of relatives computed for comparable regions for the professions.

tional groups; our data on the incomes of the public are not. It may be that, occupation by occupation, regional differences in the incomes of nonprofessional workers are of about the same magnitude as regional differences in the incomes of professional workers; that the apparently greater regional differences in the income of the public reflect differences in the industrial characteristics of the regions and hence in the occupational composition of the population; and that regions vary more in industrial characteristics than size of community classes.[13] While it is beyond the scope of this book to investigate these explanations in detail, since this would involve an intensive analysis of regional and size of community differences in the income of the public, the second explanation appears on the surface more reasonable than the first.

2 VARIABILITY OF INCOME

Variability of professional income in community size or regional groups can be studied by measuring the absolute variability of income about the arithmetic mean or median for each size of community or region; or by measuring the relative variability, the percentage deviations of individuals' incomes from the mean or median. In studying variability of incomes in each profession for the country as a whole (see Ch. 4) we noted that average income and absolute variability of income are positively associated. A graphical test of the existence of such an association between absolute variability and average income by community size groups is presented in Chart 16, and by regions, in Chart 17.

13 A third possible explanation of the wider regional differences in the income of the public than in professional income is that the former includes income from property while the latter does not; but this explanation is not supported by the available data. To test it we computed regional relatives for 1930 of salaries and wages plus other labor income plus entrepreneurial withdrawals per gainfully occupied person. These relatives showed somewhat less dispersion than the relatives for 1930 computed from per capita incomes and the latter showed approximately the same dispersion as the relatives for 1929–36 per capita income given in Table 18; nonetheless they showed considerably greater dispersion than the relatives of professional income.

CHART 16

Relation between Standard Deviation and Arithmetic Mean; and between Interquartile Difference and Median, by Size of Community

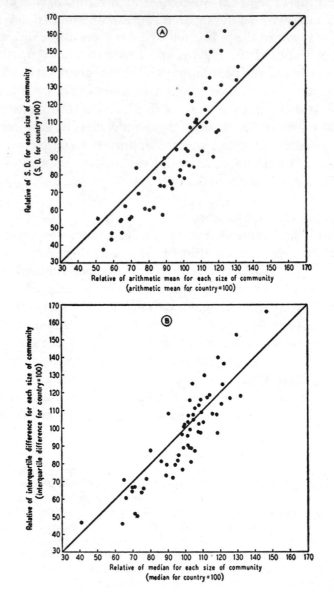

CHART 17

Relation between Standard Deviation and Arithmetic Mean; and between Interquartile Difference and Median, by Region

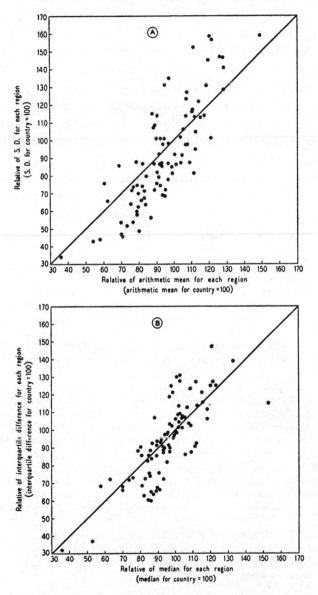

The meaning of the charts can best be indicated by describing one of the panels in detail. Each point on panel A of Chart 16 is for a particular size of community, profession, and sample. For example, the chart contains seven points based on the 1933 medical sample, one for each of the seven size of community classes. These points were computed as follows: (1) the arithmetic means for the four years covered by the sample—1929, 1930, 1931, 1932—were averaged for each size of community. This gave seven averages for this sample.[14] (2) The average for each size of community was divided by the corresponding average for the country. (3) These two steps were applied to the standard deviations, yielding ratios of the average standard deviation in each size of community to the average for the country.[15] (4) The ratio of the arithmetic mean for a size of community to the arithmetic mean for the country was plotted against the corresponding ratio of standard deviations, the former being measured on the horizontal axis, the latter on the vertical.

Dividing the size of community means and standard devia-

[14] Averages for the period covered by the sample were used instead of averages for individual years because of the high intercorrelation among the latter. Any one sample includes essentially the same individuals for each year it covers; the relations among communities of different size in one year are necessarily similar to those shown by the same sample for another year. Use of averages for each sample as a whole makes the points plotted on the charts independent.

[15] The average standard deviation for the country used as the base of the ratios was a weighted average of the standard deviations for the seven size of community classes, the weights being the average number of physicians reporting in each. This average was used instead of the actual standard deviation computed from the countrywide frequency distribution of income because the latter (1) includes the differences among as well as within size of community classes; (2) implicitly involves a different weighting system since it essentially represents a weighted average of the squares of the standard deviations for the seven size of community classes. As a result, ratios based on the actual standard deviation would have differed in 'level' from sample to sample and profession to profession.

These difficulties do not apply to the arithmetic means. Nevertheless the same procedure was followed for consistency. The resulting weighted average incomes for the country differed only slightly from those obtained by averaging the original nationwide averages.

tions by the countrywide means and standard deviations yields ratios that are comparable from sample to sample and profession to profession; consequently, points for different samples and professions can all be plotted on the same chart. Stated differently, this procedure eliminates both temporal and professional differences in level of income and absolute variability. Aside from random variation, size of community differences alone remain.[16]

Panel B of Chart 16 was constructed in the same way as panel A except that medians were used instead of means, and inter-quartile differences instead of standard deviations. Chart 17 was also constructed in the same way, except that the data are for regions.

It is clear from the charts that there are marked size of community and regional differences in absolute variability of professional income, and that these differences are highly correlated with corresponding differences in level of income. An analysis of size of community and regional differences in absolute variability would therefore duplicate the analysis of differences in level of income presented in Section 1. In consequence, we restrict our analysis to relative variability—variability measured in percentages rather than dollars.

The evidence on size of community and regional differences in relative variability is summarized in Tables 21 and 22 and Charts 18 and 19. The size of community and regional groups for the professions have been condensed to permit comparison with measures of variability for all nonrelief families computed from the National Resources Committee estimates of the distribution of income by size for the year 1935–36.[17] The

16 The size of community classes differ from profession to profession. This is relatively unimportant since the mean and standard deviation (or median and interquartile difference) represented by any point are for the same class.

17 For Table 21, giving data by size of community, the National Resources Committee rural nonfarm and farm distributions were combined simply by adding the two distributions expressed in terms of number of families in each income class. This method was not followed in grouping size of community classes for the professions. Rather a weighted average of the measures of variability was computed, the weights being the average number of returns over the period.

(Footnote continued on p. 205)

TABLE 21

Coefficient of Variation and Relative Interquartile Difference, and Relatives of Coefficient of Variation and Relative Interquartile Difference, by Size of Community

Professions and All Nonrelief Families

SIZE OF COMMUNITY	ALL NONRELIEF FAMILIES [1] 1935–36	PHYSICIANS [2] 1929–34	DENTISTS [2] 1929–34	LAWYERS [2] 1932–34	CERTIFIED PUBLIC ACCOUNTANTS [2] 1929–36	CONSULTING ENGINEERS [2] 1929–32
			Coefficient of Variation			
1,500,000 & over	1.494			1.272	.855	1.398
500,000 & over		1.305	1.002			
100,000–1,500,000	1.339			1.209	.726	1.331
100,000– 500,000		1.220	.741			
25,000– 100,000	1.288	.990	.704	1.265	.633	.995
5,000– 25,000						6.207
2,500– 25,000	1.080	.966	.550	1.079		
Under 25,000					.701	
Under 5,000						1.536
Under 2,500	1.149	1.012	.588	.794		
U. S. standardized avg.[3]	1.227	1.079	.683	1.021	.716	2.010
		Relatives of Coefficient of Variation (U. S. standardized avg. = 100)				
1,500,000 & over	121.8			124.6	119.4	69.6
500,000 & over		120.9	146.7			
100,000–1,500,000	109.1			118.4	101.4	66.2
100,000– 500,000		113.0	108.5			
25,000– 100,000	105.0	91.7	103.1	123.9	88.4	49.5
5,000– 25,000						308.8
2,500– 25,000	88.0	89.5	80.5	105.7		
Under 25,000					97.9	
Under 5,000						76.4
Under 2,500	93.6	93.8	86.1	77.8		
U. S. standardized avg.	100.0	100.0	100.0	100.0	100.0	100.0
			Relative Interquartile Difference			
1,500,000 & over	.789			1.497	.927	1.764
500,000 & over		1.242	.969			
100,000–1,500,000	.841			1.587	.749	1.539
100,000– 500,000		1.165	.827			
25,000– 100,000	.825	1.174	.818	1.534	.764	1.183
5,000– 25,000						2.708
2,500– 25,000	.883	1.097	.708	1.270		
Under 5,000						3.180
Under 25,000					.726	
Under 2,500	.927	1.282	.772	1.057		
U. S. standardized avg.[3]	.878	1.218	.807	1.290	.757	2.446

TABLE 21 (cont.)

SIZE OF COMMUNITY	ALL NONRELIEF FAMILIES[1] 1935-36	PHYSICIANS[2] 1929-34	DENTISTS[2] 1929-34	LAWYERS[2] 1932-34	CERTIFIED PUBLIC ACCOUNTANTS[2] 1929-36	CONSULTING ENGINEERS[2] 1929-32
			Relatives of Relative Interquartile Difference (U. S. standardized avg. = 100)			
1,500,000 & over	89.9			116.0	122.5	72.1
500,000 & over		102.0	120.1			
100,000–1,500,000	95.8			123.0	98.9	62.9
100,000– 500,000		95.6	102.5			
25,000– 100,000	94.0	96.4	101.4	118.9	100.9	48.4
5,000– 25,000						110.7
2,500– 25,000	100.6	90.1	87.7	98.4		
Under 25,000					95.9	
Under 5,000						130.0
Under 2,500	105.6	105.3	95.7	81.9		
U. S. standardized avg.	100.0	100.0	100.0	100.0	100.0	100.0

[1] Computed from distributions in *Consumer Incomes in the United States*, Tables 8 and 9B.
[2] The measures in this table were computed from Tables B 1b, B 4b, B 6b, B 9b, and B 11b by averaging the measures for all the years covered for each profession and combining the resulting averages into broader size of community classes, using as weights the average number of returns for the period in each size of community class.
[3] The standardized averages are weighted averages of the averages for each size of community class, the weights being the percentage of all nonrelief families in each.

tables give not only the actual measures but also relatives obtained by expressing the actual measures as percentages of a national average.[18] The charts are based on these relatives.

This gives, in general, lower measures of variability than would be obtained by combining the frequency distributions. However, test computations indicated that the difference in the results obtained by the two methods was negligible for the coefficient of variation. Though somewhat more sizable for the relative interquartile difference, the conclusions reached would not be changed if the alternative method of combining the size of community classes were used.

The measures for the professions in Table 22 for broader regions are also weighted averages of the measures for the individual regions, the weights being the average number of returns over the period, and are subject to the same qualification as the measures for broader size of community classes.

Because of the necessity of weighting by states, no frequency distributions were computed by size of community for the 1937 medical sample. In this as in all other analyses of variability, the 1937 legal sample was omitted for reasons given in Chapter 4, Section 1b.

18 The base of the relatives is in each case the weighted average of the relevant size of community or regional measures, the weights used being the same for all professions and for nonrelief families. For the size of community measures, the weights are the percentage of all nonrelief families in each size of community given in footnote 7 above. For the regional measures, the weights are the percentage of the total population residing in each region during 1929-36.

TABLE 22

Coefficient of Variation and Relative Interquartile Difference, and Relatives of Coefficient of Variation and Relative Interquartile Difference, by Region

Professions and All Nonrelief Families

REGION[1]	ALL NONRELIEF FAMILIES[2] 1935-36	PHYSI- CIANS[3] 1929-36	DENTISTS[3] 1929-34	LAWYERS[3] 1932-34	CERTIFIED PUBLIC ACCOUN- TANTS[3] 1929-36	CON- SULTING ENGI- NEERS[3] 1929-32
			Coefficient of Variation			
New England	1.475	1.002	.633	1.164	.636	1.984
North Central	1.369	1.039	.777	1.176	.830	1.489
South	1.242	1.098	.814	1.307	.671	.980
Mountain & Plains	.939	1.073	.633	1.278	.668	1.406
Pacific	1.179	1.139	.732	1.402	.560	1.100
U. S. standardized avg.[4]	1.297	1.064	.766	1.238	.739	1.335
	Relatives of Coefficient of Variation (U. S. standardized avg. = 100)					
New England	113.7	94.2	82.6	94.0	86.1	148.6
North Central	105.6	97.7	101.4	95.0	112.4	111.5
South	95.8	103.2	106.3	105.6	90.9	73.4
Mountain & Plains	72.4	100.8	82.6	103.2	90.5	105.3
Pacific	90.9	107.0	95.6	113.2	75.9	82.4
U. S. standardized avg.	100.0	100.0	100.0	100.0	100.0	100.0
			Relative Interquartile Difference			
New England	.749	1.152	.857	1.784	.879	2.551
North Central	.810	1.100	.830	1.443	.885	1.666
South	1.157	1.273	.748	1.442	.746	1.383
Mountain & Plains	.926	1.166	.751	1.354	.827	1.630
Pacific	.759	1.082	.798	1.263	.612	1.838
U. S. standardized avg.	.914	1.158	.800	1.446	.819	1.650
	Relatives of Relative Interquartile Difference (U. S. standardized avg. = 100)					
New England	81.9	99.5	107.1	123.4	107.3	154.6
North Central	88.6	95.0	103.8	99.8	108.1	101.0
South	126.6	109.9	93.5	99.7	91.1	83.8
Mountain & Plains	101.3	100.7	93.9	93.6	101.0	98.8
Pacific	83.0	93.4	99.8	87.3	74.7	111.4
U. S. standardized avg.	100.0	100.0	100.0	100.0	100.0	100.0

For professions other than engineering and law, the size of community differences in the coefficient of variation are similar in both character and magnitude from profession to profession and for the professions and all nonrelief families: the coefficient of variation tends to be greatest for the very largest communities, to decline more or less regularly to the next to the smallest size of community class, and then to rise. This pattern is confirmed by data both for more detailed size of community classes and for individual samples.[19] The coefficients of variation for lawyers display the initial decline, but not the later rise; those for engineers are exceedingly erratic, possibly because of the small number of returns on which they are based. These two professions, which show least agreement, are the only ones for which the measures in Table 21 and Chart 18 are based on a single sample.

The general character of the size of community differences is the same for the coefficient of variation as for the arithmetic mean (see Sec. 1 above): both measures tend to decline with size of community. However, there is one striking difference. While the arithmetic mean in the very smallest communities is decidedly lower than in any other size of community class, the

[19] See Appendix Tables B 1b, B 4b, B 6b, B 9b, and B 11b.

FOOTNOTES TO TABLE 22

[1] Regions are those used by the National Resources Committee. The New England and Pacific regions are the same as the corresponding Census regions; North Central includes the Middle Atlantic, the East North Central, and part of the West North Central Census regions; South includes the South Atlantic, the East South Central, and the West South Central Census regions; Mountain and Plains includes the Mountain and part of the West North Central Census regions.

[2] Computed from distributions in *Consumer Incomes in the United States*, Table 13B.

[3] The measures in this table were computed from Tables B 1a, B 4a, B 6a, B 9a, and B 11a by averaging the measures for all the years covered for each profession and combining the resulting averages into broader regions, using as weights the average number of returns for the period in each region.

[4] The standardized averages are weighted averages of the regional averages, the weights being the average percentage of the total population residing in each region, 1929–36.

CHART 18

Relatives of Coefficient of Variation and Relative Interquartile Difference by Size of Community
Professions and All Nonrelief Families

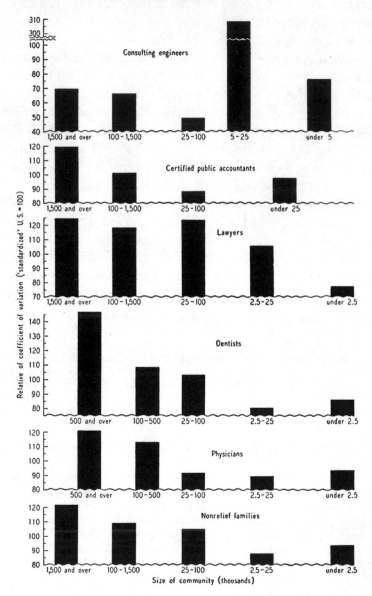

Size of community (thousands)

CHART 18 (CONCL.)

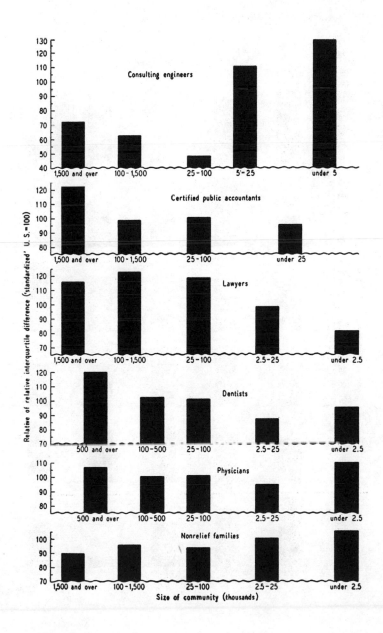

CHART 19

Relatives of Coefficient of Variation and Relative Interquartile
Difference by Region

Professions and All Nonrelief Families

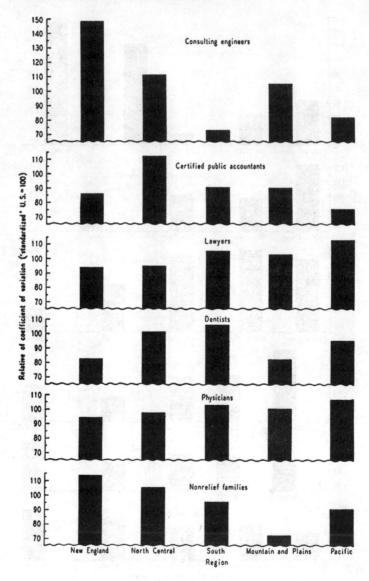

CHART 19 (CONCL.)

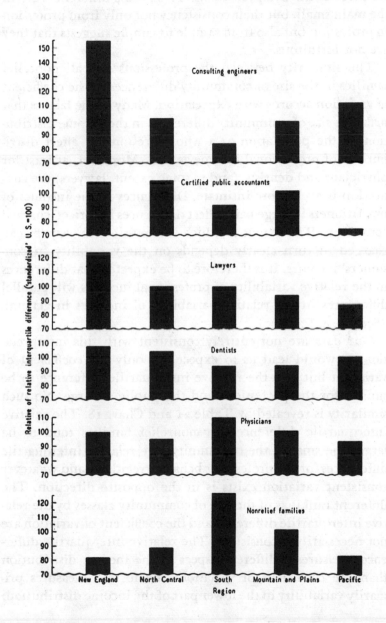

coefficient of variation is higher in the smallest than in the next to the smallest size of community class for all families and for three of the five professions. True, these differences are in the main small, but their consistency not only from profession to profession but also from sample to sample suggests that they are not fortuitous.

The similarity between the professions and all nonrelief families in the size of community differences in the coefficient of variation accords with expectation. Many of the factors that make for size of community differences in the income distribution of the population as a whole presumably affect distributions of professional income as well. Moreover, at least for physicians and dentists (and to some extent, lawyers) the connection is even more intimate. Differences in the incomes of practitioners in large part reflect differences in 'prices' charged consumers. The extent to which it is possible to vary 'prices' charged in turn clearly depends on the variability in consumers' incomes. It is therefore to be expected that differences in the relative variability of professional incomes will parallel differences in the relative variability of incomes in general. (See Ch. 4, Sec. 3.)

Our data are not entirely consistent with this interpretation. It would lead us to expect not only the coefficient of variation but also the relative interquartile difference to be similar for the professions and the public at large. No such similarity is revealed by Table 21 and Chart 18. The relative interquartile differences for nonrelief families tend to be larger the smaller the community; the relative interquartile differences for the professions behave irregularly and whatever consistent variation exists is in the opposite direction. The different rankings of the size of community classes by the relative interquartile difference and the coefficient of variation are not necessarily inconsistent. The relative interquartile difference measures a different aspect of the income distribution than the coefficient of variation: the former measures primarily variability in the lower part of the income distribution;

the latter, primarily variability in the upper part.[20] Two distributions that are identical except that one contains a few incomes higher than any in the other will have different coefficients of variation but may have the same relative interquartile differences. Presumably, this is roughly the situation in the income distributions of nonrelief families in cities of different size. The extremely high incomes tend to be found in the very large cities. In consequence, while the relative interquartile difference increases as size of community declines, the coefficient of variation declines. But why should the lower part of the income distribution of all families impress its pattern on the distributions of professional income less than the upper?

One clue to this puzzle is that the relative interquartile difference varies less from size of community to size of community than the coefficient of variation. Chance variation in the former measure might more easily hide a real relationship than chance variation in the latter.[21] Indeed it is conceivable that the relative interquartile difference for all families is the same for all size of community classes and that the observed differences in the measures reflect errors of estimate. Study of the Lorenz curves for all nonrelief families in the several size of community classes lends some support to this hypothesis: the major differences are in the upper parts, the lower parts are fairly similar. However, the evidence is far too meagre to enable us to state with any confidence that differences among the size of community classes in relative variability are restricted to the upper parts of the income distributions.

A second possibility, applicable solely to the professions

20 This statement is valid only for distributions that are sharply skewed in the same direction as income distributions.
21 However, it is also possible that with sharply skewed distributions of the kind with which we are concerned, the coefficient of variation computed by the ordinary method is subject to greater sampling variability than the relative interquartile difference, and that for this reason the coefficients of variation are more widely dispersed than the relative interquartile differences. While the consistency of the differences among the coefficients of variation argues against this interpretation, it does not negate it.

rendering services directly to the ultimate consumer, is that there tends to be a lower limit set by custom to the prices charged. At income levels below those at which higher prices are feasible, differences in the variability of consumers' incomes may be reflected primarily in the number of practitioners and may leave no impress on their income distribution. Differences in the variability of incomes of the practitioners who serve these income classes would then be attributable to factors other than the variability of consumers' incomes.

Still a third possibility is that the size of community differentials in the coefficients of variation for nonrelief families reflect the size of community differentials in the coefficients of variation for independent professional men, their salaried brethren, and independent and salaried businessmen, rather than the reverse. As we saw in Chapter 3, the incomes of independent professional families are not only higher than those of other groups but also much more variable, and this is also true of business and professional families as a group. In 1935–36 independent professional families were less than 1.5 per cent of all nonrelief families in the United States, but 17 per cent of all nonrelief families with incomes over $5,000. All entrepreneurial families—independent business and independent professional families combined—were only 11 per cent of all nonrelief families but 42 per cent of those with incomes over $5,000. Finally, business and professional families combined—salaried and independent—were 20 per-cent of all nonrelief families but almost 80 per cent of those with incomes over $5,000. Hence these groups, the variability of whose incomes might be expected to arise from much the same factors, dominate the part of the income distributions primarily responsible for differences in the coefficient of variation. Moreover, the concentration of these groups in large communities would be an additional factor tending to make the coefficient of variation decline with size of community. The wage-earning and clerical groups, on the other hand, dominate the lower part of the income distributions except in communities under 2,500 where farmers are concentrated. The relative interquartile differences for all families may reflect primarily the low variability of income for these groups. Farm families have more variable incomes than wage-earning and clerical families, which is probably the reason why the interquartile difference for all families is highest in communities under 2,500.

This third possible explanation of our results is not necessarily inconsistent with the two others mentioned; but it does suggest that we are in no position to give a satisfactory explanation, on other than purely statistical grounds, of the observed size of community differences in the variability of income.

The data on regional differences in relative variability in Table 22 and Chart 19 reveal little or no similarity among the professions or between the professions and nonrelief families, whether relative variability is measured by the coefficient of variation or the relative interquartile difference. More detailed data—for nine regions and each sample separately—confirm the absence of any similarity among the professions. If, as in Table 23, we rank the coefficients of variation and the relative interquartile differences for each sample in order of magnitude, the resulting sets of ranks are exceedingly chaotic.[22] The degree of consilience shown by the whole set of ranks of the coefficient of variation would be exceeded by chance well over half the time; that shown by the set of ranks of the relative interquartile difference, more than one-tenth the time.[23]

The absence of any similarity among the professions in regional differences in relative variability may well mean that such differences are small or nonexistent, the observed differences reflecting primarily random variation. We know that there are some regional differences, at least for the coefficient of variation. As we have repeatedly had occasion to note, the

[22] The data on which the ranks are based are given in Appendix Tables B 1a, B 4a, B 6a, B 9a, and B 11a.

[23] Probability statements based on values of χ_r^2 computed for the table of ranks. χ_r^2 is 6.3 for the coefficients of variation, 12.7 for the relative interquartile differences.

TABLE 23

Ranking of Regions by Coefficient of Variation and by Relative Interquartile Difference

	PHYSICIANS			DENTISTS		LAWYERS	CERTIFIED PUBLIC ACCOUNTANTS			CONSULTING ENGINEERS
	1933 sample	1935 sample	1937 sample	1933 sample	1935 sample	1935 sample	1933 sample	1935 sample	1937 sample	1933 sample
Ranking by Coefficient of Variation										
New England	7	5	6	6	9	6	6	5	8	1
Middle Atlantic	8	7	4	2	1	7	3	2	1	2
E. N. Central	5	1	9	4	5	5	2	1	3	5
W. N. Central	3	6	8	7	7	8	8	4	2	3
S. Atlantic	4	4	3	3	2	9	1	9	5	} 8
E. S. Central	2	3	1	8	8	3	9	8	6	
W. S. Central	6	9	7	1	6	2	5	3	7	7
Mountain	9	2	2	9	4	1	4	7	4	4
Pacific	1	8	5	5	3	4	7	6	9	6
Ranking by Relative Interquartile Difference										
New England	5	8	3	1	6	1	2	6	1	1
Middle Atlantic	7	5	6	2	1	2	1	2	7	5
E. N. Central	8	7	9	6	2	6	3	4	4	7
W. N. Central	4	6	4	5	5	5	4	7	3	4
S. Atlantic	3	4	1	3	4	4	8	8	5	} 8
E. S. Central	1	2	2	4	7	3	7	3	8	
W. S. Central	2	3	7	9	9	7	5	1	6	2
Mountain	9	1	8	8	8	8	6	5	2	6
Pacific	6	9	5	7	3	9	9	9	9	3

Ranking is from high to low. The ranks are based on averages of the relevant measures for the years covered by each sample for each region. The measures for each year are presented in Tables B 1a, B 4a, B 6a, B 9a, and B 11a.

regions differ considerably in size of community composition. Consequently, the size of community differences in the coefficient of variation noted above should be reflected in the regional measures of variability. However, in the absence of differences among communities of the same size but in different regions, this indirect effect might be fairly small and easily obscured by chance fluctuations.

Comparison of the coefficients of variation for regions and

TABLE 24

Difference between Highest and Lowest Size of Community and Regional Relatives of Coefficient of Variation and Relative Interquartile Difference

	DIFFERENCE BETWEEN HIGHEST AND LOWEST RELATIVES OF			
	COEFFICIENT OF VARIATION FOR		RELATIVE INTERQUARTILE DIFFERENCE FOR	
	Size of community classes [1]	Regions [2]	Size of community classes [1]	Regions [2]
All nonrelief families	33.8	41.3	15.7	44.7
Physicians	31.4	12.8	15.2	16.5
Dentists	66.2	23.7	32.4	13.6
Lawyers	46.8	19.2	41.1	36.1
Certified public accountants	31.0	36.5	26.6	33.4
Consulting engineers	259.3	75.2	81.6	70.8

[1] Size of community classes used in Table 21.
[2] Regions used in Table 22.

for size of community classes in general supports the hypothesis that regional differences are considerably smaller than size of community differences. The evidence is summarized in Table 24, the first two columns of which compare the difference between the highest and lowest size of community relatives of the coefficient of variation with the difference between the highest and lowest regional relatives. The ranges are comparable because, except for accountants, the number of size of community classes is the same as the number of regional classes. For four of the five professions the range of the size of community relatives is greater than the range of the regional relatives, and for all four, the former is more than twice the latter. The difference in the opposite direction for accountants is small. The range of the regional relatives for all nonrelief families, on the other hand, is greater than the range of the size of community relatives,[24] and is also greater than the range of the regional relatives for all the professions except engineering.

The ranges for the relative interquartile difference (last two columns of Table 24) are in interesting contrast to the ranges for the coefficient of variation. For three of the six groups, the range of the size of community relatives exceeds the range of the regional relatives, but for only one is the former more than twice the latter; for the other two as well as for two of the three groups showing a difference in the opposite direction, the difference is small. In general, differences between the two columns are of an order that might arise from chance alone.

The differences between the ranges for the coefficients of variation are not in themselves sufficient to establish conclusively that regional differences in the variability of professional income are small or nonexistent as compared with size of community differences.[25] But together with the low degree of consistency between different samples for the same profession, they at least establish a strong presumption in that direction. This presumption is further strengthened by its agreement with the conclusion stated earlier in this chapter that regional differences in levels of income, if they exist, are far less important

[24] However, this result seems to be inconsistent with the Lorenz curves for nonrelief families. The Lorenz curves based on the size of community distributions are not only more widely dispersed than those based on the regional distributions but are also more consistent. With one exception, the size of community Lorenz curves occupy the same order throughout their length; the regional Lorenz curves, on the other hand, change order repeatedly; their order at one end is practically the reverse of their order at the other.

[25] Testing whether the mean difference for the five professions between the two columns based on the coefficient of variation differs significantly from zero yields a Student's ratio of 1.59 with a probability between .2 and .1 of being exceeded in absolute value by chance. Taking into account the fact that the mean difference is in the expected direction would halve the probability. Student's ratio for the two columns based on the relative interquartile difference is 1.18 with a probability between .4 and .3 of being exceeded by chance.

than size of community differences. That we should again find size of community the more important category is not surprising.

3 SUMMARY

The major statistical findings of this chapter are:

1) The size of community differences in the frequency distributions of income by size are similar in character and magnitude from profession to profession and are much the same for professional workers as for the public at large.

2) The level of income tends to decline with size of community.

3) The coefficient of variation also tends to decline with size of community but is greater for the very smallest communities than for communities somewhat larger; the relative interquartile difference behaves erratically.

4) There is some similarity among the professions and between the professions and the public at large in the character, but practically none in the magnitude, of the regional differences in level of income.

5) There is little or no similarity among the professions or between the professions and the public in the magnitude or character of regional differences in variability of income.

6) Regional differences in both level and variability of income are probably greater for the public than for professional workers.

7) For the professions, size of community differences in income are decidedly greater than regional differences; for the public, the relation is uncertain.

The absence of large differences in professional income from region to region suggests that there is sufficient geographical mobility among professional workers to prevent large differences from arising or being maintained. And this, in turn, suggests that the much larger size of community differences must also be interpreted as consistent with mobility, since it seems unlikely that mobility is less among communities varying in size than among regions.

This interpretation of the differences in professional income implies a similar interpretation of the size of community differences in the income of the public, since the latter are about the same as those in professional income. The final piece to the puzzle, the regional differences in the income of the public, does not fit into its appointed place. If these differences too are attributable to mobility, as the analysis up to this point would suggest, they should be about the same as the regional differences in professional income whereas they are considerably wider. Two possible explanations of this apparently contradictory result were offered but neither was tested: greater mobility of workers in nonprofessional pursuits among communities varying in size than among regions; and the heterogeneous occupational composition of the groups to which our income data for the public relate.

APPENDIX TO CHAPTER 5

1 TESTS OF THE EXISTENCE OF REGIONAL AND SIZE OF COMMUNITY DIFFERENCES IN AVERAGE INCOME

Table 25 illustrates the kind of data needed to measure differences in the average incomes of professional men practising in different regions but in communities of the same size, or in communities varying in size but in the same region. The smallness of the sample on which the table is based makes necessary rather coarse regional and size of community groupings. As a result, the influence of size of community is not entirely eliminated from regional comparisons, and the influence of region is not entirely eliminated from size of community comparisons.

To test the existence of regional differences in average income we

TABLE 25

Arithmetic Mean Income and Number of Persons Covered, by Region and Size of Community

Physicians, 1934: 1935 Sample

SIZE OF COMMUNITY	NE	MA	ENC	WNC	SA	ESC	WSC	MT	PAC	ALL REGIONS
				Arithmetic Mean Income (dollars)						
500,000 & over	6,167	3,485	3,615	3,096	3,348	...	...	...	2,669	3,697
100,000–500,000	2,918	3,249	3,506	3,623	4,268	3,370	2,991	3,310	3,307	3,411
50,000–100,000	4,226	4,372	4,644	4,920	4,209	7,783	2,779	...	3,212	4,244
25,000– 50,000	4,704	3,732	3,899	4,789	4,631	1,176	4,305	2,668	4,304	3,966
10,000– 25,000	3,932	4,024	3,691	3,068	3,131	3,743	3,458	6,636	4,561	3,944
2,500– 10,000	2,879	3,131	3,651	3,389	2,499	1,779	3,134	3,755	2,686	3,071
Under 2,500	2,142	2,409	2,058	2,119	1,830	1,310	1,381	3,988	2,001	2,045
All size of community classes	4,010	3,400	3,377[2]	3,117[3]	3,637[4]	2,461	2,571	4,041	3,120	3,296[1]
				Number of Persons Covered						
500,000 & over	24	162	112	18	10	...	...	...	50	376
100,000–500,000	24	35	41	42	30	31	33	18	41	295
50,000–100,000	15	17	27	9	16	1	9	...	8	102
25,000– 50,000	13	17	21	7	8	3	4	9	10	92
10,000– 25,000	14	35	34	15	16	8	13	11	17	163
2,500– 10,000	11	29	24	23	11	13	9	8	10	138
Under 2,500	13	45	67	54	33	27	33	14	16	302
All size of community classes	114	340	330[2]	169[3]	125[4]	83	101	60	152	1,497[1]

[1] Includes 29 returns, reporting a total income of $54,452, for which size of community or region was unknown.

[2] Includes 4 returns, reporting a total income of $7,135, for which size of community was unknown.

[3] Includes 1 return, reporting an income of $2,191, for which size of community was unknown.

[4] Includes 1 return, reporting an income of $598, for which size of community was unknown.

rank the regions by size of average income for each size of community class (Table 26). The first section of the table gives the ranks for the size of community classes in which all regions are represented, the second for all size of community classes and the regions common to them. The two sets of ranks have been prepared from the one table of averages to overcome the difficulty

TABLE 26

Ranking of Regions by Arithmetic Mean Income, by Size of Community

Physicians, 1934: 1935 Sample

SIZE OF COMMUNITY	NE	MA	ENC	WNC	SA	ESC	WSC	MT.	PAC.
All Regions, Five Size of Community Classes									
100,000–500,000	9	7	3	2	1	4	8	5	6
25,000– 50,000	2	7	6	1	3	9	4	8	5
10,000– 25,000	4	3	6	9	8	5	7	1	2
2,500– 10,000	6	5	2	3	8	9	4	1	7
Under 2,500	3	2	5	4	7	9	8	1	6
Sum of ranks	24	24	22	19	27	36	31	16	26
Avg. rank	4.8	4.8	4.4	3.8	5.4	7.2	6.2	3.2	5.2
Six Regions, All Size of Community Classes									
500,000 & over	2	4	3	5	1				6
100,000–500,000	6	5	3	2	1				4
50,000–100,000	4	3	2	1	5				6
25,000– 50,000	2	6	5	1	3				4
10,000– 25,000	3	2	4	5	6				1
2,500– 10,000	4	3	1	2	6				5
Under 2,500	2	1	4	3	6				5
Sum of ranks	23	24	22	19	28				31
Avg. rank	3.3	3.4	3.1	2.7	4.0				4.4

Ranking is from high to low.

raised by the gaps in the latter table: 'cells' for which no observations are available.[1] To test the existence of size of community differences, we rank the size of community classes for each region

[1] Most of the gaps reflect the absence of communities of the specified size in the specified region; e.g., there is no city with a population over 500,000 in the East South Central, West South Central, or Mountain regions. A few of the gaps reflect the absence of any returns in the sample although the region contains communities of the specified size; e.g., there is one city in the Mountain region with a population between 50,000 and 100,000, but our medical sample includes no returns from it.

(Table 27). Tables 26 and 27 are, of course, both derived from Table 25.

The ranks in Table 27 display considerably more regularity than those in Table 26, suggesting that size of community differences are larger and more consistent than regional differences. To check these impressions we computed from the average ranks at

TABLE 27

Ranking of Size of Community Classes by Arithmetic Mean Income, by Region

Physicians, 1934: 1935 Sample

	500,000 & OVER	100,000–500,000	50,000–100,000	25,000–50,000	10,000–25,000	2,500–10,000	UNDER 2,500
	All Regions, Five Size of Community Classes						
New England		3		1	2	4	5
Middle Atlantic		3		2	1	4	5
E. N. Central		4		1	2	3	5
W. N. Central		2		1	4	3	5
S. Atlantic		2		1	3	4	5
E. S. Central		2		5	1	3	4
W. S. Central		4		1	2	3	5
Mountain		4		5	1	3	2
Pacific		3		2	1	4	5
Sum of ranks		27		19	17	31	41
Avg. rank		3.0		2.1	1.9	3.4	4.6
	Six Regions, All Size of Community Classes						
New England	1	5	3	2	4	6	7
Middle Atlantic	4	5	1	3	2	6	7
E. N. Central	5	6	1	2	3	4	7
W. N. Central	5	3	1	2	6	4	7
S. Atlantic	1	3	4	2	5	6	7
Pacific	6	3	4	2	1	5	7
Sum of ranks	22	25	14	13	21	31	42
Avg. rank	3.7	4.2	2.3	2.2	3.5	5.2	7.0

Ranking is from high to low.

the bottom of each section of Tables 26 and 27 a statistic designated χ_r^2 and determined the probability that the observed χ_r^2 would have been exceeded by chance, i.e., that chance alone would have produced differences among the average ranks as great as or greater than the observed differences.[2] χ_r^2 is 7.9 and 3.8 respec-

[2] See Friedman, 'The Use of Ranks to Avoid the Assumption of Normality Implicit in the Analysis of Variance'.

tively for the two parts of Table 26; either value would be exceeded by chance more frequently than once in twenty times, indicating that the observed regional differences in average rank might easily have been obtained by chance. Table 27 yields decidedly different results: χ_r^2 is 16.9 and 21.6 respectively, and these values would have been exceeded by chance less than once in a hundred times. It is unreasonable to suppose that the observed differences are attributable to chance alone.

Similar calculations were made for the other medical samples and for the other professions. All the tests are for the last year of the period covered by a particular sample.[3] In addition, joint tests of the different samples for the same profession were made by combining the sets of ranks for the different samples in one table. For example, the five sets of ranks for physicians in the first section of Table 26, and similar sets for 1932 from the 1933 sample and for 1936 from the 1937 sample were placed one under the other, yielding a final table with fifteen sets of ranks. The averages of the fifteen ranks in each column were then used to compute χ_r^2.

The results of these tests are summarized in Table 28. The values of χ_r^2 in lines 5 and 6 provide tests of size of community differences; those in lines 7 and 8, tests of regional differences. The values of χ_r^2 that would be exceeded by chance less than once in a thousand times are designated by (‡), those that would be exceeded by chance less than once in a hundred times by (†), and those that would be exceeded by chance less than once in twenty times by (*). The other values would be exceeded by chance more than once in twenty times.

The most striking feature of Table 28 is the almost complete absence of low values of χ_r^2 in lines 5 and 6, and the paucity of high values in lines 7 and 8. Only 3 of the 24 values in lines 5 and 6 but 16 of the 24 values in lines 7 and 8 are less than the value that

---

[3] Since the averages for different years from the same sample are for essentially the same individuals, they are highly intercorrelated. As a consequence, χ_r^2's computed for the different years covered by the same sample would not be independent and would add little to the information given by the χ_r^2 for a single year. Tests were made to see whether using the average income for the entire period covered by the sample would add much information or yield different results. Since practically the same results were obtained, we restricted the analysis to one year for each sample. The last year covered by each sample was used because more individuals reported for this year than for earlier years and because the data are presumably less biased.

would be exceeded by chance more than once in twenty times. These results mean that size of community differences in average income almost indisputably exist, but that the existence of regional differences is somewhat dubious.

The only low values in lines 5 and 6 are for the last accountancy sample and the engineering sample. The values for the earlier accountancy sample belie those for the last; moreover, the values for the two samples combined are higher than for either sample separately, suggesting that the size of community differences among the 1936 averages, irregular though they are, are in the same direction as those among the 1934 averages. The one value for engineers would be exceeded by chance approximately once in five times; nonetheless it is considerably larger than the value, 2.7, that reflects regional differences.[4] Moreover, the regional and size of community classes used for engineers are so few and broad that real differences might easily fail to produce a significant value of χ_r^2. These considerations as well as the results for the other professions suggest that we should not be justified in concluding that the small value of χ_r^2 reflects the absence of real size of community differences in the average income of consulting engineers.

The tests of regional differences tell a different story. None of the values for lawyers and accountants is statistically significant; nor is the one value we have for engineers.[5] Only for physicians and dentists is there any evidence that region, by itself, has a real influence on income level. For physicians, both values from the first sample and one of the values from the three samples combined would be exceeded by chance less than once in a hundred times. The test for all samples using only six regions yields a value that would be exceeded by chance more than once in twenty times. Since we are here concerned with regional differences, the test using all regions is the more important. To check the evidence afforded

---

4 The two values of χ_r^2 are comparable because both are based on the same number of degrees of freedom.

5 Not only are these values not significant on a .05 level of significance; none is even close to being significant. The two values for the separate legal samples would be exceeded by chance well over half the time, the value for the two legal samples combined about one-third the time. For accountants the three values in line 7 would be exceeded by chance more than one-third, one-tenth, and one-fifth the time respectively; the three values in line 8, one-fifth, one-third, and one-tenth the time respectively; the one value for consulting engineers would be exceeded by chance slightly more than one-half the time.

TABLE 28

Tests of the Significance of Size of Community and Regional Differences in Arithmetic Mean Income

	PHYSICIANS				DENTISTS			LAWYERS[2]			CERTIFIED PUBLIC ACCOUNTANTS[3]			CONSULTING ENGINEERS[5]
	1932	1934	1936	All samples	1932	1934	Both samples[1]	1934	1936	Both samples	1934	1936	Both samples[4]	1932
							Number of Classes							
Tests based on all regions: no. of														
1 Regions	9	9	9		9	9		9	9		9	9		4
2 Size of community classes	5	5	5		5	4		6	6		4	3		4
Tests based on all size of community classes: no. of														
3 Regions	6	6	6		6	6					6	6		4
4 Size of community classes	7	7	7		7	7					5	5		4
							Value of X_r^2							
Tests of size of community differences based on														
5 All regions	24.7‡	16.9†	15.1‡	51.5‡	23.2‡	19.1‡	33.0‡	21.7‡	16.6†	37.1‡	13.7†	4.1	14.5‡	5.1
6 All size of community classes	18.1†	21.6†	13.4*	44.7†	22.3†	18.9†	37.0‡				13.8†	5.0	14.4†	
Tests of regional differences based on														
7 All regions	25.2†	7.9†	10.9	21.3†	22.8†	13.2	26.3‡	6.8	3.7	7.8	8.1	12.2	10.6	2.7
8 All size of community classes	17.3†	3.8†	8.5	4.8	13.9*	11.8*	23.1‡				7.1	5.4	7.5	

* Greater than the value that would be exceeded by chance less than once in twenty times.

† Greater than the value that would be exceeded by chance less than once in a hundred times.

‡ Greater than the value that would be exceeded by chance less than once in a thousand times.

The values that would be exceeded by chance less than once in twenty, a hundred, and a thousand times respectively for line 5 are 9.5, 13.3, and 18.5 for physicians and the 1932 data for dentists; 7.8, 11.3, and 16.3 for the other data for dentists and for the 1934 data for accountants; 11.1, 15.1, and 20.5 for lawyers; 6.2, 8.7, and 11.6 for the 1936 data for accountants; 6.0, 9.2, and 13.8 for the two accountancy samples combined; and 7.5, 9.8, and 11.1 for engineers. For line 6 these values are 12.6, 16.8, and 22.5 for physicians and dentists; and 9.5, 13.3, and 18.5 for accountants. For line 7 they are 15.5, 20.1, and 26.1 for all professions except engineers; for engineers they are 7.5, 9.3, and 11.1. For line 8 they are 11.1, 15.1, and 20.5 for all professions. These values are derived from χ^2 tables and certain exact distributions of χ_r^2 given by Milton Friedman, 'The Use of Ranks to Avoid the Assumption of Normality Implicit in the Analysis of Variance', *Journal of the American Statistical Association*, Dec. 1937, pp. 688-9.

1 In computing the value in line 5, we used four size of community classes. In computing the value in line 7, however, we used the five size of community classes available for 1932.

2 Since for lawyers all size of community classes are represented in only two regions, we limited the analysis to all regions and six size of community classes.

3 The 1933 accountancy sample was tabulated considerably earlier than the other samples and before we became aware of the firm member bias discussed in Chapter 2. The national, regional, and size of community averages were later adjusted for this bias, but the averages for the size of community and regional cells were not. This accounts for the omission of the first accountancy sample.

The comparisons designated 'all size of community classes' are based on only five of the six size of community classes used for accountants. Since all six size of community classes are represented in only two regions, we omitted communities with populations over 1,500,000 in order to include six regions.

4 In computing the value in line 5, we used three size of community classes. In computing the value in line 7, however, we used the four size of community classes available for 1934.

5 Broader regional and size of community groups were used for consulting engineers than for the other professions. The resulting 4 x 4 table had no empty 'cells'. The regions used are New England and Middle Atlantic; East North Central and West North Central; South Atlantic, East South Central, and West South Central; Mountain and Pacific. The size of community classes are under 25,000, 25,000–100,000, 100,000–500,000, 500,000 and over.

by our data, we applied a similar test to the data of the Committee
on the Costs of Medical Care on the 1929 incomes of physicians.[6]
Unfortunately, only data on *gross* income by region and size of
community are available from this survey, while the tests so far
cited are all for *net* income. Further, our 1933 sample yields a
higher value of χ_r^2 when the regions are ranked by the size of
average gross income than when they are ranked by average net
income, suggesting that regional differences in gross income are
more marked than in net income.[7] The data of the Committee on
the Costs of Medical Care therefore give only an indirect check on
our results and may be expected to overstate the importance of
differences in *net* income. Using the nine Census regions and six
size of community classes, we obtained a value of 27.2 for χ_r^2. This
value would be exceeded by chance less than once in a thousand
times.

Table 28 gives somewhat stronger evidence of regional differences in dental incomes than in medical incomes. Not only are
three of the four values of χ_r^2 'significant', but also both values for
the two samples combined are greater than the values for the individual samples. The value obtained using all regions would be exceeded by chance less than once in a hundred times; that using all
size of community classes, less than once in a thousand times. However, it should be borne in mind in interpreting these results that
our dental data relate solely to American Dental Association members. The only conclusion that can be drawn from the evidence is
that the average income of dentists who were members of the American Dental Association in 1933 and 1935—the years the samples were
taken—and who live in the same size of community differs from
region to region. The proportion of dentists who are members of
the American Dental Association varies considerably among regions—in 1936 from 70 per cent in the Mountain region to 55 per
cent in the Middle Atlantic region—and presumably the relation
between the incomes of members and nonmembers also varies
considerably. Correction for the restriction of our samples to
members might have a sizable effect on the regional differences in

---

[6] Leven, *Incomes of Physicians*, p. 113.

[7] The values of χ_r^2 obtained from the *gross* income data for 1932 are 29.8 for
the test using all regions and 19.5 for the test using all size of community
classes. The corresponding values obtained from the *net* income data are 25.2
and 17.3 (see Table 28).

income. Unfortunately, a satisfactory correction of this bias by region and size of community is not possible.

2 REGIONAL DIFFERENCES IN THE AVERAGE INCOME OF PHYSICIANS AND DENTISTS

The averages in Tables 16 and 17 in the text of this chapter are for size of community classes that are not geographically homogeneous; and in Table 18, for regions that differ in size of community composition. In consequence, differences among the size of community averages mirror the effect of both size of community and region; and so do differences among the regional averages. The tests in the preceding section demonstrate that regional differences are small or nonexistent for lawyers, accountants, and engineers practising in communities of the same size. For these professions, therefore, the geographic heterogeneity of the size of community classes is unimportant; differences among the 'crude' size of community averages are adequate measures of differences among corresponding communities in the same region, and differences among the 'crude' regional averages are disguised size of community differences.

For physicians and dentists, 'pure' regional differences apparently exist, and hence the 'crude' size of community and regional average incomes are inaccurate measures of the income differences properly attributable to each factor. As noted in the text, the distortion in the size of community averages is negligible because regional differences are so much smaller than size of community differences. The distortion in the regional averages is more serious, and the differences among the regional averages in Table 18 cannot be interpreted as even approximate measures of differences in the incomes of individuals practising in communities of the same size but in different regions. In this section, we attempt to measure these differences more accurately.

To eliminate the influence of size of community we compute 'standardized' regional averages analogous to the standardized death rates so common in vital statistics. For each region we have averages for communities of several sizes. The averages for physicians and dentists in Table 18, and in the columns headed 'Actual' of Table 29, are weighted averages of these size of community averages, the weights being the number of physicians or dentists included in our samples and therefore varying from region to

TABLE 29

Arithmetic Mean Income Standardized with Respect to Size of Community, and Relatives of Actual and Standardized Arithmetic Mean Income, by Region

Physicians and Dentists

	ARITHMETIC MEAN INCOME [1] (dollars)				RELATIVES OF ARITHMETIC MEAN INCOME (all or six regions = 100)			
	All size of community classes		Excl. some size of community classes [2]		All size of community classes		Excl. some size of community classes [2]	
	Actual	Stand.[4]	Actual	Stand.[4]	Actual	Stand.	Actual	Stand.
				Physicians (1929–36)				
New England	4,860	4,764	4,538	4,181	116.1	113.8	117.6	108.4
Middle Atlantic	4,239	4,186	4,233	4,109	101.2	100.0	109.7	106.5
E. N. Central	4,075	4,003	3,838	3,813	97.3	95.6	99.5	98.8
W. N. Central	3,886	4,309	3,708	3,864	92.8	102.9	96.1	100.2
S. Atlantic	4,046	4,665	3,635	3,634	96.6	111.4	94.2	94.2
E. S. Central	3,174[8]		3,208	3,475			83.2	90.1
W. S. Central	3,294[3]		3,231	3,224			83.7	83.6
Mountain	4,057[8]		4,057	3,978			105.2	103.1
Pacific	4,282	4,095	4,487	4,234	102.3	97.8	116.3	109.7
All regions	4,031		3,858	3,858	100.0		100.0	100.0
Six regions	4,187	4,187				100.0		100.0

Dentists (1929-34)

New England	3,778	3,695	3,670	3,442	105.6	103.3	114.9	107.8
Middle Atlantic	4,443	4,143	3,645	3,570	123.7	115.8	114.1	111.8
E. N. Central	3,225	3,169	2,796	2,857	90.2	88.6	87.5	89.4
W. N. Central	2,843	2,954	2,763	2,930	79.5	82.6	86.5	91.7
S. Atlantic	3,657	4,037	3,498	3,368	102.2	112.9	109.5	105.4
E. S. Central	2,640[3]		2,660	2,707			83.3	84.8
W. S. Central	3,269[3]		3,299	3,128			103.3	97.9
Mountain	3,767[3]		3,354	3,322			105.0	104.0
Pacific	3,752	3,655	3,780	3,573	105.2	102.2	118.3	111.9
All regions	3,577	3,577	3,194	3,194	100.0	100.0	100.0	100.0
Six regions	3,577				100.0	100.0	100.0	100.0

[1] These averages were computed separately for each year and sample. They were linked into a continuous series by the procedure described in the footnotes to Tables B 3 and B 5. The averages for six or all regions were computed directly (i.e., they are not averages of the regional averages in this table), and are based on actual averages rather than on the weighted averages used in computing the regional standardized averages.

[2] The size of community classes excluded are 50,000–100,000 and 500,000 and over; for dentists, the 10,000–25,000 class also is excluded.

[3] Some size of community classes not represented.

[4] The standardized averages are weighted averages of the size of community averages for each region. For physicians, the weights are the estimated number of physicians in 1931 in each size of community class for the country as a whole given by R. G. Leland, *Distribution of Physicians in the United States* (American Medical Association, 1936), Table 42. For dentists, the weights are averages, for each size of community class, of the number of dentists reporting their 1932 income in the 1933 and 1935 samples.

region. We can, however, combine the size of community averages using weights that are the same from region to region. Since the resulting averages are for hypothetical regions with the same size of community composition, the influence of size of community is eliminated. Two sets of standardized averages are given in Table 29: one, for the six regions in which all the size of community classes are represented; the other, for all regions but excluding size of community classes not represented in all regions.[8]

When the influence of differences in the size of community composition of the regions is eliminated, the range between the highest and lowest relatives is reduced by between 20 and 25 per cent, as the following tabulation indicates.

	DIFFERENCE BETWEEN HIGHEST AND LOWEST RELATIVES	
	Actual	'Standardized'
Physicians		
All size of community classes	23.3	18.2
Excluding some size of community classes	34.4	26.1
Dentists		
All size of community classes	44.2	33.2
Excluding some size of community classes	35.0	27.1

[8] The size of community classes excluded are 50,000–100,000 and 500,000 and over; for dentists, the 10,000–25,000 class also is excluded. These size of community classes are excluded either because some regions contain no communities of the specified size or because for some years and regions our samples include no returns from individuals practising in communities of the specified size.

For physicians, the weights used in computing the 'standardized' averages are the estimated number of physicians in active practice in 1931 in each size of community class for the country as a whole given by Leland, *Distribution of Physicians*, Table 42. For dentists, the weights were obtained by averaging, for each size of community, the number of dentists reporting their 1932 income in the 1933 and 1935 samples.

It should be noted that the standardized averages depend on the particular weights used in combining averages for communities of different size, and that these weights are in large measure arbitrary. For example, we could have used as weights the size of community distribution of professional men in a single region, instead of in the country as a whole, and any one of the nine regions might have been used. If the regional differences are about the same for each size of community, approximately the same results should be obtained no matter what set of weights are used, so long as the same weights are used for all regions. Of course, varying the weights will increase or reduce the likelihood that peculiarities in the figures for a particular size of community will affect the standardized averages.

The two sets of standardized averages show important differences. The average income of physicians in the South Atlantic region is 11 per cent above the average for all regions according to the set for all size of community classes, but 6 per cent below the average for all regions according to the set that excludes some size of community classes. The average income of physicians in the Pacific region is 2 per cent below the average in all regions according to the first set, but 10 per cent above according to the second. Similarly, the average income of dentists in the Pacific region is 2 per cent above the average in all regions according to the first set of standardized averages, but 12 per cent above according to the second. These differences may of course reflect variation in the regional differences from size of community to size of community— a possibility we cannot test with our meagre data. But we suspect that the differences arise from random variation. In any event, the existence of such differences suggests that the averages in Table 29 are subject to a wide margin of error. The broad conclusions they suggest are probably accurate but it would be exceedingly hazardous to use them as precise measures of the difference between one region and another.

No matter which set of standardized averages we use, physicians in New England rank relatively high with an average income about 10 per cent above the average for the country; in the Middle Atlantic and West North Central regions, they seem to have average incomes above, and in the East North Central region, an average income below, the average for the country. The one set of averages for the East South Central, West South Central, and Mountain regions places the Mountain region above, and the other two regions considerably below, the average for the country. West South Central with an average income more than 15 per cent below that for the country seems to have the lowest average of any region.

The most striking feature of the standardized averages for dentists is the relatively low average income in the East South Central, East North Central, and West North Central regions, a band of states comprising roughly the 'Middle West' and 'Deep South'. The average income of dentists practising in these regions and in any specified size of community can reasonably be set at least 10 per cent below the average income of all dentists practising in the same size of community. None of the other six regions stands out so sharply. The Middle Atlantic, South Atlantic, Pacific, New England, and Mountain regions seem to have average incomes above the average for the country, and rank in approximately the order listed. The average for the Middle Atlantic region exceeds that for the country by 10 to 15 per cent; the averages for the other regions exceed that for the country by smaller margins.

To facilitate comparison between physicians and dentists, it is convenient to summarize the preceding results in more rigid fashion than is perhaps justified. In general the two groupings

	PHYSICIANS	DENTISTS
Regions with averages definitely above average for country	New England Middle Atlantic Mountain W. N. Central	Middle Atlantic S. Atlantic Pacific New England Mountain
Regions with averages whose relation to average for country is questionable	S. Atlantic Pacific	W. S. Central
Regions with averages definitely below average for country	E. N. Central E. S. Central W. S. Central	E. S. Central W. N. Central E. N. Central

are fairly similar: the first group has three regions common to the two professions, the last group two. But there are also certain fairly striking differences between the two groupings. West South Central seems by a fair margin to be the region in which physicians have the lowest average income; among dentists it is listed in the 'questionable' group. Dentists in this region apparently receive an average income about the same as the average for the country; physicians, an average income approximately 15 per cent below the average for the country. The second striking difference is in the position of the West North Central region. It is in the first group for physicians, in the last for dentists: i.e., physicians in this region appear to have an average income slightly above the average for all physicians; dentists, an average income about 10 per cent below the countrywide average.

Although too much reliance should not be placed on these differences,[9] they seem reasonable in view of the relative number of physicians and dentists. In 1936 there were 2.11 times as many

[9] They may merely reflect random variation or the bias in our averages for dentists arising from the restriction of our samples to American Dental Association members.

physicians as dentists in active practice in the United States. In the West South Central region the corresponding ratio was 3.18 and in the West North Central, 1.78.[10] In the West South Central region physicians are numerous relatively to dentists and their incomes are low relatively to dentists'; in the West North Central region the relation is reversed. These figures are merely suggestive and do not conclusively establish that the observed difference in relative incomes reflects this difference in the relative number of practitioners; indeed, one region, the East South Central, has an even higher ratio of physicians to dentists, 3.27, than the West South Central region; and one region, the Pacific, has an even lower ratio, 1.61, than the West North Central.

CHAPTER 6

Other Determinants of Professional Income

1 TRAINING AND ABILITY

THE KIND OF TRAINING individuals get and the ability they possess play a large role in determining their professional competence, connections, and opportunities; and, through these, their incomes. Unfortunately, data for measuring the influence of these important factors are almost nonexistent. The only information available on the influence of training and ability is from two fragmentary studies of lawyers, one for New York County, the other for Wisconsin. The New York County study

10 See Appendix to Chapter 4, Section 3b, for a more detailed discussion of the relation between the incomes of physicians and dentists and the number of practitioners, and for the source of these figures.

presents data, summarized in Table 30, on the incomes of
college graduates and nongraduates and of graduates of full-
and part-time law schools. The classifications are of course in-
terrelated: individuals who graduate from college are more
likely to attend a full-time law school than those who do not.

The median income of college graduates is almost 50 per
cent larger than that of noncollege graduates; similarly, the
median income of graduates of full-time law schools is about

TABLE 30

Median Income, by Prelegal Training
and by Type of Law School Attended

New York County Lawyers, 1933 and 1928–1932

	NO. OF LAWYERS REPORTING INCOME FOR		MEDIAN INCOME	
	1933	*1928–32*	*1933*	*1928–32*
			(dollars)	
Prelegal training				
College graduate	1,742	1,317	3,570	5,220
Not college graduate	1,026	795	2,480	3,570
Type of law school attended				
Full-time	1,794	1,402	3,555	5,140
Part-time	1,011	786	2,580	3,355

Survey of the Legal Profession in New York County (New York County Lawyers
Association, 1936), p. 23.

50 per cent larger than that of graduates of part-time law
schools. These results presumably indicate that more extensive
training yields higher incomes. However, the results are not
unambiguous. On the one hand, the increasing tendency for
individuals to go to college means that college graduates are
concentrated in younger age groups than other lawyers. Since
income tends to increase for a time with age (see Sec. 2), the
medians in Table 30 probably understate the difference between the incomes of college graduates and others in practice
the same number of years. On the other hand, both college
graduates and graduates of full-time law schools doubtless
come from wealthier families and have more valuable professional connections than other lawyers. The latter frequently

cannot afford to go to college and often attend part-time schools while earning their living. Hence, lawyers who received the better training would probably have earned higher incomes than their fellow lawyers even if they had received the same training as the latter.

The Wisconsin data relate 1932 incomes to the standing of individuals in their law school classes (Table 31). In general,

TABLE 31

1932 Professional Income, by Grade in Law School

Graduates of University of Wisconsin Law School

		% OF LAWYERS ATTAINING SPECIFIED GRADE IN LAW SCHOOL WHOSE 1932 INCOME WAS			
GRADE IN LAW SCHOOL	NO. OF LAWYERS REPORTING INCOME	Loss	$0– 2,000	$2,000– 4,000	Over $4,000
A	67	.0	29.9	32.8	37.3
B	143	.7	34.9	32.2	32.2
C	136	.7	41.2	32.4	25.7
D	113	.9	41.6	29.2	28.3
E	137	5.1	50.4	29.2	15.3

L. K. Garrison, 'A Survey of the Wisconsin Bar', *Wisconsin Law Review*, Feb. 1935, pp. 161–3. Data are for the graduating classes of University of Wisconsin Law School, 1904–31, excluding 1917–20.

those who received high grades in law school had better success in the practice of law than those who received low grades, although the correlation is far from close. The looseness of the relation between law school grades and income may mean that there is equally little connection between ability and income; probably, however, it means that law school grades are a poor index of the type of ability that spells success in the practice of law. High grades may measure application rather than ability, and individuals may 'loaf' in law school but work hard once they enter practice. In addition, the type of ability needed to get high grades may not be the same as the type of ability needed to make money as a lawyer.

2 NUMBER OF YEARS IN PRACTICE

The early career of an independent professional man is characterized by low earnings. Some time must elapse before his availability and competence become known—before he can attract 'practice'. To get a client is as a rule more difficult than to keep him. Once started, his practice tends to be cumulative. A satisfied client will return again and again and will recommend the practitioner to his friends or business associates. In the course of time the professional man becomes known, gains a reputation, acquires experience—that is to say, 'builds up a practice', and therefore is able to charge higher fees and to keep more fully occupied. If his reputation is good, his practice and income will continue to grow. But a limit to growth is set by the amount of business he can handle, the size of the market he serves, and the competition of fellow practitioners. This limit may come early or late in a man's professional career. But sooner or later he will have to struggle to retain his clients and to replace those he is unable to retain. And eventually, he will pass the zenith of his career. Long before his physical energies decline, he will find it increasingly difficult to retain his practice in the face of competition of younger men, trained in the latest methods and vigorously striving to make a place for themselves. Some of the more eminent, of course, will easily weather this competition and continue to increase their practice and income long after most other practitioners of their age are experiencing serious difficulty in maintaining their position. But others will find their problem intensified by poor health, while still others will voluntarily relinquish their practice in whole or in part as the urge for retirement overcomes the drive for professional advancement.

The data summarized in Table 32 and Charts 20 and 21 document this picture of an initially rapid rise in average income, followed by a slower rise, relative stability, and ultimately, a decline. In medicine and dentistry, professions in which scientific advance has been rapid and in which physical skill and dexterity are required, younger men are at an advantage and the peak income is reached fairly early—between the thirteenth and twentieth year of practice. In law, the only one of the 'business' professions for which data are available, experience and contacts are more important and physical fit-

CHART 20

Arithmetic Mean Income of Physicians and Dentists by Years in Practice

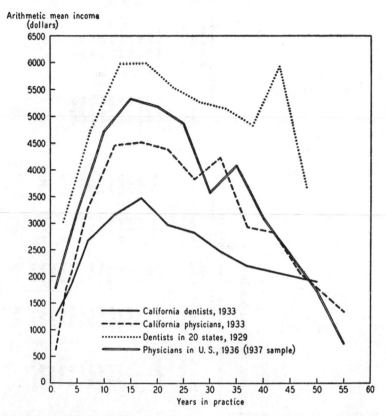

Arithmetic mean income
(dollars)

California dentists, 1933
California physicians, 1933
Dentists in 20 states, 1929
Physicians in U. S., 1936 (1937 sample)

Years in practice

The midpoint for California dentists '40 and over' class has been arbitrarily set at 50; for California physicians '50 and over', at 55.

ness secondary. In consequence, peak income is reached much later. Indeed, according to the data for New York County, the oldest lawyers have the highest median income. However, the last class—in practice 35 years and over—is fairly broad and if subdivided might well reveal a decline. Wisconsin lawyers seem to attain peak incomes between the twentieth and fortieth year of practice.

TABLE 32

Average Income, by Years in Practice

Physicians, Dentists, and Lawyers: Selected Studies

PHYSICIANS IN U. S.,[1] 1936 INCOME

Years in practice	Arith. mean income (dollars)
Under 3	1,788
3– 7	3,182
8–12	4,718
13–17	5,326
18–22	5,179
23–27	4,859
28–32	5,575
33–37	4,076
38–42	3,091
43–47	2,402
48–52	1,703
53–57	747
All	3,941
No. of returns in sample	1,409

PHYSICIANS & DENTISTS IN CALIFORNIA,[2] 1933 INCOME

	PHYSICIANS		DENTISTS	
Years in practice	Median income (dollars)	Arith. mean income	Median income (dollars)	Arith. mean income
Under 2	600	616	1,100	1,267
2	1,100	1,175	(see above)	
3	1,500	1,771	1,500	1,642
4	2,000	2,068	1,500	1,857
5– 9	2,950	3,267	2,400	2,674
10–14	3,600	4,465	2,900	3,168
15–19	3,600	4,508	3,000	3,474
20–24	3,500	4,399	2,500	2,962
25–29	2,900	3,884	2,500	2,828
30–34	3,000	4,227	2,200	2,480
35–39	2,300	2,938	2,100	2,200
40–44	1,900	2,858	1,650	1,911
45–49	1,400	2,048	(see above)	
Over 49	1,150	1,344		
All	2,700	3,572	2,500	2,769
No. of returns in sample	2,737		1,615	

DENTISTS IN 20 STATES,[3] 1929 INCOME

Year of graduation	Equiv. no. of years in practice	Median income (dollars)	Arith. mean income (dollars)
1929–25	Under 6	2,695	3,025
1924–20	6–10	4,049	4,742
1919–15	11–15	5,047	5,976
1914–10	16–20	4,982	5,995
1909–05	21–25	4,741	5,551
1904–00	26–30	4,261	5,258
1899–95	31–35	3,770	5,144
1894–90	36–40	3,765	4,899
1889–85	41–45	4,167	5,940
1884–80	46–50	3,125	3,682
All		4,094	5,011
No. of returns in sample		4,705	

LAWYERS IN NEW YORK COUNTY,[4]
1933 INCOME

Year of admission to bar	Equiv. no. of years in practice	Median income (dollars)
After 1929	Under 5	1,794
1924–29	5–10	3,164
1918–23	11–16	5,547
1911–17	17–23	6,674
1900–10	24–34	6,572
Before 1900	Over 34	6,068
All		5,364
No. of returns in sample		2,938

LAWYERS IN WISCONSIN,[5] 1930 INCOME
ARITH. MEAN INCOME OF LAWYERS PRACTISING IN

		Communities with populations of			
Years in practice	Milwaukee	Over 25,000[6]	10,000–25,000	2,000–10,000	Under 2,000
		(dollars)			
Under 5	1,772	2,224	1,983	1,937	1,709
5–9	3,196	3,849	3,764	3,184	2,509
10–19	5,035	5,264	5,218	3,223	2,946
20–29	7,846	6,950	5,495	4,286	3,422
30–34	10,415	6,201	5,652	3,759	2,512
35–39	8,853	6,553	4,425	4,290	2,235
Over 39	5,049	5,558	3,716	3,660	2,554
No. of returns in sample	812	525	186	292	161

[1] See Table 34a.
[2] California Medical-Economic Survey, Formal Report on Factual Data (California Medical Association, 1937), pp. 80, 88.
[3] Maurice Leven, Practice of Dentistry and the Incomes of Dentists in Twenty States: 1929 (University of Chicago Press, 1932), p. 135.
[4] Survey of the Legal Profession in New York County, p. 20.
[5] Garrison, 'A Survey of the Wisconsin Bar', p. 155.
[6] Excluding Milwaukee.

CHART 21

Average Income of Lawyers by Years in Practice

————————New York County, median income in 1930
Wisconsin, arithmetic mean income in 1930
— — — — —Milwaukee
————————Communities over 25,000 (excl. Milwaukee)
·················Communities of 10,000 – 25,000
══════════Communities of 2,000 – 10,000
— ·· — ·· —Communities under 2,000

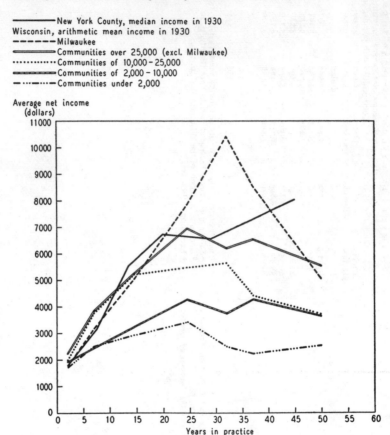

The midpoint for Wisconsin 'over 40' years in practice has been arbitrarily set at 50; for New York 'over 35', at 45.

Both the rise and decline seem larger for physicians than dentists. The factors responsible for this difference are presumably the same as those which account for the greater variability of medical than of dental incomes (see Ch. 4, Sec. 3). The most significant in the present connection is probably the greater importance attached to medical services and the consequent willingness to pay more for the services of a physician considered superior to another than for the services of a dentist considered superior.

For physicians, information on years in practice from the 1937 sample makes possible a more intensive analysis.[1] The percentage distribution of physicians by years in practice in Table 33 is bimodal. The first mode is in the 3–7 years-in-practice class; the second, in the 23–27 years-in-practice class. The class containing the second mode includes individuals who graduated from medical school about 1910. It will be recalled from Chapter 1 that the initiation shortly before this date of

[1] The available data on years in practice are not unambiguous. The question was "state the number of years you have practised medicine". No other instructions were given. Consequently it is not clear whether the respondents excluded time spent as interns or in postgraduate study, or other interruptions to practice. However, this vagueness cannot be important; with rare exceptions, the maximum possible error is one or two years. For reasons of economy, only the data on income in 1936 have been analyzed by number of years in practice.

The questionnaire sent to lawyers in 1937 contained a question on the number of years in practice, but we have made no use of the answers. We have repeatedly had occasion to question the validity of this sample; in addition, the tabulation of the answers would be exceedingly arduous because of the necessity of both adjusting for the size of community bias and weighting the individual states in combining them. An additional difficulty is the questionnaire used. It was in two parts: the upper half requested data about the legal enterprise, the lower half about the individual lawyer. Additional copies of the lower half were enclosed with questionnaires sent to firm members, who were asked to distribute them among the other members of the firm. Almost all individual practitioners who replied returned both halves; and so did most firm members who returned the upper halves. In many cases, however, additional copies of the lower half were not returned by the other firm members. There is therefore reason to suppose that the sample of completed 'lower halves' is even more biased than the entire sample.

A table of average income of lawyers by years in practice based on this 1937 Department of Commerce sample, which did not seem to us worth tabulating in that fashion, is presented in *Economics of the Legal Profession* (American Bar Association, 1938), p. 21. So far as we can gather, the figures presented are based solely on the lower half of the schedules and are not corrected for the size of community bias or the nonrandomness of the sample by states. As a consequence the average 1936 income of all lawyers computed from this table is $3,446, whereas the average we obtain for 1936 from the same sample is $5,202 (Table 10). The table shows a rising income through 28–37 years in practice, and a decline thereafter.

TABLE 33

Percentage Distribution by Years in Practice; Arithmetic Mean Income and Number of Persons Covered, by Years in Practice and Type of Practice

Physicians, 1936

YEARS IN PRACTICE	% DISTRIBUTION[1]	ARITHMETIC MEAN INCOME (dollars)				NUMBER OF PERSONS COVERED[2]			
		All physicians	General practitioners	Partial specialists	Complete specialists	All physicians	General practitioners	Partial specialists	Complete specialists
Under 3	6.7	1,788	1,770	1,722	1,896	81	37	24	20
3–7	17.3	3,182	3,124	3,085	3,540	228	114	76	38
8–12	13.8	4,718	3,813	4,571	6,133	172	63	68	41
13–17	9.9	5,326	4,071	4,908	7,312	125	37	52	36
18–22	8.2	5,179	3,500	4,744	7,499	105	34	43	28
23–27	12.1	4,859	3,261	5,032	6,742	179	72	61	46
28–32	11.2	3,575	2,605	3,980	4,558	167	71	63	33
33–37	9.1	4,076	2,538	4,282	7,155	146	62	58	26
38–42	6.6	3,091	2,257	2,766	9,085	100	58	30	12
43–47	2.8	2,402	1,967	2,236	10,749	33	19	12	2
48–52	1.6	1,703	1,169	2,403		18	12	6	
53–57	0.7	747	692	922		7	5	2	
All classes[3]	100.0	3,941	2,917	3,957	5,795	1,409	603	513	293

[1] Excludes returns for which the number of years in practice was unknown.

[2] Number of persons covered by the returns used before weighting. These numbers, therefore, cannot be used directly to esti-mate the percentage distribution of physicians by years in practice.

[3] Includes some returns for which the number of years in practice was unknown.

an intensive drive for higher standards of medical education caused a sharp decrease in medical students and graduates.

Table 33 and Chart 22 give the average 1936 incomes of all physicians, general practitioners, partial specialists, and com-

CHART 22

Arithmetic Mean Income of Physicians by Type of Practice and Years in Practice, 1936

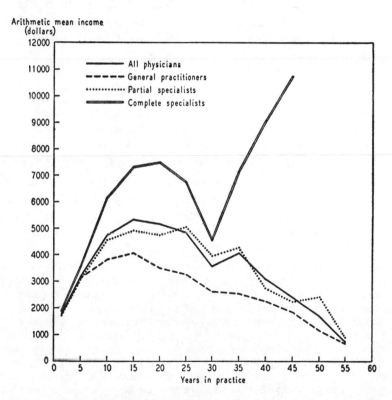

plete specialists by years in practice. According to the averages for all physicians, it takes approximately seven years for physicians to attain an average income equal to the average for the profession; another 10 or 11 years brings them to the peak; and it is then between 15 and 20 years before their incomes fall below the average for the profession. The rise is considerably steeper than the decline, and the peak income is received by physicians in practice about 17 or 18 years.[2] Strictly speaking, this pattern describes only the relative earnings in a given year of physicians in practice varying periods. However, the pattern for 1936 is very similar to corresponding patterns for the 1933 incomes of California physicians (Table 32 and Chart 20) and the 1928 gross incomes of physicians in all parts of the country.[3] This close similarity among patterns for periods as much as eight years apart suggests that they can also be interpreted as describing the change through time in the earnings of each year's entrants relative to average earnings in the profession as a whole—the earnings 'life cycle', as it were.

While in the early years incomes depend but little on type of practice, beginning with the 8–12 years-in-practice class the averages diverge considerably. The pattern for general practitioners has a peak at about 15 years, for partial specialists, at about 25 years. The peculiar pattern for complete specialists makes it impossible to select any one year as *the* peak. There is one peak at 20 years, another at 45 years, the last class for which we have data. Fluctuations that might arise from chance are so great that either the decline from 25 to 35 years or the rise thereafter might be spurious, although the smoothness of

---

[2] These statements are more precise than Chart 22 alone would justify, since averages for five-year periods are plotted on the chart. They are based on our examination of the annual averages, which suggests that the curve relating average income to number of years in practice crosses the average for the profession as a whole for the first time between 7 and 8 years and for the second time at about 33 or 34 years, and reaches a peak at about 17 or 18 years.

[3] See Leven, *Incomes of Physicians*, pp. 44–9, 114. Interestingly enough, the rise between 30 and 35 years in practice in the pattern from our data is matched by a similar rise in the pattern from the California 1933 data. There is no such rise in the pattern from the 1928 data. An examination of the averages for each year in practice rather than for the five-year intervals used in Chart 20, reveals that two of the annual averages in the 28–32 years-in-practice class are lower than any in the 33–37 years-in-practice class, and two of the latter are larger than any in the former group. The remaining three in the two groups are about equal. A rough test of the significance of the difference between the two five-year averages indicates that the observed difference would be exceeded in well over one-fifth of random samples. In view of these results and of the absence of any reasonable explanation for such a 'kink' we are disposed to attribute the coincidence between the California and our data to chance.

the decline and subsequent rise argues against such an interpretation.[4] In any event, the pattern for complete specialists has a much sharper upward 'tilt' than the pattern for partial specialists, and the latter than the pattern for general practitioners. Consequently, the percentage differences among the three groups of practitioners display a fairly uniform tendency to increase with number of years in practice. These patterns for the three groups of practitioners cannot, like the pattern for all physicians, be interpreted as describing the 'life cycle' of earnings. Young men who become physicians ordinarily remain physicians throughout the whole of their working life. Young men who start as general practitioners, however, may often later become partial specialists or complete specialists. The patterns for the different groups of practitioners naturally reflect this shift in their composition, and hence cannot be interpreted as the 'life cycle' of the earnings of a stable group. (See also Sec. 3a below.)

Chart 23 presents for each type of practitioner and each size of community the relation between average income and years in practice. The averages are given in Table 34. The tendency noted in the countrywide data for the tilt of the patterns to shift upward as we pass from general practitioners to partial specialists to complete specialists persists for the larger communities, but is, if anything, reversed for the two smallest size of community classes. In general, the amplitude of the patterns increases at first as size of community decreases, and

[4] It is difficult to make an accurate test of these statements: first, because the particular movements to be investigated are selected from many on the basis of their peculiarity; second, because the averages are weighted. However, standard errors of the differences can be computed that neglect these difficulties. The difference between the average at 20 years in practice and the average at 30 years is about twice its approximate standard error; the difference between the latter average and the average at 45 years in practice is slightly more than twice its approximate standard error; and the difference between the average at 20 years and the average at 45 years in practice is about one and a half times its standard error. If we disregard the two complications mentioned, these differences are on the borderline of 'significance'. Since both complications tend to lessen the 'significance' of the differences, it is not unreasonable to attribute the differences to chance fluctuation. It should be noted that these tests do not take into account the regularity of the averages.

CHART 23

Arithmetic Mean Income of Physicians by Type of Practice, Size of Community, and Years in Practice

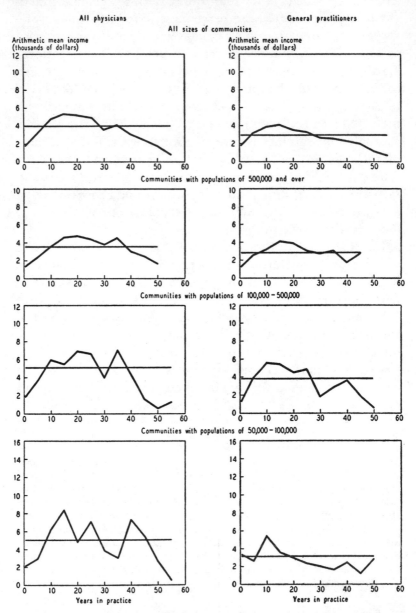

The horizontal line in each diagram represents the arithmetic mean income of all physicians of the specified type in the particular size of community.

CHART 23 (CONT.)

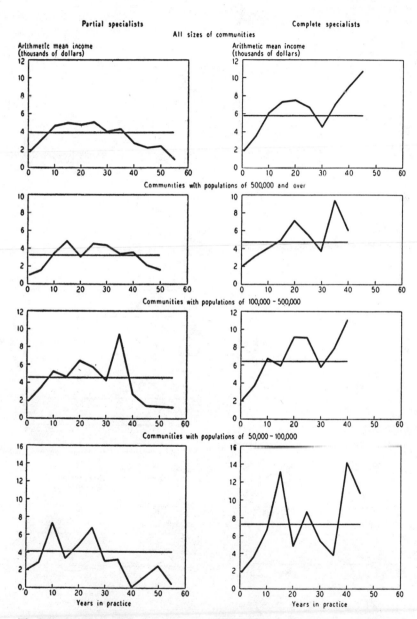

The horizontal line in each diagram represents the arithmetic mean income of all physicians of the specified type in the particular size of community.

CHART 23 (CONT.)

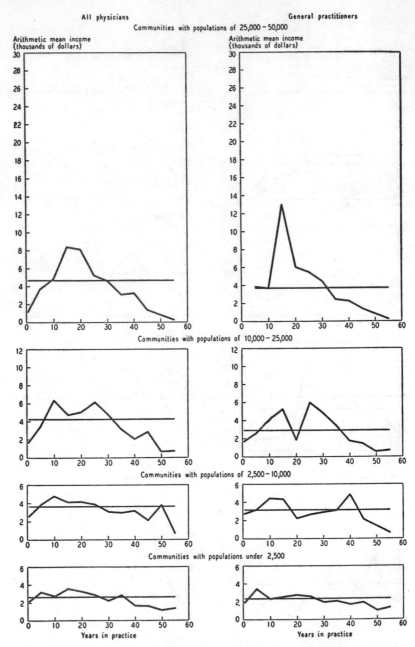

The horizontal line in each diagram represents the arithmetic mean income of all physicians of the specified type in the particular size of community.

CHART 23 (CONCL.)

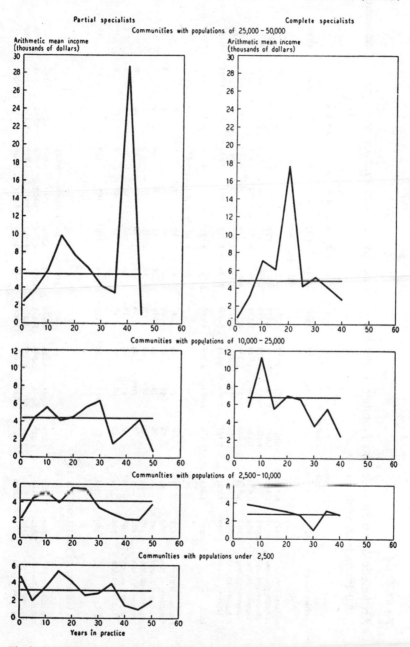

Partial specialists   Complete specialists

Communities with populations of 25,000 – 50,000

Arithmetic mean income (thousands of dollars)

Communities with populations of 10,000 – 25,000

Communities with populations of 2,500 – 10,000

Communities with populations under 2,500

Years in practice

The horizontal line in each diagram represents the arithmetic mean income of all physicians of the specified type in the particular size of community.

TABLE 34

Arithmetic Mean Income and Number of Persons Covered, by Years in Practice and Size of Community

a All Physicians, 1936

SIZE OF COMMUNITY	ALL	NOT REPORTING YEARS IN PRACTICE	REPORTING YEARS IN PRACTICE AS											
			Under 3	3-7	8-12	13-17	18-22	23-27	28-32	33-37	38-42	43-47	48-52	53-57
			Arithmetic Mean Income (dollars)											
500,000 & over	3,525	3,743	1,373	2,357	3,587	4,594	4,733	4,347	3,781	4,503	3,054	2,418	1,600	...
100,000–500,000	5,103	5,155	1,913	3,685	5,991	5,512	6,013	6,675	3,983	7,054	4,542	1,635	600	1,279
50,000–100,000	5,079	...	2,166	2,998	6,277	8,416	4,860	7,122	3,881	3,039	7,340	5,472	2,682	500
25,000– 50,000	4,679	2,086	1,110	3,745	4,819	8,387	3,121	5,220	4,599	3,074	3,228	1,331	...	200
10,000– 25,000	4,256	3,805	1,674	3,492	6,865	4,715	5,014	6,099	4,773	3,119	3,015	2,823	613	700
2,500– 10,000	3,648	3,986	2,556	3,880	4,805	4,111	4,134	3,873	3,060	2,968	3,194	2,106	3,767	640
Under 2,500	2,620	2,794	2,135	3,183	2,731	3,568	3,232	2,853	2,211	2,821	1,653	1,634	1,141	1,353
U. S.	3,941[1]	4,011	1,788	3,182	4,718	5,326	5,179	4,859[1]	3,575	4,076	3,091	2,402	1,705	747
			Number of Persons Covered [2]											
500,000 & over	241	7	18	42	42	26	22	29	22	16	10	6	1	...
100,000–500,000	265	15	22	32	28	26	26	35	24	32	19	4	1	1
50,000–100,000	97	...	6	12	12	15	7	13	8	16	4	3	2	1
25,000– 50,000	110	4	5	16	10	9	10	16	20	9	7	3	...	1
10,000– 25,000	162	5	6	30	24	15	11	16	20	16	10	6	2	1
2,500– 10,000	198	9	7	40	24	18	15	26	25	10	15	6	2	2
Under 2,500	335	8	17	56	32	18	14	43	48	47	35	5	10	2
U. S.	1,409[1]	48	81	228	172	125	105	179[1]	167	146	100	33	18	7

b General Practitioners, 1936

SIZE OF COMMUNITY	ALL	NOT REPORTING YEARS IN PRACTICE	Under 3	3-7	8-12	13-17	18-22	23-27	28-32	33-37	38-42	43-47	48-52	53-57
			Arithmetic Mean Income (dollars)											
500,000 & over	2,802	460	1,270	2,541	3,179	4,086	3,844	3,033	2,710	3,048	1,757	2,732	...	...
100,000–500,000	3,819	4,160	1,318	3,914	5,588	5,465	4,531	4,854	1,878	2,888	3,638	1,933	600	...
50,000–100,000	3,171	...	3,339	2,613	5,470	3,562	...	2,352	2,004	1,619	2,465	1,250	2,859	...
25,000– 50,000	3,701	2,250	...	3,858	3,677	13,000	6,048	5,453	4,404	2,439	2,231	1,364	...	200

Arithmetic Mean Income (dollars) (continued)

City size														
10,000– 25,000	2,923	4,935	1,663	2,574	4,128	5,231	1,832	5,957	4,805	3,454	1,744	1,432	540	700
2,500– 10,000	3,174	1,933	2,725	3,195	4,454	4,334	3,211	2,664	2,903	3,107	4,875	2,122	···	640
Under 2,500	2,381	3,583	1,890	3,473	2,329	2,530	2,754	2,584	1,938	2,087	1,675	1,910	998	1,353
U.S.	2,917	3,265	1,770	3,124	3,813	4,071	3,500	3,526	2,605	2,538	2,257	1,967	1,169	692

Number of Persons Covered [2]

City size														
500,000 & over	75	1	7	15	9	9	5	11	6	5	4	3	··	··
100,000–500,000	73	7	4	12	4	5	8	7	7	9	7	2	1	··
50,000–100,000	21	··	1	4	5	1	··	··	2	3	1	1	1	1
25,000– 50,000	41	2	··	7	5	1	4	6	6	4	5	2	··	··
10,000– 25,000	62	1	5	14	9	2	5	5	7	8	5	3	··	1
2,500– 10,000	93	3	5	17	9	9	5	14	12	5	8	4	··	1
Under 2,500	238	5	15	45	22	10	9	29	31	28	30	4	9	2
U.S.	603	30	37	114	63	57	34	72	71	62	58	19	12	5

c Partial Specialists, 1936

Arithmetic Mean Income (dollars)

City size														
500,000 & over	3,276	4,116	3,011	1,584	3,424	4,832	3,118	4,530	4,351	3,375	3,538	2,122	1,600	··
100,000–500,000	4,595	6,405	1,934	3,404	5,226	4,640	6,487	5,708	4,258	9,452	2,717	1,414	··	1,279
50,000–100,000	4,099	1,872	2,050	2,900	7,846	3,352	4,882	6,778	3,074	3,213	60	1,088	2,525	500
25,000– 50,000	5,534	3,254	2,433	3,857	5,974	9,841	7,683	5,680	6,222	3,461	28,760	4,225	700	··
10,000– 25,000	4,391	3,205	1,709	4,371	5,570	4,185	4,498	5,507	6,365	1,565	2,838	2,081	700	··
2,500– 10,000	4,165	1,145	2,200	4,434	5,156	3,950	5,598	2,602	3,418	2,702	3,154	2,081	3,767	··
Under 2,500	3,127	··	4,675	1,966	3,484	5,349	4,131	··	2,810	3,933	1,471	1,000	2,000	··
U.S.	3,957[1]	4,148	1,732	3,085	4,571	4,908	4,744	5,032[1]	3,980	4,282	2,766	2,236	2,405	922

Number of Persons Covered [2]

City size														
500,000 & over	98	2	6	15	19	13	9	8	10	7	5	5	1	··
100,000–500,000	94	3	9	10	10	6	9	14	10	11	9	2	··	··
50,000–100,000	38	··	2	4	4	6	4	5	2	8	1	··	··	··
25,000– 50,000	38	2	2	5	3	5	5	4	7	5	1	··	··	··
10,000– 25,000	61	3	1	13	9	7	3	7	5	5	4	8	··	··
2,500– 10,000	88	5	2	19	13	8	8	9	12	3	5	2	2	··
Under 2,500	95	5	2	10	10	9	5	13	17	19	5	1	1	2
U.S.	513[1]	18	24	76	68	52	43	61[1]	65	58	50	12	6	2

TABLE 34 (concl.)

d Complete Specialists, 1936

SIZE OF COMMUNITY	ALL	NOT REPORTING YEARS IN PRACTICE	REPORTING YEARS IN PRACTICE AS											
			Under 3	3–7	8–12	13–17	18–22	23–27	28–32	33–37	38–42	43–47	48–52	53–57
			Arithmetic Mean Income (dollars)											
500,000 & over	4,705	4,478	2,047	3,179	4,050	4,949	7,137	5,574	3,716	9,387	6,000	...	...	...
100,000–500,000	6,416	5,515	2,109	3,739	6,750	5,980	9,154	9,100	5,859	7,859	11,054	...	...	...
50,000–100,000	7,292	...	1,934	3,611	6,656	18,152	17,657	8,693	5,415	3,849	14,155	10,749		
25,000– 50,000	4,885	...	726	3,159	7,083	6,047	4,827	4,272	5,241	...	2,762	...		
10,000– 25,000	6,729	3,000	...	5,654	11,216	5,476	6,947	6,511	3,542	5,494	2,413	...		
2,500– 10,000	2,717	848	...	3,853	3,600	...	3,053	2,658	1,000	3,184	2,729	...		
Under 2,500	5,875	...	...	3,505	...	...	...	7,500	...	...	...	...		
U. S.	5,795	4,769	1,896	3,540	6,133	7,812	7,499	6,742	4,558	7,155	9,085	10,749		
			Number of Persons Covered [2]											
500,000 & over	68	4	5	12	14	4	8	10	6	4	1	...		
100,000–500,000	98	5	9	10	14	15	9	14	7	12	3	...		
50,000–100,000	38	...	3	4	3	6	3	6	4	5	2	2		
25,000– 50,000	31	...	3	4	2	5	1	6	7	...	3	...		
10,000– 25,000	39	1	...	3	6	6	5	6	8	3	1	...		
2,500– 10,000	17	1	...	4	2	...	2	3	1	2	2	...		
Under 2,500	2	...	...	1	...	...	...	1	...	...	...	...		
U. S.	293	11	20	38	41	36	28	46	33	26	12	2		

[1] Includes one return for which size of community was unknown.
[2] Number of persons covered by the returns used, before weighting.

These numbers, therefore, cannot be used directly to compute percentage distribution of physicians by years in practice.

then declines sharply. Little or no importance can be attached
to the initial increase: the patterns for the very large communities are based on more returns than those for communities of an intermediate size; and the differences in amplitude
may reflect merely the greater play of random variation in the
latter. The lower amplitude of the patterns for small communities may reflect the larger number of returns in such
communities for all groups except complete specialists. But
the decline in amplitude is so large that it probably cannot be
set aside.

Except for the lower amplitude of the patterns for small
communities, the most interesting feature of Chart 23 is the
fairly persistent but far from uniform tendency for the patterns to assume a greater downward tilt as size of community
decreases; i.e., for the decline in income to become steeper
relatively to the initial rise. In general, the smaller the community the sooner is the average income of all physicians sur-
passed, and the peak income received. For all physicians, the
peak income is at 20 years in the two largest size of community
classes,[5] at 15 years in the next two, at 10 years in the next two,
but at 15 years in the smallest communities. For general practitioners, the progression is somewhat less regular: 15, 10, 10,
15, 15 (or 25), 10,[6] 5. For partial specialists and complete specialists, the extreme irregularity of the patterns makes the selection of single peaks difficult, but a similar general tendency
is noticeable, particularly for complete specialists.

The difference in the 'tilt' of the patterns is reflected in
smaller differences among communities of varying size in the
average incomes of younger practitioners than in the average
incomes of older practitioners. Indeed, for the first two years-
in-practice classes in Table 34a average incomes are highest in
communities with populations of 2,500–10,000 and are not
much lower in the smallest communities. Nonetheless, the
ranking of the size of community classes by average income is

[5] For communities of 100,000–500,000 this assumes that the peak at 35 years is
to be disregarded.
[6] Disregarding peak at 40 years.

much the same for most of the years-in-practice classes separately as for all combined. Differences among the size of community classes in the distribution of physicians by years in practice seem not to be responsible for the size of community differences in average income analyzed in the preceding chapter.[7]

The relatively flat pattern in small communities is probably attributable to the absence of effective direct competition. In large communities there are many physicians and the competitive forces discussed above can operate. The young physician only recently out of medical school appeals to some because he is presumably 'up-to-date' or merely because he is 'new'; the middle-aged man, to others who regard his 'practical experience' as more than counterbalancing the possibility that he may not be familiar with the latest methods; the older man, to still others, whose choice is dominated by habituation, confidence born of long and continuous service, or respect for a reputation gained by many years of practice. The relative income status of physicians in practice varying periods depends on the relative strength of these motives; the general preference for middle-aged men leads to their receiving higher incomes. In villages, on the other hand, there are frequently only one or two physicians. Competition is almost completely ineffective. The income a physician receives depends less on his age than on other factors—the prosperity of the region in which he practises, its proximity to other places, and the like. Of course, there is some competition and hence some tendency for income to rise at first with number of years in practice. Also, the older men become partly retired and hence income eventually declines. But both the rise and decline are mild relatively to those in larger communities.

One possible explanation of the tendency for the tilt of the patterns to shift downward as size of community decreases is the concentration of young physicians in the larger communities (Table 35). In cities with over a million inhabitants more

[7] Size of community averages standardized for differences in distribution by years in practice are almost the same as the original averages.

TABLE 35

Age Distribution, by Size of Community

All Physicians, General Practitioners and Partial Specialists, and Complete Specialists, 1931: 16 States and the District of Columbia

AGE CLASSES	1,000,000 & Over	500,000– 1,000,000	250,000– 500,000	100,000– 250,000	50,000– 100,000	25,000– 50,000	10,000– 25,000	5,000– 10,000	2,500– 5,000	1,000– 2,500	Under 1,000	ALL CLASSES
All Physicians												
Under 35	28.5	27.1	22.9	21.6	20.2	15.9	15.9	14.2	14.2	12.0	10.3	21.1
35–44	27.9	25.9	25.0	27.7	24.9	23.6	23.0	20.5	18.7	16.9	14.6	23.9
45–54	21.1	21.3	23.3	23.1	26.8	26.8	25.4	25.1	26.7	25.7	24.7	23.5
55 & over	22.5	25.7	28.8	27.6	28.1	33.7	35.7	40.2	40.4	45.4	50.4	31.5
All ages	100.0	100.0	100.0	100.0	100.0	100.0	100.0	100.0	100.0	100.0	100.0	100.0
General Practitioners and Partial Specialists												
Under 35	33.4	31.3	26.7	25.8	23.3	16.9	17.3	14.8	14.6	12.0	10.3	23.2
35–44	26.2	25.2	22.2	24.7	21.5	21.5	21.8	19.9	18.4	16.7	14.4	21.9
45–54	18.7	18.8	20.6	20.2	25.3	25.4	24.2	24.3	26.2	25.6	24.5	22.0
55 & over	21.7	24.2	30.5	29.3	29.9	36.2	36.7	41.0	40.8	45.7	50.8	32.9
All ages	100.0	100.0	100.0	100.0	100.0	100.0	100.0	100.0	100.0	100.0	100.0	100.0
Complete Specialists												
Under 35	10.9	11.4	11.6	8.8	11.0	12.3	8.4	9.1	7.8	9.2	8.9	10.6
35–44	34.0	34.6	33.1	36.6	34.7	31.3	29.3	25.9	23.8	25.8	22.6	33.1
45–54	29.7	29.6	31.5	33.1	31.3	31.7	31.7	31.3	33.5	28.4	35.1	30.8
55 & over	25.4	24.4	23.8	22.5	23.0	24.7	30.6	33.7	34.9	36.6	33.4	25.5
All ages	100.0	100.0	100.0	100.0	100.0	100.0	100.0	100.0	100.0	100.0	100.0	100.0

R. G. Leland, *Distribution of Physicians in the United States* (American Medical Association, 1936), pp. 56-7. The age classes are combinations of finer classes for which the original data are presented.

than a quarter of the physicians were under 35 years of age in 1931, while fewer than a quarter were 55 or over; in places of less than a thousand inhabitants, on the other hand, only a tenth of the physicians were under 35 years of age while half were 55 or over. The exact proportions are very different for the two groups segregated—complete specialists, and general practitioners and partial specialists—but the general picture is the same.[8]

The average income of young physicians will depend not only on the preferences of the community for physicians in practice varying periods, but also on the relative number of young physicians. For any given community, the higher the proportion of young physicians, the lower their average income will tend to be relatively to the average income of older men. We have, of course, no evidence on whether or how preferences for physicians vary with size of community. But we do know that the smaller the community the better the relative income status of the young physician. And it seems reasonable to attribute this to the relative scarcity of young physicians in the small communities. Of course, this explanation must be related to the preceding discussion of the degree of competition in communities of varying size. It can be considered valid only for communities sufficiently large to permit a moderate degree of competition, say for communities over 10,000 in population.

Why are the age distributions of physicians so different in communities of different size? Two explanations may be suggested. Perhaps the less important is the increasing need for extensive equipment and adequate facilities that has tended to make large cities seem more desirable to the physician than rural communities where facilities are likely to be limited. Probably of far greater importance is the secular increase in the proportion of the nation's population living in big cities,

8 Distributions by years in practice and size of community computed from our sample suggest the same tendency. But the estimated distributions vary so much and so irregularly among size of community classes that the tendency could not be established from our data alone.

largely a result of migration from rural to urban communities. The corresponding shift in the distribution of physicians among communities of different size [9] probably took place less through actual movement of physicians already in practice than through concentration in the larger cities of physicians just entering practice. The shift in population might be expected to lead to low medical incomes in rural communities relatively to incomes in large communities, and thus provide a strong incentive for new physicians to begin practice in large communities—indeed, the proverbially low income of physicians in rural areas is amply supported by our data. The small number of new entrants who started practice in rural areas presumably led to a smaller decline, or greater rise, in incomes in those areas relative to incomes in urban communities than would otherwise have taken place. Further, it led to a relatively favorable income status of young physicians, and hence to smaller size of community differences in the average incomes of young physicians than in the average incomes of older physicians.

If our analysis is correct, and the distribution of the population among communities of different size remains fairly stationary for a moderately long period, or at least changes less rapidly than in the past, we may expect a lessening of the difference between average incomes in small and large communities, and between the age distributions of physicians in communities of different size, and as a consequence, a greater similarity in the relation between income and years in practice. It follows that while the pattern for all physicians relating income to years in practice may be interpreted as describing the 'life cycle' of earnings, the patterns for the separate size of community classes cannot be so interpreted.

Differences in age distribution are not, of course, the only cause of size of community differences in the relation between income and years in practice. Differences in clientele, the variability of physicians' incomes, the opportunity to obtain

[9] See Leland, *Distribution of Physicians*, pp. 50, 51, for evidence that such a shift has taken place.

salaried posts, and numerous other factors doubtless play a
role. Consequently, even if differences in age distribution were
eliminated, the relation between income and years in practice
might still be expected to differ among communities of varying size.

3 TYPE AND ORGANIZATION OF PRACTICE

The increasing complexity of professional activity has led to
considerable specialization. The accompanying division of
function has taken different forms in different professions. In
medicine and dentistry it has taken the form of a differentiation in the kind of service rendered by individuals practising
independently and coordinated by the impersonal mechanism
of the market place. Sharing of office space, nonprofessional
help, and equipment is frequent, but formal organization into
partnerships or firms, exceedingly rare. Few physicians or
dentists employ others; only about 20 per cent of all physicians
and dentists are salaried employees and many of these are employed by business and government. In accountancy, engineering, and to some extent law, division of function has taken the
form not only of specialization by separate professional units,
but also of larger professional units, the individual members
or employees frequently concentrating on specific fields of
practice. The larger professional units are sometimes conducted by an individual practitioner who hires other professional men as employees; more frequently, they are organized
as partnerships or firms of several independent professional
men who may or may not employ others. Our data suggest that
about a third of the accountants, almost half of the engineers,
and about a quarter of the lawyers who practise independently
are members of firms.

The form division of function has taken is primarily attributable to the type of consumer served and the nature of the
services rendered. The curative professions serve almost exclusively individuals in their capacity as ultimate consumers.
The 'unit' of professional service is therefore small and can

seldom be delegated in large part to subordinates. The individual customer usually requires only a single type of service at any time; he seldom purchases a 'bundle' of different kinds of service. The kinds of service needed can rarely be predicted or contracted for in advance. The necessary professional equipment can ordinarily be almost as efficiently and intensively utilized by one man as by many, or by a sharing arrangement that does not affect other aspects of practice. Since prestige and judgment of quality attach to the individual practitioner, little is to be gained by organization into 'firms', or by the hiring of many professional employees.

If hospitalization had developed as a private enterprise under the direct control of physicians, instead of as a semipublic enterprise under the control of nonprofit or governmental organizations, these statements would not be valid. The elaborate physical equipment and the large number of subordinates that would then have been needed might have led to a very different organization of medical practice than we now have. Firms and even incorporated enterprises might have become common. Whatever private hospitals do exist are frequently conducted by 'firms' of physicians.

The increasing complexity of medical practice and the increasing emphasis on preventive care and periodic physical examinations are giving rise to a greater need for extensive equipment as well as a greater possibility of cooperation among physicians in rendering medical services. In addition, the widespread agitation for some form of health insurance or cooperative purchase or provision of medical care is tending to enlarge the 'unit' of service purchased and to facilitate advance contractual arrangements for an assortment of specialized services. Both factors seem to be leading to an extension of the 'group' practice of medicine, and, to some extent, of dentistry as well.

Law, to a significant degree, and accountancy and consulting engineering almost exclusively, render services to business enterprises. The 'unit' of professional services tends to be larger and can more easily be delegated to subordinates than in the curative professions. In addition, individual customers are more likely to purchase a variety of services and can more easily predict and contract for them in advance. Organization into firms seems to be least frequent among lawyers, the only one of the three 'business' professions that renders a significant part of its services to individuals.

The difference in clientele that accounts for the difference in the form that division of function has taken and for the consequent difference in the size of professional units has also affected another aspect of the organization of professional activity, namely, the relative importance of independent and salaried practice. As we have seen, few independent physicians or dentists hire others as salaried employees. In addition, few users of medical or dental service need or can afford a full-time physician or dentist. Only when business enterprises or governmental bodies provide medical care for their employees or when government engages in public health activities is there an opportunity for salaried employment by nonprofessional enterprises; and even in these cases, the part-time services of a physician or dentist engaged principally in independent practice often suffices. As a result, about 80 per cent of all physicians and dentists are in independent practice. In the business professions, on the other hand, not only is salaried employment by professional units proper more common, but also the principal consumers are business enterprises and governmental bodies that can afford to hire full-time professional employees, and that use the independent professional units only for specialized services their own employees cannot render. Over nine-tenths of all engineers and accountants and auditors (certified and noncertified) and about a third of all lawyers are salaried employees.

a Type of practice

Specialization is far more widespread in medicine than in dentistry. Of the physicians listed in the 1931 Directory of the

American Medical Association, 16 per cent considered themselves complete specialists, 16 per cent, partial specialists, and 68 per cent, general practitioners.[10] According to our 1937 medical sample, the only one of our samples in which the respondent was asked type of practice,[11] 22 per cent of the physicians considered themselves complete specialists, 38 per cent, partial specialists, and 40 per cent, general practitioners.[12] The study of the Committee on the Costs of Medical Care, on the other hand, indicates that in 1929 only 3 per cent of the dentists considered themselves complete specialists, 8 per cent, partial specialists, and 89 per cent, general practitioners.[13] Unfortunately, no data are available on the trend of specialization in dentistry. While in this, as in other respects, dentistry is likely to develop in the same manner as medicine, but with a considerable lag, it is doubtful that specialization will ever be as widespread in dentistry as in medicine, since,

[10] Leland, *Distribution of Physicians*, p. 31.

[11] The actual wording of the question was:

"Indicate the type of practice in which you are engaged:

General practice ....
Specialized practice (such as surgery, neurology, obstetrics, etc.)............
Special interest with general practice (such as pediatrics, surgery, gynecology, etc.) ...."

[12] The percentage of complete specialists in our sample checks fairly closely with other estimates, but the percentage of partial specialists is considerably higher (see Table 36 and Appendix A, Sec. 2c i). This difference does not necessarily reflect bias in the sample. It may more reasonably be interpreted as a result of differences in the way the question on specialization was asked and the answers were edited, since the distinction between general practitioners and partial specialists is exceedingly vague. There are no commonly accepted objective criteria to segregate general practitioners from physicians giving 'special attention' to a subject but not limiting their practice to it. In most cases, therefore, physicians are asked to classify themselves. In a survey for Michigan, however, an attempt was made to go behind this classification by asking the public relations committee of each county medical society to classify the society's members. The results show that a considerable percentage of the physicians who classified themselves as partial specialists were considered by their colleagues to be general practitioners. See *Report of the Committee on Survey of Medical Services and Health Agencies* (Michigan State Medical Society, 1933), pp. 57–64.

[13] See Table 36, which gives also the estimates of the California Medical-Economic Survey. The two sets of estimates are very close.

in a very real sense, dentistry is itself a specialized branch of medicine. In medicine the available data suggest, though the evidence is by no means conclusive, that specialization is still increasing.[14]

In both professions, complete specialists receive higher average incomes than partial specialists, and partial specialists than general practitioners. Though the differentials cannot be estimated with any exactitude from the studies summarized in Table 36, they are sizable. In dentistry, the average income of complete specialists seems to be about 30 per cent larger than that of partial specialists, and the average income of partial specialists about 30 per cent larger than that of general practitioners. In medicine, for the period 1929–36, according to our 1937 sample, the average income of complete specialists was approximately $5,900; of partial specialists, $3,800; of general practitioners, $2,900; i.e., the average income of complete specialists was about 50 per cent larger than that of partial specialists, and the average income of partial specialists, about 30 per cent larger than that of general practitioners. These estimates of the differentials in medicine are in general between those suggested by the other two studies of medical incomes cited in the table: the estimates from the study of the Committee on the Costs of Medical Care are higher, from the California survey, lower. Although based on fewer returns, the estimates from our 1937 medical sample are probably more

[14] See Leven, *Incomes of Physicians*, pp. 50–65; H. G. Weiskotten, 'Tendencies in Medical Practice', *Journal of the Association of American Medical Colleges*, March 1932, pp. 65–85.

Dean Weiskotten's study gives data on the type of practice in 1926 of 1,834 physicians who graduated in 1915, and 1,947 who graduated in 1920 and on the type of practice in 1931 of 3,230 physicians who graduated in 1925. The data suggest that the proportion of graduates who became or who planned to become specialists was fairly stable for the classes of 1920 and 1925, and greater for both than for the class of 1915 or all physicians. The increasing specialization among physicians as a whole seems to reflect the replacement of older physicians by younger, associated with a relatively stable degree of specialization among the younger. The evidence on this point, however, is fairly meagre.

Our 1937 medical sample provides no information on changes over time in the degree of specialization, since the questionnaires requested merely the type of practice when the questionnaire was received (early 1937).

TABLE 36

Arithmetic Mean Income and Percentage Distribution, by Type of Practice

Physicians and Dentists: Selected Studies

| | PHYSICIANS | | | DENTISTS | |
	1937 sample[1] *1929–36*	Comm. on Costs of Medical Care[2] *1929*	Cal. Medical-Economic Survey[3] *1929–34*	Comm. on Costs of Medical Care[4] (20 states) *1929*	Cal. Medical-Economic Survey[3] *1929–34*
Arithmetic mean income (dollars)					
General practitioners	2,022	3,000	3,836	4,791	3,564
Partial specialists	3,777	6,100	5,060	6,129	4,847
Complete specialists	5,904	10,000	6,039	8,623	5,894
All practitioners	3,916	5,700	4,916	5,011	3,762
% excess of					
Partial specialists over general practitioners	29	56	32	28	36
Complete specialists over general practitioners	102	156	57	80	65
Complete specialists over partial specialists	56	64	19	41	22
% of practitioners who were [8]					
General practitioners	40	56	42	89	90
Partial specialists	38	21	24	8	5
Complete specialists	22	23	34	3	5
All practitioners	100	100	100	100	100
No. of returns	1,408[5]	5,380[6]	2,737[7]	4,705	1,615[7]

[1] See Tables 37, 41, and 43. Percentage distribution is for early 1937.

[2] Maurice Leven, *Incomes of Physicians* (University of Chicago Press, 1932), pp. 13, 15, 55, 109.

[3] *California Medical-Economic Survey*, pp. 73, 79, 94, 100. Percentage distributions are for 1934.

[4] Leven, *Practice of Dentistry*, pp. 14, 88, 89.

[5] Number of persons reporting 1936 income, before weighting.

[6] Estimated number of returns received, before weighting or adjusting; computed from Leven, *Incomes of Physicians*, pp. 13, 15, 109.

[7] Number of persons reporting 1933 incomes; fewer reported for other years. Percentage distribution based on 3,206 returns for physicians and 1,802 for dentists.

[8] Distributions are based on the number reporting in the last·year of the period indicated above.

TABLE 37

Arithmetic Mean Income, by Type of Practice

Physicians, 1929–1936

	1929	1930	1931	1932	1933	1934	1935	1936	Average 1929–36
Arithmetic mean income (dollars)									
General practitioners	4,096	3,571	3,067	2,404	2,266	2,478	2,584	2,914	2,922
Partial specialists	5,337	4,467	4,015	3,018	2,788	3,215	3,412	3,962	3,777
Complete specialists	8,290	7,787	6,461	4,694	4,187	4,836	5,174	5,805	5,904
% excess of									
Partial specialists over general practitioners	30.3	25.1	30.9	25.5	23.0	29.7	32.0	36.0	29.3[1]
Complete specialists over general practitioners	102.4	118.1	110.7	95.3	84.8	95.2	100.2	99.2	102.1[1]
Complete specialists over partial specialists	55.3	74.3	60.9	55.5	50.2	50.4	51.6	46.5	56.3[1]
No. of returns [2]									
General practitioners	382	359	379	401	434	531	554	603	
Partial specialists	342	325	337	365	388	450	468	512	
Complete specialists	188	183	190	207	221	256	272	293	

[1] Computed from the averages for 1929–36.

[2] Number of returns received, before weighting.

accurate than those from the other studies.[15] (The annual figures from the 1937 medical sample are given in Table 37.)

As might be expected from these differences in income level,

TABLE 38

Median and Quartile Incomes, by Type of Practice

Physicians, 1934–1936

	1934	1935	1936
		(dollars)	
		Third Quartile	
All physicians	4,290	4,473	5,056
General practitioners	3,436	3,472	3,968
Partial specialists	4,338	4,441	5,066
Complete specialists	6,113	6,902	7,775
		Median	
All physicians	2,690	2,824	3,100
General practitioners	2,221	2,220	2,484
Partial specialists	2,749	2,900	3,230
Complete specialists	3,798	4,165	4,375
		First Quartile	
All physicians	1,554	1,588	1,824
General practitioners	1,234	1,251	1,394
Partial specialists	1,798	1,806	2,014
Complete specialists	2,238	2,329	2,599

absolute variability of income is much greater for complete specialists than for partial specialists, and for partial specialists than for general practitioners (Tables 38–40). The greater part of these differences in absolute variability is accounted

[15] The estimates from the Committee on Costs of Medical Care study were obtained indirectly from data on gross income; the relation between gross and net income was derived from a study of 1928 incomes made by the American Medical Association; see Leven, *Incomes of Physicians*, p. 109. This indirect procedure might easily have introduced substantial errors. Not only are the California data for a single state, but also the percentage of complete specialists seems too high. Only 20 per cent of California physicians were listed as complete specialists in the 1931 Directory of the American Medical Association (Leland, *Distribution of Physicians*, p. 17), and only 25 per cent of the returns from California in our 1937 medical sample were from complete specialists. The relatively low percentage differences between the average incomes from the California study for complete specialists and the other two groups may reflect the inclusion of some individuals as complete specialists who should have been considered partial specialists or general practitioners.

for by the differences in income level. Relative variability is in general somewhat less for general practitioners than for the other two groups, but the difference is neither large nor consistent.

Complete specialists naturally tend to be concentrated in

TABLE 39

Measures of Variability of Income, by Type of Practice

Physicians, 1934–1936

	1934	1935	1936
Interquartile Difference (dollars)			
All physicians	2,736	2,885	3,232
General practitioners	2,202	2,221	2,574
Partial specialists	2,540	2,635	3,052
Complete specialists	3,875	4,573	5,176
Standard Deviation (dollars)			
All physicians	2,965	3,057	3,631
General practitioners	1,857	1,996	2,242
Partial specialists	2,431	2,644	3,572
Complete specialists	4,453˙	4,308	4,831
Relative Interquartile Difference			
All physicians	1.017	1.022	1.043
General practitioners	.991	1.000	1.036
Partial specialists	.924	.909	.945
Complete specialists	1.020	1.098	1.183
Ratio of Quartiles			
All physicians	2.761	2.817	2.772
General practitioners	2.784	2.775	2.846
Partial specialists	2.413	2.459	2.515
Complete specialists	2.731	2.964	2.992
Coefficient of Variation			
All physicians	.886	.862	.902
General practitioners	.733	.755	.752
Partial specialists	.739	.758	.882
Complete specialists	.903	.816	.817

the larger communities where the more extensive 'market' for professional services affords greater opportunity for division of function. In addition, specialists are more likely than general practitioners to be at the peak earnings stage of their working life. Many men begin their careers as general practitioners and become specialists only after receiving additional training and experience. On the other hand, most of the older men received their professional education before specialization had progressed very far and when formal training was less extensive than it later became. These differences between specialists and general practitioners help to explain the large differences between their average incomes. In effect, countrywide averages by type of practice compare one group in the best locations—at least in money terms—and in the prime of life with

TABLE 40

Median and Quartile Incomes, and Measures of Variability,
by Type of Practice

Dentists in 20 States, 1929:
Committee on Costs of Medical Care Study

	ALL DENTISTS	GENERAL PRACTITIONERS	PARTIAL SPECIALISTS	COMPLETE SPECIALISTS
Third quartile (dollars)	6,203	5,955	7,222	11,765
Median (dollars)	4,094	3,989	4,756	6,980
First quartile (dollars)	2,669	2,618	3,031	4,422
Interquartile difference (dollars)	3,534	3,337	4,191	7,343
Standard deviation (dollars)	4,080	3,476	5,930	6,781
Relative interquartile difference	.863	.837	.881	1.052
Coefficient of variation	.808	.728	.952	.764
No. of returns	4,705	4,189	377	139

Computed from frequency distributions in Leven, *Practice of Dentistry*, p. 88.

another containing many who are in poorer locations and who are just getting started or are on the verge of retiring.

Limitations of data make it necessary to restrict further analysis of these factors to physicians. Both Table 41, based on our sample, and Table 42, based on a comprehensive count of the 1931 Directory of the American Medical Association, indicate that the percentage of all physicians who are specialists varies markedly among communities of different size. According to our sample, slightly over 38 per cent of all physicians in communities with populations of 50,000–500,000 considered

TABLE 41

Distribution by Type of Practice,
by Size of Community and by Region

Physicians, 1936

| | % OF PHYSICIANS WHO WERE | | |
Size of community	General practitioners	Partial specialists	Complete specialists
500,000 & over	30.8	41.6	27.6
100,000–500,000	25.2	36.3	38.5
50,000–100,000	24.8	37.1	38.1
25,000– 50,000	38.0	37.8	24.2
10,000– 25,000	41.7	38.0	20.3
2,500– 10,000	44.8	50.1	5.1
Under 2,500	71.9	27.0	1.0
Region			
New England	40.3	36.8	22.9
Middle Atlantic	33.0	44.0	23.0
E. N. Central	48.7	32.8	18.5
W. N. Central	47.8	28.3	24.0
S. Atlantic	39.0	37.8	23.2
E. S. Central	48.7	36.0	15.3
W. S. Central	32.6	42.2	25.2
Mountain	44.5	37.4	18.1
Pacific	33.1	43.2	23.6
U. S.	40.2	38.0	21.9

TABLE 42

Distribution by Type of Practice, by Size of Community

Physicians Listed in 1931 Directory
of American Medical Association

| | % OF PHYSICIANS WHO WERE | | | |
Size of community	General practitioners & partial specialists		Complete specialists	
1,000,000 & over	79.1	} 77.7	20.9	} 22.3
500,000–1,000,000	74.7		25.3	
250,000– 500,000	74.9	} 75.3	25.1	} 24.7
100,000– 250,000	75.8		24.2	
50,000– 100,000	76.3	76.3	23.7	23.7
25,000– 50,000	79.8	79.8	20.2	20.2
10,000– 25,000	84.0	84.0	16.0	16.0
5,000– 10,000	88.8	} 91.2	11.2	} 8.8
2,500– 5,000	93.6		6.4	
1,000– 2,500	97.2	} 97.7	2.8	} 2.3
Under 1,000	98.0		2.0	

Leland, *Distribution of Physicians*, p. 31.

themselves complete specialists while only 25 per cent considered themselves general practitioners. In communities under 2,500 on the other hand, only 1 per cent considered themselves complete specialists, while over 70 per cent considered themselves general practitioners. Perhaps the most surprising feature of the tables is the lower percentage of complete specialists in the largest communities than in communities of an intermediate size.[16] For the other classes, the percentage of complete specialists declines consistently with size of community.

Size of community differences in the average income of each

[16] The lower percentage of complete specialists in the largest communities is not accounted for by differences among the size of community classes in the distribution of physicians by number of years in practice; for each years-in-practice class separately, the percentage of complete specialists tends to be lower in the largest communities than in those of intermediate size.

To test this point we computed from the 1937 sample the percentage of all physicians who are complete specialists for each size of community and 9 classes by number of years in practice (in practice 2 years or less, 3 to 7 years, 8 to 12 years, . . . , 38 to 42 years). In 7 of the 9 years-in-practice classes the percentage of complete specialists was less in communities over 500,000 in population than in either of the next two size of community classes. The exceptions were the 8–12 and 23–27 years-in-practice classes. Standardized percentages, using as weights the distribution of all physicians in the United States by number of years in practice, were also computed. They differ only slightly from the percentages in Table 41.

More extensive data for 16 states and the District of Columbia on the age distribution of physicians in 1931 by type of practice and size of community yield a similar conclusion (Leland, *Distribution of Physicians*, pp. 56–7). Data are given for two groups: 'general practice or special attention' and 'specialists'. The latter group may be taken to correspond to our 'complete specialists'. Data are given for 12 five-year age classes between 20 and 80 (20–24, 25–29, etc.) and for a final class of 80 and up, and for the size of community classes in Table 42. In 6 of the 12 age classes for which there were complete specialists in all or almost all size of community classes, the percentage of complete specialists in communities over 500,000 was less than in communities between 100,000 and 500,000 or between 50,000 and 100,000; in only three classes was the percentage of complete specialists in communities over 500,000 greater than in either of the other two size of community classes. Standardized percentages using the age distribution of all physicians in the country as weights differed little in magnitude or order from the original percentages. It is significant, however, that the three age classes in which the largest communities had the highest percentage of specialists included the older physicians, the age classes being 55–59, 65–69, and 70–74.

TABLE 43

Arithmetic Mean Income, Relatives of Arithmetic Mean Income, and Number of Persons Covered, by Size of Community and by Region

All Physicians, General Practitioners, Partial Specialists, and Complete Specialists

	ARITHMETIC MEAN INCOME,[1] 1929-36 (dollars)				RELATIVES OF ARITHMETIC MEAN INCOME (U.S. = 100)				NUMBER OF PERSONS COVERED,[2] 1936			
	All physi-cians	General practi-tioners	Partial special-ists	Complete special-ists	All physi-cians	General practi-tioners	Partial special-ists	Complete special-ists	All physi-cians	General practi-tioners	Partial special-ists	Complete special-ists
Size of community												
500,000 & over	3,875	3,230	3,439	5,268	99.0	110.5	91.1	89.2	241	75	98	68
100,000-500,000	5,026	3,683	4,310	6,708	128.3	126.0	114.1	113.6	265	73	94	98
50,000-100,000	4,826	3,153	3,860	6,778	123.2	107.9	102.2	114.8	97	21	38	38
25,000- 50,000	4,486	3,336	5,029	5,275	114.6	114.2	133.1	89.3	110	41	38	31
10,000- 25,000	4,024	3,054	3,859	5,804	102.8	104.5	102.2	98.3	162	62	61	39
2,500- 10,000	3,530	3,377	3,711	3,032	90.1	115.6	98.3	51.4	197	93	87	17
Under 2,500	2,448	2,170	3,131	3,672	62.5	74.3	82.9	62.2	335	238	95	2
Region												
New England	4,745	3,426	4,406	7,142	121.2	117.2	116.7	121.0	131	62	39	30
Middle Atlantic	4,062	2,782	3,598	6,041	103.7	95.2	97.9	102.3	207	69	91	47
E. N. Central	3,852	3,147	3,890	5,602	97.9	107.7	103.0	94.9	197	98	62	37
W. N. Central	3,310	2,580	2,916	5,376	84.5	88.3	77.2	91.1	182	88	50	44
S. Atlantic	4,235	3,042	4,648	5,762	108.1	104.1	123.1	97.6	155	64	56	35
E. S. Central	3,038	2,476	3,406	4,955	77.6	84.7	90.2	83.9	70	33	27	10
W. S. Central	3,387	1,800	2,984	5,996	86.5	61.6	79.0	101.6	106	35	46	25
Mountain	4,284	3,029	4,287	7,144	109.4	103.7	113.5	121.0	199	96	74	29
Pacific	4,231	3,919	3,996	5,166	108.0	134.1	105.8	87.5	161	58	67	36
U. S.[3]	3,916	2,922	3,777	5,904	100.0	100.0	100.0	100.0	1,408	603	512	298

[1] Computed by adding the averages for the years covered by the sample and dividing by the number of years—8.

[2] Number of persons covered by the returns used, before weighting.

[3] Includes 1 return for which size of community was unknown.

of the three groups of physicians are similar in character, though in general somewhat smaller in magnitude, than the corresponding differences in the average income of all physicians (Table 43). The peak income of general practitioners is in the same size of community class as the peak income of all practitioners—communities with populations between 100,000 and 500,000. The peak income of partial specialists is in the 25,000–50,000 class and of complete specialists, in the 50,000–100,000 class. However, the average income of complete specialists is only a trifle smaller in the 100,000–500,000 class than in the 50,000–100,000 class, and is considerably larger in either than in any other class. In general, average incomes are lowest in the smallest communities. The one exception—complete specialists—is hardly significant in view of the few complete specialists in our sample for the two smallest size of community classes. The variation in average income from one size of community class to the next is less regular for each type of practitioner than for all physicians. Presumably, this, too, is attributable to the fewness of the returns on which the separate averages are based. As a result, little confidence can be attached to the exact quantitative differences in the table.

Standardized averages provide a simple and efficient tool for eliminating the effect of differences in the location of the several types of physicians. Table 44 gives standardized averages for general practitioners, partial specialists, and complete specialists for 1929–36. They are weighted combinations of the size of community averages, the weights being the total number of physicians of all types in the corresponding size of community class.[17] The use of the same weights for all types of practice eliminates the influence of size of community.[18]

17 The total number of physicians in each size of community class was taken from Leland, *Distribution of Physicians*, and is for 1931, the latest year for which such figures are available.
18 The standardized averages do not eliminate the influence of regional variation in the distribution of physicians by type of practice except as such variation reflects differences in the size of community composition of the regions. Experimental computations for 1936 indicated that eliminating the influence of regional variation would affect the averages but slightly and the differences

The correction for the influence of size of community sharply reduces the income differentials. The difference between the original averages for complete specialists and general practitioners is 102 per cent; for complete specialists and partial specialists, 56 per cent; for partial specialists and general practitioners, 29 per cent (Table 37, averages for 1929–36). The corresponding differences between the standardized averages are 64, 36, and 20 per cent. Roughly a third of the difference between the original averages is attributable to the concentration of specialists in the larger communities. The remaining two-thirds measures the difference between the average incomes of physicians differing in type of practice but practising in communities of the same size.

The countrywide standardized averages might of course conceal important differences among size of community classes or regions in the relative incomes of the three types of practitioners. To test whether there are any consistent differences we computed, for each size of community in each region, the ratios between the average 1936 incomes of complete specialists and partial specialists, complete specialists and general practitioners, and partial specialists and general practitioners. We found no evidence that these ratios differed significantly among communities of varying size or among regions.[19] How-

---

among the averages even less. These computations were made by weighting the average income of each type of practitioner in each size of community and regional 'cell' by the total number of physicians in that 'cell' as shown by Leland. The averages for the different types of practice were made comparable by excluding those cells in which there were no returns for one or more types of practice. The resulting standardized averages are $3,114 for general practitioners, $4,035 for partial specialists, and $5,587 for complete specialists. All are somewhat higher than the averages in Table 44 because the excluded cells included mainly the smaller communities. According to these averages the income of complete specialists exceeds that of general practitioners by 79.4 per cent, and of partial specialists by 38.5 per cent, while the income of partial specialists exceeds that of general practitioners by 29.6 per cent. The corresponding figures from Table 44 are 78.1, 39.0, and 28.2.

19 The existence of regional or size of community differences was tested by an analysis of ranks of the same sort as that used in the Appendix to Chapter 5 to test the significance of regional and size of community differences in average income.

TABLE 44

Arithmetic Mean Income Standardized with Respect to Size of Community, by Type of Practice

Physicians, 1929–1936

	1929	1930	1931	1932	1933	1934	1935	1936	Average 1929–36
'Standardized' arithmetic mean income [1] *(dollars)*									
General practitioners	4,391	3,850	3,328	2,563	2,392	2,589	2,681	3,044	3,105
Partial specialists	5,292	4,432	3,984	2,993	2,775	3,169	3,356	3,901	3,738
Complete specialists	8,041	6,311	5,130	3,787	3,493	3,979	4,673	5,421	5,104
% excess of									
Partial specialists over general practitioners	20.5	15.1	19.7	16.8	16.0	22.4	25.2	28.2	20.4 [2]
Complete specialists over general practitioners	83.1	63.9	54.1	47.8	46.0	53.7	74.3	78.1	64.4 [2]
Complete specialists over partial specialists	51.9	42.4	28.8	26.5	25.9	25.6	39.2	39.0	36.5 [2]

[1] Weighted averages of averages for size of community classes. For all years and types of practice, weights are the total number of physicians in each size of community class in 1931 (see Leland, *Distribution of Physicians*).

[2] Computed from the average incomes in the first three lines.

ever, many of the 'cells' contained few returns. Consequently, the ratios show erratic fluctuations that may have prevented small but real discrepancies from being detected.[20]

Table 45 and Chart 24 show the relation between number of years in practice and type of practice. The percentage of general practitioners declines at first, reaching a trough of about 28 per cent in the 13–17 years-in-practice class, and rises thereafter. The percentage of complete specialists, on the other hand, rises at first, reaching a peak of about 30 per cent in the 18–22 years-in-practice class, and declines thereafter. The percentage of partial specialists fluctuates irregularly around 38 per cent. The striking feature of the chart is the exceedingly small percentage of specialists among physicians who have been in practice more than 37 years. In part, this merely reflects the relatively large percentage of the older physicians who practise in small communities in which specialization is rare. But this is not the whole story. In com-

[20] The frequency distributions of the ratios for individual size of community and regional cells indicate the wide variability of the ratios. The frequency distributions are given below. I stands for average income and the subscripts c, p, and g, for complete specialists, partial specialists, and general practitioners respectively.

NO. OF SIZE OF COMMUNITY AND REGIONAL CELLS
FOR WHICH INDICATED RATIOS FALL BETWEEN
SPECIFIED VALUES

VALUE OF RATIOS	$\dfrac{I_c}{I_g}$	$\dfrac{I_c}{I_p}$	$\dfrac{I_p}{I_g}$
0 – .5	3	3	1
.5–1.0	6	7	11
1.0–1.5	11	18	21
1.5–2.0	5	10	11
2.0–2.5	10	3	7
2.5–3.0	4	3	2
3.0–3.5	3	1	..
3.5–4.0	3	..	..
4.0–4.5	..	..	1
4.5–5.0	1	..	..
Over 5	..	1	..
All values	46	46	54

The differences in the total number of cells arise from the absence in some cells of returns from one or more types of practitioner.

munities of each size, there is the same tendency toward a drastic decline in the percentage of specialists. The basic reason seems rather to be that mentioned earlier: the substantial improvement in the standards of medical training since 1910 which implemented the increasing need for specialists arising from the rapid progress of medical science.

For 1936, we have computed average incomes by number of years in practice and can therefore estimate the influence of the concentration of complete specialists in the intermedi-

TABLE 45

Distribution by Type of Practice, by Years in Practice

Physicians, 1936

YEARS IN PRACTICE	% OF ALL PHYSICIANS WHO WERE		
	General practitioners	Partial specialists	Complete specialists
Under 3	42.9	31.2	25.9
3– 7	47.4	35.4	17.2
8–12	33.8	40.4	25.8
13–17	28.5	44.3	27.3
18–22	31.2	38.8	29.9
23–27	37.1	34.5	28.3
28–32	38.5	39.8	21.6
33–37	40.7	41.8	17.5
38–42	55.4	35.0	9.6
43–47	56.9	39.3	3.7
48–52	56.7	43.3	
53–57	76.2	23.8	

In computing the percentages, returns for which number of years in practice was unknown were excluded. The actual number of persons reporting in each class is shown in Table 34b, c, and d.

ate years-in-practice classes in which average incomes are relatively high. The accompanying table compares the percentage differences among average incomes standardized for differences in the distribution of the various types of practitioner not only by size of community but also by years in practice [21] with the

21 The actual standardized averages are: complete specialists, $5,504, partial specialists, $4,204, and general practitioners, $3,486. These averages are based only on those size of community and years-in-practice classes containing returns from all three types of practitioner. They are weighted averages of the average incomes in such cells, the weights being the estimated number of physicians of all types in each cell.

percentage differences previously presented for 1936. The
third line of this table gives estimates of the percentage difference between the incomes of physicians in communities

| | PERCENTAGE EXCESS IN 1936 AVERAGE INCOME OF | | |
	COMPLETE SPECIALISTS OVER GENERAL PRACTITIONERS	COMPLETE SPECIALISTS OVER PARTIAL SPECIALISTS	PARTIAL SPECIALISTS OVER GENERAL PRACTITIONERS
Original averages	99.2	46.5	36.0
Averages standardized with respect to distribution by:			
Size of community	78.1	39.0	28.2
Size of community and no. of years in practice	57.9	30.9	20.6

of the same size and in practice the same number of years but
differing in type of practice. Correction for the influence of
number of years in practice reduces the percentage differences
by about the same amount as correction for the influence of
size of community. The final differences are much more moderate than the differences among the original averages.

Presumably, the differences that remain are largely attributable to differences in training and skill. Physicians who
specialize often get additional training; frequently they become specialists because they have been successful and have
attained good reputations as general practitioners. Hence,
men who specialize would probably earn higher incomes as
general practitioners than those who remain general practitioners. The higher income of specialists is probably not a
transitory phenomenon that will lead to or be eliminated by
a rush to specialization; but rather a permanent concomitant
of a segregation of practitioners by criteria related to their
chances of success.[22]

[22] This interpretation is supported by the apparent temporal stability in the
proportion of graduates who become or plan to become specialists suggested
by Weiskotten's study (see footnote 14).

The growing tendency in recent years to formalize the distinctions among
types of practitioner by establishing boards to 'certify' specialists in particular
fields may introduce an additional element of rigidity.

CHART 24

Distribution of Physicians by Type of Practice,
by Years in Practice

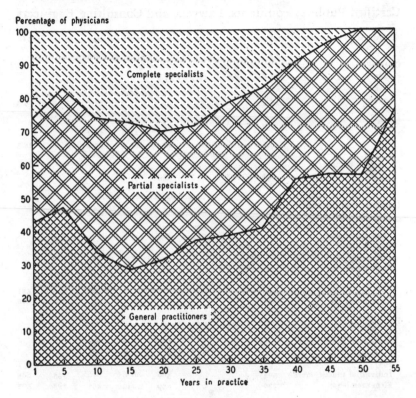

Percentage of physicians

b Organization of independent practice

A classification of lawyers, accountants, and engineers into firm
members and individual practitioners is much less clear-cut
from an analytical point of view than a classification of physicians and dentists into complete specialists, partial specialists,
and general practitioners. On the whole, firm members are
more likely to specialize than individual practitioners; but
there are many firm members who specialize little if at all
and there are many individual practitioners who restrict prac-

TABLE 46

Percentage of Persons in Independent Practice Who are Members of Firms and Number of Persons Covered

Certified Public Accountants, Lawyers, and Consulting Engineers

PROFESSION & SAMPLE	1929	1930	1931	1932	1933	1934	1935	1936
				% Who are Members of Firms				
Certified public accountants								
1933	48.8	48.3	47.3	47.3				
1935				32.1	31.5	30.2		
1937	35.9					30.7	32.5	35.3
Lawyers								
1935				23.8	23.0	22.7		
1937	28.7			28.3	25.3	25.1	26.3	25.3
Consulting engineers								
1933	44.2	44.3	43.5	43.5				
				Number of Persons Covered *				
Certified public accountants								
1933								
Individual practitioners	373	393	409	426				
Firm members	590	609	611	637				
1935								
Individual practitioners				792	842	883		
Firm members				623	647	635		
1937								
Individual practitioners	343					506	525	531
Firm members	346					395	446	512
Lawyers								
1935								
Individual practitioners				694	743	771		
Firm members				575	589	606		
1937								
Individual practitioners	504			566	696	676	733	865
Firm members	220			239	249	253	283	303
Consulting engineers								
1933								
Individual practitioners	263	268	269	268				
Firm members	208	213	207	206				

* Number of persons covered by returns used, before weighting or adjusting. These numbers, therefore, cannot be used to compute percentage of persons who are members of firms.

tice to small segments of the entire field. With these qualifications, a classification by organization of practice is essentially similar to a classification by type of practice. Like specialists and for the same reasons, firm members are concentrated in the larger communities, are seldom in the initial stages of their careers, and tend to receive higher average incomes than other members of the profession in the same community and of the same age.

The percentage of all practitioners who are members of firms, as estimated from our samples, is given in Table 46 for each year and profession.[23] The different accountancy samples yield widely divergent estimates of the percentage of firm members. According to the 1933 sample, slightly under 50 per cent of all practitioners are firm members; according to the other two samples, only slightly over 30 per cent. This difference is much too large to be attributed to chance fluctuation; [24] and it cannot be interpreted as reflecting a marked decline in the percentage of firm members, since for 1932 and

[23] Information on the number of members in a firm was requested separately for each year for which income information was obtained.

[24] Because of the weighting introduced to correct for the firm member bias, it is difficult to make a logically valid test of the significance of the differences among the successive samples in the estimated proportion of firm members. As an approximate test we computed χ^2 for the accompanying table.

SAMPLE AND YEAR FOR WHICH INCOME WAS REPORTED	ACTUAL NO. OF INDIVIDUAL PRACTITIONERS REPORTING INCOME	NO. OF FIRM MEMBERS WEIGHTED TO CORRECT FOR FIRM MEMBER BIAS	TOTAL
1933 sample for 1932	426	382	808
1935 sample for 1934	883	383	1,266
1937 sample for 1936	531	289	820
Total	1,840	1,054	2,894

The next to the last column gives our estimates of the number of firm members who would have replied if the questionnaire had requested information about the individual recipient rather than the firm of which he is a member. The logical difficulty with using these estimates is that they are actually based on fewer separate returns, and hence are less accurate than the numbers alone might suggest. Their use tends to accentuate the significance of the differences. However, since χ^2 is 63.8, while a value of 13.8 would be exceeded only once in a thousand times, it seems clear that allowance for this difficulty would leave the differences statistically significant.

1929 we have estimates from two samples.[25] We are forced to conclude that the difference is attributable to a bias in one or more of our accountancy samples. In view of the marked agreement between the second sample, the largest of the three, and the latest sample, we are disposed to set the proportion of all certified public accountants who are members of firms at about one-third.

In all three professions the proportion of firm members seems to have decreased somewhat from 1929 to 1932. In the two professions for which the data cover a longer period—law and accountancy—this decrease continues until 1934. From then to 1936 the proportion of firm members increases. These changes are all exceedingly small, but their consistency is a reason for believing that they reflect the facts accurately. Moreover, it seems reasonable that firms are more likely to disintegrate and less likely to be formed when economic conditions are becoming worse than when they are improving.

Table 47 reveals that the average incomes of firm members are considerably higher than those of individual practitioners. The differentials vary considerably from sample to sample. This time the second sample of accountants disagrees with the other two; the first and third samples suggest that the average income of firm members is about 25 or 30 per cent larger than the average income of individual practitioners; the second sample, that it is almost 60 per cent larger. For lawyers, the

[25] The lapse of time between the dates at which the two samples were chosen might well have led to an underestimate of the proportion of firm members in the overlapping year from the later sample and an overestimate from the earlier sample, for reasons discussed in Chapter 2. The proportion of firm members would presumably be relatively high among individuals retiring from practice between say, 1933—when the first sample was chosen—and 1935—when the second sample was chosen—and relatively low among individuals inadvertently excluded from the 1933 sampling list because of recent entry into the profession. But it is hardly credible that this factor could account for so large a difference as that between the 1932 estimates from the 1933 and 1935 samples since only two years separated the dates at which these samples were chosen. It is somewhat more reasonable, though still exceedingly doubtful, that the difference between the 1929 estimates from the 1933 and 1937 samples can be explained in this way.

TABLE 47

Arithmetic Mean Income, by Organization of Practice

Certified Public Accountants, Lawyers, and Consulting Engineers

PROFESSION & SAMPLE	1929	1930	1931	1932	1933	1934	1935	1936
				Arithmetic Mean Income (dollars)				
Certified public accountants								
1933								
Individual practitioners	6,941	6,289	5,282	4,313				
Firm members	8,962	8,414	6,951	5,294				
1935								
Individual practitioners					3,544	3,275	3,664	
Firm members					5,643	5,213	5,682	
1937								
Individual practitioners	5,469					3,620	3,817	4,248
Firm members	6,552					4,803	4,926	5,120
Lawyers								
1935								
Individual practitioners					2,883	2,515	2,656	
Firm members					5,511	5,048	5,260	
1937								
Individual practitioners	5,762				3,205	2,826	2,848	2,996	3,189
Firm members	13,973				10,613	9,859	9,706	9,844	11,153
Consulting engineers								
1933								
Individual practitioners	8,535	7,472	4,943	2,483				
Firm members	16,019	13,264	7,114	3,940				
				% by which Arithmetic Mean Income of Firm Members Exceeds				
				Arithmetic Mean Income of Individual Practitioners				
Certified public accountants								
1933		29.1	33.8	31.6	22.7			
1935					59.2	59.2	55.1	
1937		19.8				32.7	29.1	20.5
Lawyers								
1935					91.2	100.7	98.0	
1937		142.5			231.1	248.9	240.8	228.6	249.7
Consulting engineers								
1933		87.7	77.5	43.9	58.7			

1935 sample suggests a difference of about 100 per cent; the 1937 sample, if we ignore the comparison for 1929, a differ ence of almost 250 per cent.[26] The one sample for consulting engineers suggests a difference between 40 and 90 per cent. While there is some overlapping among the several professions it seems clear that the difference between firm members and individuals is greatest for lawyers and least for accountants.

According to the measures in Tables 48 and 49, absolute

[26] However, if the one extreme questionnaire repeatedly mentioned is eliminated, the difference is reduced to about 125 per cent.

TABLE 48

Median and Quartile Incomes, by Organization of Practice

Certified Public Accountants, Lawyers, and Consulting Engineers

	1933 SAMPLES				1935 SAMPLES			1937 SAMPLES		
	1929	1930	1931	1932	1932	1933	1934	1934	1935	1936
					(dollars)					
Third Quartile										
Certified public accountants										
All	9,308	8,560	7,326	5,993	5,029	4,724	5,232	4,967	5,073	5,687
Individual practitioners	8,565	7,670	6,252	5,486	4,325	3,908	4,541	4,494	4,754	5,384
Firm members	9,968	9,372	8,268	6,509	6,565	6,031	6,502	5,926	5,989	6,295
Lawyers										
All					4,339	3,620	3,936			
Individual practitioners					3,334	3,010	3,192			
Firm members					7,008	6,241	7,108			
Consulting engineers										
All	14,805	11,721	8,631	4,785						
Individual practitioners	10,650	9,384	6,411	3,955						
Firm members	18,800	14,896	12,500	5,735						
Median										
Certified public accountants										
All	6,116	5,647	4,780	4,017	3,336	3,129	3,515	3,858	3,460	3,963
Individual practitioners	5,186	5,000	4,157	3,509	2,884	2,763	3,122	3,099	3,290	3,660
Firm members	6,727	6,322	5,411	4,452	4,624	4,288	4,876	4,292	4,069	4,514

Lawyers				
All	7,943	6,016	4,041	2,178
Individual practitioners	6,414	5,125	3,190	1,524
Firm members	9,545	6,841	6,125	3,800
Consulting engineers				
All	3,570	2,719	1,456	33
Individual practitioners	2,769	2,000	570	0
Firm members	4,867	4,343	2,553	575
Certified public accountants				
All	4,099	3,883	3,217	2,541
Individual practitioners	3,629	3,297	2,789	2,294
Firm members	4,394	4,380	3,776	2,985

First Quartile

Lawyers						
All	2,218	1,906	2,028	2,296	2,479	2,684
Individual practitioners	1,900	1,581	1,747	2,143	2,804	2,532
Firm members	4,004	3,275	3,742	2,747	2,861	3,111
Certified public accountants						
All	2,235	2,127	2,356			
Individual practitioners	1,975	1,936	2,074			
Firm members	3,162	2,886	3,236			
Lawyers						
All	1,140	982	967			
Individual practitioners	970	840	854			
Firm members	2,149	1,778	1,892			
Consulting engineers						

TABLE 49

Measures of Variability of Income, by Organization of Practice

Certified Public Accountants, Lawyers, and Consulting Engineers

	1933 SAMPLES				1935 SAMPLES			1937 SAMPLES		
	1929	1930	1931	1932	1932	1933	1934	1934	1935	1936
Interquartile Difference (dollars)										
Certified public accountants										
All	5,209	4,677	4,109	3,452	2,794	2,597	2,876	2,671	2,594	3,003
Individual practitioners	4,936	4,373	3,463	3,192	2,350	1,972	2,467	2,351	2,450	2,852
Firm members	5,574	4,992	4,492	3,524	3,403	3,145	3,266	3,179	3,128	3,184
Lawyers										
All					3,199	2,638	2,969			
Individual practitioners					2,364	2,170	2,338			
Firm members					4,859	4,463	5,216			
Consulting engineers										
All	11,235	9,002	7,175	4,752						
Individual practitioners	7,881	7,384	5,841	3,955						
Firm members	13,933	10,553	9,847	5,160						
Standard Deviation (dollars)										
Certified public accountants										
All	6,723	6,410	5,152	3,708	3,568	3,360	3,483	3,072	3,334	3,240
Individual practitioners	5,810	4,856	4,407	3,266	3,211	2,937	3,019	2,866	2,925	3,103
Firm members	7,481	7,534	5,819	4,075	3,881	3,815	4,023	3,352	3,956	3,410
Lawyers										
All					4,369	4,368	4,164			
Individual practitioners					3,921	3,859	3,713			
Firm members					5,099	5,306	4,921			
Consulting engineers										
All	14,580	16,669	9,010	6,462						
Individual practitioners	10,363	10,724	9,391	6,139						
Firm members	17,580	21,615	8,455	6,835						

Relative Interquartile Difference

	1	2	3	4	5	6	7	8	9	10
Certified public accountants										
All	.852	.828	.860	.859	.838	.830	.818	.795	.750	.758
Individual practitioners	.952	.874	.832	.910	.815	.714	.790	.759	.745	.779
Firm members	.829	.790	.830	.792	.736	.733	.670	.741	.769	.705
Lawyers										
All					1.442	1.384	1.464			
Individual practitioners					1.244	1.373	1.338			
Firm members					1.214	1.363	1.394			
Consulting engineers										
All	1.414	1.496	1.776	2.182						
Individual practitioners	1.228	1.440	1.830	2.596						
Firm members	1.400	1.543	1.508	1.564						

Ratio of Quartiles

	1	2	3	4	5	6	7	8	9	10
Certified public accountants										
All	2.271	2.204	2.279	2.357	2.250	2.221	2.221	2.163	2.046	2.119
Individual practitioners	2.360	2.326	2.242	2.391	2.190	2.019	2.189	2.097	2.063	2.126
Firm members	2.269	2.140	2.190	2.181	2.076	2.090	2.009	2.157	2.093	2.023
Lawyers										
All					3.806	3.686	4.070			
Individual practitioners					3.437	3.583	3.738			
Firm members					3.261	3.510	3.757			
Consulting engineers										
All	4.147	4.311	5.928	145.000						
Individual practitioners	3.846	4.692	11.247	∞						
Firm members	3.863	3.430	4.712	9.974						

Coefficient of Variation *

	1	2	3	4	5	6	7	8	9	10
Certified public accountants										
All	.843	.865	.843	.768	.840	.854	.803	.761	.784	.700
Individual practitioners	.837	.772	.834	.757	.893	.883	.811	.780	.750	.717
Firm members	.834	.883	.836	.765	.691	.727	.698	.691	.793	.659

TABLE 49 (concl.)

Coefficient of Variation* (cont.)

	1933 SAMPLES				1935 SAMPLES			1937 SAMPLES		
	1929	1930	1931	1932	1932	1933	1934	1934	1935	1936
Lawyers										
All					1.236	1.390	1.266			
Individual practitioners					1.340	1.508	1.377			
Firm members					.930	1.040	.929			
Consulting engineers										
All	1.231	1.647	1.548	2.124						
Individual practitioners	1.214	1.435	1.900	2.472						
Firm members	1.120	1.636	1.239	1.759						

ASSUMED CORRELATION	1933 SAMPLES				1935 SAMPLES			1937 SAMPLES		
	1929	1930	1931	1932	1932	1933	1934	1934	1935	1936
Accountants										
.5	.962	1.019	.965	.883	.797	.839	.805	.797	.915	.760
0	1.179	1.249	1.182	1.082	.977	1.028	.987	.977	1.121	.932
Lawyers										
.5					1.073	1.200	1.072			
0					1.315	1.471	1.314			
Engineers										
.5	1.292	1.888	1.430	2.030						
0	1.584	2.313	1.752	2.487						

* Under the assumptions outlined in the footnote to Table 13 we can estimate roughly the effect, on the coefficient of variation, of the downward bias arising from dividing the income of a firm equally among its members. If all firms contained two members, and if there were no correlation between the incomes of members of the same firm, the 'true' standard deviation for firm members, and consequently the 'true' coefficient of variation, would tend to be 1.41 (square root of 2) times the measures as we compute them. If the correlation were .5, the correction factor would be 1.15. Applying these factors gives the accompanying results for the coefficients of variation for firm members.

variability of income is larger for firm members than for individual practitioners but relative variability is smaller. The measures for firm members are, however, much affected by the downward bias discussed in Chapter 4, Section 1b. Its elimina-

TABLE 50

Percentage of Persons in Independent Practice Who Are Members of Firms, by Size of Community and by Region

Certified Public Accountants, Lawyers, and Consulting Engineers

% WHO ARE MEMBERS OF FIRMS [1]

	Certified public accountants			Lawyers		Consulting engineers
Size of community	1932	1934	1936	1934	1936	1932
1,500,000 & over	53.0	30.9	33.5	23.1	33.3	57.7
500,000–1,500,000	39.0	33.4	34.9	4.6	22.3	42.1
250,000– 500,000	55.8	37.1	47.0	23.4	31.0	37.2
100,000– 250,000	46.3	35.0	30.5	30.6	18.9	29.7
25,000– 100,000	51.1	25.4	40.2	30.0	34.0	45.7
10,000– 25,000				27.1	23.0	
2,500– 10,000	} 11.3	12.2	22.1	23.9	20.3	} 16.3
Under 2,500				17.8	11.0	
Region						
New England	42.7	33.6	34.3	22.0	18.6	46.5
Middle Atlantic	49.6	30.4	34.3	20.8	18.8	53.6
E. N. Central	53.3	37.0	41.0	21.0	38.0	39.7
W. N. Central	48.8	42.0	54.7	27.3	18.4	40.0
S. Atlantic	34.2	20.3	34.1	21.5	25.9	} 25.0
E. S. Central	45.4	32.1	31.5	33.2	9.7	
W. S. Central	56.6	26.2	35.1	30.5	20.8	40.0
Mountain	56.9	22.1	33.5	19.9	19.5	40.0
Pacific	36.7	22.3	24.0	15.5	39.9	31.4
U. S.[2]	47.3	30.2	35.3	22.7	25.3	43.5

[1] Percentages are based on numbers reporting for the last year covered by each sample.
[2] Includes a few returns for which size of community or region was unknown.

tion would increase the difference in absolute variability, but might well erase or even reverse the observed difference in relative variability.[27]

Organization into firms is least frequent in small communities (Table 50). There is little difference among the profes-

[27] Rough estimates of coefficients of variation corrected for this bias are given in the footnote to Table 49. For accountants the coefficients of variation for individual practitioners are below both sets of corrected coefficients for firm members for the first and third samples, and between the two sets for the second sample. For lawyers the coefficients of variation for individual practitioners exceed both sets of corrected coefficients for firm members. For engineers the coefficients for individual practitioners are below both sets of corrected

sions in this respect. Except for the single erratic value from the 1935 legal sample, firm members are uniformly least numerous in communities with populations of less than 25,000; the variation among the other size of community classes in the percentage of firm members seems to be random. The regional differences in the percentage of firm members, while larger than can be accounted for by chance, are in general less consistent from profession to profession than the differences among the size of community classes.[28]

In the smallest communities, where firms are few, the advantage of organization into firms is apparently least; indeed, according to three of the six samples for which data are given in Table 51, firm members in the smallest communities actu-

coefficients for firm members for two years, between them for one, and above them for one. This evidence suggests that, in accountancy, relative variability of income is greater for firm members than for individual practitioners; in law, the situation is reversed, and in engineering, relative variability is about the same for individual practitioners and firm members. The roughness of our estimates of the corrected coefficients of variation, the margin of error attaching to the original measures, and the neglect of other measures of variability mean that these conclusions must be considered exceedingly tentative.

28 To test the significance of the differences between the distributions of individual practitioners and firm members by size of community and region we used the χ^2 test. In each case χ^2 was computed from a table giving in one column the number of individual practitioners in the sample in each size of community (or region), and in a second column, the number of firm members.

For accountants we used the actual number of individual practitioners, but the number of firm members weighted to correct for the firm member bias. For the 1935 legal sample, we used the number of firm members weighted to correct for the firm member bias but we adjusted neither the number of individuals nor the number of firm members for the size of community bias. The original number of individuals and of firm members was used for the 1937 legal sample, no adjustment being made for either the size of community bias or the nonrandomness of the sample by states. The use of figures for lawyers not adjusted for the size of community bias and the nonrandomness of the 1937 sample by states is partly justified by the 'null' hypothesis being tested—namely, that the proportion of firm members is the same in all regions or in all size of community classes. In any event, this procedure is almost unavoidable if any attempt is to be made to interpret the results in probability terms. The sample of consulting engineers is the only one that raises no problems, since it is subject to no biases for which we have attempted to adjust. The values of χ^2 are summarized in the accompanying table. For reasons given in footnote 24, the procedure used led to overestimates of the significance of the differences,

ally have lower average income than individual practitioners. There is some indication that the advantage of organization into firms increases consistently with size of community. Consulting engineers seem to be an exception to this statement; but no reliance can be placed on the figure in Table 51 for consulting engineers in communities under 25,000. The firm

---

since in all cases, the number of firm members is greater than the number of separate returns for firm members.

TEST OF SIGNIFICANCE OF DIFFERENCE BETWEEN
DISTRIBUTIONS OF FIRM MEMBERS AND OF
INDIVIDUAL PRACTITIONERS BY

| | SIZE OF COMMUNITY | | REGION | |
	No. of degrees of freedom	χ^2	No. of degrees of freedom	χ^2
Certified public accountants				
1933 sample for 1932	5	38.0‡	8	14.9
1935 sample for 1934	5	26.2‡	8	21.9†
1937 sample for 1936	5	14.9*	8	13.7
All samples	5	64.6‡	8	38.4‡
Lawyers				
1935 sample for 1934	7	23.3†	8	9.1
1937 sample for 1936	7	44.4‡	8	32.2‡
Both samples	7	45.3‡	8	14.9
Consulting engineers				
1933 sample for 1932	5	27.4‡	7	18.8†

* Greater than the value that would be exceeded by chance once in twenty times.

† Greater than the value that would be exceeded by chance once in a hundred times.

‡ Greater than the value that would be exceeded by chance once in a thousand times.

For 5 degrees of freedom these values are 11.070, 15.086, and 20.517 respectively; for 7 degrees of freedom, 14.067, 18.475, 24.322; for 8 degrees of freedom, 15.507, 20.090, 26.125.

On this showing, the significance of the difference between the distribution of firm members and individuals by size of community is indisputable, even though large allowance is made for deficiencies in the tests. The differences between the regional distributions are less marked, though it seems fairly certain that on the whole they are larger than could be expected from chance alone. In each comparison the value of χ^2 is greater for the size of community distributions than for the regional, although more degrees of freedom are available for the latter.

member average used in deriving this figure is based on only one firm for the two years that are responsible for its relatively high value.[29]

As already suggested, it seems reasonable to interpret these results in terms of the clientele to whom services are rendered.

TABLE 51

Difference between Arithmetic Mean Income of Firm Members and of Individual Practitioners

Certified Public Accountants, Lawyers, and Consulting Engineers

| | % BY WHICH ARITHMETIC MEAN INCOME OF FIRM MEMBERS EXCEEDS ARITHMETIC MEAN INCOME OF INDIVIDUAL PRACTITIONERS [1] | | | | | |
| | Certified public accountants | | | Lawyers | | Consulting engineers |
Size of community	1929–32	1932–34	1934–36	1932–34	1934–36	1929–32
1,500,000 & over	40.8	88.5	36.0	197.9	456.1	82.8
500,000–1,500,000	17.6	80.2	59.5	336.1	195.9	87.3
250,000– 500,000	40.5	70.1	33.3	99.1	168.3	−18.4
100,000– 250,000	11.8	29.3	2.4	65.4	34.6	−1.4
25,000– 100,000	−0.4	13.9	−9.1	90.4	128.8	−38.8
10,000– 25,000				11.2	109.5	
2,500– 10,000	} −5.9	−1.5	18.9	63.7	47.8	} 208.8
Under 2,500				38.9	−28.0	
Region						
New England	51.8	48.2	35.6	296.8	232.9	61.8
Middle Atlantic	31.5	79.0	35.2	117.1	209.4	95.6
E. N. Central	34.8	38.8	10.2	115.7	437.1	−25.1
W. N. Central	−14.4	43.4	34.7	46.3	24.2	64.9
S. Atlantic	35.9	17.4	−2.1	66.2	185.6	} −16.3
E. S. Central	47.6	78.3	64.5	83.4	181.7	
W. S. Central	13.2	74.0	33.2	94.0	−28.2	−52.9
Mountain	4.0	66.9	87.6	57.9	31.5	−64.8
Pacific	16.8	42.4	9.3	70.8	169.1	9.0
U. S.[2]	29.8	57.8	27.1	96.4	239.9	72.1

[1] For all professions, percentage difference is computed from simple unweighted averages of the annual averages.
[2] Based on averages that include a few returns for which size of community or region was unknown.

In small communities much more than in large, the clientele is likely to be composed of small businesses and individual consumers; and the 'unit' of service is likely to be small and personal. Organization into firms is less advantageous and less frequent.

The difference between the average incomes of firm mem-

[29] The percentage differences for the individual years are of interest in this connection: 1929, 474.5; 1930, 167.2; 1931, −342.5; 1932, −181.9.

bers and individual practitioners in communities of the same size is in general less than the difference between the country-wide averages. (Compare Tables 47 and 52.) For accountants, correction for the influence of size of community reduces the difference between the incomes of firm members and indi-

TABLE 52

Difference between Arithmetic Mean Incomes of Firm Members and of Individual Practitioners, Based on Averages Standardized with Respect to Size of Community

Certified Public Accountants, Lawyers, and Consulting Engineers

	% BY WHICH STANDARDIZED ARITHMETIC MEAN INCOME OF FIRM MEMBERS EXCEEDS STANDARDIZED ARITHMETIC MEAN INCOME OF INDIVIDUAL PRACTITIONERS [1]							
PROFESSION & SAMPLE	*1929*	*1930*	*1931*	*1932*	*1933*	*1934*	*1935*	*1936*
Certified public accountants [2]								
1933	25.1	32.7	24.6	15.5				
1935				53.3	54.3	51.2		
1937						30.6	27.9	19.6
Lawyers [3]								
1935				102.0	108.9	105.2		
1937						142.1	138.5	169.0
Consulting engineers [4]								
1933	94.4	54.6	10.1	39.3				

[1] The standardized averages from which the percentage differences are computed are weighted averages of the averages for the size of community classes. The same weights are used for both individual practitioners and firm members.
[2] The weights used in computing the standardized averages are, for each size of community class, the total number of accountants, adjusted for the firm member bias, in both the 1935 and 1937 samples who reported 1934 incomes.
[3] The weights used in computing the standardized averages are, for each size of community class, the total number of lawyers, adjusted for the size of community and firm member biases, in the 1935 sample who reported 1934 incomes.
[4] The weights used in computing the standardized averages are, for each size of community class, the total number of engineers reporting 1932 incomes.

vidual practitioners only slightly: in 1936, the year for which the reduction is least, from 20.5 to 19.6, but in the 1932 averages from the 1933 sample, the year and sample for which the reduction is greatest, from 22.7 to 15.5, i.e., by almost a third. The correction for the influence of size of community actually increases the differential shown by the first legal sample. This anomalous result is entirely accounted for by one size of community class—500,000–1,500,000. The percentage of firm members in this class in the 1935 sample is exceedingly low—4.6 per cent in 1934—but the average income of the firm members reporting was 323 per cent higher than the average income of the individual practitioners.[30] The 1937 legal sample yields a very different result; correction for the influence of size of community reduces the differential by a third. As usual, the engineering sample yields erratic results: the differential

TABLE 53

Distribution by Organization of Practice
and Year of Admission to Bar

New York County Lawyers, 1933

YEAR OF ADMISSION TO BAR	NO. IN SAMPLE IN INDEPENDENT PRACTICE	NUMBER OF		% FIRM MEMBERS ARE OF ALL LAWYERS IN INDEPENDENT PRACTICE
		INDIVIDUAL PRACTITIONERS	FIRM MEMBERS	
1930–1934	730	583	147	20.1
1924–1929	1,023	747	276	27.0
1918–1923	433	275	158	36.5
1911–1917	377	230	147	39.0
1900–1910	508	339	169	33.3
Before 1900	257	152	105	40.9
All years	3,328	2,326	1,002	30.1

Survey of the Legal Profession in New York County, p. 28.

in 1929 is increased from 88 to 94 per cent; the differential in 1931 is reduced from 44 to 10 per cent.

We have evidence on the relation between organization of practice and number of years in practice only for lawyers. A study of New York County lawyers indicates that the percentage of firm members at first increases sharply with number of years in practice and then remains fairly constant (Table 53). Studies of young lawyers in California and Wisconsin confirm the initial sharp rise.[31] As we saw in Section 2, the average in-

30 The number of firm members in that class in 1934, weighted for the firm member bias, was 5.
31 See summary of results for California and Wisconsin lawyers in Economics of the Legal Profession, p. 48.

come of lawyers in the years-in-practice groups in which firm members are most numerous is considerably higher than in the years-in-practice groups in which firm members are fewest. Consequently, the difference between the average incomes of individual practitioners and firm members in practice the same number of years would be considerably smaller than the difference between the countrywide averages; or between the averages standardized with respect to size of community distribution. Unfortunately, the available data are too meagre for even rough estimates of the quantitative effect of this factor.

c Salaried and independent practice

As noted above, independent practice is likely to dominate professions that serve primarily individuals; salaried practice, professions that serve primarily business enterprises and public agencies. Accordingly, independent practice is dominant among physicians and dentists and the numerically small groups of authors, composers, etc. In contrast to these are accountants, engineers, chemists, metallurgists, etc., groups in which independent practice is relatively rare. Certified public accountants may seem an exception, since they are predominantly individual practitioners. However, as previously noted, they belong to the same professional group as the large number of accountants and auditors employed by business firms and government. In any profession that is largely salaried, some men, either because of superior skill or for other reasons, find it advantageous to practise without an attachment to a business or governmental organization. Consulting engineers, economists, chemists, etc., are other examples of such auxiliary groups of independent practitioners.

Law serves individuals, business enterprises, and governmental agencies, and in consequence occupies an intermediate position between these two groups. Initially dominated by independent practice, it has become increasingly salaried as large business enterprises have grown in importance and the government's role as an employer has expanded.

The independent practitioner must make a larger capital investment in equipment, expense of building up a practice, etc., than the salaried man, and must assume a greater risk. These factors that would tend to make the average income of the independent practitioner larger than the average income of the salaried man [32] are common to all professions. In addition, in medicine and dentistry, and to a considerable extent, law, salaried employment is ordinarily a step toward independent practice. Salaried employees are therefore likely to be younger than independent practitioners and to include a larger proportion of men who have not yet reached their peak earnings. The salaried employee of a physician, dentist, or lawyer is unlikely to receive more than his employer, though of course he may receive more than other independent practitioners. Since prestige plays so large a role in attracting custom, the salaried man will find it advantageous to enter independent practice as he gains experience and acquires a reputation on his own account.

In accountancy and engineering, most men are salaried employees throughout their professional career. The independent practitioners are an auxiliary group. The business enterprises and governmental agencies that are the major consumers of the services of these professions are likely to purchase from independent practitioners solely highly specialized services: services that their own professional employees cannot render and that are required in such small amounts that it is not profitable to employ additional full-time employees; or services that they would prefer to have performed by outside agencies whose findings will be respected as objective and impartial (e.g., an independent audit). Independent practitioners in these professions are likely to be recruited from men who have done particularly well as salaried employees and have be-

[32] Independent practice may, of course, have greater appeal for other reasons than the expectation of larger pecuniary returns. But it may be hazarded that the 'net advantages' are not so clearly or generally on the side of independent practice as to affect the general tenor of this analysis.

come fairly well known; men who would earn relatively high incomes as salaried employees.[33]

The relative status of the salaried and independent groups may be reversed during cyclical depressions when large numbers of previously salaried individuals may become unemployed and enter independent practice because they find it impossible to obtain salaried employment. Such a condition is unlikely to become chronic, however, unless there is a definitely inferior group of professionally trained persons who can manage to stay in private practice but would not be hired by employers, or unless competition plays little or no role in the pricing of professional services; for otherwise competition, slow and halting though its workings may be, will tend to drive down salaries until the situation again approaches that outlined above.

The incomes of independent practitioners are likely to be not only higher but also more variable than those of salaried employees. Independent practitioners are likely to be a heterogeneous group, including at the one extreme, some men who are in independent practice as a temporary expedient because they cannot get a salaried post, at the other extreme, men who render highly specialized services for which no one consumer can provide an adequate outlet. Salaried employees are ordinarily a more homogeneous group: a man is not likely to be employed at all unless he is worth the usual 'starting' salary; and while in time he may have a fairly responsible and well-paid position, he is unlikely to become a 'top' executive unless he subordinates professional work to general managerial activity. Two other factors, touched on in Chapter 4, Section 3, also make for greater variability of income from independent practice. In the first place, the incomes of independent practitioners include an element of entrepreneurial return, a typi-

[33] Of course, these considerations apply only to men engaged in rendering services strictly related to their specialty; they do not apply to men trained, for example, as lawyers or accountants, who become corporate executives or occupy other posts in which they perform tasks largely unconnected with their particular profession.

cally variable element greatly subject to 'random' influences. In the second place, 'nonrational' factors, which make for wide variation in consumers' judgments of the quality of the services rendered by different men, affect independent practitioners more than salaried employees since the former are more likely to sell services to individuals and in small quantities.

The National Resources Committee estimates of the distribution of income by size, cited in Chapter 3, tend to support these statements. The arithmetic mean income of independent professional families in 1935–36 was more than twice that of salaried professional families, and the variability of income was greater among independent than among salaried families (Table 8 and Chart 3). However, these data are for all professions combined, whereas the considerations just presented apply to each profession separately. The larger and more variable incomes of independent professional families may merely mean that independent practitioners are concentrated in those professions in which incomes are largest and most variable. They do not necessarily mean that independent practitioners receive larger and more variable incomes than salaried men in the same profession.

The estimates summarized in Table 54 bear more directly on the relative income of salaried and independent practitioners in the same profession, but are based on much smaller samples. They indicate that salaried employees tend to have lower arithmetic mean incomes than their independent brethren but may have higher median incomes. This difference reflects, of course, a greater skewness in the distribution of income from independent practice. In general, the data on which the estimates in Table 54 are based show greater variability of income from independent practice than from salaried employment. The available data, though hardly adequate to establish the conclusions suggested by the considerations outlined above, are entirely consistent with them.

TABLE 54

Arithmetic Mean and Median Incomes of Salaried Employees
and Independent Practitioners

Physicians and Lawyers: Selected Studies

	YEAR TO WHICH ESTIMATES RELATE	NO. OF RETURNS	ARITH. MEAN INCOME	MEDIAN INCOME
Physicians			(dollars)	
American Medical Association Study [1]	1928			
Salaried		853	5,428	4,718
Independent		5,475	6,499	4,938
Committee on the Costs of Medical Care, 'accepted' estimate [2]	1929			
Salaried		....[6]	4,524	4,213
Independent		....[6]	5,467	3,705
California Medical-Economic Survey [3]	1933			
Full-time salaried [4]		....[6]	3,345	3,000
Full- & part-time salaried		....[6]	3,674	3,300
All physicians		2,737	3,572	2,700
Lawyers				
New York County Study [5]	1933			
Employed in law offices on 'salary basis'		320	4,316	3,400
All employed in law offices		558	4,011	2,885
Independent		2,667	6,664	3,210

[1] Leven, *Incomes of Physicians*, p. 105.
[2] *Ibid.*, p. 20. The 'accepted' estimate is based on the American Medical Association study and data for special groups of salaried physicians.
[3] *California Medical-Economic Survey*, pp. 90 and 94.
[4] Estimates of 1934 salary.
[5] *Survey of the Legal Profession in New York County*, pp. 18, 34. This report does not contain arithmetic averages for any group, or medians for salaried employees. We computed them from frequency distributions. The lawyers employed on other than a 'salary basis' presumably receive commissions or perquisites. The averages are for total professional income, not only income from salaried employment.
[6] Data not available.

CHAPTER 7

The Stability of Relative
Income Status

So FAR attention has been restricted to factors that might explain why different professional men receive different incomes in the same year, why one man earns $10,000, another only $1,000. We have tried to account for these differences in terms of differences in attributes of individuals: the professions they practise, where they practise, the type and organization of their practices, the number of years they have practised, and their training and ability. Except for number of years in practice, these attributes are all relatively permanent. A man's ability and training remain the same except for changes connected with experience. He usually practises in the same community year after year and rarely changes the type or organization of his practice. Consequently, if factors like these were alone responsible for income differences, men in practice the same number of years would have the same positions in an array of practitioners by size of income—the same relative income status —year after year. True, their incomes in dollars would rise and fall with ups and downs in the fortunes of the economy and the profession as a whole, but these changes would affect all alike and leave their relative positions unaltered.

Of course, individuals do not have the same relative income status year after year. Some who rank high in one year rank low in another, and conversely. As just noted, these differences in relative income status can be ascribed only in small part to changes in the attributes considered in preceding chapters. They must be ascribed largely to accidental occurrences that impinge on the individual in one year but not in another: a stroke of good fortune may suddenly improve his status, a stroke of bad fortune may blight his career. This chapter is concerned with the effect of such accidental occurrences on the relative income status of the same individual in different years.

1 THE INCOMES OF THE SAME INDIVIDUALS IN DIFFERENT YEARS

The changes in relative income status that actually occur are illustrated by Table 55, which shows the incomes of 1,020 dentists in 1932 and 1934. Since the average income of the whole group is almost identical in the two years and variability of income does not differ widely,[1] the same actual income would imply approximately the same relative income status. Consequently, if there had been no changes in relative income status, all observations would fall in the diagonal cells printed in bold face in the table. In fact, only about a third of the observations are in the diagonal cells. And even some of the dentists whose incomes fall in the diagonal cells may have experienced a change in relative income status too small to move them from one income class to another. The two-thirds whose incomes are not in the diagonal cells clearly experienced a change in relative income status. For example, of the 138 dentists who had 1932 incomes between $1,000 and $1,500, one had a loss in 1934, another, an income between $4,000 and $5,000.

A simple summary measure of the degree of stability of relative income status shown by Table 55 is given by the coefficient of correlation between incomes in the two years.[2] The stronger the tendency for individuals to maintain their income status,

1 The average income is $2,738 in 1932 and $2,726 in 1934; the standard deviation, $2,363 and $2,096 respectively.

Table 55 gives the total number of dentists as 1,020.5, and the number in one cell as 11.5. The explanation of the fraction is that, for the 1935 and 1937 samples, a return reporting income for only part of the year was counted as the fraction of the year it covered. See the explanatory note at the beginning of Appendix B.

2 Since we are interested in shifts in relative position, the rank difference correlation might be preferable. Two sets of data might yield identical rank difference correlations but very different product moment correlations if both relationships were not linear. However, this difficulty is unimportant for our data (see below). Moreover, the rank difference correlation would be more arduous to compute with the large number of observations available.

TABLE 55

Relation between 1932 and 1934 Incomes
Dentists, 1935 Sample

INCOME IN 1932 (thousands of dollars)	NUMBER OF DENTISTS WHOSE INCOME (THOUSANDS OF DOLLARS) IN 1934 WAS																					ALL CLASSES	
	* −1 to 0	0	.001 to .5	.5 to 1	1 to 1.5	1.5 to 2	2 to 2.5	2.5 to 3	3 to 3.5	3.5 to 4	4 to 5	5 to 6	6 to 7	7 to 8	8 to 9	9 to 10	10 to 12	12 to 14	16 to 18	18 to 20	25 to 30	* No.	Arith. mean income[1] in 1934 (dollars)
−2 to −1	1	1																				2	−125
−1 to 0	2		1																			3	−250
0	1	8	1																			10	250
.001 − .5		1	10	11.5	7	2	2															33.5	683
.5 − 1		1	6	39	24	11	9	2	1													89	1,082
1 − 1.5			1	20	61	33	44	18	8	1												138	1,504
1.5 − 2				5	31	49	55	31	16	11	1											152	1,928
2 − 2.5					6	37	24	34	27	17	11					1	1					159	2,387
2.5 − 3					2	9	12	15	23	14	7	7	1	1								122	2,957
3 − 3.5					1	2	10	13	9	10	11	1										81	3,167
3.5 − 4					1	1	6	8	11	17	24	9										53	3,282
4 − 5					1	1	4	4	9	11	24	9	2									80	3,975
5 − 6							2	8	11	10	6	1	1	1	1							33	5,189
6 − 7								4	3	3	5	7	3	1	1	1	1					23	5,728
7 − 8								2	2	1	3	1	2	1	1							18	5,986
8 − 9											1	1	2	1	1	1						7	6,558
9 − 10											1	1		1	1							4	9,125
10 − 12												1		2	1	1						3	10,000
12 − 14														1	1	2		2				5	11,500
14 − 16																						1	11,000
16 − 18																		1	1			1	17,000
18 − 20																		1	1			1	17,000
20 − 25																							
25 − 30																				1		1	19,000
30 − 40																					1	1	27,500
All classes	6	12	23	76.5	134	146	165	122	106	76	67	36	20	7	6	6	6	2	2	1	1	1020.5	
Arith. mean income[1] in 1932 (dollars)	−42	375	685	861	1,349	1,770	2,335	2,650	3,177	3,586	4,216	5,653	6,200	7,500	7,667	9,250	11,333	13,000	18,000	22,500	35,000		

* The 1934 income classes '−2,000 to −1,000', '14,000–16,000', '20,000–25,000', and '30,000–40,000' have been omitted from this table for lack of space. No dentists reported income in 1934 in these classes.

[1] Averages computed from frequency distributions in this table, not from reported incomes.

i.e., the less shifting, the larger will be the correlation coefficient, and conversely. The correlation coefficient is not affected by changes in income level from one year to the next, since it depends on the differences between individuals' incomes and the average income in the profession.

The correlation coefficient for Table 55 is .907. Similar correlation coefficients for all pairs of years for which we have prepared correlation tables like Table 55 [3] are given in Table 56.

Except for consulting engineers, the correlation coefficients in Table 56 are all high, indicating a marked degree of stability in the positions that individuals occupy in an array of professional men by size of income. The coefficients are not sufficiently consistent from group to group or sample to sample to make possible an unambiguous ranking of the professions by variability of income status. The major differences are, however, clear. The correlation coefficients are largest for physicians and dentists and smallest for engineers. There is perhaps some tendency for the coefficients to be larger for physicians than for dentists, and for accountants than for lawyers, but the differences are slight and irregular and deserve little confidence. The temporal differences are even less consistent than the differences among professions. For example, the 1932–33 correlation is the lowest consecutive-year correlation for physicians and accountants, but the highest for dentists. Moreover, the temporal differences among the correlation coefficients are in general much smaller than the differences among the professions.[4]

[3] See the general note to Table 56 for the reasons why we excluded some pairs of years for some professions and restricted the analysis for certified public accountants, lawyers, and consulting engineers to individual practitioners.

[4] The statistical significance of the difference between the correlation coefficients can, of course, be tested in the usual fashion by transforming the correlation coefficients into $z = \frac{1}{2}\log_e \frac{1+r}{1-r}$, and making use of the fact that the standard deviation of z is $1/\sqrt{n-3}$. However, this test assumes that the basic data are normally distributed, an assumption to which our data patently do not conform. For this reason, we preferred to base our conclusions on the con-

One possible explanation of the greater stability of relative income status in the curative professions, medicine and dentistry, than in the business professions, is that it reflects a difference in the strength of competitive forces. In professions like medicine and dentistry that serve the ultimate consumer, custom may well play a more important role than in professions that serve primarily business enterprises. A consumer usually has 'his' physician or dentist from whom he is not easily won away. He is unlikely to 'shop around' extensively, and ordinarily has little competence to judge the technical quality of the services he purchases. 'Reputation' and 'renown' play a large part in his choice, and, in the main, reputations are not made or lost overnight. The enterprises that purchase services of the business professions are more addicted to rational calculation than the ultimate consumer. They are in a better position to judge the quality of services; they experiment more, seeking the best services at the lowest prices. They often purchase professional services in fairly large quantities and it is worth their while to devote a good deal of attention to getting the best 'buy'. Individuals who gain a reputation not justified by their professional competence are more likely to lose it than in the curative professions. Individuals who have been undervalued are more likely to gain the reputation they deserve.

The contrast just drawn is of course not sharp and definite. In business as in private life, custom guides day to day affairs. Firms have 'their' accountants just as individuals have 'their'

---

sistency of the differences among the correlation coefficients rather than on their statistical significance as determined by the above test.

If the test of significance is applied, it will be found that the relatively large size of the samples on which the coefficients are based leads to significant differences between almost all pairs of coefficients in Table 56. For example, the difference between the (transformed values of the) 1933–34 correlation coefficients for physicians and dentists is more than twice its standard error; between the 1932–33 correlation coefficients, more than three times the standard error. Similarly, the difference between the correlation coefficients for physicians for 1929–30 and 1932–33 is more than twice its standard error; and the difference between the coefficients for physicians for 1932–33 and 1933–34, more than five times its standard error.

TABLE 56

Correlation Coefficients between Incomes in Different Years, and Number of Returns Correlated

YEARS CORRELATED	PHYSICIANS	DENTISTS	LAWYERS[2]	CERTIFIED PUBLIC ACCOUNTANTS	CONSULTING ENGINEERS
				(individual practitioners)	
			Correlation Coefficient		
Consecutive years					
1929 & 1930 [1]	.932	.887		.901	.672
1932 & 1933	.920	.939	.834[3]	.848[4]	
1933 & 1934	.947	.936	.854[3]	.858[4]	
1934 & 1935				.906	
1935 & 1936				.868	
Nonconsecutive years, 1 year intervening					
1929 & 1931 [1]	.939	.843		.786	.628
1932 & 1934	.889	.907	.795[3]	.731[4]	
1934 & 1936				.826	
Nonconsecutive years, 2 years intervening					
1929 & 1932 [1]	.877	.761		.821	.521
			Number of Returns Correlated		
Consecutive years					
1929 & 1930	2,120	1,219		368	257
1932 & 1933	1,379	1,020	685[5]	783[5]	
1933 & 1934	1,446	1,057	730[5]	831[5]	
1934 & 1935				491	
1935 & 1936				505	
Nonconsecutive years, 1 year intervening					
1929 & 1931	2,110	1,220		365	251
1932 & 1934	1,381	1,020	674[5]	776[5]	
1934 & 1936				472	
Nonconsecutive years, 2 years intervening					
1929 & 1932	2,094	1,216		362	246

Several features of the table require explanation. (1) Not all the correlation coefficients that could have been computed from the 1933 samples are presented. Our initial analysis of these samples was later judged erroneous. It was possible, however, to use the results to approximate the correlation coefficients between 1929 and each of the other years by the method described in footnote 1. In view of the inevitable interdependence among the correlation coefficients computed

TABLE 56, NOTES (cont.)

from the same sample for different pairs of years, we decided that the large amount of labor needed to compute the correlation coefficients for the other pairs of years was not justified. To test the accuracy of the approximate method used to compute the correlation coefficient for the 1933 samples, we applied the same procedure to the 1935 accountancy sample with the accompanying results (the extreme case noted in footnote 4 is excluded throughout).

Correlation Coefficient

	USUAL PROCEDURE	APPROXIMATE METHOD, USING REGRESSION OF	
YEARS CORRELATED		LATER ON EARLIER YEAR	EARLIER ON LATER YEAR
1932 & 1933	.848	.836	.882
1933 & 1934	.858	.853	.862
1932 & 1934	.731	.752	.782

The agreement is, on the whole, good.

(2) No correlation coefficients are presented for the 1937 medical and legal samples because they are nonrandom among states. To have weighted the states before combining them as we did in computing the other measures presented for these samples, would have required inordinate labor and yielded results not easily susceptible to the kind of statistical analysis presented in the Appendix to this chapter. On the other hand, considerable ambiguity would have attached to correlation coefficients computed without correcting for the bias.

(3) This general rule of making no computations involving correction for biases also accounts for the restriction of our analysis of the legal and accountancy samples to individual practitioners. The data for firm members are subject to a twofold bias: (a) the sampling bias that led to overrepresentation of large firms; (b) the bias in measures of variability arising because the income of the firm as a whole, not of each member, was reported. The first bias but not the second could have been corrected by weighting.

(4) Likewise, correlation coefficients were computed only for consulting engineers who were individual practitioners although the data for engineers are subject to the second bias alone. For the 1933 accountancy and engineering samples, we have some evidence on the effect of excluding firm members since correlation coefficients were computed for both individual and all practitioners. In computing coefficients for all practitioners, the accountancy sample was not corrected for the firm member bias. The exclusion of firm members has little

Correlation Coefficient

	ACCOUNTANTS		ENGINEERS	
	Individual		Individual	
YEARS CORRELATED	practitioners	All	practitioners	All
1929 & 1930	.901	.873	.672	.680
1929 & 1931	.786	.697	.628	.509
1929 & 1932	.821	.665	.521	.367

effect on the correlation coefficients for consecutive pairs of years but alters markedly the other correlation coefficients.

TABLE 56, NOTES (concl.)

(5) We departed from our general rule of not analyzing samples that require weighting of parts to correct for bias only in analyzing the 1935 legal sample. This sample, it will be recalled, is subject to a size of community bias. In its analysis for the present purpose, we used the original data and did not correct for the size of community bias. This departure is explained by a desire to include some results for lawyers and by our inability to discover any respect in which the correlation coefficient would be seriously affected by not correcting for the size of community bias. It seems reasonable, however, that it is affected in some fashion. Consequently, less confidence should be attached to the coefficients for lawyers than for the other professions.

(6) Both dental samples are restricted to American Dental Association members. Since the resulting bias has not been adjusted for, any conclusions about dentists must be interpreted as referring to members alone.

[1] Correlation coefficients computed indirectly. Practitioners were arrayed by size of 1929 net income. For each decile of this array, average net income for each year 1929–32 was computed. Straight line regression equations were computed between average incomes for each year 1930–32 and average 1929 incomes. The slope of each equation was multiplied by the ratio of the standard deviation of income in 1929 to the standard deviation of income in the year considered, the standard deviations being based on the entire frequency distribution of income. The product is the figure entered in this table. For accountants and engineers, the deciles were computed from an array of all practitioners including firm members. The number of individual practitioners thus varied from decile to decile. The actual numbers in the deciles were used as weights in computing the regression equations.

[2] Correlation coefficients computed without correcting for size of community bias.

[3] Excludes one extreme return reporting an income of $8,357 in 1932; $50,471 in 1933; $3,165 in 1934. Correlation coefficients including this return are: 1932 and 1933, .759; 1933 and 1934, .757; 1932 and 1934, .794.

[4] Excludes one extreme return reporting an income of $41,000 in 1932; —$19,000 in 1933; $13,000 in 1934. Correlation coefficients including this return are: 1932 and 1933, .596; 1933 and 1934, .793; 1932 and 1934, .696.

[5] Excludes return omitted in computing correlation coefficient.

physicians. And 'nepotism' or 'favoritism' involving the purchase of an inferior service in preference to a superior one are by no means absent. Nevertheless, it is probably true that custom reigns more widely in private life than in business affairs, and this may be the reason why professional status, though relatively stable in all professions, is more stable in the curative than in the business professions.

The correlation coefficients in Table 56 are classified into three groups: for consecutive years, nonconsecutive years with one year intervening, and nonconsecutive years with two years intervening. As is to be expected, the correlation coefficients between nonconsecutive years are in general smaller than between consecutive years: shifts in income status are likely to be greater and to affect more people the longer the period considered. A more important question is whether the shifts over long periods are a random cumulation of the year to year shifts. If they were, the correlation coefficients between nonconsecutive years would be the product of the correlation coefficients for the intervening pairs of consecutive years. For example, the correlation coefficient between physicians' incomes in 1932 and 1933 is .920, and between their incomes in 1933 and 1934, .947. If the shifts in successive pairs of years were independent, the correlation coefficient between incomes in 1932 and 1934 would be .920 x .947 or .871; in fact, it is .889, indicating that the income status of physicians over the three years is more stable than the degree of shifting from one year to the next would suggest.

Stated in somewhat different terms, the question posed in the preceding paragraph is: among a group of individuals with the same incomes in, say, 1933, which are most likely to experience a rise in income in 1934? Those for whom the 1933 income represents an increase from 1932 or those for whom it represents a decrease? The answer is given by the partial correlation coefficient between incomes in one year and the second succeeding year, income in the intervening year being the variable eliminated.

	PARTIAL CORRELATION COEFFICIENT BETWEEN INCOMES IN	
	1932 AND 1934, INCOME IN 1933 BEING THE VARIABLE ELIMINATED	1934 AND 1936, INCOME IN 1935 BEING THE VARIABLE ELIMINATED
Medicine	.141	
Dentistry	.232	
Law	.288	
Accountancy	.0125	.188

All the correlation coefficients are positive. The conclusion suggested for physicians by the example worked out above is therefore confirmed for the other professions: there is a tendency for individuals whose income status changes to regain their initial positions. This tendency is, however, slight. The partial correlation coefficients are all below 0.3, the simple correlation coefficients are all above 0.7.

The smallness of the partial correlation coefficients probably reflects two forces working in opposite directions. On the one hand, the natural life cycle of earnings makes for a negative correlation. Young men just beginning practice tend to have steadily rising incomes; older men, in some professions at least, steadily falling ones.[5] On the other hand, individuals in practice the same length of time tend to return to the same position after reverses or successes. The observed correlation coefficients are positive, suggesting that the second tendency is stronger, at least for periods as brief as that covered by our analysis.

The last column and the last row of Table 55 give a more detailed summary of the interrelations between incomes in 1932 and 1934. The last column gives the average 1934 income of the dentists in each 1932 income class. For example, dentists whose 1932 incomes were between $500 and $1,000 had an average income of $1,082 in 1934; dentists whose 1932 incomes were between $7,000 and $8,000 had an average income of $5,986 in 1934. Similarly, the last row gives the average 1932 income of each 1934 income class. Averages like those in the last column and row of Table 55 are plotted in Chart 25 for other professions and pairs of years.

The chart contains 42 diagrams, each showing the average income in one year of ten classes obtained by grouping individuals by their incomes in another year. To illustrate, the first diagram depicts the relation between incomes of physicians in 1929 and 1932. The grouping is by 1929 income. The or-

5 This makes for a negative partial correlation because, of a group of persons whose incomes are the same in one year, those persons will tend to have higher incomes in the next year who had lower incomes in the preceding year, and conversely; i.e., those who have risen to this level will continue to rise and those who have fallen to this level will continue to fall.

CHART 25

Relation between Incomes of Same Individuals in Different Years

(Scales represent income in thousands of dollars in designated years)

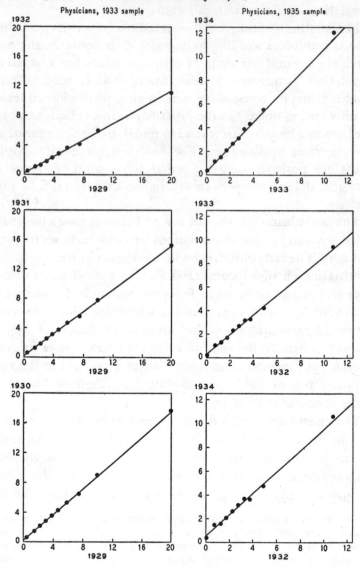

CHART 25 (CONT.)

(Scales represent income in thousands of dollars in designated years)

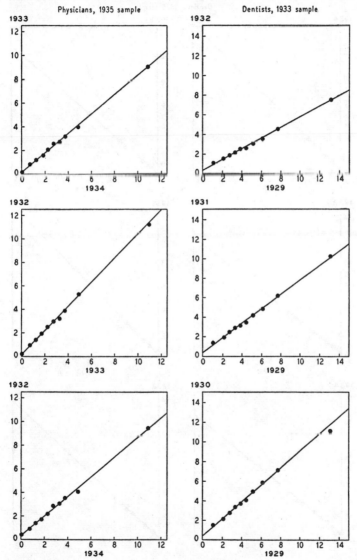

CHART 25 (CONT.)

(Scales represent income in thousands of dollars in designated years)

Dentists, 1935 sample

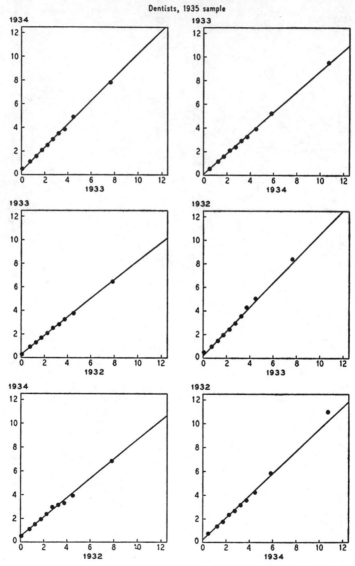

CHART 25 (CONT.)

(Scales represent income in thousands of dollars in designated years)

Lawyers, 1935 sample

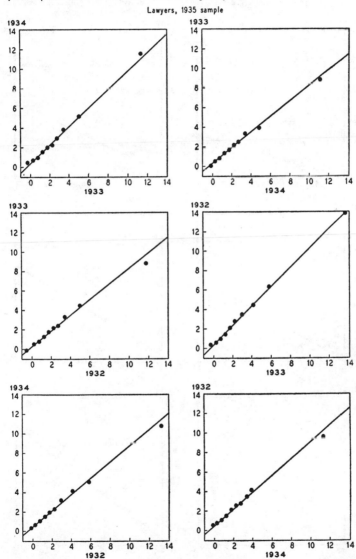

CHART 25 (CONT.)

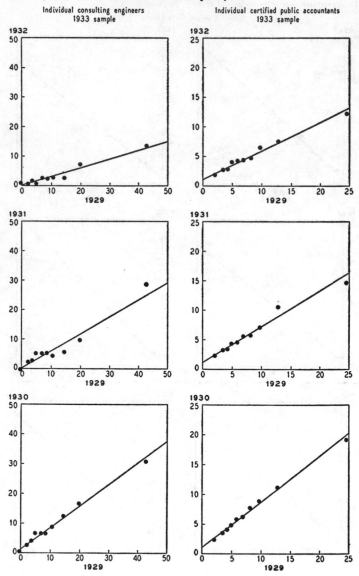

(Scales represent income in thousands of dollars in designated years)

Individual consulting engineers
1933 sample

Individual certified public accountants
1933 sample

CHART 25 (CONT.)

(Scales represent income in thousands of dollars in designated years)

Individual certified public accountants
1935 sample

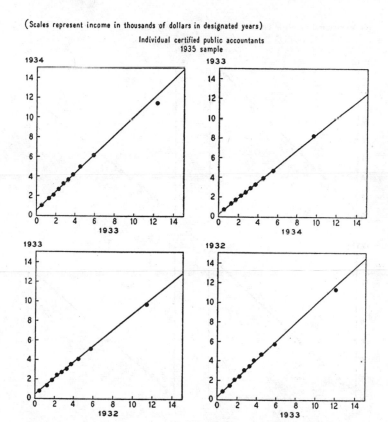

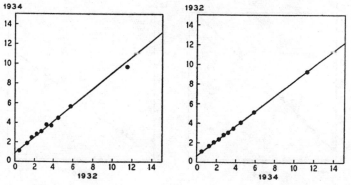

CHART 25 (CONCL.)

(Scales represent income in thousands of dollars in designated years)

Individual certified public accountants
1937 sample

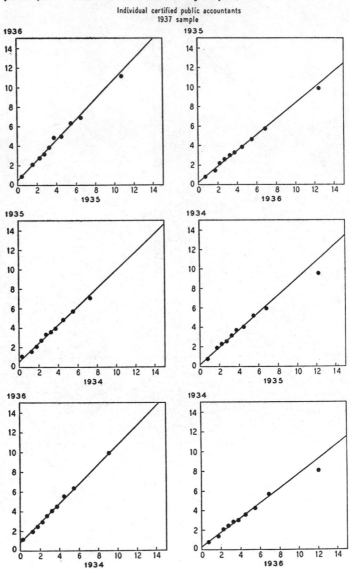

dinate of any point (the vertical distance between the point and the horizontal axis) is the average income in 1932 of the 1929 income class whose average income in 1929 is given by the corresponding abscissa (the horizontal distance between the point and the vertical axis). In all diagrams, income in the year that serves as the basis for grouping the practitioners (in the diagram just cited, 1929) is measured along the horizontal axis. In order to limit the disturbing influence of sampling fluctuations, the income classes for which points are plotted are sometimes broader than those used in the correlation tables. In the main, this is true only of the lowest, highest, and less frequently, next to the highest income classes.[6] In addition to the actual averages, regression lines computed from the correlation tables are plotted on the chart. For the 1933 samples, the lines are based on the plotted points; for the other samples, on data for the finer class intervals. (The constants of the regression equations are given in Table 60, Section 1a of the Appendix to this chapter.[7])

[6] In obtaining the classes plotted, we subdivided none of the finer class intervals except in the analysis of the 1933 samples. For these samples, each class contains almost exactly the same number of practitioners. There is more variation among the classes for the other samples but, with few exceptions, the largest class contains fewer than three times as many practitioners as the smallest. It should be noted that if any set of observations falls on a straight line, their means will fall on the same straight line.

[7] For the 1933 samples the equations of the straight lines were computed from the ten pairs of means by the usual least squares procedure. For the other samples, however, this procedure was not followed. As we show below, the standard deviation of income in year 2 is not the same for all year 1 income classes: at first it decreases with income in year 1, then increases very rapidly. Consequently, the different income classes were weighted inversely to their estimated variances in computing the equations of the straight lines. See Section 1 of the Appendix to this chapter for a more detailed explanation of the method used in obtaining the weights.

The use of weights means that the regression equations plotted in Chart 25 for the 1935 and 1937 samples are not entirely consistent with the correlation coefficients in Table 56, since the correlation coefficients were computed in the usual fashion. The reason for this difference in procedure is that we have been unable to find a logically sound method for taking the unequal variances of the different income classes into account in estimating the correlation coefficient. We cannot see that the difference in procedure introduces any bias into our results. It means simply that a less accurate method of estimation has

The broad conclusion suggested by the diagrams is that the straight lines fit the points remarkably well. Of course, few of the points fall exactly on the straight lines, but the deviations are small and, of more importance, appear randomly distributed about the lines. The one tolerably clear exception to this generalization is in the diagrams for accountants; the last point is almost uniformly below the fitted line, and the first two points are very frequently below, i.e., there is some indication that the regression is concave to the horizontal axis. Though the deviations are small, the last point is below the line in 14, the first in 9, and the second in 10 of the 15 accountancy diagrams. The only other profession displaying anything like the same degree of consistent departure from the fitted lines is law, for which the first point is above the line in all six diagrams. However, this is the only point showing consistent departure; and since all six diagrams are based on the same sample, little importance should be attached to this phenomenon. Accountancy is the one profession for which data based on all three samples are presented. The analysis for medicine and dentistry is restricted to two samples, and for law and engineering, to one.

---

been used to obtain the correlation coefficients than to obtain the regression equations.

The geometric mean of the two weighted regression coefficients gives one possible alternative estimate of the correlation coefficient. This method seems reasonable by analogy to the relations when all observations are given equal weight. However, since we have been unable to find any other justification of its validity, we have not used the method. It yields results very similar to those obtained by the usual procedure, as the accompanying comparison indicates (r = correlation coefficient by usual procedure, r' = geometric mean of weighted regression coefficients).

YEARS COMPARED	PHYSICIANS r	r'	DENTISTS r	r'	LAWYERS r	r'	ACCOUNTANTS r	r'
1932 and 1933	.920	.931	.939	.909	.834	.893	.848	.880
1933 and 1934	.947	.934	.936	.920	.854	.869	.858	.889
1932 and 1934	.889	.874	.907	.874	.795	.849	.731	.793
1934 and 1935							.906	.906
1935 and 1936							.868	.921
1934 and 1936							.826	.863

For reasons explained in detail in Section 1 of the Appendix to this chapter, it is difficult to make an exact statistical test of the hypothesis that the regressions are linear. Since the results of the tests there made are seriously affected by personal judgments, the basis for which cannot be fully presented, we have preferred to rest our case on the diagrams in Chart 25 and on the lack of consistency among the deviations of the points from the lines. Moreover, whether or not the deviations are greater than can reasonably be attributed to chance, they are so small that they could scarcely be considered 'significant' in any other than the statistical sense of that term.

The diagrams in Chart 25 summarize the relation between the average incomes in two years of individuals classified by their incomes in one of those years. To complete the description of the correlation tables, we must investigate the variability about these averages, the extent to which individuals in the same income class in one year are dispersed in another year. We use the standard deviation as a measure of absolute variability, the coefficient of variation as a measure of relative variability.

Chart 26 summarizes the relation between the standard deviation of income in one year and the size of income in another. It contains five sections—four based on the 1935 medical, dental, legal, and accountancy samples, and one based on the 1937 accountancy sample. Each section was prepared as follows: (1) Standard deviations of income in each year were computed for groups of practitioners classified by their incomes in each of the other years. For example, the standard deviation of 1934 income was computed for each 1932 and each 1933 income class; the standard deviation of 1933 income, for each 1932 and each 1934 income class; and the standard deviation of 1932 income, for each 1933 and each 1934 income class. This yielded six sets of standard deviations—two sets for each of the three years. In each case the fine class intervals, rather than the broad ones plotted in Chart 25, were used. (2) The standard deviations were expressed as ratios to a standard deviation obtained

CHART 26

Relation between Absolute Variability and Size of Income in Base Year

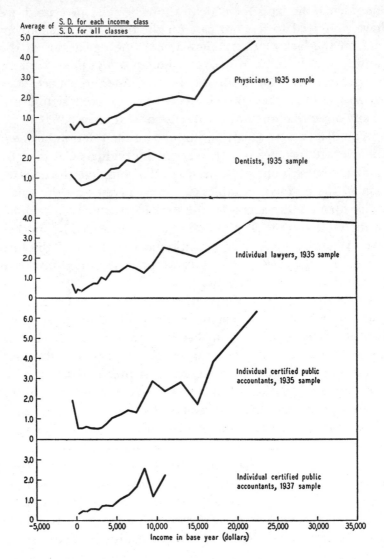

Average of $\dfrac{\text{S. D. for each income class}}{\text{S. D. for all classes}}$

Physicians, 1935 sample

Dentists, 1935 sample

Individual lawyers, 1935 sample

Individual certified public accountants, 1935 sample

Individual certified public accountants, 1937 sample

Income in base year (dollars)

by combining all income classes.[8] This was done to eliminate differences in the levels of the six sets of standard deviations. The levels differed, first, because of differences from year to year in the absolute variability of the income distribution as a whole, second, because four sets of standard deviations were for incomes in a year immediately following or preceding the 'base' year while two sets were for incomes in a year two years before or after the 'base' year. The latter naturally tended to be greater than the former. (3) The six ratios for the same dollar income class were then averaged; e.g., the six ratios for the income class $1,000–$1,500. Fewer than six ratios were available for those income classes which in some years included either no practitioners or only one. No averages were struck for such classes. The use of the same dollar income classes for the different years is somewhat questionable because of changes in average professional income and hence in the position of each income class relative to the average. However, the changes in average income are small relatively to the range of income classes plotted. The possible refinement in the results hardly justified the arbitrariness of any alternative procedure. (4) These average ratios are plotted in the chart against the income classes to which they refer. The average ratios are measured along the vertical axis, the income classes along the horizontal. The income classes in the base year are not all the same width: the higher classes tend to be wider than the lower. Consequently, there is a bias toward greater variability in the higher income classes.

The lines in Chart 26 tell much the same story. Absolute variability at first falls for a short distance, then rises at an increasing rate throughout the rest of the range. The falling portion covers primarily the negative and extremely low posi-

---

[8] This average standard deviation was not a simple arithmetic average. It was the root mean square of the deviations of the observations about the class means. In other words, the sum of the squares of the observations about the class mean was computed for each class; these sums were added for all classes and the total divided by the total number of degrees of freedom (the number of observations minus the number of income classes). The square root of the quotient gave the standard deviation used as the base of the ratios.

tive income classes. This is, of course, reasonable. If individuals were to remain in these classes for any length of time they would almost certainly be forced out of professional practice entirely. The fact that they remain in practice means that years in which they lose money or receive negligible incomes are the exception rather than the rule. Nor is the large increase in dispersion as income increases surprising in view of the results of earlier chapters. We have almost uniformly found a positive relation between absolute variability and income level: the higher the income level, the greater the absolute variability. True, in Chart 26 the standard deviation of income is plotted against average income in a different year. But we found earlier in this chapter that there is a fairly close positive relation between incomes in the two years.

Chart 27, based on coefficients of variation instead of standard deviations, differs from Chart 26 in two other respects: (1) The figures plotted are the averages of the actual coefficients of variation rather than of ratios of the coefficients of variation to an average coefficient for all income classes. (2) Each figure plotted is the average of four instead of six coefficients of variation, the four used being those that refer to incomes in a year immediately following or preceding the 'base' year. Both changes were made for the same reason. Dividing the standard deviations by the average income eliminated the larger part of the differences in the level of the standard deviations. The four sets of coefficients of variation used were consequently at almost the same level. The other two sets—those for years two years before or after the 'base' year—were, however, on a higher level. Instead of correcting for differences in level so that all six sets could be combined, we analyzed only the four directly comparable sets. The two excluded sets yield curves similar to those in Chart 27. The coefficients of variation on which Chart 27 is based were obtained by dividing the standard deviation by the mean income for the same year; e.g., the coefficients of variation of 1932 income for 1933 income classes were obtained by dividing the standard deviation of 1932 income for each 1933 income class

CHART 27

Relation between Relative Variability and Size of Income in Base Year

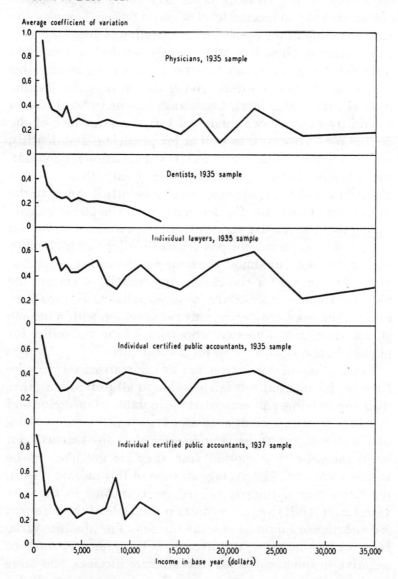

Average coefficient of variation

Physicians, 1935 sample

Dentists, 1935 sample

Individual lawyers, 1935 sample

Individual certified public accountants, 1935 sample

Individual certified public accountants, 1937 sample

Income in base year (dollars)

by the average 1932 income of the same 1933 income class.

The initial decrease and then approximate constancy in the standard deviation as the mean income increases naturally reflects itself in an even more rapid decrease in the coefficients of variation. At an income level of about $2,000, however, the rate of decline in the coefficient of variation is drastically curtailed. Among physicians and dentists the decline continues thereafter but at a very much slower pace. Among accountants it apparently ceases entirely, giving way to irregular fluctuations about a stable level. Correction for the upward bias in variability noted above might lead to a continuance of the decline for accountants as well as for physicians and dentists. After the $2,000 point, the coefficients of variation for accountants are about the same as or somewhat greater than those for physicians, and these, in turn, are consistently larger than the coefficients of variation for dentists. Yet in Chapter 3 we concluded that the relative variability of the income distribution as a whole was greater for physicians than for either accountants or dentists, but almost the same for the two latter professions. The reason for the change in order is, of course, the higher correlation coefficients for physicians and dentists than for accountants. Considering only the variation within income groups eliminates a greater proportion of the variability for physicians and dentists than for accountants.

The findings of this section may be summarized very briefly. Relative income status is fairly stable in all professions other than engineering, and somewhat more stable in medicine and dentistry than in accountancy and law: while a group of individuals who are in the same income class one year will not be in the same class another year, they are not likely to be widely dispersed. The average income of this income class in the latter year is linearly related to its income in the base year, i.e., it tends to equal a constant multiple of the base year income plus or minus a constant amount. The absolute variability of income about this average is large for very small or negative incomes, small for intermediate incomes, and large for large incomes; relative variability decreases sharply for base year incomes below $2,000, and thereafter either remains constant or declines more slowly.

2 AN INTERPRETATION OF THE LINEAR REGRESSIONS

The results of the preceding section have an important bearing on whether the degree of stability of relative income status that characterizes a profession also characterizes separate income classes; stated differently, whether the uncertainties and accidental occurrences that accompany economic change affect with equal strength those who rank high in a profession and those who rank low. One significant interpretation of 'equal effect' can be shown to imply linear regression between incomes in different years, and conversely. We have already seen that the observed regressions are very nearly linear.

A man's relative income status in any two years will be determined in part by factors that are common to the two years: personal attributes such as training, ability, personality; attributes of the man's practice such as its location, type, organization; and accidental influences whose effects are present in both years. Superimposed on these factors are transitory influences that affect his income in only one of the two years; influences that are likely to be interpreted by the man affected as 'accidental' or 'chance' occurrences, though in reality they may be the result of definite causal factors at work, and may even reappear at intervals associated, for example, with cyclical fluctuations in general business activity. Let us call the part of a man's income determined by the first set of factors the 'permanent' component, and the part determined by the second set, the 'transitory' component. The magnitude of the two components will depend on the period covered. Factors that are 'permanent' for a particular pair of years may not be for a longer period, or a different pair of years; factors that are 'transitory' change correspondingly; lengthening the period considered will in general increase the range of factors considered 'transitory'. The separation could be fixed and constant only for a man's whole career treated as a unit.

When we ask whether the stability of relative income status

is the same for all income classes, or whether economic change affects all income classes alike, it seems clear that implicitly we are thinking not of classes determined by actual income but of classes determined by what we have called the permanent component of income. Surely, there is little point in asking whether men who have very high incomes this year because they happen to have been the beneficiaries of strokes of good fortune are affected more by the occurrences that accompany economic change than the men who have low incomes this year because they have had bad 'luck'. The relevant question would seem to be whether the men whose personal and professional attributes would tend to make their relative income status high are more affected by these occurrences than other professional men.

There is of course no way of isolating the permanent and transitory components of the income of a particular man. We can measure only his actual income, and we can classify men only by their actual incomes. The difference between the average income of men in the same actual income class and the average income in the profession as a whole will consist of two parts: (1) the difference between the average permanent components for these men and for the profession as a whole, and (2) the average transitory component. (The average transitory component for the profession as a whole can, without loss of generality, be defined as zero since we are interested in relative income status.) If the permanent and transitory components of a man's income are uncorrelated [9] then both parts of the difference between the average income of an income class and the average income of the profession will tend to have

[9] Zero correlation between permanent and transitory components does not necessarily imply that the absolute value of the transitory component is the same no matter what the size of the permanent component. For example, suppose the transitory component was equally likely to be either $+10$ per cent of the permanent component or -10 per cent. The correlation between the transitory and permanent components would be zero, since the average transitory component would be the same (i.e., zero) for all values of the permanent component. The absolute value of the transitory component would be a fixed proportion of the permanent component.

the same sign; e.g., an income class above the average for the profession will tend to have an average permanent component above the average permanent component for the profession and a positive average transitory component.[10] In other words, an income class above the average in any year has on the whole been favorably affected by transitory factors, and conversely.

While we cannot isolate the transitory component of the income of a particular man, we can isolate the average transitory component of the average income of an income class. Suppose we have data on the incomes of the same men in two years (say 1932 and 1933) in which the average income in the profession as a whole is the same. (This assumption about average income will be removed presently; it is made here merely to simplify exposition.) For any 1932 income class,

average income in 1932 = average permanent component
in 1932 + average transitory
component in 1932.

If, as assumed above, the transitory and permanent components are uncorrelated, the average transitory component for this 1932 income class will be zero in 1933. It is not zero in 1932 because 1932 transitory components helped to determine the 1932 income class into which the individuals were grouped. But such a grouping is entirely random with respect to 1933 transitory components, since by definition these are not present in 1932. Consequently, for the same 1932 income class,

average income in 1933 = average permanent component
in 1933.

[10] Let x = income of an individual,

p = permanent component of his income,

t = transitory component of his income,

$\bar{x}$ = average income for profession as a whole,

$\bar{p} = \bar{x}$ = average permanent component for profession as a whole,

$\bar{t} = 0$ = average transitory component for profession as a whole,

r = correlation coefficient between variables indicated by subscripts.

Then

$x = p + t$.

If $r_{pt} = 0$, then r_{xp} and r_{xt} are greater than zero, from which it follows that the average value of p and t corresponding to an x greater than $\bar{x}$ will be greater than $\bar{p}$ and $\bar{t}$ respectively.

In two years in which average income in the profession is the same, it seems not unreasonable to assume that the permanent component is the same for each man separately. If we make this assumption, then

average income in 1933 = average permanent component
in 1932.

It follows that the difference between the average incomes in 1932 and 1933 of a 1932 income class measures the average transitory component in 1932. This average transitory component divided by the difference between the average 1932 income of the 1932 income class and the average 1932 income in the profession measures the proportion of the latter difference that can be attributed to transitory factors. If this proportion is the same for all income classes we can say that they are affected equally by the occurrences that accompany economic change. The above reasoning applies equally well in reverse: the difference between the average incomes in 1933 and 1932 of a 1933 income class measures the average transitory component in 1933. It should be recalled, however, that the result obtained in this way will not be the same as the average transitory component in 1933 computed from data for, say, 1934. The former measures the effect of forces present in 1933 but not in 1932; the latter, the effect of forces present in 1933 but not in 1934.

We can remove the assumption that the average income in the profession is the same in the two years compared by broadening the assumption made above about the relation between permanent components in different years. Instead of assuming them equal we can assume that the permanent component changes in the same proportion as average income in the profession.[11] We can then correct the average 1932 income of a

11 This assumption implies that the relative variability of the permanent component among all members of the profession is constant in different years. Any change in the relative variability of actual incomes is attributed to a change in the strength of transitory forces. There is no reason why the relative variability of the permanent component must remain constant. It is perfectly possible that what we have called the permanent forces might not have effects

1932 income class for the change in the average income in the profession. For example, if average income in the profession is 10 per cent lower in 1933 than in 1932, the average 1932 income of each 1932 income class can be reduced by 10 per

---

that were constant or that changed in proportion to the change in the average income in the profession. In that case, the variability of the permanent component might change from year to year. The likelihood of such changes taking place is increased if the data used are for a group that includes individuals in practice different numbers of years. 'Experience' is a permanent factor that obviously does not have constant effects. It would be preferable, therefore, to analyze each years-in-practice group separately. Unfortunately, we cannot do so with our data.

An alternative assumption that could be made is that the relative variability of the permanent component is proportional to the relative variability of actual income. If relative variability is measured by the coefficient of variation, this is equivalent to assuming that the standard deviation of the permanent component is proportional to the standard deviation of actual income, since the average permanent component for the profession is equal to average income. If permanent and transitory components are uncorrelated, this would imply that the standard deviation of the permanent component is also proportional to the standard deviation of the transitory component. This does not seem reasonable. It seems better to use an assumption that permits the transitory components to contribute a greater proportion of the variability of actual incomes in some years than in others.

The formula for the proportion contributed by the transitory factors under the alternative assumption (hereafter called the variability assumption) can be derived as follows:

Let x_{11}, p_{11}, t_{11} be the average income, permanent component, and transitory component, respectively, in year 1 of a year 1 income class;

x_{21}, p_{21}, t_{21} be the average income, permanent component, and transitory component, respectively, in year 2 of a year 1 income class.

Let $\bar{x}_1$, $\bar{x}_2$ be the average income of the profession in years 1 and 2, respectively (these will also be the average permanent components in the profession);

s_1, s_2 the standard deviation of income in years 1 and 2, respectively;

K'_1 the proportion contributed by the transitory factor in year 1 as computed under the variability assumption.

Then

$$p_{11} - \bar{x}_1 = (p_{21} - \bar{x}_2)\frac{s_1}{s_2} = (x_{21} - \bar{x}_2)\frac{s_1}{s_2},$$

$$(1) \qquad t_{11} = x_{11} - p_{11} = x_{11} - \bar{x}_1 - (x_{21} - \bar{x}_2)\frac{s_1}{s_2},$$

$$K'_1 = \frac{t_{11}}{x_{11} - \bar{x}_1} = 1 - \frac{x_{21} - \bar{x}_2}{x_{11} - \bar{x}_1} \cdot \frac{s_1}{s_2}.$$

The corresponding formula under the assumption stated in the text (hereafter called the mean assumption) can be derived in similar fashion. Let K_1

cent and then compared directly with the 1933 average income of the same class.[12]

The computation of the average transitory component is illustrated in Table 57. Column 7 gives the percentage contributed by the transitory component to the deviation of each 1932 income class from the 1932 average income of all dentists. Though computed with the aid of 1933 data, these percentages refer to 1932: e.g., in 1932, 13 per cent of the difference between the average income of dentists who received between $500 and $1,000 and the average income of all dentists is accounted for by transitory factors not present in 1933. The very high figure for the $2,500–$3,000 class (182) should be attributed little importance; it is for an income class whose average income was nearly the same as the average income of all dentists; consequently, both the permanent and transitory components are small and sampling errors might lead to wide variation in the percentage attributed to either component. The rest of the percentages are fairly similar, ranging from 7

---

represent the proportion contributed by the transitory factor in year 1 as computed under the mean assumption.

Then

$$p_{11} - \bar{x}_1 = (p_{21} - \bar{x}_2)\frac{\bar{x}_1}{\bar{x}_2} = (x_{21} - \bar{x}_2)\frac{\bar{x}_1}{\bar{x}_2},$$

$$(2) \qquad t_{11} = x_{11} - p_{11} = x_{11} - \bar{x}_1 - (x_{21} - \bar{x}_2)\frac{\bar{x}_1}{\bar{x}_2},$$

$$K_1 = \frac{t_{11}}{x_{11} - \bar{x}_1} = 1 - \frac{x_{21} - \bar{x}_2}{x_{11} - \bar{x}_1}\cdot\frac{\bar{x}_1}{\bar{x}_2}.$$

It is clear from (1) and (2) that if K is the same for all income classes, so is K', since s_1, s_2, and $\bar{x}_1$, and $\bar{x}_2$ do not vary from income class to income class. Hence, the two assumptions lead to the identical criterion of 'equal effect', although they do not give the same value for the magnitude of the contribution of transitory factors unless the coefficient of variation is identical in the two years compared.

12 In the symbols of the preceding footnote the formula described in the text is

$$K_1 = \frac{x_{11}\dfrac{\bar{x}_2}{\bar{x}_1} - x_{21}}{x_{11}\dfrac{\bar{x}_2}{\bar{x}_1} - \bar{x}_2}.$$

This formula can be derived from formula (2) by clearing fractions and then dividing numerator and denominator by $\bar{x}_1$.

TABLE 57

Computation of Transitory Component in Deviation
of Average 1932 Income for 1932 Income Classes
from Average Income for Profession

Dentists, 1935 Sample

1932 INCOME CLASSES	AVG. INCOME IN		1932 corrected for change in avg. for profession	AVG. TRANSITORY COMPONENT IN 1932	DEVIATION OF 1932 CORRECTED AVG. FROM AVG. FOR PROFESSION	TRANSITORY COMPONENT AS % OF TOTAL DEVIATION
	1932	1933				
(1)	(2)	(3)	(4)	(5)	(6)	(7)
		(dollars)				
−2,000 to 500	83	244	74	−170	−2,422	7.0
500 to 1,000	750	901	670	−231	−1,826	12.7
1,000 to 1,500	1,250	1,268	1,117	−151	−1,379	10.9
1,500 to 2,000	1,750	1,663	1,563	−100	−933	10.7
2,000 to 2,500	2,250	2,078	2,011	−67	−485	13.8
2,500 to 3,000	2,750	2,527	2,458	−69	−38	181.6
3,000 to 3,500	3,250	2,818	2,904	+86	+408	21.1
3,500 to 4,000	3,750	3,226	3,351	+125	+855	14.6
4,000 to 5,000	4,500	3,794	4,021	+227	+1,525	14.9
5,000 to 40,000	7,843	6,475	7,009	+534	+4,513	11.8
All classes	2,793	2,496	2,496			

Col. 4 = col. 2 × 2,496/2,793   Col. 6 = col. 4 − 2,496
Col. 5 = col. 4 − col. 3   Col. 7 = 100 × (col. 5/col. 6)

to 21, with all except two between 11 and 15, and varying
erratically from class to class. On this showing we should be inclined to conclude that all income classes were affected roughly
in the same degree.[13]

[13] A common fallacy is to regard all income classes as having been affected
'equally' only if the transitory component is zero. Individuals are classified by
the size of their income in the base year, say 1932, and the average income of
these classes computed for future years. Divergent movements in these averages are interpreted as reflecting a differential effect of the change in total
income. For example, a larger decline in the average income of the upper
1932 income classes from 1932 to 1933 than in the average income of the lower
1932 income classes, would be interpreted as meaning that the upper income
classes 'suffered' most from the decline in total income. According to this test,
all income classes are affected equally if the average income of each income
class changes in the same proportion as the average income of all classes, i.e.,
if the transitory component is zero.

As the discussion above indicates, this test would be valid only if individuals
were classified by the permanent component of their income. It is completely
fallacious as actually applied. (See Harold Hotelling, review of Howard
Secrist, 'The Triumph of Mediocrity in Business', *Journal of the American*

If the percentages in column 7 were equal, the averages in column 3 plotted against those in column 2 would fall on a straight line. Chart 28 serves to illustrate this point. Let us measure income in one year, say 1932, along the horizontal axis and income in 1933, along the vertical axis. Any point in the chart describes the income position of an individual or an income class in the two years. Suppose OM_1 is the average income of the profession in 1932 and OM_2 the average income in 1933, so that the point M represents the average incomes in the two years. Let point B represent the average 1932 and 1933 incomes of a particular income class, so that OA is the average income of this class in 1932, AB, its average income in 1933. Then AC will be the corrected average 1932 income (comparable to the figures in column 4 of Table 57). The transitory component in 1932 will be measured by BC, the permanent component by AB (or expressed as a deviation from the average permanent component for the profession, by BD), the total deviation from the average for the profession by CD, and

---

Statistical Association, Dec. 1933, pp. 463–5, and the subsequent discussion, *ibid.*, June 1934, pp. 196–200.) An alternative statement of the argument of the text indicates the essential fallacy. Suppose the actual figures on incomes are replaced by ranks. Let us give a rank of 1 to the lowest 1932 income, a rank of 2 to the next lowest income, and so on; and repeat the process for future years. Consider the nine individuals with the lowest 1932 incomes. Their average 1932 rank is obviously 5. Their average rank in 1933 can clearly be no less than 5; it will be 5 only if these same individuals have the lowest incomes in 1933; if there is any shifting in relative income status their average rank must of necessity increase. Similarly, if the average rank of the group of individuals with the highest incomes in 1932 changes at all from 1932 to 1933, it must of necessity decrease.

Nothing essential is altered by using actual incomes rather than ranks. The fact that individuals 'wander', that their relative income status shifts from one year to the next, means that the 'extreme' 1932 income classes will be less extreme in 1933 than in 1932; that the 1932 average incomes of 1932 income classes will tend to be more divergent than their 1933 average incomes. Strictly speaking, this is necessarily true only if the coefficient of variation does not increase from 1932 to 1933. The precise statement is that the 1933 average incomes of 1932 income classes necessarily diverge less than the 1933 average incomes of 1933 income classes. If the divergence among the latter is considerably greater than the divergence among the 1932 average incomes of 1932 income classes, it is possible for the 1933 average incomes of 1932 income classes to diverge more than the 1932 average incomes of the 1932 income classes.

CHART 28

Illustration of Transitory Component

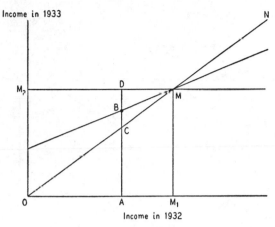

Income in 1932

the transitory component as a proportion of the total deviation by BC/CD. If this proportion were constant as A moved along the horizontal axis it is clear that the point B would generate a straight line.[14]

[14] Let x_{11} and x_{21} represent the abscissa and the ordinate, respectively, of the point B, and $\bar{x}_1$ and $\bar{x}_2$ the mean incomes in years 1 and 2, i.e., $\bar{x}_1 = OM_1$, and $\bar{x}_2 = OM_2$. (These are the symbols defined in footnote 11 above.) Then

$$AC = \frac{\bar{x}_2}{\bar{x}_1} x_{11},$$

$$BC = AB - AC = x_{21} - \frac{\bar{x}_2}{\bar{x}_1} x_{11},$$

$$CD = AD - AC = \bar{x}_2 - \frac{\bar{x}_2}{\bar{x}_1} x_{11},$$

$$\frac{BC}{CD} = \frac{x_{21} - \frac{\bar{x}_2}{\bar{x}_1} x_{11}}{\bar{x}_2 - \frac{\bar{x}_2}{\bar{x}_1} x_{11}}.$$

Setting the right hand member of this expression equal to K_1, multiplying both sides of the equation by the denominator of the fraction, and rearranging, gives:

$$x_{21} = K_1 \bar{x}_2 + \frac{\bar{x}_2}{\bar{x}_1} (1 - K_1) x_{11}.$$

It follows that if K_1 is a constant, x_{21} is linearly related to x_{11}. It is obvious that the converse is also true, namely, that if the regression is a straight line, then

CHART 29

Illustration of Different Types of Regression

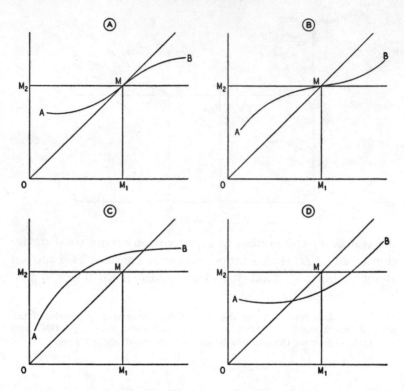

If the regression is not linear, the strength of the transitory factors differs from income class to income class. Several possible types of regression are illustrated in Chart 29. The regression AB in panel A depicts a case in which transitory factors

----

the proportion attributed to the transitory component is the same for all income classes. Further, since K'_1 is the same for all income classes when K_1 is (see footnote 11), the variability assumption also implies a straight line when the proportion attributed to the transitory factors is the same for all income classes. The only difference is that the mean assumption measures the proportion contributed by the transitory factors from the line, $y = \dfrac{\bar{x}_2}{\bar{x}_1} x_{11}$; the variability assumption from the line, $y = \bar{x}_2 + \dfrac{s_2}{s_1}(x_{11} - \bar{x}_1)$.

are relatively strongest in the extreme income classes; regression AB in panel B, one in which the transitory factors are relatively strongest in the intermediate income classes; the regression AB in panel C, one in which the transitory factors are relatively weakest in the low income classes, relatively strongest in the high income classes; the regression AB in panel D, one in which the transitory factors are relatively strongest in the low income classes, relatively weakest in the high income classes. It is perfectly possible for the regression of 1933 income on 1932 income to be linear but the regression of 1932 income on 1933 income, nonlinear. This would in no way be contradictory. It would merely imply, if our line of reasoning is valid, that transitory factors were equally important in all classes in 1932 but not in 1933.

We found in Section 1 that the regressions between incomes in different years are approximately linear. Accountants constitute the only exception. For them, there is some indication that transitory forces were relatively weaker in the low income classes and relatively stronger in the high income classes than in the intermediate classes. For the remaining professions, we can conclude that transitory forces affect all income classes equally. It follows that a single figure will suffice to indicate for all income classes the percentage of the difference between the average income of an income class and the average income in the profession that can be attributed to the transitory component. This figure can be computed from the average incomes in the profession in the two years and the slope of the regression line.[15] For the illustrative example in Table 57 it is

15 Let b_{21} represent the slope of the regression line of year 2 on year 1. Then, from the equation in the preceding footnote containing K_1,

$$b_{21} = \frac{\bar{x}_2}{\bar{x}_1}(1 - K_1), \text{ or}$$

$$(1) \quad K_1 = 1 - b_{21}\frac{\bar{x}_1}{\bar{x}_2},$$

where K_1 is the proportion attributed to the transitory component. The equation in the preceding footnote also suggests an alternative method of computing K_1. If a is the intercept of the regression line, then

11.5 per cent. Similar figures for other years and professions are given in Table 58.

Table 58 brings out clearly the effect of the choice of the years compared on the size of the transitory component. For example, about 4 per cent of the deviation of the average income of each income class from the average income of all physicians is accounted for in 1933 by transitory factors, if these are defined as factors present in 1933 but not in 1932; about 9 per cent is accounted for by transitory factors, if these are defined as factors present in 1933 but not in 1934. As would be expected, the transitory component is uniformly larger if the comparison year is one year removed from the base year than if it immediately precedes or follows the base year.

$$a = K_1 \bar{x}_2, \text{ or}$$

$$(2) \quad K_1 = \frac{a}{\bar{x}_2}.$$

The first formula for K_1 can be derived from this one by substituting for a its equivalent,

$$\bar{x}_2 - b_{21} \bar{x}_1.$$

From equation (1) of footnote 11 it can be shown that under the variability assumption

$$(3) \quad K'_1 = 1 - b_{21}\frac{s_1}{s_2}.$$

If the regression is fitted by least squares

$$(4) \quad b_{21} = r\frac{s_2}{s_1},$$

where r is the correlation coefficient. Hence,

$$(5) \quad K'_1 = 1 - r.$$

It follows that if K'_2 is the proportionate contribution of the transitory component in year 2 computed from data for years 1 and 2 under the variability assumption,

$$K'_1 = K'_2.$$

I.e., if we use the variability assumption, transitory factors must be attributed the same strength in the two years. This was pointed out in somewhat different form in footnote 11.

As was also implied in that footnote, under the mean assumption $K_1 \gtreqless K_2$ if $V_1 \gtreqless V_2$, where V is the coefficient of variation for the profession in the year designated by the subscript. This can be shown by substituting (4) into (1), and the formula for b_{12} corresponding to (4) into the formula for K_2 corresponding to (1).

TABLE 58

Percentage Contribution of Transitory Component
to Deviation of Average Income for Each Income Class
from Average Income for Profession

		PERCENTAGE CONTRIBUTION OF TRANSITORY COMPONENT			
BASE YEAR	COMPARISON YEAR	Physicians	Dentists	Lawyers	Certified public accountants
1932	1933	10.0	11.5	9.7	14.0
1933	1932	3.7	6.70	11.7	10.1
1933	1934	9.0	12.4	15.5	13.0
1934	1933	4.2	3.4	10.7	9.1
1932	1934	15.7	18.0	14.5	22.4
1934	1932	9.5	6.71	15.8	19.0
1934	1935				14.7
1935	1934				3.8
1935	1936				9.6
1936	1935				6.2
1934	1936				19.4
1936	1934				7.5

Percentage contributions computed from formula (1) of footnote 15, using
weighted b's in Table 60 and actual means.

There is nothing in the arithmetic of the computation that
makes such a result inevitable; indeed, the arithmetic does not
preclude negative percentage contributions, though no sen-
sible meaning could be attributed to them. Our failure to get
any illogical results is evidence in support of the assumptions
on which the analysis is based.[16]

Our earlier finding that transitory factors are more important for lawyers and accountants than for physicians and dentists is reflected in the percentage contributions: in four of the
six possible comparisons, the percentage contribution is less

[16] Had we used the original b's instead of the weighted b's in computing the
percentage contributions, we would have gotten two negative contributions,
both for dentists, base year 1934. (See footnote 7 for the reason we computed
weighted b's.) The use of the weighted b's also explains why there are no
entries in Table 58 for years prior to 1932.

Negative contributions are impossible if the variability assumption is used
in place of the mean assumption. This is obvious from equation (5) in footnote
15.

for physicians and dentists than for either lawyers or accountants; in the other two, the percentage contributions for physicians and dentists are between those for lawyers and accountants. In three of the four professions, the factors present in 1932 but not in 1933 were more important than those present in 1933 but not in 1932; in all four, the latter were less important than those present in 1933 but not in 1934, and these in turn were more important than those present in 1934 but not in 1933.[17] Apparently there were some factors associated with the downswing that carried over into 1932 but not through 1933; some did carry over into 1933, but were apparently eliminated in the course of the upswing that followed. This interpretation is confirmed by the percentage contributions for accountants for the later years, which are on the whole lower than those for the earlier years.

APPENDIX TO CHAPTER 7

1 STATISTICAL TESTS OF THE LINEARITY OF REGRESSION BETWEEN INCOME IN TWO YEARS

Linearity of regression is ordinarily tested by an analysis of variance that is equivalent to testing the significance of the difference between the squared correlation ratio and the squared correlation coefficient. The observations are grouped by the value of the independent variable (here, income in the base

17 Despite the statement in the last paragraph of footnote 15 these changes do not parallel the changes in the coefficient of variation. The reason is that the percentage contribution is based on the weighted b's, which are not given by formula (4) of footnote 15 if the correlation coefficient and standard deviations are computed from the original data. It is interesting that the changes described in the text are slightly more consistent than those in the coefficients of variation.

year), and the mean value of the dependent variable (income in the other year) is computed for each class. Two estimates of variance are then computed. (1) The difference between each class mean and the corresponding ordinate of a regression equation fitted by the ordinary least squares procedure is squared, multiplied by the number of observations on which the mean is based, and summed for all base year income classes. The resulting sum of squares divided by the proper number of degrees of freedom (two fewer than the number of classes) gives an estimate of variance based on the deviations of the means about the regression. (2) The difference between each observation and the mean of the class in which it falls is squared and summed for all observations. The resulting sum of squares divided by the proper number of degrees of freedom (the number of observations minus the number of classes) gives an estimate of variance based on the deviations of the observations about the class means.[1]

If a linear regression adequately describes the relation between the two variables, the deviations of the class means from the regression reflect chance fluctuation alone; consequently, the variance of the means about the regression should be equal to the variance of the observations about the means. Of course, the two are rarely exactly equal. Whether the linear regression is adequate thus turns on whether the first estimate of variance exceeds the second by more than can reasonably be attributed to chance alone. The ratio of the first variance to the second, called the analysis of variance ratio and denoted by F, fluctuates in repeated random samples from a normal universe in a known manner; published tables give the values of F that would be exceeded by chance in 20, 5, 1, and 0.1 per cent of random samples for many pairs of degrees of freedom.[2]

Values of the analysis of variance ratio computed in the manner described are given for the 1935 medical, dental, and legal samples, and for the 1935 and 1937 accountancy samples in the columns of Table 59 headed 'original'. At the bottom of the table are the approximate values of F that would be exceeded by chance in 5,

1 In practice, of course, short-cut methods are used to compute the two sums of squares; see R. A. Fisher, *Statistical Methods for Research Workers* (London: Oliver and Boyd, 1925), Sec. 44, 45, 46.
2 R. A. Fisher and F. Yates, *Statistical Tables for Biological, Agricultural, and Medical Research* (London: Oliver and Boyd, 1938), Table V.

TABLE 59

Tests of Linearity of Regression between Incomes in Different Years

Physicians, Dentists, Lawyers, and Certified Public Accountants

ANALYSIS OF VARIANCE RATIO (F)

REGRESSION	PHYSICIANS Original	Weighted	DENTISTS Original	Weighted	LAWYERS [1] Original	Weighted	CERTIFIED PUBLIC ACCOUNTANTS [2] Original	Weighted
1933 on 1932	4.32	1.23	5.13	.84	7.37	2.60	5.61	1.11
1932 on 1933	31.69	1.88	5.54	1.47	6.52	1.41	3.03	.72
1934 on 1933	9.55	1.02	4.22	.89	15.80	1.20	7.30	.63
1933 on 1934	8.54	1.87	7.92	1.49	9.93	1.06	5.24	1.64
1934 on 1932	7.22	.68	2.81	1.17	10.68	1.23	5.16	1.26
1932 on 1934	5.78	1.13	5.51	1.20	7.02	.92	1.05	.63
1935 on 1934							9.99	10.29
1934 on 1935							4.66	.94
1936 on 1935							5.54	1.05
1935 on 1936							1.18	1.09
1936 on 1934							6.14	8.08
1934 on 1936							3.45	.78

PROPORTION OF RANDOM SAMPLES IN WHICH VALUE OF F WOULD BE EXCEEDED	APPROXIMATE VALUE OF F THAT WOULD BE EXCEEDED BY CHANCE [3]
1 in 20	1.55
1 in 100	1.85
1 in 1,000	2.20

[1] Individual practitioners only. Excludes in both original and weighted analysis for 1932–33 and 1933–34 one return reporting an income of $8,357 in 1932; $50,471 in 1933; $3,165 in 1934.

[2] Individual practitioners only. Excludes in both original and weighted analysis for the 1935 sample one return reporting an income of $41,000 in 1932; −$19,000 in 1933; $13,000 in 1934.

[3] Precise values of F vary because of differences in the number of degrees of freedom. They are slightly lower for physicians and slightly higher for the other professions. However, in no case would the probability attached to a variance ratio be altered by using the exact significance values. The number of degrees of freedom for means about the regression varies from 25 to 28 for physicians, 19 to 22 for dentists, 21 to 24 for lawyers, and 20 to 22 for accountants (both samples). The number of degrees of freedom for observations about the means varies from 1,350 to 1,416 for physicians, 996 to 1,036 for dentists, 650 to 705 for lawyers, 752 to 809 for the 1935 accountancy sample, and 450 to 483 for the 1937 accountancy sample.

1, and 0.1 per cent of random samples.[3] All except two of the thirty variance ratios are larger than the value of F that would be exceeded by chance in one in a thousand random samples, and most

[3] The values are 'approximate' because the number of degrees of freedom for the means about the regression and for the observations about the means are not the same for all professions and regressions. The variation in the number of degrees of freedom is too slight to justify giving separate significance values of F for each regression or profession. The use of exact significance values would not alter the probability attached to any variance ratio.

of them are very much larger. If the variance ratios were taken at face value we should be forced to conclude that the regression between incomes in two years is very definitely not linear.

The variance ratios cannot, however, be taken at face value. The significance values of F at the bottom of Table 59 that were used as the basis of comparison are computed on the assumption that the variance of the observations about the means is the same for all classes and that the observations are drawn from a normal universe. Consequently, in comparing the computed F's with these significance values we are in effect testing the composite hypothesis that (1) the regression is linear, (2) the variance of the observations about the means is the same for all classes, and (3) the observations in each class are a random sample from a normal universe. Chart 26 demonstrates conclusively that the variance of the observations about the means is not the same for all income classes and Chart 1 and Table 12 as well as the frequency distributions in Appendix B, suggest strongly that the distribution of the observations is far from normal.[4] Consequently, the high values of F may reflect the failure of these two conditions to be satisfied rather than nonlinearity of regression.

a Effect of unequal variances

The description of how the two estimates of variance are computed makes it clear that the contribution of each class to the sum of the squares of the observations about class means is proportional to the number of observations in the class minus one, but that all classes contribute equally to the sum of the squares of the means about the regression.[5] Chart 26 demonstrates that after a brief

[4] The evidence on nonnormality cited is not conclusive since it pertains to the distribution as a whole, whereas the relevant question in the present connection is the distribution of the observations within each base year income class. Inspection of these distributions tends to confirm the indication given by the distribution for each year as a whole: they too are definitely not normal but tend to be skewed.

[5] There is no inconsistency between this statement and the fact that the square of the difference between the class mean and the corresponding ordinate of the regression equation is multiplied by the number of observations on which the mean is based. The square of the difference between the class mean and the regression equation gives an estimate of the variance of a mean; the variance of a mean is the variance of an individual observation divided by the number of observations on which the mean is based; multiplication by the number of ob-

initial decline, the variance of the observations about the class mean increases consistently with the base year income. Moreover, the number of observations in an income class at first increases and then decreases with income so that the low and intermediate income classes include the most observations. Consequently, the high income classes, which have few observations, receive a much greater weight in the variance of the means about the regression than in the variance of the observations about the means. Since the high income classes have large variances, the former variance would consequently tend to exceed the latter, and the analysis of variance ratio would tend to exceed unity, even though the means differed from the regressions solely because of chance fluctuations.

If we knew the relations among the variances of the different income classes, we could correct for this bias in the F's and test the hypothesis of linearity without assuming equal variance by weighting both the sums of the squares within classes and the squared differences between the class means and the regression by numbers proportional to the reciprocals of the class variances.[6] Since we do not know the relations among the variances of the different income classes, we estimated them from the data. Forced on us by our lack of knowledge, this procedure is not entirely accurate since estimating the relations among the variances uses up an unknown number of degrees of freedom, for which no allowance was made.

---

servations merely converts an estimate of the variance of a mean into an estimate of the variance of an individual observation. The essential point in the present connection is rather that each additional class increases by one the number of degrees of freedom of means about the regression, but increases the number of degrees of freedom of observations about means by the number of observations in the class minus one.

[6] Let $\sigma_i^2 = w_i \sigma_0^2$, where σ_i^2 is the 'true' variance of the i-th income class, and σ_0^2, the 'true' variance of an income class selected as the base. The sum of squared deviations of the observations in the i-th class from their mean divided by $n_i - 1$, where n_i is the number of observations in the i-th class, is an estimate of σ_i^2 based on $n_i - 1$ degrees of freedom. The squared deviation of the class mean from the regression multiplied by n_i is also an estimate of σ_i^2 if the 'true' regression is linear. If divided by w_i, these estimates are converted into estimates of σ_0^2, which, by definition and unlike σ_i^2, is constant for all income classes. Consequently, the weighted sum of squared deviations about the class means divided by the total number of degrees of freedom within classes and the weighted sum of squared deviations of means about the regression divided by the corresponding number of degrees of freedom both give estimates of the same thing, namely σ_0^2, if $1/w_i$ is used as the weight for the i-th class.

The method used to estimate the relations among the variances was to construct a chart for each sample similar to the sections of Chart 26 but based on class variances rather than standard deviations, and giving the points for each year rather than their average. The variance of each income class was expressed as a ratio to the mean variance for all classes, i.e., as a ratio to the denominator of the corresponding analysis of variance ratio in the columns of Table 59 headed 'original', and plotted against the midpoint of the proper base year income class. A free hand curve was drawn through the resulting scatter and extended to cover very high or very low income classes containing a single observation and therefore giving no estimates of the class variance though contributing to the sum of the squares of the class means about the regression.[7] The ordinates of the free hand curve corresponding to the successive income classes were read from the graphs and their reciprocals used as weights. The use of a single curve for all regressions from the same sample minimizes the number of degrees of freedom used in obtaining the weights. At the same time, the scatter about the final free hand curve was usually very large and the curve often had to be extrapolated a considerable distance in order to get weights for all income classes. In consequence, a large element of personal judgment entered into the determination of the weights and seriously limits the confidence that can be attached to the results.

The inequality of the class variances not only imparts an upward bias to the analysis of variance ratios but also renders the regressions computed by the ordinary least squares method inappropriate. A new set of regression equations was therefore computed by weighting the observations by the reciprocals of the ordinates of the free hand curve described in the preceding paragraph, i.e., by weighting the observations inversely to their estimated variances. These are the regressions plotted in Chart 25. The constants of both the original and weighted regressions are given in Table 60.

The weights from the free hand curves fitted to the variances and the weighted regressions make it possible to compute analysis of variance ratios that are independent of the assumption that the class variance is the same for all income classes. These analysis of

[7] We resorted to the use of free hand curves only after considerable experimentation with fitting mathematical functions to the class variances. No relatively simple function gave anything approaching an adequate fit.

TABLE 60

Constants of Original and Weighted Regression Equations

	CONSTANTS [1]			
	Original		Weighted	
REGRESSION	a	b	a	b
Physicians				
1930 on 1929	169	.876		
1931 on 1929	237	.749		
1932 on 1929	243	.546		
1933 on 1932	217	.866	285	.841
1932 on 1933	278	.976	136	1.031
1934 on 1933	154	1.108	259	1.057
1933 on 1934	174	.809	124	.825
1934 on 1932	309	.984	522	.912
1932 on 1934	413	.804	312	.837
Dentists				
1930 on 1929	389	.875		
1931 on 1929	353	.749		
1932 on 1929	355	.541		
1933 on 1932	235	.810	286	.791
1932 on 1933	74	1.090	160	1.044
1934 on 1933	395	.963	329	.979
1933 on 1934	—45	.910	81	.864
1934 on 1932	535	.804	503	.816
1932 on 1934	—49	1.022	167	.937
Lawyers [2]				
1933 on 1932	440	.726	258	.795
1932 on 1933	451	.957	289	1.004
1934 on 1933	274	1.000	366	.940
1933 on 1934	464	.730	283	.804
1934 on 1932	445	.818	425	.833
1932 on 1934	729	.770	473	.865
Certified Public Accountants [3]				
1930 on 1929	1,048	.769		
1931 on 1929	1,197	.605		
1932 on 1929	1,152	.480		
1933 on 1932	497	.818	489	.824
1932 on 1933	562	.879	379	.939
1934 on 1933	681	.909	524	.969
1933 on 1934	330	.808	291	.816
1934 on 1932	1,085	.754	889	.823
1932 on 1934	883	.708	666	.764
1935 on 1934	731	.890	561	.933
1934 on 1935	629	.755	228	.880

TABLE 60 (cont.)

	CONSTANTS [1]			
	Original		Weighted	
REGRESSION	a	b	a	b
Certified Public Accountants [3] (cont.)				
1936 on 1935	831	.931	461	1.038
1935 on 1936	277	.808	262	.817
1936 on 1934	978	.963	818	.998
1934 on 1936	439	.708	304	.747
Consulting Engineers [4]				
1930 on 1929	1,436	.724		
1931 on 1929	165	.585		
1932 on 1929	195	.302		

[1] General equation: $y = a + bx$, where $x =$ independent variable (income in base year); $y =$ dependent variable (income in other year); $a =$ intercept; $b =$ slope.

[2] Individual practitioners only. In computing both original and weighted constants for the 1932–33 and 1933–34 regressions, we excluded one return reporting an income of \$8,357 in 1932; \$50,471 in 1933; \$3,165 in 1934.

[3] Individual practitioners only. In computing both original and weighted constants for the 1935 sample, we excluded one return reporting an income of \$41,000 in 1932; — \$19,000 in 1933; \$13,000 in 1934.

[4] Individual practitioners only.

variance ratios are given in the columns of Table 59 headed 'weighted'. As already implied, these F's were obtained by the same procedure as the original F's except that the class means were expressed as deviations from the weighted regressions and that both the sum of the squares of the observations about the means and the sum of the squares of means about the regressions are weighted sums. All except two of the weighted F's are smaller than the original F's and most of the former are a small fraction of the latter. Whereas 28 of the 30 original F's are larger than the value of F that would be exceeded by chance in less than one in a thousand random samples, only three of the weighted F's are so large; two of the other 27 weighted F's would be exceeded by chance in less than one in a hundred random samples, and one, in less than one in twenty. The remaining 24 values would be exceeded by chance more than once in twenty times and hence are entirely consistent with the hypothesis that the regressions are linear. Moreover, the two largest weighted F's—those for the 1935 on 1934 and 1936 on

1934 accountancy regressions—reflect not a consistent departure from linearity but the wide deviations from the regressions of two of the almost 500 observations on which they are based. If these two observations are eliminated, the F's are reduced from 10.29 and 8.09 to 1.19 and .97 respectively.[8]

The weighted analysis strongly suggests that linearity of regression is the rule and that the high values of the original F's reflect the inequality of class variances rather than nonlinearity of the regressions. However, for the time being at least, this conclusion too must be accepted with the greatest reservation. For just as the extremely high values of the original F's reflect the inequality of the variances, so the low values of the weighted F's may conceivably reflect the nonnormality of the income distributions—the third element of our original three-pronged hypothesis.

b Effect of nonnormality

Several studies suggest that the effect of nonnormality on the analysis of variance is not serious.[9] However, since they related to effects of moderate departures from normality, whereas our data are markedly nonnormal, they do not justify the assumption that our results are equally little affected.

Unfortunately, we know no way of correcting adequately for the influence of nonnormality without more exact knowledge of the distribution of income for base year income classes than we possess, i.e., without knowing the equation of a mathematical formula that adequately describes these distributions. Some indirect indication of the possible effect of nonnormality is given by the efficiency of the ordinary estimate of variance for data whose logarithms are normally distributed. In the discussion in footnote 2 to Chapter 3 it was noted that though the logarithmic normal

[8] The two observations eliminated have the values: (1) 1934, $0; 1935, $7,856; 1936, $8,331; (2) 1934, —$5,903; 1935, $8,744; 1936, $5,926. The results of eliminating each observation separately are as follows:

	F FOR	
	1935 on 1934	1936 on 1934
Eliminating return (1)	2.70	1.60
Eliminating return (2)	9.26	7.86

[9] See E. S. Pearson, 'The Analysis of Variance in Cases of Non-normal Variation', *Biometrika*, 1931; and T. Eden and F. Yates, 'On the Validity of Fisher's *z* Test When Applied to an Actual Example of Non-normal Data', *Journal of Agricultural Science*, Jan. 1933.

curve does not describe income distributions adequately, it is probably better than any of the other curves suggested.

Let x represent the original observations and y their natural logarithms (i.e., logarithms to the base e); let μ_y and σ_y be the 'true' mean and standard deviation respectively of the logarithms of the observations, i.e., of the normal curve according to which the logarithms are distributed; and μ_x and σ_x the 'true' mean and standard deviation respectively of the observations themselves. The best estimates [10] of μ_y and σ_y from a sample of observations are given by the usual formulae:

(1) Estimate of $\mu_y = \dfrac{\Sigma y}{n} = \dfrac{\Sigma \log x}{n} = \bar{y} = \overline{\log x}$;

(2) Estimate of $\sigma_y = \sqrt{\dfrac{\Sigma(y - \bar{y}^2)}{n - 1}} = \sqrt{\dfrac{\Sigma(\log x - \overline{\log x})^2}{n - 1}} = s_y$,

where n is the number of observations in the sample. The best estimates of μ_x and σ_x are not, however, given by the usual formulae but by

(3) Estimate of $\mu_x = e^{\bar{y} + \frac{s_y^2}{2}} = \bar{x}$;

(4) Estimate of $\sigma_x = \left(e^{\bar{y} + \frac{s_y^2}{2}} \right) \sqrt{e^{s_y^2} - 1} = s_x$.

That is, the logarithm to the base e of the best estimate of the mean of x is the mean of the logarithms plus one-half the variance of the logarithms; to get the best estimate of the standard deviation of x we must find the value whose logarithm to the base e is the variance of the logarithms, subtract unity, take the square root, and multiply by the best estimate of the mean of x obtained as just described.[11]

[10] In what follows the 'best estimates' will be interpreted as the maximum likelihood estimates.

[11] If common instead of natural logarithms are used, i.e., if the logarithms are taken to the base 10 instead of to the base e, the formulae for the best estimates of μ_x and σ_x become:

Estimate of $\mu_x = 10^{\bar{y} + 1.151295\, s_y^2}$

Estimate of $\sigma_x = 10^{\bar{y} + 1.151295\, s_y^2} \sqrt{10^{2.30259\, s_y^2} - 1}$,

where $\bar{y}$ and s_y^2 are computed by the ordinary formulae from the common logarithms of the observations.

The efficiency of an estimate of a parameter is defined as the ratio of the variance of the best estimate of the parameter to the variance of the estimate under consideration. Let $\bar{x}'$ and s'_x be estimates of the mean and standard deviations of the observations computed by the usual formulae (i.e., formulae like (1) and (2) but applied to the original observations). It can be shown that the efficiency of $\bar{x}'$ is given by

$$(5) \quad \frac{\sigma_{\bar{x}}^2}{\sigma_{\bar{x}'}^2} = \frac{\sigma_y^2 + \frac{\sigma_y^4}{2}}{e^{\sigma_y^2} - 1} ;$$

the efficiency of $(s'_x)^2$, i.e., of the estimate of the variance of the original observations computed by the usual formula, by

$$(6) \quad \frac{\sigma_{s_x^2}^2}{\sigma_{(s'_x)^2}^2} = \frac{2\,\sigma_y^2\left[2(e^{\sigma_y^2} - 1)^2 + (2e^{\sigma_y^2} - 1)^2\,\sigma_y^2\right]}{e^{6\,\sigma_y^2} - 4\,e^{3\,\sigma_y^2} - e^{2\,\sigma_y^2} + 8\,e^{\sigma_y^2} - 4}.$$

As equations (5) and (6) indicate, the efficiency of the ordinary estimates of the mean and variance of observations from a logarithmically normal population depends on the variance of that population. It is, consequently, impossible to give any general indication of their efficiency. However, in the course of experimenting with alternative methods of testing the linearity of the regressions we computed the variance of the logarithms of the observations about their class means for the 1933 on 1934 accountancy regression. For this special case [12] the efficiency of the ordinary estimate is approximately 99.5 per cent for the mean and 80 per cent for the variance. The loss of information through using the ordinary estimate is negligible for the mean, but sizable for the variance.[13]

The possible inefficiency of the ordinary estimate of variance, if the observations are drawn from a logarithmically normal population, strongly suggests, though it does not conclusively demonstrate, that an analysis of variance of the type used above is an

[12] The mean intraclass variance of the logarithms to the base e is .14135 for income classes above \$1,500. This figure is used in the text in estimating the efficiency of the mean and variance.

[13] If the mean variance of the logarithms is estimated for income classes above \$500, instead of above \$1,500, as in the preceding footnote, it becomes .26738. The efficiency of the mean is then 99 per cent, but of the variance only 59 per cent.

inefficient test of linearity. But whether or not this deduction can validly be made, it is clear that marked departures from normality can affect greatly the validity of statistical tests based on variances; and that in consequence, little confidence can be placed in the results of tests assuming normality when, as in the present instance, the data to which they are applied are known to deviate widely from normality.

c An alternative test of linearity [14]

A test of linearity that is independent of the assumptions of equal class variance and normal distributions can be based on the diagrams of Chart 25. Each diagram of Chart 25 shows ten points and a regression equation fitted to them. We can ask whether there is any consistency in the deviations of the points from the different regressions for the same profession.

An example designed to answer this question is Table 61, based on the nine regressions for physicians. Each column corresponds to one point on the diagrams of Chart 25—column 1 to the first point, column 2 to the second, and so on. Each row of the table is for a particular regression. The pluses and minuses indicate whether the point is above or below the relevant regression; a zero indicates that the point falls exactly on the regression line.[15] At the bottom of the table are entered the number of pluses and minuses in each row, and the total number of pluses and minuses in the table.

If the regressions are not really linear we should expect the points to differ systematically from the straight line. For example, if the true regression were convex to the horizontal axis, the first few points and the last few points should be consistently above the fitted straight line, and the intermediate points consistently below. This would be reflected in a preponderance of pluses in the first few columns of Table 61, of minuses in the intermediate columns, and of pluses in the last few columns. On the other hand, if regressions deviate little from linearity, the pluses and minuses should be randomly distributed; the proportion of pluses in each column should be approximately the same as in the whole table. To test

[14] This test was suggested by a procedure applied to an analogous problem by G. H. Moore and W. A. Wallis.
[15] At least, to the number of significant figures to which we have carried our computations.

whether the pluses and minuses are randomly distributed among the columns we can treat the two rows giving the number of pluses and minuses in each column as a two-by-ten contingency table, compute χ^2 for the table, and see how frequently the observed value of χ^2 would be exceeded by chance.[16] For Table 61, χ^2 is 14.6 and would be exceeded by chance in about one-tenth of random samples. The table gives no evidence of consistent departure from linearity.

TABLE 61

Test of Consistency of Deviation of Points from Regressions

Physicians

REGRESSION	SIGN OF DEVIATION FROM REGRESSION OF POINT NUMBER										TOTAL
	1	*2*	*3*	*4*	*5*	*6*	*7*	*8*	*9*	*10*	
1930 on 1929	+	−	o	+	+	−	+	−	+	o	
1931 on 1929	+	−	−	+	+	+	+	−	+	+	
1932 on 1929	+	−	−	−	+	+	+	−	+	−	
1933 on 1932	−	+	−	−	+	+	+	−	−	+	
1932 on 1933	+	+	−	−	+	+	−	+	−	−	
1934 on 1933	+	+	−	−	−	−	+	+	+	+	
1933 on 1934	+	+	+	+	+	+	−	−	−	−	
1934 on 1932	−	+	−	−	+	+	+	−	−	+	
1932 on 1934	+	−	+	−	−	+	−	+	−	+	
Number of +'s	7	5	2.5	3	7	7	6	2	5	5.5	50
Number of −'s	2	4	6.5	6	2	2	3	7	4	3.5	40
Total	9	9	9	9	9	9	9	9	9		

Weighted regressions for 1935 sample; regressions fitted to ten plotted points for 1933 sample.

Before presenting the results for the other professions, we note one limitation of this test. While it makes no assumption about normality or equal variance it does assume that the items in each column are independent. Our data do not satisfy this assumption. The different regressions for any one sample are based on data for essentially the same individuals. Even more serious is the interdependence among the regressions for which the base year is the same; for these, each base year income class includes essentially the same individuals. For example, both the 1933 on 1932 and 1934 on 1932 regressions summarize the average incomes of individuals grouped by their 1932 income. If the individuals in a particular

16 See Fisher, *Statistical Methods for Research Workers*, Sec. 21.

1932 income class have an abnormally high average income in 1933 there is some reason to suppose that they will have an abnormally high income also in 1934. This interdependence among the items in the same class tends to make for a concentration of pluses or minuses and hence imparts an upward bias to χ^2.

The importance of this interdependence is revealed by pairing the regressions from the same sample in two ways: first, into pairs with the same base year, e.g., the regressions 1933 on 1932, and 1934 on 1932, the regressions 1932 on 1933, and 1934 on 1933, and so on; second, into pairs with different base years but the same second year, e.g., the regressions 1932 on 1933, and 1932 on 1934, the regressions 1933 on 1932, and 1933 on 1934, and so on. For each pair we can count the points for which the signs entered in tables like Table 61 agree. For example, the 1933 on 1932, and 1934 on 1932 regressions for physicians agree in sign for all ten points. If this is done for all professions and all pairs of regressions from the 1935 and 1937 samples, the number of agreements in sign is 101 out of 150 for pairs with the same base year but only 76 out of 150 for pairs with different base years.[17] The effect of the interdependence is far from negligible.

The values of χ^2 computed from tables similar to Table 61, and the probability that each would be exceeded by chance, follow.[18] In view of the bias toward large values of χ^2 arising from the

PROFESSION	χ^2	PROBABILITY OF BEING EXCEEDED BY CHANCE
Physicians	14.6	.10
Dentists	18.2	.03
Lawyers	18.2	.03
Certified public accountants	24.5	.004

interdependence of regressions from the same sample, only the χ^2 for accountants, for whom this bias is least since data are available from three samples, seems sufficiently large to establish even a presumption in favor of nonlinearity. The χ^2 for both dentists and lawyers are indeed larger than the values we should ordinarily be willing to attribute to chance, but both are very close to the ordinary borderline of significance—a probability of .05—and, in

---

17 The difference between 101 and 76 is about three times its standard error.
18 No χ^2 is given for engineers since only three regressions are available.

addition, the χ^2 for lawyers is based on a single sample and hence is most subject to bias.

We are thus led to the conclusion enunciated in the text of this chapter; namely, that accountancy is the one profession for which there is a tolerably clear indication that the regression is not linear.

2   THE ANALYSIS OF CHANGES IN RELATIVE INCOME STATUS FOR PERIODS LONGER THAN TWO YEARS

Section 2 of this chapter outlines a procedure for interpreting changes in relative income status between any two years. The present section sketches a generalization of this procedure applicable to a period of any length. This generalized procedure is embodied in an appendix rather than in the text; first, because it is tentative and intended to be suggestive rather than definitive, second, because our data are not entirely suited to its application.

The dichotomy between permanent and transitory components of a man's income, as was noted above, necessarily does violence to the facts. An accurate description of the factors determining a man's income must substitute a continuum for the dichotomy. This continuum is bounded at one extreme by 'truly' permanent factors—those that affect a man's income throughout his career— and at the other by the 'truly' transitory—those that affect his income only during a single time unit, where a time unit is the shortest period during which it seems desirable to measure income, in our case, a year, but conceivably a month, a week, a day, an hour, or even a minute. Between these extremes fall what may be called 'quasi-permanent' factors, factors whose effects neither disappear at once nor last throughout a man's career. The quasi-permanent factors can be ordered according to the length of time during which their effects persist: two-year factors, three-year factors, etc.

A man's income can then be conceived as the sum of the parts attributable to each set of factors:

$$\text{Income in any year} = \text{permanent component} \\ + \text{quasi-permanent component} \\ + \text{transitory component.}$$

The quasi-permanent component in any year can in turn be expressed as:

Quasi-permanent component = (two-year component ending this year

+ three-year component ending this year

+ four-year component ending this year

+ etc.)

+ (two-year component ending next year

+ three-year component ending next year

+ four-year component ending next year

+ etc.)

+ (three-year component ending year after next

+ four-year component ending year after next

+ etc.)

+ etc.

This framework classifies factors affecting income according to the length of time during which their effects are present and the year in which their effects come to an end. How far the classification is carried depends on the period covered by the analysis. For example, if a three-year period is considered, the classification would stop with two-year components. A three-year component ending in the third year of the period would be permanent for these three years, a three-year component ending in the second year of the period would be equivalent to a two-year component ending in that year, and so on.

We can symbolize these relations for a three-year period (years 1, 2, and 3) as follows:

$$(1) \quad \begin{aligned} x'_1 &= p'_1 + t'_1 + q'_{11} + q'_{12}; \\ x'_2 &= p'_2 + t'_2 \qquad\quad + q'_{22} + q'_{23}; \\ x'_3 &= p'_3 + t'_3 \qquad\qquad\qquad + q'_{33} + q'_{34}, \end{aligned}$$

where x' is income; p', the component that is permanent for the three years considered; t', the transitory component; q', the quasi-permanent component, in this case, a two-year component; the subscripts to x', p', and t' denote the year in which the income, permanent component, and transitory component are received; the first subscript to q' denotes the year in which it is received, and the second, the year in which the component ends (i.e., the last year in which income is affected by the factors responsible for this component).

As already noted, the components that summarize the effects of factors present in two of the three years, for example, q'_{12} and q'_{22}, may include the final (or for q'_{23} and q'_{33}, the initial) effects of factors present for more than two years. From the point of view of the three years, however, these partial effects are indistinguishable from two-year effects proper. In the same way, data for this three-year period alone would never permit the segregation of those effects in year 1 that are a carry-over from preceding years but do not continue into the future (q'_{11}) from the purely transitory effects (t'_1); q'_{11} and t'_1, and in similar fashion q'_{34} and t'_3, will necessarily be merged in the data. We split the component present in year 1 (or year 3) but not in the other two years into two parts in order to get comparable components for different years. What will appear from the data to be transitory for year 1 ($q'_{11} + t'_1$) or for year 3 ($q'_{34} + t'_3$) is not comparable with what will appear from the data to be transitory for year 2 (t'_2).

It follows from the considerations just advanced that lengthening the period to four years, which would involve introducing three-year components, will leave the content of t'_1, t'_2, and t'_3 unchanged, but will reduce the content of the p' and q' terms, i.e., of the permanent and quasi-permanent components. It follows also that while we might hope from data for three years to segregate the permanent, quasi-permanent, and transitory components of year 2 incomes, we cannot do so for year 1 or year 3 unless we assume each component equally important in all years; otherwise, the quasi-permanent and transitory components will be merged.

Our analysis has so far precisely paralleled the two-year analysis in Section 2 of this chapter. At this point we part company with that analysis for a time. Instead of attempting to segregate the different components for a particular income class, we shall outline a procedure for estimating the average importance of each component for all income classes combined. This will lead to an alternative interpretation of the percentage contributions presented in Table 58. We shall then return to the problem of segregating the components for each income class separately. As in the analysis in the text of the chapter, however, some assumption about the relation between permanent (and quasi-permanent) components in different years must be made. We shall consider two alternative assumptions: the one used in the text of the chapter, designated the 'mean assumption'; and the one used in footnotes 11, 14, and 15 of the chapter, designated the 'variability assumption'.

a The mean assumption

For a group of men in practice the same number of years it seems reasonable to assume that the permanent and quasi-permanent components change in proportion to the change in the arithmetic mean income of the group as a whole; i.e., that factors common to several years would, if they alone were present, lead to a constant ratio between a man's income and average income in the profession. This ratio could then serve as a measure of relative income status. The same assumption would not seem reasonable for a group of men in practice varying numbers of years. Permanent forces whose effects depend on 'experience' would then lead to changes in income ratios: the ratios would tend to rise over time for the younger men, and to fall for older men past their peak earnings. Even for men in practice the same number of years the assumption is doubtless not entirely valid. The 'earnings life cycle' probably depends in a consistent fashion on other permanent factors; for example, it is probably different for physicians who specialize than for physicians who engage in general practice. However, eliminating the influence of differences in the number of years in practice probably eliminates most of the changes in the permanent and quasi-permanent components not related to changes in general economic conditions in the profession.

i *The procedure.*[19] In symbols, the mean assumption can be written:

$$\frac{p_1'}{x_1'} = \frac{p_2'}{x_2'} = \frac{p_3'}{x_3'} = p;$$

$$(2) \quad \frac{q_{12}'}{x_1'} = \frac{q_{22}'}{x_2'} = q_2;$$

$$\frac{q_{23}'}{x_2'} = \frac{q_{33}'}{x_3'} = q_3,$$

[19] The reader not interested in the derivation of the procedure should pass directly to Section 2a ii below.

where $\bar{x}'$ is the arithmetic mean income in the year indicated by the subscript. Dividing the equations (1) by the corresponding mean incomes, we have

$$(3) \quad \begin{aligned} x_1 &= p + t_1 + q_1 + q_2; \\ x_2 &= p + t_2 + q_2 + q_3; \\ x_3 &= p + t_3 + q_3 + q_4, \end{aligned}$$

where $x = x'/\bar{x}'$; $t = t'/\bar{x}'$, the subscripts indicating the year; and $q_1 = q'_{11}/\bar{x}'_1$; $q_4 = q'_{34}/\bar{x}'_3$.

If the different components of the income of any year are uncorrelated (i.e., if $r_{pt} = r_{pq} = r_{tq} = r_{q_1 q_2} = r_{q_2 q_3} = r_{q_3 q_4} = 0$, where r is the correlation coefficient between the variables indicated by the subscripts), then

$$(4) \quad s^2_{x_1} = s^2_p + s^2_{t_1} + s^2_{q_1} + s^2_{q_2};$$

$$(5) \quad s^2_{x_2} = s^2_p + s^2_{t_2} + s^2_{q_2} + s^2_{q_3};$$

$$(6) \quad s^2_{x_3} = s^2_p + s^2_{t_3} + s^2_{q_3} + s^2_{q_4},$$

where s stands for the standard deviation of the variable indicated by the subscript. The standard deviation of the income ratio (x) is of course equal to the coefficient of variation of actual income (x').

If further, the transitory components in different years are uncorrelated (i.e., $r_{t_1 t_2} = r_{t_1 t_3} = r_{t_2 t_3} = 0$), then

$$(7) \quad r_{x_1 x_2} s_{x_1} s_{x_2} = s^2_p + s^2_{q_2};$$

$$(8) \quad r_{x_2 x_3} s_{x_2} s_{x_3} = s^2_p + s^2_{q_3};$$

$$(9) \quad r_{x_1 x_3} s_{x_1} s_{x_3} = s^2_p.$$

From equations (4) through (9),

$$(10) \quad s^2_p = r_{x_1 x_3} s_{x_1} s_{x_3} = (9);$$

$$(11) \quad s^2_{q_2} = r_{x_1 x_2} s_{x_1} s_{x_2} - r_{x_1 x_3} s_{x_1} s_{x_3} = (7) - (9);$$

$$(12) \quad s^2_{q_3} = r_{x_2 x_3} s_{x_2} s_{x_3} - r_{x_1 x_3} s_{x_1} s_{x_3} = (8) - (9);$$

$$(13) \quad s^2_{t_2} = s^2_{x_2} - s^2_p - s^2_{q_2} - s^2_{q_3} = (5) - (7) - (12);$$

$$(14) \quad s^2_{t_1} + s^2_{q_1} = s^2_{x_1} - s^2_p - s^2_{q_2} = (4) - (10) - (11);$$

$$(15) \quad s^2_{t_3} + s^2_{q_4} = s^2_{x_3} - s^2_p - s^2_{q_3} = (6) - (10) - (12).$$

If now we designate the proportionate contribution of the permanent, quasi-permanent, and transitory components to the total variance of income in any year as P, Q, and T, indicating the year by subscripts, we have

$$(16) \quad P_1 = \frac{s_p^2}{s_{x_1}^2} = \frac{(10)}{(4)};$$

$$(17) \quad P_2 = \frac{s_p^2}{s_{x_2}^2} = \frac{(10)}{(5)};$$

$$(18) \quad P_3 = \frac{s_p^2}{s_{x_3}^2} = \frac{(10)}{(6)};$$

$$(19) \quad T_2 = \frac{s_{t_2}^2}{s_{x_2}^2} = \frac{(13)}{(5)};$$

$$(20) \quad Q_2 = \frac{s_{q_2}^2 + s_{q_3}^2}{s_{x_2}^2} = 1 - P_2 - T_2 = 1 - (17) - (19).$$

As was implied in the discussion above, we cannot segregate the transitory from the quasi-permanent component for years 1 and 3. But we can derive

$$(21) \quad T_1 + Q_1 = 1 - P_1 = 1 - (16);$$
$$(22) \quad T_3 + Q_3 = 1 - P_3 = 1 - (18).$$

These proportionate contributions can be derived from statistical data on the incomes in three successive years of a group of professional men in practice the same number of years, since s_x^2 is given by the square of the coefficient of variation of actual income, and the correlation coefficient between income ratios in two years is numerically identical with the correlation coefficient between actual incomes.[20]

20 Instead of using income ratios, we could have used logarithms and assumed that the deviations of the logarithms of the permanent components from their mean were identical in different years, and similarly for the quasi-permanent components. This set of assumptions would lead to the same equations that we obtained, except that the correlation coefficients between dollar incomes would be replaced by the correlation coefficients between the logarithms of income and the coefficients of variation by the standard deviations of the logarithms. The use of logarithms has some advantages, since it may well be more reasonable to assume that logarithmic components are additive and uncorrelated than to assume that dollar components are.

The relation between these results and those presented in Section 2 of the text of this chapter can be seen most easily if we express P_1 in terms of the regression coefficient. It can easily be shown that

$$P_1 = b_{31}\frac{\bar{x}'_1}{\bar{x}'_3},$$

from which,

$$Q_1 + T_1 = 1 - b_{31}\frac{\bar{x}'_1}{\bar{x}'_3}.$$

This is the formula used in computing the percentage contribution of the component considered transitory for years 1 and 3 (see footnote 15 of the text). It follows that the percentages attributed to the transitory and permanent components in Table 58, there interpreted as contributions to the deviation of the mean income of each income class from the mean income in the profession, can also be interpreted as the percentages of the total variance of income attributable to the two components.[21]

Equations (16) through (22) enable us to compute the percentage contribution of the different components to the variance of the income distribution as a whole. We cannot get an equally detailed breakdown for separate income classes. Let a bar over each symbol designate an arithmetic mean, and a subscript to the left of the symbol, the year that serves as a basis for grouping the individuals. For example, $_1\bar{x}_2$ will stand for the average income ratio in year 2 of a year 1 income class. If the transitory and quasi-permanent components are defined so that their average for all individuals is zero, then not only the average income ratio but also the average permanent component expressed as a ratio to the average income (p) will be unity for the income distribution as a whole. We can then write the following sets of equations:

$$(23) \quad _1\bar{x}_1 = {_1\bar{p}} + {_1\bar{t}_1} + {_1\bar{q}_1} + {_1\bar{q}_2};$$
$$(24) \quad _1\bar{x}_2 = {_1\bar{p}} + {_1\bar{q}_2};$$
$$(25) \quad _1\bar{x}_3 = {_1\bar{p}};$$
$$(26) \quad _2\bar{x}_1 = {_2\bar{p}} + {_2\bar{q}_2};$$
$$(27) \quad _2\bar{x}_2 = {_2\bar{p}} + {_2\bar{t}_2} + {_2\bar{q}_2} + {_2\bar{q}_3};$$

21 Formulae (17) to (22) can also be expressed in terms of the regression coefficients.

$$(28) \quad {}_2\bar{x}_3 = {}_2\bar{p} + {}_2\bar{q}_3;$$
$$(29) \quad {}_3\bar{x}_1 = {}_3\bar{p};$$
$$(30) \quad {}_3\bar{x}_2 = {}_3\bar{p} + {}_3\bar{q}_3;$$
$$(31) \quad {}_3\bar{x}_3 = {}_3\bar{p} + {}_3\bar{t}_3 + {}_3\bar{q}_3 + {}_3\bar{q}_4.$$

It follows that for year 1 and year 3 income classes we can isolate the permanent component and one part of the quasi-permanent component but not the transitory component; for year 2 income classes we cannot isolate the permanent component alone, but can only get it in combination with part of the quasi-permanent component. To compute percentage contributions the isolated parts should be expressed as deviations from their mean for the distribution as a whole (unity for p, zero for t and q) and divided by the deviation of the average income ratio in the base year from the average income ratio for the distribution as a whole (unity). In actual computation it would be more convenient to use dollar incomes and the procedure outlined in Table 57. By analogy with the analysis of Section 2 of the text of this chapter, if the percentage contributions of the components that can be isolated are the same for all classes, the regression equations will be linear. In that case, formulae (16) through (22) will measure the percentage contributions for separate income classes as well as for the distribution as a whole.

ii *Illustrative computations of percentage contributions.* The logic of the preceding analysis calls for its application to data for individuals in practice the same number of years. Unfortunately, our data do not satisfy this requirement. Number of years in practice was reported only on the 1937 medical sample, and we have not prepared correlation tables for this sample because of the adjustments that would have been necessary. Despite this defect, we have thought it desirable to use our data to illustrate the kinds of results that can be obtained by the technique outlined above.

The blank spaces in Table 62, which summarizes the numerical results, are for components whose contribution cannot be isolated from data for three years. One 'nonsense' result was obtained, for the 1934 incomes of dentists. The percentage of the total variance attributable to the permanent component turns out to be over 100 per cent, an absurd but not arithmetically impossible result.

TABLE 62

Percentage of Total Variance Attributable to Permanent,
Quasi-permanent, and Transitory Components

Computed under Mean Assumption

PROFESSION & YEAR	PERMANENT COMPONENT	% OF TOTAL VARIANCE ATTRIBUTABLE TO QUASI-PERMANENT COMPONENT Carried over from preceding year	Carrying over into following year	TRANSITORY COMPONENT
Physicians				
1932	91		1	
1933	87	1	7	5
1934	87	7		
Dentists				
1932	80		10	
1933	85	11	1	3
1934	100.5	1		
Lawyers *				
1932	82		1	
1933	83	1	6	10
1934	75	6		
Certified public accountants * 1935 sample				
1932	71		14	
1933	66	13	16	5
1934	73	17		
1937 sample				
1934	77		13	
1935	77	13	5	5
1936	87	5		

* Individual practitioners only.

This result may reflect errors in our data, the grouping of individuals in practice varying numbers of years, or the falsity of the assumptions on which the theoretical framework rests. The absence of any other 'nonsense' results gives some grounds for accepting the first interpretation.[22]

The transitory component is more important than the quasi-permanent component in law, less important in medicine, dentistry, and accountancy. Moreover, the transitory component contributes about the same percentage to the total variance in the three last professions—about 5 per cent. Differences among these professions in the stability of relative income status apparently reflect primarily differences in the strength of quasi-permanent forces. The lesser stability of relative income status in law than in medicine or dentistry, on the other hand, reflects primarily the greater strength of transitory forces. Apparently, the incomes of lawyers were affected by sizable random influences in 1933.

This analysis would be much more illuminating if we could name the specific factors that are included in the purely formal categories of permanent, quasi-permanent, and transitory factors, and isolate the contribution of each. It is probably not possible to do so for the transitory factors; these are likely to be largely 'chance' influences that have no counterpart in objectively determinable attributes of the individual or his practice, although this need not always be the case. There is more likelihood of naming the factors considered 'permanent' or 'quasi-permanent'. Indeed, the earlier chapters of this book, as already noted, are largely concerned with measuring the influence of specific permanent factors. Using our results for physicians, we can exemplify the

22 However, another 'nonsense' result would have been obtained if we had used an alternative value of the coefficient of variation for accountants. Because our basic correlation analysis was for pairs of years, we had two coefficients of variation for each year. For example, for 1933 we had one coefficient of variation computed from data for individuals who reported their 1932 and 1933 incomes, another computed from data for the slightly different group who reported their 1933 and 1934 incomes. We used the square of the larger of the two coefficients of variation as the base of the percentages. Had we used the smaller coefficients of variation for the 1933 incomes of accountants, the percentage attributable to the transitory component would have been — 0.6. An accurate analysis would call for the use of data only for individuals who reported their incomes in all three years.

kind of breakdown of the total variability of income that would be desired:

> *Percentage of total variance of 1933 incomes of physicians attributable to:*
>
> | | | |
> |---|---|---|
> | Size of community, number of years in practice, and type of practice [23] | 22 | |
> | Other factors present in all three years, 1932–34 | 65 | |
> | All 'permanent' factors | | 87 |
> | | | |
> | Factors present in | | |
> | 1932 and 1933 but not 1934 | 1 | |
> | 1933 and 1934 but not 1932 | 7 | |
> | All 'quasi-permanent' factors | | 8 |
> | | | |
> | Transitory factors present in 1933 but not 1932 or 1934 | | 5 |
> | | | |
> | All factors | | 100 |

The 65 per cent attributable to 'other factors present in all three years' may in part reflect chance forces whose influence was present in all three years; in the main, however, it is a measure of the extent to which we have failed in our attempt to isolate permanent factors. It presumably reflects primarily the influence of factors that we have either neglected to consider or whose contribution we have not been able to measure (e.g., training and ability). Ideally, the 22 per cent attributable to size of community, years in practice, and type of practice should be segregated into the parts attributable to each.[24]

[23] We have arbitrarily assumed that the percentage contributed by these factors is the same for 1933 as for 1936, the only year for which we analyzed number of years in practice. The standard deviation of the 1936 incomes of physicians, computed from the 1937 medical sample, is $3,631. If the variation associated with size of community, number of years in practice, and type of practice is eliminated, the standard deviation is reduced to $3,214; i.e., this is the average standard deviation of incomes for physicians in the same size of community, in practice the same number of years, and engaged in the same type of practice. The percentage cited above, 22, was computed from these standard deviations by squaring them, subtracting the smaller square from the larger, and dividing the difference by the larger square.

[24] The variance of each factor that would be computed in an analysis of variance would not be the appropriate variance for such a breakdown for two reasons: first, the variance among, say, size of community classes includes the variance of the other factors as well; second, and more important, even eliminating the variance of the other factors, the part that is left is an estimate of the variance among the size of community income components of not all individuals in the

b The variability assumption

The variability assumption is that both the standard deviation of the permanent component and the standard deviation of the quasi-permanent component are proportional to the standard deviation of actual income.

i *The procedure.* In the symbols used above, except that s here denotes the standard deviation of actual income in the year designated by the subscript, the variability assumption is:

$$(32) \quad \frac{p'_1 - \bar{x}'_1}{s_1} = \frac{p'_2 - \bar{x}'_2}{s_2} = \frac{p'_3 - \bar{x}'_3}{s_3};$$

$$(33) \quad \frac{q'_{12}}{s_1} = \frac{q'_{22}}{s_2};$$

$$(34) \quad \frac{q'_{23}}{s_2} = \frac{q'_{33}}{s_3}.$$

It follows from this assumption that the proportionate contribution of the permanent components, though not necessarily the breakdown of the remainder between quasi-permanent and transitory components, will be equal in all years. By a method similar to that used in the last section these proportionate contributions, if the different components are uncorrelated, can be shown to be:

$$(35) \qquad P^* = r_{13};$$

$$(36) \qquad Q^*_2 = r_{12} + r_{23} - 2r_{13};$$

$$(37) \qquad T^*_2 = 1 - r_{12} - r_{23} + r_{13};$$

$$(38) \quad T^*_1 + Q^*_1 = T^*_3 + Q^*_3 = 1 - r_{13}.$$

The starred symbols have the same meaning as the unstarred symbols previously used, except that they are computed under the variability assumption; r is the correlation coefficient between actual incomes in the years indicated by the subscripts. The breakdown of Q^*_2 into the proportionate contributions of q'_{22} and q'_{23} is given by:

$$(39) \quad Q^*_{22} = r_{12} - r_{13};$$

$$(40) \quad Q^*_{23} = r_{23} - r_{13}.$$

---

profession but a hypothetical sample containing one individual in each size of community class. For both reasons, the variance among size of community classes will tend to be too large.

We have preferred the 'mean assumption' because it does not seem reasonable to assume that the percentage contribution of the permanent factors is the same in all years.

ii *Illustrative computations of percentage contributions.* The results obtained by using the variability assumption do not differ greatly from those obtained by using the mean assumption (compare Table 63 with Table 62). The transitory component is again

TABLE 63

Percentage of Total Variance Attributable to Permanent, Quasi-permanent, and Transitory Components

Computed under Variability Assumption

PROFESSION & YEAR	PERMANENT COMPONENT [1]	% OF TOTAL VARIANCE ATTRIBUTABLE TO QUASI-PERMANENT COMPONENT		TRANSITORY COMPONENT
		Carried over from preceding year	Carrying over into following year	
1933				
Physicians	89	3	6	2
Dentists	91	3	3	3
Lawyers [2]	79	4	6	11
Certified public accountants [2]	73	12	13	2
1935				
Certified public accountants [2]	83	8	4	5

[1] Percentage attributable to permanent component same in 1932 and 1934 as in 1933 and same in 1934 and 1936 as in 1935.
[2] Individual practitioners only.

smaller than the quasi-permanent component in medicine, dentistry, and accountancy, and larger than the latter in law. The transitory component is more important in law than in any other profession and about equally important in medicine, dentistry, and accountancy. No 'nonsense' results were obtained, though it is arithmetically possible to get negative results for all except the permanent component. In one respect the results under the variability assumption seem more reasonable than the results under the mean assumption: the percentages attributed to the two parts of the quasi-permanent component are less widely divergent.

CHAPTER 8

Temporal Changes in Income

THE PRECEDING CHAPTER is concerned with relative income status, the position a man occupies in an array of practitioners by size of income; this chapter, with actual income, the number of dollars he receives for his services. Both are important to the professional man: relative income status, as a measure of professional success; actual income, as the determinant of his standard of living.

Changes in a man's actual income depend not only on changes in his relative income status but also on changes in the income of his profession as a whole. The latter, in turn, depend on changes in general economic activity and on the sensitivity to them of economic conditions within the profession. It has often been supposed that the professions are relatively sheltered; that professional workers are less affected by cyclical movements in economic activity than other workers. The data presented below demonstrate that this supposition is not tenable, at least for independent professional men and for the single cycle our data cover. True, independent professional men are less likely to become completely unemployed than salaried professional or nonprofessional workers, and hence the losses entailed by a decline in average income may be more evenly distributed among them; but their average income changes as much as that of other workers.

1 CHANGES IN AVERAGE INCOME

We have previously noted the close similarity among the professions other than consulting engineering in the patterns of temporal change in average income (Ch. 4, Chart 7). This impression is confirmed by two sets of indices of average net income, one with 1929 and the other with 1933 as the base, computed by chaining the averages from the various samples for each profession (Chart 30 and Table 64). There are, in-

TABLE 64

Indices of Arithmetic Mean Income

Professions and All Gainfully Occupied Persons

	1929	1930	1931	1932	1933	1934	1935	1936
				1929 = 100				
Physicians								
All samples [1]	100.0	89.1	77.1	58.0	53.5	61.5	65.1	74.0
1937 sample [2]	100.0	88.8	76.4	57.6	52.8	59.6	63.2	71.8
Dentists [3]	100.0	93.9	80.2	59.2	52.2	57.1		
Lawyers								
Both samples [4]	100.0			65.3	57.7	60.5	63.5	68.9
1937 sample [5]	100.0			65.3	56.7	56.3	59.1	64.1
Certified public accountants [6]	100.0	92.3	76.6	60.3	55.6	61.1	64.0	69.9
Consulting engineers	100.0	84.8	49.7	26.3				
Employee compensation plus entrepreneurial withdrawals per gainfully occupied person [7]	100.0	90.8	76.6	60.7	56.7	63.1	67.1	73.6
				1933 = 100				
Physicians								
All samples [1]	186.8	166.4	144.1	108.4	100.0	115.0	121.8	138.5
1937 sample [2]	189.2	168.0	144.6	109.0	100.0	112.8	119.5	135.9
Dentists [3]	191.8	180.1	153.8	113.6	100.0	109.6		
Lawyers								
Both samples [4]	173.5			113.3	100.0	104.9	110.1	119.5
1937 sample [5]	176.3			115.2	100.0	99.2	104.1	113.0
Certified public accountants [6]	180.2	166.3	138.0	108.6	100.0	110.0	115.3	125.8
Employee compensation plus entrepreneurial withdrawals per gainfully occupied person [7]	176.5	160.2	135.2	107.2	100.0	111.3	118.5	129.9

[1] 1933 sample used for 1929–32; 1935 sample for 1932–34; 1937 sample for 1934–36. In deriving the index the arithmetic mean incomes for each sample in Table 10 were expressed as percentages of the mean incomes for the initial year for which the sample was to be used. The percentages from the 1935 sample were then multiplied by the 1932 percentage from the 1933 sample and the percentages from the 1937 sample by the percentage from the preceding step for 1934. This gave the index with 1929 as the base. The index with 1933 as the base and the indices for the other professions were derived similarly.

[2] 1937 sample used for the entire period 1929–36.

[3] See footnote 1; 1933 sample used for 1929–32; 1935 sample for 1932–34.

[4] See footnote 1; 1937 sample used for 1929, 1932, and 1934–36; 1935 sample for 1932–34.

[5] 1937 sample used for 1929 and 1932–36.

[6] See footnote 1; 1933 sample used for 1929–32; 1935 sample for 1932–34; 1937 sample for 1934–36.

[7] Estimates of employee compensation and entrepreneurial withdrawals for 1929–36 by Simon Kuznets, *National Income and Its Composition,* 1919–1938 (National Bureau of Economic Research, 1941), Table 68. Total number of gainfully occupied persons in the United States by Daniel Carson, *Labor Supply and Employment* (National Research Project, mimeo., Nov. 1939).

CHART 30

Indices of Arithmetic Mean Income for Five Professions and Indices of Employee Compensation plus Entrepreneurial Withdrawals per Gainfully Occupied Worker

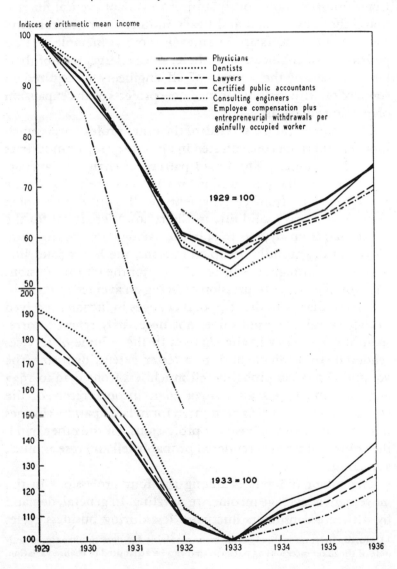

deed, differences in detail but the movements are so similar that it is questionable whether the minor differences ought to be attributed to anything except chance variation.[1]

The precipitous fall in the incomes of consulting engineers is not surprising. The demand for services of engineers comes from industries notoriously subject to violent cyclical fluctuations—the construction and heavy industries in general. And consulting engineers are in an even more vulnerable cyclical position than engineers as a whole, since a larger part of their services than of the services of all engineers is required in connection with the initiation of new projects or the expansion of existing enterprises.

The demand for the services of the other professions is much broader and is not concentrated in any one group of industries or final consumers. The broad pattern of change in average net income in these professions resembles closely that in the average income from employment of all gainfully occupied persons (the heavy solid line in Chart 30). Were it not for the milder fall from 1932 to 1933 in the average income from employment of gainfully occupied persons, the heavy solid line would pass through the cluster of lines for the four professions and would give the impression of being an average of them.

This similarity in the temporal changes in incomes received in the several professions does not necessarily reflect a corresponding similarity in the changes in the volume of services rendered. In medicine and, to a lesser extent, dentistry, the volume of services probably fell much less from 1929 to 1933 and rose much less after 1933 than income received, the changes in income being accounted for in large part by changes in collections. In the business professions, on the other hand, the volume of services rendered probably fell and rose as much as income.

The minor differences among the four professions in the movement of average income are puzzling. In general, demand by ultimate consumers fluctuates less during business cycles

1 Unfortunately, no method seems to be available for determining the magnitude of the differences among patterns that can be attributed to chance variation.

than demand by business firms. We should, therefore, expect the incomes of physicians and dentists, who serve ultimate consumers, to fall less from 1929 to 1933 and rise less from 1933 to 1936 than the incomes of accountants and lawyers, who serve in large part business firms. Yet the relative fall in average income from 1929 to 1933 is slightly larger for physicians and dentists than for lawyers and certified public accountants; and the relative rise from 1933 to 1936 is larger for physicians (no data are available for dentists) than for lawyers and accountants. Whether these differences are to be attributed to the character of the services provided by accountants and lawyers, to an increase in the demand for their services in connection with failure and reorganization of business firms during depression, or to the peculiarities of the samples used, we cannot tell.

From the indices on a 1929 base, one might conclude that the minor differences among the professions are larger during the recovery from 1933 to 1936 than during the preceding downswing. However, the indices on a 1933 base indicate that this is merely a result of the general tendency of relatives on a fixed base to diverge. There is little reason for concluding that the movements of average income are any more divergent among the professions during the rising phase of the cycle than during the declining.

2 CHANGES IN VARIABILITY OF INCOME

In general, absolute variability decreased in all professions from 1929 to 1933 and increased from 1933 to 1936, i.e., it changed in the same direction as average income (Chart 31). The decrease is considerably more marked than the subsequent increase, and indeed the evidence for the increase, while fairly conclusive, is by no means unmixed. Changes in absolute variability, like changes in average income, are of much the same magnitude in all professions other than engineering.

The several measures of relative variability summarized in Chart 9, reproduced here in Chart 32, tell a less simple and straightforward story. Only for engineering can we say with any confidence just what our data show, let alone what the

CHART 31

Two Measures of Absolute Variability of Income

——— Physicians   —·—·—· Lawyers   —··—··— Consulting engineers
············· Dentists   — — — Certified public accountants

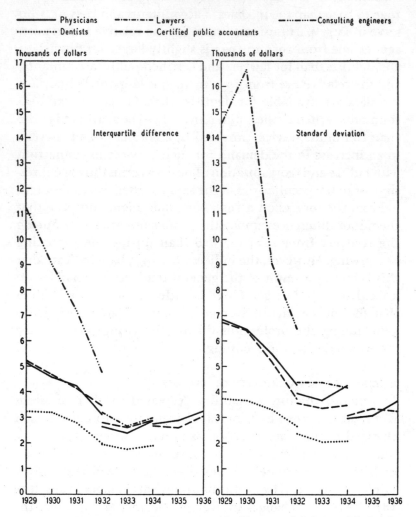

'true' changes were: all measures indicate a fairly rapid rise in relative variability from 1929 to 1932. All we can say with confidence about the other professions is that changes in relative variability were not large; in other words, differences in average income account for the largest part of the temporal

CHART 32

Two Measures of Relative Variability of Income

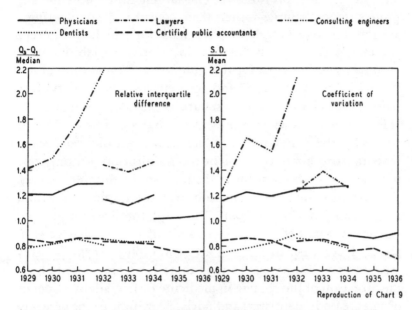

Reproduction of Chart 9

changes in absolute variability. This statement, based on changes within the period covered by individual samples, may seem to be contradicted by the differences among the successive samples for the same profession: the 'level' of the measures varies from sample to sample and is in general lower for the samples covering 1934–36 than for the samples covering 1932–34. The successive samples for the same profession overlap, and for the overlapping year two measures are plotted on the chart, one from the earlier sample, the other, from the later sample. The difference between them cannot be interpreted as a temporal change, since both are for the same year; it must be interpreted as arising either from sampling error or bias. It follows that differences in the level of the measures from successive samples cannot be interpreted as reflecting temporal changes in variability. Evidence on temporal changes is given solely by differences among measures from the same sample.

In addition to measures summarized in Chart 32 (and Table 13) we have the results of a study of Lorenz curves for the various samples and professions. The largest differences for any profession or sample—other than consulting engineering—are for the 1933 sample of physicians, for which the Lorenz curves suggest a steady increase in relative variability from 1929 to 1932. Yet even for this sample the largest vertical difference between the 1929 and 1932 curves, when the two are plotted on a chart ten inches square, is three-tenths of an inch. It is thus obvious why we present no charts giving the Lorenz curves for the same profession and sample for different years: if reduced to a size convenient for publication, on only one or two would it be possible to distinguish the different curves.

If we combine the information from the Lorenz curves and the measures in Chart 32 (and Table 13), there is some, but by no means unmixed, evidence of a slight rise in relative variability from 1929 to 1932 in all professions, except possibly accountancy. From 1932 to 1933 there is no agreement about the direction of the change in medicine or law, slight evidence of a decrease in dentistry, and fairly clear indications of an increase in accountancy. From 1933 to 1934 inequality seems to increase in medicine, and to decrease in dentistry and accountancy; 'no agreement' is again the verdict for law. From 1934 to 1935 the evidence favors a slight increase in inequality in medicine and a slight decrease in accountancy.

The general tendency for relative variability to increase from 1929 to 1932, when average incomes were falling rapidly in all professions, suggests the hypothesis that relative variability moves inversely to the income level. Of the later samples, only those for accountancy support this hypothesis. Those for law and dentistry are neutral, but those for medicine definitely contradict the hypothesis. In short, the only simple hypothesis about the relation of relative variability to general business conditions and average income that seems consistent with our findings is that there is none and that the observed differences are chance phenomena.

3 CHANGES IN INCOME BY SIZE OF COMMUNITY

The countrywide changes in average professional income described earlier naturally dominate income changes in communities of different size. The familiar pattern of a fall from 1929 to 1933 and a rise thereafter is repeated time and again in Chart 33, which presents, by size of community classes, average incomes obtained by combining the different samples for each profession.[2] Since the income scale of Chart 33 is logarithmic, equal distances represent equal percentage changes. The rough parallelism of the lines in each panel indicates that temporal changes in the average income of professional workers practising in communities varying in size are alike not only in direction but also in relative magnitude. The least regular patterns of change are displayed by lawyers and consulting engineers. The data are perhaps less satisfactory for law than for any other profession; the data for consulting engineering cover only 1929–32 and include very few returns for the two size of community classes that show the greatest departures (communities under 5,000 and between 5,000 and 25,000 in population).

In the other professions the departures from parallelism, though minor, do not seem entirely random. Table 65 suggests that the fall was somewhat larger and the subsequent rise somewhat smaller in large cities than in small.[3] The evidence is by no means clear-cut or conclusive. It is strongest for account-

[2] See notes to Tables B 3, B 5, B 8, B 10, and B 11 for methods used to combine the samples.

[3] Table 65 measures changes in income between fixed dates, rather than between the high and low years for each community class. However, average income reached its trough in a year other than 1933 in only three of the twenty-eight series for which computations were made; average income in the initial year (1929 or 1932) was higher than in any other year prior to the trough in all series; and average income in the terminal year (1934 or 1936) was higher than in any other year subsequent to the trough in all but one instance. Consequently the results obtained by using fixed dates are virtually identical with those which would have been obtained by using the high and low years determined for each size of community class separately. It should be noted that, because of the limited periods our data cover, 'high' as used here is not synonymous with 'cyclical peak', though 'low' is synonymous with 'cyclical trough'.

CHART 33

Arithmetic Mean Income by Size of Community

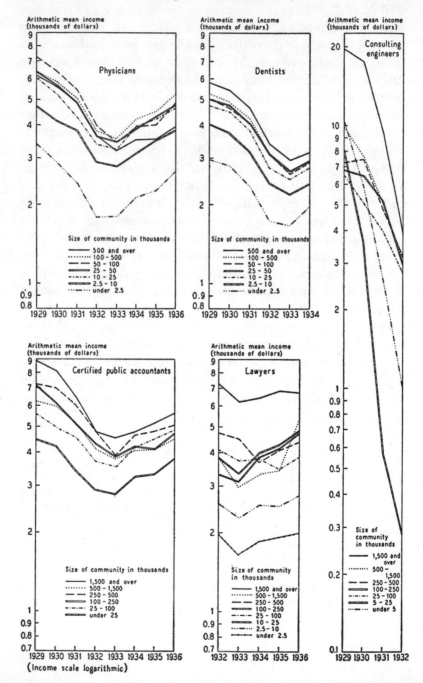

Arithmetic mean income
(thousands of dollars)

Physicians

Size of community in thousands
——— 500 and over
·········· 100 - 500
– – – 50 - 100
–·–·– 25 - 50
–··–··– 10 - 25
▬▬▬ 2.5 - 10
········· under 2.5

Arithmetic mean income
(thousands of dollars)

Dentists

Size of community in thousands
——— 500 and over
·········· 100 - 500
– – – 50 - 100
–·–·– 25 - 50
–··–··– 10 - 25
▬▬▬ 2.5 - 10
········· under 2.5

Arithmetic mean income
(thousands of dollars)

Consulting
engineers

Arithmetic mean income
(thousands of dollars)

Certified public accountants

Size of community in thousands
——— 1,500 and over
·········· 500 - 1,500
– – – 250 - 500
▬▬▬ 100 - 250
–·–·– 25 - 100
········· under 25

Arithmetic mean income
(thousands of dollars)

Lawyers

Size of community
in thousands
——— 1,500 and over
·········· 500 - 1,500
– – – 250 - 500
▬▬▬ 100 - 250
–·–·– 25 - 100
–··–··– 10 - 25
▬▬▬ 2.5 - 10
········· under 2.5

Size of
community
in thousands
——— 1,500 and
          over
·········· 500 -
          1,500
– – – 250 - 500
–·–·– 100 - 250
–··–··– 25 - 100
▬▬▬ 5 - 25
········· under 5

(Income scale logarithmic)

TABLE 65

Change in Arithmetic Mean Income, by Size of Community

Average for Period Covered = 100

SIZE OF COMMUNITY	PHYSICIANS	DENTISTS	CERTIFIED PUBLIC ACCOUNTANTS	LAWYERS
			Decline [1]	
	1929–33	*1929–33*	*1929–33*	*1932–33*
1,500,000 & over	} 69.4	} 67.5	71.1	15.1
500,000–1,500,000			51.9	23.3
250,000– 500,000	} 58.9	} 68.5	62.1	5.6
100,000– 250,000			66.0	5.1
50,000– 100,000	78.2	64.6	} 45.9	} 9.6
25,000– 50,000	63.6	62.2		
10,000– 25,000	63.7	64.2	} 48.6	11.6
2,500– 10,000	55.8	62.5		11.5
Under 2,500	64.9	57.1		16.8
U. S.	64.2	64.9	61.4	12.1
			Rise [1]	
	1933–36	*1933–34*	*1933–36*	*1933–36*
1,500,000 & over	} 17.4	} 4.8	17.5	8.2
500,000–1,500,000			14.7	59.9
250,000– 500,000	} 34.5	} 7.0	21.8	−2.8 [2]
100,000– 250,000			16.9	42.0
50,000– 100,000	29.4	7.6	} 29.9	} 4.0
25,000– 50,000	28.6	6.3		
10,000– 25,000	31.7	7.7	} 28.5	36.5
2,500– 10,000	29.1	6.7		18.6
Under 2,500	35.7	12.3		18.1
U. S.	28.4	6.8	19.8	17.7
			Decline and Rise [3]	
	1929–36	*1929–34*	*1929–36*	*1932–36*
1,500,000 & over	} 86.8	} 72.3	88.6	23.3
500,000–1,500,000			66.6	83.2
250,000– 500,000	} 93.4	} 75.5	83.9	2.8
100,000– 250,000			82.9	47.1
50,000– 100,000	107.6	72.2	} 75.8	} 13.6
25,000– 50,000	92.2	68.5		
10,000– 25,000	95.4	71.9	} 77.1	48.1
2,500– 10,000	82.9	69.2		30.1
Under 2,500	100.6	69.4		34.9
U. S.	92.6	71.7	81.2	29.8

[1] Based on arithmetic means in Tables B 3, B 5, B 8, B 10, and B 11 expressed as relatives of averages for the period in Table 16.

[2] Negative because mean income declined from 1933 to 1936.

[3] 'Decline and rise' is sum of percentage decline and percentage rise.

ants, whose average income fell more and rose less in each of the four largest size of community classes than in either of the two smallest. The evidence for dentists, though less uniform, is still fairly convincing. Average income fell most in communities over 100,000 and rose least in communities over 500,000; it fell least and rose most in communities under 2,500. The evidence is most uncertain and mixed for physicians. Taken alone it would hardly justify any conclusion. However, what differences there are in income movement are in the same general direction as in the other two professions.

The smaller rise in the larger communities tends to counterbalance the greater fall, so that the total cyclical movement in average income, measured roughly in Table 65 by summing the percentage rise and the percentage fall, shows little tendency to vary consistently with size of community. True, for both dentists and accountants the total rise and fall shows a slight tendency to decrease with size of community. However, the data for dentists extend only to 1934; consequently, the total rise and fall includes all of the cyclical fall, but only a small part of the cyclical rise, which presumably continued after 1934. The total rise and fall therefore reproduces the tendency for the fall to be least in small communities.

The data thus suggest that the amplitude of the cyclical movement proper was much the same in all size of community classes but was superimposed on divergent underlying trends, the smaller communities in general displaying trends that were upward relatively to the trends in the larger communities. Since average incomes in general decrease with size of community, the divergent trends imply a lessening of income differences among communities of varying size.

A more sensitive test of this point is provided by Chart 34, designed to bring into sharp relief the differential behavior of income in the several size of community classes. The data plotted on the chart were obtained by expressing the average income in each size of community class in each year as a percentage of the countrywide average. Hence, if percentage changes in income had been identical in all size of community

CHART 34

Relatives of Arithmetic Mean Income by Size of Community

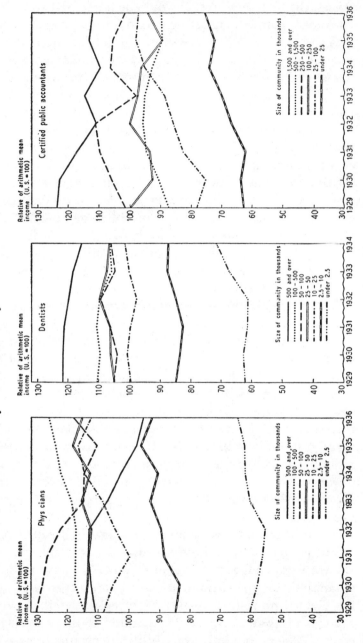

classes, the lines on the chart would be horizontal and parallel. Of course, perfect parallelism would hardly be expected with data such as ours, which are subject to large sampling fluctuations. The point at issue is rather whether there is any general tendency for the lines to converge. As the preceding analysis would lead us to expect, the charts do show such a tendency, most marked for accountants and least marked for physicians.

Two possible explanations can be advanced, with some evidence in support of each. The convergent tendency may reflect changes peculiar to the specific professions. In discussing the relation between medical income and number of years in practice for communities of varying size, we concluded that the concentration of young physicians in large communities is tending to decrease the difference between average incomes in small and large communities (Ch. 6). Similar tendencies may be operative in the other professions. On the other hand, the convergent tendency may reflect a common outside influence, a similar decrease in the size of community differences in the average income of the public at large. For example, the very large increase in farm aid in recent years may well have led to an improvement in the relative economic position of rural areas. The section that follows indicates that, at least for physicians and dentists, regional differences in the temporal behavior of average professional income are correlated with corresponding differences in the temporal behavior of the average income of the public. It seems not unreasonable to assume that what holds for regions holds also for communities of varying size, especially since regional differences in average income reflect primarily regional differences in degree of urbanization.

A complete analysis of temporal changes in the distribution of income by size would require an analysis of changes in the variability as well as the level of income. We have made such an analysis for the various size of community groups, but it has yielded no results worth presenting in detail. As always, changes in absolute variability parallel those in average income. Changes in relative variability are erratic; there is little or no consistency among different measures for the same profession and even less consistency among professions. A corresponding analysis for regions yields similar negative results; consequently, the next section, like this one, is devoted entirely to income levels.

4 CHANGES IN INCOME BY GEOGRAPHIC REGION

While the dominant impression conveyed by Chart 35 [4] is one of similarity in temporal changes in income, comparison with Chart 33 suggests that there is less similarity among regions than among communities of varying size. In part this is an optical illusion. Average incomes differ more among communities of varying size than among regions; in consequence, the lines are spread more widely on Chart 33 than on Chart 35 and can diverge more without intersecting. But comparison of Table 66 with Table 65 indicates that the smaller degree of uniformity is more than an optical illusion. The percentage changes in average income vary more among regions than among communities of varying size; and the difference is greater than could be accounted for by the larger number of regions than of size of community classes.

The exceedingly erratic changes in legal incomes and the short time span covered by the data for engineers again make it necessary to confine detailed analysis to physicians, dentists, and accountants. These three professions display considerable similarity in regional income changes. The fall from 1929–33 was apparently severest in the East North Central, Middle Atlantic, and West North Central regions, and mildest in the South Atlantic, East South Central, and New England regions. The subsequent rise was greatest in the East South Central, East North Central, and West South Central regions and least in the Middle Atlantic and New England regions. As these groupings indicate, there was little relation between the magnitude of the fall and the magnitude of the rise. For example, the fall in income was severe in both the Middle At-

4 See notes to Tables B 3, B 5, B 8, B 10, and B 11 for methods used to combine the samples.

CHART 35

Arithmetic Mean Income by Region

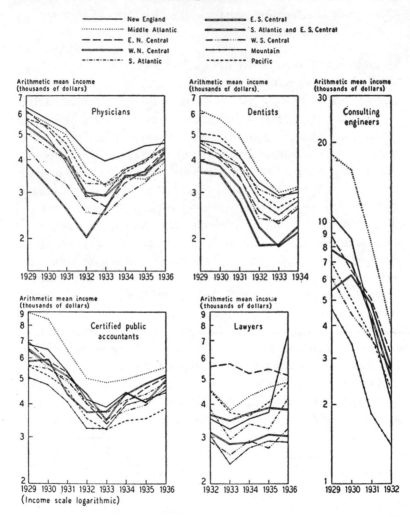

New England
Middle Atlantic
E. N. Central
W. N. Central
S. Atlantic

E. S. Central
S. Atlantic and E. S. Central
W. S. Central
Mountain
Pacific

lantic and East North Central regions, but the rise was small in the former and large in the latter.

The absence of any uniform relation between the fall and subsequent rise makes for wide differences in the amplitude of the cyclical movement, as measured by the sum of the percent-

TABLE 66

Change in Arithmetic Mean Income, by Region
Average for Period Covered = 100

	PHYSICIANS[1]	DENTISTS[1]	CERTIFIED PUBLIC ACCOUNTANTS[1]	LAWYERS[1]	ALL PERSONS (per capita)[2]
			Decline		
	1929–33	*1929–33*	*1929–33*	*1932–33*	*1929–33*
New England	48.5	48.9	57.8	7.3	47.4
Middle Atlantic	68.8	71.6	67.2	16.6	58.2
E. N. Central	85.6	67.7	71.8	—2.0[3]	71.4
W. N. Central	63.4	73.3	61.5	9.7	61.2
S. Atlantic	44.4	51.3	40.7	24.3	49.8
E. S. Central	39.3	63.1	43.9	4.7	73.1
W. S. Central	59.5	69.8	62.9	10.3	63.1
Mountain	66.9	55.3	44.4	23.3	56.8
Pacific	57.9	64.0	57.5	18.7	57.7
U. S.	64.2	64.9	61.4	12.1	60.5
			Rise		
	1933–36	*1933–34*	*1933–36*	*1933–36*	*1933–36*
New England	13.6	2.2	12.8	95.9	20.9
Middle Atlantic	11.1	3.2	11.0	23.8	22.7
E. N. Central	40.5	9.5	35.1	—9.8[4]	38.1
W. N. Central	28.9	8.3	29.9	6.7	34.4
S. Atlantic	37.8	6.4	24.0	35.0	36.0
E. S. Central	52.5	11.5	29.9	9.2	44.5
W. S. Central	44.0	9.8	26.0	22.2	34.9
Mountain	36.7	9.6	28.8	17.8	41.8
Pacific	26.6	6.6	15.7	26.8	33.9
U. S.	28.4	6.8	19.8	17.7	31.1
			Decline and Rise[5]		
	1929–36	*1929–34*	*1929–36*	*1932–36*	*1929–36*
New England	62.1	50.5	70.6	103.2	68.3
Middle Atlantic	79.9	74.8	78.2	40.4	80.9
E. N. Central	126.1	77.2	106.9	—11.8[6]	109.5
W. N. Central	92.3	81.6	91.4	16.4	95.6
S. Atlantic	82.2	57.7	64.7	59.3	85.8
E. S. Central	91.8	74.6	73.8	13.9	117.6
W. S. Central	103.5	79.6	88.9	32.5	98.0
Mountain	103.6	64.9	73.2	41.1	98.6
Pacific	84.5	70.6	73.2	45.5	91.6
U. S.	92.6	71.7	81.2	29.8	91.6

[1] Based on arithmetic means in Tables B 3, B 5, B 8, B 10, and B 11 expressed as relatives of averages for the period in Table 18.
[2] Based on series for regions computed from averages for states in R. R. Nathan and J. L. Martin, *State Income Payments, 1929–37* (U. S. Department of Commerce, 1939).
[3] Negative because mean income rose from 1932 to 1933.
[4] Negative because mean income declined from 1933 to 1936.
[5] 'Decline and rise' is sum of percentage decline and percentage rise.
[6] Negative because series moved inversely.

age rise and percentage fall. The differences among regions, unlike those among communities of varying size seem to reflect real differences in cyclical behavior. The amplitude of the cyclical movement appears to have been largest in a band of states running down the center of the country—the East North Central, West North Central, and West South Central regions —and smallest in the South Atlantic and New England states.

These differences in the cyclical behavior of average income apparently characterize not only the professions but also the public at large (last column of Table 66). Though there are differences in detail, the regions displaying the largest movements in professional income in the main also display the largest movements in the income of the public. A more detailed test of the relation suggested by Table 66 is provided by Chart 36, which compares the year-to-year changes in professional income with the year-to-year changes in the income of the public at large. In order to eliminate the influence of changes in the countrywide average income, the percentage change in each region is expressed as a percentage of the countrywide change. The straight diagonal lines in the charts are arbitrarily drawn so as to pass through (0,0) and (100,100); they typify a situation in which the percentage change in professional income would be identical with that in the income of the public at large.

The panels for physicians and dentists confirm the relation suggested by Table 66: there is a decided positive correlation between changes in professional income and changes in the income of the public. The panel for accountants, on the other hand, displays no correlation: the distribution of points appears haphazard. This difference between accountants and the curative professions, though surprising in the light of Table 66 which suggests a correlation between accountants and the public at large no less close than between the other two professions and the public, is consistent with previously noted differences among the professions. Medicine and dentistry serve the public directly; the demand for their services is necessarily intimately related to the incomes of the individuals residing

CHART 36

Relation between Relatives of Regional Changes from One Year to the Next in Professional Income and in per Capita Income Regional Change for U. S. = 100

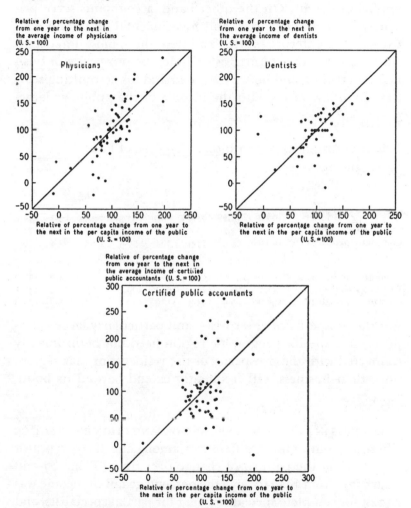

In all three panels each point represents a single region and a single pair of successive years. In the panel for physicians, one extreme observation (112, — 351) has been omitted; in the panel for certified public accountants, two extreme observations (69, — 163), (119, — 188) have been omitted.

in the region in which they practise. Unless counterbalanced by changes in the number of practitioners, changes in the income of the public will tend to be reflected in changes in medical and dental income, and over such short periods as our data cover, substantial changes in the number of practitioners are unlikely to occur. On the other hand, accountants serve primarily business enterprises and governmental units, and relatively large enterprises are doubtless their most important customers. For the country as a whole, the prosperity of business enterprises, and hence their demand for accounting services, doubtless varies with the income of the public at large.

TABLE 67

Indices of Arithmetic Mean Income, by Type of Practice
Physicians, 1929–1936

	1929	1930	1931	1932	1933	1934	1935	1936
				1929 = 100				
General practitioners	100.0	87.2	74.9	58.7	55.3	60.5	63.1	71.1
Partial specialists	100.0	83.7	75.2	56.5	52.2	60.2	63.9	74.2
Complete specialists	100.0	93.9	77.9	56.6	50.5	58.3	62.4	70.0
				1933 = 100				
General practitioners	180.8	157.6	135.3	106.1	100.0	109.4	114.0	128.6
Partial specialists	191.6	160.3	144.1	108.2	100.0	115.3	122.4	142.1
Complete specialists	198.0	185.9	154.3	112.1	100.0	115.4	123.6	138.6

But the prosperity of enterprises, and particularly large enterprises, in a specific geographic region need not be intimately connected with the prosperity of the residents of that region, since their business will frequently extend beyond its boundaries.

5 CHANGES IN INCOME BY TYPE AND ORGANIZATION OF PRACTICE
There are only minor differences among the three types of physicians in the pattern of change over time (Table 67 and Chart 37). From 1929 to 1933 the percentage fall in income was largest for complete specialists, next for partial specialists, and smallest for general practitioners. The percentage rise from 1933 to 1936 was about the same for complete and partial specialists; but larger for both than for general practitioners.

CHART 37

Indices of Arithmetic Mean Income by Type of Practice
Physicians, 1937 Sample

Indices of arithmetic mean income

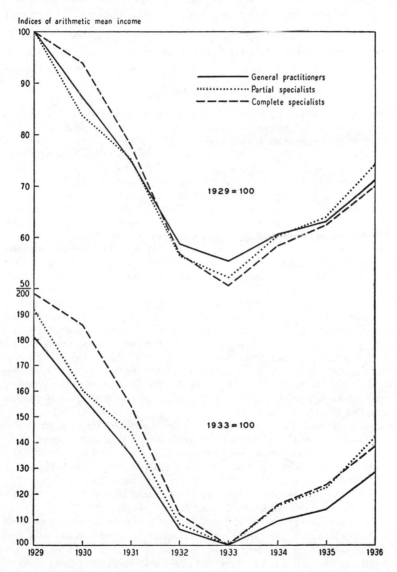

Over the whole period, 1929–36, the incomes of both partial specialists and general practitioners seem to have risen relatively to the incomes of complete specialists, more markedly for partial specialists than for general practitioners. This apparent narrowing of the gap between the incomes of general practitioners and complete specialists may be a product of an increasing tendency toward specialization. On the other hand, it may be no more than a statistical resultant of classifying physicians by their status in 1936 or 1937.[5]

5 In the main, shifts in type of practice are from general practice to specialization, either partial or complete, rather than the reverse. As a result, the group of physicians who in 1936 were general practitioners includes relatively few who were specialists in earlier years; it excludes a larger number who were specialists in 1936 but had been general practitioners during the earlier part of the period 1929–36. Presumably the average income of these individuals was higher than the income of those who remained general practitioners over the whole period. It follows that the average income for an earlier year of individuals who were general practitioners in 1936 will tend to be lower than the average income of all individuals who were general practitioners in that year, and that this bias is larger the farther back we go from 1936. The trend over the period 1929–36 in the incomes of individuals who were general practitioners in 1936 will have an upward bias relatively to the trend in the income of all general practitioners.

Similarly, the fact that individuals are more likely to change from partial specialization to complete specialization than to change from the latter to the former, imparts an upward bias to the trend in the income of individuals who were partial specialists in 1936 relatively to the trend in the income of all partial specialists in each year. Moreover, this bias is accentuated by the inclusion as partial specialists of individuals who were general practitioners during some of the earlier years of the period. Presumably, the average income of these individuals, while larger than that of all general practitioners, was less than that of all partial specialists.

Nor is the trend in the income of complete specialists exempt from an upward bias. Included in the ranks of complete specialists in 1936 are some individuals who in earlier years were partial specialists or general practitioners and who had an average income lower than that of all complete specialists.

Classifying practitioners by their status in 1936 might thus be expected to impart an upward bias to the trend in the income of *each* of the three groups. This bias would presumably be greatest for partial specialists.

The observed changes over the period 1929–36 in the relative income levels of the three groups are entirely consistent with the biases just discussed and may conceivably be completely accounted for by them. The incomes of the physicians who were partial specialists in 1936 rose relatively to the incomes of both of the other groups; and this is what we should expect on the basis of our

TABLE 68

Indices of Arithmetic Mean Income, by Organization of Practice
Certified Public Accountants, Lawyers, and Consulting Engineers

	1929	1930	1931	1932	1933	1934	1935	1936
				1929 = 100				
Certified public accountants [1]								
Individual practitioners	100.0	90.6	76.1	62.1	57.4	64.2	67.7	75.4
Firm members	100.0	93.9	77.6	59.1	54.5	59.5	61.0	63.4
Lawyers, both samples [2]								
Individual practitioners	100.0			55.6	48.5	51.2	53.9	57.4
Firm members	100.0			76.0	69.6	72.5	73.5	83.3
Lawyers, 1937 sample [3]								
Individual practitioners	100.0			55.6	49.0	49.4	52.0	55.5
Firm members	100.0			76.0	70.6	69.5	70.4	79.8
Consulting engineers								
Individual practitioners	100.0	87.5	57.9	29.1				
Firm members	100.0	82.8	44.4	24.6				
				1933 = 100				
Certified public accountants [1]								
Individual practitioners	174.1	157.8	132.5	108.2	100.0	111.9	117.9	131.3
Firm members	183.3	172.1	142.2	108.3	100.0	109.0	111.8	116.2
Lawyers, both samples [2]								
Individual practitioners	206.1			114.6	100.0	105.6	111.1	118.3
Firm members	143.7			109.2	100.0	104.2	105.7	119.7
Lawyers, 1937 sample [3]								
Individual practitioners	204.1			113.5	100.0	100.8	106.1	112.8
Firm members	141.6			107.6	100.0	98.4	99.7	113.1

[1] 1933 sample used for 1929–32; 1935 sample for 1932–34; 1937 sample for 1934–36. See footnote 1 to Table 64 for method of combining samples.
[2] 1937 sample used for 1929, 1932, and 1934–36; 1935 sample used for 1932–34.
[3] 1937 sample used for 1929 and 1932–36.

The differences between firm members and individual practitioners in the movement of average income are also of doubtful significance (Table 68 and Chart 38). For both accountants and engineers, the relative fall in income from 1929 to 1933 was larger for firm members than for individual practitioners. For lawyers, on the other hand, the relative fall seems to have been larger for individuals. However, this difference is considerably more questionable than the differences for the other

---

analysis even if the relative incomes of all partial specialists had remained unchanged. Similarly the apparent rise in the income of general practitioners relative to the income of complete specialists might be accounted for by a greater proportionate shift from general practice to specialization than from general practice and partial specialization to complete specialization.

CHART 38

Indices of Arithmetic Mean Income by Organization of Practice
Certified Public Accountants, Consulting Engineers, and Lawyers

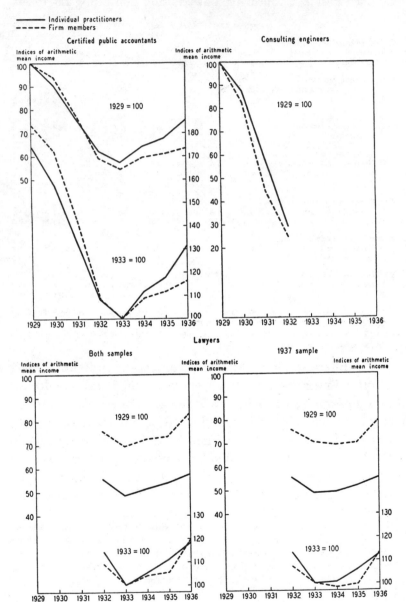

professions, since it is based on a sample which not only is particularly suspect, but in addition was selected at a date further removed from 1929 than the dates at which the samples for the other professions were selected.[6] For accountants, the average income of individual practitioners not only fell less from 1929 to 1933 but also rose more from 1933 to 1936, i.e., the economic fortunes of individual practitioners improved relatively to those of firm members during 1929–36.

Our data for lawyers tell a very confused story about the relative fate of firm members and individual practitioners from 1933 to 1936. For the full period, 1929–36, the average income of firm members appears to have risen a trifle more than that of individual practitioners. But this is entirely attributable to a very much greater rise from 1935 to 1936. Both from 1933 to 1934, and from 1934 to 1935, the individual practitioners' incomes rose more rapidly. Indeed, according to the 1937 sample, the incomes of firm members actually fell from 1933 to 1934.

Our data, therefore, yield no general conclusions about the relative behavior of the incomes of firm members and individual practitioners during the 1929–36 cycle. From the evidence for consulting engineers and accountants alone we should be tempted to conclude that firm members, and hence the larger and more affluent enterprises, suffered more from the depression than individual practitioners. But the validity of this conclusion is called into question not only because among lawyers the individual practitioners seem to have suffered more; but also because the relatively greater rise in the incomes of individual accountants during the upswing of the

6 The upward bias in the trend of incomes produced by asking information for a period of time from a sample selected at the end of the period would presumably be larger for firm members than for individual practitioners. The former are likely to be considerably older on the average than the latter and hence more likely to retire. The greater upward bias in the trend in the incomes of firm members might lead to a spurious rise in the average incomes of firm members relative to the average incomes of individual practitioners. For example, the relative fall in income from 1929 to 1934 according to the 1937 accountancy sample is larger for firm members than for individuals, although the 1933 accountancy sample indicates the reverse.

cycle suggests that the less rapid fall in their incomes during
1929–33 may reflect secular rather than cyclical influences. As
for the impact of revival, we cannot draw a valid conclusion
even for lawyers, let alone for the professions in general.

CHAPTER 9

Summary

1 PROFESSIONAL WORKERS AND OTHERS—NUMBERS AND EARN-INGS (CH. 3)

OF THE 50 million persons listed in the 1930 Census as gainfully occupied, only 3 million were professional workers.
Some 500,000 were independent practitioners; the rest, salaried employees of private enterprises or governmental agencies. Judged by earnings, the 3 million professional workers
are a fortunate group. Their earnings, though less equally distributed than those of nonprofessional workers, are between
two and three times as large. A small part of this difference in
average earnings reflects the concentration of professional
workers in large communities. The average earnings of professional workers are apparently between 85 and 180 per cent
larger than those of nonprofessional workers in communities
of the same size, rather than between 100 and 200 per cent
larger, as suggested by the nationwide averages.

The long and intensive training needed for professional
work involves not only direct expenses for tuition fees, books,
and the like, but also the postponement of the date when the
worker can begin to earn an income. It is difficult to estimate

precisely the difference in earnings that would compensate
for the professional man's capital investment, but available
data suggest that, at a maximum, he would have to earn 70
per cent more than the nonprofessional worker to make the
two pursuits equally attractive financially. Evidently, the
extra returns from a professional career exceed the extra costs.

The difference between extra returns and extra costs may
reflect a higher level of ability of professional workers, or certain nonpecuniary advantages of their work. But there is
some basis for supposing that at least in part it reflects the
fact that professional workers constitute a 'noncompeting'
group. The social and economic stratification of the population leaves only limited groups really free to enter the professions. A young man must not only have the ability to
practise a profession and must not only want to enter it; he
must also be able to finance his training and be cognizant of
opportunities; and both his entry into the profession and his
success in it will be greatly facilitated if he has the proper background and connections.

These factors have apparently led to underinvestment in
professional training. Unlike high returns on capital invested
in machinery, high returns on capital invested in professional
training need not lead to an increase in investment. Capital
invested in human beings is not separable from the individual
and cannot be bought and sold on the open market. Individuals might invest in themselves, their children, or their
protégés, even though they did not expect the added income
to repay the cost; no investor in search of profit would invest
in the education of strangers even though a high return to the
latter were expected. The amount invested in professional
training will depend less on expected returns than on the number of persons who have or can get the money to finance their
training. If they are few, relatively to the demand for the services of professional workers, underinvestment will result; in
the contrary case, overinvestment.

These remarks apply, of course, solely to voluntary investment by prospective practitioners themselves, their parents,

or their direct benefactors. They take no account of the large expenditures on education by government and private philanthropists, expenditures that in part at least are made necessary by the absence of any automatic tendency for profit-seeking investment to equate the return on capital invested in professional training to the return on capital invested elsewhere.

2 EARNINGS FROM INDEPENDENT PRACTICE AND FROM SALARIED EMPLOYMENT (CH. 6)

Independent practice of a profession tends to be more lucrative than salaried employment; while professional workers, independent and salaried, earn on the average between two and three times as much as all other workers, independent practitioners alone earn about four times as much. In large measure, the high average earnings of independent practitioners reflect their concentration in the better-paid professions. But there is also some evidence that, profession by profession, independent practitioners receive larger arithmetic mean earnings than their salaried brethren. The earnings of independent practitioners are less equally distributed than those of salaried workers: a larger proportion of independent than of salaried workers receive very low earnings, a larger proportion, very high earnings.

Independent practice tends to predominate in professions that sell services primarily to ultimate consumers (e.g., medicine, dentistry); salaried employment, in professions that sell services primarily to business enterprises and governmental agencies (e.g., engineering, accountancy). In the former, salaried employment is often a step toward independent practice, partaking of an apprenticeship, and might be expected to yield lower earnings. In the latter, on the other hand, salaried employment is the usual life career. Independent practice is engaged in primarily by the more highly skilled and better-known members of the profession who render specialized services that the employees of the business enterprises or governmental agencies cannot perform and that are required in amounts too small to justify the full-time employment of high-salaried men. Consulting engineers and independent certified public accountants are examples of such auxiliary professional groups.

3 AVERAGE LEVEL OF INCOME IN THE FIVE PROFESSIONS (CH. 4)
Of the five professional groups we study in detail, consulting engineers and certified public accountants receive the largest average incomes from independent practice. The Department of Commerce data on which our detailed analysis is based do not permit a satisfactory estimate of the absolute level of income of consulting engineers, though they do enable us to rank them relatively to other professional groups. The data suggest that the average (arithmetic mean) earnings of independent certified public accountants were about $5,300 during 1929–34 ($5,200 during 1929–36), of physicians, about $4,100 during 1929–34 ($4,000 during 1929–36), and of dentists, about $3,100. Lawyers had average net earnings about the same as, or somewhat larger than, physicians; the data do not permit a satisfactory estimate of the absolute level.

As already implied, the high earnings of consulting engineers and independent certified public accountants are easily explained by the character of these small and select segments of broader professional groups. Neither consulting engineers nor independent certified public accountants are comparable to independent practitioners in law, medicine, and dentistry, professions in which independent practice predominates. On the other hand, medicine and dentistry, the two remaining professions for which our data permit intensive analysis, are comparable. They are closely related, serve much the same public, and require similar abilities and training. The proportion of physicians and dentists in salaried employment is small, probably well under one-fifth, and is about the same in both professions. Consequently, it is decidedly more difficult to explain the sizable difference between average earnings in medicine and dentistry, a difference of $1,000, or almost a third of the dental average. Moreover, this difference between the nationwide averages understates the difference between physicians and dentists in the same community and in practice the same number of years.

Factors associated with the free working of supply and demand do not account for the whole difference between average earnings of physicians and dentists. If they did, the numbers seeking to enter the two professions would be approximately in proportion to the numbers already in the professions. In fact, three and a half to four times as many persons were seeking in recent years to become physicians as were seeking to become dentists, although the total number of physicians is only slightly more than twice the number of dentists. At existing levels of remuneration, prospective practitioners apparently consider medicine more attractive than dentistry: were entry into the two professions equally easy, there would be a tendency for the number of physicians to increase relatively to the number of dentists and for the gap between average incomes in the two professions to narrow. But entry is not equally easy. There has been only a minor increase in the number of physicians relatively to the number of dentists from 1930 to 1940, in contrast with a marked decline in the ratio from 1910 to 1920 and 1920 to 1930. The gap between average incomes in the two professions showed no tendency to narrow during the period covered by our data. Part of the difference between the average incomes of physicians and dentists is therefore attributable to the greater difficulty of entry into medicine.

It is not easy to assess the quantitative importance of each of the factors responsible for the difference in average incomes. The factors are numerous and varied, many are vague and subjective, and their effects are merged. The cost of the three years additional training required of physicians is the only one whose influence is at all susceptible to quantitative measurement. We estimate that alone it would account for not more than a 17 per cent differential in average incomes. We have tried to evaluate the influence of the remaining factors associated with the free working of supply and demand—the greater variability of income in medicine than in dentistry, the nonpecuniary advantages and disadvantages of the two professions, and the conditions of demand for their services—by combining personal judgment, theoretical analysis, and such meagre empirical data as are relevant and available. We hazard the guess that on balance these factors alone would lead to lower average income in medicine than in dentistry, partly counterbalancing the influence of extra costs of medical training. If this guess is correct, completely free and moderately rational choice of profession could at most account for a 17 per cent difference between average incomes in medicine and dentistry. The observed difference is over 32 per cent. Thus about half of the observed difference seems attributable to greater difficulty of entry into medicine. This difficulty is encountered when individuals apply for admission to medical schools. In recent years between 40 and 50 per cent have been refused. Some, of course, apply again in later years, but the available data suggest that approximately a third of all who seek admittance to medical schools are never admitted. The corresponding percentages for dentistry are much smaller.

The difference in ease of entry is open to three interpretations. It may reflect, first, a public policy of raising the standards of medical practice to levels that create a shortage in the relative supply of 'innate abilities' needed for the medical as compared with the dental profession; second, a related public policy of raising the standards of medical training to levels that are difficult for medical schools to meet and that make it impossible for the accredited schools to handle large numbers of students; or, third, a deliberate policy of limiting the number of entrants in order to keep down the total number of physicians, that is, to prevent 'overcrowding' of the profession. We are in no position to judge the relative importance of these possible causes of the greater difficulty of entry into medicine.

4 VARIABILITY OF INCOME IN THE FIVE PROFESSIONS (CH. 4)

The five professions differ not only in level of income but also in the extent to which the incomes of individuals vary about the average. In the accompanying tabulation the professions are ranked in the order of the level, absolute variability (variability measured in dollars), and relative variability (variability measured in percentages of average income) of annual income.

RANKING OF PROFESSIONS IN DECREASING ORDER OF

LEVEL OF INCOME	ABSOLUTE VARIABILITY	RELATIVE VARIABILITY
Consulting engineering	Consulting engineering	Consulting engineering
Certified public	Law	Law
accountancy	Certified public	Medicine
Law	accountancy and	Certified public
Medicine	Medicine	accountancy
Dentistry	Dentistry	Dentistry

Except for the position of certified public accountancy, the three rankings are identical. We are inclined to regard this similarity among the rankings, striking though it is, as coincidental, since we can find no reasonable explanation for it. The variability of income among practitioners is determined primarily by the degree to which their services vary in quality, as judged by consumers; the importance attributed by consumers to securing services considered superior in quality and hence the premium they are willing to pay to the man they consider 'better'; and the variability among consumers in resources and hence in the prices they can afford to pay. None of these seems intimately connected with the factors that determine the level of income.

5 STABILITY OF RELATIVE INCOME STATUS (CH. 4 AND 7)

The same variability of *annual* income in two professions may reflect different underlying circumstances. In one profession each individual may, year after year, occupy the same relative position in an array of practitioners by size of income. In another, the relative status of individuals may shift widely from year to year, so that many who are at the top in one year are at the bottom the next, and conversely. In the first profession, the variability of annual income would be essentially the same as, and would provide a reasonably good measure of, the variability of income for a longer period. In the second, the variability of annual income would greatly overstate lasting or long-run variability.

All our professions are characterized by a considerable degree of stability of relative income status. An individual's income rises and falls with the ups and downs in the fortunes of the economy and of the profession as a whole; but his relative income status changes little from year to year. The variability of income for a two- or three-year period is not much smaller than the variability of annual income. Moreover, the stability of relative income status is even greater over long periods than would be suggested by a comparison of incomes in successive years. Individuals tend to return to the same relative position after reverses or successes. Stability of relative income status is greatest in professions like medicine and dentistry in which custom is so important, and somewhat less in the 'business' professions in which competitive forces have larger scope.

In all the professions except possibly accountancy there appears to be a linear relation between the average incomes in different years of groups of individuals classified by their incomes in one of those years. One interpretation of this finding is that the transitory forces leading to changes from year to year in the relative income status of individuals affect all income classes alike.

6 FACTORS DETERMINING SIZE OF EARNINGS WITHIN THE PRO-
   FESSIONS

As we have seen, the profession an individual chooses has a decided effect on the income he can expect to earn, the range of income he can consider possible, and the stability of income he can hope to attain. But the choice of a profession by no means determines his income uniquely. It depends in addition on where he practises, how long he has practised, the kind of practice he engages in, how he organizes his practice, and his ability, social and business connections, personality, and good fortune. Adequate statistical analysis is possible for a few of the many factors that determine his income: location, type of practice, organization of practice, and number of years in practice.

Though each has a significant influence on average income, even taken all together these factors account for only a small part of the marked inequality of income that characterizes independent professional practice. There are so many other factors making for inequality that individuals who have the same number of years' experience and engage in practice of the same type or organization in the same community receive incomes that vary almost as much as the incomes of all members of the profession.

The effect of the factors studied on the stability of relative income status is similarly limited. Professional men typically remain in the same community for long periods and rarely change the type or organization of their practices. Differences in income arising from differences in location, type, or organization of practice tend to persist and to lead to stability in the ranking of individuals by size of income. On the other hand, differences in income arising from differences in number of years in practice militate against stability: individuals become older and gain experience, and tend to shift upward or downward. However, it is doubtful that the factors enumerated exercise any greater influence on the stability of relative income status than on the variability of annual income.

a Location of practice (Ch. 5)

Of the many features characterizing the location of practice, we have concentrated on two: size of community and geographic region. The paucity of data forced the use of broad categories even for these two characteristics. We have generally used six to eight size of community classes and the nine Census regions.

The size of the community in which an individual practises has a much greater effect on his income than the region in which that community is located. Not only are regional differences in average income smaller than size of community differences, but also they are largely attributable to regional differences in degree of urbanization. Indeed, for the professions other than medicine and dentistry, this appears to be the whole story: the regional differences in average income not accounted for by differences in degree of urbanization apparently reflect sampling fluctuations.

In general, average income increases consistently with the size of community. Medicine constitutes the one exception: medical incomes are higher in middle-sized than in very large cities. In all professions, the most striking disparity is between communities with populations under 2,500 and those with populations over 10,000; average incomes in the former are one-half to two-thirds as large as average incomes in the latter. Communities between these two groups in population are also between them in income. The variability of income displays a much less consistent relation to size of community. One measure of relative variability, the coefficient of variation, tends to decline with size of community for most of the range, but to be larger for the smallest communities than for somewhat bigger ones. Another measure, the relative interquartile difference, displays no consistent relation to size of community. Neither measure displays consistent regional differences.

The absence of substantial regional differences in average income suggests that there is sufficient geographic mobility to prevent them from arising or being maintained. If this is the case, size of community differences cannot easily be attributed to immobility. Mobility among large, middle-sized, and small communities in the same region is probably at least as great as among regions. The size of community differences in income must therefore reflect either the concentration of abler men in the large cities or nonpecuniary advantages of small communities.

The size of community differences in professional income are similar, both in direction and magnitude, to the corresponding differences in the income of the public at large. This parallelism of results suggests a parallelism of causes. If the differences in professional income are interpreted as reflecting mobility rather than immobility, it seems reasonable to interpret the differences in the income of the public in like manner. This would imply that regional differences in the income of the public also reflect mobility and hence should be similar to those in professional income, since professional and other workers would be unlikely to agree in their evaluations of the nonpecuniary advantages of communities of different size but disagree in their evaluations of the nonpecuniary advantages of regions. This conclusion is not supported by the data. Regional differences in professional income display some similarity in direction to the corresponding differences in the income of the public at large, but practically none in magnitude. The income of the public at large seems to vary more from region to region than the income of professional workers. There are several possible explanations of this apparently contradictory result; to decide which, if any, is valid would require a more intensive analysis of this problem than we have made.

b Specialization (Ch. 6)

The complex character of professional activity has occasioned specialization in all professions. In medicine and dentistry specialization has taken the form of a limitation in the kind of service rendered by individuals practising independently and coordinated by the impersonal mechanism of the market. Sharing of office space, nonprofessional help, and some types of equipment is frequent, but formal organization into partnerships or firms is rare. In law, accountancy, and engineering, specialization by separate professional units has been supplemented by the formation of larger units, or firms, the individual members or employees frequently concentrating on specific fields of practice. Our data suggest that about a quarter of the lawyers, a third of the accountants, and almost half of the consulting engineers who practise independently are members of firms.

Specialization is far more widespread in medicine than in dentistry. About one-fifth of all physicians in independent practice consider themselves complete specialists and almost two-fifths, partial specialists. Only about 3 per cent of all dentists in independent practice consider themselves complete specialists, and fewer than 10 per cent, partial specialists. In both professions complete specialists receive higher average incomes than partial specialists, and partial specialists than general practitioners. In dentistry complete specialists receive an average income about 30 per cent larger than that of partial specialists and 70 per cent larger than that of general practitioners. In medicine complete specialists receive an average income more than 50 per cent larger than that of partial specialists and twice that of general practitioners. According to the Department of Commerce data for physicians, the average income for 1929–36 of complete specialists was approximately $5,900; of partial specialists, $3,800; and of general practitioners, $2,900.

The differences among these countrywide averages mirror the effect not only of specialization but also of location and experience. Complete specialists are concentrated in the larger cities and in the middle age group. In effect, the averages for complete specialists and general practitioners compare one group in the most lucrative locations and the prime of life with another containing many who are in poorer locations and who are just getting started or are on the verge of retiring. Averages computed for physicians living in the same community and in practice the same number of years would show a difference of about 30 rather than 50 per cent between complete and partial specialists and of 60 rather than 100 per cent between complete specialists and general practitioners. Presumably the differences that remain are largely attributable to differences in training and skill and are a permanent concomitant of a segregation of physicians by criteria related to their chances of success, rather than a transitory phenomenon that will be eliminated by or would give rise to an influx into the specialties.

c Organization of practice (Ch. 6)
A classification of lawyers, accountants, and engineers into firm members and individual practitioners, though much less clear-cut analytically than a classification of physicians and

dentists into specialists and general practitioners, is yet essentially similar. Like specialists, and for the same reasons, firm members are concentrated in the larger cities, are seldom in the initial stages of their careers, and receive higher average incomes than other members of the profession in the same community and of the same age. According to countrywide figures, the average income of firm members exceeds that of individual practitioners by about 100 per cent in law, 40 to 90 per cent in engineering, and 25 to 60 per cent in accountancy. Unfortunately, from the available data we cannot estimate how much these differences would be reduced by allowing for differences in location and experience.

d Years in practice (Ch. 6)
The relation between income and number of years in practice is similar in all professions: income rises for a time and then declines. In medicine and dentistry, professions in which scientific advance has been rapid and physical skill and dexterity are required, younger men are at an advantage and the peak income is reached fairly early—between the thirteenth and twentieth year of practice. In law, the only one of the 'business' professions for which data are available, experience and contacts are more important and physical fitness secondary. In consequence, the peak income is reached much later—probably between the twentieth and fortieth year of practice.

For physicians, the data make possible a more detailed analysis of the relation between income and number of years in practice. It takes about 7 years for beginning physicians to attain an average income equal to the average for the profession; another 10 or 11 years brings them to the peak; and it is then between 15 and 20 years before their average income falls below the average for the profession. The patterns for different types of physicians vary in important respects from the pattern for all physicians just described. Though at first average income is about the same in all types of practice, after an initial period of 8 to 12 years the averages diverge considerably. The rise is larger for complete than for partial specialists and for partial specialists than for general practitioners. General practitioners reach their peak income somewhat earlier than all physicians; the other two groups somewhat later. The percentage differences among the incomes of the three groups thus display a fairly uniform tendency to increase with number of years in practice.

The relation between the income of physicians and number of years in practice is not the same for all size of community classes: the initial rise and the later fall are larger, and the rise is sharper relatively to the fall, in large communities than in small. The relatively flat pattern in small communities is probably attributable to the absence of effective direct competition. The tendency for the rise to be more rapid relatively to the fall in the large communities appears in part attributable to the concentration of young physicians in large communities.

7   CHANGES IN INCOME FROM 1929 TO 1936 (CH. 8)
The average earnings of physicians, dentists, lawyers, and certified public accountants fell from 1929 to 1933 and rose from 1933 to 1936. For consulting engineers, we have data only for 1929–32. During this period, they experienced a much sharper decline in average earnings than other independent professional men. Both the fall and the rise in average earnings in the other four professions were about the same in percentage terms as the contemporaneous changes in the average earnings of all gainfully occupied workers. In this cycle, at least, professional earnings were neither more nor less stable over time than earnings in other pursuits.

Temporal changes in average earnings in the professions paralleled corresponding changes in the income of the public not only for the country as a whole, but also for separate regions. Short-run changes in income from independent professional practice seem to reflect primarily changes in general economic activity and consequently in the prosperity of the consumers of professional services.

Variability of income measured in dollars displayed temporal changes similar to those in average income. Variability measured in percentage terms changed erratically. The evidence on this point is confused and difficult to interpret, but the only conclusion that seems justified is that relative variability changed in no consistent or regular fashion with changes in general economic conditions.

8 INCOME FROM INDEPENDENT PROFESSIONAL PRACTICE AND
   TOTAL INCOME

Most of the conclusions summarized in this chapter relate to net income from independent professional practice, not to the total income of professional men in independent practice. For most professional men in independent practice, income from practice is by far the major source of income. But often there are other sources—salaried professional or nonprofessional employment, property, etc. Whether the variability of total income will be larger or smaller than the variability of income from independent practice depends on the relation between this part of total income and the rest.

Interprofessional comparisons also might be affected by the inclusion of income from sources other than independent practice. Opportunity to obtain such income obviously varies from profession to profession; and so may the relation between income from independent practice and from other sources. This problem of the composition of income, of how different sources of income combine, is relevant not only to studies of professional groups but also to all studies of the distribution of income by size. Fortunately, the exceedingly meagre data that have been available on the problem are being greatly supplemented by recent and current studies.

DIRECTOR'S COMMENT

by

C. Reinold Noyes

CERTAIN reservations seem to me to be required with regard to the scientific validity of some of the points made in this study.

1) The average income in all professions is compared with the average income in "all other pursuits" (p. 68), after allowance is made for amortizing the higher costs of education and the shorter span of working life in the former. The average of professional incomes is shown to be 85-180% higher, while amortization for higher 'cost of production' is estimated to require a difference of only 70%. The professional group is stated to be a "fortunate" (p. 390) and "non-competing" (p. 391) group with an average income which appears to be significantly higher than the "equilibrium level."

The figures show a very wide range of incomes within both the professional and the non-professional groups. Roughly we may say that they run from zero to $50,000 a year in the professions, and from zero to $500,000 a year in other pursuits.[1] Evidently, many other causes make for differences in income besides differences in cost of education. The latter are assumed to work on the average only as between the groups. But these other causes must also work between the groups. If the equilibrium level were to be equality of average incomes in the two groups, after allowing for differences in 'cost of production,' it would be necessary to suppose that the average effect of all other causes making for differences in income is precisely the same for both groups. Not only is there no evidence

[1] The round figure of $50,000 for the professions is taken from the Appendix to this study; that for other pursuits is taken from the figures published periodically by the Treasury Department for payments for services by corporations.

that this is the case, but it seems that it would be quite impossible to assemble evidence to prove it. *A priori,* it is unlikely that any such wide miscellany of forces operating in two fields would ever produce the same average effects in both. Nor, as a matter of common observation, do we usually expect such a result among income classes. There is a wide difference between the average income of motion picture stars and of longshoremen, for instance, which certainly cannot be accounted for by differences in cost of educational requirements.

Some, or perhaps all, of these other causes making for differences of income within as well as between income classes are mentioned by the authors. Among these are differences in ability, etc. No effort is made, nor probably could be, to appraise the distribution of effects of these other causes upon the two groups. But, without such measurement, there is no ground for rejecting the possibility that, if these other causes (*excluding* social and legal ease of entry) were measured they would warrant an average level of incomes in the professions, as compared with that of other pursuits, much higher than it is now. So far as we can know from these data incomes in the professions may be well *below* the equilibrium level.

It is true, as the authors say, that there are social and legal obstacles to entry into professional practice which do not exist, at least to the same extent, in most other pursuits. Thus it is also possible that these obstacles restrict entry to, reduce the number in, and thus raise the level of incomes in the professions above what they would be in the absence of these obstacles. (See pp. 93-4.) Nevertheless, without proof that the higher level of incomes in the professions is not wholly accounted for, or more than accounted for, by greater ability, etc., it does not seem justifiable to treat the relative difficulty of entry as the cause, or even as one of the chief causes, of the difference in average income levels. If a zoölogist were to find that, on the average, herbivora are 365 mm. (let us say) taller than carnivora, would he be justified in concluding that the sole reason, or even a chief reason, is the advantages of a vegetarian diet?

It may be that professional men constitute a "fortunate," "non-competing" group, with incomes considerably higher than the "equilibrium level." On the other hand, so far as the evidence presented here is concerned, one would have equal warrant for concluding that they are an unfortunate group, subject to excessive competition due to over-crowding, and composed of men who have rejected the opportunity to earn much larger incomes in other pursuits only because they were determined to dedicate themselves to social service rather than to pecuniary rewards. One is left quite free to arrive at either of these extreme verdicts, or one anywhere between them.

2) When it comes to the similar contrast which the authors set up between the medical and dental professions, an attempt is made to establish a *ceteris paribus*. That is, it is assumed that the two professions require much the same type and degree of ability, etc., so that other causes of differences in average incomes (above) should operate about equally in both (pp. 136 and 393). If it is necessary to meet such a requirement for determining what ought to be equilibrium levels of average income in this case, it was equally necessary to do so in the case of professions vs. other pursuits. The difficulty would be that there could be hardly any warrant for the assumption, in the first case, that other pursuits require, on the average, much the same type and degree of ability as the professions do.

3) It is doubtful that competent opinion would support the assumption that medicine and dentistry require much the same type and degree of ability, etc. Without disparaging dentistry, particularly in view of the enormous scientific advances it has made in the last few decades, it seems hardly proper to equate the manual skill required of a dentist to that required of a surgeon or the dentist's necessary fund of scientific knowledge and experience to that of a diagnostician or a neurologist.

4) The authors use average incomes in their contrast between medicine and dentistry. In medicine they estimate the average to be 32% higher than in dentistry. But both the median and the first quartile incomes are approximately the same in the two professions. The difference between the ratios of average and of median and first quartile incomes is accounted for by the fact that there is a considerable group of large incomes in medicine, while the higher incomes in dentistry are both much smaller and much fewer (pp. 111-2 and 128). The large incomes in medicine are presumably obtained by those who succeed in building up large practices and even in charging higher fees in free competition with all other physicians. That argues either a peculiarity in demand or one in supply, or both, which apparently does not exist in dentistry to anywhere near the same degree. To the extent that the peculiarity in supply is due to exceptional ability at the top in medicine which does not exist in dentistry, the assumption of equal average abilities (3, above) is not justified unless there is also an assumption that this is offset by a range of much lower abilities in medicine. To the extent that the peculiarity of demand is due to 'differentiation' of product, its higher price and larger sales cannot be attributed to lack of freedom of entry into the profession, for the whole existing profession is free to compete for these large and high-priced practices. On either basis the only portion of the medical profession that might be called non-competitive is the great rank and file. But the medians and first quartiles show that the great rank and file in medicine receive about the same income as the great rank and file of dentists. Thus there is no evidence of disequilibrium in income levels as between the two professions, after eliminating those who represent a peculiarity of supply or are able to take advantage of a peculiarity in demand which exist in much greater degree in one than they do in the other profession.

5) Approached in another way, which somewhat cuts across the last, there is the matter of specialists. In both professions the average income of specialists is considerably higher than

that of general practitioners (p. 264). But since specialists
bulk large in medicine and are relatively few in dentistry
(pp. 263-4), the result is that, while the average income of
all physicians is higher than that of all dentists, the average
income of general practitioners is about the same in both.
Specialists have been for the most part recruited from general practice. At least, for one practising in either profession,
there is complete freedom of entry into the specialties. They
are then strictly competitive.[2] Thus, again, there is no evidence of disequilibrium in income levels as between the two
professions when those are eliminated in each profession who
succeeded, in open competition, in becoming specialists.

6) It seems logical to conclude from the points made in
sections 4 and 5 above that there is one sector—or two sectors—
in the medical profession the incomes in which are responsible for the fact that the average income is higher in medicine
than in dentistry. The existence of this sector—or these sectors—either

(a) makes the requirements for the two professions incom-
parable on a *ceteris paribus* basis, if it is due to a peculiarity
of supply, or

(b) is the outcome of free competition within the medical
profession to meet a peculiarity of demand.

On neither explanation can the existence of these sectors be ascribed to greater difficulty of entry into the profession as a whole. The remainder of the two professions, whose
incomes might be affected by differences in freedom of entry,
are about on a parity so far as average income is concerned.
Therefore it is more difficult to accept the authors' conclusion
in the contrast between medicine and dentistry than it was
to accept the first one with regard to the contrast between
the professions as a whole and other pursuits. There the aver-

2 The authors say, "Presumably, the differences that remain are largely attributable to differences in training and skill and are a permanent concomitant
of a segregation of physicians by criteria related to their chances of success,
rather than a transitory phenomenon that will be eliminated by or would
give rise to an influx into the specialties" (p. 401).

age for the professions was certainly higher and the question concerned only comparability. Here, when a reasonable degree of comparability is attained, the averages seem to be about the same. If, then, we were to accept the authors' general conclusions in Chapter 4, Section 2 [3] and in Chapter 9, it would seem to be necessary to suppose that 'equilibrium levels' between physicians and dentists would involve a lower average income for the great rank and file and for general practitioners in medicine than for the corresponding classes of dentists.

[3] And particularly that "the observed difference in incomes is therefore apparently greater than the 'equilibrium' difference" (pp. 124-5).

The Reliability of the Department
of Commerce Samples

THIS APPENDIX discusses in detail the reliability of the data on which the greater part of our analysis is based. These data were collected by the U. S. Department of Commerce as part of a study of the size of national income. Chapter 2 describes the samples we have used and summarizes the conclusions reached in this Appendix.

The relatively small size of the samples (see column 10 of Table 4) makes it specially important to investigate thoroughly their representativeness, to determine the biases to which they may be subject, and to find ways of eliminating these biases. We shall attempt to do this (1) by examining in detail the sampling methods used; and (2) by comparing (a) the distribution of the samples with the distribution of the universe, (b) different samples covering the same year with one another, (c) the Department of Commerce samples with other studies of the incomes of professional men.[1]

1 THE SAMPLING METHOD

The process of obtaining a sample involves first, the designation of a list of names to serve as the basis for sampling; second, the choice of the persons on the list to whom questionnaires are sent; third, the return of the questionnaires by the respondents; and fourth, the editing of the returned questionnaires before final use. Biases may enter at each stage: the list may be defective, the method of choosing names may not yield a truly 'random' sample, those who reply may differ from those who fail to reply, the answers of those

---

1 Most of the computations cited in this Appendix do not incorporate minor revisions of the basic data made at a fairly late stage in the study. Correction of the computations would have altered none of the conclusions and hence did not seem justified. In consequence, however, there are minor discrepancies between some of the measures cited in this Appendix and supposedly identical measures in the text, text tables, or tables of Appendix B.

who reply may have a systematic bias, and the questionnaires rejected in the process of editing may differ systematically from those retained.

a The lists employed

i *The incompleteness of the lists for the earlier years.* All questionnaires requested information on income for several years from a sample of professional men selected from a list presumed to be comprehensive for the end of the period. For example, the questionnaires mailed to physicians in 1933 requested information on income for the four years 1929–32. These questionnaires were sent to a sample selected from a list of physicians in practice in 1932. Even if such a sample were entirely random for 1932 it would not be random for 1929, since the list would exclude the names of men who were in practice in 1929 but who died, retired, or left the profession for other reasons, between 1929 and 1932. The longer the period between the year for which information is requested and the year for which the list is comprehensive, the more incomplete the list will tend to be.

The resulting bias in average income depends not only on the number of men who leave the profession and hence are omitted from the list but also on their average income. If their average income were equal to the average income in the profession as a whole, there would be no bias; if it were higher than the average income in the profession, the sample average would tend to be too low; and conversely.

Since termination of independent professional practice is usually due to death or retirement, the persons omitted from the list are likely to be concentrated in the relatively high age groups. The average age of professional men at the time of death is about 69 years.[2] The average age of those omitted because of death was, therefore, less than 69 in the year in question—i.e., in one of the earlier years when they were in practice. The average age of those omitted because they retired or left the profession for other reasons was almost certainly still lower.

From the evidence in Chapter 6, it appears that average income rises for a time with increasing experience and then falls, eventu-

2 Clark, *Life Earnings in Selected Occupations,* p. 150. This is the expected average age at death of males who were 20 in 1930.

ally dropping below the average for the profession as a whole. In medicine and dentistry the average for the profession is reached after 33 or 34 years in practice, i.e., by men about 55 or 60 years old. In the other professions the rise continues longer and the fall is less rapid, so that the average for the profession is not reached until considerably later. These statements, based on data for all persons in practice, may not be valid for persons destined to leave practice in the next few years. Some men may be in a position to retire because their earnings have been better than average; others may retire or leave practice because they have been receiving such low incomes that there is no incentive for them to remain in practice.

While this evidence does not yield a clear-cut conclusion, it does suggest that those omitted from the list are concentrated in age groups whose average income is about the same as or somewhat higher than the average for the profession. If this is so, and if the average income at each age of men in practice can be assumed valid for men destined to leave practice in the next few years, the sample averages for the earlier years might be expected to be somewhat too low. Since the persons omitted from the list are likely to be more numerous and, on the average, younger the longer the period between the year for which income information is requested and the year for which the list is comprehensive, the bias in the sample averages will tend to be greatest for the earliest year covered. Hence the incompleteness of the list not only affects the absolute level of average income but also imparts an upward bias to the trend of average income over time.

In practice, this tendency is accentuated by the fact that a list purporting to be comprehensive for a given year rarely is. New entrants into a profession are difficult to trace and are almost always inadequately covered. Since the average income of new entrants is considerably below the average for the profession, their underrepresentation tends to make the sample average for the terminal year too high.

The existence of an upward bias in the trend of income over time is confirmed by our data. Such a bias would mean that the earlier of two samples for the same profession would tend to yield a higher average for an overlapping year. We show below (Sec. 2b) that this tendency is reflected in our data after correction is made for the specific biases discussed later. In the absence of detailed data on the persons omitted from the list, it has not been possible to correct the data for this bias.

ii *The inclusion of persons not in independent practice.* All lists of professional men from which the samples were selected include not only men in independent practice but also salaried employees and persons not in professional practice.[3] Although the questionnaires emphasized that information was desired solely from men in independent practice, some of the returned questionnaires contained notations indicating that this instruction had been disregarded. It is unlikely, however, that a large number of persons not in independent practice are included in the final sample, since the many items on the questionnaires applicable only to persons in independent practice facilitated the identification of questionnaires inadvertently returned by others. Except for the elimination of questionable returns in the process of editing, no attempt has been made to correct the data for the inclusion of persons not in independent practice.

The inclusion of salaried employees on the list from which the sample was selected introduced an additional bias into the 1937 accountancy sample. The questionnaire for this sample differed from the questionnaires for the other accountancy samples and the other professions in that it requested a recipient who was a salaried employee of an accounting firm to hand the questionnaire to his employer. Consequently, an accountant with salaried professional employees would be more likely to be included in the final sample than an accountant without such employees. This would make for an overrepresentation of the more affluent accountants since accountants who have professional employees are likely to receive higher incomes than other accountants. Two bits of evidence suggest that this bias is unimportant. First, the 1937 accountancy sample yielded lower average incomes for the overlapping years than the earlier samples (Table 5). Second, it seems likely that a larger proportion of firms than of individual practitioners employ other accountants; yet the proportion of firm members in the 1937 sam-

[3] In addition, the lists include the names of some retired or deceased persons. Replies by the retired persons for the years prior to retirement would tend to counteract the bias discussed in the preceding section. In fact, however, it is clear from the returned questionnaires that most retired persons either do not reply or return the questionnaires with notations that they have retired but with no information for years prior to retirement.

ple is about the same as in the 1935 sample and decidedly lower than in the 1933 sample (Table 46).

iii *The medical, legal, and accountancy lists.* The lists used in selecting the medical, legal, and accountancy samples—the Directory of the American Medical Association, the *Martindale-Hubbell Law Directory,* and the mailing list of the American Society of Certified Public Accountants—seem excellent apart from the general defects already noted. Since in all three professions the right to practise is limited to individuals licensed by the state, the inclusion of new practitioners is relatively easy. The number of names on these lists checks very closely with the totals recorded in other sources.[4]

iv *The dental list.* The list used for dentists was restricted to members of the American Dental Association, which included only about 46 per cent of the dentists in practice when our samples were taken.[5] It is clear from the available evidence that members

[4] The 1931 medical directory lists 156,339 physicians; the 1930 *Census of Population,* 153,803. The 1930 issue of the legal directory (relating to lawyers in practice in 1929) lists 141,501 lawyers; the 1930 Census, 139,059 as engaged in professional service. (The Martindale-Hubbell directory makes no attempt to list lawyers employed by nonlegal enterprises. This explains why the comparison is made with the number of lawyers listed by the Census as engaged in professional service.) The mailing list of the American Society of Certified Public Accountants included between 13,000 and 15,000 names during the period in question. The American Institute of Accountants (with which the Society recently merged) estimated that there were approximately 16,500 certified public accountants in 1937.

[5] The estimate of 46 per cent is based on (1) data supplied by the American Dental Association on the number of members in 1932 and 1934, and (2) estimates of the total number of dentists in the United States in 1932 and 1934. The estimates of the total number of dentists are based on straight-line interpolation between 71,055, the number of dentists listed in the *Census of Population* for 1930, and 75,225, the estimate of the number of dentists in 1936 given in Table 1. The years 1932 and 1934 were used because our samples were drawn from the membership lists for those years.

According to these data, 45.5 per cent of all dentists were members in 1932 and 47.2 in 1934. The figure we use, 46.2, is an average of the two, with the 1932 and 1934 figures weighted respectively 4 and 3, the number of years covered by the corresponding samples.

These estimates are for all dentists, whereas our interest centers in independent practitioners. Some indication of the maximum error involved in using the same percentage for independent practitioners can be obtained by assuming that *all* members are in independent practice, and accepting unpub-

of the American Dental Association are not representative of all dentists. In a study of 1929 incomes made in 1930 and covering slightly over 5,000 dentists in twenty states, Leven found "that the net incomes of those who reported themselves as members were, on the average 30 per cent higher than those of the dentists who did not claim membership".[6] In a study made in California in 1934 and based on approximately 1,600 returns, the 1933 average net professional income of members of the American Dental Association was found to be 33.4 per cent higher than that of nonmembers.[7] Both percentages are based on fairly large samples. Their closeness, while not conclusive as to their reliability, gives some reason for confidence in them.

However, neither figure can be used, without further investigation, to adjust the average incomes from our samples. In both studies a dentist was classified as a member or nonmember on the basis of his answer to a question requesting him to indicate the societies to which he belonged. Leven found a wide discrepancy between the membership records of the American Dental Association and the information supplied by the dentists themselves: 49 per cent of the dentists in the 20 states covered by Leven's sample were carried on the membership rolls of the Association in 1929, whereas Leven estimates that 68 per cent would have classified themselves as members if all had returned questionnaires.[8] The California figures show a similar discrepancy. The discrepancy is presumably attributable to three groups: individuals who were formerly members of the Association but had been dropped for nonpayment of dues or for other reasons; individuals belonging to local or other dental societies but not to the national association;

---

lished estimates by the American Dental Association of the total number of dentists in independent practice (these estimates seem, if anything, slightly too low). These assumptions yield 57.8 as the percentage of independent practitioners who were members. Assuming that a smaller proportion of members than of nonmembers are in independent practice would of course yield a figure below 46.2 per cent; but there seems no particular numerical assumption that deserves special recognition as setting a lower limit.

6 *Practice of Dentistry*, p. 200.

7 *California Medical-Economic Survey*, Table 71. The average income of members was $3,022; of nonmembers, $2,265. These averages are based on 1,074 members and 541 nonmembers.

8 *Practice of Dentistry*, pp. 12, 200.

individuals who had become members so recently that their names had not been entered on the membership rolls.

Since our samples were chosen from the membership rolls of the American Dental Association, only individuals listed as members by the Association could have been included. Hence, the relevant figure for our purposes is the percentage excess of the average income of this group of members over the average income of other dentists. The data available from the two studies cited do not yield a precise estimate of this figure. The best we can do is to set limits within which it may reasonably be supposed to lie. On the basis of Leven's figures, these limits are 17 and 42 per cent; on the basis of the California figures, they are 20 and 50 per cent. More or less arbitrarily, we have selected 30 per cent as the best estimate of the percentage excess of the average income of dentists on the membership rolls of the Association over the average income of other dentists.[9]

Since, as already indicated, approximately 46 per cent of all dentists were on the membership rolls of the American Dental Association when our samples were selected, a difference of 30 per cent between the incomes of members and nonmembers would imply that the average income of all dentists is 87.6 per cent of the average income of members alone. The final estimates of the average incomes of dentists given in Table 11 were computed by using this correction factor to adjust for the restriction of the samples

[9] Let k be the percentage excess of the average income of dentists on the membership rolls of the Association over the average income of the remaining dentists; x_m, the average income of dentists on the membership rolls of the Association; x_q, the average income of dentists who classify themselves as members but are not on the membership rolls of the Association; and x_n, the average income of all other dentists. The relation between k and the figure of 30 per cent cited by Leven or the figure of 33.4 per cent from the California study depends on the relation of x_q to x_m and x_n, and on the relative size of the three groups. According to Leven's figures, if x_q were equal to x_m, k would equal 17 per cent. On the other hand, if x_q were equal to x_n, k would equal 42 per cent. According to the California figures, these two extreme assumptions would give values of k of about 20 and 50 per cent respectively. Presumably, the correct value of k lies between these two extremes, since the self-designated members appear to be somewhat of a mixture of the other two groups and might be expected to have an average income between x_m and x_n. The figure of 30 per cent selected for k implies, on the basis of Leven's figures, that x_q is approximately 12 per cent greater than x_n and 17 per cent less than x_m; on the basis of the California figures, that x_q is 21 per cent greater than x_n and 13 per cent less than x_m.

to members.[10] This is the only table in which corrected data are presented. The data for dentists in all other tables should be interpreted as referring solely to members of the American Dental Association.

The correction factor used to adjust for the bias in average income is admittedly based on slender evidence. However, a recent study, the results of which became available only after our estimates had been made—and, indeed, published [11]—provides striking confirmation of their validity. This study was made by the Department of Commerce and is based on a sample of over 7,000 dentists. The sample was similar to those we analyze but covered both members and nonmembers. According to this study the average income of nonsalaried dentists was $4,267 in 1929, and $2,188 in 1933.[12] Our final estimates (Table 11) are $4,176 for 1929, and $2,178 for 1933; i.e., the difference is about 2 per cent for 1929, and less than 0.5 per cent for 1933.

The exclusion of nonmembers presumably affects not only average income but also other aspects of the frequency distribution of income by size. In particular it seems reasonable to expect that the

[10] Since the two figures on which the correction factor of .876 is based cannot be determined exactly but are selected from a range of possible values, it is of interest to investigate the effect on the correction factor of choosing different values. In the following table the values actually used are italicized; the other hypothetical values are approximately the largest and smallest values that, on the basis of the preceding analysis, could reasonably have been used.

PERCENTAGE DIFFERENCE BETWEEN INCOMES OF MEMBERS AND NON-MEMBERS (k) TAKEN AS	VALUE OF THE CORRECTON FACTOR IF PERCENTAGE OF MEMBERS IS TAKEN AS		
	40	46.2	60
20	.900	.910	.933
30	.862	.876	.908
40	.829	.846	.886

[11] Incomes from Independent Professional Practice, 1929–1936, *Bulletin 72–73* (National Bureau of Economic Research, 1939), p. 10.

[12] Lasken, 'Incomes of Dentists and Osteopathic Physicians', Table 2. The returns included a disproportionately large number of members. Consequently the averages cited represent weighted averages of the incomes of members and nonmembers, the weights being the estimated total number in each group. Because of a marked increase in the membership of the American Dental Association between the dates when the samples we analyze were taken—1933 and 1935 —and the date the later Department of Commerce sample was taken—1938—it is not possible to make a direct comparison between the percentage excess of the average income of members that we have used and that shown by the later sample.

frequency distribution will be more concentrated and less 'skew' than if a more comprehensive list had been employed. Unfortunately, no way could be found to correct for these deficiencies.

v *The engineering list.* The list used for consulting engineers appears seriously defective. It was compiled with the aid of the American Engineering Council, representatives of which examined the directories of four national engineering societies and checked the names of engineers thought to be consultants. The number of names obtained in this way totaled 3,286; yet, according to Table 1, there were in 1930 approximately 10,000 consultants. The list clearly excludes consultants who were not members of engineering societies. In addition, it excludes engineers whose status as consultants was not known by the persons who examined the directories. Both deficiencies operate in the same direction— to exclude the less prominent and well-known. Since these individuals might be expected to receive relatively low incomes, the final sample has a definite, and possibly fairly substantial, upward bias. Unfortunately, it has not been feasible to adjust the data for this bias.

b The selection of the persons to whom questionnaires were sent
A questionnaire was sent to every *n*-th dentist on the list of the American Dental Association. This procedure is entirely valid and should yield a 'random' sample of the list employed, though, for reasons noted in the preceding section, not of the universe of dentists. Similarly, no bias could have been introduced into the engineering sample at this stage, since a questionnaire was mailed to every person whose name was on the list. The method of selecting the persons to whom questionnaires were sent was less straightforward for the other professions and introduced a number of significant biases.

i *The nonrandomness of the 1937 medical and legal samples by states.* For both physicians and lawyers, questionnaires were sent to persons selected by taking a specified number of names from each page of the relevant professional directory. For the 1933 and 1935 medical samples and the 1935 legal sample, the same number of names was taken from each page. For the 1937 medical and legal samples, however, the number of names per page was deliberately varied from state to state.[13] These two samples are therefore admittedly nonrandom as among states. To correct for this nonrandomness, all computations for these two samples have been made for each state separately, and the results weighted by the estimated total number of practitioners before being combined. (More exactly, each return has been weighted by the ratio of the estimated total number of practitioners in the state to the number in the sample for that state.)

For physicians, the weights used are the estimated number of physicians in active practice in each state in 1936.[14] The weights therefore include salaried physicians as well as those in independent practice whereas we use them in connection with data for independent practitioners alone. The proportion of all physicians in active practice in the United States in 1929 who were salaried employees has been estimated as about 15 per cent.[15] It is doubtful, therefore, that the inclusion of salaried physicians greatly affects the percentage allocation of the total among states; and, it is solely the latter, of course, that is relevant from the point of view of weighting. In any event, there are no data that could be used to estimate the proportion of salaried physicians by states.

For lawyers, the weights used are the number of lawyers in each state listed in the 1936 *Martindale-Hubbell Law Directory*.[16] This directory lists lawyers in practice in 1935 and includes salaried lawyers as well as independent practitioners. There seems little reason to suppose, however, that either deficiency seriously af-

[13] Since these samples were taken with the expectation that the data would be used in an analysis of income by states, it was desired to have a sample for each state sufficiently large to be used for this purpose. The same sampling ratio for all states would have necessitated a larger total sample than was feasible. Consequently, the sampling ratio was varied from state to state, a larger proportion of names being taken for smaller states.

[14] The estimate for each state was derived by multiplying the number of physicians in that state listed in the 1936 Directory of the American Medical Association (this count is given in the directory itself) by the 1931 ratio for the same state of the number of physicians in active practice to the total number of physicians. These ratios were based on Leland (*Distribution of Physicians*, p. 17) who gives, for each state, the total number of physicians listed in the 1931 directory, and the number listed as in active practice, retired, and not in practice. This tabulation is the most recent available.

[15] Leven, *Incomes of Physicians*, pp. 103–4.

[16] These figures were furnished by Martindale-Hubbell.

fects the relative weight assigned each state. And, as for physicians, there is no feasible alternative.

ii *The size of community bias in the medical and legal samples.* The selection of a specified number of names from each page of a directory—the procedure followed for physicians and lawyers—will yield a 'random' sample only if all pages contain the same number of names or if any variation in the number of names per page is independent of the characteristics to be studied. Examination of the medical and legal directories reveals that they satisfy neither requirement. The number of names per page varies considerably, and the variation is associated with size of community, which, in turn, is associated with income.

In both directories, the names of professional men are listed by communities. The communities are separated by a blank space and the name of each community and some information about it are given. More space per page is needed for this purpose, and hence less space remains for the listing of names, the smaller the communities listed on a page. By itself this would tend to make the number of names per page less for small communities than for large ones.

In the Directory of the American Medical Association, this tendency is more than counterbalanced by another: the number of lines devoted to each physician varies and tends to be greater for large communities. There are two reasons for this. First, a physician in a large community is likely to have a longer address, since it includes a street and number whereas the post office designation is ordinarily sufficient for a physician in a small community. Second, the medical directory lists the professional societies [17] of which the physician is a member, and, if he is a specialist, indicates by symbols his specialty. Specialists and members of the professional societies listed are concentrated in the larger communities.

The average number of names per column [18] of the medical directory is shown in Table A 1 for communities of various size. The number of names per column is approximately the same for all communities over 10,000 in population, but is considerably less

[17] Other than the American Medical Association, membership in which is designated by printing the name in capital letters, but in the same size type.
[18] There are three columns to a page.

in these communities than in smaller ones.[19] Such variation clearly tends to introduce a bias into a sample chosen by taking the same number of names from each page: communities for which the total number of names per page is relatively large tend to be underrepresented. Small communities therefore tend to be underrepresented in the medical samples.

TABLE A 1

Average Number of Names per Column of the Directory of the American Medical Association, by Size of Community

SIZE OF COMMUNITY (1930 Census)	AVG. NO. OF NAMES PER COLUMN
500,000 & over	44
100,000–500,000	45
50,000–100,000	47
25,000– 50,000	44
10,000– 25,000	46
2,500– 10,000	62
Under 2,500	54

Count of sample columns from 1936 Directory of the American Medical Association. In all, 70 columns containing 3,293 names were counted.

Though the variation in the number of names per page is small, the expected bias is revealed by a comparison of the distribution of the samples by size of community class with the corresponding distribution of all physicians. This comparison shows a slight underrepresentation of communities under 10,000 in population.[20]

[19] The differences between the averages in the two smallest community classes and the others cannot be attributed to chance. The significance of the differences among the mean values for the seven groups was tested by the analysis of variance. A value of 9.7 was obtained for F, the ratio of the mean square between groups to the mean square within groups. For the number of degrees of freedom available, a value of 3.1 would be exceeded by chance only once in a hundred times. On the other hand, the differences among the first five classes are not significant. The value of F for these five classes alone was 0.9.

[20] Leland, *Distribution of Physicians*, Table 42, gives the distribution of physicians in active practice in 1931 by size of community, based on a count of the 1931 Directory of the American Medical Association. The distributions by size of community of the physicians reporting income for 1932 in both the 1933 and 1935 samples were compared with this 1931 distribution for all physicians. (No attempt was made to compare the 1937 sample because of its nonrandomness among states.)

The effect of correcting for the size of community bias was tested by correct-

Comprehensive data are available, at least for 1931, on the distribution of physicians by size of community and geographic region.[21] These data could be used to correct for the size of community bias by weighting the sample data for each size of community class by the corresponding number of physicians in the universe. Before deciding to make this correction, however, a test was made, using 1932 arithmetic mean incomes from both the 1933 and 1935 samples, in order to see how much these would be altered by the correction. This test, summarized in Table A 2, suggests that the weighting does improve the results, but that the improvement is so slight as not to be worth the labor involved.[22]

---

ing the sample distributions on the basis of Table A 1 (see footnote 24 for the exact method used), adjusting the totals for the corrected distribution to make them equal to the totals for the uncorrected distributions, and computing χ^2 between the sample distributions and the distribution of all physicians. The smaller the value of χ^2, the less the discrepancy between the sample and the universe. For both samples, the correction for the size of community bias lessens the discrepancy between the sample and the universe.

	VALUE OF χ^2 FOR	
	1933 sample	1935 sample
Not corrected	65.77	16.96
Corrected	39.87	14.01

21 *Ibid.*

22 Table A 2 gives for the United States and the nine Census regions the unweighted and weighted arithmetic mean incomes and the difference between them. The unweighted means exceed the weighted means for the United States in both samples, for six out of nine regions in the 1933 sample, and for five out of nine, in the 1935 sample. Moreover, in both samples, the positive differences are, on the average, considerably larger in absolute value than the negative differences. These results conform to expectation. The two community classes that have the largest number of names per page and hence should be underrepresented in the sample include the smallest communities, in which the average income of physicians is relatively low (see Ch. 5). The use of correct weights should therefore raise the mean income.

Table A 2 therefore affords additional evidence of the existence of the size of community bias. At the same time, the difference between the weighted and unweighted means are all small. The correction raises the mean for the country from the 1933 sample by slightly over two per cent and the corresponding mean from the 1935 sample by about one-tenth of one per cent. The differences are not much larger for individual regions, for which the number of returns is much smaller and hence the possibility of random variation much greater. Comparable means from the two samples differ considerably more than weighted and unweighted means from the same sample.

TABLE A 2

Effect of Size of Community Bias on Arithmetic Mean Income

Physicians, 1932: 1933 and 1935 Samples

	1 9 3 3 S A M P L E				1 9 3 5 S A M P L E			
	No. of returns	Arithmetic mean income in 1932 (dollars)		Difference between unweighted and weighted means	No. of returns	Arithmetic mean income in 1932 (dollars)		Difference between unweighted and weighted means
		Unweighted	Weighted[1]			Unweighted	Weighted[1]	
New England	160	4,676	4,712	−36	104	4,161	4,121	+40
Middle Atlantic	480	3,977	3,907	+70	316	3,725	3,784	−59
E. N. Central	490	2,781	2,718	+63	301	3,089	3,107	−18
W. N. Central	242	3,599	3,656	−57	164	2,736	2,723	+13
S. Atlantic	233	3,406	3,214	+192	110	3,217	3,294	−77
E. S. Central	136	2,313	2,319	−6	76	1,434	1,410	+24
W. S. Central	173	2,646	2,494	+152	96	2,216	2,222	−6
Mountain	64	2,250	2,062	+188	57	3,198	2,957	+241
Pacific	282	4,202	4,025	+177	142	3,038	2,950	+88
U. S.	2,288[2]	3,434	3,347	+87	1,392[3]	3,107	3,104	+3

[1] Weights used are the number of physicians in 1931 in each region and size of community. R. G. Leland, *Distribution of Physicians in the United States* (American Medical Association, 1936), Table 42.

[2] Includes 28 returns for which either size of community or region was unknown.

[3] Includes 26 returns for which either size of community or region was unknown.

Hence the original sample has been used and no attempt has been made to correct for the size of community bias.

In the *Martindale-Hubbell Law Directory*, the tendency for the number of names per page to be greater for large communities than for small ones because of the space needed to separate communities and to describe them is reinforced by the variation in the amount of space allotted individual lawyers or firms: some names are printed in larger type than others, and some names are followed by a brief statement describing the activities of the lawyer

TABLE A 3

Average Number of Names per Page of the
Martindale-Hubbell Law Directory, by Size of Community

SIZE OF COMMUNITY (1930 Census)	AVG. NO. OF NAMES PER PAGE
1,500,000 & over	148
500,000–1,500,000	141
250,000– 500,000	131
100,000– 250,000	109
Under 100,000 *	86

For communities over 500,000 with the exception of Milwaukee, Martindale-Hubbell supplied the number of lawyers listed in the 1936 directory. A count was made of the number of pages assigned each of these communities in the 1936 directory, and the number of names per page computed by division. The averages for the other size of community classes are based on counts of sample pages selected from the 1937 directory. In all, 47 pages containing 4,369 names were counted.

* In the substantive analysis by size of community, this class is broken down into four classes: 25,000–100,000, 10,000–25,000, 2,500–10,000, and under 2,500. There seemed, however, to be no significant differences among these classes in the average number of names per page. Hence, they were grouped together for the present purpose.

or firm and listing the members and associates of the firm. This larger amount of space is allotted only to lawyers who have been in practice a certain number of years and who have attained prominence in their communities. It so happens that the proportion of lawyers allotted the larger amount of space is higher in small communities than in large ones, presumably as a result of the concentration in large cities of both young lawyers and salaried lawyers.

These two factors make for wide differences in the average number of names per page. As Table A 3 shows, the average number of names per page decreases consistently with size of community and is 72 per cent larger for communities over 1,500,000 in population than for communities under 100,000. These differences are very much larger than in the medical directory and in the opposite direction. They might be expected to lead to a considerable underrepresentation of lawyers in large communities.

In order to eliminate this considerable bias, the data for both legal samples were grouped by size of community and all computations made for such groups.[23] In combining the size of community classes an adjustment was made on the basis of Table A 3.[24]

The conclusions that the two legal samples are subject to bias and that Table A 3 can be used to correct this bias, have so far been based solely on *a priori* reasoning. These conclusions should be tested empirically before being accepted, first, because other factors might conceivably have counteracted the presumed bias, second, because the analysis has been entirely in terms of the sample of questionnaires sent out, whereas the corrections must be applied to the sample of questionnaires returned.

Unfortunately, there are no comprehensive data on the number of lawyers by size of community with which to compare the distributions of the samples.[25] Indeed, if such data were available,

[23] In practice, the data for the 1935 sample were grouped by size of community and region, and for the 1937 sample, because of the necessity of weighting by states, by both size of community and state.

[24] This adjustment was made by multiplying the number of questionnaires in each size of community class by a factor proportional to the average number of names per page in Table A 3. For example, to get the same proportionate sample as from communities under 100,000, the sample from communities over 1,500,000 should have been 1.72 $(\frac{148}{86})$ times as large as it actually was. In order to adjust the sample, it is therefore necessary to treat each questionnaire from a community over 1,500,000 as if it represented 1.72 questionnaires; and similarly for other size of community classes. In combining averages, the average for each size of community was weighted by the adjusted number of questionnaires. In combining frequency distributions by size of income, the adjusted number of questionnaires, rather than the original number, was added for each income class.

[25] Offhand, it may seem that such data could be compiled from the *Census of Population*, at least for communities above 25,000. The main reason they cannot is that the Census classifies lawyers by residence, whereas the questionnaires were mailed to the business address. A comparison of the number of lawyers listed in the *Martindale-Hubbell Law Directory* for some of the larger cities with the number listed in the Census reveals large differences. For example, the

the bias could be corrected more adequately and directly: each size of community class could be weighted by the total number of lawyers in that class. In the absence of more comprehensive data, we have relied on a count made available by Martindale-Hubbell of the lawyers listed in the 1936 directory for each state and each city over 500,000 except Milwaukee. For the nine states containing one or more of these cities, the distribution of all lawyers by size of community classes was compared with the distribution of the sample both before and after correction for the size of community bias. This comparison confirms both the existence of the bias and the validity of the correction based on Table A 3.[26] A similar

---

Census gives a total of 1,898 lawyers for Boston, Martindale-Hubbell, 4,374. Yet the totals for the state of Massachusetts agree very well; the Census total is 6,940, the directory total, 7,150. This difference is, of course, consistent; the Census gives smaller totals for large communities and larger totals for small communities. Two additional minor difficulties are that the Census includes lawyers employed by both legal and nonlegal enterprises, and that it is for 1930, whereas the earlier of the two samples was mailed in 1933.

26 For each of the nine states, the questionnaires from the 1935 sample reporting income in 1934 and the questionnaires from the 1937 sample reporting income in 1936 were grouped into the size of community classes in Table A 3. These distributions were then adjusted for the firm member bias discussed in Sec. 1b iv. Both the adjusted and the unadjusted distributions were then corrected for the size of community bias by the method outlined in footnote 24 above.

This procedure gave four distributions by size of community for each state and each sample: (1) not corrected for the size of community bias and not adjusted for the firm member bias, (2) not corrected but adjusted, (3) corrected but not adjusted, (4) corrected and adjusted. In order to make the four distributions comparable, their totals were made equal to the unadjusted and uncorrected total number of returns. The size of community classes were then combined to conform with the classification available for the universe; namely, communities over 1,500,000, 500,000–1,500,000, and under 500,000.

Even if the samples were entirely 'random', the ratio of the sample to the estimated universe should decrease as size of community increases, since the estimated number of lawyers includes not only independent but also salaried lawyers, and these tend to be concentrated in the larger communities. The resulting discrepancy between the sample and the universe is in the same direction as that arising from the size of community bias. Hence, while sample distributions corrected for the size of community bias should conform more closely to the estimated distribution of the universe than uncorrected distributions, they should still differ significantly from it.

Comparison of the four distributions for each state and sample with the distribution of the universe reveals that in practically all cases the discrepancy between the uncorrected distributions and the universe is in the expected

conclusion emerges if the distribution of all lawyers by states is

———

direction, and that correction for the size of community bias tends to reduce but not to eliminate the discrepancy. As a single objective measure of the extent of the discrepancy, χ^2 was computed for each of the four distributions available for each sample and each state (except Maryland, for which the sample was too small). The larger the value of χ^2, the greater the discrepancy between the sample and the universe. Hence the correction is to be considered successful if the corrected distributions yield smaller values of χ^2 than the uncorrected. (Since the totals of all distributions were arbitrarily made the same, the values of χ^2 measure solely the extent of the discrepancy between the distribution of the sample and of the universe.)

	NUMBER OF STATES IN WHICH	
	χ^2 for corrected distribution smaller than for uncorrected (i.e. correction successful)	χ^2 for corrected distribution larger than for uncorrected (i.e. correction unsuccessful)
1935 sample		
Not adjusted for firm member bias	7	1
Adjusted for firm member bias	8	0
1937 sample		
Not adjusted for firm member bias	4	4
Adjusted for firm member bias	7	1

On the whole, the correction was clearly successful. Moreover, since a correction introduced at random would be as likely to raise χ^2 as to lower it, the differences shown in the above table cannot reasonably be attributed to chance alone. Adding the values of χ^2 for the separate states yields a similar conclusion.

	SUM OF THE VALUES OF χ^2 FOR EIGHT STATES			
	1935 sample		*1937 sample*	
	Not adjusted for firm member bias	Adjusted for firm member bias	Not adjusted for firm member bias	Adjusted for firm member bias
Not corrected	169.67	169.22	38.47	40.98
Corrected	85.78	82.58	28.95	18.10

One final computation may be cited. For the 1935 sample, the distributions for nine states were combined, and χ^2 computed for each of the four sample distributions.

	χ^2 FOR NINE STATES, 1935 SAMPLE	
	Not adjusted for firm member bias	Adjusted for firm member bias
Not corrected	173.3	169.8
Corrected	79.3	77.0

This computation, like the others, indicates that the correction lessened the discrepancy between the sample and the universe. A similar computation for the 1937 sample could not validly be made, since the sample is not random among

compared with the distribution of the sample before and after correction for the size of community bias.[27]

iii *The overrepresentation of certain types of physicians and lawyers.* In selecting the medical and legal samples, the particular names taken from each page of the directory were determined by laying a straight edge marked off at equally spaced intervals along a column of names. The names that fell opposite the marks were included in the sample. The probability of a particular person being chosen is therefore proportional to the space his listing occupies. A person whose listing occupies two lines has twice as large a chance of being included in the sample as a person whose listing occupies only one line.[28] As noted in the preceding section, in both the medical and legal directories the number of lines devoted to each person varies. In the medical directory the variation is fairly limited: many names require one line and few names more than three. In the legal directory, on the other hand, the variation is much greater: from one line to ten or fifteen or even, occasionally, more.

The samples for both professions, but especially for lawyers, will therefore tend to overrepresent persons whose listings occupy

---

states. It should be noted that except for the unadjusted and uncorrected distributions, the probability of the computed χ^2 being exceeded by chance cannot be judged by the use of the ordinary sampling distribution of χ^2. The reason is that the totals of the remaining distributions were arbitrarily adjusted to equal the totals for the unweighted and uncorrected ones. Nor is there any sampling distribution available for testing the significance of the differences between the values of χ^2 computed in this way.

[27] As in the preceding footnote, χ^2 was used as a measure of the discrepancy and the totals of the sample distributions were arbitrarily made the same. Because the 1937 sample is not random among states, the test could be made only for the 1935 sample.

χ^2 FOR 1935 SAMPLE BY STATES

	Not adjusted for firm member bias	Adjusted for firm member bias
Not corrected	325.3	256.4
Corrected	239.3	176.9

[28] The statement that the probability of a particular person being chosen is proportional to the space his listing occupies is precise only for listings requiring a smaller number of lines than the space between the markings on the straight edge. Every person whose listing occupies more space than this must be chosen; the probability that he will be included in the sample is therefore unity no matter how much space his listing occupies.

more than the average amount of space.[29] As noted above, in the medical samples, these will tend to be specialists and physicians with long addresses; in the legal sample, the older and more prominent lawyers. Since both groups tend to have incomes higher than the average for all practitioners, the income data from the samples may be expected to have an upward bias.

Comparison of the percentage of specialists in the 1937 medical sample—the only sample for which this information is available—with the percentage indicated by other studies does not confirm the existence of this suspected bias (see Sec. 2c below). Similarly, comparison of our legal samples with studies of lawyers in Wisconsin and New York County fails to confirm its existence, since average incomes from our samples are lower than averages from the other studies. However, these tests are fragmentary and unsatisfactory and cannot be taken as establishing the absence of this bias. Unfortunately we have been unable to make more adequate tests. No correction has been made for this bias.

iv *The firm member bias in the legal and accountancy samples.* The legal and accountancy samples were selected from lists of persons, not of professional units (i.e., firms plus individual practitioners), but each person to whom a questionnaire was sent was requested, if a member of a firm, to reply for the firm as a whole. By the procedure followed, a firm had a greater chance of being included in the sample than an individual practitioner, since it was included if *any one* of its members was included; and the larger the firm, the greater its chance of being included. For example, suppose that a 2 per cent sample is taken from a universe of 5,000 individual practitioners and 5,000 members of two-member firms. The sample of persons to whom questionnaires are sent will tend to include 100 individual practitioners and 100 firm members. If all who receive questionnaires reply and if no firm has more than one of its members in the sample,[30] the questionnaires returned

29 Any variation in the amount of space devoted to each person that is associated with size of community has already been allowed for in the preceding section. What is relevant here is solely the variation among persons in communities of the same size.

30 On the average, with the assumed figures, one firm would have both members selected: the probability of a particular person being selected is 1/50; of both members of a firm being selected, this number squared, or 1/2500; and there are assumed to be 2,500 firms.

will cover 100 individual practitioners and 200 firm members, since each firm member will reply not only for himself but also for his partner. The final sample will include twice as many firm members as individual practitioners, although there are an equal number of each in the assumed universe.

It follows that the method of selecting lawyers and accountants to whom questionnaires were to be sent, combined with the wording of the questionnaires, yield 'outgoing' samples that contain a known proportionate excess of firm members.[31] If, like the legal samples, the sample is small relatively to the universe, it will tend to contain approximately twice as many members of two-member firms, three times as many members of three-member firms, and so on, as it should for a representative sample. If, like the accountancy samples, the sample is fairly large relatively to the universe, the proportionate excess will be smaller, but still considerable.[32]

The overrepresentation of firm members in the 'outgoing' sample might be expected to lead to a similar overrepresentation in the sample of questionnaires returned—the 'incoming' sample. Whether the overrepresentation will be larger or smaller in the

[31] This bias does not affect the medical and dental samples because almost all physicians and dentists practise as individuals. It does not affect the engineering sample because questionnaires were sent to all persons on the list; consequently, every member of every firm on the list received a questionnaire.

[32] Let p be the proportion of all names on the list included in the sample and let $q = 1 - p$. Then q is the probability that a particular name will not be included in the sample, q^m, the probability that none of m specified names will be included, and $1 - q^m$, the probability that at least one of m specified names will be included, i.e., the probability that at least one member of a firm of m members, and hence the firm itself, will be included. If p is small, q^m is approximately equal to $1 - mp$, as can be seen by expanding $(1 - p)^m$. In this case, $1 - q^m = mp$. Since p is the proportion of individual practitioners included in the sample, it follows that if the sample is small relatively to the universe, the proportion of firms of size m in the sample will be m times the proportion of individual practitioners in the sample. Since $1 - mp$ is always less than q^m, $1 - q^m$ is always less than mp and $(1 - q^m)/p$ is always less than m. The difference is negligible when p is small, but increases as p increases. The difference reflects the increasing possibility that more than one member of the firm will be included in the sample. At the limit, when p is unity, i.e., when a 100 per cent sample is taken, q is zero, and $1 - q^m$ is unity, or equal to p. The formulae in this footnote are valid so long as the universe is fairly large. Otherwise, a slight correction is needed. See *Money Disbursements of Wage Earners and Clerical Workers in Five Cities in the West North Central-Mountain Region, 1934–36*, U. S. Bureau of Labor Statistics Bulletin 641, pp. 384–90.

incoming than in the outgoing sample depends on the relative proportion of firm members and of individual practitioners who refuse to reply.[33] Since we have no information on these proportions, we have tested the existence and magnitude of the presumed bias indirectly.

For lawyers, we have placed major reliance on a comparison between the estimated percentage of all lawyers who are firm members and the percentage of lawyers in our samples who are firm members, before and after correction for the firm member bias. The estimate of the percentage of all lawyers who are firm members is based on a sample count of the 1933 *Martindale-Hubbell Law Directory*.[34] Unfortunately the directory listings do not permit an entirely satisfactory classification. They distinguish between firm members and other lawyers, but not between lawyers in independent practice and salaried employees.[35] A survey made by the New

[33] If the probability that a firm will refuse to reply were independent of the number of members of the firm who received questionnaires and equal to the probability that an individual practitioner will refuse, it can easily be shown that the proportionate excess of firms of each size would be the same in the incoming as in the outgoing sample, i.e., that the probability of a firm of m members being included in the incoming sample is given by the formulae of the preceding footnote, with p, as there, equal to the ratio of the number of individual practitioners in the *outgoing* sample to the number in the universe. If the probability that a particular member of a firm will refuse were the same as the probability that an individual practitioner will refuse, and if, when more than one member of a firm received questionnaires, the probabilities that the different members would refuse were independent of one another (implying that a firm is more likely to reply the more members receive questionnaires), it can be shown that the probability that a firm of m members will be included in the incoming sample is different from the probability that it will be included in the outgoing sample and is given by the formulae of the preceding footnote, with p equal to the ratio of the number of individual practitioners in the *incoming* sample to the number in the universe. There is little basis on which to choose between these alternative sets of assumptions. Moreover, other plausible assumptions would give different results.

[34] The sample count included every 50th page of the directory. While involving much less work, such a sample is, of course, subject to larger sampling errors than one including every 50th name, because of the larger size of the sampling unit and consequently the smaller number of units. At the same time, it is not subject to any of the biases arising from taking the same number of names from each page.

[35] Only lawyers employed by other lawyers or by legal firms are listed in the directory, which makes no attempt to list lawyers employed by nonlegal enterprises.

York County Lawyers Association indicates that approximately 20 per cent of all lawyers in active practice in New York County are employed by legal firms.[36] Since the percentage of salaried employees is probably at least as large in New York County as elsewhere, we have used this figure to convert the results of the sample count into an upper estimate of the percentage of all lawyers who are firm members. The percentage computed directly from the sample count gives a lower limit.

The 1935 legal sample was adjusted for the firm member bias by weighting the number of members of two-member firms by one-half, the number of members of three-member firms by one-third, etc. The sum of these weighted numbers was used as the corrected number of firm members.[37] The 1937 legal sample was adjusted in the same way, except that more nearly exact weights were used and that the weights varied from state to state. This was necessary because in some states questionnaires were mailed to a sizable proportion of all lawyers.[38]

The comparison between the estimated percentage of firm members in the universe and the percentage computed from the samples (Table A 4) reveals that the 1935 sample conforms to expectations but the 1937 sample does not. The unadjusted percentage of firm members in the 1935 sample is much higher than the estimated percentage in the universe; the adjusted percentage of firm members, a trifle lower.[39] This indication of a firm member bias in the 1935 legal sample is confirmed by a comparison between the distribution of all lawyers by states and the distribution of the

[36] *Survey of the Legal Profession in New York County*, p. 12. The exact percentage is 21.14.

[37] The adjustment was made separately for each size of community class in order to correct for the size of community bias.

[38] The adjustment was made separately for each size of community class in each state in order to correct for the size of community bias and the nonrandomness among states.

[39] As a measure of the discrepancy between the estimated percentage of firm members in the universe and the percentage in the sample, we can use χ^2 computed from a 2x2 table giving the number of firm members and individuals counted in the directory and the corresponding numbers in the sample. The value of χ^2 before allowance for the inclusion of salaried employees in the directory is 174.6 for the unadjusted sample numbers, and .59 for the adjusted ones. The corresponding values of χ^2, after allowance for the inclusion of salaried employees, are 71.1 and 19.3, respectively.

TABLE A 4

Test of Existence of Firm Member Bias

Lawyers, 1935 and 1937 Samples

	NO. OF INDE-PENDENT PRACTITIONERS	% OF INDEPENDENT PRACTITIONERS CLASSIFIED AS FIRM MEMBERS
Sample from 1933 *Martindale-Hubbell Law Directory*	3,109	24.0–30.0 [1]
1935 sample [2]		
Not adjusted for firm member bias	1,332 [6]	44.5
Adjusted for firm member bias [3]	933 [7]	23.0
1937 sample [4]		
Not adjusted for firm member bias	1,168 [6]	25.3
Adjusted for firm member bias [5]		12.9

[1] Lower limit assumes that no salaried employees are included in the directory. The upper limit assumes that 20 per cent of all practitioners in the directory were salaried employees and that these were all included in the sample count as individual practitioners.

[2] Compilation is of schedules reporting net income for 1933.

[3] Each size of firm was weighted by the reciprocal of the number of members.

[4] Compilation is of schedules reporting net income for 1936.

[5] Because the sampling ratio varied from state to state, different weights were used for each state. The weights used were $p/(1 - q^m)$, where p is the proportion of names in the particular state to whom questionnaires were sent, $q = 1 - p$, and m is the number of members in the firm.

[6] Total number of persons represented on questionnaires before correction for size of community or firm member bias.

[7] Total number of persons represented on questionnaires after adjustment for firm member bias but before correction for size of community bias.

1935 sample by states, before and after adjustment for the firm member bias. There is much closer agreement after adjustment than before adjustment.[40]

The unadjusted percentage of firm members in the 1937 legal sample is about the same as the estimated percentage in the universe; the adjusted percentages, very much lower. Adjustment for the presumed firm member bias, which yields closer agreement for the 1935 sample, has exactly the opposite effect on the 1937 sample. This difference between the two samples is puzzling; and we have

[40] See the values of χ^2 given in footnote 27 above.

been unable to explain it satisfactorily.[41] Hence the 1937 sample must be viewed with considerable scepticism.

In the light of these results, we have corrected the 1935 sample for the firm member bias by weighting each size firm by the reciprocal of the number of members in that size firm,[42] but have made no attempt to correct the 1937 sample. For the 1937 sample, firm members and individual practitioners have been combined without weighting.

For accountants, the absence of any evidence on the proportion of firm members rules out the kind of test for the existence of the presumed firm member bias in the incoming sample that we used for lawyers. We have relied instead on two even more indirect tests, both of which indicate that the bias in the outgoing samples is also present in the incoming samples.

The more satisfactory of these tests is based on data for New York State alone. (However, New York contains almost one-third of all certified public accountants.) These data were derived from sample counts of (1) the New York section of the 1933 yearbook

[41] The only explanation that has occurred to us hinges on the content and form of the questionnaires. The questionnaire sent out in 1935 covered a single sheet and requested information solely about the legal enterprise—individual practitioner or firm, as the case might be. It therefore requested the same information from and involved the same amount of trouble for individual practitioners and firm members. The questionnaire sent out in 1937, on the other hand, was in two parts; the top part requested information about the enterprise, the bottom part about the practitioner. Both parts were to be filled out by individual practitioners. A firm member was supposed to fill out the top part for the firm as a whole, the bottom part for himself. Additional copies of the bottom part were enclosed and were to be filled out by firm members other than the one who received the questionnaire. (See Appendix C.) The trouble involved was therefore greater for a firm member than for an individual practitioner, since the former was asked to distribute additional copies of the bottom part. In addition, there may have been a reluctance to return the questionnaire unless all firm members filled out the bottom part; refusal by a single firm member might have resulted in a refusal by the firm as a whole.

Both factors would tend to make the refusal rate for firm members higher relatively to the refusal rate for individuals in the 1937 sample than in the 1935 sample. It seems dubious, however, that this factor alone could have produced a difference in results as great as that reflected in Table A 4.

[42] These are not the exact weights, which, according to footnote 32, would be $p/(1 - q^m)$. For a sample as small as the legal sample, however, the difference between the two sets of weights is so slight that the gain in accuracy through the use of exact weights would not repay the extra labor involved.

of the American Institute of Accountants and (2) the 1938 register of the New York State Society of Certified Public Accountants.[43] Both lists contain enough information to permit the identification of persons in independent practice and of firm members. On the basis of this sample count, we estimated the number of certified public accountants in independent practice who were members of (1) the Institute, (2) the Society, (3) both the Institute and the Society, (4) the Institute but not the Society, (5) the Society but not the Institute. For each group, we estimated the percentage who were firm members. (See first five lines of Table A 5.)

Like most professional associations, these two include the more prominent and affluent practitioners. In accountancy, they would tend to include a larger proportion of firm members than of individual practitioners, since, on the average, firm members receive higher incomes and are older than individual practitioners (see Ch. 6, Sec. 3). At the time the count was made, the Institute was more biased in this direction than the New York State Society,[44] as is clear from the first two lines of Table A 5. The difference is even greater between accountants who were members of both associations and of only one: 71 per cent of the independent practitioners who belonged to both associations were firm members; but only about 40 per cent of those who belonged to one association. *A priori*, the percentage of firm members might be expected to be still smaller among certified public accountants who belonged to neither the Society nor the Institute.

This suggests a method of testing whether our samples overrepresent firm members: we can construct from our samples two estimates of the percentage of firm members among accountants who belonged to neither association—one, before adjusting the samples for the presumed firm member bias, a second, after adjusting the samples—and see which appears more consistent with this *a priori* presumption. These estimates, given in Table A 5, were computed as follows. The percentage of firm members in the original sample was applied to the estimated total number of certified public accountants in independent practice in New York State. This gave the total number of firm members and of individual

[43] Every third page of the former and every tenth page of the latter was included in the sample count.

[44] The Institute has since merged with the American Society of Certified Public Accountants.

practitioners in the state. Subtracting the number of firm members
and of individual practitioners who belonged to one or both of the
associations (as estimated from the sample counts) gave the number
of firm members and of individual practitioners who belonged to
neither association. The percentages in the column headed 'unadjusted' are based on these numbers. This process was then re-

TABLE A 5

Test of the Existence of Firm Member Bias

Certified Public Accountants

CERTIFIED PUBLIC ACCOUNTANTS IN NEW YORK STATE WHO BELONG TO	ESTIMATED % OF INDEPENDENT CERTIFIED PUBLIC ACCOUNTANTS WHO ARE MEMBERS OF FIRMS	
American Institute of Accountants *	63.1	
N. Y. State Society of Certified Public Accountants *	47.8	
Both Institute and Society	71.1	
Institute but not Society	37.8	
Society but not Institute	42.4	
	Samples	
Neither Institute nor Society: estimate based on	*Unadjusted*	*Adjusted*
1937 sample for 1936	49.5	24.0
1937 sample for 1934	43.3	18.8
1935 sample for 1934	38.9	16.7
All certified public accountants: estimate based on		
1937 sample for 1936	48.3	34.9
1937 sample for 1934	45.0	32.2
1935 sample for 1934	42.7	31.1

* Data derived from sample counts of the New York section of the 1933 yearbook of the American Institute of Accountants and the 1938 register of the
New York State Society of Certified Public Accountants, respectively.

peated, except that the percentage of firm members applied to
the estimated total number of accountants was based not on the
original samples but on the samples after adjustment for the presumed firm member bias.[45] This yielded the percentages in the
column headed 'adjusted'.

Table A 5 shows that accepting the original sample as valid

[45] The adjustment was made by weighting the number of members of firms of
each size by $p/(1 - q^m)$, where p is the proportion of names included in the
outgoing sample, q is $1 - p$, and m is the number of members in the firm. For the
1933 and 1935 samples p was taken as 0.5, for the 1937 sample, as 0.4. See footnote 32 above.

contradicts the *a priori* presumption stated above, since the percentage of firm members among certified public accountants who belonged to neither association is as large as or larger than the corresponding percentage among accountants who belonged to only one association. On the other hand, adjusting for the firm member bias yields percentages that are consistent with expectations: the percentage of firm members is uniformly smaller among accountants who belonged to neither association than among accountants who belonged to only one. This test therefore confirms the existence of the presumed bias in all samples.

The second test involved a comparison of the frequency distributions by size of firm computed from two different samples covering the same year. Two comparisons were made for each of two years: one, between distributions not adjusted for the firm member bias; a second, between distributions adjusted for this bias. For both years, the adjusted distributions differed less from one another than the unadjusted.[46]

These tests give no reason for doubting the existence of the firm member bias in any of the samples. Consequently, all three accountancy samples have been adjusted for the firm member bias by weighting each size firm inversely to the overrepresentation theoretically to be expected in the outgoing sample.[47]

c The return of questionnaires by the respondents
The problem of selecting a random 'outgoing' sample, to which Sections a and b have been devoted, is common to all investigations using samples, whether in the social, biological, or physical sciences. It is a problem treated extensively in the literature of

[46] χ^2 was used as a measure of the discrepancy between the two distributions. In order to make the χ^2's comparable, the totals of the adjusted distributions were made equal to the totals of the unadjusted distributions.

SAMPLES COMPARED	NO. OF DEGREES OF FREEDOM	VALUES OF χ^2 Unadjusted distributions	Adjusted distributions
1935 sample and 1933 sample for 1932 (i.e., for persons reporting income in 1932)	4	74.92	67.91
1937 sample and 1935 sample for 1934	5	26.96	16.48

[47] See footnote 45 for the weights used.

theoretical statistics, one that is susceptible to *a priori* analysis of the type suggested by the familiar model of balls in an urn.

In most fields other than the social sciences, the representativeness of the sample is determined entirely by its method of selection. Not so in the social sciences. If a ball is drawn from an urn it cannot refuse to become a member of a sample; but if an individual is sent a questionnaire, he can refuse to reply. The outgoing sample may be completely random, yet the incoming sample hopelessly biased if the persons who reply differ significantly and consistently from those who fail to reply.

Not only does the representativeness of a sample in the social sciences depend on the behavior of the objects sampled; so also may the validity of the information obtained. A ball chosen from an urn cannot tell the investigator that it is black when it is really white. The investigator may make a mistake; but his errors ordinarily are his own and subject to check. An individual asked to state his net income from independent professional practice may state his gross income, his income from both independent and salaried practice, or his income less personal expenses; if he thinks his answer will affect policy, he may deliberately overstate or understate his income; and so on.

This distinction between the outgoing and incoming samples that is so important for samples like ours has received little attention in the theoretical literature of statistics, first, because it does not arise in the kinds of samples with which theoretical statisticians have been mainly concerned, second, because it is not susceptible to *a priori* analysis. Whether individuals who reply differ from those who do not reply and whether the answers of those who reply are subject only to random errors or to consistent and biased errors are essentially empirical questions, the answers to which will depend greatly on the particular circumstances surrounding the inquiry—the agency sponsoring it, the purpose of the inquiry, the way the questions are worded, the methods used to encourage replies, and so on.

Unfortunately, there is little empirical evidence directly relevant to these questions. Our own samples give some; and prior studies of professional income add a bit more.

The only evidence from our samples on the characteristics of persons who fail to reply is provided by the 1937 medical and legal samples, for which we know the number of questionnaires sent to persons in each state, as well as the number returned.[48]

These data reveal fairly conclusively that the refusal ratio (the ratio of questionnaires not returned to questionnaires sent) differs significantly among states.[49] Moreover, differences among the refusal ratios are fairly similar for the two professions: states that have a high proportion of refusals among physicians also tend to have a high proportion of refusals among lawyers.[50]

The question immediately arises whether the proportion of persons in a particular state who refuse to reply is correlated with the average income of the persons who do reply. Such a correlation between states would suggest a similar correlation within states. For example, if the average income of those who replied were relatively high in states that have a high proportion of refusals, it would seem reasonable to conclude that within each state separately persons with high incomes are less likely to reply than persons with low incomes.[51] For the 1937 medical and legal sam-

[48] Offhand, a comparison between the distribution by states, regions, etc., of the returned questionnaires and the corresponding estimated distribution of the universe might seem to provide evidence on the nature of the refusal bias. However, discrepancies revealed by such comparisons are the product of errors in the list employed, the method of selecting the sample, and the estimates of the universe as well as of differences in the willingness of various groups to reply. To disentangle the resultant composite is an almost impossible task. Such comparisons are valuable as evidence on the over-all reliability of the data, and are used for this purpose in Section 2a below.

[49] The discrepancy between the geographic distributions of the returned questionnaires and the questionnaires sent was measured by computing χ^2 between the two distributions.

	NO. OF DEGREES OF FREEDOM *	χ^2	PROBABILITY THAT OBSERVED VALUE OF χ^2 WOULD HAVE BEEN EXCEEDED BY CHANCE
1937 medical sample	48	118.73	less than .00000005
1937 legal sample	47	95.86	less than .00005

* One less than the number of classes in the distribution. For the medical sample, the classes were the forty-eight states and the District of Columbia. For the legal sample, Delaware could not be included separately because there were too few questionnaires.

[50] The rank difference correlation between the refusal ratios for physicians and lawyers is .435 with a standard error of .144.

[51] This test is not vitiated by the use of sample rather than population average incomes unless (a) there is a significant relationship between income and willingness to reply and (b) this relationship differs among states (or other units),

ples, the correlation between the refusal ratio and average income is negligible, suggesting that willingness to reply is not related to income.[52]

For the particular samples analyzed—the 1937 medical and legal samples—the variation in the refusal ratio among states is of no importance, since these samples have been weighted by states. The findings are important for the inferences they suggest about the remaining samples and about the factors leading to refusals within states. For the other samples also, the refusal ratio presumably varies significantly among states and the incoming samples cannot be expected to be entirely representative of the universe even if the outgoing samples are. However, in the absence of any correlation with average income, the variation in the refusal ratio does not of itself introduce a bias into the average incomes computed from the samples. And the two samples analyzed give no direct indication of such a correlation between states; hence no indirect indication of such a correlation within states.

---

being direct in some and inverse in others. If the relationship is similar in all states, the sample averages will give the correct ranking of states by income. For example, suppose in all states nine-tenths of the individuals with incomes over $5,000 but only half of those with incomes below $5,000 refuse to reply; and suppose that the percentage of individuals with incomes over $5,000 is larger in state A than in state B. The sample averages will have a downward bias for both states, and this bias will be larger for state A than for state B. Nevertheless, the sample average for state A will be larger than the sample average for state B.

52 The rank difference correlation between the refusal ratio and average income is $+.023$ for physicians, and $-.064$ for lawyers. The standard error of each is .144.

Another hypothesis tested was that differences among the refusal ratios were related to the political complexion of the states. Since the questionnaires were distributed by a government agency it might be supposed that persons in sympathy with the administration would be more likely to respond than persons not in sympathy with it. This hypothesis was tested by computing for both lawyers and physicians rank difference correlations first, between the refusal ratio and the percentage that the democratic presidential vote in 1936 was of the total vote, and second, between the refusal ratio and the change from 1932 to 1936 in the percentage that the democratic presidential vote was of the total vote. For physicians, the correlations obtained were $-.04$ and $+.05$ respectively; for lawyers, $+.08$ and $+.07$. None of these is significant, since the standard error of each is .146. While these correlations do not support the hypothesis, it should be noted that the refusal ratios were correlated with the political complexion of all voters in the state, whereas the relevant correlation would be with the political complexion of the specific professional group; and the former may be a poor index of the latter.

The evidence from our samples on the characteristics of those who fail to reply can be supplemented by evidence from three other studies of professional income—the studies of the 1929 incomes of physicians and dentists made by the Committee on the Costs of Medical Care, and the California Medical-Economic Survey sponsored by the California Medical Association.

For physicians, the Committee on the Costs of Medical Care made both a nationwide study and intensive surveys of particular communities. In connection with one of the latter—on incomes of Vermont physicians—"a supplementary study of a sample taken from the physicians who failed for one reason or another to participate in the state-wide survey disclosed the fact that the 57 per cent [who participated] were fairly representative of the total." [53] The nationwide sample of the Committee on the Costs of Medical Care yielded somewhat different results. A follow-up letter was sent to a sample of the physicians who failed to reply to the original questionnaire. "A comparison between the data received on the first letter and those received in response to the follow-up letter, for the same areas, show important differences in the two subsamples. The second contains a larger proportion of small incomes and its median income is about $1,000 lower than the median of the first returns." [54] Leven is disposed to explain this difference as being "due, to some extent at least, to the nature of the appeal in the follow-up letter. The physicians were urged to make returns even though they felt that their collections and charges in 1929 and 1930 were typical neither of their own practice nor of the incomes of physicians in general. This . . . undoubtedly resulted in returns from a disproportionately high number of those whose incomes were low because of special circumstances—sickness, old age, partial retirement, and the like." [55]

In the dental survey of the Committee on the Costs of Medical

[53] Leven, *Incomes of Physicians,* p. 8. In a footnote to this statement Leven indicates that "a test study was made in three Vermont communities. The gross incomes of the physicians who had not returned the mailed questionnaire were obtained by personal contact and, by adding these to the returns procured by mail, a 100 per cent sample was made available. The additional data changed the average by only $25. The reasons for the physicians' failure to reply to the mailed questionnaire were tabulated and it was established that failure to reply was not in any way associated with the size of income."

[54] *Ibid.,* p. 13.

[55] *Ibid.,* p. 14.

Care, questionnaires were sent to a 25 per cent sample of a presumably comprehensive list of all dentists in twenty states. Usable questionnaires were returned by 66 per cent of those circularized. The representativeness of this group was tested by comparing their age distribution with that of all dentists, by comparing the percentage of the respondents who were members of the American Dental Association or component societies with the corresponding percentage for all dentists, and, for three states, by obtaining independent estimates of the gross incomes of dentists who failed to reply.

The first test suggested that the only serious discrepancy was in the most recent graduating class, which seemed to be underrepresented in the sample. However, it is not clear whether this reflected a defect in the list used for sampling [56] or the unwillingness of young men to reply. In any event, correction of the sample for this deficiency would have lowered the estimated average income by only 1.4 per cent.[57]

The second test indicated that a larger proportion of members than of nonmembers replied. Since members have higher incomes than nonmembers, this bias resulted in an underrepresentation of dentists with low incomes.[58] The third test yielded similar results. In each of three states, Colorado, Georgia, and Wisconsin, the average gross income based on both the replies to questionnaires and the estimates of local dental committees for dentists who failed to reply was lower than the average based on the questionnaire data alone. The difference varied from $28 or less than one-half of one per cent to almost $500 or about eight per cent.[59]

It is clear that in this study of the Committee on the Costs of Medical Care, the refusal ratio was larger among dentists with low incomes than among dentists with high incomes, although the difference was not great. It is doubtful, however, that this result can be generalized. The study was conducted under the auspices of the American Dental Association; in addition, several of the devices used to stimulate replies must have been more effective with members of dental societies than with nonmembers. For ex-

---

56 See Sec. 1a i above.

57 Leven, *Practice of Dentistry*, p. 199.

58 *Ibid.*, p. 200. The indicated correction in the average net income of all general practitioners was about 1.5 per cent.

59 *Ibid.*, p. 203.

ample, special letters were sent by officers of various state societies; committees of component societies solicited individuals who had not replied; the purpose and plans of the study were presented and discussed at society meetings; and articles about the study appeared in a variety of dental journals.[60] That under these circumstances a larger percentage of members than of nonmembers should have replied is not surprising, and this in turn might explain the smaller percentage of returns from individuals with low incomes.[61]

The California Medical-Economic Survey sent two successive follow-up letters to physicians and dentists who did not return the original questionnaire. On the whole, the three successive samples differ little for either physicians or dentists. There are no significant differences among the arithmetic mean incomes, median incomes, standard deviations, or income distributions themselves.[62] The one consistent difference among the samples is that for both

---

[60] *Ibid.*, pp. 210–2.

[61] Unfortunately no data are available to test this hypothesis. The data published for the three states do not segregate members from nonmembers and it is therefore impossible to determine whether the lower average income for all dentists is due solely to a greater weighting of nonmembers.

[62] The measures for the different samples are summarized in the accompanying table.

		PHYSICIANS			DENTISTS	
		Arithmetic mean	Standard deviation of income		Arithmetic mean	Standard deviation of income
INDIVIDUALS REPLYING TO	Median income	income	distribution income	Median income	income	distribution
			(dollars)			
Original letter	2,700	3,651	3,523	2,300	2,745	1,918
First follow-up	2,700	3,483	3,311	2,400	2,710	1,836
Second follow-up	2,500	3,497	3,426	2,700	3,071	1,964
All letters	2,700	3,572		2,500	2,769	

California Medical-Economic Survey, pp. 71, 74. The standard deviations were computed from the frequency distributions.

The significance of the differences among the arithmetic mean incomes for each profession was tested by the analysis of variance and found not significant. In each set of standard deviations even the largest and smallest do not differ significantly and hence the whole set scarcely can.

The significance of the differences among the frequency distributions was tested by the χ^2 test. For physicians, χ^2 is 25.96; the number of degrees of freedom, 22; and the probability of the observed χ^2 being exceeded by chance, .25. For dentists the corresponding figures are 15.01, 14, and .38. For neither are the differences larger than might have been expected from chance.

physicians and dentists the percentage of general practitioners among those replying was larger for each successive letter; but even these differences are quantitatively so small that they do not appear to be statistically significant.

Though too meagre to justify a definite conclusion, the evidence presented on this important question of the refusal bias suggests first, that there are significant geographical differences among the percentage refusing to reply; second, that these differences are not associated with geographical differences in income; third, that while within each community or region there may be differences between the willingness of different income groups to respond, these differences cannot be large; and fourth, that if such differences do exist, the lower income groups are probably the least willing to reply.

The evidence from our samples on the second of the questions noted above—namely, the accuracy of the answers of those who reply—is qualitative rather than quantitative, and derives from a detailed study of individual questionnaires. This study suggests a number of possible sources of bias in the replies, none of which appear to be particularly serious.

Perhaps the most important source of bias arises from requesting information on income for a number of years. The difficulty of answering accurately for all years tends toward the insertion of approximate incomes, and, even more important, toward the insertion of the same or very nearly the same income for each year. While this tendency may not affect the average for the period as a whole, it does damp fluctuations in income over the period. This tendency is, of course, more important the longer the period for which information is requested. It therefore affects most the samples collected in 1937.

Some respondents seem to have been confused about the meaning of 'gross' and 'net' professional income and of 'professional expenses' to be deducted from the former in arriving at the latter. Although the instructions were fairly explicit even in the first set of questionnaires, and were made increasingly detailed and precise in each succeeding set, there are indications that some respondents included nonprofessional income and salaries from professional work with income from independent professional practice, or deducted living expenses as well as strictly professional expenses in deriving net income, or interpreted 'net' in the sense of 'net taxable income'. However, relatively few questionnaires seem to have been affected by such errors. So far as they affect the final results, they probably, on balance, make for a downward bias in net income.

The examination of the schedules suggests that the answers of accountants and dentists are probably most accurate, and those of lawyers and physicians least accurate. Because of the shorter period covered, the two earlier sets of questionnaires—those sent out in 1933 and 1935—are probably more accurate than the last set—those sent out in 1937.

d The editing of the questionnaires
The last possible source of bias in obtaining the sample of usable questionnaires is the processing of returned questionnaires before their actual use in the statistical analysis—the weeding out of the 'unusable' returns and the correction of 'obvious' errors. Many unusable questionnaires offer no serious problem—the respondent will have made a notation to the effect that he is 'not in practice', 'employed on salary', 'retired', or that he has reported income from 'incidental part-time work'; gross income will be less than net income; gross income less reported expenses will not equal net income; a firm member will indicate that he is reporting solely his own income; etc. Other questionnaires cannot be classified so simply. There is an inevitable tendency to regard as suspect a questionnaire that deviates widely in any respect from other questionnaires or from what is expected on the basis of other knowledge. The real problem of editing is how to decide whether each of these is really an error or simply an 'extreme' case. If, implicitly or explicitly, the rule 'exclude wherever doubtful' is followed, the extremes will inevitably tend to be eliminated, with resulting biases depending on their characteristics. On the other hand, if the rule 'include wherever doubtful' is followed, the extremes will be included, but so also will the erroneous returns.

The choice between these alternatives is necessarily arbitrary. Both involve errors of unknown magnitude and direction. In editing the present samples, an attempt was made to steer between the Scylla of excluding doubtful cases and the Charybdis of including them; but the course followed varied somewhat for the different samples. The 1933 samples were edited by different persons and at a different time than the later samples. In the editing

TABLE A 6

Number of Questionnaires Returned

Number Usable, and Number not Usable, by Reasons

SAMPLE & YEAR SENT OUT	TOTAL [1]	USABLE [2]	NOT USABLE	NOT USABLE BECAUSE			
				Deceased or retired	Not in independent practice [3]	No usable information	Other reasons [4]
Physicians							
1 (1933)	2,882	2,438	444	103	215	65	61
2 (1935)	1,686	1,588	98	17	66	14	1
3 (1937)	1,647	1,577	70	10	9	50	1
Dentists							
1 (1933)	1,609	1,499	110	8	68	20	14
2 (1935)	1,171	1,122	49	11	20	6	12
Lawyers							
1 (1935)	1,161	1,050	111	22	68	9	12
2 (1937)	1,260	1,063	197	18	79	91	9
Certified public accountants							
1 (1933)	977	679	298	21	171	19	87
2 (1935)	1,255	1,062	193	14	143	12	24
3 (1937)	853	752	101	15	57	19	10
Consulting engineers							
1 (1933)	804	415	389	59	227	43	60

[1] Excludes questionnaires returned by post office as undeliverable.
[2] Includes all questionnaires containing any usable information. The numbers in this column are therefore somewhat larger than the numbers on which most of the results in the text are based.
[3] Includes questionnaires on which the respondent indicated he was a salaried employee or 'not in public practice'. For accountants and engineers also includes questionnaires for incorporated firms.
[4] Includes questionnaires rejected for miscellaneous reasons such as: respondent indicated independent professional activity was purely incidental to other full-time work; questionnaire duplicated another returned by member of the same firm; respondent practised outside continental United States.

of the 1933 samples, Scylla exercised the stronger attraction while in the editing of the later samples the course was set somewhat closer to Charybdis. This difference is brought out clearly by Table A 6, which gives data on the number of questionnaires discarded for various reasons. For each of the professions for which more than one sample was taken, the percentage of schedules discarded is largest for the 1933 sample.

It is doubtful that the difference in procedure could have led to serious discrepancies between the samples; or either procedure to a considerable bias in any one sample. Many of the questionnaires discarded were eliminated on the basis of explicit annotations on the returns. Most of the remainder, those in the discarding of which the judgment factor was decisive, are included in the category entitled 'no usable information', and even in the earlier samples are relatively few. The major differences among the professions are in the category 'not in independent practice' and these accord with the known characteristics of the professions: salaried employment is most frequent in accountancy and engineering, the two professions that show the largest percentage of questionnaires discarded for this reason.

2 TESTS OF THE RELIABILITY OF THE DATA

An examination of sampling methods can, at best, establish a presumption that certain biases are present and certain others, absent. But even though no biases are discovered, or whatever biases are discovered can be corrected, the final sample cannot be judged free from bias or the data accepted as accurate and reliable. If we can think of a dozen possible sources of bias, it would be naive to suppose that there were not a hundred overlooked. This need for additional tests of the reliability of our data is enhanced by our inability to evaluate properly certain recognized possible sources of bias—for example, differences between persons who return questionnaires and those who do not. We have applied three types of tests to our data: (a) comparison of the distribution of each sample by geographic units with the estimated distribution of all practitioners; (b) comparison of different samples for the same profession with one another; (c) comparison of our samples with other studies.

a Comparison with geographic distribution of all practitioners

The comparisons that we have made between the distributions of the samples and the estimated distributions of all practitioners are summarized in Table A 7. For physicians, the distributions compared are by size of community class and region; [63] for dentists, lawyers, and certified public accountants, by states. No compari-

[63] We have used the nine Census regions and seven size of community classes (see Ch. 5, footnote 3). The total number of classes is less than 63 because all size of community classes are not represented in all regions and because some classes containing few returns were combined for the χ^2 analysis.

TABLE A 7

Comparison between Distributions of Samples by Geographic Units and Estimated Distributions of All Practitioners

Physicians, Dentists, Lawyers, and Certified Public Accountants

PROFESSION & SAMPLE (1)	GEOGRAPHIC UNITS (2)	UNIVERSE WITH WHICH SAMPLE IS COMPARED (3)	NO. OF DEGREES OF FREEDOM (4)	χ^2 (5)	P [1] (6)
Physicians					
1933	Region and size of community	No. in 1931 [2]	57	236.47	less than .000000001
	Regions only	"	8	55.55	less than .000001
	Size of community only	"	6	65.77	less than .0000001
	Size of community within each region [3]	"	49	164.50	less than .000000001
1935	Region and size of community	"	54	103.80	.00003
	Region only	"	8	31.29	.0001
	Size of community only	"	6	16.96	.009
	Size of community within each region [3]	"	46	71.37	.008
Dentists					
1933	States	Membership in A.D.A., Dec. 31, 1935 [4]	40	130.98	less than .000000001
	"	*No. from Census of Population,* 1930	40	179.07	"
1935	"	Membership in A.D.A., Dec. 31, 1935 [4]	33	86.99	.0000001
		No. on Apr. 1, 1936 [5]	33	135.11	less than .000000001
Lawyers					
1935	States	No. in 1935 [6]	40	325.26	"
Certified Public Accountants					
1935	States	No. in 1937 [7]	30	89.43	.00000006
1937	"	"	30	143.31	less than .000000001

[1] *P* is the probability that the observed χ^2 would be exceeded by chance.
[2] Leland, *Distribution of Physicians,* Table 42.
[3] χ^2 was computed separately for each region, and the resulting values summed.
[4] R. P. Thomas, 'Dental Survey', *Journal of the American Dental Association and the Dental Cosmos,* Jan. 1938, p. 158.
[5] *Ibid.,* p. 155. The figure for Illinois was reduced from 11,370 to 6,000 to correct for an obvious overestimate. See notes to Table 1, Ch. 1.
[6] Based on a count of the *Martindale-Hubbell Law Directory* for 1936 made available by Martindale-Hubbell.
[7] Estimates made by American Institute of Accountants.

sons have been made for consulting engineers, since there are no data on the number of consulting engineers either by regions and size of community classes, or by states.

As a measure of the discrepancy between the sample and universe distributions, we use the statistic χ^2, entered in column 5 of Table A 7. The values of χ^2 are not directly comparable, since they are affected by the number of classes in the distributions. They can be compared by reference to column 6, which gives P, the probability that the observed values of χ^2 would be exceeded by chance. The smaller the probability, the larger the discrepancy between the sample and universe distributions.

For all professions, the estimated distributions of the universe have been compared with the original sample distributions, before correction for biases. The original distributions have been used because values of χ^2 based on the corrected distributions cannot be interpreted in probability terms. In judging Table A 7, however, it should be borne in mind that the discrepancies it reveals for lawyers and accountants are partly explained by the size of community and firm member biases noted above, and that the data on which the substantive analysis in the text is based have been corrected for these biases.[64] No comparisons have been made for the 1937 legal and medical samples because they are not random among states.

The striking feature of Table A 7 is the extreme discrepancies between the sample and universe distributions. The two differ least, as measured by the probabilities associated with χ^2, for the 1935 medical sample. Yet even for this sample, the largest value of P is .009, i.e., the discrepancy between the size of community distributions of the sample and universe is so large that it would be exceeded by chance alone only 9 times in a thousand. For the other medical sample and the other professions, the smallest discrepancy is so large that it would be exceeded by chance alone less than one time in a million.

[64] Comparisons for lawyers and accountants based on both the original and adjusted distributions have already been presented above (see footnotes 26, 27, and 46). For accountants the differences between the comparisons based on the original distributions and those based on the adjusted distributions are relatively small, but for lawyers adjustment for the firm member and size of community biases accounted for almost half of the discrepancy between the sample and the universe.

These large discrepancies are not subject to a clear and un-ambiguous interpretation; they may reflect errors not in the samples but in the estimated distributions of the universe. The samples supposedly include only persons in independent prac-tice; the available data on the distribution of all practitioners uniformly include not only persons in independent practice but also salaried employees and some persons who are not in practice either because they have retired or for other reasons. Moreover, the distributions of all practitioners are estimates subject to a con-siderable margin of error and are available for the year in which the sample was chosen for only three comparisons. The inclusion of salaried employees is the most serious deficiency: they not only number almost one-sixth of all physicians and dentists and almost one-third of all lawyers and certified public accountants, but also are more concentrated in large and prosperous communities.

The comparisons in Table A 7 for dentists are instructive in indicating the importance of using the correct universe. Though our samples were restricted to members of the American Dental Association, they were compared with both members and all dentists. For each sample, χ^2 is lower for the former comparison—27 per cent lower for the 1933 sample, 36 per cent lower for the 1935 sample.[65]

Errors in the estimated distributions of all practitioners may therefore explain part, possibly a large part, of the observed dis-crepancies between the sample and universe distributions. It seems unlikely, however, that they are entirely responsible for these dis-crepancies. If they were, the discrepancies might be expected to be least for physicians and dentists, the professions which contain fewest salaried employees. Yet, according to Table A 7, the dis-crepancies are of about the same order of magnitude for these pro-fessions as for lawyers and accountants.

For each profession included in Table A 7, we can compute the ratio of the number of practitioners in the sample from a par-ticular state to the estimated total number of practitioners in that state. The existence of discrepancies between the sample and uni-verse distributions means that these ratios vary from state to state. To the extent that the discrepancies reflect factors common to all professions, the ratios for different professions will be corre-

[65] The χ^2's are directly comparable because the number of degrees of freedom is the same.

lated. The inclusion of salaried employees in the estimated total number of practitioners is one such factor, since salaried employees in the different professions are presumably concentrated in the same states. Similarly there may be some factors affecting the willingness of individuals to reply that differ in strength from state to state but affect all professions alike.[66]

To test the correlation, the ratios for each of the four professions were ranked in order of magnitude.[67] Though by no means identical, the four sets of ranks show a degree of similarity that would be exceeded by chance only 16 times in 100,000. The measure of similarity, χ_r^2, is almost half as large as its maximum possible value, i.e., as the value that it would attain if the ranks were identical.[68] This finding suggests first, that much of the apparent nonrepresentativeness of the samples is attributable to factors affecting all samples alike, such as errors in the estimated distributions of all practitioners or general forces affecting willingness to reply; second, that such factors are not entirely responsible for the apparent nonrepresentativeness of the samples; and third, that much of the apparent nonrepresentativeness is attributable to factors affecting particular professions or samples rather than to factors affecting all professions and samples alike.

The nonrepresentativeness of our samples means that no great confidence can be placed in our data on the number and proportion of professional men in various states, regions, or size of community classes. This presumptive unreliability of the geographic distributions of our samples is in itself not serious, since we have little interest in using our samples to study the geographic distribution of professional men. But it inevitably arouses suspicion

[66] Since the data were collected by a government agency, the attitude toward the party in power might be such a factor.

[67] Ratios based on the 1935 samples were used for all professions. For dentists, the number of members of the American Dental Association rather than the total number of dentists was the denominator of the ratio. For accountants, the numerator of the ratio was the number of accountants in the sample after correction for the firm member bias, and for lawyers, the number of lawyers in the sample after correction for both the firm member and size of community biases.

[68] For the test of similarity, see Friedman, 'The Use of Ranks', pp. 675–701, especially pp. 675–80, 694–5. The value of χ_r^2 is 77.37; the mean value on the chance hypothesis, 46; and its standard deviation, 8.31. The probability stated above assumes χ_r^2 normally distributed. The value of χ_r^2 that would be obtained if the ranks were identical is 184.

about the reliability of the data on average income or the distribution of income by size. If the states (or other geographic units) underrepresented in the samples tended to have relatively many professional men with low incomes, income data for groups of states would have an upward bias, and conversely. Moreover, if there were such a bias for groups of states, it would be reasonable to infer a similar bias within each state separately.

Fortunately, there appears to be no correlation between average income and biases in the geographic distributions of the samples. Rank difference correlation coefficients between the sample average income and the ratio of the sample to the estimated universe are uniformly small (Table A 8).[69] Four of the eight coefficients computed are less than their standard errors, and all are less than twice their standard errors; i.e., all might easily reflect merely chance variation.[70] This result was foreshadowed by similar correlations described in Section 1c, and it is confirmed by others described below. The apparent absence of any relation between average income and the biases in the geographic distribution of our samples suggests that income figures for groups of states will not be contaminated by the non-randomness of the geographic distributions; such figures will of course be subject to random errors but not, on this score at least, to bias.

[69] For physicians, the correlations were computed both by states and by region and size of community; for the other professions, only by states. See footnote 51 for a discussion of the validity of the test.

[70] Despite the risk of attempting to explain too much, it may be worth noting that the observed coefficients are entirely consistent with known biases in the samples and known deficiencies in the estimates of the universe. The medical sample underrepresents small communities, where incomes are relatively low. Hence, this factor alone would tend to produce a positive correlation between average income and the ratio of the sample to the universe, when the correlation is by region and size of community. Both observed correlations of this type for physicians are positive. In all professions, salaried employees tend to be concentrated in large and prosperous communities, where incomes are relatively high. Our estimates of the universe are too large, and our ratios of sample to universe too low, for states that contain many salaried employees. This factor, then, would tend to produce a negative correlation. Four of the five coefficients for the professions other than medicine are negative. For physicians, the known bias in the sample would be less important relatively to the deficiencies in the universe in a distribution by states than in a distribution by region and size of community. The correlation coefficient for physicians by states not only is less than by region and size of community, but also is negative.

TABLE A 8

Rank Difference Correlation Coefficients between Sample Average Income and Ratio of Sample to Universe

Physicians, Dentists, Lawyers, and Certified Public Accountants

PROFESSION & SAMPLE (1)	GEOGRAPHIC UNITS (2)	UNIVERSE (3)	YEAR OF AVERAGE INCOME (4)	NO. OF ITEMS CORRELATED (5)	RANK DIFFERENCE CORRELATION COEFFICIENT (6)	STANDARD ERROR (7)
Physicians						
1933	Region and size of community	No. in 1931 [1]	1932	59	.239	.131
1935	"	"	1932	59	.138	.131
1935	States	No. in active practice, 1934 [2]	1934	49	—.013	.144
Dentists						
1933	"	Membership in A.D.A., Dec. 31, 1935 [3]	1932	49	—.216	.144
1935	"	"	1934	49	—.245	.144
Lawyers [4]						
1935	"	No. in 1935 [5]	1934	47	—.057	.147
Certified public accountants [6]						
1935	States	No. in 1937 [7]	1934	47	.073	.147
1937	"	"	1936	47	—.112	.147

[1] Leland, *Distribution of Physicians*, Table 42.
[2] Total number of physicians in each state as given in the Directory of the American Medical Association, multiplied by 1931 ratio for that state of total number of physicians in active practice to total number of physicians (Leland, Table 14).
[3] Thomas, 'Dental Survey', p. 158.
[4] The ratios of sample to universe are based on the number of individuals in the sample after correction for firm member and size of community biases. Average income is solely for individual practitioners.
[5] Based on a count of *Martindale-Hubbell Law Directory* for 1936 made available by Martindale-Hubbell.
[6] The ratios of sample to universe are based on the number of individuals in the sample after correction for firm member bias.
[7] Estimates made by American Institute of Accountants.

For physicians, the availability of data from the 1937 sample on type of practice permits one additional comparison with the universe. According to this sample, 22 per cent of all physicians considered themselves complete specialists, 38 per cent, partial specialists, and 40 per cent, general practitioners. According to a comprehensive count of the 1931 Directory of the American Medical Association, 16.5 per cent of all physicians in active practice were complete specialists, 15.6 gave 'special attention' to a subject, and 67.9 per cent were in general practice.[71] The large difference between our sample and the directory count in the percentage classified as partial specialists is of little significance, since the distinction between partial specialists and general practitioners is extremely vague.[72] Of more interest is the considerably higher percentage classified as complete specialists in the sample. One possible explanation is the bias, noted in Section 1b iii, which is due to selecting the sample by laying a straight edge marked off at equally spaced intervals along a column of names. However, this explanation is contradicted by the comparisons made below between our samples and other studies that presumably do not have this bias. The percentage of complete specialists in our sample is fairly close to the percentage in the other studies and for three of four comparisons is below rather than above the latter. The observed difference may therefore more reasonably be attributed to (1) a general tendency for specialists to be more willing to reply, (2) a difference in the wording and interpretation of the question on type of practice, (3) the inclusion among those listed in the directory as 'in active practice' of some persons who have retired or are not in practice and who tend to be classified as general practitioners, (4) the inclusion in the directory count of unclassified nonmembers as general practitioners,[73] or (5) an increase in the percentage of specialists from 1931 to 1936. Though there is no evidence on the relative importance of these factors, the slight tendency for the percentage of specialists to be smaller in our sample than in other samples suggests that point (1), if it applies at all, probably applies to our samples less than to the others. This would be consistent with the fact that the other studies were all conducted by medical associations and hence probably evoked a better response from members, who include a larger percentage of specialists than of general practitioners.

b Comparison of different samples for the same profession
Two or three independent samples are available for each profession other than engineering. These samples cover spans of years that overlap. Comparisons between the distributions of the

71 See Leland, *Distribution of Physicians*, p. 32.
72 See footnote 12 of Ch. 6.
73 See Leland, *Distribution of Physicians*, p. 17.

samples for the overlapping years reveal larger discrepancies than can reasonably be attributed to chance alone (Table A 9).[74] At the same time, the discrepancies are considerably smaller than those between the sample and universe distributions (compare Tables A 7 and A 9). In part, the smaller discrepancies merely confirm our earlier finding that a large part of the observed discrepancies between the sample and universe distributions is attributable to errors in the estimated distributions of the universe or

TABLE A 9

Comparisons between Distributions of Successive Samples for Overlapping Years

Physicians, Dentists, and Certified Public Accountants

PROFESSION & SAMPLES COMPARED (1)	GEOGRAPHIC UNITS (2)	YEAR OF COMPARISON (3)	NO. OF DEGREES OF FREEDOM (4)	χ^2 (5)	P [1] (6)
Physicians					
1933 & 1935	States	1932	36	54.59	.022
	Size of community	1932	6	14.12	.029
Dentists					
1933 & 1935	States	1932	31	66.67	.00009
Certified public accountants [2]					
1933 & 1935	States	1932	34	48.52	.047
1937 & 1935	"	1934	29	39.03	.10

[1] P is the probability that the observed χ^2 would be exceeded by chance.
[2] Comparisons are between distributions not corrected for firm member bias.

to general forces affecting all samples alike. In part, also, they are explained by the fact that similar methods were used to choose the different samples for the same profession. Deficiencies in the sampling methods would affect all samples alike and hence would not produce discrepancies among them.

The observed discrepancies must reflect either changes in the willingness of individuals to reply that were not uniform for all states (or other units), or differences in the universes from which the samples were drawn. Differences in the universe can hardly be important for physicians or accountants since the samples for

[74] No comparison was made for law because the 1937 legal sample is not random among states. For the same reason, the 1937 medical sample was not compared with the other medical samples.

these professions were chosen from comprehensive lists at intervals of only two years, and the distribution of all persons in the professions is very stable. The dental samples, on the other hand, were chosen from the membership lists of the American Dental Association, which experienced a decline in membership of about 8 per cent from 1932 to 1933 and then an increase of about 15 per cent from 1933 to 1934.[75] The decline and subsequent growth were doubtless not the same in all states. This greater change in the universe may be the reason why the dental samples differ more from one another than the samples for the other professions.

The relatively small discrepancies between the geographic distributions of the samples appear uncorrelated with differences between average incomes. For each pair of samples in Table A 9, we have computed rank difference correlation coefficients by states between (a) the ratio of the number in one sample to the number in the other and (b) the difference between the average incomes from the two samples. The correlation coefficients are uniformly small (Table A 10). Three are smaller than their standard errors, and the fourth is only slightly larger than its standard error.

The differences between the nationwide average incomes for years covered by more than one sample for the same profession confirm the bias discussed in Section 1a i. It was suggested there that requesting information for a period of years from a sample chosen from a list presumed to be comprehensive for the end of the period would tend to impart an upward bias to the trend of income over time. In consequence, the earlier of two samples would tend to yield a higher average for an overlapping year. Seven of the ten differences summarized in Table 5 (Ch. 2) are in the expected direction, and two of the three exceptions are for lawyers, for whom the 1937 sample is suspect on other grounds (see Sec. 1b iv above). Except for one of the accountancy comparisons, the positive differences are moderate, the largest being 13 per cent. Even the 35 per cent difference between the 1929 averages from the 1933 and 1937 accountancy samples is not disturbing since the bias in question should be larger the longer the time elapsing between the selection of the samples, and between these dates and the date for which the comparison is made. It is fair to conclude, there-

[75] Based on data from the American Dental Association. These changes are *net*. Others may well have taken place and may have affected the distribution of members by states.

fore, that these comparisons give no evidence of the existence of
any biases other than those already noted.

A more detailed comparison between the average incomes from
successive samples is summarized in Chart A 1, which contains
three panels. The panels for physicians and dentists compare the
1932 average incomes from the 1933 and 1935 samples; the panel
for accountants compares the 1934 average incomes from the

TABLE A 10

Rank Difference Correlation Coefficients between the Ratio of the
Number of Persons in One Sample to the Number in Another
Sample for the Same Profession and the Difference in Average
Income, by States

Physicians, Dentists, and Certified Public Accountants

PROFESSION & SAMPLES COMPARED	YEAR OF COMPARISON	NO. OF STATES	RANK DIFFERENCE CORRELATION COEFFICIENT	STANDARD ERROR
(1)	(2)	(3)	(4)	(5)
Physicians				
1935 & 1933	1932	48	.1383	.1459
Dentists				
1935 & 1933	1932	48	—.23	.1459
Certified public accountants *				
1935 & 1933	1932	46	.0944	.149
1937 & 1935	1934	46	.1148	.149

* The first correlation is based on the original number of persons, uncorrected
for the firm member bias, and on average incomes, also uncorrected. The second
correlation is based on the number of persons after correction for the firm member bias, and on the average incomes of individuals practising alone (i.e., on
averages that exclude firm members).

1935 and 1937 samples.[76] Each point in the chart is for an individual state. The vertical distance of the point from the zero axis
measures the difference between the two averages for a state (the
average from the earlier sample minus the average from the later
sample); the horizontal distance, the total number of persons from
that state who reported their incomes in the two samples.

[76] The panel for accountants refers solely to individuals practising alone, i.e.,
excludes firm members. The latter were excluded because of the firm member
bias.

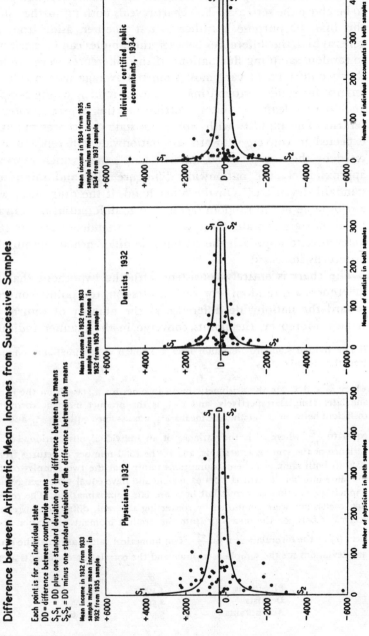

CHART A 1

Difference between Arithmetic Mean Incomes from Successive Samples

Each point is for an individual state
DD = difference between countrywide means
S_1S_1 = DD plus one standard deviation of the difference between the means
S_2S_2 = DD minus one standard deviation of the difference between the means

Mean income in 1932 from 1933 sample minus mean income in 1932 from 1935 sample

Mean income in 1932 from 1933 sample minus mean income in 1932 from 1935 sample

Mean income in 1934 from 1935 sample minus mean income in 1934 from 1937 sample

Physicians, 1932

Dentists, 1932

Individual certified public accountants, 1934

The general bias arising from the time elapsing between the selection of the samples is reflected in the tendency for the points to be above the zero axis. The chart reveals nothing further about this bias. Its purpose is rather to test whether, aside from this general bias, the differences between the samples can be attributed to random sampling fluctuations. If the differences were random, they would tend to vary most from the average nationwide difference for states contributing the fewest returns to the samples, and to vary least for states contributing the largest number of returns. The rapidity with which the state differences might be expected to converge toward the nationwide difference is indicated by the heavy curved lines in each panel, which represent approximately the nationwide difference plus and minus one standard deviation.[77] On the other hand, if the differences were attributable not to random factors but to differential biases varying from state to state, there would be no tendency for the state differences to approach the nationwide difference as the number of returns increased.

The chart is entirely consistent with the hypothesis that the differences are random. For each profession, the points converge toward the nationwide difference as the number of returns increases. Moreover, the points converge in the manner indicated

[77] The plotted standard deviation lines are rough approximations computed from the formula

$$\sigma^2_{\bar{x}_1 - \bar{x}_2} = \sigma^2_{\bar{x}_1} + \sigma^2_{\bar{x}_2} - 2r_{\bar{x}_1 \bar{x}_2} \sigma_{\bar{x}_1} \sigma_{\bar{x}_2},$$

where $\bar{x}_1$ and $\bar{x}_2$ are the arithmetic mean incomes for a state from the earlier and later samples respectively, and $r_{\bar{x}_1 \bar{x}_2}$ is the product moment correlation coefficient between the arithmetic means. $\sigma^2_{\bar{x}_1}$ was assumed equal to $\sigma^2_{\bar{x}_2}$ and each equal to $\frac{2\sigma^2}{n}$, where σ^2 is the variance of an individual observation, i.e., the variance of the sample as a whole, and n, the total number of returns from a state in both samples. These assumptions imply that the two samples contain the same number of returns from each state and have equal variances. Neither implicit 'assumption is correct but both are fair approximations. The correlation coefficients were computed by converting the rank difference correlation coefficient between the means (r') into the product moment correlation coefficient (r) by the formula $r = 2 \sin \frac{\pi r'}{6}$. The numerical values assigned the standard deviations for the sample as a whole and the correlation coefficients are:

	σ	r
Physicians	4,100	.6
Dentists	2,500	.5
Accountants	3,300	.6

by the standard deviation lines, and their distribution about these lines does not deviate significantly from the distribution that random factors would produce.[78] The chart therefore gives no evidence that, aside from the general bias noted, there are any other biases that affect the successive samples for the same profession differently.

c Comparison of our samples with other studies

Data on professional income for the period covered by our samples are rare. There are a fair number of studies for physicians and dentists, two fragmentary studies for lawyers, one for consulting engineers, and none for certified public accountants. Three of these studies are sufficiently extensive to warrant and permit detailed comparison with our data. These are the studies of the 1929 incomes of physicians and of dentists made under the auspices of the Committee on the Costs of Medical Care; and the California Medical-Economic Survey, which covered both physicians and dentists for the years 1929–34. Only very general comparison with the other studies is feasible.

i *Incomes of physicians in 1929.* Data on 1929 income was obtained by the Committee on the Costs of Medical Care from over 5,000 physicians in independent practice who replied to a questionnaire mailed to 20,000 physicians throughout the nation. The results of this study were presented and analyzed by Leven.[79] His book includes, in addition, a brief analysis of more than 6,000 questionnaires obtained by the American Medical Association in

[78] The observed distributions of the differences compared with the expected distributions, computed on the assumption that the differences are normally distributed, are:

	NUMBER OF DIFFERENCES FOR					
	PHYSICIANS		DENTISTS		ACCOUNTANTS	
DIFFERENCE	Observed	Expected	Observed	Expected	Observed	Expected
Larger than σ	12	7.6	11	7.8	7	7.3
σ to mean	9	16.4	13	16.7	15	15.7
Mean to — σ	16	16.4	17	16.7	16	15.7
Less than — σ	11	7.6	8	7.8	8	7.3
Total	48	48	49	49	46	46

The discrepancy between observed and expected distributions is greatest for physicians. Yet even this discrepancy would be exceeded by chance alone more than one time in 20.

[79] *Incomes of Physicians.*

a study, restricted mainly to its members, covering 1928. The questionnaires used by the Committee on the Costs of Medical Care asked only for gross income; net income was estimated on the basis of the relation between net and gross income revealed by the American Medical Association sample.

Arithmetic mean and median gross and net incomes from the other samples are reasonably consistent with those from ours (Table A 11). The averages from the American Medical Association sample are uniformly highest, as might be expected from its overrepresentation of members. The averages from our 1933 sample (referred to in the table as the Department of Commerce sample) are somewhat higher than those from the Committee's sample, although, on *a priori* grounds, the differences might be expected to be in the opposite direction. Our sample was taken at a later date and hence should have a downward bias relatively to the Committee's. However, the differences are small—the largest is less than four per cent—and, for the arithmetic means, are only slightly larger than their standard errors.[80] Moreover, the averages presented by Leven are weighted averages of the averages for size of community classes, the weights being the estimated total number of physicians in each size of community class. This adjustment was made because the Committee's sample seemed to underrepresent both very small and very large communities. The average gross income yielded directly by the sample can be computed from the data Leven presents and is given in Table A 11. It is almost identical with the average from our 1933 sample.[81]

The distribution of the Committee's sample by size of gross income differs somewhat from the corresponding distribution for 1929 of our 1933 sample. Although the standard deviations of the two distributions are very close, $11,790 for the Committee's sample and $11,835 for our sample,[82] the observed difference between the distributions as a whole would be exceeded by chance

[80] The standard error of the difference between the arithmetic means is approximately $300 for gross income and $173 for net income.

[81] It was noted in Sec. 1b ii above that our samples underrepresent the smaller communities. The resulting upward bias in average income seemed too slight to justify correction. This upward bias may, however, have been larger in 1929 than in 1932, the year for which it was tested, and may partly explain the failure of our averages to be below those from the Committe's sample.

[82] The difference between the two standard deviations is not statistically significant.

TABLE A 11

Arithmetic Mean and Median Gross and Net Incomes Physicians: Department of Commerce, Committee on Costs of Medical Care, and American Medical Association Samples

SAMPLE	YEAR	NO. OF RETURNS	ARITHMETIC MEAN			MEDIAN		
			ACTUAL	DIFFERENCE FROM 1933 D. OF C. SAMPLE		ACTUAL	DIFFERENCE FROM 1933 D. OF C. SAMPLE	
				Absolute	Percentage		Absolute	Percentage
(1)	(2)	(3)	(4) (dollars)	(5) (dollars)	(6)	(7) (dollars)	(8) (dollars)	(9)
			Gross Income					
Dept. of Commerce, 1933	1929	2,226	9,778			7,275		
American Medical Association	1928	5,475	10,440	+662	+6.8	8,090	+815	+11.2
Comm. on Costs of Med. Care								
Original	1929	5,380[1]	9,764[2]	−14	−.1			
Weighted by size of community	1929	5,380[1]	9,461	−317	−3.2	7,026	−249	−3.4
			Net Income					
Dept. of Commerce, 1933	1929	2,139	5,916			4,223		
Dept. of Commerce, 1937	1929	912[3]	5,493[4]	−423	−7.2	4,938	+715	+16.9
American Medical Association	1928	5,475	6,499	+583	+9.9			
Comm. on Costs of Med. Care, weighted by size of community	1929	5,380	5,700	−216	−3.7	4,100	−123	−2.9

Maurice Leven, *Incomes of Physicians* (University of Chicago Press, 1932), pp. 20, 24, 105, 109, 111.

[1] Leven cites a figure of 6,980. But this is adjusted to allow for individuals who failed to reply and to whom no follow-up letter was sent. The figure given above, 5,380, is an estimate of the actual number of returns on which the averages are based. It is derived from *Incomes of Physicians*, pp. 13, 15, and 109.

[2] Computed from *ibid.*, p. 111.

[3] Actual number of returns before weighting.

[4] Weighted average of the state averages.

CHART A 2

Distribution of Gross Income by Size

Physicians, 1929: Committee on Costs of Medical Care
and Department of Commerce Samples

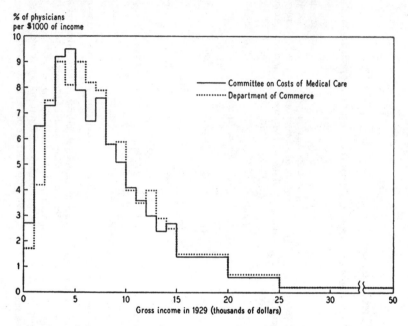

alone less than one time in a thousand.[83] The difference between
the two distributions is therefore *statistically* significant. At the
same time, as Chart A 2 shows, the difference is so small that it
is hardly significant in any other sense.[84] The Committee's sample
contains relatively more very low incomes and relatively fewer
intermediate incomes. These differences may reflect the underrepresentation of small communities in our sample. The distributions of net income differ somewhat more than the distributions
of gross income, but since the Committee's distribution of net income was derived from its distribution of gross income by using
ratios of net income to gross income, this comparison is of slight
importance.

[83] χ^2 is 46.8, with 18 degrees of freedom.
[84] The reason so minor a difference is statistically significant is, of course, that
the samples are so large.

Comparison is possible not only between the nationwide data from the two samples but also between the arithmetic mean gross incomes in each size of community class within each region. While our size of community classes are not identical with those used by Leven, the differences are slight.[85] Chart A 3, constructed in the same way as Chart A 1, summarizes the comparison. Each point in the chart is for a size of community and regional cell, or for a size of community class or region as a whole. The vertical distance of the point from the zero axis measures the difference between the average from the Committee's sample and the average from our sample; the horizontal distance, the square root of the number of physicians in our sample. The heavy curved lines include a range of one standard deviation on either side of the zero axis, since zero is the expected difference on the hypothesis that the two samples represent the same universe.[86] If the differences between the samples reflected sampling fluctuation alone, the points should converge toward the zero axis as the number of returns increased. On the other hand, if the differences reflected bias, there

[85] The two classifications differ at the extremes. We use the classes under 2,500, and 2,500–10,000, whereas Leven uses under 5,000, and 5,000–10,000; at the other extreme, Leven uses the classes 500,000–1,000,000, and 1,000,000 and over, whereas we use the one class, 500,000 and over. Since Leven does not give the number of returns in each cell, we were unable to combine his class intervals. Consequently we compared our class 500,000 and over with his class 500,000–1,000,000 and at the lower extreme compared the overlapping class intervals.

[86] The standard deviation is approximate. Since Leven does not give the number of returns in each cell, the standard deviation is computed on the assumption that the ratio of the number in the Committee's sample to the number in our sample is the same for each cell as for the entire country. For simplicity, the standard deviation of an individual observation is assumed equal for the two samples, an assumption that is approximately correct. On these assumptions, the standard deviation of the difference between the averages in any cell is

$$\frac{\sigma}{\sqrt{n_1}} \sqrt{\frac{p+1}{p} - \frac{2r}{\sqrt{p}}}$$

where σ is the standard deviation of an individual observation, i.e., the standard deviation of the sample, p is the ratio of the number in the Committee's sample to the number in our sample, and r is the correlation between the cell averages from the two samples. σ was taken as $11,790, p as 2.46, and r as .64. The product moment correlation coefficient was estimated from the rank difference correlation coefficient.

Difference between Arithmetic Mean Gross Incomes from Committee
on Costs of Medical Care and Department of Commerce Samples

Physicians, 1929

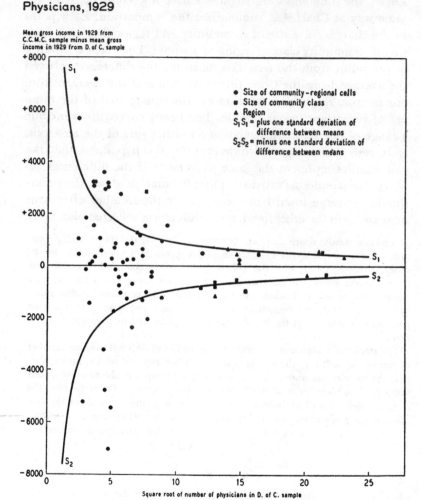

Mean gross income in 1929 from
C.C.M.C. sample minus mean gross
income in 1929 from D. of C. sample

Square root of number of physicians in D. of C. sample

would be no tendency for the points to converge. It is clear from
the chart that the points do converge in the manner indicated by
the standard deviation lines. The distribution of the points
about the standard deviation lines does not differ significantly from

the distribution that chance alone would produce.[87] Interestingly enough, the average from the Committee's sample is larger than the average from our sample for more than half the cells, 37 out of 59, although the difference between the nationwide averages is in the opposite direction.

Both the Committee's sample and our 1937 sample furnish data on the percentage of physicians who consider themselves general practitioners, partial specialists, and complete specialists. While

	PERCENTAGE OF ALL PHYSICIANS	
	Comm. on Costs of Med. Care	1937 D. of C. sample
General practitioners	56.7	38.6
Partial specialists	20.7	39.9
General practitioners and partial specialists	77.4	78.5
Complete specialists	22.6	21.5
Total	100.0	100.0

the percentage of physicians who classified themselves as complete specialists is very similar for the two samples, the division of the other physicians between general practitioners and partial specialists is very different. However, as noted above, the vagueness of the distinction between the general practitioner and the partial specialist makes this difference of little significance.

These comparisons between our medical samples and that of the Committee on the Costs of Medical Care are comforting. The samples are remarkably similar in practically all respects despite marked differences between the agencies conducting the surveys, the dates at which they were made, the sampling methods, and the questionnaires used.

ii *Incomes of dentists in 1929*. The study of dental incomes in 1929 made by the American Dental Association in cooperation

[87] The expected and observed distributions of the points for the individual cells are:

	OBSERVED	EXPECTED
Larger than σ	12	9.4
σ to 0	25	20.1
0 to $-\sigma$	13	20.1
Less than $-\sigma$	9	9.4
Total	59	59.0

χ^2 between the observed and expected is 4.46 and would be exceeded by chance in more than one-fifth of random samples. The regional and size of community averages are, of course, not independent of the averages for the separate cells and hence have been excluded from the above comparison.

with the Committee on the Costs of Medical Care is less directly comparable with our samples than the Committee's study of the incomes of physicians. A minor difficulty is that the Committee's dental study was restricted to 20 states. About 9,000 dentists were circularized in these states and over 5,000 returns containing usable information on income obtained. A more important difficulty is that our sample is restricted to members of the American Dental Association, whereas the Committee's sample is not.

To facilitate comparability, arithmetic mean net and gross incomes in 1929 have been computed from our 1933 sample for the twenty states covered by the Committee's sample and have been corrected for the restriction of our sample to members (Table A 12). The corrected averages were computed from the original averages by multiplying the latter by the correction factor derived in Section 1a iv for the country as a whole. The same correction factor was used for both net and gross income, though it was derived from net income data alone. Consequently, the estimate of the average gross income of all dentists is even rougher than the estimate of the average net income.

Table A 12 also includes two sets of averages from the Committee's sample: the original averages derived directly from the sample; and the final estimates for the 20 states presented by Leven, who was responsible for the analysis of the dental sample as well as the medical sample. These final estimates embody two adjustments. First, the net incomes of dentists who reported gross income but not net income were estimated on the basis of the relationship between net income and gross income revealed by the remaining returns, and these estimated net incomes were added to the original sample.[88] Second, a correction was made for the inclusion in the sample of a larger percentage of members than of nonmembers.

The final estimates from the Committee's sample are somewhat higher than those from our sample, as might be expected from the general tendency for the earlier of two samples to yield a higher average for the overlapping year. The average net income is $373, or 8.4 per cent, higher; the average gross income, $508, or 6.7 per

[88] No such adjustment was made for the Department of Commerce sample. However, the percentage of respondents who reported gross income but not net income was five times as large in the Committee's sample as in the Department of Commerce sample.

TABLE A 12

Arithmetic Mean Gross and Net Incomes

Dentists in 20 States: Department of Commerce and Committee on Costs of Medical Care Samples, 1929

	GROSS INCOME		NET INCOME	
	No. of returns	Arith. mean income (dollars)	No. of returns	Arith. mean income (dollars)
Dept. of Commerce 1933 sample, for 20 states covered by Comm. on Costs of Med. Care sample				
Original	879	8,702	855	5,076
Adjusted for restriction to Amer. Dental Assn. members [1]		7,623		4,447
Comm. on Costs of Med. Care sample for 20 states				
Original [2]	5,493	8,279	4,705	5,011
Final estimate (corrected for returns giving gross income but not net income and for overrepresentation of members) [3]		8,131		4,820

[1] Averages in first line multiplied by .876.
[2] Maurice Leven, *Practice of Dentistry and the Incomes of Dentists in Twenty States: 1929* (University of Chicago Press, 1932), pp. 75–7.
[3] *Ibid.*, p. 207.

cent, higher. Part of this difference is doubtless due to the underrepresentation of new entrants in the Committee's sample noted by Leven.[89] His final estimates do not allow for this underrepresentation, although he indicates that correction for it would lower the average net income by about $65.[90] The rest of the difference in net income, $308, is slightly less than twice its standard error, while, even without correction for this factor, the difference in gross income is also slightly less than twice its standard error.[91] On the whole, then, the agreement is fairly good.

[89] *Practice of Dentistry,* p. 199.
[90] *Ibid.* Leven states that this would be the effect on the income of *general practitioners.* However, since 89 per cent of the dentists were general practitioners the same figure may without serious error be used for all dentists.
[91] The standard error of the difference between the means is $155 for net income, and $271 for gross income.

The difficulty of correcting characteristics other than the arithmetic mean for the restriction of the Department of Commerce sample to members makes precise comparison of the samples with respect to these characteristics impossible. The uncorrected frequency distributions of net and gross income by size naturally differ more than would be expected from chance alone; so also do the distributions of the samples by states.[92] As Chart A 4 indicates, the differences between the frequency distributions of net and gross income are consistent with the tendency for nonmembers to have lower incomes than members. The distribution from the Committee's sample includes relatively more low incomes and relatively fewer intermediate incomes. This divergence appears more marked in the gross income distribution than in the net income distribution because of the wider dispersion of the former; it is definitely present in both. Both the gross and net income distributions from the Committee's samples have smaller standard deviations than the corresponding distributions from our sample.[93] Though not particularly large in magnitude, this difference is in the opposite direction from what might be expected. As noted in

[92] The values of χ^2 and the number of degrees of freedom for these comparisons are as follows:

	χ^2	NO. OF DEGREES OF FREEDOM
Distributions of income by size		
Gross income	50.1	19
Net income (C.C.M.C. original distribution)	30.9	18
Net income (C.C.M.C. distribution adjusted to include dentists reporting gross but not net income)	35.8	18
Distributions of returns by states	74.9	19

For 19 degrees of freedom χ^2 will exceed 30.14 once in twenty times from chance; 36.19, once in a hundred times; and 43.82, once in a thousand times. For 18 degrees of freedom the corresponding values are 28.87, 34.80, and 42.31. The C.C.M.C. distributions were taken from *Practice of Dentistry*, pp. 84, 88, 189. The Department of Commerce distributions compared with them include only dentists in the 20 states covered by the C.C.M.C. study.

[93] The values of the standard deviations are:

	COMM. ON THE COSTS OF MED. CARE	DEPT. OF COMMERCE
	(dollars)	
Gross income	6,817	7,456
Net income	4,107	4,217

The difference between the standard deviations is statistically significant for gross income but not for net.

Distributions of Gross and Net Income by Size

Dentists in 20 States, 1929: Committee on Costs of Medical Care and Department of Commerce Samples

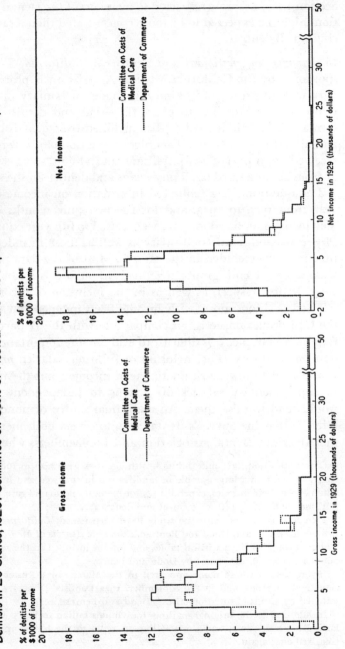

Section 1a iv, a sample restricted to members of the Dental Association might be expected to be more concentrated than a sample including all dentists.

iii *Incomes of physicians and dentists in California.* The study sponsored by the California Medical Association is probably the most intensive study of its kind ever made. In January 1935, questionnaires were mailed to every physician and dentist in California.[94] The initial mailing list included over 9,000 physicians and almost 6,000 dentists. Completed questionnaires were finally received from over 3,000 physicians and almost 2,000 dentists,[95] or from about a third of all physicians and dentists in the state.

The questionnaires requested information on income for each year from 1929 to 1933, and for the first nine months of 1934. The incomes reported for 1934 were raised to full-year equivalents. Physicians and dentists on salary as well as those in independent practice were included in the sample. Most of the data presented seem to be for both groups together, although this is not entirely clear. In this respect, as well as in the inclusion of income from salaried positions along with income from independent practice, the California sample is not comparable with the Department of Commerce sample. It is difficult to evaluate the importance of this noncomparability. The inclusion of full-time salaried employees would tend to lower arithmetic mean incomes; but the inclusion of supplementary salaries of persons in independent practice would tend to raise them. An additional source of noncomparability is that the Survey's dental sample covers both members of the American Dental Association and nonmembers, whereas our

[94] Osteopaths, hospitals, and public health agencies were also included in the study. In addition a large sample of families was interviewed and information obtained on their incomes, expenditures for medical and dental care and other purposes, and their need for medical and dental care.

Two reports dealing with the study have been issued: *California Medical-Economic Survey,* and Dodd and Penrose, *Economic Aspects of Medical Service.* The first contains the statistical tables and graphs included in the second, but none of the text of the report by Dodd and Penrose.

"Every person whose name appeared in the March, 1934 Roster of Physicians and Surgeons, and in the September, 1933 Dentists' Directory, . . . was solicited by means of questionnaires", Dodd and Penrose, p. 8.

[95] In addition to the original mailing, individuals failing to reply were circularized a second time; and those failing to reply to the follow-up were circularized once again.

sample covers members only. This is less serious, however, than may appear, since members were overrepresented in the Survey's dental sample.[96]

Our 1933 sample of California physicians yields average gross incomes between $847 and $1,321 *higher* than the corresponding averages from the Survey (Table A 13). Our later medical samples, on the other hand, yield average gross incomes between $203 and $1,278 *lower* than the corresponding averages from the Survey. While these differences seem fairly large, the number of physicians in our samples for California is so small that all of the differences might easily have arisen from chance.[97] Moreover, that the earlier sample is higher, and the later samples lower accords with what might be expected from the oft-repeated characteristics of samples taken at different dates.

The differences between the average net incomes from the two studies are naturally similar to the differences between the average gross incomes. The averages from our 1933 sample are higher, and from our 1935 and 1937 samples lower, than the corresponding averages from the Survey. The differences between the 1933 sample and the Survey are again sufficiently small to be attributable to sampling fluctuations.[98] The differences between the later samples and the Survey, however, cannot be interpreted in this way. The smallest of the three differences for the 1935 sample is 2.2 times its standard error; the largest, 3.4 times its standard error.[99] Three

[96] Dodd and Penrose infer that members are seriously overrepresented from the fact that 66.5 per cent of the respondents reported themselves as members, whereas, according to the Association's records, only 41.3 per cent belonged to the American Dental Association. This discrepancy may, however, merely reflect the tendency noted by Leven for individuals not listed on the Association's membership rolls to report themselves as members. (See Sec. 1a iv above; Leven, *Practice of Dentistry*, pp. 200–1; Dodd and Penrose, p. 170.) It seems likely that both factors were at work, and hence that the overrepresentation of members, while present, is less serious than Dodd and Penrose believe.

[97] The standard error of the difference between the means is larger than $540 for the 1933 sample, $720 for the 1935 sample, and $970 for the 1937 sample.

[98] The relevant standard error is larger than $210.

[99] The relevant standard error is about $270. The smaller standard error for net income than for gross income explains why the differences between the average net incomes are, and the differences between the average gross incomes are not, statistically significant even though the former are numerically smaller than the latter.

TABLE A 13

Arithmetic Mean Gross and Net Incomes, and Number of Persons Covered

California Physicians: Department of Commerce Samples and California Medical-Economic Survey, 1929–1934

	1929	1930	1931	1932	1933	1934
			Gross Income			
Arithmetic mean (dollars)						
Cal. Med.-Ec. Survey	11,049	10,092	8,868	7,195	6,456	6,911
Dept. of Commerce						
1933 sample	11,896	11,021	10,189	8,177		
1935 sample				6,067	5,537	5,940
1937 sample	9,771	9,610	8,649	6,686	6,253	6,607
Difference between means (dollars)						
Cal. Med.-Ec. Survey minus						
Dept. of Commerce						
1933 sample	−847	−929	−1,321	−982		
1935 sample				+1,128	+919	+971
1937 sample	+1,278	+482	+219	+509	+203	+304
Number of persons covered						
Cal. Med.-Ec. Survey	1,154	1,212	1,285	1,361	1,470	1,381
Dept. of Commerce						
1933 sample	202	214	219	223		
1935 sample				111	115	119
1937 sample	52	52	54	62	68	76
			Net Income			
Arithmetic mean (dollars)						
Cal. Med.-Ec. Survey	6,657	5,984	5,069	4,146	3,572	4,068
Dept. of Commerce						
1933 sample	6,680	6,166	5,500	4,308		
1935 sample				3,157	2,969	3,254
1937 sample	5,336	5,221	4,424	3,104	3,061	3,489
Difference between means (dollars)						
Cal. Med.-Ec. Survey minus						
Dept. of Commerce						
1933 sample	−23	−182	−431	−162		
1935 sample				+989	+603	+814
1937 sample	+1,321	+763	+645	+1,042	+511	+579
Number of persons covered						
Cal. Med.-Ec. Survey	1,445	1,524	1,643	1,756	2,737	1,871
Dept. of Commerce						
1933 sample	200	210	215	216		
1935 sample				110	112	115
1937 sample	49	47	50	56	60	76

California Medical-Economic Survey, Formal Report on Factual Data (California Medical Association, 1937), pp. 94-5.

of the six differences for the 1937 sample are less than twice their standard errors, but the other three are all more than twice their standard errors.[100] The later date at which the 1937 sample was selected makes the differences between it and the Survey understandable. But this explanation will not serve for the 1935 sample.

Comparison of the distributions of net income by size supports the view that the 1933 sample does not differ significantly from the Survey but that the 1935 sample does. While the discrepancy between the 1929 distributions of income from the two studies would be exceeded by chance more than half the time, the discrepancy between the 1933 distributions from our 1935 sample and the Survey would be exceeded by chance less than one time in a hundred.[101] We have been unable to find any explanation of the difference between our 1935 sample and the Survey.[102]

The percentage of complete specialists in our 1937 sample, 25 per cent, is considerably lower than the percentage in the Survey, 34 per cent. So far as this discrepancy represents more than a difference in the interpretation of the term 'complete specialists', it reflects upon the adequacy of the Survey data rather than ours, since only 20 per cent of California physicians were listed as complete specialists in the 1931 Directory of the American Medical Association.[103]

The average gross and net incomes of California dentists (Table A 14) give no reason to suspect the reliability of either of our dental samples. The original averages from our samples are consistently above the corresponding averages from the Survey, as is to be expected from the restriction of our samples to American Dental Association members. With two exceptions, the averages

[100] The relevant standard error is larger than $360.
[101] χ^2 for the 1929 distributions is 10.6 with 12 degrees of freedom; a χ^2 of 11.3 would be exceeded by chance half the time. χ^2 for the 1933 distributions is 15.4 with 5 degrees of freedom; a χ^2 of 15.1 would be exceeded by chance only once in a hundred times.
[102] One hypothesis tested was that the difference was attributable to a discrepancy between the distributions of the samples by size of community. However, there appears to be no such discrepancy. χ^2 between the size of community distributions is 5.5 with 5 degrees of freedom; the probability of this value being exceeded by chance is 0.4.
[103] See Leland, *Incomes of Physicians*, p. 17.

TABLE A 14

Arithmetic Mean Gross and Net Incomes, and
Number of Persons Covered

California Dentists: Department of Commerce Samples and
California Medical-Economic Survey, 1929–1934

	1929	1930	1931	1932	1933	1934
			Gross Income			
Arithmetic mean (dollars)						
Cal. Med.-Ec. Survey	8,680	8,308	7,163	5,633	4,936	5,444
Dept. of Commerce, original						
1933 sample	9,591	9,439	8,416	6,436		
1935 sample				6,027	5,406	5,719
Dept. of Commerce, adjusted for restriction to members of Amer. Dental Assn.*						
1933 sample	8,296	8,165	7,280	5,567		
1935 sample				5,213	4,676	4,947
Difference between means (dollars)						
Cal. Med.-Ec. Survey minus						
Dept. of Commerce, original						
1933 sample	−911	−1,131	−1,253	−803		
1935 sample				−394	−470	−275
Dept. of Commerce, adjusted						
1933 sample	+384	+143	−117	+66		
1935 sample				+420	+260	+497
Number of persons covered						
Cal. Med.-Ec. Survey	720	781	839	894	965	866
Dept. of Commerce						
1933 sample	110	122	125	129		
1935 sample				93	99	99
			Net Income			
Arithmetic mean (dollars)						
Cal. Med.-Ec. Survey	5,095	4,772	3,968	3,012	2,769	2,956
Dept. of Commerce, original						
1933 sample	5,408	5,478	4,721	3,299		
1935 sample				3,247	2,792	3,023
Dept. of Commerce, adjusted for restriction to members of Amer. Dental Assn.*						
1933 sample	4,678	4,738	4,084	2,854		
1935 sample				2,809	2,415	2,615
Difference between means (dollars)						
Cal. Med.-Ec. Survey minus						
Dept. of Commerce, original						
1933 sample	−313	−706	−753	−287		
1935 sample				−235	−23	−67
Dept. of Commerce, adjusted						
1933 sample	+417	+34	−116	+158		
1935 sample				+203	+354	+341

* Original arithmetic means multiplied by .865. This yields arithmetic mean of a hypothetical sample containing the same percentage of American Dental Association members as listed on the 1933 membership rolls (41.3 per cent) on the assumption that the average income of members exceeds that of nonmembers by 30 per cent.

TABLE A 14 (cont.)

	1929	1930	1931	1932	1933	1934
Number of persons covered			*Net income* (cont.)			
Cal. Med.-Ec. Survey	852	920	979	1,048	1,615	976
Dept. of Commerce						
1933 sample	108	118	121	128		
1935 sample				93	100	100

California Medical-Economic Survey, pp. 99–100.

corrected for this bias are below those from the Survey. The dif
ferences are all sufficiently small to be attributable to sampling
fluctuations.[104] Moreover, the Survey overrepresents members and
hence has a slight upward bias. Since the correction applied to our
samples purports to make full allowance for their restriction to
members, the upward bias in the Survey data would explain the
lower corrected averages from our samples.[105]

Comparisons of the distributions of the samples by size of community and by size of net income on the whole confirm the absence
of any significant differences between our samples and the Survey.[106]

In sum, the only significant discrepancy revealed by these comparisons is between our 1935 medical sample and the Survey. This
sample appears, at least for California, to have a downward bias
of some importance.

iv *Other studies of the incomes of physicians.* Three additional
studies of medical incomes with which our samples can be compared are for Wisconsin, Michigan, and Utah.

The Wisconsin study, made by a committee of the State Medical
Society, covered 1930 incomes as reported on state income tax re-

[104] Minimum estimates of the relevant standard errors of the difference between
the arithmetic mean gross incomes are $400 for the 1933 sample and $430 for
the 1935 sample; of the difference between the arithmetic mean net incomes,
$220 for the 1933 sample and $230 for the 1935 sample.

[105] See footnote 96 above. The correction we make accepts the estimate of 41.3
per cent cited in the Survey as the percentage of dentists who were members of
the dental association in 1933 (see *California Medical-Economic Survey*, p. 73).
The basis of our estimate of 30 per cent as the excess of the income of members
over that of nonmembers is given in Sec. 1a iv above.

[106] A comparison of the distribution of the samples in 1933 by size of community yields a χ^2 of 2.9 with 5 degrees of freedom. The probability of this value

turns filed by physicians.[107] *Ordinarily, studies based on income tax returns are subject to a serious upward bias because they omit persons whose incomes were below the exemption limit. This difficulty is, however, less serious for Wisconsin than for most other states because a much larger percentage of persons are required to file returns.[108] Income tax returns were found for 2,129 of an estimated 2,836 physicians in active practice. The committee in charge of the study estimated that considerably fewer than 500 of the 707 physicians omitted failed to file because of low incomes. The downward bias arising from the tendency toward understatement of income on tax returns probably offsets, in this study at least, most if not all of the upward bias arising from the omission of persons who did not file tax returns.

Our samples agree remarkably well with the Wisconsin study (Table A 15). The largest difference between the arithmetic means for all physicians is between mean net incomes from the Wisconsin

---

being exceeded by chance is 0.7. The results of the comparisons of the net income distributions are as follows:

	NO. OF DEGREES OF FREEDOM	χ^2	PROBABILITY THAT χ^2 WOULD BE EXCEEDED BY CHANCE
Cal. Med.-Ec. Survey compared with 1933 sample			
1929	8	9.2	.3
1930	9	10.7	.3
1931	8	6.6	.6
1932	7	4.5	.7
Cal. Med.-Ec. Survey compared with 1935 sample			
1932	6	9.4	.15
1933	6	4.6	.6

This last set of results, though showing no significant differences, is somewhat disturbing since the distributions from the Department of Commerce samples were not corrected for the restriction of the samples to members.

107 The results of the study appear in *Wisconsin Medical Journal*, Supplement, Dec. 1932, pp. 939–67.

108 The exemption limits in Wisconsin in 1930 were $800 for single individuals and $1,600 for married persons. In addition, the income tax authorities can request returns from any individual, regardless of his income. Typically, the assessors retain on their mailing lists individuals who have paid a tax in any of the preceding few years.

study and our 1933 sample; and even this difference, $408, might easily have arisen from chance.[109] Despite the slenderness of our sample, the averages for the separate groups of physicians—general practitioners and partial specialists, and complete specialists—are

TABLE A 15

Arithmetic Mean Gross and Net Incomes, and
Number of Persons Covered

Wisconsin Physicians: Department of Commerce Samples and
Study of Wisconsin State Medical Society, 1930

	GROSS INCOME			NET INCOME		
	All physi-cians	General prac-titioners and partial special-ists	Complete special-ists	All physi-cians	General prac-titioners and partial special-ists	Complete special-ists
Arithmetic mean income (dollars)						
Wisconsin study	7,553	5,323	12,468	4,704	2,945	8,542
Dept. of Commerce samples for Wisconsin						
1933 sample	7,767			4,296		
1937 sample	7,575	5,515	12,932	4,555	2,986	8,318
Number of persons covered						
Wisconsin study	2,129	1,460	669	2,129	1,460	669
Dept. of Commerce samples for Wisconsin						
1933 sample	43			42		
1937 sample	18	13	5	17	12	5

Wisconsin Medical Journal, Supplement, Dec. 1932, pp. 939–67.

very close. Finally, the percentage of physicians in our 1937 sample who designated themselves complete specialists—28 to 30 per cent —is almost exactly the same as the percentage of physicians in the Wisconsin sample who were listed as complete specialists—31 per cent.

The Michigan data are from a questionnaire survey conducted by the State Medical Society.[110] Information on 1931 income was

109 The standard error of the difference between the arithmetic mean net incomes is approximately $600 for the 1933 sample and $1,000 for the 1937 sample. The corresponding standard errors for gross income are even larger.
110 See *Report of the Committee on Survey of Medical Services and Health Agencies* (Michigan State Medical Society, 1933), Ch. V, VI.

TABLE A 16

Arithmetic Mean Gross and Net Incomes, and
Number of Persons Covered

Michigan Physicians: Department of Commerce Samples and
Study of Michigan State Medical Society, 1929 and 1931

	GROSS INCOME		NET INCOME	
	1929	*1931*	*1929*	*1931*
Arithmetic mean income (dollars)				
Michigan study				
All returns	9,976	6,590	6,306	3,876
Returns reporting for both 1929 and 1931	9,976	7,546	6,306	4,497
Dept. of Commerce samples for Michigan				
1933 sample	9,997	7,188	6,801	4,282
1937 sample	10,385	7,000	5,722	4,293
Number of persons covered				
Michigan study				
All returns	592	1,289	592	1,289
Returns reporting for both 1929 and 1931	592	592	592	592
Dept. of Commerce samples for Michigan				
1933 sample	73	78	74	78
1937 sample	13	15	13	13

Report of the Committee on Medical Services and Health Agencies (Michigan
State Medical Society, 1933), Ch. V, VI.

reported by 1,289 of the almost 5,000 physicians estimated to be in
private practice. Only 592 of these, however, reported income in
1929. The average incomes from this study are reasonably similar
to those from our samples for Michigan (Table A 16). The differences vary from $21 to about $600 and all are well within the range
of sampling variation.[111]

The Utah data are from a questionnaire survey made by the
Utah State Medical Association and cover 1929–31, and 1933.[112]
Although returns were received from only 94 physicians, these
constitute almost a fifth of all physicians practising in the state.
Of the three studies under discussion, this is the only one with
which our data fail to check satisfactorily. While the 1937 and

111 The standard error of the difference between the arithmetic mean net incomes is approximately $500 for the 1933 sample and $1,000 for the 1937 sample.
The corresponding standard errors for gross income are even larger.
112 See *A Survey of Medical Services and Facilities of the State of Utah—1934,
December* (Utah State Medical Association).

1935 samples do not differ from the Utah sample more than might be expected from chance, the 1933 sample does (Table A 17).[113] The arithmetic mean net incomes from our 1933 sample are substantially below those from the Utah study in all three years for which the comparison can be made. The difference is $2,826 for 1929, $1,964 for 1930, and $1,836 for 1931. Each difference is considerably more than twice its standard error. While the arithmetic mean gross incomes differ somewhat less, those from our 1933 sample are consistently lower. It seems clear that the 1933 sample for Utah has a sizable downward bias. The other samples seem satisfactory. A further test of the 1937 sample is that the percentage of physicians reporting themselves as complete specialists, 17 per cent, is almost identical with the corresponding percentage from the Utah study, 16 per cent.

v *Incomes of dentists in Minnesota.* As part of a general study of the economics of dentistry in Minnesota, the University Relations Committee, comprising representatives from the State Dental Association and the University of Minnesota School of Dentistry, obtained completed questionnaires from about 600 of the 2,000 dentists in Minnesota.[114] The questionnaires asked for gross and net income in 1933 and 1934. Our 1935 dental sample checks closely with this more extensive sample (Table A 18). The original arithmetic means from our sample are slightly higher than those from the Minnesota study. However, these are not entirely comparable since our sample is restricted to American Dental Association members. Arithmetic means corrected for this bias are between $100 and $160 lower than the corresponding averages from the Minnesota study. These differences are all well within the range of sampling fluctuation;[115] moreover, since the Minnesota

113 The approximate standard errors of the differences between arithmetic mean net incomes are:

    1933 sample: 1929, $1,000; 1930, $800; 1931, $450;
    1935 sample: 1933, $500;
    1937 sample: 1929, $630; 1930, $530; 1931, $300; 1933, $300.

The corresponding standard errors for gross income are larger.

114 See 'Report of the University Relations Committee', *North-West Dentistry*, April 1936, pp. 79–88.

115 Approximate standard errors of the differences are: net income, $200; gross income, $300.

TABLE A 17

Arithmetic Mean Gross and Net Incomes, and
Number of Persons Covered

Utah Physicians: Department of Commerce Samples and
Utah State Medical Association Study, 1929–1931 and 1933

	1929	1930	1931	1933
		Gross Income		
Arithmetic mean income (dollars)				
Utah study	9,644	8,683	7,151	5,661
Dept. of Commerce sample for Utah				
1933 sample	8,073	6,984	5,688	
1935 sample				5,428
1937 sample	9,994	9,248	7,940	5,853
Number of persons covered				
Utah study	94	94	94	94
Dept. of Commerce sample for Utah				
1933 sample	10	11	11	
1935 sample				8
1937 sample	31	27	28	31
		Net Income		
Arithmetic mean income (dollars)				
Utah study	6,532	5,202	4,139	3,038
Dept. of Commerce sample for Utah				
1933 sample	3,706	3,238	2,303	
1935 sample				3,032
1937 sample	6,883	5,702	4,685	3,369
Number of persons covered				
Utah study	94	94	94	94
Dept. of Commerce sample for Utah				
1933 sample	11	11	11	
1935 sample				8
1937 sample	29	27	28	30

A Survey of Medical Services and Facilities of the State of Utah—1934, December (Utah State Medical Association).

study was sponsored by the State Dental Association, it is likely that it overrepresents Association members. The quartiles and medians, as well as the arithmetic means, are similar. These measures are not corrected for the restriction of our sample to members. Presumably for this reason, the measures from our sample are higher in eight out of twelve comparisons.

TABLE A 18

Arithmetic Mean, Median, and Quartile Gross and Net Incomes, and Number of Persons Covered

Minnesota Dentists: Department of Commerce 1935 Sample and Study of Minnesota University Relations Committee, 1933–1934

	GROSS INCOME		NET INCOME	
	1933	1934	1933	1934
Arithmetic mean income (dollars)				
Minnesota study	3,739	3,981	2,149	2,378
Dept. of Commerce 1935 sample for Minnesota				
Original	3,886	4,205	2,168	2,394
Adjusted for restriction to members *	3,593	3,889	2,005	2,214
First quartile (dollars)				
Minnesota study	2,350	2,496	1,304	1,507
Dept. of Commerce 1935 sample for				
Minnesota	2,500	2,375	1,357	1,250
Median (dollars)				
Minnesota study	3,426	3,695	1,992	2,260
Dept. of Commerce 1935 sample for				
Minnesota	3,666	3,500	2,115	2,400
Third quartile (dollars)				
Minnesota study	4,759	5,073	2,822	3,112
Dept. of Commerce 1935 sample for				
Minnesota	4,900	5,875	2,500	3,416
Number of persons covered				
Minnesota study	600	600	600	600
Dept. of Commerce 1935 sample for				
Minnesota	44	49	42	47

'Report of the University Relations Committee', *North-West Dentistry*, April 1936, pp. 79–88.

* Original averages multiplied by .925. This correction factor assumes that 67.4 per cent of all dentists in Minnesota are members and that the income of members is 30 per cent greater than that of nonmembers. The percentage of members is based on Thomas, 'Dental Survey', pp. 155, 158.

vi *Incomes of lawyers*. The only studies of legal incomes with which we have compared our data are for Wisconsin and New York County.

The Wisconsin study was conducted by Dean Lloyd K. Garrison and, like the Wisconsin study of physicians' incomes, is based on income tax returns.[116] Returns were found for 2,161 of an esti-

116 See 'Survey of the Wisconsin Bar', pp. 150–61.

mated total of 3,027 lawyers. The percentage of lawyers for whom returns were not found is somewhat larger than the corresponding percentage of physicians, and hence the resulting upward bias may be somewhat larger. Although primarily restricted to lawyers in independent practice, some lawyers in salaried posts were included. The study covers the period 1927–32, but since we have no data for lawyers prior to 1932 the comparison is necessarily limited to that year. The arithmetic mean net income from our 1935 sample is very close to that from Garrison's sample—it is less

TABLE A 19

Arithmetic Mean Net Income, and Number of Persons Covered

Wisconsin Lawyers: Department of Commerce Samples
and Garrison's Sample, 1932

	NO. OF PERSONS COVERED	ARITH. MEAN NET INCOME, 1932 (dollars)
Garrison's sample	2,161	3,517
Dept. of Commerce sample for Wisconsin		
1935 sample	45[1]	3,327[2]
1937 sample	13[1]	1,865[3]

L. K. Garrison, 'A Survey of the Wisconsin Bar', *Wisconsin Law Review*, Feb. 1935.

[1] Number of individuals before weighting.
[2] Weighted for firm member and size of community bias.
[3] Weighted for size of community bias. No replies were received from Wisconsin firms.

than $200 below the latter (Table A 19). The average from the 1937 sample, on the other hand, is almost $1,700 lower. Although the variability of the incomes of lawyers is large and consequently very sizable differences might arise from chance in a sample containing so few as 13 lawyers,[117] these results seem to support our earlier conclusion that the 1937 legal sample is considerably less reliable than the 1935 sample.

The data for New York County, on the other hand, indicate exactly the opposite, since the 1937 sample agrees with the New York County sample better than the 1935 sample (Table A 20).

[117] The standard error of the difference between the means is about $1,000 for the 1937 sample and $700 for the 1935 sample.

The New York data were compiled from questionnaires sent to all lawyers in New York County (i.e., Manhattan).[118] Data on 1933 income were reported by 3,210 of an estimated total of 15,000 lawyers.[119] Of these, 2,667 specified that they were in 'private practice'. The New York survey was restricted to Manhattan and included income from salaried employment as well as from independent practice, whereas our samples are for all five boroughs of New York City and cover only income from independent prac-

TABLE A 20

Arithmetic Mean and Median Net Incomes,
and Number of Persons Covered

New York Lawyers: Department of Commerce Samples
and New York County Sample, 1933

	NO. OF PERSONS COVERED	NET INCOME IN 1933 Arith. mean (dollars)	Median
New York County sample for lawyers in private practice [1]	2,667	6,664	3,210
Dept. of Commerce samples for New York City			
1935 sample [2]	51	3,897	2,000
1937 sample	52	5,961	2,750

[1] Survey of the Legal Profession in New York County (New York County Lawyers Association, 1936), p. 18. Arithmetic mean is not presented but was computed by us from frequency distribution.
[2] Number of persons covered represents actual number for whom information was reported. The mean and median incomes are corrected for firm member bias.

tice. These discrepancies between the samples may possibly account for the $703 difference between the arithmetic means from our 1937 sample and the New York County study; they are hardly sufficient to account for the $2,767 excess of the latter over the mean from our 1935 sample. However, an examination of the variability of income makes this difference appear less serious. The variability of income is so large that, for a sample the size of our 1935 sample, a difference of $2,767 would be exceeded by chance alone

118 See Survey of the Legal Profession in New York County.
119 19,000 questionnaires were mailed.

between 9 and 16 times in a hundred.[120] The observed difference
may therefore be attributable to sampling fluctuations. An additional check on our samples is that they show about the same percentage division of lawyers between individual practitioners and
firm members as the New York County study. According to the
latter, 70 per cent of all lawyers in New York County are individual practitioners and 30 per cent are firm members.[121] According to our 1935 sample, 66 per cent of all lawyers are individual
practitioners; according to our 1937 sample, 69 per cent.[122]

vii *Incomes of consulting engineers.* The Bureau of Labor Statistics has recently published the results of an intensive study of the
incomes of engineers.[123] This study covered engineers of all types,
among them independent consultants. Questionnaires were sent
to 173,151 professional engineers, 52,589 of whom replied. Data
on income were requested for 1929, 1932, and 1934. Unfortunately,
few data were prepared for consulting engineers separately. The
only data on the income of consulting engineers in the final report
are the median, quartiles, and first and ninth deciles of 'monthly
engineering earnings'. In Table A 21 we have converted the
medians and quartiles into annual earnings by simply multiplying
by 12. This would clearly be an invalid conversion if the initial
data were really full-time monthly earnings, the information requested, since annual earnings depend not only on the monthly
rate but also on the fullness of employment. However, as the
Bureau of Labor Statistics report states, "it is questionable if such
a thing as a rate of compensation can be applied to this field of
engineering service [consulting engineering], for, unlike the other

120 The reason for the range is that the mean from our sample is a weighted
mean and hence its standard error is difficult to compute exactly. The figures
cited are based on a standard error between $1,650 and $1,980.
121 *Survey of the Legal Profession in New York County*, p. 12. The data on
which these percentages are based include all lawyers who reported organization of practice, whether or not they reported net income.
122 This comparison is an additional check on our conclusion (Sec. 1b iv) that
the 1935 sample requires correction for a firm member bias but the 1937 sample
does not. The percentage cited for the 1935 sample is corrected; the percentage
for the 1937 sample is not. The uncorrected percentage from the 1935 sample
is 45; the corrected percentage from the 1937 sample, 86.
123 Andrew Fraser, Jr. under the direction of A. F. Hinrichs, *Employment and
Earnings in the Engineering Profession, 1929 to 1934*, Bul. 682 (Bureau of
Labor Statistics, 1941).

TABLE A 21

Quartile and Median Net Incomes,
and Number of Persons Covered

Consulting Engineers: Department of Commerce and
Bureau of Labor Statistics Samples, 1929 and 1932

	1929		*1932*	
	Dept. of Commerce sample	BLS sample*	Dept. of Commerce sample	BLS sample*
Third quartile (dollars)	14,805	8,772	4,785	5,160
Median (dollars)	7,943	5,268	2,178	2,940
First quartile (dollars)	3,570	3,492	33	1,728
No. of persons covered	471	997	474	1,059

Andrew Fraser, Jr., *Employment and Earnings in the Engineering Profession,
1929 to 1934,* Bul. 682 (Bureau of Labor Statistics, 1941), pp. 184, 189.

* Medians and quartiles are corresponding measures for 'monthly engineering
earnings' multiplied by 12.

kinds of engineering employment, the rates reported were almost
necessarily derived directly from the earned annual incomes reported".[124] Despite this comment, the conversion may still not be
entirely valid since some consulting engineers may have entered
the amount normally earned during a month of reasonably full
employment. Any error in the conversion would presumably be
much more serious for 1932 than for 1929. Since the questionnaire was designed primarily for salaried employees, no explicit
instructions were given that net rather than gross income be
entered.[125] In consequence, some engineers may have reported
gross income.

There is little similarity between the measures from the two
samples. The measures from our sample are higher for 1929 but
lower for 1932. The differences for 1929 are consistent with the

[124] *Ibid.,* p. 187.
[125] The actual question was:
    "Earned income (please give data for each year):
       From salaries or personal services in both engineering and nonengi-
       neering work
       Average monthly rate from engineering work for time actually em-
       ployed". *Ibid.,* p. 215.

known upward bias in our consulting engineering sample arising
from the inadequacy of the sampling list (see Sec. 1a v). The differences for 1932, however, are in the opposite direction. Conceivably, these may reflect the incorrectness of computing the annual
measures by multiplying the measures for 'monthly engineering
earnings' by 12; measures computed directly from the Bureau of
Labor Statistics data on annual earnings might be lower than
those from our sample. We have been unable to test this possible
explanation.

Supplementary Material

This appendix supplements the text tables by presenting in detail the data on which many of the tables are based. It includes three kinds of data: (1) Frequency or percentage distributions of income by size for all professions by region and by size of community; for physicians by type of practice; for lawyers, accountants, and engineers, by organization of practice. Distributions are presented for each year covered by each sample, with two important exceptions: (a) the distributions for the 1937 medical and accountancy samples are for 1934–36 only; (b) none are presented for the 1937 legal sample. (See Ch. 4, footnote 8, for explanation of these omissions.) (2) Measures computed from the distributions: quartiles, median, interquartile difference, standard deviation, relative interquartile difference, and coefficient of variation. For the 1933 medical and dental samples some of these measures are not entirely consistent with other data for these samples. After the distributions had been computed, several errors were found in the original returns. The arithmetic means and all measures for the United States are corrected for these errors; but the other measures computed from the distributions are not. These corrections are the 'final revisions' referred to in the footnotes to the tables. (3) Final estimates of arithmetic mean income by region and by size of community for all professions; and arithmetic mean income by region and by size of community for physicians and lawyers, for all the years covered by the 1937 samples. These final estimates were computed by combining the different samples for the same profession. The text tables give only the averages over the period covered by all the samples; this appendix, the averages for individual years.

Because of biases discussed in Chapter 2 and Appendix A (over-representation of firm members in the legal and accountancy samples, size of community bias in the legal samples, and the non-randomness among the states in the 1937 medical sample), it was necessary to weight the returns before computing frequency distributions. For these samples, the measures computed from the

489

distributions are based on the weighted frequency distributions. Since the latter have no independent meaning, we present instead the percentage distributions computed from them. However, the total number of individuals shown on the tables is the actual number before any weighting or adjusting. Applying the percentages to these numbers will give neither the weighted frequency distributions nor the actual number of returns in each class. Since the data for individual certified public accountants did not have to be adjusted for any biases, the part of Table B 9 c dealing with individual practitioners gives the actual number in each income class.

All samples included some returns on which income was reported for only part of either the first or the last year covered by the return. In the 1933 samples these part-year returns were converted to full-year returns by raising the reported income proportionately, i.e., by dividing the reported income by the fraction of the year it represented. In the 1935 and 1937 samples the part-year returns were treated as such; the arithmetic means were computed by using the actual income reported on a part-year return and counting the return as the fraction of the year it covered. The frequency distributions were computed by placing the return in the class into which it would have fallen had the report been for a full year, but counting the return as the fraction of the year it covered.

The following abbreviations are used in the tables presenting distributions and measures computed from the distributions:

A.M.	arithmetic mean	I.D.	interquartile difference
Q_3	third quartile	S.D.	standard deviation
Md	median	R.I.D.	relative interquartile difference
Q_1	first quartile	V	coefficient of variation

TABLE B1

Distribution of Income of Physicians by Size and Measures Computed from the Distributions

a   By Region, 1929-1936

1929 (1933 SAMPLE)[6]

INCOME CLASSES (dollars)	NE	MA	ENC	WNC	SA	ESC	WSC	MT.	PAC.	U.S.[2]
Under -2,000										
-2,000 to -1,000[5]		4							1.3	8.2
-1,000 to 0[5]	3		3		6	2	6		2.7	21.8
0										
1 to 500	5	10	12	3	8	9	4	4	10	67
500 to 1,000	1	12	14	5	10	10	2	2	8	68
1,000 to 1,500	9	21	23	16	16	10	24	5	12	137
1,500 to 2,000	6	18	30	15	21	18	17	2	14	143
2,000 to 2,500	10	27	32	22	14	12	10	6	14	147
2,500 to 3,000	10	25	35	18	16	7	11	3	8	135
3,000 to 3,500	6	24	35	18	10	10	5	4	13	128
3,500 to 4,000	17	32	31	8	16	4	11	5	20	145
4,000 to 5,000	11	49	58	23	21	13	18	2	33	230
5,000 to 6,000	12	40	41	19	19	13	11	9	22	188
6,000 to 7,000	16	29	30	16	11	3	8	6	19	141
7,000 to 8,000	9	25	18	10	6	5	10	3	16	102
8,000 to 9,000	4	25	23	13	9	4	5	4	9	97
9,000 to 10,000	6	14	15	9	5		4	1	13	70
10,000 to 12,000	11	24	21	5	7	3	6		13	92
12,000 to 14,000	4	19	15	7	7	4	5		8	69
14,000 to 16,000	4	12	7	5	2	1	2	1	8	42
16,000 to 18,000	3	9	4	4		2	2	1	5	30
18,000 to 20,000		5	5	2	1				1	14
20,000 to 25,000	7	5	4	4	3				3	26
25,000 to 30,000	3	3	2	1			2			11
30,000 to 40,000		1	1	2	3	1			5	13
40,000 to 50,000		2	1		1					4
50,000 and over		1	1	2		1			1	6
No. of physicians covered	157	436	461	227	212	132	163	58	259	2,135
A.M.[7] (dollars)	6,791	6,490	5,764	6,454	5,263	4,359	4,651	4,398	6,888	5,916

Measures computed from the distributions[8]

Absolute (dollars)

	NE	MA	ENC	WNC	SA	ESC	WSC	MT.	PAC.	U.S.
Q_3	8,725	8,420	7,150	7,675	6,100	5,090	6,150	6,100	8,117	7,374
Md	5,050	4,912	4,167	4,220	3,725	2,850	3,575	3,925	4,829	4,223
Q_1	2,725	2,856	2,516	2,308	1,808	1,536	1,725	2,050	2,742	2,253
I.D.	6,000	5,564	4,634	5,367	4,292	3,554	4,425	4,050	5,375	5,121
S.D.	5,970	6,157	6,077	7,919	5,964	5,972	4,463	3,270	9,902	6,855

Relative

	NE	MA	ENC	WNC	SA	ESC	WSC	MT.	PAC.	U.S.
R.I.D.	1.188	1.133	1.112	1.272	1.152	1.247	1.238	1.032	1.113	1.213
V^1	.897	.946	1.073	1.245	1.166	1.373	.964	.743	1.457	1.159

For footnotes see p.569.

TABLE B1a (cont.)

1930 (1933 SAMPLE)[6]

INCOME CLASSES (dollars)	NE	MA	ENC	WNC	SA	ESC	WSC	MT.	PAC.	U.S.[2]
Under -2,000[5]						1.6				2
-2,000 to -1,000[5]		3.7			4	1.6	3.6			12.2
-1,000 to 0[5]	8	7.3	4		4	4.8	5.4	1	3	38.8
0										
1 to 500	3	8	19	2	9	11	5	4	10	73
500 to 1,000	4	15	29	13	13	13	10	4	5	110
1,000 to 1,500	8	30	21	27	25	14	21	2	18	170
1,500 to 2,000	8	20	39	19	18	10	18	9	11	152
2,000 to 2,500	7	29	48	17	12	13	12	5	17	161
2,500 to 3,000	15	28	31	20	17	9	12	3	11	149
3,000 to 3,500	11	23	41	14	13	10	14	2	27	156
3,500 to 4,000	9	39	30	14	11	10	7	5	18	144
4,000 to 5,000	17	44	50	22	28	10	14	11	34	233
5,000 to 6,000	12	46	34	18	15	6	9	8	25	175
6,000 to 7,000	14	32	32	12	10	5	13	1	14	136
7,000 to 8,000	6	30	24	13	7	1	4	4	11	104
8,000 to 9,000	8	17	11	9	7	6	3	1	11	73
9,000 to 10,000	4	12	15	7	2	3	6	1	7	57
10,000 to 12,000	8	25	15	6	7	2	6	2	22	94
12,000 to 14,000	6	11	9	8	2	2	1	1	9	49
14,000 to 16,000	1	12	9	2	6	1	2		7	40
16,000 to 18,000	2	7	3	1	2		1		1	17
18,000 to 20,000	1	3	5	3	1				1	14
20,000 to 25,000	7	8	3	2	3		1		4	28
25,000 to 30,000	1	3		2	2	1			2	11
30,000 to 40,000		2	2	1	1				2	8
40,000 to 50,000	1	1				1				3
50,000 and over			1	2					1	4
No. of physicians covered	161	456	475	234	219	136	168	64	271	2,214
A.M.[7] (dollars)	6,184	5,882	5,022	5,685	4,691	3,629	3,786	3,864	6,474	5,270

Measures computed from the distributions[8]

Absolute (dollars)

	NE	MA	ENC	WNC	SA	ESC	WSC	MT.	PAC.	U.S.
Q_3	7,725	7,456	6,219	6,800	5,488	4,183	5,550	5,063	7,950	6,559
Md	4,367	4,394	3,555	3,579	3,350	2,450	2,775	3,825	4,450	3,798
Q_1	2,569	2,538	2,060	1,933	1,503	1,083	1,438	1,783	2,725	1,981
I.D.	5,156	4,918	4,159	4,867	3,985	3,100	4,112	3,280	5,225	4,578
S.D.	6,019	5,502	5,538	7,452	5,296	5,249	3,640	2,842	10,274	6,448

Relative

	NE	MA	ENC	WNC	SA	ESC	WSC	MT.	PAC.	U.S.
R.I.D.	1.181	1.117	1.170	1.360	1.190	1.265	1.482	.858	1.174	1.205
V^1	.988	.929	1.122	1.331	1.136	1.454	.959	.736	1.594	1.224

For footnotes see p. 569.

TABLE B1a (cont.)

1931 (1933 SAMPLE)[6]

INCOME CLASSES (dollars)	NE	MA	ENC	WNC	SA	ESC	WSC	MT.	PAC.	U.S.[2]
Under -2,000[5]			1.4						1.4	3.8
-2,000 to -1,000[5]		2.2	3		3.3	1.6	3			11.2
-1,000 to 0[5]	7	8.8	8.6	1	6.7	8.4	6		5.6	53
1 to 500	2	18	20	6	14	18	8	4	8	103
500 to 1,000	8	26	30	16	23	14	19	5	18	161
1,000 to 1,500	10	27	41	25	24	14	19	9	17	193
1,500 to 2,000	7	23	38	22	17	19	15	3	18	163
2,000 to 2,500	15	29	43	23	22	10	17	9	20	189
2,500 to 3,000	9	27	44	15	13	11	14	4	19	159
3,000 to 3,500	14	39	54	20	15	8	7	5	19	181
3,500 to 4,000	10	31	30	15	12	6	10	6	22	143
4,000 to 5,000	14	55	41	22	19	7	17	9	32	218
5,000 to 6,000	12	37	35	15	15	7	10	3	21	157
6,000 to 7,000	10	38	24	17	7	4	5	2	11	121
7,000 to 8,000	7	21	20	9	11	2	6	2	13	94
8,000 to 9,000	9	12	10	4	4	4	5	2	13	63
9,000 to 10,000	5	15	12	5	5	2	2	1	9	57
10,000 to 12,000	5	15	10	9	2	2	5		13	61
12,000 to 14,000	3	17	9	4	8	1	2		9	53
14,000 to 16,000		8	5	2	2		3		4	24
16,000 to 18,000	5	7	1	1						14
18,000 to 20,000	3	1	2	2	1				2	11
20,000 to 25,000	4	6	1	3	4	1			6	25
25,000 to 30,000		4	1	1	1					7
30,000 to 40,000	1	1		1	1	1			1	6
40,000 to 50,000										
50,000 and over			1	1					1	3
No. of physicians covered	160	467	485	239	230	141	173	64	283	2,274
A.M.[7] (dollars)	5,658	5,294	4,067	4,880	4,197	2,956	3,391	3,037	5,591	4,564

Measures computed from the distributions[8]

Absolute (dollars)

	NE	MA	ENC	WNC	SA	ESC	WSC	MT.	PAC.	U.S.
Q_3	7,433	6,769	5,138	5,988	5,167	3,575	4,612	4,125	7,038	5,827
Md	3,925	4,040	3,074	3,200	2,836	1,850	2,500	2,825	3,914	3,275
Q_1	2,093	2,171	1,746	1,775	1,150	725	1,125	1,450	2,046	1,600
I.D.	5,340	4,598	3,392	4,213	4,017	2,850	3,487	2,675	4,992	4,227
S.D.	5,630	4,978	4,691	6,341	4,837	4,001	3,279	2,160	8,170	5,473

Relative

	NE	MA	ENC	WNC	SA	ESC	WSC	MT.	PAC.	U.S.
R.I.D.	1.361	1.138	1.103	1.317	1.416	1.541	1.395	.947	1.275	1.291
V^1	1.012	.940	1.157	1.308	1.174	1.387	.969	.696	1.485	1.199

For footnotes see p.569.

TABLE B 1a (cont.)

1932 (1933 SAMPLE)[6]

INCOME CLASSES (dollars)	NE	MA	ENC	WNC	SA	ESC	WSC	MT.	PAC.	U.S.[2]
Under −2,000[5]		1.6	1.4				2.5		2.5	7.6
−2,000 to −1,000[5]		3.2	1.4	1	3.7	2.7	2.5		1.3	13.9
−1,000 to 0[5]	5	11.2	14.2	5	7.3	12.3	5	1	15.2	80.5
1 to 500	8	29	40	12	17	24	12	11	15	171
500 to 1,000	12	30	40	29	27	9	21	5	18	194
1,000 to 1,500	8	35	70	29	28	19	18	8	17	235
1,500 to 2,000	14	35	61	27	27	23	22	8	25	246
2,000 to 2,500	17	43	54	21	20	9	25	7	24	225
2,500 to 3,000	12	42	41	16	18	6	8	6	28	178
3,000 to 3,500	6	40	42	25	15	11	10	1	25	177
3,500 to 4,000	11	26	14	18	7	3	12	5	11	107
4,000 to 5,000	17	48	28	12	17	4	13	5	27	175
5,000 to 6,000	8	40	25	11	10	2	1	4	19	121
6,000 to 7,000	12	18	17	7	7	4	8	1	14	90
7,000 to 8,000	5	10	11	8	5	4	3	1	8	56
8,000 to 9,000	8	16	11	4	3	2	4		6	54
9,000 to 10,000	3	5	8	3	1	1	2		4	27
10,000 to 12,000	3	14	1	5	6	1	3		9	42
12,000 to 14,000	3	9	2	1	2				7	24
14,000 to 16,000	2	4	2	1					1	10
16,000 to 18,000	5	4		3	4		1		3	20
18,000 to 20,000		3	1		3				3	10
20,000 to 25,000	3	2	1	1	1	1				9
25,000 to 30,000		1		1	1	1				4
30,000 to 40,000		1								1
40,000 to 50,000										
50,000 and over				1					1	2
No. of physicians covered	162	471	486	241	230	139	173	63	284	2,280
A.M.[7] (dollars)	4,676	3,977	2,781	3,599	3,406	2,313	2,646	2,250	4,202	3,434

Measures computed from the distributions[8]

Absolute (dollars)

	NE	MA	ENC	WNC	SA	ESC	WSC	MT.	PAC.	U.S.
Q_3	6,400	5,089	3,500	3,965	4,100	2,888	3,663	3,538	5,175	4,267
Md	3,475	3,050	2,104	2,400	2,079	1,543	2,057	1,950	2,850	2,400
Q_1	1,757	1,603	1,133	1,231	1,033	406	1,011	925	1,531	1,163
I.D.	3,643	3,486	2,367	2,734	3,067	2,482	2,652	2,613	3,644	3,104
S.D.	4,515	4,153	2,671	5,318	4,148	3,551	2,651	1,755	6,311	4,270

Relative

	NE	MA	ENC	WNC	SA	ESC	WSC	MT.	PAC.	U.S.
R.I.D.	1.336	1.143	1.125	1.139	1.475	1.609	1.289	1.340	1.279	1.293
V^1	.980	1.026	.955	1.481	1.237	1.557	.994	.776	1.524	1.243

For footnotes see p.569.

1932 (1935 SAMPLE)

INCOME CLASSES (dollars)	NE	MA	ENC	WNC	SA	ESC	WSC	MT.	PAC.	U.S.[z]
Under -2,000			1							1
-2,000 to -1,000		1				1				2
-1,000 to 0	2	7	3	1	.21		1	1	1	16.21
0	2	11.08	15	3	7	11	8	2	6.25	66.33
1 to 500	2	11	19	10	7	9	5	6	6	77
500 to 1,000	9	18	25	26	11	13	13.5	8	6	133.5
1,000 to 1,500	8	28	32	22	14	16	15	4	21	164
1,500 to 2,000	11	26	48	13	13	11.5	8	5	12	151.5
2,000 to 2,500	13	41	39	22	11	2	14	9	15	170
2,500 to 3,000	8	20	26	9	8	3	6	5	22	110
3,000 to 3,500	9	25	23	15	9	3	5	3	13	106
3,500 to 4,000	6	25	12	8	4	2	5	3	12	79
4,000 to 5,000	12	22	19	15	8	2	5	5	7	95
5,000 to 6,000	3	22	9	5	4	1	7	1	4	57
6,000 to 7,000	1	12	6	8			1	1	7	36
7,000 to 8,000	5	13	9		4	1			3	35
8,000 to 9,000	3	11	3	3	3		1		2	26
9,000 to 10,000	1	3	3		1	1		1	1	11
10,000 to 12,000	3	8	2	1	2		1	1	1	19
12,000 to 14,000		5.42	2	2	2				1	12.42
14,000 to 16,000	2	3	1	1					1	8
16,000 to 18,000	1	1							1	3
18,000 to 20,000		1			1					2
20,000 to 25,000	2	1	1		1			1		6
25,000 to 30,000										
30,000 to 40,000	1		1					1		3
40,000 to 50,000			1							1
50,000 and over			1							1
No. of physicians covered	104	315.5	301	164	110.21	76.5	95.5	57	142.25	1,391.96
A.M. (dollars)	4,161	3,725	3,073	2,736	3,198	1,434	2,216	3,198	3,038	3,107

Measures computed from the distributions

Absolute (dollars)

	NE	MA	ENC	WNC	SA	ESC	WSC	MT.	PAC.	U.S.
Q_3	4,667	5,070	3,386	3,625	3,806	1,821	3,112	3,458	3,685	3,791
Md	2,812	2,867	2,096	2,159	2,132	1,133	1,828	2,139	2,588	2,247
Q_1	1,636	1,554	1,192	1,022	1,084	396	866	828	1,388	1,158
I.D.	3,031	3,516	2,194	2,603	2,722	1,425	2,246	2,630	2,297	2,633
S.D.	5,125	3,437	5,404	2,473	3,644	1,679	1,958	5,426	2,701	3,947

Relative

	NE	MA	ENC	WNC	SA	ESC	WSC	MT.	PAC.	U.S.
R.I.D.	1.078	1.226	1.047	1.206	1.277	1.258	1.229	1.230	.888	1.172
V^1	1.190	.909	1.715	.903	1.136	1.146	.875	1.643	.877	1.250

For footnotes see p.569.

TABLE B1a (cont.)

1933 (1935 SAMPLE)

INCOME CLASSES (dollars)	NE	MA	ENC	WNC	SA	ESC	WSC	MT.	PAC.	U.S.[2]
Under -2,000		3								3
-2,000 to -1,000		1	1					1		3
-1,000 to 0	3	2	2	2	1	1			2	13
0	3	12	13.33	4	6	11	6	2	10	68.33
1 to 500	4.75	21	21.33	9	7	9	7	8	5	95.08
500 to 1,000	11	26	36	25	14	11	14	6	10	157
1,000 to 1,500	7	33	41	24	11	15	17	5	17	178
1,500 to 2,000	15	29	45	16	18	11	11	7	14	169
2,000 to 2,500	8	35	39	15	9	4	8	8	17	146
2,500 to 3,000	15	35	25	18	12	7	9	3	21	146
3,000 to 3,500	6	30	29	14	9	5	7	3	14	120
3,500 to 4,000	7	16	11	11	8	1	5	1	13	74
4,000 to 5,000	9	19	16	7	7	3	8	8	7	84
5,000 to 6,000	4	18	14	11	4		4		4	60
6,000 to 7,000	3	16	6	4		1	2	3	3	38
7,000 to 8,000	1	8	4	1	5	1		1	3	24
8,000 to 9,000	3	10	3	1	2		1		1	21
9,000 to 10,000	3	3	2		1				1	10
10,000 to 12,000	2	4	3		2				2	13
12,000 to 14,000		6			1			1	1	9
14,000 to 16,000	1	2								3
16,000 to 18,000			1	2	1					4
18,000 to 20,000	1								1	2
20,000 to 25,000	2	1		1		1		1		6
25,000 to 30,000	1									1
30,000 to 40,000			2					1		3
40,000 to 50,000					1					1
50,000 and over			1							1
No. of physicians covered	109.75	330	315.66	165	119	81	99	59	146	1,452.41
A.M. (dollars)	3,785	3,166	2,748	2,653	3,174	1,822	2,169	3,249	2,815	2,867

Measures computed from the distributions

Absolute (dollars)

	NE	MA	ENC	WNC	SA	ESC	WSC	MT.	PAC.	U.S.
Q_3	4,284	4,237	3,226	3,384	3,640	2,344	3,160	4,031	3,482	3,462
Md	2,604	2,543	1,980	2,084	2,139	1,284	1,750	2,031	2,441	2,137
Q_1	1,406	1,265	1,064	1,026	1,080	458	920	812	1,280	1,068
I.D.	2,878	2,972	2,162	2,358	2,560	1,886	2,240	3,219	2,202	2,394
S.D.	4,621	3,126	4,375	2,815	4,754	2,734	1,705	5,422	2,598	3,675

Relative

	NE	MA	ENC	WNC	SA	ESC	WSC	MT.	PAC.	U.S.
R.I.D.	1.105	1.169	1.092	1.131	1.197	1.469	1.280	1.585	.902	1.120
V^1	1.208	.963	1.557	1.059	1.473	1.515	.780	1.615	.923	1.265

For footnotes see p.569.

TABLE B1a (cont.)

1934 (1935 SAMPLE)

INCOME CLASSES (dollars)	NE	MA	ENC	WNC	SA	ESC	WSC	MT.	PAC.	U.S.[2]
Under -2,000		2						1		3
-2,000 to -1,000		1								1
-1,000 to 0	3	3	3	2	1			1	1	14
0	1	13	12	4	6	8	4	1	7	57
1 to 500	5	19	19.83	7	8.33	6	6	7	6	86.16
500 to 1,000	6	25	31	22	11	13	11	4	9	137
1,000 to 1,500	13	34	36	19	13	13	16	6	18.33	176.33
1,500 to 2,000	12	28	34	18.58	11	13	14	5	15	153.58
2,000 to 2,500	12	43	39	16	10	3	10	5	19	159
2,500 to 3,000	10	28	29	11	7	8	8	3	17	122
3,000 to 3,500	6	27	24	19	12	4	7	4	14	120
3,500 to 4,000	9	19	19	6	9	4	5	3	10	85
4,000 to 5,000	15	25	23	16	13	4	7	7	12	123
5,000 to 6,000	3	15	16	9	6	3	5	4	8	70
6,000 to 7,000	5	18	14	5	2		3	3	4	55
7,000 to 8,000	1	11	6	2	2	2	2		3	29
8,000 to 9,000		7	4	1	3		1	3	2	21
9,000 to 10,000	4	5	4	4	4		1		1	23
10,000 to 12,000	4	8	5	3	2			1	4	27
12,000 to 14,000		3	1		2		1		1	8
14,000 to 16,000	1	4	1	1		1				8
16,000 to 18,000		1	2	1						4
18,000 to 20,000	2									2
20,000 to 25,000	1							1	1	3
25,000 to 30,000		1		1	1					3
30,000 to 40,000	1		1		1	1				4
40,000 to 50,000			1					1		2
50,000 and over		1								1
No. of physicians covered	114	340	325.83	167.58	124.33	83	101	60	152.33	1,497.07
A.M. (dollars)	4,010	3,400	3,377	3,117	3,637	2,461	2,571	4,041	3,120	3,296

Measures computed from the distributions

Absolute (dollars)

	NE	MA	ENC	WNC	SA	ESC	WSC	MT.	PAC.	U.S.
Q_3	4,284	4,520	3,936	4,069	4,378	2,890	3,482	4,714	3,896	4,073
Md	2,750	2,536	2,348	2,350	2,630	1,558	1,982	2,500	2,524	2,378
Q_1	1,708	1,324	1,217	1,182	1,182	760	1,133	1,084	1,412	1,216
I.D.	2,576	3,196	2,719	2,887	3,196	2,130	2,349	3,630	2,484	2,857
S.D.	4,840	3,369	5,548	3,320	4,525	4,198	2,224	6,446	2,905	4,250

Relative

	NE	MA	ENC	WNC	SA	ESC	WSC	MT.	PAC.	U.S.
R.I.D.	.937	1.260	1.158	1.229	1.215	1.367	1.185	1.452	.984	1.201
V^1	1.185	.979	1.617	1.046	1.241	1.687	.848	1.629	.918	1.276

For footnotes see p.569.

TABLE B 1a (cont.)

1934 (1937 SAMPLE)[9]

INCOME CLASSES (dollars)	NE	MA	ENC	WNC	SA	ESC	WSC	MT.	PAC.	U.S.
Under -2,000						0.5				0.03
-2,000 to -1,000										
-1,000 to 0		1.2		0.8	0.1				1.5	0.5
0	3.6	4.3	3.1	1.5	2.2		3.0	3.1	3.0	3.0
1 to 500	2.9	2.2	2.7	4.4	3.6	1.7	4.1	3.1	0.5	2.7
500 to 1,000	1.0	7.1	5.7	12.3	5.8	13.1	10.5	7.5	8.5	7.5
1,000 to 1,500	11.6	8.8	8.0	8.7	9.9	21.8	14.8	7.3	10.6	10.3
1,500 to 2,000	10.8	7.2	7.3	13.8	9.9	9.6	8.7	9.8	10.8	9.1
2,000 to 2,500	14.0	10.5	15.7	11.0	13.1	17.0	16.9	11.6	9.0	13.0
2,500 to 3,000	8.1	13.3	9.6	9.5	9.7	4.5	7.9	11.8	11.8	10.3
3,000 to 3,500	9.1	10.5	11.1	11.0	8.5		5.4	11.1	6.0	9.0
3,500 to 4,000	3.9	3.7	10.3	4.4	3.6	8.3	10.6	3.9	8.6	6.4
4,000 to 5,000	12.1	13.6	11.3	10.3	7.8	12.3	8.9	11.9	10.0	11.3
5,000 to 6,000	5.0	6.6	6.1	3.1	9.0	4.1	1.2	3.9	2.5	5.3
6,000 to 7,000	3.6	4.6	3.9	3.3	4.5		3.1	5.5	2.4	3.7
7,000 to 8,000	2.0	4.1	1.2	3.1	3.1		2.4	2.1	4.0	2.7
8,000 to 9,000	2.1	0.6	1.4	1.8	1.4			1.3	1.0	1.0
9,000 to 10,000	2.9		0.5		3.6	2.1		1.2	2.9	1.1
10,000 to 12,000	2.7	0.6		1.1	1.9			0.8	3.7	1.0
12,000 to 14,000	2.2		0.9		1.0	2.5		0.8	2.7	0.8
14,000 to 16,000	2.4					2.5	2.0	2.7		0.5
16,000 to 18,000		0.6	1.1		1.3		0.5		0.7	0.5
18,000 to 20,000										
20,000 to 25,000										
25,000 to 30,000									0.4	0.01
30,000 to 40,000		0.6								0.1
40,000 to 50,000										
50,000 and over										
No. of physicians covered	116.42	180	177.5	165	132.67	56.25	95	175.5	139.50	1,237.84
A.M. (dollars)	3,873	3,269	3,249	2,773	3,652	2,947	2,733	3,575	3,599	3,276

Measures computed from the distributions

Absolute (dollars)

	NE	MA	ENC	WNC	SA	ESC	WSC	MT.	PAC.	U.S.
Q_3	4,821	4,449	4,134	3,732	5,091	3,905	3,676	4,484	4,478	4,290
Md	2,874	2,826	2,890	2,392	2,778	2,094	2,262	2,824	2,762	2,690
Q_1	1,772	1,600	1,878	1,350	1,772	1,222	1,249	1,706	1,948	1,554
I.D.	3,049	2,849	2,256	2,382	3,319	2,683	2,427	2,778	2,530	2,736
S.D.	3,323	3,291	2,512	2,110	2,909	3,097	2,598	3,340	3,227	2,965

Relative

	NE	MA	ENC	WNC	SA	ESC	WSC	MT.	PAC.	U.S.
R.I.D.	1.061	1.008	.781	.996	1.195	1.281	1.073	.984	.916	1.017
V^1	.846	.982	.759	.744	.783	1.031	.920	.919	.874	.886

For footnotes see p. 569.

1935 (1937 SAMPLE)[9]

INCOME CLASSES (dollars)	NE	MA	ENC	WNC	SA	ESC	WSC	MT.	PAC.	U.S.
Under -2,000										
-2,000 to -1,000										
-1,000 to 0		0.5	0.4	2.2		1.6			0.1	0.5
0	2.3	3.0	1.9	1.4	3.1		2.1	2.0	2.6	2.3
1 to 500	3.4	3.8	1.3	3.8	3.4	0.9	1.1	2.7	2.9	2.7
500 to 1,000	0.2	10.6	5.5	10.4	2.4	14.6	10.4	5.9	6.0	7.5
1,000 to 1,500	9.1	9.3	8.9	10.0	11.3	18.3	12.0	4.8	10.4	10.2
1,500 to 2,000	12.8	6.4	10.7	12.9	12.2	10.5	9.2	14.3	9.9	10.1
2,000 to 2,500	12.0	7.8	7.9	14.4	13.6	11.4	16.0	7.8	10.7	10.5
2,500 to 3,000	12.3	11.1	8.4	5.0	10.1	12.8	8.0	10.2	8.8	9.5
3,000 to 3,500	7.3	9.3	15.0	8.3	3.5		11.4	11.9	7.3	9.2
3,500 to 4,000	3.0	9.0	7.8	7.6	5.7	10.5	4.3	7.2	3.3	7.0
4,000 to 5,000	10.1	11.4	13.2	11.4	9.6	8.2	13.6	10.2	14.2	11.7
5,000 to 6,000	6.7	4.9	3.3	3.8	4.6	3.7	3.6	3.9	6.3	4.5
6,000 to 7,000	4.7	5.2	4.7	1.9	4.4		1.9	5.0	1.0	3.7
7,000 to 8,000	3.1	4.5	3.7	2.4	4.6		0.5	4.7	1.7	3.2
8,000 to 9,000	4.1	0.7	1.5	1.3	4.0	1.7	1.2	2.6	4.1	2.0
9,000 to 10,000	0.4	0.5	1.0	0.4	1.0	1.7	2.4	1.0	1.8	1.0
10,000 to 12,000	3.8	1.0	3.1	1.8	2.7			1.7	3.2	2.0
12,000 to 14,000	2.3		0.6	0.2	0.9	2.0	1.9	2.3	4.2	1.1
14,000 to 16,000	0.6		0.6		0.9				0.6	0.3
16,000 to 18,000		0.5	0.5	0.8	1.9		0.5	1.4		0.6
18,000 to 20,000	1.9					2.0				0.3
20,000 to 25,000		0.5							1.0	0.2
25,000 to 30,000										
30,000 to 40,000								0.4		0.01
40,000 to 50,000										
50,000 and over										
No. of physicians covered	118	191.5	183	165.5	142.5	65	94	191	143	1,293.5
A.M. (dollars)	4,181	3,224	3,642	2,938	3,835	2,953	3,048	3,909	3,955	3,470

Measures computed from the distributions

Absolute (dollars)

	NE	MA	ENC	WNC	SA	ESC	WSC	MT.	PAC.	U.S.
Q_3	5,192	4,367	4,547	3,938	5,014	3,730	4,043	4,806	4,919	4,473
Md	2,914	2,887	3,168	2,322	2,696	2,176	2,478	3,098	2,926	2,824
Q_1	1,891	1,382	1,827	1,361	1,698	1,215	1,478	1,837	1,652	1,588
I.D.	3,301	2,985	2,720	2,577	3,316	2,519	2,565	2,969	3,267	2,885
S.D.	3,630	2,758	2,780	2,569	3,429	3,260	2,550	3,661	3,754	3,057

Relative

	NE	MA	ENC	WNC	SA	ESC	WSC	MT.	PAC.	U.S.
R.I.D.	1.133	1.034	.859	1.110	1.230	1.157	1.035	.958	1.117	1.022
V^1	.862	.834	.751	.861	.874	1.072	.814	.916	.916	.862

For footnotes see p. 569.

T A B L E B1a (concl.)

1936 (1937 SAMPLE)[9]

INCOME CLASSES (dollars)	NE	MA	ENC	WNC	SA	ESC	WSC	MT.	PAC.	U.S.
Under -2,000										
-2,000 to -1,000										
-1,000 to 0	1.0	0.9	0.5	0.7					0.2	0.5
0	1.7	0.5	1.2	1.0	2.9		0.8	1.7	2.3	1.2
1 to 500	2.0	4.7	1.2	6.4	1.6	3.3	2.3	5.0	0.9	3.0
500 to 1,000	3.5	9.1	7.5	7.3	4.4	9.9	8.3	4.1	3.7	7.0
1,000 to 1,500	3.8	7.3	4.8	13.3	6.0	10.9	7.7	4.7	11.2	7.5
1,500 to 2,000	12.4	7.3	7.1	8.5	12.3	9.8	9.2	9.2	9.6	8.9
2,000 to 2,500	14.3	12.6	8.8	10.3	12.3	13.4	9.3	9.4	10.2	11.2
2,500 to 3,000	12.1	9.4	7.1	7.5	7.1	9.1	14.8	11.7	7.3	9.0
3,000 to 3,500	8.8	6.6	10.4	11.0	8.3	9.0	8.5	4.9	7.6	8.5
3,500 to 4,000	2.3	9.5	8.4	6.0	2.6	3.3	9.3	12.3	5.1	7.0
4,000 to 5,000	11.0	9.8	12.4	9.4	8.8	15.3	10.2	9.1	12.2	10.8
5,000 to 6,000	5.4	7.9	12.5	4.4	7.0	5.4	2.9	6.7	6.5	7.5
6,000 to 7,000	3.5	5.6	1.9	4.0	2.0	1.9	5.6	3.1	2.8	3.6
7,000 to 8,000	3.6	2.8	2.7	2.7	7.7		4.9	6.6	1.6	3.4
8,000 to 9,000	3.9	2.6	4.2	3.7	6.2	1.6	1.5	2.1	4.3	3.5
9,000 to 10,000	0.2	0.9	2.7	1.2	2.1			1.9	3.7	1.5
10,000 to 12,000	5.6	0.5	3.6	0.8	4.2	3.3	1.6	1.7	3.2	2.5
12,000 to 14,000	0.8	0.9	0.9	0.4	0.8		1.0	2.0	5.2	1.2
14,000 to 16,000	2.2		0.6	0.7	0.5			0.4	1.6	0.6
16,000 to 18,000	2.1		1.1	0.4	1.9	1.9	2.1	2.1	0.5	1.0
18,000 to 20,000				.0.3				0.3		0.04
20,000 to 25,000		0.5	0.5		0.6	1.9		0.5		0.4
25,000 to 30,000		0.5						0.4		0.1
30,000 to 40,000										
40,000 to 50,000					0.8					0.1
50,000 and over										
No. of physicians covered	130.79	297	196.75	182	155.5	70	106	199	160.92	1,407.96
A.M. (dollars)	4,268	3,496	4,291	3,274	4,700	3,591	3,663	4,331	4,397	3,944

Measures computed from the distributions

Absolute (dollars)

	NE	MA	ENC	WNC	SA	ESC	WSC	MT.	PAC.	U.S.
Q_3	5,416	4,719	5,448	4,319	6,901	4,406	4,474	5,441	5,683	5,056
Md	2,972	2,902	3,586	2,670	3,209	2,642	2,922	3,435	3,288	3,100
Q_1	2,026	1,671	2,153	1,362	1,913	1,544	1,824	2,020	1,841	1,824
I.D.	3,390	3,048	3,295	2,957	4,988	2,862	2,650	3,421	3,842	3,232
S.D.	3,717	3,180	3,362	2,869	5,173	3,889	3,060	3,985	3,697	3,631

Relative

	NE	MA	ENC	WNC	SA	ESC	WSC	MT.	PAC.	U.S.
R.I.D.	1.141	1.050	.919	1.107	1.554	1.083	.907	.996	1.168	1.043
V^i	.853	.888	.772	.861	1.071	1.050	.824	.903	.822	.902

For footnotes see p.569.

TABLE B1 (cont.)

b   By Size of Community, 1929-1934

1929 (1933 SAMPLE)[6]

Communities with populations (in thousands) of

INCOME CLASSES (dollars)	500 & over	100 to 500	50 to 100	25 to 50	10 to 25	2.5 to 10	under 2.5	.U.S.[2]
Under -2,000								
-2,000 to -1,000[5]	4.7	1.4						8.2
-1,000 to 0[5]	2.3	5.6	1	2	1	2	8	21.8
0								
1 to 500	19	8	3	4	5	7	19	67
500 to 1,000	10	4	5	4	6	6	29	68
1,000 to 1,500	25	20	6	12	15	12	46	137
1,500 to 2,000	31	18	4	7	14	18	49	143
2,000 to 2,500	35	23	10	12	8	15	44	147
2,500 to 3,000	29	26	11	10	10	15	32	135
3,000 to 3,500	31	23	8	11	12	7	33	128
3,500 to 4,000	33	34	13	18	9	17	20	145
4,000 to 5,000	52	53	15	19	31	30	28	230
5,000 to 6,000	46	36	10	21	17	26	30	188
6,000 to 7,000	38	31	17	13	17	9	13	141
7,000 to 8,000	18	27	7	12	13	13	12	102
8,000 to 9,000	30	22	10	5	9	10	10	97
9,000 to 10,000	14	12	11	12	8	7	3	70
10,000 to 12,000	27	24	11	7	9	3	9	92
12,000 to 14,000	17	22	5	7	12	4	2	69
14,000 to 16,000	11	10	7	5	7	1	1	42
16,000 to 18,000	12	5	3	4	2	2	2	30
18,000 to 20,000	77	1	1		4	1		14
20,000 to 25,000	6	6	5	4	2	3		26
25,000 to 30,000	4	5	1	1				11
30,000 to 40,000	4	5	1	2	1			13
40,000 to 50,000	2			1		1		4
50,000 and over	2	3					1	6
No. of physicians covered	510	425	165	193	212	209	391	2,135
A.M.[7] (dollars)	6,606	7,126	7,113	6,491	6,171	5,062	3,186	5,916

Measures computed from the distributions[8]

Absolute (dollars)

	500 & over	100 to 500	50 to 100	25 to 50	10 to 25	2.5 to 10	under 2.5	.U.S.
Q_3	8,200	8,350	9,170	8,025	8,150	6,250	4,444	7,374
Md	4,681	4,925	5,533	4,800	4,650	4,086	2,508	4,223
Q_1	2,508	3,009	3,338	2,869	2,775	2,288	1,453	2,253
I.D.	5,692	5,341	5,832	5,156	5,375	3,962	2,991	5,121
S.D.	7,190	9,384	5,764	6,093	5,107	4,915	3,680	6,855

Relative

	500 & over	100 to 500	50 to 100	25 to 50	10 to 25	2.5 to 10	under 2.5	.U.S.
R.I.D.	1.216	1.084	1.054	1.074	1.156	.970	1.193	1.213
V^1	1.102	1.332	.827	.949	.834	.977	1.101	1.159

For footnotes see p. 569.

TABLE B1b (cont.)

1930 (1933 SAMPLE)[6]

Communities with populations (in thousands) of

INCOME CLASSES (dollars)	500 & over	100 to 500	50 to 100	25 to 50	10 to 25	2.5 to 10	under 2.5	U.S.[2]
Under -2,000[5]		2.4						2
-2,000 to -1,000[5]	4	2.4					5.3	12.2
-1,000 to 0[5]	6	7.2		.5	8	3	8.7	38.8
0								
1 to 500	20	9	4	3	5	5	25	73
500 to 1,000	22	12	4	5	9	11	43	110
1,000 to 1,500	34	23	7	12	16	19	55	170
1,500 to 2,000	37	23	7	8	12	19	46	152
2,000 to 2,500	36	33	10	11	7	17	46	161
2,500 to 3,000	28	27	12	22	13	14	30	149
3,000 to 3,500	33	33	11	13	20	16	29	156
3,500 to 4,000	29	26	12	19	16	18	23	144
4,000 to 5,000	57	55	22	20	20	25	31	233
5,000 to 6,000	44	29	11	26	23	16	24	175
6,000 to 7,000	36	26	15	12	13	18	13	136
7,000 to 8,000	27	24	9	7	14	9	10	104
8,000 to 9,000	19	19	12	4	11	2	6	73
9,000 to 10,000	8	19	6	8	8	6	2	57
10,000 to 12,000	27	30	5	9	11	6	5	94
12,000 to 14,000	17	12	8	3	7	2		49
14,000 to 16,000	13	8	5	5	5	3	1	40
16,000 to 18,000	6	4		3	2	1	1	17
18,000 to 20,000	5	4	2	1	1	1	1	14
20,000 to 25,000	8	7	4	5	2	2		28
25,000 to 30,000	3	5	1	1		1		11
30,000 to 40,000	4	1	1	1	1			8
40,000 to 50,000	2	1						3
50,000 and over	1	2					1	4
No. of physicians covered	526	444	168	203	224	214	405	2,214
A.M.[7] (dollars)	5,963	6,522	6,235	5,733	5,350	4,439	2,726	5,270

Measures computed from the distributions[8]

Absolute (dollars)

Q_3	7,240	8,043	8,167	6,838	7,375	5,650	3,832	6,559
Md	4,158	4,356	4,850	4,100	4,081	3,558	2,117	3,798
Q_1	2,082	2,492	2,950	2,663	2,450	1,940	1,086	1,981
I.D.	5,158	5,551	5,217	4,175	4,925	3,710	2,746	4,578
S.D.	6,788	9,480	5,126	5,193	4,466	4,074	3,378	6,448

Relative

R.I.D.	1.241	1.274	1.076	1.018	1.207	1.043	1.297	1.205
V^1	1.148	1.474	.816	.914	.840	.917	1.175	1.224

For footnotes see p. 569.

1931 (1933 SAMPLE)[o]

Communities with populations (in thousands) of

INCOME CLASSES (dollars)	500 & over	100 to 500	50 to 100	25 to 50	10 to 25	2.5 to 10	under 2.5	U.S.[2]
Under -2,000[5]	1.5	1.7						3.8
-2,000 to -1,000[5]	1.5	3.4	1		2.3		2.3	11.2
-1,000 to 0[5]	12	11.9	1	4	4.7	7	13.7	53
1 to 500	20	11	7	4	11	7	38	103
500 to 1,000	37	17	8	15	11	12	59	161
1,000 to 1,500	43	31	8	10	18	16	60	193
1,500 to 2,000	30	26	16	9	15	23	43	163
2,000 to 2,500	40	33	13	20	21	19	42	189
2,500 to 3,000	35	28	14	13	17	20	29	159
3,000 to 3,500	46	32	13	25	20	13	31	181
3,500 to 4,000	25	34	13	16	14	19	21	143
4,000 to 5,000	50	59	14	24	26	19	24	218
5,000 to 6,000	47	28	13	13	15	22	17	157
6,000 to 7,000	31	27	9	12	13	12	14	121
7,000 to 8,000	28	21	8	5	16	7	6	94
8,000 to 9,000	17	24	6	7	5	1	3	63
9,000 to 10,000	15	15	7	4	8	5	2	57
10,000 to 12,000	15	20	8	9	3	4	2	61
12,000 to 14,000	17	11	4	6	8	6	1	53
14,000 to 16,000	6	6	5	2	3	2		24
16,000 to 18,000	4	4	4	1	1			14
18,000 to 20,000	6	1	1	2	1			11
20,000 to 25,000	7	10	1	4	2	1		25
25,000 to 30,000	4	1		1		1		7
30,000 to 40,000	3	1	1				1	6
40,000 to 50,000								
50,000 and over	1	2						3
No. of physicians covered	542	459	175	206	235	216	409	2,274
A.M.[7] (dollars)	5,206	5,646	5,331	4,952	4,395	4,085	2,285	4,564

Measures computed from the distributions[8]

Absolute (dollars)

	500 & over	100 to 500	50 to 100	25 to 50	10 to 25	2.5 to 10	under 2.5	U.S.[2]
Q_3	6,371	7,219	7,070	6,200	6,088	5,150	3,357	5,827
Md	3,592	4,010	3,680	3,570	3,400	3,090	1,833	3,275
Q_1	1,814	2,132	2,041	2,200	1,792	1,738	878	1,600
I.D.	4,557	5,087	5,029	4,000	4,296	3,412	2,479	4,227
S.D.	5,980	7,656	4,827	4,718	3,956	3,702	2,660	5,473

Relative

	500 & over	100 to 500	50 to 100	25 to 50	10 to 25	2.5 to 10	under 2.5	U.S.[2]
R.I.D.	1.269	1.269	1.367	1.120	1.264	1.104	1.352	1.291
V^1	1.152	1.375	.916	.961	.898	.923	1.111	1.199

For footnotes see p.569.

TABLE B1b (cont.)

1932 (1933 SAMPLE)[6]

Communities with populations (in thousands) of

INCOME CLASSES (dollars)	500 & over	100 to 500	50 to 100	25 to 50	10 to 25	2.5 to 10	under 2.5	U.S.[2]
Under -2,000[5]	1.2	2.1	1		1.8		1.5	7.6
-2,000 to -1,000[5]	3.6	2.1	1		1.8		4.7	13.9
-1,000 to 0[5]	22.2	12.8	5	7	5.4	8	18.8	80.5
0								
1 to 500	37	22	9	10	17	12	61	171
500 to 1,000	30	31	14	14	20	14	68	194
1,000 to 1,500	55	40	11	16	20	29	61	235
1,500 to 2,000	52	43	20	21	23	34	49	246
2,000 to 2,500	51	43	17	20	23	24	42	225
2,500 to 3,000	49	42	11	22	16	17	20	178
3,000 to 3,500	37	44	14	20	20	11	29	177
3,500 to 4,000	24	18	15	10	9	16	15	107
4,000 to 5,000	47	37	8	19	24	16	20	175
5,000 to 6,000	35	21	13	15	16	11	9	121
6,000 to 7,000	18	29	7	6	11	12	5	90
7,000 to 8,000	15	8	11	7	8	3	3	56
8,000 to 9,000	17	21	8	2	5		1	54
9,000 to 10,000	6	10	3	3	5			27
10,000 to 12,000	13	13	2	4	3	6	1	42
12,000 to 14,000	7	3	3	4	3	4		24
14,000 to 16,000	3	4	1	1	1			10
16,000 to 18,000	8	6	2	4				20
18,000 to 20,000	1	5	1	1	1	1		10
20,000 to 25,000	5	2			1	1		9
25,000 to 30,000	2	1					1	4
30,000 to 40,000	1							1
40,000 to 50,000								
50,000 and over	1	1						2
No. of physicians covered	541	461	177	206	235	219	410	2,280
A.M.[7] (dollars)	3,909	4,238	3,873	3,698	3,464	3,106	1,694	3,434

Measures computed from the distributions[8]

Absolute (dollars)

	500 & over	100 to 500	50 to 100	25 to 50	10 to 25	2.5 to 10	under 2.5	U.S.
Q_3	4,931	5,253	5,375	4,600	4,858	3,895	2,550	4,267
Md	2,650	2,877	3,000	2,694	2,633	2,280	1,405	2,400
Q_1	1,353	1,596	1,625	1,571	1,283	1,381	577	1,163
I.D.	3,578	3,657	3,750	3,029	3,575	2,514	1,973	3,104
S.D.	5,039	5,649	3,582	3,549	3,207	3,155	2,064	4,270

Relative

	500 & over	100 to 500	50 to 100	25 to 50	10 to 25	2.5 to 10	under 2.5	U.S.
R.I.D.	1.350	1.271	1.250	1.124	1.358	1.103	1.404	1.293
V^1	1.279	1.342	.929	.951	.939	1.008	1.154	1.243

For footnotes see p.569.

TABLE B1b (cont.)

1932 (1935 SAMPLE)

Communities with populations (in thousands) of

INCOME CLASSES (dollars)	500 & over	100 to 500	50 to 100	25 to 10	10 to 25	2.5 to 10	under 2.5	U.S.[2]
Under -2,000							1	1
-2,000 to -1,000	1	1						2
-1,000 to 0	5	2	21	3		1	5	16.21
0	12.08	11	4	6	6	5.25	21	66.33
1 to 500	43	12	1	5	3	6	25	77
500 to 1,000	29	23	9	4	12	9	43.5	133.5
1,000 to 1,500	38	35	10	2	17	8	50	164
1,500 to 2,000	31	28	9	9.5	14	17	39	151.5
2,000 to 2,500	40	29	12	10	23	18	34	170
2,500 to 3,000	30	24	7	6	11	12	17	110
3,000 to 3,500	26	28	7	8	11	11	14	106
3,500 to 4,000	27	13	4	4	12	9	8	79
4,000 to 5,000	16	28	9	6	15	12	9	95
5,000 to 6,000	10	14	4	4	6	8	10	57
6,000 to 7,000	10	7	2	4	6	3	3	36
7,000 to 8,000	13	3	4	5	6	2	2	35
8,000 to 9,000	8	7	5		4	2		26
9,000 to 10,000	2	4	1	1	2	1		11
10,000 to 12,000	11	4	1	3				19
12,000 to 14,000	7.42	1	1	2	1			12.42
14,000 to 16,000	3	1	3			1		8
16,000 to 18,000	1			2				3
18,000 to 20,000		1			1			2
20,000 to 25,000	4	1	1					6
25,000 to 30,000								
30,000 to 40,000	2				1			3
40,000 to 50,000			1					1
50,000 and over	1							1
No. of physicians covered	350.5	277	96.21	84.5	151	125.25	281.5	1,391.96
A.M. (dollars)	3,831	3,083	4,267	3,723	3,394	2,855	1,723	3,107

Measures computed from the distributions

Absolute (dollars)

	500 & over	100 to 500	50 to 100	25 to 10	10 to 25	2.5 to 10	under 2.5	U.S.
Q_3	4,050	4,062	4,994	4,980	4,283	3,872	2,392	3,791
Md	2,452	2,457	2,706	2,729	2,522	2,454	1,452	2,247
Q_1	1,231	1,290	1,492	1,559	1,492	1,560	712	1,158
I.D.	2,819	2,772	3,502	3,421	2,791	2,312	1,680	2,633
S.D.	5,549	2,906	5,644	3,683	3,686	2,221	1,527	3,947

Relative

	500 & over	100 to 500	50 to 100	25 to 10	10 to 25	2.5 to 10	under 2.5	U.S.
R.I.D.	1.150	1.128	1.294	1.254	1.107	.942	1.157	1.172
V[1]	1.425	.932	1.294	.982	1.065	.763	.872	1.250

For footnotes see p. 569.

TABLE B1b (cont.)

1933 (1935 SAMPLE)

Communities with populations (in thousands) of

INCOME CLASSES (dollars)	500 & over	100 to 500	50 to 100	25 to 50	10 to 25	2.5 to 10	under 2.5	U.S.[2]
Under -2,000	1					2		3
-2,000 to -1,000	1			1			1	3
-1,000 to 0	3	4		3			3	13
0	18.33	10	3	5	7	4	20	68.33
1 to 500	29.33	18	4	6.75	4	5	25	95.08
500 to 1,000	37	28	8	3	16	13	48	157
1,000 to 1,500	38	33	9	5	13	15	57	178
1,500 to 2,000	41	26	14	9	19	20	37	169
2,000 to 2,500	36	33	9	6	16	17	26	146
2,500 to 3,000	33	35	10	10	19	9	29	146
3,000 to 3,500	34	27	8	10	12	12	14	120
3,500 to 4,000	15	14	7	4	11	12	10	74
4,000 to 5,000	12	22	8	3	16	8	15	84
5,000 to 6,000	16	13	3	5	9	7	6	60
6,000 to 7,000	15	9	2	5	3	1	3	38
7,000 to 8,000	8	2	4	3	6	1		24
8,000 to 9,000	6	4	5	3	1	2		21
9,000 to 10,000	4	1	1	2	1	1		10
10,000 to 12,000	7	4	1			1		13
12,000 to 14,000	4		1	1	2	1		9
14,000 to 16,000	1		2					3
16,000 to 18,000	2	2						4
18,000 to 20,000	1			1				2
20,000 to 25,000	1	2		1	1	1		6
25,000 to 30,000	1							1
30,000 to 40,000	1		1		1			3
40,000 to 50,000	1							1
50,000 and over	1							1
No. of physicians covered	367.66	287	100	86.75	157	132	294	1,452.41
A.M. (dollars)	3,352	2,881	3,699	3,530	3,253	2,743	1,734	2,867

Measures computed from the distributions

Absolute (dollars)

	500 & over	100 to 500	50 to 100	25 to 50	10 to 25	2.5 to 10	under 2.5	U.S.
Q_3	3,636	3,544	4,375	4,770	4,047	3,584	2,560	3,462
Md	2,210	2,371	2,650	2,732	2,592	2,206	1,438	2,137
Q_1	1,030	1,178	1,536	1,294	1,471	1,300	755	1,068
I.D.	2,606	2,366	2,839	3,476	2,576	2,284	1,805	2,394
S.D.	5,074	2,915	4,366	3,798	3,721	2,883	1,402	3,675

Relative

	500 & over	100 to 500	50 to 100	25 to 50	10 to 25	2.5 to 10	under 2.5	U.S.
R.I.D.	1.179	.998	1.071	1.272	.994	1.035	1.255	1.120
V^1	1,486	1.006	1.151	1.075	1.127	1.048	.798	1.265

For footnotes see p. 569.

1934 (1935 SAMPLE)

Communities with populations (in thousands) of

INCOME CLASSES (dollars)	500 & over	100 to 500	50 to 100	25 to 50	10 to 25	2.5 to 10	under 2.5	U.S.[2]
Under -2,000				1		2		3
-2,000 to -1,000	1							1
-1,000 to 0	4	2		3		1	4	14
0	18	6	4	4	4	3	17	57
1 to 500	23	17.33	4	3	7	7	22.83	86.16
500 to 1,000	30	22	9	6	7	9	49	137
1,000 to 1,500	38	38	10.33	4	16	11	51	176.33
1,500 to 2,000	40	26	2	10	16	22	34.58	153.58
2,000 to 2,500	45	29	11	9	20	15	28	159
2,500 to 3,000	35	28	10	6	10	9	23	122
3,000 to 3,500	23	25	8	6	18	13	24	120
3,500 to 4,000	17	18	7	6	12	12	12	85
4,000 to 5,000	27	32	12	8	14	13	16	123
5,000 to 6,000	12	18	3	6	12	6	12	70
6,000 to 7,000	19	9	5	5	9	6	1	55
7,000 to 8,000	9	6	2	3	4	4	1	29
8,000 to 9,000	6	3	4	3	2		3	21
9,000 to 10,000	7	3	5	2	3	1	2	23
10,000 to 12,000	8	6	1	3	5	3	1	27
12,000 to 14,000	3	2		2	1			8
14,000 to 16,000	4		3		1			8
16,000 to 18,000	1	2	1					4
18,000 to 20,000	1			1				2
20,000 to 25,000	1	1		1				3
25,000 to 30,000		1			1	1		3
30,000 to 40,000	2	1	1					4
40,000 to 50,000	1				1			2
50,000 and over	1							1
No. of physicians covered	376	295.33	102.33	92	163	138	301.41	1,497.07
A.M. (dollars)	3,697	3,411	4,244	3,966	3,944	3,071	2,045	3,296

Measures computed from the distributions

Absolute (dollars)

Q_3	4,296	4,318	4,952	5,500	4,875	3,979	2,927	4,073
Md	2,378	2,631	3,052	3,000	3,042	2,466	1,600	2,378
Q_1	1,237	1,348	1,416	1,600	1,711	1,534	822	1,216
I.D.	3,059	2,970	3,536	3,900	3,164	2,445	2,105	2,857
S.D.	5,786	3,710	4,627	4,029	4,616	3,153	1,799	4,250

Relative

R.I.D.	1.286	1.129	1.159	1.300	1.040	.991	1.316	1.201
V^1	1.545	1.079	1.085	1.001	1.158	1.015	.872	1.276

For footnotes see p.569.

TABLE B1 (concl.)

c   By Type of Practice,   1934-1936

(1937 SAMPLE)[9]

INCOME CLASSES (dollars)	GENERAL PRACTITIONERS			PARTIAL SPECIALISTS			COMPLETE SPECIALISTS		
	1934	1935	1936	1934	1935	1936	1934	1935	1936
Under -2,000								0.1	
-2,000 to -1,000									
-1,000 to 0	0.5	0.3	0.7	0.5	0.5	0.3	0.6	1.1	0.4
0	3.3	2.5	0.8	2.7	2.5	1.7	2.9	1.6	1.2
1 to 500	4.3	4.1	5.0	2.3	1.9	2.3	0.7	1.7	0.6
500 to 1,000	9.0	10.8	10.2	7.7	6.5	5.5	4.4	3.2	3.9
1,000 to 1,500	16.9	14.5	10.6	6.7	7.6	6.4	4.5	6.7	3.8
1,500 to 2,000	10.8	12.6	11.9	8.6	9.9	8.4	6.8	5.8	4.0
2,000 to 2,500	11.8	11.9	11.2	15.7	11.0	11.8	10.4	7.4	10.0
2,500 to 3,000	11.2	8.5	10.6	11.7	12.8	9.3	6.0	5.8	5.4
3,000 to 3,500	8.3	10.4	8.6	9.0	8.1	9.1	10.2	8.7	7.3
3,500 to 4,000	7.3	6.3	5.8	5.9	8.5	7.2	5.6	5.6	8.7
4,000 to 5,000	9.9	8.7	8.5	12.4	13.3	12.3	11.9	4.3	12.3
5,000 to 6,000	1.7	2.6	7.0	6.3	5.1	8.4	9.9	6.9	6.9
6,000 to 7,000	2.1	2.3	2.9	2.8	3.5	3.8	8.2	6.8	4.5
7,000 to 8,000	1.3	2.4	1.9	3.3	3.3	2.5	4.2	4.5	7.7
8,000 to 9,000	0.8	1.1	2.3	0.9	1.5	4.1	1.7	4.4	4.6
9,000 to 10,000	0.1	0.3	0.9	2.0	0.6	1.2	1.4	3.0	3.3
10,000 to 12,000	0.6	0.3	0.5	0.4	2.4	3.3	2.9	4.3	4.7
12,000 to 14,000	0.2	0.4	0.6	0.7	0.6	0.7	2.3	3.2	3.2
14,000 to 16,000		0.04	0.03	0.1	0.4	0.5	2.4	0.7	1.7
16,000 to 18,000				0.4	0.3	0.8	2.2	2.2	3.2
18,000 to 20,000						0.2		1.1	0.2
20,000 to 25,000								0.9	1.8
25,000 to 30,000				0.03		0.03			0.6
30,000 to 40,000					0.03		0.7		
40,000 to 50,000						0.2			
50,000 and over									
No. of physicians covered	531.42	553.5	602.70	450.5	468.5	512.25	255.92	271.5	292.92
A.M. (dollars)	2,478	2,584	2,914	3,215	3,412	3,962	4,836	5,174	5,805

Measures computed from the distributions

Absolute (dollars)

Q_3	3,436	3,472	3,968	4,338	4,441	5,066	6,113	6,902	7,775
Md	2,221	2,220	2,484	2,749	2,900	3,230	3,798	4,165	4,375
Q_1	1,234	1,251	1,394	1,798	1,806	2,014	2,238	2,329	2,599
I.D.	2,202	2,221	2,574	2,540	2,635	3,052	3,875	4,573	5,176
S.D.	1,857	1,996	2,242	2,431	2,644	3,572	4,453	4,308	4,831

Relative

R.I.D.	.991	1.000	1.036	.924	.909	.945	1.020	1.098	1.183
V^1	.733	.755	.752	.739	.758	.882	.903	.816	.817

For footnotes see p. 569.

TABLE B2

Arithmetic Mean Income of Physicians and Number of Physicians Covered, 1929-1936;
1937 Sample[9]

By Region and by Size of Community

	1929	1930	1931	1932	1933	1934	1935	1936
REGION				ARITHMETIC MEAN INCOME (dollars)				
New England	6,171	5,840	5,455	4,179	3,989	3,873	4,181	4,268
Middle Atlantic	5,939	5,416	4,557	3,500	3,097	3,269	3,224	3,496
N. Central	5,230	4,554	3,934	3,024	2,736	3,249	3,642	4,291
W. N. Central	4,831	4,219	3,450	2,641	2,356	2,773	2,938	3,274
S. Atlantic	6,087	4,921	4,573	3,161	2,950	3,652	3,835	4,700
E. S. Central	3,915	3,295	2,937	2,334	2,331	2,947	2,953	3,591
W. S. Central	4,867	4,158	3,448	2,695	2,487	2,733	3,048	3,663
Mountain	6,211	5,499	4,478	3,233	3,032	3,575	3,909	4,331
Pacific	5,620	5,463	4,525	3,196	3,090	3,599	3,955	4,397
SIZE OF COMMUNITY								
500,000 & over	5,571	4,965	4,438	3,223	2,889	3,172	3,192	3,547
100,000 - 500,000	7,286	6,214	5,534	4,051	3,532	4,099	4,405	5,084
50,000 - 100,000	6,536	6,567	4,876	3,735	3,506	4,109	4,192	5,087
25,000 - 50,000	6,340	5,545	4,624	3,473	3,241	3,790	4,214	4,663
10,000 - 25,000	4,949	4,680	4,194	3,298	3,317	3,610	3,889	4,251
2,500 - 10,000	5,095	4,241	3,631	2,729	2,555	2,978	3,350	3,659
Under 2,500	3,490	2,853	2,450	1,955	1,884	2,096	2,228	2,625
U.S.	5,493	4,878	4,199	3,165	2,903	3,276	3,470	3,944
REGION				NUMBER OF PHYSICIANS COVERED[4]				
New England	85	83	85	92	96	116	118	131
Middle Atlantic	119	118	126	139	154	180	192	207
E. N. Central	130	124	131	142	156	178	183	197
W. N. Central	138	134	141	144	148	165	166	182
S. Atlantic	90	84	89	102	112	133	142	156
E. S. Central	41	40	40	43	48	56	65	70
W. S. Central	75	67	65	71	74	95	94	106
Mountain	133	121	128	132	138	176	191	199
Pacific	101	96	100	108	118	140	143	161
SIZE OF COMMUNITY								
500,000 & over	154	154	158	175	188	213	225	241
100,000 - 500,000	166	159	162	178	192	223	234	265
50,000 - 100,000	70	68	77	78	77	88	94	97
25,000 - 50,000	78	73	76	80	86	99	101	110
10,000 - 25,000	90	84	87	101	116	142	148	162
2,500 - 10,000	127	119	121	134	141	174	179	197
Under 2,500	227	209	224	224	242	298	311	335
U.S.	912	867	906	972	1,043	1,238	1,294	1,408

For footnotes see p. 569.

TABLE B3

Final Estimates of Arithmetic Mean Income of Physicians, 1929–1936

By Region and by Size of Community

	1929	1930	1931	1932	1933	1934	1935	1936
REGION					(dollars)			
New England	6,302	5,738	5,250	4,339	3,947	4,182	4,515	4,609
Middle Atlantic	6,093	5,523	4,971	3,734	3,174	3,408	3,361	3,645
E. N. Central	6,133	5,343	4,327	2,959	2,646	3,252	3,645	4,295
W. N. Central	5,365	4,726	4,057	2,992	2,901	3,409	3,612	4,025
S. Atlantic	5,030	4,483	4,011	3,255	3,231	3,702	3,888	4,764
E. S. Central	3,820	3,180	2,590	2,027	2,575	3,479	3,486	4,239
W. S. Central	4,428	3,604	3,228	2,519	2,466	2,923	3,260	3,918
Mountain	5,657	4,970	3,906	2,894	2,940	3,657	3,999	4,430
Pacific	5,703	5,360	4,629	3,479	3,224	3,573	3,926	4,365
SIZE OF COMMUNITY								
500,000 & over	6,175	5,574	4,866	3,654	3,197	3,526	3,548	3,943
100,000 – 500,000	6,374	5,834	5,050	3,791	3,543	4,194	4,507	5,202
50,000 – 100,000	7,269	6,372	5,448	3,958	3,431	3,937	4,017	4,874
25,000 – 50,000	6,373	5,629	4,862	3,631	3,443	3,868	4,301	4,759
10,000 – 25,000	6,030	5,228	4,295	3,385	3,244	3,934	4,238	4,633
2,500 – 10,000	4,721	4,140	3,810	2,897	2,783	3,116	3,505	3,829
Under 2,500	3,368	2,882	2,416	1,791	1,802	2,126	2,260	2,663
U.S.	5,573	4,965	4,300	3,235	2,985	3,431	3,633	4,129

These final estimates were computed from arithmetic means presented in Tables B1a, B1b, and B2. The arithmetic means for 1932 from the 1933, 1935, and 1937 samples were averaged. This average was then extrapolated back to 1929 on the basis of the 1933 sample, forward to 1934 on the basis of the 1935 sample, and from 1934 to 1936 on the basis of the 1937 sample. The averages for the 1937 sample are weighted averages of the state averages.

For footnotes see p. 569.

TABLE B4

Distribution of Income of Dentists by Size and Measures Computed from the Distributions[a]

a   By Region, 1929–1934

1929 (1933 SAMPLE)[6]

INCOME CLASSES (dollars)	NE	MA	ENC	WNC	SA	ESC	WSC	MT.	PAC.	U.S.[2]
Under –2,000									1	1
–2,000 to –1,000			1							1
–1,000 to 0	1									1
0										
1 to 500	1	2	5	4	3		2	1	4	22
500 to 1,000	1	1	5	7	3		1		2	21
1,000 to 1,500	7	3	12	11	8	2	2	1	3	51
1,500 to 2,000	4	11	21	12	7	8	3	3	8	77
2,000 to 2,500	6	10	24	22	11	6	4	4	2	91
2,500 to 3,000	13	15	30	22	8	4	4	5	9	111
3,000 to 3,500	11	17	31	23	10	4	6	11	16	132
3,500 to 4,000	7	24	34	18	10	3	10	4	13	124
4,000 to 5,000	15	33	37	34	14	11	17	4	30	197
5,000 to 6,000	6	45	33	22	17	2	7	9	17	159
6,000 to 7,000	12	27	14	12	3	2	2	3	12	88
7,000 to 8,000	12	19	14	9	3	2	2	2	14	77
8,000 to 9,000	6	11	8	3	8	1	4	2	5	48
9,000 to 10,000	2	9	12	2	3		2	1	3	34
10,000 to 12,000	4	16	13					3	7	44
12,000 to 14,000	1	7	4	4	2				1	20
14,000 to 16,000		6	3		2				1	12
16,000 to 18,000		2	1						3	6
18,000 to 20,000		2		1				1		4
20,000 to 25,000	2	3	2						1	8
25,000 to 30,000		2								2
30,000 to 40,000						1		1		2
40,000 to 50,000		1								1
50,000 and over										
No. of dentists covered	111	266	304	206	113	45	68	53	152	1,334
A.M.[7] (dollars)	5,044	6,365	4,746	3,995	4,626	3,514	4,946	4,478	5,225	4,969

Measures computed from the distributions[8]

Absolute (dollars)

	NE	MA	ENC	WNC	SA	ESC	WSC	MT.	PAC.	U.S.
Q_3	6,752	7,378	5,750	5,005	5,578	4,490	5,016	5,364	6,760	6,003
Md	4,355	5,267	3,855	3,515	3,815	3,165	4,150	3,725	4,491	4,080
Q_1	2,768	3,802	2,570	2,408	2,342	2,006	3,045	2,922	3,275	2,802
I.D.	3,985	3,575	3,180	2,598	3,235	2,484	1,971	2,441	3,485	3,201
S.D.	3,456	4,662	3,316	2,561	3,841	1,743	4,930	2,348	3,392	3,706

Relative

	NE	MA	ENC	WNC	SA	ESC	WSC	MT.	PAC.	U.S.
R.I.D.	.915	.679	.737	.739	.848	.785	.475	.656	.776	.785
V^1	.685	.734	.702	.641	.830	.496	.997	.524	.649	.746

For footnotes see p. 569.

TABLE B4a (cont.)

1930 (1933 SAMPLE)[6]

INCOME CLASSES (dollars)	NE	MA	ENC	WNC	SA	ESC	WSC	MT.	PAC.	U.S.[2]
Under -2,000										
-2,000 to -1,000										
-1,000 to 0		2	1	1			1			5
0										
1 to 500	1	2	4	2	2		1	1	3	17
500 to 1,000	3		9	13	7			1		33
1,000 to 1,500	8	6	15	12	10	5	3	2	8	70
1,500 to 2,000	3	12	24	17	4	6	5	4	10	86
2,000 to 2,500	8	11	34	21	9	6	1	5	10	105
2,500 to 3,000	12	15	24	21	9	3	10	8	12	119
3,000 to 3,500	10	28	36	23	10	5	13	5	14	146
3,500 to 4,000	13	21	30	25	12	8	5	5	14	134
4,000 to 5,000	12	49	41	34	14	5	14	8	30	208
5,000 to 6,000	9	32	34	15	16	3	7	5	19	142
6,000 to 7,000	9	22	14	17	6	1	4	5	9	88
7,000 to 8,000	11	26	13	5	8	1	2	1	10	77
8,000 to 9,000	6	11	7	2	4	2	1	3	10	46
9,000 to 10,000	3	5	5	1	2	1		1	5	23
10,000 to 12,000		15	7	3			1	1	4	31
12,000 to 14,000	2	5	8	4	2			1		24
14,000 to 16,000	1	5	2	1					2	11
16,000 to 18,000		2	1						1	4
18,000 to 20,000	1	1	1				1		1	5
20,000 to 25,000	1	2							2	5
25,000 to 30,000					1					1
30,000 to 40,000		1					1			2
40,000 to 50,000										
50,000 and over		1								1
No. of dentists covered	113	274	310	217	116	46	70	56	164	1,383
A.M.[7] (dollars)	4,906	5,921	4,297	3,827	4,274	3,489	4,478	4,223	5,098	4,664

Measures computed from the distributions.[8]

Absolute (dollars)

	NE	MA	ENC	WNC	SA	ESC	WSC	MT.	PAC.	U.S.
Q_3	6,412	7,232	5,375	4,738	5,569	4,305	4,995	5,524	6,230	5,794
Md	3,965	4,760	3,550	3,405	3,735	3,230	3,575	3,640	4,375	3,911
Q_1	2,680	3,352	2,302	2,198	2,195	2,002	2,805	2,520	2,960	2,599
I.D.	3,732	3,880	3,072	2,540	3,374	2,302	2,190	3,004	3,270	3,195
S.D.	3,491	5,061	2,964	2,485	3,233	1,942	4,322	2,463	3,503	3,653

Relative

	NE	MA	ENC	WNC	SA	ESC	WSC	MT.	PAC.	U.S.
R.I.D.	.941	.815	.866	.746	.903	.713	.613	.825	.747	.817
V^1	.717	.856	.691	.649	.751	.557	.965	.583	.687	.783

For footnotes see p. 569.

1931 (1933 SAMPLE)[6]

INCOME CLASSES (dollars)	NE	MA	ENC	WNC	SA	ESC	WSC	MT.	PAC.	U.S.[2]
Under -2,000										
-2,000 to -1,000		1								1
-1,000 to 0		1	3	1		-	1			6
0										
1 to 500	1	2	6	6	1		1	1	2	21
500 to 1,000	6	2	16	20	6	2	3	2	4	61
1,000 to 1,500	6	11	19	14	14	8	6	1	10	92
1,500 to 2,000	5	15	36	30	5	5	6	4	15	123
2,000 to 2,500	15	23	37	26	15	10	8	9	12	158
2,500 to 3,000	11	22	40	27	15	8	15	7	14	159
3,000 to 3,500	9	33	36	23	18	2	5	5	25	157
3,500 to 4,000	9	31	23	19	9	3	8	5	16	123
4,000 to 5,000	15	36	38	33	12	2	8	7	24	178
5,000 to 6,000	14	25	19	12	11	4	2	7	13	108
6,000 to 7,000	10	20	14	4	8	1	2	1	14	74
7,000 to 8,000	4	18	7	5	3	1	1	5	5	49
8,000 to 9,000	3	17	3				1	1	3	29
9,000 to 10,000	1	4	5	3	1		1		2	17
10,000 to 12,000	2	7	9		3			1	3	26
12,000 to 14,000	1	6	3	4	1				1	17
14,000 to 16,000	2	2	1						4	9
16,000 to 18,000			1							1
18,000 to 20,000	1	2					1			4
20,000 to 25,000		1		1					1	3
25,000 to 30,000										
30,000 to 40,000							1			1
40,000 to 50,000										
50,000 and over		1								1
No. of dentists covered	115	280	316	227	123	46	70	56	168	1,418
A.M.[7] (dollars)	4,404	5,114	3,635	3,154	3,731	2,715	3,693	3,894	4,318	3,986

Measures computed from the distributions[8]

Absolute (dollars)

	NE	MA	ENC	WNC	SA	ESC	WSC	MT.	PAC.	U.S.
Q_3	5,542	6,480	4,383	4,076	4,522	3,025	3,925	5,110	5,250	4,885
Md	3,615	3,980	3,001	2,795	3,235	2,140	2,840	3,475	3,554	3,238
Q_1	2,376	2,885	1,980	1,774	2,148	1,545	2,005	2,289	2,380	2,111
I.D.	3,166	3,595	2,403	2,302	2,375	1,480	1,920	2,821	2,870	2,774
S.D.	3,040	4,636	2,628	2,174	2,912	1,547	4,163	2,183	3,051	3,294

Relative

	NE	MA	ENC	WNC	SA	ESC	WSC	MT.	PAC.	U.S.
R.I.D.	.876	.903	.801	.824	.734	.692	.676	.812	.808	.857
V^1	.695	.908	.723	.689	.776	.570	1.127	.561	.707	.826

For footnotes see p. 569.

TABLE B4a (cont.)

1932 (1933 SAMPLE)[6]

INCOME CLASSES (dollars)	NE	MA	ENC	WNC	SA	ESC	WSC	MT.	PAC.	U.S.[2]
Under -2,000						1				1
-2,000 to -1,000										
-1,000 to 0			5	3			1		1	10
0										
1 to 500	3	10	8	9	1	4	1	2	3	42
500 to 1,000	4	15	27	31	13	6	6	2	11	117
1,000 to 1,500	13	22	38	34	14	10	12	6	15	168
1,500 to 2,000	11	27	55	45	17	8	15	5	22	210
2,000 to 2,500	17	30	44	25	21	6	14	13	37	208
2,500 to 3,000	9	38	51	32	15	7	11	6	17	187
3,000 to 3,500	12	35	24	20	12	3	3	11	20	141
3,500 to 4,000	10	20	14	14	4	1	2	2	9	76
4,000 to 5,000	12	29	24	10	7	2	1	1	13	100
5,000 to 6,000	14	22	9	3	10	1	2	4	9	74
6,000 to 7,000	4	13	7	4	5	1	1	2	7	45
7,000 to 8,000	4	10	7	1	1			2	1	26
8,000 to 9,000	1	5	2							8
9,000 to 10,000	2	2	3		2				4	14
10,000 to 12,000		5	1	2	1		1		1	12
12,000 to 14,000		1	3						1	5
14,000 to 16,000	1	2							1	4
16,000 to 18,000		1								1
18,000 to 20,000										
20,000 to 25,000					1		1			2
25,000 to 30,000										
30,000 to 40,000										
40,000 to 50,000										
50,000 and over		1								1
No. of dentists covered	117	288	322	233	124	50	71	56	172	1,452
A.M.[7] (dollars)	3,485	3,759	2,700	2,235	3,023	1,860	2,569	2,874	3,080	2,943

Measures computed from the distributions[8]

Absolute (dollars)

	NE	MA	ENC	WNC	SA	ESC	WSC	MT.	PAC.	U.S.[2]
Q_3	4,638	4,760	3,315	2,908	3,490	2,695	2,690	3,305	3,705	3,512
Md	3,115	3,005	2,295	1,902	2,390	1,647	2,005	2,521	2,464	2,414
Q_1	1,850	1,956	1,515	1,202	1,640	1,005	1,440	1,835	1,815	1,558
I.D.	2,788	2,803	1,800	1,705	1,850	1,690	1,250	1,470	1,890	1,954
S.D.	2,217	3,966	1,993	1,527	2,607	1,464	2,982	1,637	2,255	2,637

Relative

	NE	MA	ENC	WNC	SA	ESC	WSC	MT.	PAC.	U.S.[2]
R.I.D.	.895	.933	.784	.897	.774	1.026	.623	.583	.767	.809
V^i	.640	1.056	.734	.683	.858	.787	1.161	.570	.732	.896

For footnotes see p. 569.

1932 (1935 SAMPLE)

INCOME CLASSES (dollars)	NE	MA	ENC	WNC	SA	ESC	WSC	MT.	PAC.	U.S.[2]
Under -2,000										
-2,000 to -1,000		2								2
-1,000 to 0		1	1	1						3
0	1	1	3	1	2			1	1	10
1 to 500	1	3	11.5	7	1		1	2	6	34.5
500 to 1,000	3	10	28	19	6	6	5	4	7	91
1,000 to 1,500	5	17	46	23	9	6	6	6	19	138
1,500 to 2,000	11	22	41	24	10	8	10	4	20	152
2,000 to 2,500	8	19	36	30	16	4	10	14	22	160
2,500 to 3,000	6	21	39	16	10		4	7	16	122
3,000 to 3,500	7	16	14	13	7	3	3	9	9	81
3,500 to 4,000	4	11	12	8	2	1	3	5	7	53
4,000 to 5,000	10	25	21	7	4	1	2	2	7	80
5,000 to 6,000	4	10	9	3	2	1	1	1	2	33
6,000 to 7,000	2	7	5	1	2		1		6	24
7,000 to 8,000	1	6	1	2	3				5	18
8,000 to 9,000		2	1		1			1	2	7
9,000 to 10,000	1	2							1	4
10,000 to 12,000		2			1					3
12,000 to 14,000		3	1		1					5
14,000 to 16,000								1		1
16,000 to 18,000									1	1
18,000 to 20,000		1								1
20,000 to 25,000					1					1
25,000 to 30,000										
30,000 to 40,000		1								1
40,000 to 50,000										
50,000 and over										
No. of dentists covered	64	182	271.5	155	78	30	46	57	131	1,025.5
A.M. (dollars)	3,063	3,490	2,383	2,190	3,158	1,911	2,222	2,682	2,854	2,704

Measures computed from the distributions

Absolute (dollars)

	NE	MA	ENC	WNC	SA	ESC	WSC	MT.	PAC.	U.S.
Q_3	4,200	4,460	2,976	2,852	3,322	2,312	2,812	3,264	3,403	3,352
Md	2,750	2,834	2,073	2,042	2,344	1,688	2,050	2,410	2,284	2,260
Q_1	1,772	1,716	1,265	1,234	1,575	1,125	1,458	1,656	1,494	1,420
I.D.	2,428	2,744	1,711	1,618	1,747	1,187	1,354	1,608	1,909	1,932
S.D.	1,793	3,549	1,728	1,361	3,182	1,150	1,262	2,141	2,307	2,363

Relative

	NE	MA	ENC	WNC	SA	ESC	WSC	MT.	PAC.	U.S.
R.I.D.	.883	.968	.825	.792	.745	.703	.660	.667	.836	.855
V^1	.582	.996	.715	.621	1.006	.590	.555	.788	.802	.864

For footnotes see p.569.

TABLE B4a (cont.)

1933 (1935 SAMPLE)

INCOME CLASSES (dollars)	NE	MA	ENC	WNC	SA	ESC	WSC	MT.	PAC.	U.S.[2]
Under -2,000		1								1
-2,000 to -1,000										
-1,000 to 0		2.38	2	1			1			16.5
0	2	4	2.5	3	2				2	1
1 to 500	2	7	12.33	9	2		1	3	6	42.33
500 to 1,000	2	15.25	33	26	5	6	6	6	13	115.25
1,000 to 1,500	8.42	24	53	24	12	8	4	4	23	162.42
1,500 to 2,000	8	29.33	39	31	9	4	9	9	17	157.33
2,000 to 2,500	10	19	49	28	15	6	14	14	25	181
2,500 to 3,000	11	20	27	14.58	6	2	7	8	16	114.58
3,000 to 3,500	9	22	14	12	9	3	2	7	10	89
3,500 to 4,000	5	8	19	5	4			2	9	52
4,000 to 5,000	6	17	5	5	6	1	2	3	9	54
5,000 to 6,000		5	9		1	1	1	2	4	23
6,000 to 7,000	5	6	4	2	5				1	23
7,000 to 8,000		3	2		1				2	8
8,000 to 9,000		1			1		1		1	4
9,000 to 10,000		1							1	2
10,000 to 12,000		3	1					1		5
12,000 to 14,000										
14,000 to 16,000										
16,000 to 18,000									1	1
18,000 to 20,000		1								1
20,000 to 25,000					1					1
25,000 to 30,000		1								1
30,000 to 40,000										
40,000 to 50,000										
50,000 and over										
No. of dentists covered	68.42	189.96	271.83	160.58	79	31	48	61	139	1,060.79
A.M. (dollars)	2,726	2,881	2,139	1,853	2,917	1,922	2,163	2,379	2,525	2,381

Measures computed from the distributions

Absolute (dollars)

	NE	MA	ENC	WNC	SA	ESC	WSC	MT.	PAC.	U.S.
Q_3	3,439	3,466	2,742	2,464	3,458	2,438	2,572	2,984	3,162	2,996
Md	2,582	2,316	1,924	1,779	2,316	1,688	2,107	2,232	2,190	2,080
Q_1	1,668	1,372	1,171	1,024	1,448	1,110	1,500	1,514	1,320	1,260
I.D.	1,771	2,094	1,571	1,440	2,010	1,328	1,072	1,470	1,842	1,736
S.D.	1,534	2,993	1,485	1,137	2,829	1,115	1,403	1,655	2,037	2,025

Relative

	NE	MA	ENC	WNC	SA	ESC	WSC	MT.	PAC.	U.S.
R.I.D.	.686	.904	.817	.809	.868	.787	.509	.659	.841	.835
V[1]	.562	1.030	.688	.605	.959	.574	.640	.695	.797	.843

For footnotes see p.569.

1934 (1935 SAMPLE)

INCOME CLASSES (dollars)	NE	MA	ENC	WNC	SA	EEC	WSC	MT.	PAC.	U.S.[2]
Under -2,000										
-2,000 to -1,000										
-1,000 to 0		3	1	1				1		6
0	2	4	2.42	2	3			1	1	15.42
1 to 500		10	7.46	8	3		2	1	4	35.46
500 to 1,000	3	13	38	22	2	2	4	5	9.42	100.42
1,000 to 1,500	10	18	39	29	10	9	6	4	19	147
1,500 to 2,000	8	28	40.46	23	9	7	8	8	25	156.46
2,000 to 2,500	10	23.25	50	29.42	15	4	11	8	21	174.67
2,500 to 3,000	10	24	28	22	8	2	6	11	15	128
3,000 to 3,500	6	21	27	13	8	3	7	10	14	110
3,500 to 4,000	8	20	16	8	8	2	2	5	7	76
4,000 to 5,000	10	13.87	17	9	5	1	2	3	8	69.87
5,000 to 6,000	3	6	7	2	2		2	2	13	37
6,000 to 7,000		8	6	2	3				1	20
7,000 to 8,000	1	2	1		1	1		1		7
8,000 to 9,000	1	1	1		2				1	6
9,000 to 10,000		2	3		1					6
10,000 to 12,000		2			1		1	1	1	6
12,000 to 14,000		1	1							2
14,000 to 16,000										
16,000 to 18,000		1							1	2
18,000 to 20,000					1					1
20,000 to 25,000										
25,000 to 30,000		1								1
30,000 to 40,000										
40,000 to 50,000										
50,000 and over										
No. of dentists covered	72	202.12	285.34	170.42	82	31	51	61	140.42	1,107.3
A.M. (dollars)	2,803	3,015	2,428	2,078	3,154	2,230	2,459	2,692	2,766	2,609

Measures computed from the distributions

Absolute (dollars)

	NE	MA	ENC	WNC	SA	EEC	WSC	MT.	PAC.	U.S.
Q_3	3,812	3,684	3,142	2,804	3,719	2,812	3,090	3,338	3,390	3,304
Md	2,650	2,538	2,144	2,004	2,466	1,822	2,250	2,614	2,280	2,266
Q_1	1,688	1,545	1,288	1,166	1,639	1,320	1,547	1,703	1,534	1,408
I.D.	2,124	2,139	1,854	1,638	2,080	1,492	1,543	1,635	1,856	1,896
S.D.	1,571	2,888	1,728	1,257	2,749	1,344	1,672	1,745	2,058	2,066

Relative

	NE	MA	ENC	WNC	SA	EEC	WSC	MT.	PAC.	U.S.
R.I.D.	.802	.843	.865	.817	.843	.819	.686	.625	.814	.837
V^1	.550	.952	.706	.599	.870	.606	.669	.645	.748	.787

For footnotes see p.569.

TABLE B 4 (cont.)

b   By Size of Community, 1929-1934

1929 (1933 SAMPLE)[6]

Communities with populations (in thousands) of

INCOME CLASSES (dollars)	500 & over	100 to 500	50 to 100	25 to 50	10 to 25	2.5 to 10	under 2.5	U.S.[2]
Under -2,000	1							1
-2,000 to -1,000	1							1
-1,000 to 0							1	1
0								
1 to 500	6	3	3		3	4	3	22
500 to 1,000	4	3		2	2	2	7	21
1,000 to 1,500	6	7	4	3	6	5	18	51
1,500 to 2,000	16	13	6	3	10	10	19	77
2,000 to 2,500	15	12	5	6	10	19	22	91
2,500 to 3,000	15	14	5	13	16	21	26	111
3,000 to 3,500	22	26	8	9	21	20	23	132
3,500 to 4,000	32	14	9	13	14	20	21	124
4,000 to 5,000	34	37	21	17	25	36	25	197
5,000 to 6,000	37	23	11	17	35	22	13	159
6,000 to 7,000	18	18	5	15	15	13	3	88
7,000 to 8,000	24	13	7	12	6	13	2	77
8,000 to 9,000	12	16	2	5	7	2	4	48
9,000 to 10,000	10	10	4	1	4	2	3	34
10,000 to 12,000	18	8	3	6	6	2		44
12,000 to 14,000	9	4	1	4		1		20
14,000 to 16,000	6	2	2	1		1		12
16,000 to 18,000	4		2					6
18,000 to 20,000		2	2					4
20,000 to 25,000	6			1	1			8
25,000 to 30,000	2							2
30,000 to 40,000	1	1						2
40,000 to 50,000	1							1
50,000 and over								
No. of dentists covered	300	226	100	128	181	193	190	1,334
A.M.[7] (dollars)	6,215	5,372	5,321	5,438	4,654	4,148	3,170	4,969

Measures computed from the distributions[8]

Absolute (dollars)

	500 & over	100 to 500	50 to 100	25 to 50	10 to 25	2.5 to 10	under 2.5	U.S.
Q_3	7,685	6,885	6,320	6,829	5,755	5,370	4,008	6,003
Md	4,943	4,565	4,380	4,645	4,455	3,912	2,985	4,080
Q_1	3,283	3,009	3,060	3,360	2,906	2,652	1,935	2,802
I.D.	4,402	3,876	3,260	3,469	2,849	2,718	2,073	3,201
S.D.	5,175	3,876	3,812	3,139	2,556	2,174	1,821	3,706

Relative

	500 & over	100 to 500	50 to 100	25 to 50	10 to 25	2.5 to 10	under 2.5	U.S.
R.I.D.	.891	.849	.744	.747	.640	.695	.694	.785
V^1	.833	.724	.711	.579	.549	.523	.570	.746

For footnotes see p. 569.

1930 (1933 SAMPLE)[6]

Communities with populations (in thousands) of

INCOME CLASSES (dollars)	500 & over	100 to 500	50 to 100	25 to 50	10 to 25	2.5 to 10	under 2.5	U.S.[2]
Under -2,000								
-2,000 to -1,000								
-1,000 to 0	1		1	2			1	5
0								
1 to 500	2	3	1	1	2	3	4	17
500 to 1,000	9	4	3	2	1	5	9	33
1,000 to 1,500	9	12	3	4	12	7	22	70
1,500 to 2,000	14	14	7	4	13	15	18	86
2,000 to 2,500	19	13	8	8	12	23	22	105
2,500 to 3,000	17	14	4	11	18	21	29	119
3,000 to 3,500	25	26	14	14	16	21	28	146
3,500 to 4,000	34	19	7	9	17	28	19	134
4,000 to 5,000	49	38	18	18	31	27	26	208
5,000 to 6,000	33	23	13	15	28	23	5	142
6,000 to 7,000	14	19	7	13	18	11	5	88
7,000 to 8,000	25	17	5	11	7	9	3	77
8,000 to 9,000	14	11	1	7	4	4	5	46
9,000 to 10,000	9	6	2	2	3	1		23
10,000 to 12,000	13	7	2	3	5	1		31
12,000 to 14,000	8	5	3	4		1	1	24
14,000 to 16,000	6	2	1	2				11
16,000 to 18,000	2		2					4
18,000 to 20,000	2	1	1	1				5
20,000 to 25,000	4				1			5
25,000 to 30,000	1							1
30,000 to 40,000	1	1						2
40,000 to 50,000								
50,000 and over	1							1
No. of dentists covered	312	235	103	131	188	200	197	1,383
A.M.[7] (dollars)	5,830	5,001	4,941	5,163	4,817	3,834	3,005	4,664

Measures computed from the distributions[8]

Absolute (dollars)

Q_3	7,180	6,318	5,695	6,665	5,540	4,934	3,902	5,794
Md	4,355	4,405	4,068	4,435	4,130	3,585	2,842	3,911
Q_1	3,080	2,950	2,764	3,004	2,625	2,411	1,800	2,599
I.D.	4,100	3,368	2,931	3,661	2,915	2,522	2,102	3,195
S.D.	5,316	3,514	3,585	3,220	2,570	1,994	1,836	3,653

Relative

R.I.D.	.941	.765	.721	.825	.706	.704	.740	.817
V^1	.912	.700	.732	.624	.583	.522	.599	.783

For footnotes see p.569.

TABLE B 4b (cont.)

1931 (1933 SAMPLE)[6]

Communities with populations (in thousands) of

INCOME CLASSES (dollars)	500 & over	100 to 500	50 to 100	25 to 50	10 to 25	2.5 to 10	under 2.5	U.S.[2]
Under −2,000								
−2,000 to −1,000			1					1
−1,000 to 0		1			1	3	1	6
0								
1 to 500	6	3	1	4		2	4	21
500 to 1,000	10	11	5	2	3	9	21	61
1,000 to 1,500	14	13	7	6	11	11	27	92
1,500 to 2,000	22	18	6	4	21	29	21	123
2,000 to 2,500	31	21	12	15	18	23	35	158
2,500 to 3,000	23	19	9	12	30	35	31	159
3,000 to 3,500	46	24	14	15	15	21	21	157
3,500 to 4,000	25	23	10	10	23	18	14	123
4,000 to 5,000	34	37	18	21	28	27	10	178
5,000 to 6,000	28	21	5	15	21	13	4	108
6,000 to 7,000	19	15	4	12	9	9	6	74
7,000 to 8,000	16	9	3	7	6	5	3	49
8,000 to 9,000	10	7	1	4	4	1	1	29
9,000 to 10,000	4	4	3	2	3		1	17
10,000 to 12,000	12	7	2	2		2		26
12,000 to 14,000	8	3	3	2				17
14,000 to 16,000	3	2	3	1				9
16,000 to 18,000	1							1
18,000 to 20,000	3	1						4
20,000 to 25,000	3							3
25,000 to 30,000								
30,000 to 40,000		1						1
40,000 to 50,000								
50,000 and over	1							1
No. of dentists covered	319	240	107	134	193	208	200	1,418
A.M.[7] (dollars)	4,972	4,319	4,321	4,421	3,744	3,241	2,515	3,986

Measures computed from the distributions[8]

Absolute (dollars)

Q_3	6,001	5,265	4,780	5,715	4,879	4,215	3,199	4,885
Md	3,582	3,705	3,305	3,965	3,395	2,891	2,295	3,238
Q_1	2,438	2,370	2,258	2,508	2,375	1,964	1,405	2,111
I.D.	3,563	2,895	2,522	3,207	2,504	2,251	1,794	2,774
S.D.	4,918	3,316	3,220	2,672	1,854	1,834	1,585	3,294

Relative

R.I.D.	.995	.781	.763	.809	.738	.779	.782	.857
V^1	.989	.761	.760	.602	.496	.569	.619	.826

For footnotes see p.569.

1932 (1933 SAMPLE)[6]

Communities with populations (in thousands) of

INCOME CLASSES (dollars)	500 & over	100 to 500	50 to 100	25 to 50	10 to 25	2.5 to 10	under 2.5	U.S.[7]
Under –2,000		1						1
–2,000 to –1,000								
–1,000 to 0	3	3			1	1	2	10
0								
1 to 500	6	5	6	8	2	6	8	42
500 to 1,000	21	16	10	4	14	18	32	117
1,000 to 1,500	29	17	8	12	30	23	45	168
1,500 to 2,000	37	31	11	10	29	39	48	210
2,000 to 2,500	42	40	17	17	27	37	27	208
2,500 to 3,000	44	27	13	20	27	34	21	187
3,000 to 3,500	34	25	13	15	25	18	10	141
3,500 to 4,000	15	19	10	5	10	13	4	76
4,000 to 5,000	34	19	6	12	13	12	3	100
5,000 to 6,000	18	14	3	15	14	4	6	74
6,000 to 7,000	17	11	2	6	3	3	2	45
7,000 to 8,000	11	6		4	1	2	2	26
8,000 to 9,000	1	2	2	3				8
9,000 to 10,000	2	4	2	3	1	1		14
10,000 to 12,000	5	2	3	1				12
12,000 to 14,000	2		3					5
14,000 to 16,000	3				1			4
16,000 to 18,000	1							1
18,000 to 20,000								
20,000 to 25,000	1	1						2
25,000 to 30,000								
30,000 to 40,000								
40,000 to 50,000								
50,000 and over	1							1
No. of dentists covered	327	243	109	135	198	211	210·	1,452
A.M.[7] (dollars)	3,626	3,164	3,283	3,369	2,709	2,456	1,854	2,943

Measures computed from the distributions[8]

Absolute (dollars)

	500 & over	100 to 500	50 to 100	25 to 50	10 to 25	2.5 to 10	under 2.5	U.S.
Q_3	4,388	3,926	3,712	4,850	3,352	3,040	2,402	2,512
Md	2,822	2,745	2,522	2,868	2,483	2,215	1,703	2,414
Q_1	1,797	1,967	1,625	1,930	1,565	1,554	1,102	1,558
I.D.	2,591	2,159	2,088	2,920	1,787	1,486	1,299	1,954
S.D.	3,997	2,472	2,732	2,182	1,693	1,362	1,261	2,637

Relative

	500 & over	100 to 500	50 to 100	25 to 50	10 to 25	2.5 to 10	under 2.5	U.S.
R.I.D.	.918	.787	.828	1.018	.720	.671	.763	.809
V^1	1.102	.769	.846	.641	.626	.563	.660	.896

For footnotes see p. 569.

TABLE B4b (cont.)

1932 (1935 SAMPLE)

Communities with populations (in thousands) of

INCOME CLASSES (dollars)	500 & over	100 to 500	50 to 100	25 to 50	10 to 25	2.5 to 10	under 2.5	U.S.[2]
Under -2,000								
-2,000 to -1,000	1		1					2
-1,000 to 0	1						2	3
0	1	2	3	1	1	1	1	10
1 to 500	9	4	3	4.5	2	3	9	34.5
500 to 1,000	25	11	4	8	7	9	24	91
1,000 to 1,500	26	21	14	9	13	22	32	138
1,500 to 2,000	29	29	13	11	17	29	22	152
2,000 to 2,500	33	24	13	15	24	26	24	160
2,500 to 3,000	27	21	10	14	17	19	11	122
3,000 to 3,500	19	17	8	11	12	9	5	81
3,500 to 4,000	8	9	5	11	6	12	2	53
4,000 to 5,000	23	15	12	7	11	8	3	80
5,000 to 6,000	13	8	3	1	6	2		33
6,000 to 7,000	7	2	2	5	6	2		24
7,000 to 8,000	7	5	2	1	3			18
8,000 to 9,000	2	4	1					7
9,000 to 10,000	1	1	1	1				4
10,000 to 12,000	2	1						3
12,000 to 14,000		2	2	1				5
14,000 to 16,000		1						1
16,000 to 18,000	1							1
18,000 to 20,000	1							1
20,000 to 25,000	1							1
25,000 to 30,000								
30,000 to 40,000	1							1
40,000 to 50,000								
50,000 and over								
No. of dentists covered	238	177	97	100.5	125	142	135	1025.5
A.M. (dollars)	3,142	3,035	2,900	2,826	2,822	2,333	1,609	2,704

Measures computed from the distributions

Absolute (dollars)

Q_3	3,969	3,708	3,875	3,586	3,562	2,934	2,234	3,352
Md	2,409	2,448	2,404	2,562	2,469	2,134	1,492	2,260
Q_1	1,432	1,608	1,473	1,619	1,742	1,508	953	1,420
I.D.	2,537	2,100	2,402	1,967	1,820	1,426	1,281	1,932
S.D.	3,446	2,394	2,376	1,965	1,646	1,200	951	2,363

Relative

R.I.D.	1.053	.858	.999	.768	.737	.668	.859	.855
V^1	1.083	.778	.804	.689	.575	.515	.586	.864

For footnotes see p.569.

1933 (1935 SAMPLE)

Communities with populations (in thousands) of

INCOME CLASSES (dollars)	500 & over	100 to 500	50 to 100	25 to 50	10 to 25	2.5 to 10	under 2.5	U.S.[2]
Under -2,000	1							1
-2,000 to -1,000								
-1,000 to 0	2.38	2	1				1	6.38
0	4.5	2	4	2	1	1	2	16.5
1 to 500	11.33	6	2	5	7	4	7	42.33
500 to 1,000	28.25	17	11	11	7	13	25	115.25
1,000 to 1,500	34	27	14	13	19.42	18	35	162.42
1,500 to 2,000	31	25	8	16	16	32	27.33	157.33
2,000 to 2,500	26	32	21	16	27	37	21	181
2,500 to 3,000	32	19.58	10	15	14	12	9	114.58
3,000 to 3,500	17	16	9	12	8	18	8	89
3,500 to 4,000	18	6	4	4	11	7	2	52
4,000 to 5,000	18	10	6	8	9	3		54
5,000 to 6,000	8	6	3	2	2	2		23
6,000 to 7,000	5	7	3	1	7			23
7,000 to 8,000	5	2		1				8
8,000 to 9,000	1	2			1			4
9,000 to 10,000	1			1				2
10,000 to 12,000		2	2	1				5
12,000 to 14,000								
14,000 to 16,000								
16,000 to 18,000	1							1
18,000 to 20,000	1							1
20,000 to 25,000	1							1
25,000 to 30,000	1							1
30,000 to 40,000								
40,000 to 50,000								
50,000 and over								
No. of dentists covered	247.46	181.58	98	108	129.42	147	137.33	1,060.79
A.M. (dollars)	2,734	2,577	2,447	2,435	2,545	2,125	1,560	2,381

Measures computed from the distributions

Absolute (dollars)

	500 & over	100 to 500	50 to 100	25 to 50	10 to 25	2.5 to 10	under 2.5	U.S.
Q_3	3,446	3,175	3,139	3,125	3,352	2,719	2,135	2,996
Md	2,216	2,184	2,214	2,219	2,264	2,074	1,481	2,080
Q_1	1,212	1,340	1,232	1,346	1,447	1,512	986	1,260
I.D.	2,234	1,835	1,907	1,779	1,905	1,207	1,149	1,736
S.D.	3,028	1,910	1,920	1,743	1,593	1,002	841	2,025

Relative

	500 & over	100 to 500	50 to 100	25 to 50	10 to 25	2.5 to 10	under 2.5	U.S.
R.I.D.	1.008	.840	.861	.802	.841	.582	.776	.835
V^1	1.096	.740	.772	.706	.622	.468	.532	.843

For footnotes see p. 569.

TABLE B 4b (concl.)

1934 (1935 SAMPLE)

Communities with populations (in thousands) of

INCOME CLASSES (dollars)	500 & over	100 to 500	50 to 100	25 to 50	10 to 25	2.5 to 10	under 2.5	U.S.[2]
Under -2,000								
-2,000 to -1,000								
-1,000 to 0	2	1	1			1	1	6
0	4	1	3	1.42	2	1	3	15.42
1 to 500	13	5	2	1.46	4	5	5	35.46
500 to 1,000	21	13.42	8	15	7	14	20	100.42
1,000 to 1,500	35	26	13	6	8	23	33	147
1,500 to 2,000	32	28	10	19.46	26	11	30	156.46
2,000 to 2,500	31	33	16	18	19.42	35	19.25	174.67
2,500 to 3,000	31	15	12	14	14	24	16	128
3,000 to 3,500	18	17	13	12	19	22	8	110
3,500 to 4,000	16	16	5	8	13	11	7	76
4,000 to 5,000	20	13	9	10	7	6.87	3	69.87
5,000 to 6,000	11	11	2	6	6	1		37
6,000 to 7,000	8	3	3		4	2		20
7,000 to 8,000	3	3			1			7
8,000 to 9,000	2	2			2			6
9,000 to 10,000	2	2	2					6
10,000 to 12,000	1	3		1	1			6
12,000 to 14,000			1	1				2
14,000 to 16,000								
16,000 to 18,000	2							2
18,000 to 20,000	1							1
20,000 to 25,000								
25,000 to 30,000	1							1
30,000 to 40,000								
40,000 to 50,000								
50,000 and over								
No. of dentists covered	254	192.42	100	113.34	133.42	156.87	145.25	1,107.3
A.M. (dollars)	2,926	2,841	2,710	2,650	2,821	2,318	1,815	2,609

Measures computed from the distributions

Absolute (dollars)

Q_3	3,610	3,653	3,384	3,402	3,524	3,083	2,440	3,304
Md	2,322	2,330	2,406	2,370	2,510	2,335	1,677	2,266
Q_1	1,336	1,530	1,423	1,614	1,738	1,396	1,110	1,408
I.D.	2,274	2,123	1,961	1,788	1,786	1,687	1,330	1,896
S.D.	2,930	2,051	2,026	1,823	1,760	1,192	992	2,066

Relative

R.I.D.	.979	.911	.815	.754	.712	.772	.793	.837
V^1	1.001	.714	.743	.681	.617	.511	.549	.787

For footnotes see p.569.

TABLE B5

Final Estimates of Arithmetic Mean Income of Dentists[3], 1929–1934

By Region and by Size of Community

	1929	1930	1931	1932	1933	1934
REGION			(dollars)			
New England	4,739	4,609	4,137	3,274	2,914	2,996
Middle Atlantic	6,156	5,708	4,930	3,624	2,992	3,131
E. N. Central	4,468	4,046	3,422	2,542	2,282	2,590
W. N. Central	3,954	3,788	3,122	2,212	1,872	2,108
S. Atlantic	4,729	4,369	3,814	3,090	2,854	3,086
E. S. Central	3,563	3,538	2,753	1,886	1,897	2,201
W. S. Central	4,613	4,176	3,444	2,396	2,332	2,652
Mountain	4,328	4,082	3,764	2,778	2,464	2,788
Pacific	5,033	4,911	4,160	2,967	2,625	2,876
SIZE OF COMMUNITY						
500,000 & over	5,800	5,441	4,640	3,384	2,945	3,151
100,000 – 500,000	5,263	4,900	4,232	3,100	2,632	2,902
50,000 – 100,000	5,011	4,654	4,070	3,092	2,609	2,890
25,000 – 50,000	5,001	4,748	4,065	3,098	2,669	2,905
10,000 – 25,000	4,752	4,510	3,823	2,766	2,495	2,765
2,500 – 10,000	4,043	3,737	3,159	2,394	2,181	2,379
Under 2,500	2,961	2,807	2,350	1,732	1,679	1,954
U.S.	4,768	4,475	3,825	2,824	2,487	2,725

These final estimates were computed from arithmetic means presented in Tables B 4 a and B 4 b. The arithmetic means for 1932 from the 1933 and 1935 samples were averaged. This average was then extrapolated back to 1929 on the basis of the 1933 sample and forward to 1934 on the basis of the 1935 sample.

For footnotes see p.569.

TABLE B6

Distribution of Income of Lawyers by Size and Measures Computed from the Distributions

a By Region, 1932-1934

1932 (1935 SAMPLE)[10]

INCOME CLASSES (dollars)	NE	MA	ENC	WNC	SA	ESC	WSC	MT.	PAC.	U.S.[2]
Under -2,000		0.8								0.2
-2,000 to -1,000									1.1	0.1
-1,000 to 0	2.2	1.1						3.8	1.5	0.6
0		1.2	1.6	1.2	2.7		6.9	5.6	2.9	2.1
1 to 500	12.2	2.9	4.5	11.2	11.8	5.5	6.9	8.7	7.5	7.1
500 to 1,000	5.6	9.3	16.6	8.3	8.6	13.7	18.2	9.9	6.5	11.4
1,000 to 1,500	11.6	11.5	10.2	16.3	11.8	13.2	10.7	15.5	14.4	12.7
1,500 to 2,000	15.0	6.0	12.4	11.4	9.5	19.6	10.1	7.4	12.5	11.3
2,000 to 2,500	8.2	10.6	10.9	11.7	8.6	11.9	10.4	5.0	13.3	10.5
2,500 to 3,000	2.2	9.0	9.0	6.9	6.7	9.1	5.5	14.9	5.6	7.6
3,000 to 3,500	7.3	7.5	5.3	5.6	3.2		7.1	8.1	4.2	5.5
3,500 to 4,000	4.3	3.4	5.8	2.0	4.5	4.1	4.4		3.3	3.8
4,000 to 5,000	6.2	10.0	4.8	4.7	7.2		6.9	2.5	7.6	6.2
5,000 to 6,000	7.7	7.3	3.7	6.9	7.5	5.4	1.1	2.5	2.4	5.2
6,000 to 7,000	4.3	1.2	6.4	4.6	4.1		1.4	8.7	2.9	3.6
7,000 to 8,000	5.9	4.3	1.8	5.1		1.3	2.5	5.0	1.4	3.0
8,000 to 9,000		1.5	1.3	2.4	2.5		1.1		3.9	1.7
9,000 to 10,000	2.6	1.2	2.1	0.6	3.8	2.3	1.1			1.5
10,000 to 12,000	2.2	4.2	1.2	0.6	2.3	1.8	1.4		1.8	1.9
12,000 to 14,000		0.4			1.4	2.8	1.7		0.9	0.6
14,000 to 16,000		1.4	0.8			4.6				0.7
16,000 to 18,000		1.5	0.7		1.1					0.6
18,000 to 20,000		0.6			1.4					0.3
20,000 to 25,000		3.0			1.4	2.3	1.7		1.4	1.2
25,000 to 30,000	2.8		0.8	0.6		1.8	1.1			0.6
30,000 to 40,000								2.5		0.2
40,000 to 50,000										
50,000 and over										
No. of lawyers covered[a]	80	220	243	214	129	84	128	51	109	1,269
A.M. (dollars)	3,812	4,323	3,218	2,891	3,845	4,185	3,063	3,207	2,935	3,508

Measures computed from the distributions

Absolute (dollars)

	NE	MA	ENC	WNC	SA	ESC	WSC	MT.	PAC.	U.S.
Q_3	5,062	5,233	3,882	4,098	5,060	3,744	3,446	3,260	3,584	4,339
Md	2,217	2,870	2,213	2,068	2,328	1,948	1,864	1,934	1,961	2,218
Q_1	1,220	1,422	1,110*	1,132	1,082	1,220	810	848	1,192	1,140
I.D.	3,842	3,811	2,772	2,966	3,978	2,524	2,636	2,412	2,392	3,199
S.D.	4,805	4,990	3,558	3,035	4,336	5,687	4,444	5,509	3,438	4,369

Relative

	NE	MA	ENC	WNC	SA	ESC	WSC	MT.	PAC.	U.S.
R.I.D.	1.733	1.328	1.253	1.434	1.709	1.296	1.414	1.247	1.220	1.442
V^1	1.270	1.142	1.101	1.024	1.132	1.347	1.418	1.701	1.160	1.236

For footnotes see p. 569.

1933 (1935 SAMPLE)[10]

INCOME CLASSES (dollars)	NE	MA	ENC	WNC	SA	ESC	WSC	MT.	PAC.	U.S.[2]
Under −2,000										
−2,000 to −1,000		2.5							1.1	0.6
−1,000 to 0		0.7		0.9				3.4	1.4	0.6
0		1.6	2.9	2.2	1.7		5.3	2.2	4.1	2.5
1 to 500	11.2	4.2	7.8	11.6	13.7	10.9	9.1	10.5	10.4	9.1
500 to 1,000	9.8	12.7	15.1	10.9	10.1	16.6	15.9	15.5	8.7	12.7
1,000 to 2,500	12.1	12.5	17.9	16.4	10.3	21.4	16.4	18.2	22.4	16.3
1,500 to 2,000	12.8	10.6	6.7	13.2	10.0	9.6	10.8	8.8	10.6	10.1
2,000 to 2,500	10.6	11.0	8.5	7.6	10.3	10.1	10.6	13.2	11.0	9.9
2,500 to 3,000	8.3	5.9	7.2	7.1	10.0	1.7	4.0	6.6	8.5	6.7
3,000 to 3,500		5.5	7.9	5.2	5.6	3.5	9.0	2.2	5.4	5.7
3,500 to 4,000	1.6	3.8	3.9	3.9	3.0	3.9	2.0		2.7	3.2
4,000 to 5,000	7.8	4.9	5.2	7.7	4.3	5.2	5.3	7.2	6.7	5.7
5,000 to 6,000	11.0	7.0	5.2	5.6	8.8	1.7	1.3	2.2	1.7	5.7
6,000 to 7,000	1.6	6.1	3.8	1.4	1.7		2.5	2.2		2.8
7,000 to 8,000	5.9	1.1	1.6	1.1	2.4		1.3	2.2	1.7	1.6
8,000 to 9,000	2.5	1.9	0.4	0.9	4.3					1.2
9,000 to 10,000		1.2		1.1					1.3	0.5
10,000 to 12,000	2.1	0.5	2.9	0.8	1.3	.4.4		3.4	0.9	1.5
12,000 to 14,000		1.8	1.0	0.6	1.1	2.2	3.8			1.2
14,000 to 16,000		0.7			1.3	2.6	1.5			0.5
16,000 to 18,000		1.2	0.7	0.8		4.4				0.7
18,000 to 20,000		1.3						2.2		0.3
20,000 to 25,000	2.7	0.4		0.6						0.4
25,000 to 30,000		0.7					1.0			0.2
30,000 to 40,000			0.7			1.7			1.3	0.4
40,000 to 50,000										
50,000 and over			0.6							0.1
No. of lawyers covered[a]	81	229	253	229	134	87	137	56	115	1,332
A.M. (dollars)	3,477	3,624	3,283	2,622	2,981	3,989	2,749	2,521	2,429	3,096

Measures computed from the distributions

Absolute (dollars)

	NE	MA	ENC	WNC	SA	ESC	WSC	MT.	PAC.	U.S.
Q_3	5,069	4,813	3,636	3,466	4,057	3,660	3,156	2,740	2,808	3,620
Md	2,192	2,232	1,972	1,797	2,204	1,558	1,650	1,510	1,586	1,906
Q_1	1,164	1,130	974	970	976	926	883	787	956	982
I.D.	3,905	3,683	2,662	2,496	3,081	2,734	2,323	1,953	1,852	2,638
S.D.	4,017	4,418	5,467	3,000	2,953	6,088	3,938	3,406	4,212	4,368

Relative

	NE	MA	ENC	WNC	SA	ESC	WSC	MT.	PAC.	U.S.
R.I.D.	1.781	1.650	1.350	1.389	1.398	1.755	1.408	1.293	1.168	1.384
V^1	1.133	1.209	1.639	1.119	.973	1.532	1.393	1.311	1.690	1.390

For footnotes see p. 569.

TABLE B6a (concl.)

1934 (1935 SAMPLE)[10]

INCOME CLASSES (dollars)	NE	MA	ENC	WNC	SA	ESC	WSC	MT.	PAC.	U.S.[2]
Under -2,000										
-2,000 to -1,000									2.5	0.2
-1,000 to 0		0.7	0.4	0.5		4.2				0.5
0	1.9	1.8	2.5	1.6	1.7		5.2	4.2	5.5	2.6
1 to 500	5.5	5.2	6.7	10.8	9.6	7.1	6.9	19.5	10.9	8.1
500 to 1,000	12.2	10.0	17.1	15.7	9.2	8.3	20.3	8.9	20.1	14.4
1,000 to 1,500	15.3	11.5	14.0	11.8	9.2	21.1	7.1	11.5	8.9	12.2
1,500 to 2,000	15.3	13.1	9.6	12.1	8.8	7.9	14.1	8.3	10.9	11.3
2,000 to 2,500	1.5	10.1	7.2	8.5	11.9	12.0	8.9	14.6	6.9	8.7
2,500 to 3,000	9.5	4.8	6.2	7.6	6.2	5.8	7.1	8.3	11.7	7.0
3,000 to 3,500	5.4	6.4	6.2	6.0	9.9	5.0	7.6	6.3	6.6	6.5
3,500 to 4,000	3.4	3.0	4.4	4.7	5.3	3.3	1.9	5.3	2.2	3.7
4,000 to 5,000	5.9	8.3	8.9	4.9	8.2	5.8	5.5	2.1	3.3	6.5
5,000 to 6,000	3.0	4.0	4.1	4.8	4.6		5.2	2.1	2.5	3.8
6,000 to 7,000	3.4	3.4	3.2	4.3	3.1	5.0	3.3		0.8	3.1
7,000 to 8,000	5.0	4.2	2.0	1.6	2.7	1.7	0.9	2.1	2.2	2.5
8,000 to 9,000	2.3	2.6	2.9	0.5	4.7				1.3	1.9
9,000 to 10,000	3.4	1.7	0.5	2.9	0.8		0.9		0.8	1.3
10,000 to 12,000	2.5	2.3	1.1	1.1	0.8		1.4	4.7	1.4	1.5
12,000 to 14,000		0.4	1.2				2.6			0.6
14,000 to 16,000		2.5	1.1		1.1	6.3				1.1
16,000 to 18,000	1.9	0.4	0.7							0.3
18,000 to 20,000	2.5	2.3			2.1	5.0				1.0
20,000 to 25,000		0.4		0.5					1.3	0.4
25,000 to 30,000		0.7								0.1
30,000 to 40,000						1.7		2.1		0.2
40,000 to 50,000										
50,000 and over							0.9			0.1
No. of lawyers covered[a]	84	233	263	240	141	90	142	58	115	1,377
A.M. (dollars)	3,789	4,084	3,019	2,658	3,413	4,255	3,084	2,889	2,365	3,248

measures computed from the distributions

Absolute (dollars)

	NE	MA	ENC	WNC	SA	ESC	WSC	MT.	PAC.	U.S.
Q_3	4,843	5,019	4,087	3,540	4,379	4,069	3,362	2,976	2,898	3,936
Md	1,994	2,380	1,984	1,898	2,482	2,062	1,872	1,852	1,600	2,028
Q_1	1,176	1,318	951	885	1,244	1,130	816	574	654	967
I.D.	3,667	3,701	3,136	2,655	3,135	2,939	2,546	2,402	2,244	2,969
S.D.	4,118	4,675	3,101	2,783	3,505	6,355	5,679	5,281	3,204	4,164

Relative

	NE	MA	ENC	WNC	SA	ESC	WSC	MT.	PAC.	U.S.
R.I.D.	1.839	1.555	1.581	1.399	1.263	1.425	1.360	1.297	1.402	1.464
V^1	1.088	1.130	1.022	1.024	1.008	1.458	1.806	1.773	1.355	1.266

For footnotes see p.569.

TABLE B6 (cont.)

b   By Size of Community, 1932-1934

1932 (1935 SAMPLE)[10]

Communities with populations (in thousands) of

INCOME CLASSES (dollars)	1,500 & over	500 to 1,500	250 to 500	100 to 250	25 to 100	10 to 25	2.5 to 10	under 2.5	U.S.[2]
Under -2,000	1.3								0.2
-2,000 to -1,000				1.0					0.1
-1,000 to 0		1.6	1.9	1.0		0.9			0.6
0	1.3	1.6	1.9	2.0	2.1	2.7	2.6	2.7	2.1
1 to 500	3.8	6.6	8.0	4.0	9.0	6.3	7.2	10.6	7.1
500 to 1,000	11.4	6.6	9.6	15.0	7.8	10.0	15.0	11.9	11.4
1,000 to 1,500	10.1	11.5	10.5	14.0	9.9	10.9	11.8	20.5	12.7
1,500 to 2,000	6.3	19.7	11.8	3.0	13.4	10.4	11.1	15.2	11.3
2,000 to 2,500	13.9	6.6	10.5	7.0	6.4	11.8	11.8	15.2	10.5
2,500 to 3,000	8.9	11.5	5.7	6.0	6.4	8.1	7.2	8.6	7.6
3,000 to 3,500	5.1	3.3	6.7	5.0	4.9	7.2	7.8	4.0	5.5
3,500 to 4,000	3.8	3.3	1.9	6.0	7.1	0.9	5.2	2.0	3.8
4,000 to 5,000	2.5	11.5	5.7	8.0	4.9	11.8	5.2	4.0	6.2
5,000 to 6,000	10.1	3.3	3.8	6.0	7.1	4.5	5.9	1.3	5.2
6,000 to 7,000	2.5	3.3	3.8	6.0	5.7	2.7	2.6	2.7	3.6
7,000 to 8,000	2.5	1.5	3.7	3.0	3.5	6.3	3.9		3.0
8,000 to 9,000	1.3	4.9	1.9	2.0	2.1	0.9	0.7	0.7	1.7
9,000 to 10,000	1.3	1.6	1.9	3.0	3.5	0.9			1.5
10,000 to 12,000	5.1		1.9	4.0	2.8	0.9	0.7		1.9
12,000 to 14,000			2.9				0.7	0.7	0.6
14,000 to 16,000	1.3		1.0	1.0	0.7	0.9	0.7		0.7
16,000 to 18,000	2.5		1.0	1.0					0.6
18,000 to 20,000			1.0	1.0					0.3
20,000 to 25,000	3.8		2.9	1.0	1.2				1.2
25,000 to 30,000	1.3	1.6			1.4	0.9			0.6
30,000 to 40,000						0.9			0.2
40,000 to 50,000									
50,000 and over									
No. of lawyers covered[4]	111	71	161	160	217	156	194	183	1,269
A.M. (dollars)	4,701	3,300	4,176	3,787	4,004	3,480	2,664	1,931	3,508

Measures computed from the distributions.

Absolute (dollars)

Q_3	5,656	4,239	4,177	5,500	5,434	4,490	3,547	2,462	4,339
Md	2,607	2,181	2,300	2,750	2,610	2,269	2,097	1,641	2,218
Q_1	1,360	1,373	1,172	1,072	1,308	1,234	1,007	992	1,140
I.D.	4,296	2,866	4,005	4,428	4,126	3,256	2,540	1,470	3,199
S.D.	5,968	3,876	4,943	4,155	4,561	4,583	2,431	1,719	4,369

Relative

R.I.D.	1.648	1.314	1.741	1.610	1.581	1.435	1.211	.896	1.442
V^1	1.272	1.179	1.188	1.045	1.134	1.289	.894	.864	1.236

For footnotes see p.569.

TABLE B 6b (cont.)

1933 (1935 SAMPLE)[10]

Communities with populations (in thousands) of

INCOME CLASSES (dollars)	1,500 & over	500 to 1,500	250 to 500	100 to 250	25 to 100	10 to 25	2.5 to 10	under 2.5	U.S.[2]
Under -2,000									
-2,000 to -1,000	1.2		1.7	1.0		0.8			0.6
-1,000 to 0	1.2	3.0	0.9						0.6
0	1.7	3.0	2.6	1.0	3.3 -	2.5	1.3	3.7	2.5
1 to 500	1.2	9.1	9.5	9.1	11.1	8.7	11.4	11.7	9.1
500 to 1,000	14.7	6.7	13.8	14.1	9.8	10.6	11.4	18.5	12.7
1,000 to 1,500	18.4	19.3	15.5	11.1	9.8	14.4	19.0	20.4	16.3
1,500 to 2,000	11.1	10.7	9.5	4.0	11.7	12.3	9.5	12.3	10.1
2,000 to 2,500	8.6	15.2	8.6	7.0	9.8	10.1	10.8	9.9	9.9
2,500 to 3,000	6.1	6.1	6.0	6.8	4.4	5.9	9.5	9.3	6.7
3,000 to 3,500	6.1	4.6	1.7	6.0	5.9	5.1	7.6	8.6	5.7
3,500 to 4,000	2.5	6.1	2.6	2.0	5.2	4.2	3.2	1.2	3.2
4,000 to 5,000	3.7	4.6	4.3	11.8	7.8	10.1	3.8	2.5	5.7
5,000 to 6,000	3.7	6.1	4.3	13.0	4.6	5.9	5.7	1.2	5.2
6,000 to 7,000	6.1	1.5	2.6	1.0	2.6	3.4	5.1		2.8
7,000 to 8,000	1.2	1.5	0.9	4.0	3.3	3.4			1.6
8,000 to 9,000	2.5	1.5	2.6		2.0			0.6	1.2
9,000 to 10,000	1.2		0.9		1.3		0.6		0.5
10,000 to 12,000	1.2		5.2	2.0	2.0		0.6		1.5
12,000 to 14,000			0.9	5.0	2.6	0.8	0.6		1.2
14,000 to 16,000	1.2		2.6						0.5
16,000 to 18,000	2.5		1.7		1.3				0.7
18,000 to 20,000	1.2			1.0		0.8			0.3
20,000 to 25,000		1.5			1.3				0.4
25,000 to 30,000	1.2				0.7				0.2
30,000 to 40,000	1.2		0.9			0.8			0.4
40,000 to 50,000									
50,000 and over			0.9						0.1
No. of lawyers covered[4]	111	75	174	160	234	165	204	193	1,332
A.M. (dollars)	4,044	2,550	3,966	3,560	3,647	3,049	2,362	1,621	3,096

Measures computed from the distributions

Absolute (dollars)

	1,500 & over	500 to 1,500	250 to 500	100 to 250	25 to 100	10 to 25	2.5 to 10	under 2.5	U.S.
Q_3	4,274	3,264	4,600	5,834	4,274	4,036	3,146	2,422	3,620
Md	2,207	1,940	1,818	2,702	2,228	2,036	1,866	1,394	1,906
Q_1	1,131	1,096	875	995	1,048	1,082	1,025	758	982
I.D.	3,143	2,168	3,725	4,839	3,226	2,954	2,121	1,664	2,638
S.D.	5,835	3,097	6,577	3,560	4,420	3,959	2,095	1,268	4,368

Relative

	1,500 & over	500 to 1,500	250 to 500	100 to 250	25 to 100	10 to 25	2.5 to 10	under 2.5	U.S.
R.I.D.	1.424	1.118	2.049	1.791	1.448	1.451	1.137	1.194	1.384
V	1.427	1.194	1.630	.984	1.194	1.311	.869	.757	·1.390

For footnotes see p. 569.

1934 (1935 SAMPLE)[10]

Communities with populations (in thousands) of

INCOME CLASSES (dollars)	1,500 & over	500 to 1,500	250 to 500	100 to 250	25 to 100	10 to 25	2.5 to 10	under 2.5	U.S.[2]
Under -2,000									
-2,000 to -1,000		1.5		1.0					0.2
-1,000 to 0			1.6		0.6		0.6	0.6	0.5
0	1.2	4.6	3.2	3.0	2.5	1.6	2.5	2.4	2.6
1 to 500	6.2	10.8	12.1	5.0	6.1	6.5	7.4	10.7	8.1
500 to 1,000	8.3	10.8	20.2	11.9	16.6	13.0	13.5	15.7	14.4
1,000 to 1,500	13.6	7.7	8.1	13.9	9.8	10.5	12.3	18.4	12.2
1,500 to 2,000	13.6	13.8	10.5	5.9	9.8	10.1	10.4	16.0	11.3
2,000 to 2,500	6.2	7.7	5.6	5.0	11.7	8.9	14.1	10.1	8.7
2,500 to 3,000	6.2	10.8	5.6	5.0	3.7	9.7	7.4	9.5	7.0
3,000 to 3,500	6.2	7.7	6.5	5.0	6.8	4.0	11.0	5.3	6.5
3,500 to 4,000	2.5	1.5	4.0	3.0	4.8	5.7	3.7	4.2	3.7
4,000 to 5,000	11.2	10.8	4.8	10.9	6.1	6.5	3.1	3.0	6.5
5,000 to 6,000	3.7	1.5	2.4	3.9	3.7	8.1	6.1	1.8	3.8
6,000 to 7,000	2.5	1.5	0.8	5.9	4.9	4.9	3.7	1.8	3.1
7,000 to 8,000	3.7	4.6	2.4	3.9	2.5	2.4	1.2	0.6	2.5
8,000 to 9,000	3.7		3.2	2.0	1.8	3.2	1.2		1.9
9,000 to 10,000	1.2		1.6	4.0	3.1	0.8			1.3
10,000 to 12,000	2.5	3.1	1.6	2.0	1.8	1.6	0.6		1.5
12,000 to 14,000	1.2		0.8	2.0	0.6				0.6
14,000 to 16,000	2.5		1.6	4.0	0.6	0.8			1.1
16,000 to 18,000	1.2			1.0			0.6		0.3
18,000 to 20,000	1.2	1.5	2.4	2.0	0.6		0.6		1.0
20,000 to 25,000			0.8		1.2				0.4
25,000 to 30,000	1.2								0.1
30,000 to 40,000						1.6			0.2
40,000 to 50,000									
50,000 and over					0.6				0.1
No. of lawyers covered[a]	113	74	183	161	247	173	209	201	1,377
A.M. (dollars)	4,213	2,825	3,241	4,398	3,720	3,622	2,629	1,815	3,248

Measures computed from the distributions

Absolute (dollars)

	1,500 & over	500 to 1,500	250 to 500	100 to 250	25 to 100	10 to 25	2.5 to 10	under 2.5	U.S.
Q_3	4,982	3,475	3,062	6,145	4,429	4,766	3,312	2,558	3,936
Md	2,568	2,050	1,731	2,946	2,195	2,466	2,120	1,570	2,028
Q_1	1,341	875	700	1,151	976	1,188	1,044	861	967
I.D.	3,641	2,600	2,362	4,994	3,453	3,578	2,268	1,697	2,969
S.D.	4,766	3,154	4,330	4,497	5,467	4,820	2,601	1,419	4,164

Relative

	1,500 & over	500 to 1,500	250 to 500	100 to 250	25 to 100	10 to 25	2.5 to 10	under 2.5	U.S.
R.I.D.	1.418	1.268	1.365	1.695	1.573	1.451	1.070	1.081	1.464
V^1	1.117	1.108	1.321	1.015	1.467	1.307	.975	.762	1.266

For footnotes see p. 569.

TABLE B6 (concl.)

c   By Organization of Practice, 1932–1934

(1935 SAMPLE)[10]

| INCOME CLASSES | INDIVIDUAL PRACTITIONERS | | | FIRM MEMBERS | | |
(dollars)	1932	1933	1934	1932	1933	1934
Under –2,000	0.2					
–2,000 to –1,000	0.2	0.8	0.3			
–1,000 to 0	0.8	0.7	0.5			0.4
0	2.8	3.1	3.2		0.4	0.8
1 to 500	8.4	10.4	9.9	2.9	4.9	2.2
500 to 1,000	13.5	14.7	15.7	4.6	5.9	10.2
1,000 to 1,500	14.8	18.6	14.2	5.8	8.6	5.6
1,500 to 2,000	11.7	10.3	12.6	9.9	9.5	6.9
2,000 to 2,500	11.8	10.1	8.7	6.4	9.3	8.8
2,500 to 3,000	7.3	6.2	7.4	8.6	8.6	5.9
3,000 to 3,500	5.3	5.9	6.8	6.3	5.2	5.8
3,500 to 4,000	3.3	3.0	2.7	5.6	4.0	7.0
4,000 to 5,000	4.4	4.4	5.9	11.8	10.4	8.8
5,000 to 6,000	5.0	4.7	2.7	5.8	7.1	7.5
6,000 to 7,000	2.4	2.1	2.8	7.4	5.1	4.1
7,000 to 8,000	1.3	1.1	2.0	8.3	3.4	4.2
8,000 to 9,000	1.7	0.9	0.8	1.5	2.1	5.6
9,000 to 10,000	1.1	0.4	0.9	2.7	0.9	2.6
10,000 to 12,000	1.2	0.8	1.1	4.2	3.9	3.1
12,000 to 14,000	0.4	0.2		1.2	4.5	2.5
14,000 to 16,000	0.5	0.3	0.7	1.4	1.2	2.6
16,000 to 18,000	0.2	0.2		1.8	2.6	1.5
18,000 to 20,000	0.2	0.3	0.5	0.5	0.6	2.8
20,000 to 25,000	0.9	0.3	0.4	2.1	0.6	0.4
25,000 to 30,000	0.4	0.1		1.3	0.6	0.6
30,000 to 40,000	0.2	0.3	0.2		0.6	
40,000 to 50,000						
50,000 and over		0.2	0.1			
No. of lawyers covered[a]	694	743	771	575	589	606
A.M. (dollars)	2,883	2,515	2,656	5,511	5,048	5,260

Measures computed from the distributions

Absolute (dollars)

Q_3	3,334	3,010	3,192	7,008	6,241	7,108
Md	1,900	1,581	1,747	4,004	3,275	3,742
Q_1	970	840	854	2,149	1,778	1,892
I.D.	2,364	2,170	2,338	4,859	4,463	5,216
S.D.	3,921	3,859	3,713	5,099	5,306	4,921

Relative

R.I.D.	1.244	1.373	1.338	1.214	1.363	1.394
V^i	1.340	1.508	1.377	.930	1.040	.929

For footnotes see p.569.

TABLE B7

Arithmetic Mean Income of Lawyers and Number of Lawyers Covered, 1932-1936; 1937 Sample[ii]

By Region and by Size of Community

	1932	1933	1934	1935	1936
REGION		*ARITHMETIC MEAN INCOME (dollars)*			
New England	4,076	3,694	3,223	3,419	6,707
Middle Atlantic	5,451	4,930	4,484	4,859	5,078
E. N. Central	8,764	7,100	7,464	7,747	7,358
W. N. Central	4,250	3,334	3,063	3,285	3,236
S. Atlantic	2,574	3,118	3,338	3,209	4,130
E. S. Central	3,442	2,527	3,132	3,274	3,222
W. S. Central	2,587	2,353	2,723	2,561	3,022
Mountain	2,390	2,151	2,575	2,732	2,716
Pacific	6,155	5,351	4,866	5,466	6,491
SIZE OF COMMUNITY					
1,500,000 & over	10,891	8,648	8,737	9,264	9,130
500,000 - 1,500,000	4,637	3,849	3,769	3,927	5,971
250,000 - 500,000	4,935	5,010	4,135	4,580	4,927
100,000 - 250,000	3,595	3,171	3,286	3,553	4,036
25,000 - 100,000	3,697	4,312	3,874	3,548	3,952
10,000 - 25,000	4,561	3,694	4,334	4,664	5,261
2,500 - 10,000	2,742	2,360	2,461	2,439	2,667
Under 2,500	2,073	1,925	1,890	1,969	2,035
U.S.	5,303	4,604	4,567	4,795	5,202
REGION		*NUMBER OF LAWYERS COVERED*[ii]			
New England	59	67	68	75	95
Middle Atlantic	126	149	149	156	174
E. N. Central	121	142	135	151	180
W. N. Central	133	155	157	172	197
S. Atlantic	77	90	87	103	113
E. S. Central	49	53	53	53	61
W. S. Central	44	58	48	59	73
Mountain	105	127	125	136	159
Pacific	91	104	107	111	116
SIZE OF COMMUNITY					
1,500,000 & over	79	93	93	101	117
500,000 - 1,500,000	53	64	62	68	80
250,000 - 500,000	105	117	114	129	139
100,000 - 250,000	81	97	89	96	109
25,000 - 100,000	109	127	130	138	157
10,000 - 25,000	112	127	126	130	148
2,500 - 10,000	148	170	171	190	219
Under 2,500	118	150	144	164	199
U.S.	805	945	929	1,016	1,168

For footnotes see p.569.

TABLE B8

Final Estimates of Arithmetic Mean Income of Lawyers, 1932-1936

By Region and by Size of Community

REGION	1932	1933	1934 (dollars)	1935	1936
New England	3,527	3,217	3,506	3,719	7,296
Middle Atlantic	4,535	3,801	4,284	4,642	4,852
E. N. Central	5,588	5,700	5,242	5,441	5,168
W. N. Central	3,111	2,821	2,860	3,067	3,022
S. Atlantic	3,803	2,949	3,376	3,246	4,177
E. S. Central	3,633	3,463	3,694	3,861	3,800
W. S. Central	2,884	2,589	2,904	2,731	3,223
Mountain	3,033	2,384	2,732	2,899	2,882
Pacific	4,488	3,714	3,616	4,062	4,824

SIZE OF COMMUNITY					
1,500,000 & over	7,225	6,215	6,475	6,866	6,766
500,000 - 1,500,000	3,851	2,976	3,297	3,435	5,223
250,000 - 500,000	4,752	4,513	3,688	4,085	4,394
100,000 - 250,000	3,308	3,110	3,842	4,154	4,719
25,000 - 100,000	4,087	3,722	3,797	2,477	3,873
10,000 - 25,000	3,822	3,349	3,978	4,281	4,829
2,500 - 10,000	2,579	2,287	2,545	2,522	2,758
Under 2,500	1,970	1,654	1,852	1,929	1,994

These final estimates were computed from arithmetic means presented in Tables B 6a, B 6b, and B 7. The arithmetic means for 1934 from the 1935 and 1937 samples were averaged. This average was then extrapolated back to 1932 on the basis of the 1935 sample and forward to 1936 on the basis of the 1937 sample. The averages from the 1937 sample are weighted averages of the averages for each state. The averages for the 1935 sample are adjusted for the firm member bias. Both samples have been adjusted for the size of community bias.

For footnotes see p. 569.

TABLE B 9

Distribution of Income of Certified Public Accountants by Size and Measures Computed from the Distributions, 1929-1936

a   By Region

1929 (1933 SAMPLE)

INCOME CLASSES (dollars)	NE	MA	ENC	WNC	SA	ESC	WSC	MT.	PAC.	U.S.[2]
Under -2,000										
-2,000 to -1,000										
-1,000 to 0										
0										
1 to 500	1.5									0.1
500 to 1,000		0.4				3.3			1.3	0.4
1,000 to 1,500	2.0	0.4	4.5				2.7			1.3
1,500 to 2,000	3.0	0.4	2.4					6.2		1.1
2,000 to 2,500	6.0	1.4	6.7		10.2		6.4	3.1	4.6	4.2
2,500 to 3,000	1.5	3.8	1.6	6.7	8.5		6.4	8.4	2.9	3.8
3,000 to 3,500	3.0	7.1	6.6	3.0	4.8	3.3	10.0		7.5	5.9
3,500 to 4,000	9.4	5.2	1.8	12.7	3.7	10.0	11.7	15.6	8.3	6.8
4,000 to 5,000	9.5	9.7	14.3	12.7	15.3	35.6	13.0	18.8	21.6	14.3
5,000 to 6,000	13.9	9.0	8.2	18.7	18.0	10.0	4.1	4.1	13.8	10.9
6,000 to 7,000	7.0	9.9	12.0	3.0	11.4	14.4	8.3	16.6	16.3	10.7
7,000 to 8,000	12.6	3.8	5.8	5.2	7.9	3.3	11.1	7.3	5.4	6.1
8,000 to 9,000	8.8	7.4	11.1	10.4	4.8	3.3	6.3	3.1	6.4	7.8
9,000 to 10,000	4.0	5.5	5.1	10.5			7.5	9.5	5.4	5.2
10,000 to 12,000	4.5	7.5	5.8	11.9	7.0	13.4	2.1		2.5	6.1
12,000 to 14,000	3.5	8.0	2.9	5.2	1.6	3.3	2.1			4.0
14,000 to 16,000	1.5	3.6	3.9				3.5	4.1	2.7	2.7
16,000 to 18,000	4.0	2.5	3.8		4.8		2.1			2.4
18,000 to 20,000		3.4						3.1	1.3	1.3
20,000 to 25,000	1.5	4.0	2.7							1.9
25,000 to 30,000	3.2	2.5			2.1		2.7			1.4
30,000 to 40,000		3.1								1.0
40,000 to 50,000			0.8 *							0.2
50,000 and over		1.4								0.4
No. of accountants covered[a]	88	314	168	56	78	38	68	42	104	963
A.M. (dollars)	7,533	10,416	7,513	6,730	6,470	6,147	6,556	6,093	5,905	7,926

Measures computed from the distributions

Absolute (dollars)

	NE	MA	ENC	WNC	SA	ESC	WSC	MT.	PAC.	U.S.
Q_3	8,662	12,870	9,005	9,252	7,396	6,885	8,198	7,291	6,919	9,308
Md	6,064	7,683	6,334	5,801	5,418	4,936	4,980	4,886	5,274	6,116
Q_1	3,935	4,629	4,104	4,210	3,710	4,235	3,470	3,732	4,018	4,099
I.D.	4,727	8,241	4,901	5,042	3,686	2,650	4,728	3,559	2,901	5,209
S.D.	5,485	9,417	5,707	2,973	4,640	2,790	4,952	3,721	2,988	6,723

Relative

	NE	MA	ENC	WNC	SA	ESC	WSC	MT.	PAC.	U.S.
R.I.D.	.780	1.073	.774	.869	.680	.537	.949	.728	.550	.852
V^1	.735	.894	.758	.436	.709	.463	.742	.613	.505	.843

For footnotes see p. 569.

TABLE B9a (cont.)

1930 (1933 SAMPLE)

INCOME CLASSES (dollars)	NE	MA	ENC	WNC	SA	ESC	WSC	MT.	PAC.	U.S.[2]
Under -2,000										
-2,000 to -1,000										
-1,000 to 0		0.6	0.7							0.3
0										
1 to 500	1.4	0.4				3.1				0.4
500 to 1,000			2.2	6.4	1.5				1.3	1.1
1,000 to 1,500		2.2	5.5				5.0	2.9		2.1
1,500 to 2,000	1.4	1.4	4.1		2.9			2.9	1.3	1.8
2,000 to 2,500	4.3	2.2	3.5				6.4	6.7	6.4	3.1
2,500 to 3,000	5.7	1.2	6.0	8.4	2.0	3.1	5.0	2.9	3.8	3.8
3,000 to 3,500	10.5	4.8	6.2	6.3	16.9	6.2	8.2	9.6	12.7	8.0
3,500 to 4,000	1.9	6.8	4.5	6.3	7.4	5.3	7.4	10.5	3.8	5.8
4,000 to 5,000	20.6	9.1	13.2	15.3	14.3	32.2	25.7	14.5	21.2	15.4
5,000 to 6,000	6.7	7.7	14.0	16.0	20.2	9.4	11.6	22.2	22.5	12.8
6,000 to 7,000	9.4	10.0	6.5	10.6	13.5	10.4	8.6	3.8	10.2	9.3
7,000 to 8,000	8.7	11.5	7.2	7.7		10.4	5.0	5.7	1.3	7.7
8,000 to 9,000	6.7	4.1	8.7	5.7	8.4	3.1	5.0	3.8	9.9	6.2
9,000 to 10,000	8.4	4.8	3.8	4.2	2.5		4.3	11.6		4.3
10,000 to 12,000	2.9	8.4	4.9	6.3	5.5	12.5	2.1		1.3	5.5
12,000 to 14,000	4.8	6.1	1.5	7.0	1.5				1.3	3.4
14,000 to 16,000		3.9	2.7			4.2	3.6			2.1
16,000 to 18,000	1.4	3.0	2.0		1.5				3.3	1.9
18,000 to 20,000		1.8	0.7							0.7
20,000 to 25,000		3.2					2.1			1.2
25,000 to 30,000	5.0	2.1	1.3					2.9		1.5
30,000 to 40,000		2.9								0.9
40,000 to 50,000		1.6	0.7		2.0					0.8
50,000 and over										
No. of accountants covered[a]	89	327	181	61	84	42	65	46	106	1,002
A.M. (dollars)	7,200	9,761	6,384	5,935	6,316	6,231	5,593	5,708	5,457	7,314

Measures computed from the distributions

Absolute (dollars)

	NE	MA	ENC	WNC	SA	ESC	WSC	MT.	PAC.	U.S.
Q₃	8,621	11,924	8,154	7,753	6,729	7,500	6,664	6,759	6,212	8,560
Md	5,595	7,310	5,290	5,459	5,252	4,999	4,703	5,003	4,982	5,647
Q₁	3,905	4,590	3,238	3,818	3,616	4,223	3,533	3,505	3,484	3,883
I.D.	4,716	7,334	4,916	3,935	3,113	3,277	3,131	3,254	2,728	4,677
S.D.	5,604	8,400	5,576	2,755	6,133	3,126	3,783	4,361	2,979	6,410

Relative

	NE	MA	ENC	WNC	SA	ESC	WSC	MT.	PAC.	U.S.
R.I.D.	.843	1.003	.929	.721	.593	.656	.666	.650	.548	.828
V[1]	.781	.848	.858	.457	.949	.505	.663	.753	.543	.865

For footnotes see p. 569.

TABLE B9a (cont.)

1931 (1933 SAMPLE)

INCOME CLASSES (dollars)	NE	MA	ENC	WNC	SA	ESC	WSC	MT.	PAC.	U.S.[2]
Under -2,000			2.0							0.3
-2,000 to -1,000			1.3			3.1				0.3
-1,000 to 0			2.9	3.4						0.7
0										
1 to 500		0.5			2.7	3.1	2.0			0.7
500 to 1,000		1.2	3.8					2.9		1.2
1,000 to 1,500	2.9	1.9	3.1				4.7	5.7	3.8	2.6
1,500 to 2,000		5.2	5.9	2.0	4.1		4.0	3.8	2.5	3.9
2,000 to 2,500	5.7	3.6	4.4	8.6	4.6	3.1	12.8	9.6	10.2	5.8
2,500 to 3,000	10.0	6.9	3.1	8.0	10.2	3.1	4.7	5.7	7.8	6.6
3,000 to 3,500	6.2	3.1	8.8	6.6	7.3	17.8	7.8	7.8	9.0	6.7
3,500 to 4,000	8.6	8.3	6.4	11.3	13.2	6.2	9.0	17.2	7.4	8.8
4,000 to 5,000	18.2	11.5	15.6	16.1	24.2	17.7	14.2	3.8	23.6	15.9
5,000 to 6,000	8.8	8.3	10.5	6.6	9.6	17.7	13.8	21.1	15.2	10.8
6,000 to 7,000	11.4	8.7	7.9	11.3	10.3	8.4	8.7	6.7	5.3	8.8
7,000 to 8,000	7.8	5.8	4.4	8.6	2.7	15.6	10.1	2.9	2.5	5.8
8,000 to 9,000	7.2	5.4	5.5	6.0	1.4	4.2		4.9	4.3	4.7
9,000 to 10,000	2.9	5.0	1.8	6.0					1.2	2.7
10,000 to 12,000	1.9	7.8	4.6	2.7	2.7		2.0	4.9	2.9	4.5
12,000 to 14,000	1.9	8.1			3.7				4.4	3.6
14,000 to 16,000	5.0	1.3		2.7			3.5			1.3
16,000 to 18,000		1.9	4.7		1.4		2.7			1.7
18,000 to 20,000	1.4		1.0							0.3
20,000 to 25,000		2.1						2.9		0.8
25,000 to 30,000		2.4	1.5							1.0
30,000 to 40,000		0.9	0.8							0.4
40,000 to 50,000										
50,000 and over					1.8					0.2
No. of accountants covered[4]	89	336	173	64	90	42	67	46	103	1,020
A.M. (dollars)	5,929	7,519	5,799	5,361	5,739	4,592	5,005	4,923	4,854	6,072

Measures computed from the distributions

Absolute (dollars)

	NE	MA	ENC	WNC	SA	ESC	WSC	MT.	PAC.	U.S.
Q_3	7,407	9,905	6,927	7,107	5,903	6,381	6,228	5,871	5,705	7,326
Md	4,909	5,936	4,540	4,621	4,325	4,766	4,352	3,918	4,395	4,780
Q_1	3,508	3,654	2,776	3,223	3,232	3,352	2,656	2,759	3,038	3,217
I.D.	3,899	6,251	4,151	3,884	2,671	3,029	3,572	3,112	2,667	4,109
S.D.	3,568	5,990	5,582	2,999	6,941	2,183	3,474	3,849	2,708	5,152

Relative

	NE	MA	ENC	WNC	SA	ESC	WSC	MT.	PAC.	U.S.
R.I.D.	.794	1.053	.914	.841	.618	.636	.821	.794	.607	.860
V^1	.599	.790	.968	.564	1.203	.458	.686	.766	.553	.843

For footnotes see p.569.

TABLE B9a (cont.)

1932 (1933 SAMPLE)

INCOME CLASSES (dollars)	NE	MA	ENC	WNC	SA	ESC	WSC	MT.	PAC.	U.S.[2]
Under -2,000									1.2	0.1
-2,000 to -1,000	1.3	4.5	0.7							1.6
-1,000 to 0		0.7						2.9		0.2
0				3.4						0.2
1 to 500	1.8	0.9	2.1			3.0	1.9			1.1
500 to 1,000		1.7	3.6	4.6	1.4		1.9	5.7	1.2	2.1
1,000 to 1,500	1.3	3.7	2.8	2.0	2.7	3.0	2.5	3.8	2.3	3.0
1,500 to 2,000	4.0	5.0	5.4	9.2	10.2	6.1	8.2	9.6	12.7	7.1
2,000 to 2,500	12.4	7.2	10.1	6.6	8.2	16.3	9.7	6.7	9.4	8.9
2,500 to 3,000	11.6	5.4	7.9	4.6	8.7	10.1	6.3	11.6	15.9	8.3
3,000 to 3,500	11.1	5.6	12.8	5.3	10.1	12.1	16.9	13.4	15.0	10.1
3,500 to 4,000	10.2	5.4	8.9	4.6	12.3	7.1	1.9		7.7	7.1
4,000 to 5,000	9.3	15.1	18.9	15.1	17.5	13.2	29.2	15.5	7.0	15.6
5,000 to 6,000	9.2	6.6	13.0	17.1	12.7	8.2	5.7	11.5	10.4	9.7
6,000 to 7,000	9.1	6.0	1.9	10.5	8.8	10.1	6.9	10.7	10.4	7.0
7,000 to 8,000	7.3	7.1	4.0	3.9	2.7	10.7	1.9		3.5	5.0
8,000 to 9,000	2.3	6.8		6.6			1.9			2.9
9,000 to 10,000	1.8	3.0	2.4	2.6					2.5	2.0
10,000 to 12,000	4.2	6.4	1.7	3.9			1.9		1.2	3.3
12,000 to 14,000	3.1	3.5	0.9							1.6
14,000 to 16,000		2.0	0.9		2.7		3.2			1.2
16,000 to 18,000		1.4								0.4
18,000 to 20,000		1.2	0.9					2.9		0.7
20,000 to 25,000		1.5	1.2							0.7
25,000 to 30,000					1.8					0.2
30,000 to 40,000										
40,000 to 50,000										
50,000 and over										
No. of accountants covered[4]	95	341	196	64	89	43	73	46	108	1,063
A.M. (dollars)	4,659	5,816	4,384	4,577	4,622	3,932	4,235	3,900	3,752	4,777

Measures computed from the distributions

Absolute (dollars)

	NE	MA	ENC	WNC	SA	ESC	WSC	MT.	PAC.	U.S.
Q_3	6,297	8,131	5,152	6,246	5,299	5,492	4,882	5,003	5,273	5,993
Md	3,816	4,707	3,719	4,646	3,851	3,470	4,027	3,360	3,249	4,017
Q_1	2,678	2,694	2,478	2,446	2,639	2,394	2,570	2,222	2,413	2,541
I.D.	3,619	5,437	2,674	3,800	2,660	3,098	2,312	2,781	2,860	3,452
S.D.	2,889	4,616	3,538	2,665	3,947	1,748	2,749	3,139	2,175	3,708

Relative

	NE	MA	ENC	WNC	SA	ESC	WSC	MT.	PAC.	U.S.
R.I.D.	.948	1.155	.719	.818	.691	.893	.574	.828	.880	.859
V^1	.614	.786	.802	.570	.855	.441	.642	.798	.568	.768

For footnotes see p.569.

1932 (1935 SAMPLE)

INCOME CLASSES (dollars)	NE	MA	ENC	WNC	SA	ESC	WSC	MT.	PAC.	U.S.[2]
Under -2,000		0.2								0.1
-2,000 to -1,000	1.3									0.1
-1,000 to 0					0.9		2.0		0.8	0.3
0			0.8							0.1
1 to 500	1.6	1.2	3.2	4.8	0.9	4.3		2.4	0.8	1.9
500 to 1,000	1.3	2.5	4.5	2.0	0.9	2.2	5.9	9.7	8.8	3.6
1,000 to 1,500	14.5	4.1	5.0	2.0	6.4	2.2	12.5	7.3	2.1	5.3
1,500 to 2,000	6.6	8.4	9.8	14.3	10.7	10.8	7.9	7.3	6.5	8.6
2,000 to 2,500	14.5	10.4	10.9	9.5	17.0	13.0	3.9	9.7	11.8	10.7
2,500 to 3,000	11.8	12.7	9.4	5.6	12.4	12.9	11.2	15.3	19.3	12.4
3,000 to 3,500	6.6	8.7	12.0	11.6	12.6	8.6	9.9	7.3	11.6	10.2
3,500 to 4,000	10.9	5.1	8.5	2.0	7.3	8.6	3.9	10.5	13.2	7.4
4,000 to 5,000	9.1	13.7	15.8	24.0	14.1	14.3	19.3	11.3	9.0	14.0
5,000 to 6,000	4.1	11.1	7.4	9.7	4.7	8.7	3.9	11.3	7.4	8.9
6,000 to 7,000	1.8	4.9	3.5	5.5	5.3		7.9	5.6	3.8	4.6
7,000 to 8,000	3.5	2.1	4.1	2.0	2.6				1.7	2.3
8,000 to 9,000		2.7		2.0	1.5	11.6		2.4		2.0
9,000 to 10,000	5.4	2.0	1.5			2.9				1.1
10,000 to 12,000	2.6	2.2	0.9	2.7	1.8		6.2		1.1	2.0
12,000 to 14,000		1.7	1.7	2.0			2.0			1.3
14,000 to 16,000		2.6			0.9		3.4		0.8	1.3
16,000 to 18,000		0.9	0.5							0.4
18,000 to 20,000		2.3								0.9
20,000 to 25,000		0.2	0.2						1.1	0.2
25,000 to 30,000		0.2								0.1
30,000 to 40,000										
40,000 to 50,000			0.5							0.1
50,000 and over										
No. of accountants covered[a]	96	529	285	63	130	56	61	46	133	1,415
A.M. (dollars)	4,067	4,925	3,868	3,991	3,555	3,823	4,232	3,243	3,545	4,218

Measures computed from the distributions

Absolute (dollars)

	NE	MA	ENC	WNC	SA	ESC	WSC	MT.	PAC.	U.S.
Q_3	5,082	5,722	4,695	4,960	4,418	4,871	4,917	4,500	3,998	4,029
Md	3,246	3,678	3,266	3,526	3,034	3,274	3,332	2,948	2,994	3,336
Q_1	2,142	2,412	2,071	2,096	2,155	2,216	1,791	1,889	2,248	2,235
I.D.	2,940	3,310	2,624	2,864	2,263	2,655	3,126	2,611	1,750	2,794
S.D.	2,962	4,162	3,848	2,547	2,247	2,371	3,467	1,857	2,883	3,568

Relative

	NE	MA	ENC	WNC	SA	ESC	WSC	MT.	PAC.	U.S.
R.I.D.	.906	.900	.803	.812	.746	.811	.938	.886	.585	.838
V^1	.731	.840	.980	.637	.629	.612	.818	.569	.809	.840

For footnotes see p. 569.

TABLE B9a (cont.)

1933 (1935 SAMPLE)

INCOME CLASSES (dollars)	NE	MA	ENC	WNC	SA	ESC	WSC	MT.	PAC.	U.S.[2]
Under -2,000			0.4							0.1
-2,000 to -1,000										
-1,000 to 0		0.2			0.8					0.2
0			0.7							0.2
1 to 500	3.9	1.5	3.0	5.5	0.8		2.0	7.6	1.8	2.2
500 to 1,000	6.1	3.1	6.4	4.3	3.2	4.3	9.8	2.5	4.6	4.4
1,000 to 1,500	6.9	4.5	7.6	11.0	6.2	4.3	6.5	7.6	1.5	5.5
1,500 to 2,000	3.5	6.9	9.0	5.5	13.2	18.3	13.7	5.1	12.9	8.9
2,000 to 2,500	12.5	13.6	15.3	9.8	15.7	2.2	10.4	10.2	20.7	13.8
2,500 to 3,000	11.6	12.5	9.1	11.7	9.7	18.8	5.9	18.6	15.7	11.9
3,000 to 3,500	9.5	8.9	12.8	12.0	12.2	13.0	13.0	13.6	10.0	10.8
3,500 to 4,000	12.1	8.1	8.0	15.0	9.2	2.2	2.0	7.6	11.6	8.7
4,000 to 5,000	8.2	12.6	12.1	12.3	14.5	10.1	9.4	2.5	6.8	11.5
5,000 to 6,000	10.2	7.8	8.4	9.2	6.8	2.9	10.4	18.6	5.4	8.0
6,000 to 7,000	6.0	5.0	2.7		2.4	10.1	8.5	5.9	5.5	4.5
7,000 to 8,000	4.0	0.5	1.3		2.7	8.8			0.8	1.5
8,000 to 9,000		1.2		1.8			8.6		0.8	1.1
9,000 to 10,000		3.4	1.0		0.8	2.9				1.7
10,000 to 12,000	4.0	2.6	0.4		0.8	2.2			1.8	1.6
12,000 to 14,000	1.3	1.2	1.0	1.8	0.8					0.9
14,000 to 16,000		1.4	0.4							0.6
16,000 to 18,000		2.9								1.1
18,000 to 20,000		0.2								0.1
20,000 to 25,000		1.5								0.5
25,000 to 30,000		0.2	0.4							0.2
30,000 to 40,000										
40,000 to 50,000										
50,000 and over										
No. of accountants covered[a]	96	555	302	69	143	56	61	44	147	1,489
A.M. (dollars)	3,791	4,742	3,240	3,171	3,299	3,840	3,587	3,238	3,212	3,886

Measures computed from the distributions

Absolute (dollars)

	NE	MA	ENC	WNC	SA	ESC	WSC	MT.	PAC.	U.S.
Q_3	5,031	5,389	4,227	4,012	4,268	5,615	5,241	4,418	3,830	4,724
Md	3,287	3,431	2,921	3,090	3,013	3,077	3,071	2,954	2,768	3,129
Q_1	2,184	2,323	1,883	1,876	2,024	1,946	1,748	2,104	2,100	2,127
I.D.	2,847	3,066	2,344	2,136	2,244	3,669	3,493	2,314	1,730	2,597
S.D.	2,575	4,327	3,062	2,099	2,005	2,422	2,307	1,744	1,864	3,360

Relative

	NE	MA	ENC	WNC	SA	ESC	WSC	MT.	PAC.	U.S.
R.I.D.	.866	.894	.802	.691	.745	1.192	1.137	.783	.625	.830
V^1	.676	.898	.937	.650	.598	.618	.647	.542	.578	.854

For footnotes see p. 569.

TABLE B 9 a (cont.)

1934 (1935 SAMPLE)

INCOME CLASSES (dollars)	NE	MA	ENC	WNC	SA	ESC	WSC	MT.	PAC.	U.S.[2]
Under -2,000										
-2,000 to -1,000										
-1,000 to 0		0.4		1.8					0.8	0.3
0										
1 to 500	2.5	1.3	2.9	1.8	1.6		1.8	7.1		1.8
500 to 1,000	3.8	2.9	5.5	5.3	4.3	6.2	5.5	7.1	4.8	4.2
1,000 to 1,500	2.5	3.7	5.6	7.6	3.0		3.7	2.4	2.3	3.7
1,500 to 2,000	5.4	6.3	8.8	10.5	11.6	10.3	11.7	7.1	9.7	8.1
2,000 to 2,500	3.8	10.5	10.2	5.3	6.7	2.1	12.3	7.1	15.4	9.5
2,500 to 3,000	13.4	10.9	11.6	7.0	14.5	10.5	11.1	15.0	10.4	11.6
3,000 to 3,500	7.2	12.0	9.9	10.6	8.0	13.8	3.7	7.1	13.0	10.5
3,500 to 4,000	13.8	7.5	4.4	6.4	13.9	8.9	8.7	4.7	11.4	8.3
4,000 to 5,000	16.1	13.8	11.8	13.6	16.7	22.7	10.5	18.1	18.0	14.6
5,000 to 6,000	14.2	10.4	13.6	16.0	7.2	2.1	9.8	7.9	5.3	10.2
6,000 to 7,000	6.8	5.4	6.2	6.4	4.6	7.5	15.1	6.3	4.9	6.0
7,000 to 8,000	5.4	1.5	1.8		4.3		1.8	3.1	0.8	1.9
8,000 to 9,000	1.3	1.8	3.2	1.8	1.6	2.7	2.5	2.4	1.5	2.2
9,000 to 10,000		1.6	2.1		1.9	9.0			1.8	1.7
10,000 to 12,000		2.3		2.3		2.1		2.4		1.2
12,000 to 14,000	3.9	3.1	0.8	1.8						1.7
14,000 to 16,000		0.2				2.1	1.8			0.2
16,000 to 18,000		1.7	0.4		0.2			2.4		0.8
18,000 to 20,000		0.5	0.6	1.8						0.4
20,000 to 25,000		2.1								0.8
25,000 to 30,000			0.4							0.1
30,000 to 40,000		0.2								0.1
40,000 to 50,000										
50,000 and over										
No. of accountants covered[3]	95	567	307	71	143	59	63	47	149	1,518
A.M. (dollars)	4,312	4,872	3,924	4,031	3,685	4,493	3,866	3,990	3,478	4,274

Measures computed from the distributions

Absolute (dollars)

	NE	MA	ENC	WNC	SA	ESC	WSC	MT.	PAC.	U.S.
Q_3	5,467	5,555	5,302	4,158	4,688	5,238	5,617	4,968	4,404	5,232
Md	3,916	3,638	3,266	3,510	3,514	3,900	3,512	3,306	3,258	3,515
Q_1	2,764	2,500	2,106	1,908	2,339	2,808	2,092	2,098	2,242	2,356
I.D.	2,703	3,055	3,196	3,250	2,349	2,430	3,525	2,870	2,162	2,876
S.D.	2,522	4,430	3,089	3,205	2,049	2,913	2,688	3,067	1,784	3,483

Relative

	NE	MA	ENC	WNC	SA	ESC	WSC	MT.	PAC.	U.S.
R.I.D.	.690	.840	.979	.926	.668	.623	1.004	.868	.664	.818
V[1]	.582	.892	.773	.783	.550	.634	.682	.775	.511	.803

For footnotes see p.569.

TABLE B9a (cont.)

1934 (1937 SAMPLE)

INCOME CLASSES (dollars)	NE	MA	ENC	WNC	SA	ESC	WSC	MT.	PAC.	U.S.[2]
Under -2,000		0.4								0.1
-2,000 to -1,000			1.2							0.2
-1,000 to 0		0.4					2.2			0.3
0		0.4								0.1
1 to 500	2.5	0.4	3.2		4.7	5.9		14.2	4.5	2.6
500 to 1,000	2.5	4.3			2.5		4.5	7.1		2.6
1,000 to 1,500	5.0	6.1	5.5		3.3	8.8		3.6	4.5	5.1
1,500 to 2,000	10.5	5.0	8.6	9.5	7.7	2.9	6.7	8.0	10.5	7.1
2,000 to 2,500	9.9	12.7	12.6	3.2	7.5	6.6	20.4	11.6	12.4	11.6
2,500 to 3,000	8.0	12.7	12.2	15.1	12.4	12.5	10.6	3.6	19.2	12.5
3,000 to 3,500	7.4	11.8	10.4	15.1	10.7	11.7	8.9	7.1	11.3	10.9
3,500 to 4,000	10.5	7.3	2.8	6.3	9.1		15.8	17.8	17.3	8.4
4,000 to 5,000	9.9	12.7	17.1	14.2	16.3	31.7	9.1	8.0	9.0	14.0
5,000 to 6,000	15.7	10.4	10.2	10.2	8.6	5.9	6.7	8.9	1.5	9.1
6,000 to 7,000	7.6	3.6	9.8	10.2	5.7		7.8		1.5	5.2
7,000 to 8,000	5.6	2.8	1.0		5.9	2.9	2.2	6.6	4.9	3.2
8,000 to 9,000	2.5	1.2	1.6	3.2	1.1		2.8	3.6	1.5	1.6
9,000 to 10,000		0.7	1.2		2.2	11.1			1.9	1.4
10,000 to 12,000	2.5	2.8	1.8		1.4		2.2			1.8
12,000 to 14,000		0.9		3.2	1.1					0.6
14,000 to 16,000		1.2								0.4
16,000 to 18,000		1.1								0.4
18,000 to 20,000			0.8	3.9						0.3
20,000 to 25,000		0.4								0.1
25,000 to 30,000		0.8								0.3
30,000 to 40,000										
40,000 to 50,000										
50,000 and over										
No. of accountants covered[a]	50	327	168	40	111	42	55	34	74	901
A.M. (dollars)	4,056	4,285	3,862	4,613	3,966	4,000	3,607	3,154	3,274	3,984

Measures computed from the distributions.

Absolute (dollars)

	NE	MA	ENC	WNC	SA	ESC	WSC	MT.	PAC.	U.S.
Q_3	5,560	5,097	5,068	5,280	5,105	4,838	4,644	4,252	3,864	4,967
Md	3,700	3,332	3,322	3,596	3,571	4,049	3,310	3,136	2,970	3,358
Q_1	2,231	2,320	2,258	2,710	2,456	2,531	2,284	1,505	2,220	2,296
I.D.	3,329	2,777	2,810	2,570	2,649	2,307	2,360	2,747	1,644	2,671
S.D.	2,289	3,860	2,584	3,710	2,408	2,454	2,151	2,226	1,854	3,072

Relative

	NE	MA	ENC	WNC	SA	ESC	WSC	MT.	PAC.	U.S.
R.I.D.	.900	.833	.846	.715	.742	.570	.713	.876	.554	.795
V^1	.565	.891	.660	.782	.600	.603	.580	.701	.556	.761

For footnotes see p.569.

TABLE B 9 a (cont.)

1935 (1937 SAMPLE)

INCOME CLASSES (dollars)	NE	MA	ENC	WNC	SA	ESC	WSC	MT.	PAC.	U.S.[2]
Under -2,000										
-2,000 to -1,000										
-1,000 to 0		0.4	0.8							0.3
0										
1 to 500	4.8	0.7	2.3		3.5		6.2	9.6	3.0	2.4
500 to 1,000	2.2	3.0				2.9	4.1	6.4	2.7	2.1
1,000 to 1,500	6.5	3.7	3.8	8.2	4.5	8.6		3.2	5.4	4.3
1,500 to 2,000	4.8	7.6	8.4	10.3	3.5	5.7	10.3	9.6	2.5	6.9
2,000 to 2,500	14.0	10.0	8.7	3.9	11.8		13.4	11.2	6.7	9.4
2,500 to 3,000	17.8	9.1	11.6	9.0	9.0	9.3	6.2	7.2	24.8	11.3
3,000 to 3,500	6.5	15.2	11.0	23.3	13.3	15.0	9.8	19.1	21.2	14.5
3,500 to 4,000		9.6	10.8	8.4	10.1	5.7	6.2		10.2	8.5
4,000 to 5,000	9.2	16.7	13.2	10.4	14.1	27.9	18.0	14.4	8.4	14.7
5,000 to 6,000	13.0	6.4	7.6	5.8	10.1	5.7	8.3	7.2	9.4	7.8
6,000 to 7,000	14.3	5.8	6.6	8.4	8.1	5.7	7.2	6.4	2.7	6.6
7,000 to 8,000	4.8	2.9	5.3	9.0	4.8		8.2		1.3	3.9
8,000 to 9,000	2.2	1.4	3.0		1.1					1.3
9,000 to 10,000		0.4	2.3		2.0	6.4		5.9	1.7	1.4
10,000 to 12,000		2.9	1.5		3.2	7.2	2.1			2.1
12,000 to 14,000		0.7	1.7		1.1					0.7
14,000 to 16,000		0.8								0.3
16,000 to 18,000		0.4	0.8	3.2						0.4
18,000 to 20,000		0.9								0.3
20,000 to 25,000		0.4	0.8							0.3
25,000 to 30,000										
30,000 to 40,000		0.9								0.3
40,000 to 50,000										
50,000 and over										
No. of accountants covered[a]	59	341	176	52	116	43	61	38	85	971
A.M. (dollars)	3,732	4,511	4,382	4,231	4,185	4,376	3,800	3,308	3,325	4,177

Measures computed from the distributions

Absolute (dollars)

	NE	MA	ENC	WNC	SA	ESC	WSC	MT.	PAC.	U.S.
Q_3	5,713	4,940	5,605	5,247	5,519	5,004	5,118	4,612	3,930	5,073
Md	2,997	3,518	3,666	3,397	3,720	4,105	3,502	3,076	3,118	3,460
Q_1	2,238	2,482	2,550	2,640	2,599	2,925	2,166	2,806	2,594	2,479
I.D.	3,475	2,458	3,055	2,607	2,920	2,079	2,952	2,806	1,336	2,594
S.D.	2,142	4,328	3,170	2,952	2,467	2,686	2,249	2,297	1,627	3,334

Relative

	NE	MA	ENC	WNC	SA	ESC	WSC	MT.	PAC.	U.S.
R.I.D.	1.159	.699	.833	.767	.785	.506	.843	.912	.428	.750
V^1	.562	.944	.708	.695	.575	.594	.587	.683	.482	.784

For footnotes see p. 569.

TABLE B9a (concl.)

1936 (1937 SAMPLE)

INCOME CLASSES (dollars)	NE	MA	ENC	WNC	SA	ESC	WSC	MT.	PAC.	U.S.[2]
Under -2,000										
-2,000 to -1,000									1.2	0.1
-1,000 to 0			0.7							0.1
0										
1 to 500	4.2	0.3	3.0		3.6			12.7		1.8
500 to 1,000		2.5	1.8		2.6	5.3	5.6	3.2	2.5	2.5
1,000 to 1,500	4.2	3.5	3.2	3.1	3.6	2.7	1.9		3.7	3.2
1,500 to 2,000	6.4	4.3	4.5	13.0	4.1	5.3	7.9	12.7	5.6	5.6
2,000 to 2,500	14.3	6.9	8.1	3.8	8.8	5.3	7.4	7.1	12.8	8.2
2,500 to 3,000	11.1	12.7	6.8	9.4	6.4		7.9	7.1	11.5	9.5
3,000 to 3,500	2.1	11.1	10.5	9.9	13.1	18.7	5.6	9.5	14.6	10.9
3,500 to 4,000	8.5	8.7	7.9	8.2	4.6	13.1	8.4	13.5	12.1	8.7
4,000 to 5,000	11.1	17.6	17.2	18.6	14.7	12.1	18.6	6.3	14.0	15.9
5,000 to 6,000	14.0	12.0	11.9	5.6	13.3	8.0	15.9	15.0	14.0	12.3
6,000 to 7,000	12.2	5.4	4.7	3.1	5.4	14.0	8.9	7.1	2.5	6.0
7,000 to 8,000	9.6	4.4	8.2	14.2	9.0		4.6		2.5	5.8
8,000 to 9,000	2.1	3.1	1.8		3.3			5.8	1.2	2.3
9,000 to 10,000		0.7	2.3		2.9	8.7	3.7		1.6	1.8
10,000 to 12,000		2.0	2.5	8.0	2.3	6.7	3.7			2.4
12,000 to 14,000		1.8	1.1		1.0					0.9
14,000 to 16,000		1.5	2.3							0.9
16,000 to 18,000		0.4			1.0					0.3
18,000 to 20,000			0.7							0.1
20,000 to 25,000			0.7	3.1						0.3
25,000 to 30,000		1.1								0.4
30,000 to 40,000										
40,000 to 50,000										
50,000 and over										
No. of accountants covered[4]	59	368	188	55	124	48	68	39	93	1,043
A.M. (dollars)	4,145	4,757	4,817	5,133	4,619	4,714	4,491	3,498	3,633	4,556

Measures computed from the distributions

Absolute (dollars)

	NE	MA	ENC	WNC	SA	ESC	WSC	MT.	PAC.	U.S.
Q_3	5,923	5,613	5,948	7,025	6,019	6,313	5,744	5,198	4,771	5,687
Md	3,947	3,999	4,199	4,142	4,298	3,980	4,291	3,382	3,430	3,963
Q_1	2,354	2,793	2,760	2,774	2,676	3,169	2,644	1,862	2,464	2,684
I.D.	3,569	2,820	3,188	4,251	3,343	3,144	3,100	3,336	2,307	3,003
S.D.	2,135	3,700	3,534	4,040	2,885	2,756	2,398	2,212	1,818	3,240

Relative

	NE	MA	ENC	WNC	SA	ESC	WSC	MT.	PAC.	U.S.
R.I.D.	.904	.705	.759	1.026	.794	.790	.722	.986	.673	.758
V^i	.514	.764	.717	.772	.618	.569	.535	.629	.493	.700

For footnotes see p.569.

TABLE B 9 (cont.)

b   By Size of Community

1929 (1933 SAMPLE)

Communities with populations (in thousands) of

INCOME CLASSES (dollars)	1,500 & over	500 to 1,500	250 to 500	100 to 250	25 to 100	under 25	U.S.[7]
Under -2,000							
-2,000 to -1,000							
-1,000 to 0							
0							
1 to 500		0.8					0.1
500 to 1,000		1.6		1.1			0.4
1,000 to 1,500	1.9	0.8	1.1	2.6			1.3
1,500 to 2,000	0.4	1.6	0.8	2.3	0.9	2.2	1.1
2,000 to 2,500	1.8	1.9	6.5	6.9	7.9	2.2	4.2
2,500 to 3,000	3.2	1.9	1.7	2.3	9.5	8.9	3.8
3,000 to 3,500	6.3	6.6		6.9	7.8	11.2	5.9
3,500 to 4,000	4.6	5.5	10.7	4.9	10.3	7.5	6.8
4,000 to 5,000	8.0	19.9	17.8	13.0	13.0	27.7	14.3
5,000 to 6,000	6.9	15.1	13.1	12.4	8.9	14.2	10.9
6,000 to 7,000	11.8	9.1	12.9	11.7	7.2	11.2	10.7
7,000 to 8,000	4.7	9.8	2.0	10.6	8.4	2.2	6.1
8,000 to 9,000	10.5	5.3	5.0	4.5	10.0	5.2	7.8
9,000 to 10,000	5.9	5.2	5.9	4.9	4.1	3.0	5.2
10,000 to 12,000	6.8	5.8	8.5	5.3	4.8	2.2	6.1
12,000 to 14,000	8.7	0.8	2.8	1.5	2.8		4.0
14,000 to 16,000	3.2	3.4	4.5	1.1	1.2		2.7
16,000 to 18,000	3.8	2.2	1.1	2.3	1.9		2.4
18,000 to 20,000	2.4	0.8	0.8	1.1		2.2	1.3
20,000 to 25,000	4.5	0.8	1.4				1.9
25,000 to 30,000	2.0	0.8	1.1	2.4	1.2		1.4
30,000 to 40,000	1.4		1.4	2.3			1.0
40,000 to 50,000			0.8				0.2
50,000 and over	1.3						0.4
No. of accountants covered[a]	334	159	159	114	140	50	963
A.M. (dollars)	10,010	6,724	7,979	7,318	6,214	5,220	7,926

Measures computed from the distributions

Absolute (dollars)

Q_3	12,504	8,036	9,599	8,089	8,109	6,098	9,308
Md	8,030	5,607	5,873	5,815	5,061	4,648	6,116
Q_1	4,839	4,206	4,235	3,800	3,422	3,527	4,099
I.D.	7,665	3,830	5,364	4,283	4,687	2,571	5,209
S.D.	8,560	4,275	6,623	6,366	4,078	2,856	6,723

Relative

R.I.D.	.955	.683	.913	.737	.926	.553	.852
V^i	.848	.632	.832	.864	.653	.539	.843

For footnotes see p. 569.

TABLE B9b (cont.)

1930 (1933 SAMPLE)

Communities with populations (in thousands) of

INCOME CLASSES (dollars)	1,500 & over	500 to 1,500	250 to 500	100 to 250	25 to 100	under 25	U.S.[2]
Under -2,000							
-2,000 to -1,000							
-1,000 to 0	0.5			1.1			0.3
0							
1 to 500	0.4	0.8		1.1			0.4
500 to 1,000	0.4	1.6	3.1		1.2		1.1
1,000 to 1,500	2.6	1.6	2.8	2.1	0.9	2.2	2.1
1,500 to 2,000	1.7	1.6	1.7	2.1	2.1	2.2	1.8
2,000 to 2,500	2.7	3.2	2.5	3.2	2.7	7.4	3.1
2,500 to 3,000	2.6	1.6	3.1	4.6	8.0	4.4	3.8
3,000 to 3,500	5.5	5.8	5.9	8.0	15.0	17.8	8.0
3,500 to 4,000	4.1	7.2	2.8	9.4	6.4	10.5	5.8
4,000 to 5,000	10.2	20.0	17.4	19.5	15.8	15.5	15.4
5,000 to 6,000	7.8	17.6	11.0	17.8	13.1	23.7	12.8
6,000 to 7,000	9.7	9.5	11.4	8.9	8.4	4.4	9.3
7,000 to 8,000	11.5	5.1	4.8	1.1	9.8	4.4	7.7
8,000 to 9,000	6.7	9.1	4.2	6.2	5.6	3.0	6.2
9,000 to 10,000	5.3	2.4	6.4	5.1	3.0		4.3
10,000 to 12,000	7.0	3.2	10.0	2.1	4.2	2.2	5.5
12,000 to 14,000	5.7	4.2	2.8		1.8		3.4
14,000 to 16,000	2.9		4.5	2.1	1.2		2.1
16,000 to 18,000	3.1	3.6	0.8	1.1			1.9
18,000 to 20,000	1.7			1.1			0.7
20,000 to 25,000	1.9	0.8	1.4		0.9		1.2
25,000 to 30,000	1.6	1.1	1.4	3.4		2.2	1.5
30,000 to 40,000	2.7						0.9
40,000 to 50,000	1.5		2.0				0.8
50,000 and over							
No. of accountants covered[4]	356	161	159	121	149	49	1,002
A.M. (dollars)	9,174	6,441	7,672	6,279	5,529	4,904	7,314

Measures computed from the distributions

Absolute (dollars)

	1,500 & over	500 to 1,500	250 to 500	100 to 250	25 to 100	under 25	U.S.[2]
Q_3	10,902	7,894	9,683	6,674	7,147	5,318	8,560
Md	7,144	5,376	5,972	4,937	4,871	4,354	5,647
Q_1	4,434	4,815	4,178	3,643	3,340	3,246	3,883
I.D.	6,468	3,079	5,505	3,031	3,807	2,072	4,677
S.D.	8,074	4,288	7,082	5,106	3,178	3,861	6,410

Relative

	1,500 & over	500 to 1,500	250 to 500	100 to 250	25 to 100	under 25	U.S.[2]
R.I.D.	.905	.573	.922	.614	.782	.476	.828
V^1	.870	.660	.901	.815	.567	.764	.865

For footnotes see p.569.

1931 (1933 SAMPLE)

Communities with populations (in thousands) of

INCOME CLASSES (dollars)	1,500 & over	500 to 1,500	250 to 500	100 to 250	25 to 100	under 25	U.S.[2]
Under -2,000	1.0						0.3
-2,000 to -1,000	0.7		0.8				0.3
-1,000 to 0	1.4		1.4				0.7
1 to 500	0.5		0.8	3.1			0.7
500 to 1,000	0.4	3.3		2.1		4.1	1.2
1,000 to 1,500	1.8	1.6	3.6	4.1	1.7	2.0	2.6
1,500 to 2,000	4.6	1.6	4.0	3.1	5.7	2.7	3.9
2,000 to 2,500	4.8	2.4	4.3	5.5	6.9	23.1	5.8
2,500 to 3,000	4.3	6.5	6.9	5.5	12.2	8.2	6.6
3,000 to 3,500	4.8	7.4	5.1	9.7	7.5	11.6	6.7
3,500 to 4,000	8.1	9.8	8.5	9.4	9.4	10.2	8.8
4,000 to 5,000	12.7	25.8	15.8	15.9	11.5	15.0	15.9
5,000 to 6,000	7.1	11.7	9.9	14.7	14.7	12.9	10.8
6,000 to 7,000	9.0	7.8	8.1	6.2	13.5	4.1	8.8
7,000 to 8,000	5.7	4.3	8.9	5.5	7.1		5.8
8,000 to 9,000	4.6	7.2	7.1	2.8	1.7	4.1	4.7
9,000 to 10,000	4.9	0.8	1.6	3.1	1.7		2.7
10,000 to 12,000	7.6	2.2	4.3	4.2	2.9		4.5
12,000 to 14,000	6.9	4.0	1.1	2.1	1.5		3.6
14,000 to 16,000	0.9	1.9	2.4	2.2			1.3
16,000 to 18,000	3.2		2.2		2.0		1.7
18,000 to 20,000	0.5	0.8					0.3
20,000 to 25,000	2.0					2.0	0.8
25,000 to 30,000	1.6	0.8	1.4	1.0			1.0
30,000 to 40,000	0.8		0.8				0.4
40,000 to 50,000							
50,000 and over			1.1				0.2
No. of accountants covered[4]	354	156	167	127	153	53	1,020
A.M. (dollars)	7,268	5,589	6,599	5,259	5,050	3,968	6,072

Measures computed from the distributions

Absolute (dollars)

Q_3	9,715	6,620	7,651	6,325	6,401	4,873	7,326
Md	5,687	4,673	4,927	4,479	4,573	3,425	4,780
Q_1	3,544	3,610	3,323	3,089	2,940	2,350	3,217
I.D.	6,171	3,010	4,328	3,236	3,461	2,523	4,109
S.D.	5,948	3,740	6,907	3,840	2,927	3,164	5,152

Relative

R.I.D.	1.085	.644	.878	.722	.757	.737	.860
V^1	.816	.660	1.041	.728	.574	.779	.843

For footnotes see p.569.

TABLE B9b (cont.)

1932 (1933 SAMPLE)

Communities with populations (in thousands) of

INCOME CLASSES (dollars)	1,500 & over	500 to 1,500	250 to 500	100 to 250	25 to 100	under 25	U.S.[2]
Under -2,000		0.7					0.1
-2,000 to -1,000	4.7	0.7					1.6
-1,000 to 0				1.0		2.0	0.2
0			1.2				0.2
1 to 500	0.8	1.0	2.2	1.0	1.1		1.1
500 to 1,000	2.4	1.5	1.0	2.1	0.8	7.9	2.1
1,000 to 1,500	3.2	3.7	2.4	2.1	1.7	4.6	3.0
1,500 to 2,000	4.8	5.9	8.2	5.5	11.6	9.9	7.1
2,000 to 2,500	8.5	5.9	6.6	9.4	9.6	23.8	8.9
2,500 to 3,000	7.2	10.8	5.6	10.8	11.0	3.9	8.3
3,000 to 3,500	6.7	8.8	10.5	16.9	10.2	17.7	10.1
3,500 to 4,000	6.3	11.5	5.8	4.5	8.1	5.9	7.1
4,000 to 5,000	14.1	15.1	17.5	16.7	17.6	7.9	15.6
5,000 to 6,000	6.9	10.2	13.7	11.8	11.1	6.6	9.7
6,000 to 7,000	6.0	11.6	6.9	3.8	8.2	3.9	7.0
7,000 to 8,000	6.3	3.9	5.7	6.4	4.2		5.0
8,000 to 9,000	4.1	1.5	2.4	2.8	3.1	2.0	2.9
9,000 to 10,000	3.4	2.5	1.7			2.0	2.0
10,000 to 12,000	5.6	2.2	2.9	3.2	0.8		3.3
12,000 to 14,000	3.4	1.7	1.0				1.6
14,000 to 16,000	2.4		1.2	1.0	0.8		1.2
16,000 to 18,000	1.4						0.4
18,000 to 20,000	1.3	0.7				2.0	0.7
20,000 to 25,000	0.4		2.5	1.0			0.7
25,000 to 30,000			1.0				0.2
30,000 to 40,000							
40,000 to 50,000							
50,000 and over							
No. of accountants covered[a]	358	170	192	127	154	54	1,063
A.M. (dollars)	5,412	4,449	5,252	4,420	4,117	3,355	4,777

Measures computed from the distributions

Absolute (dollars)

Q_3	7,532	5,918	6,040	5,428	5,294	3,942	5,993
Md	4,373	3,978	4,370	3,633	3,744	2,944	4,017
Q_1	2,538	2,760	2,802	2,678	2,506	2,014	2,541
I.D.	4,994	3,158	3,238	2,750	2,788	1,928	3,452
S.D.	4,338	2,871	4,465	3,100	2,204	2,913	3,708

Relative

R.I.D.	1.142	.794	.741	.757	.745	.655	.859
V^1	.794	.633	.844	.694	.535	.851	.768

For footnotes see p.569.

1932 (1935 SAMPLE)

Communities with populations (in thousands) of

INCOME CLASSES (dollars)	1,500 & over	500 to 1,500	250 to 500	100 to 250	25 to 100	under 25	U.S.[2]
Under -2,000	0.2						0.1
-2,000 to -1,000		0.6					0.1
-1,000 to 0		0.6	1.3				0.3
0	0.4			1			0.1
1 to 500	0.9	1.4	2.2	0.9	2.4	6.5	1.9
500 to 1,000	3.7	3.2	2.7	2.1	2.4	10.2	3.6
1,000 to 1,500	4.9	8.1	4.7	4.4	3.8	7.2	5.3
1,500 to 2,000	8.0	8.3	6.7	6.3	14.2	9.6	8.6
2,000 to 2,500	10.9	7.9	9.3	12.6	11.8	13.0	10.7
2,500 to 3,000	12.0	11.2	11.3	10.4	15.3	18.0	12.4
3,000 to 3,500	10.0	12.7	5.8	13.1	10.2	11.0	10.2
3,500 to 4,000	5.4	11.9	3.8	7.3	9.4	6.5	7.4
4,000 to 5,000	12.3	13.1	20.0	18.8	12.6	10.9	14.0
5,000 to 6,000	9.7	5.3	12.7	12.8	6.3	3.1	8.9
6,000 to 7,000	5.4	6.6	3.0	0.9	6.3	1.0	4.6
7,000 to 8,000	2.6	2.6	3.4	1.5	1.2	1.0	2.3
8,000 to 9,000	2.3	1.4	4.7	0.9	1.4	1.0	2.0
9,000 to 10,000	1.9		1.6	0.7	1.2		1.1
10,000 to 12,000	2.0	2.0	2.2	5.1	0.6		2.0
12,000 to 14,000	2.0	1.2	1.6	0.7		1.0	1.3
14,000 to 16,000	2.7	0.6	1.1	0.7			1.3
16,000 to 18,000	0.7	0.6			0.6		0.4
18,000 to 20,000	1.9		1.1				0.9
20,000 to 25,000		0.8		0.7	0.3		0.2
25,000 to 30,000	0.2						0.1
30,000 to 40,000							
40,000 to 50,000			0.7				0.1
50,000 and over							
No. of accountants covered[a]	525	207	190	179	193	105	1,415
A.M. (dollars)	4,728	3,942	4,769	4,226	3,559	2,704	4,218

Measures computed from the distributions

Absolute (dollars)

Q_3	5,663	4,695	5,557	4,950	4,428	3,482	5,029
Md	3,452	3,343	4,105	3,512	3,002	2,600	3,336
Q_1	2,315	2,176	2,394	2,448	2,090	1,562	2,235
I.D.	3,348	2,519	3,163	2,502	2,338	1,920	2,794
S.D.	4,012	3,145	4,619	2,976	2,405	1,884	3,568

Relative

R.I.D.	.970	.754	.771	.712	.779	.738	.838
V^i	.842	.793	.966	.702	.674	.682	.840

For footnotes see p.569.

TABLE B9b (cont.)

1933 (1935 SAMPLE)

Communities with populations (in thousands) of

INCOME CLASSES (dollars)	1,500 & over	500 to 1,500	250 to 500	100 to 250	25 to 100	under 25	U.S.[2]
Under -2,000			0.6				0.1
-2,000 to -1,000							
-1,000 to 0	0.2	0.5					0.2
0	0.4						0.2
1 to 500	1.6	1.8	1.3	2.0	2.9	6.7	2.2
500 to 1,000	4.4	5.1	3.9	3.8	4.7	5.1	4.4
1,000 to 1,500	6.2	3.3	5.1	5.3	5.5	8.0	5.5
1,500 to 2,000	7.3	8.3	7.3	7.4	10.3	19.5	8.9
2,000 to 2,500	12.9	13.4	13.3	15.6	16.5	14.3	13.8
2,500 to 3,000	13.1	14.1	9.8	6.4	13.7	11.8	11.9
3,000 to 3,500	9.7	15.1	5.5	14.9	11.5	8.3	10.8
3,500 to 4,000	6.5	8.0	9.7	12.8	9.2	10.5	8.7
4,000 to 5,000	11.7	8.6	15.8	12.5	10.0	7.0	11.5
5,000 to 6,000	7.7	10.8	12.3	3.7	7.4	6.0	8.0
6,000 to 7,000	4.5	5.8	3.9	6.4	3.5	2.9	4.5
7,000 to 8,000	0.5	1.1	4.8	2.0	1.2		1.5
8,000 to 9,000	1.0	0.5	2.4	1.8			1.1
9,000 to 10,000	2.8		1.7	1.3	2.0		1.7
10,000 to 12,000	2.4	2.4	0.9	2.1	0.6		1.6
12,000 to 14,000	1.7		0.6	1.3			0.9
14,000 to 16,000	0.9	0.5	1.1		0.6		0.6
16,000 to 18,000	2.7			0.7			1.1
18,000 to 20,000		0.5					0.1
20,000 to 25,000	1.5						0.5
25,000 to 30,000	0.2				0.6		0.2
30,000 to 40,000							
40,000 to 50,000							
50,000 and over							
No. of accountants covered[a]	550	224	197	190	199	112	1,489
A.M. (dollars)	4,501	3,610	3,883	3,796	3,393	2,606	3,886

Measures computed from the distributions.

Absolute (dollars)

	1,500 & over	500 to 1,500	250 to 500	100 to 250	25 to 100	under 25	U.S.
Q_3	5,123	4,611	5,214	4,442	4,041	3,567	4,724
Md	3,198	3,114	3,662	3,270	2,872	2,378	3,129
Q_1	2,188	2,220	2,254	2,210	2,050	1,636	2,127
I.D.	2,935	2,391	2,960	2,232	1,991	1,931	2,597
S.D.	4,263	2,470	3,122	2,606	2,771	1,489	3,360

Relative

	1,500 & over	500 to 1,500	250 to 500	100 to 250	25 to 100	under 25	U.S.
R.I.D.	.918	.768	.808	.683	.693	.812	.830
V^1	.934	.679	.796	.678	.808	.564	.854

For footnotes see p.569.

1934 (1935 SAMPLE)

Communities with populations (in thousands) of

INCOME CLASSES (dollars)	1,500 & over	500 to 1,500	250 to 500	100 to 250	25 to 100	under 25	U.S.[2]
Under -2,000							
-2,000 to -1,000							
-1,000 to 0	0.2		1.2				0.3
0							
1 to 500	1.7	1.1	0.6	1.3	1.7	5.4	1.8
500 to 1,000	3.6	4.0	3.7	3.8	4.7	8.4	4.2
1,000 to 1,500	4.6	2.9	3.1	1.3	5.0	3.9	3.7
1,500 to 2,000	7.4	8.9	4.9	6.5	10.3	14.3	8.1
2,000 to 2,500	10.7	9.3	8.4	9.9	7.0	13.0	9.5
2,500 to 3,000	10.6	13.8	9.7	14.9	8.7	13.4	11.6
3,000 to 3,500	12.4	8.9	7.6	9.2	9.8	12.0	10.5
3,500 to 4,000	5.7	8.2	8.5	13.2	11.9	6.6	8.3
4,000 to 5,000	12.9	18.0	13.6	14.3	17.3	13.7	14.6
5,000 to 6,000	8.9	13.0	14.6	13.4	8.5	2.7	10.2
6,000 to 7,000	6.4	5.5	10.9	4.9	5.3	1.8	6.0
7,000 to 8,000	1.8	1.8	2.7	0.6	2.8	2.1	1.9
8,000 to 9,000	2.6	0.5	2.9	1.3	3.6		2.2
9,000 to 10,000	1.8	2.8	3.5	1.5			1.7
10,000 to 12,000	1.6	0.5	0.8	0.6	0.8	1.8	1.2
12,000 to 14,000	3.1		1.4	2.0	0.6		1.7
14,000 to 16,000		0.5		0.6	0.6		0.2
16,000 to 18,000	1.7				0.7	0.9	0.8
18,000 to 20,000	0.8		0.6				0.4
20,000 to 25,000	1.6		1.1	0.6			0.8
25,000 to 30,000					0.6		0.1
30,000 to 40,000	0.2						0.1
40,000 to 50,000							
50,000 and over							
No. of accountants covered[a]	558	225	205	190	203	120	1,518
A.M. (dollars)	4,734	3,868	4,623	4,131	4,003	3,033	4,274

Measures computed from the distributions

Absolute (dollars)

Q_3	5,622	4,988	5,929	5,048	4,911	3,848	5,232
Md	3,468	3,564	4,160	3,618	3,614	2,687	3,515
Q_1	2,337	2,436	2,655	2,576	2,232	1,758	2,356
I.D.	3,285	2,552	3,274	2,472	2,679	2,090	2,876
S.D.	4,335	2,138	3,282	2,805	3,095	2,306	3,483

Relative

R.I.D.	.947	.716	.787	.683	.741	.778	.818
V^1	.898	.550	.697	.675	.758	.753	.803

For footnotes see p.569.

TABLE B9b (cont.)

1934 (1937 SAMPLE)

Communities with populations (in thousands) of

INCOME CLASSES (dollars)	1,500 & over	500 to 1,500	250 to 500	100 to 250	25 to 100	under 25	U.S.
Under -2,000				1.3			0.1
-2,000 to -1,000	0.6						0.2
-1,000 to 0	0.4		1.0				0.3
0	0.4						0.1
1 to 500	0.4	3.7	1.0	4.2	1.7	12.5	2.6
500 to 1,000	3.0		1.0	2.9	3.8	4.7	2.6
1,000 to 1,500	6.3	4.7	5.2	1.3	3.6	7.8	5.1
1,500 to 2,000	5.4	13.8	4.7	3.2	9.9	6.2	7.1
2,000 to 2,500	13.5	8.7	11.6	11.5	8.7	13.7	11.6
2,500 to 3,000	12.5	13.3	13.1	9.3	10.5	18.0	12.5
3,000 to 3,500	10.5	8.0	13.1	13.2	10.9	11.3	10.9
3,500 to 4,000	5.9	13.8	5.2	10.9	10.3	7.8	8.4
4,000 to 5,000	14.9	11.7	17.6	16.0	17.1		14.0
5,000 to 6,000	10.3	6.5	6.4	12.8	9.1	8.2	9.1
6,000 to 7,000	6.0	4.5	4.4	3.8	5.9	4.7	5.2
7,000 to 8,000	2.8	3.3	6.2	1.6	2.5	3.5	3.2
8,000 to 9,000	1.6	1.9	1.0	1.3	2.7		1.6
9,000 to 10,000	0.8	2.6	5.0		0.8		1.4
10,000 to 12,000	1.2	2.4	1.0	4.2	1.7	1.6	1.8
12,000 to 14,000	0.5		2.3		0.8		0.6
14,000 to 16,000	1.2						0.4
16,000 to 18,000	1.1						0.4
18,000 to 20,000		1.2		1.3			0.3
20,000 to 25,000				1.3			0.1
25,000 to 30,000	0.8						0.3
30,000 to 40,000							
40,000 to 50,000							
50,000 and over							
No. of accountants covered[a]	328	138	122	93	150	70	901
A.M. (dollars)	4,200	3,934	4,193	4,179	3,835	2,891	3,984

Measures computed from the distributions

Absolute (dollars)

Q_3	5,127	4,767	5,207	5,100	4,918	3,549	4,967
Md	3,361	3,363	3,469	3,646	3,550	2,640	3,358
Q_1	2,319	2,158	2,512	2,536	2,352	1,501	2,296
I.D.	2,808	2,609	2,695	2,564	2,566	2,048	2,671
S.D.	3,542	2,815	2,649	3,638	2,265	2,109	3,072

Relative

R.I.D.	.835	.776	.777	.703	.723	.776	.795
V[1]	.836	.711	.621	.851	.577	.721	.761

For footnotes see p.569.

1935 (1937 SAMPLE)

Communities with populations (in thousands) of

INCOME CLASSES (dollars)	1,500 & over	500 to 1,500	250 to 500	100 to 250	25 to 100	under 25	U.S.
Under -2,000							
-2,000 to -1,000							
-1,000 to 0	0.4	0.8					0.3
0							
1 to 500	0.7	1.9	1.0	3.9	1.6	11.8	2.4
500 to 1,000	2.2	1.7	1.0	2.7		7.2	2.1
1,000 to 1,500	3.7	5.0	1.9	1.2	6.5	9.0	4.3
1,500 to 2,000	8.5	6.1	10.1	2.4	5.9	4.3	6.9
2,000 to 2,500	10.0	10.6	2.2	15.1	9.9	8.3	9.4
2,500 to 3,000	10.1	13.9	15.1	7.8	8.3	15.0	11.3
3,000 to 3,500	12.6	16.1	20.4	10.3	16.6	11.8	14.5
3,500 to 4,000	9.4	8.9	7.3	10.6	5.9	8.6	8.5
4,000 to 5,000	16.5	11.7	7.6	20.5	17.8	10.7	14.7
5,000 to 6,000	7.0	8.4	11.3	7.9	9.7	1.4	7.8
6,000 to 7,000	6.0	7.9	6.2	6.9	9.1	2.9	6.6
7,000 to 8,000	3.5	1.9	5.4	5.1	3.3	6.1	3.9
8,000 to 9,000	1.4	0.8	1.9	1.2		2.9	1.3
9,000 to 10,000	1.5	1.1	4.0		1.5		1.4
10,000 to 12,000	2.7	0.8	3.4	1.8	2.4		2.1
12,000 to 14,000	0.8			2.4	0.8		0.7
14,000 to 16,000	0.4		1.2				0.3
16,000 to 18,000	0.5	1.1			0.8		0.4
18,000 to 20,000	0.4	1.3					0.3
20,000 to 25,000	0.8						0.3
25,000 to 30,000							
30,000 to 40,000	0.9						0.3
40,000 to 50,000							
50,000 and over							
No. of accountants covered[4]	343	151	138	100	157	80	971
A.M. (dollars)	4,548	3,974	4,367	4,067	4,146	2,962	4,177

Measures computed from the distributions

Absolute (dollars)

	1,500 & over	500 to 1,500	250 to 500	100 to 250	25 to 100	under 25	U.S.
Q_3	5,130	4,854	5,746	5,536	5,258	3,942	5,073
Md	3,598	3,310	3,458	3,808	3,603	2,815	3,460
Q_1	2,480	2,447	2,790	2,488	2,569	1,336	2,479
I.D.	2,650	2,407	2,956	3,048	2,689	2,606	2,594
S.D.	4,305	2,908	2,676	2,462	2,510	2,120	3,334

Relative

	1,500 & over	500 to 1,500	250 to 500	100 to 250	25 to 100	under 25	U.S.
R.I.D.	.737	.727	.855	.800	.746	.926	.750
V^1	.930	.728	.597	.588	.596	.700	.784

For footnotes see p.569.

TABLE B9b (concl.)

1936 (1937 SAMPLE)

Communities with populations (in thousands) of

INCOME CLASSES (dollars)	1,500 & over	500 to 1,500	250 to 500	100 to 250	25 to 100	under 25	U.S.
Under -2,000							
-2,000 to -1,000		0.8					0.1
-1,000 to 0		0.8					0.1
0							
1 to 500	1.0			3.0	0.8	11.5	1.8
500 to 1,000	2.5	1.6	3.2	1.2	3.4	2.8	2.5
1,000 to 1,500	2.8	4.0	1.8	3.2	4.7	3.1	3.2
1,500 to 2,000	4.5	6.3	6.4	2.3	6.6	9.7	5.6
2,000 to 2,500	8.3	13.3	7.5	8.2	3.9	7.3	8.2
2,500 to 3,000	11.7	10.7	2.0	10.8	7.5	21.8	9.5
3,000 to 3,500	10.0	5.0	19.2	4.7	17.0	8.7	10.9
3,500 to 4,000	8.4	8.3	14.8	4.1	6.3	11.8	8.7
4,000 to 5,000	15.9	19.4	8.4	25.2	12.3	16.9	15.9
5,000 to 6,000	11.3	11.7	14.0	15.8	14.7	6.3	12.3
6,000 to 7,000	5.4	5.4	4.5	7.6	10.3	1.4	6.0
7,000 to 8,000	5.3	5.4	7.3	7.3	5.8	4.5	5.8
8,000 to 9,000	3.4	1.6	4.6	1.8			2.3
9,000 to 10,000	1.5	1.0	2.9	1.2	2.1	2.8	1.8
10,000 to 12,000	2.5	2.6	2.3	1.5	3.0	1.4	2.4
12,000 to 14,000	2.0			1.2	0.8		0.9
14,000 to 16,000	2.1	1.2					0.9
16,000 to 18,000			1.1		0.8		0.3
18,000 to 20,000				1.2			0.1
20,000 to 25,000	0.3	1.0					0.3
25,000 to 30,000	1.1						0.4
30,000 to 40,000							
40,000 to 50,000							
50,000 and over							
No. of accountants covered[a]	367	161	154	104	174	83	1,043
A.M. (dollars)	4,920	4,349	4,594	4,669	4,486	3,377	4,556

Measures computed from the distributions

Absolute (dollars)

Q_3	5,881	5,415	5,839	5,787	5,851	4,488	5,687
Md	4,055	3,954	3,834	4,500	3,984	3,217	3,963
Q_1	2,752	2,432	3,106	2,831	2,872	1,892	2,684
I.D.	3,129	2,983	2,733	2,956	2,979	2,596	3,003
S.D.	3,921	3,112	2,663	2,760	2,636	2,262	3,240

Relative

R.I.D.	.772	.754	.713	.657	.748	.807	.758
V[1]	.780	.705	.571	.584	.584	.660	.700

For footnotes see p.569.

TABLE B9 (cont.)

c   By Organization of Practice

INDIVIDUAL PRACTITIONERS

INCOME CLASSES (dollars)	1933 SAMPLE				1935 SAMPLE			1937 SAMPLE		
	1929	1930	1931	1932	1932	1933	1934	1934	1935	1936
Under -2,000				1	1	1		1		
-2,000 to -1,000				1	2	1				1
-1,000 to 0		1	2	2	3	3	4	2	2	1
0								1		
1 to 500	1	3	4	6	18	26	23	18	15	12
500 to 1,000	3	5	9	11	39.67	51.71	48.25	15	15	15
1,000 to 1,500	5	10	14	20	52.5	58.5	39	31.42	27	17.5
1,500 to 2,000	8	9	16	43	87.25	80.75	92	40	40	36.25
2,000 to 2,500	17	18	36	42	106	137	98.92	63	53.17	46
2,500 to 3,000	19	19	34	40	114.25	120	112	69.75	63	59
3,000 to 3,500	29	43	33	44	79	94.83	100	59	82	62
3,500 to 4,000	30	22	37	32	61	72	76	48	44.08	48
4,000 to 5,000	56	60	60	55	97.17	78.17	128	63	70	77
5,000 to 6,000	45	51	49	39	55	47.5	61	35.75	39	59.33
6,000 to 7,000	29	39	30	23	18	26	35	20	28.08	32
7,000 to 8,000	23	21	18	21	14	6	15	8.83	16	22
8,000 to 9,000	26	21	14	11	7	7	16	9	10	10
9,000 to 10,000	14	15	15	7	8	6	7	4	2	9
10,000 to 12,000	25	18	13	15	11	10	7	9	10	10
12,000 to 14,000	14	15	9	3	7	5	8	2	4	5
14,000 to 16,000	9	7	2	4	3	2	3		1	3
16,000 to 18,000	5	6	5	1	5	4.67	4	3	1	1
18,000 to 20,000	5	1	1	2	1	1	1	1	1	1
20,000 to 25,000	4	4	2	2	1.5	2	3	1	1	1
25,000 to 30,000	2	3	4		1	2	1	1		2
30,000 to 40,000	2	1	1					1	1	
40,000 to 50,000	1	1			1					
50,000 and over	1									
No. of accountants covered	373	393	409	426	792.34	842.13	883.17	505.75	525.33	530.08
A.M. (dollars)	6,941	6,289	5,282	4,313	3,544	3,275	3,664	3,620	3,817	4,248

Measures computed from the distributions

Absolute (dollars)

Q_3	8,565	7,670	6,252	5,486	4,325	3,908	4,541	4,494	4,754	5,384
Md	5,186	5,000	4,157	3,509	2,884	2,763	3,122	3,099	3,290	3,660
Q_1	3,629	3,297	2,789	2,294	1,975	1,936	2,074	2,143	2,304	2,532
I.D.	4,936	4,373	3,463	3,192	2,350	1,972	2,467	2,351	2,450	2,852
S.D.	5,810	4,856	4,407	3,266	3,211	2,937	3,019	2,866	2,925	3,103

Relative

R.I.D.	.952	.874	.832	.910	.815	.714	.790	.759	.745	.779
V^1	.837	.772	.834	.757	.893	.883	.811	.780	.750	.717

For footnotes see p.569.

TABLE B9c (concl.)

FIRM MEMBERS

INCOME CLASSES (dollars)	1933 SAMPLE				1935 SAMPLE			1937 SAMPLE		
	1929	1930	1931	1932	1932	1933	1934	1934	1935	1936
Under -2,000			0.7							
-2,000 to -1,000			0.5	3.0				0.7		
-1,000 to 0		0.4	0.9							
0				0.4	0.5	0.4				
1 to 500			0.4	0.7	1.1	0.3		0.6	1.5	1.0
500 to 1,000		0.8		1.5	0.7	0.7	1.4	1.7	0.5	1.8
1,000 to 1,500	1.2	1.7	1.7	1.0	2.4	2.4	2.0	2.5	2.6	3.1
1,500 to 2,000		1.3	3.8	3.7	3.5	7.3	2.5	5.3	5.4	3.3
2,000 to 2,500	3.7	1.5	2.5	7.9	5.2	8.5	6.1	9.6	8.0	7.2
2,500 to 3,000	2.6	2.7	4.7	7.0	8.2	6.9	8.9	9.6	9.7	6.4
3,000 to 3,500	3.9	4.9	5.1	9.8	10.7	9.6	8.4	9.1	12.3	9.5
3,500 to 4,000	5.4	5.9	8.6	6.6	6.7	9.2	7.7	5.9	8.8	8.1
4,000 to 5,000	13.7	15.5	17.2	18.6	17.8	16.1	14.7	17.3	17.6	18.4
5,000 to 6,000	9.5	12.7	9.5	10.4	12.9	13.3	17.8	13.7	8.7	14.3
6,000 to 7,000	13.8	8.6	10.5	8.7	9.6	7.6	10.8	8.0	9.3	5.8
7,000 to 8,000	6.2	10.3	7.3	5.2	3.4	3.2	2.4	6.5	5.7	8.9
8,000 to 9,000	8.6	7.2	6.1	3.2	4.5	1.6	3.1	1.1		3.0
9,000 to 10,000	6.6	4.7	1.6	2.3	1.4	3.8	3.8	2.9	3.7	1.9
10,000 to 12,000	5.4	6.5	6.0	3.1	3.4	2.7	2.2	1.8	2.6	3.2
12,000 to 14,000	4.4	2.9	5.1	2.5	2.1	1.5	3.6	1.1	0.5	1.0
14,000 to 16,000	3.0	2.5	2.1	1.6	3.3	1.4		1.4		1.6
16,000 to 18,000	3.4	2.4	2.2	0.7		2.2	1.7		1.0	0.4
18,000 to 20,000	1.3	1.2	0.4	0.9	2.4		1.0	0.6	0.6	
20,000 to 25,000	2.7	1.3	1.2	0.9	0.4	1.2	1.8		0.5	0.4
25,000 to 30,000	2.4	2.2	1.0	0.3				0.6		0.4
30,000 to 40,000	1.5	1.6	0.6						0.6	
40,000 to 50,000		1.4								
50,000 and over	0.6		0.4							
No. of accountants covered[a]	590	609	611	637	623	647	635	395	446	512
A.M. (dollars)	8,962	8,414	6,951	5,294	5,643	5,213	5,682	4,803	4,926	5,120

Measures computed from the distributions

Absolute (dollars)

Q_3	9,968	9,372	8,268	6,509	6,565	6,031	6,502	5,926	5,989	6,295
Md	6,727	6,322	5,411	4,452	4,624	4,288	4,876	4,292	4,069	4,514
Q_1	4,394	4,380	3,776	2,985	3,162	2,886	3,236	2,747	2,861	3,111
I.D.	5,574	4,992	4,492	3,524	3,403	3,145	3,266	3,179	3,128	3,184
S.D.	7,481	7,534	5,819	4,075	3,881	3,815	4,023	3,352	3,956	3,410

Relative

R.I.D.	.829	.790	.830	.792	.736	.733	.670	.741	.769	.705
V^1	.834	.883	.836	.765	.691	.727	.698	.691	.793	.659

For footnotes see p.569.

TABLE B 10

Final Estimates of Arithmetic Mean Income of Certified Public Accountants[12], 1929–1936
By Region and by Size of Community

	1929	1930	1931	1932	1933	1934	1935	1936
REGION				(dollars)				
New England	6,765	6,466	5,325	4,184	3,900	4,436	4,082	4,533
Middle Atlantic	8,998	8,432	6,495	5,024	4,837	4,970	5,232	5,517
E. N. Central	6,889	5,854	5,318	4,020	3,367	4,078	4,627	5,086
W. N. Central	6,437	5,677	5,128	4,378	3,478	4,422	4,056	4,920
S. Atlantic	5,601	5,467	4,968	4,001	3,713	4,147	4,376	4,830
E. S. Central	5,816	5,895	4,344	3,720	3,737	4,372	4,783	5,152
W. S. Central	6,406	5,465	4,890	4,138	3,507	3,780	3,982	4,706
Mountain	5,056	4,736	4,085	3,236	3,231	3,981	4,175	4,415
Pacific	5,579	5,156	4,586	3,545	3,212	3,478	3,532	3,859
SIZE OF COMMUNITY								
1,500,000 & over	8,837	8,099	6,417	4,778	4,549	4,784	5,180	5,604
500,000 – 1,500,000	6,246	5,984	5,192	4,133	3,785	4,055	4,096	4,483
250,000 – 500,000	7,265	6,985	6,008	4,782	3,894	4,636	4,828	4,079
100,000 – 250,000	7,131	6,118	5,125	4,307	3,869	4,210	4,097	4,704
25,000 – 100,000	5,577	4,962	4,532	3,695	3,523	4,156	4,493	4,861
Under 25,000	4,479	4,208	3,405	2,879	2,775	3,229	3,308	3,772
U.S.	7,149	6,597	5,477	4,309	3,970	4,366	4,578	4,993

These final estimates were computed from arithmetic means presented in Tables B 9 a and
B 9 b. The arithmetic mean for 1934 from the 1937 sample was extrapolated to 1932 on the
basis of the 1935 sample. The resultant figure and the arithmetic means for 1932 from
the 1935 and 1937 samples were averaged. This average was then extrapolated back to
1929 on the basis of the 1933 sample, forward to 1934 on the basis of the 1935 sample, and
from 1934 to 1936 on the basis of the 1937 sample.

For footnotes see p. 569.

TABLE B 11

Distribution of Income of Consulting Engineers by Size and Measures Computed from the Distributions, 1929-1932

a   By Region

1929 (1933 SAMPLE)

INCOME CLASSES (dollars)	NE	MA	ENC	WNC	SA and ESC	WSC	MT.	PAC.	U.S.
Under -2,000[5]	3	3		6	1		1		13.7
-2,000 to -1,000[5]		1						2	2.8
-1,000 to 0[5]	1	2	2						5.5
0									
1 to 500	2	3						1	6
500 to 1,000	1	1	1		1	1		2	7
1,000 to 1,500	1	6	2		1			2	12
1,500 to 2,000		2	3	1	1		2	3	12
2,000 to 2,500		3	2	3	1	1		3	13
2,500 to 3,000	3	5	2	5	3	3	3	6	30
3,000 to 3,500	2	4	1		3			3	13
3,500 to 4,000	2	4	1		3	1		4	15
4,000 to 5,000		7	5	4	5	5		10	36
5,000 to 6,000	1	2	8	3	2		1	7	24
6,000 to 7,000		9	5		4	2		3	23
7,000 to 8,000	4	10	2		2	1		5	24
8,000 to 9,000	4	21	3	2	2			7	39
9,000 to 10,000	4	9		1	1			3	18
10,000 to 12,000	2	18	6	1	2			5	35
12,000 to 14,000	1	9		4	1		1	5	20
14,000 to 16,000	13	5			3		1	1	23
16,000 to 18,000	1	3	2	2	4	1		2	15
18,000 to 20,000	1	7	3					4	15
20,000 to 25,000		7	3			1		1	12
25,000 to 30,000		12	2						14
30,000 to 40,000	4	15		1	1				21
40,000 to 50,000		8	1						9
50,000 and over		13							13
No. of engineers covered	50	189	54	33	41	16	9	79	471
A.M. (dollars)	10,500	17,961	8,768	5,459	7,763	6,076	4,604	6,921	11,840

Measures computed from the distributions

Absolute (dollars)

	NE	MA	ENC	WNC	SA and ESC	WSC	MT.	PAC.	U.S.
Q_3	15,000	25,310	11,166	9,750	10,750	6,500	5,750	9,417	14,805
Md	9,250	10,278	6,000	4,375	5,750	4,400	2,750	5,500	7,943
Q_1	3,375	6,472	3,750	2,208	3,375	2,833	1,812	3,125	3,570
I.D.	11,625	18,838	7,416	6,842	7,375	3,667	3,938	6,292	11,235
S.D.	9,466	19,404	8,576	8,120	6,639	5,508	4,989	5,196	14,580

Relative

	NE	MA	ENC	WNC	SA and ESC	WSC	MT.	PAC.	U.S.
R.I.D.	1.257	1.833	1.236	1.564	1.283	.833	1.432	1.144	1.414
V^1	.906	1.090	.948	1.438	.859	.904	1.096	.746	1.231

For footnotes see p.569.

1930 (1933 SAMPLE)

INCOME CLASSES (dollars)	NE	MA	ENC	WNC	SA and ESC	WSC	MT.	PAC.	U.S.
Under -2,000[5]	1.3	6.3	2					1.3	10.1
-2,000 to -1,000[5]	6.4	1.4		2	1		1	1.4	14.5
-1,000 to 0[5]	1.3	4.3	2	1				6.3	14.4
0									
1 to 500	2	3	1					8	14
500 to 1,000		3	3				2	3	11
1,000 to 1,500	2	2	1	1	1			1	8
1,500 to 2,000	1	3	4	1	2	2	3	2	18
2,000 to 2,500	1	4	1	4	3	5		2	20
2,500 to 3,000		2	2	3	2	2		4	15
3,000 to 3,500	4	4	1	2	1				12
3,500 to 4,000	1	3	2		1	1	1	5	14
4,000 to 5,000	2	15	11	4	4	4	1	10	51
5,000 to 6,000		14	8	3	1			9	35
6,000 to 7,000	4	11	2	1	6			11	35
7,000 to 8,000		12		2	3			4	23
8,000 to 9,000	4	14	3		5			1	27
9,000 to 10,000	2	7	1		1			5	16
10,000 to 12,000	1	16		3	4			3	27
12,000 to 14,000	1	5	2		1	1		3	13
14,000 to 16,000	11	15	3				1	4	34
16,000 to 18,000	1	4	3	1	1	1		1	12
18,000 to 20,000	1	1	1		2				5
20,000 to 25,000		17	1	3					21
25,000 to 30,000		2							2
30,000 to 40,000	3	10	1						14
40,000 to 50,000		4							4
50,000 and over		11							11
No. of engineers covered	50	194	57	31	39	16	9	85	481
A.M. (dollars)	8,592	15,654	6,506	6,217	6,921	4,411	3,407	5,022	10,037

Measures computed from the distribution

Absolute (dollars)

Q_3	14,636	16,250	8,250	7,625	8,850	4,500	3,875	6,977	11,721
Md	6,750	8,643	4,864	4,375	6,583	2,750	1,750	4,850	6,016
Q_1	1,375	4,833	2,562	2,344	3,375	2,200	812	1,562	2,719
I.D.	13,261	11,417	5,688	5,281	5,475	2,300	3,063	5,415	9,002
S.D.	10,595	23,875	6,772	6,530	4,596	4,150	4,492	4,533	16,669

Relative

R.I.D.	1.965	1.321	1.170	1.207	.832	.836	1.750	1.116	1.496
V^1	1.253	1.692	1.033	1.029	.660	.922	1.418	.895	1.647

For footnotes see p. 569.

TABLE B11a (cont.)

1931 (1933 SAMPLE)

INCOME CLASSES (dollars)	NE	MA	ENC	WNC	SA and ESC	WSC	MT.	PAC.	U.S.
Under -2,000[5]	9.4	13.8	4.7	3			1	4.6	33.7
-2,000 to -1,000[5]	1.2	1.4		2					5.6
-1,000 to 0[5]	2.4	5.8	1.3	1	3	1		10.4	26.7
0									
1 to 500	2	9	3		2	2	2	4	24
500 to 1,000	1	4	2		2			3	12
1,000 to 1,500	2	5		4	2		1	4	18
1,500 to 2,000	2	6	6	3	2	2		8	29
2,000 to 2,500	2	3	2	1	1	2	1	7	19
2,500 to 3,000		7	2		4		2	3	18
3,000 to 3,500	6	5	5		3	1	1	9	30
3,500 to 4,000		11			3	2		4	20
4,000 to 5,000	2	4	4	2	4	2	1	5	24
5,000 to 6,000	2	18	8	1	1	2		2	34
6,000 to 7,000	1	11	5	2	2			3	24
7,000 to 8,000		2	2	5	2			7	18
8,000 to 9,000		12	2	3	1			7	25
9,000 to 10,000	3	10	2		2			2	19
10,000 to 12,000	2	9	1	1				1	14
12,000 to 14,000	10	6	4		1			3	24
14,000 to 16,000	1	17	1		1	1		1	22
16,000 to 18,000		10			1				11
18,000 to 20,000	1	6							7
20,000 to 25,000		5		2					7
25,000 to 30,000		6							6
30,000 to 40,000		2							2
40,000 to 50,000			1						1
50,000 and over		2							2
No. of engineers covered	50	191	56	30	37	15	9	88	476
A.M. (dollars)	4,141	8,496	5,055	4,837	4,350	3,517	1,840	3,565	5,887

Measures computed from the distributions.

Absolute (dollars)

	NE	MA	ENC	WNC	SA and ESC	WSC	MT.	PAC.	U.S.
Q_3	11,500	14,030	6,800	7,700	6,375	4,625	2,938	6,667	8,631
Md	3,250	6,227	4,500	4,500	3,416	3,250	2,250	2,500	4,041
Q_1	-208	2,458	1,750	1,180	1,562	1,688	312	1,000	1,456
I.D.	11,708	11,572	5,050	6,520	4,813	2,937	2,626	5,667	7,175
S.D.	7,798	11,712	7,331	7,312	4,129	3,547	1,863	4,408	9,010

Relative

	NE	MA	ENC	WNC	SA and ESC	WSC	MT.	PAC.	U.S.
R.I.D.	3.602	1.858	1.122	1.449	1.409	.904	1.167	2.267	1.776
V^1	1.995	1.379	1.489	1.756	.927	.990	1.104	1.289	1.548

For footnotes see p.569.

1932 (1933 SAMPLE)

INCOME CLASSES (dollars)	NE	MA	ENC	WNC	SA and ESC	WSC	MT.	PAC.	U.S.
Under -2,000[5]	6.4	21.9	2.7		1.5		1	5.9	41.5
-2,000 to -1,000[5]	2.3	8.5	5.3	1.3	1.5	1		5.8	23.3
-1,000 to 0[5]	5.3	15.6	—	7.7	3	1		7.3	40.2
0									
1 to 500		8	8	3	2	5	3	10	39
500 to 1,000	1	10	5	1	1	1	2	6	27
1,000 to 1,500	2	10	4	2	2		2	4	26
1,500 to 2,000	3	13	6	1	3			7	33
2,000 to 2,500	2	8	3	1	7	1		7	29
2,500 to 3,000	4	6			1			2	13
3,000 to 3,500	2	11	3	3	3	1		5	28
3,500 to 4,000	2	8	11	2	3	2		1	29
4,000 to 5,000	1	18	1	4	2		2	2	30
5,000 to 6,000		14	2		1	1		9	27
6,000 to 7,000		2	1		2			3	8
7,000 to 8,000	3	2	1	1	2			5	14
8,000 to 9,000	8	2	1					1	12
9,000 to 10,000		2						5	7
10,000 to 12,000	1	3		1		2			7
12,000 to 14,000		3	1		1				5
14,000 to 16,000		14	1	2					17
16,000 to 18,000		4							4
18,000 to 20,000		6	1						7
20,000 to 25,000		4							4
25,000 to 30,000		1							1
30,000 to 40,000		1	1						2
40,000 to 50,000									
50,000 and over									
No. of engineers covered	43	196	58	30	36	15	10	86	474
A.M. (dollars)	2,074	3,996	3,088	2,761	2,521	2,702	1,410	2,293	3,116

Measures computed from the distributions.

Absolute (dollars)

	NE	MA	ENC	WNC	SA and ESC	WSC	MT.	PAC.	U.S.
Q_3	7,417	5,643	3,796	4,125	3,834	3,812	1,375	5,167	4,785
Md	2,375	2,750	1,834	1,500	2,286	750	750	1,786	2,178
Q_1	-613	188	406	-195	1,000	175	250	125	33
I.D.	8,030	5,455	3,390	4,320	2,834	3,637	1,125	5,042	4,752
S.D.	6,726	8,030	5,737	4,237	3,406	3,742	2,056	3,453	6,462

Relative

	NE	MA	ENC	WNC	SA and ESC	WSC	MT.	PAC.	U.S.
R.I.D.	3.381	1.984	1.848	2.880	1.240	4.849	1.500	2.823	2.182
V^i	3.783	2.019	1.809	1.479	1.364	1.386	1.909	1.469	2.124

For footnotes see p. 569.

TABLE B 11 (cont.)

b   By Size of Community

1929 (1933 SAMPLE)

Communities with populations (in thousands) of

INCOME CLASSES (dollars)	1,500 & over	500 to 1,500	250 to 500	100 to 250	25 to 100	5 to 25	under 5	U.S.
Under -2,000[5]	3	3	8				1	13.7
-2,000 to -1,000[5]	1	1						2.8
-1,000 to 0[5]	1	1		2			1	5.5
1 to 500	1	2	1			1	1	6
500 to 1,000	1	2	1	2	1			7
1,000 to 1,500	6	3			1	1	1	12
1,500 to 2,000	2	3	2		4	1		12
2,000 to 2,500	3	2	5	1	1		1	13
2,500 to 3,000	3	8	5	6	8			30
3,000 to 3,500	4	3	3	2		1		13
3,500 to 4,000		4	1	1	5	2	2	15
4,000 to 5,000	6	6	8	6	6	2	2	36
5,000 to 6,000		6	8	2	5	2	1	24
6,000 to 7,000	10	1	6		3	3		23
7,000 to 8,000	9	6	5	1	3			24
8,000 to 9,000	9	15	5	6	2	1	1	39
9,000 to 10,000	5	9		3			1	18
10,000 to 12,000	14	6	6	3	1	2	3	35
12,000 to 14,000	7	9	1		1		2	20
14,000 to 16,000	5	14	1	2			1	23
16,000 to 18,000	2	4	7		1		1	15
18,000 to 20,000	5	6		2	2			15
20,000 to 25,000	5	1	4	1	1			12
25,000 to 30,000	14							14
30,000 to 40,000	15	2	1		1		2	21
40,000 to 50,000	6		1			2		9
50,000 and over	11	2						13
No. of engineers covered	148	119	79	40	46	20	19	471
A.M. (dollars)	19,591	9,835	7,284	6,901	6,479	8,093	10,297	11,840

Measures computed from the distributions

Absolute (dollars)

Q_3	28,215	13,834	10,416	9,333	7,167	7,500	13,250	14,805
Md	11,428	8,567	5,688	5,000	4,500	5,000	9,500	7,943
Q_1	6,600	3,719	2,775	2,916	2,781	2,500	3,938	3,570
I.D.	21,615	10,115	7,641	6,417	4,386	5,000	9,312	11,235
S.D.	20,382	9,479	8,405	5,336	6,448	12,667	9,533	14,580

Relative

R.I.D.	1.891	1.181	1.343	1.283	.975	1.000	.980	1.414
V[1]	1.054	.971	1.123	.768	.982	1.492	.885	1.231

For footnotes see p.569.

1930 (1933 SAMPLE)

Communities with populations (in thousands) of

INCOME CLASSES (dollars)	1,500 & over	500 to 1,500	250 to 500	100 to 250	25 to 100	5 to 25	under 5	U.S.
Under -2,000[5]	9.25	1				1		10.1
-2,000 to -1,000[5]		6	2	4		1		14.5
-1,000 to 0[5]	1.75	6	4			1	2	14.4
0								
1 to 500		8	2	1	2	1		14
500 to 1,000	5	2			2	2		11
1,000 to 1,500	1	2	2	2	1			8
1,500 to 2,000		2	5	1	7	3		18
2,000 to 2,500	4	1	3	5	3	1	3	20
2,500 to 3,000		3	2	2	5	3		15
3,000 to 3,500	5	2	1		2		2	12
3,500 to 4,000	5	6	2		1			14
4,000 to 5,000	9	6	18	3	12	1	2	51
5,000 to 6,000	12	11	3	1	5	1	2	35
6,000 to 7,000	2	16	8	4	1	1	3	35
7,000 to 8,000	7	8	6	1	1			23
8,000 to 9,000	11	3	4	5	2	1	1	27
9,000 to 10,000	2	7	2	2		1	2	16
10,000 to 12,000	13	4	6		1	3		27
12,000 to 14,000	2	6	2		1		2	13
14,000 to 16,000	14	15	2	3				34
16,000 to 18,000	3	2	2	1	3		1	12
18,000 to 20,000	1		2	1	1			5
20,000 to 25,000	18	2	1					21
25,000 to 30,000	2							2
30,000 to 40,000	8	4	1	1				14
40,000 to 50,000	4							4
50,000 and over	10		1					11
No. of engineers covered	149	123	81	37	50	21	20	481
A.M. (dollars)	17,459	7,600	7,487	6,484	5,075	3,569	5,839	10,037

Measures computed from the distributions

Absolute (dollars)

Q_3	21,320	11,124	8,688	8,750	5,500	6,750	9,000	11,721
Md	10,076	6,344	4,972	5,500	4,167	2,584	5,500	6,016
Q_1	4,694	2,958	3,125	2,125	2,084	812	2,750	2,719
I.D.	16,626	8,166	5,563	6,625	3,416	5,938	6,250	9,002
S.D.	26,284	7,441	10,431	7,048	4,450	4,507	4,456	16,669

Relative

R.I.D.	1.650	1.287	1.119	1.205	.820	2.298	1.136	1.496
V^1	1.506	.974	1.377	1.063	.880	1.241	.729	1.647

For footnotes see p.569.

TABLE B11b (cont.)

1931 (1933 SAMPLE)

Communities with populations (in thousands) of

INCOME CLASSES (dollars)	1,500 & over	500 to 1,500	250 to 500	100 to 250	25 to 100	5 to 25	under 5	U.S.
Under -2,000[5]	13.4	14.8	4.8			3		33.7
-2,000 to -1,000[5]	1.8		2.8	1.2				5.6
-1,000 to 0[5]	1.8	8.2	1.4	3.8	2	2	5	26.7
0								
1 to 500	6	3	2	1	6	5	1	24
500 to 1,000	1	1	3		2	1	4	12
1,000 to 1,500	3	5	4	2	2	1	1	18
1,500 to 2,000	3	6	5	2	7	3	3	29
2,000 to 2,500	3	5	4	2	3		2	19
2,500 to 3,000	8	3	2	3	1	1		18
3,000 to 3,500	4	9	10	3	3	1		30
3,500 to 4,000	5	6	7	2				20
4,000 to 5,000	3	7	8	3	2		1	24
5,000 to 6,000	8	10	3	2	9		2	34
6,000 to 7,000	8	9		2	5			24
7,000 to 8,000	2	7	8			1		18
8,000 to 9,000	9	9	3	4				25
9,000 to 10,000	7		3	1	2	4	2	19
10,000 to 12,000	5	5	1		3			14
12,000 to 14,000	7	13	1	2			1	24
14,000 to 16,000	16	2	2	1	1			22
16,000 to 18,000	9		1	1				11
18,000 to 20,000	6			1				7
20,000 to 25,000	5	2						7
25,000 to 30,000	3	2	1					6
30,000 to 40,000	2							2
40,000 to 50,000			1					1
50,000 and over	2							2
No. of engineers covered	142	127	78	37	48	22	22	476
A.M. (dollars)	9,420	5,035	4,778	5,193	3,975	574	2,572	5,887

Measures computed from the distributions

Absolute (dollars)

Q_3	14,938	8,139	7,188	8,188	5,889	3,250	4,500	8,631
Md.	8,000	4,357	3,500	3,625	3,166	1,000	1,500	4,041
Q_1	2,656	1,475	1,650	1,812	1,500	50	250	1,456
I.D.	12,282	6,664	5,538	6,376	4,389	3,200	4,250	7,175
S.D.	7,935	6,784	7,202	4,992	3,504	7,018	3,663	9,010

Relative

R.I.D.	1.535	1.529	1.582	1.759	1.386	3.200	2.833	1.776
V[1]	.849	1.399	1.587	.969	.867	9.761	1.360	1.548

For footnotes see p.569.

1932 (1933 SAMPLE)

Communities with populations (in thousands) of

INCOME CLASSES (dollars)	1,500 & over	500 to 1,500	250 to 500	100 to 250	25 to 100	5 to 25	under 5	U.S.
Under -2,000[5]	18.1	14.2	3.3			3	2.3	41.5
-2,000 to -1,000[5]	8.5	5.3	4.5	1.3	1	2	2.4	23.3
-1,000 to 0[5]	12.4	6.5	9.2	2.7	4	2	2.3	40.2
0								
1 to 500	5	4	11	2	8	4	5	39
500 to 1,000	10	2	8	1	3	3		27
1,000 to 1,500	6	7	2	4	3	3	1	26
1,500 to 2,000	5	16	3	2	3	1	3	33
2,000 to 2,500	5	7	7	6	2	1	1	29
2,500 to 3,000	2	3		4	4			13
3,000 to 3,500	14	6	5	2	1			28
3,500 to 4,000	5	7	5	4	7		1	29
4,000 to 5,000	11	6	7	1	4		1	30
5,000 to 6,000	10	7	2	5	2	1		27
6,000 to 7,000	2	3		1	1		1	8
7,000 to 8,000	1	8	2		1	1	1	14
8,000 to 9,000	2	9				1		12
9,000 to 10,000	2	5						7
10,000 to 12,000	3	1	3					7
12,000 to 14,000	1		3		1			5
14,000 to 16,000	14	2	1					17
16,000 to 18,000	4							4
18,000 to 20,000	6				1			7
20,000 to 25,000	1	2		1				4
25,000 to 30,000			1					1
30,000 to 40,000	1		1					2
40,000 to 50,000								
50,000 and over								
No. of engineers covered	149	121	78	37	46	22	21	474
A.M. (dollars)	3,928	3,134	3,161	2,997	2,767	286	1,024	3,116

Measures computed from the distributions

Absolute (dollars)

Q_3	5,975	5,964	4,071	3,844	3,893	1,416	1,958	4,785
Md	3,090	2,393	1,666	2,458	2,250	500	350	2,178
Q_1	-141	562	114	1,281	406	-750	-761	33
I.D.	6,116	5,402	3,957	2,563	3,487	2,166	2,719	4,752
S.D.	8,411	5,807	6,097	3,773	3,529	3,885	2,848	6,462

Relative

R.I.D.	1.979	2.257	2.375	1.043	1.550	4.332	7.769	2.182
V^1	2.184	1.927	1.932	1.231	1.251	12.333	3.168	2.124

For footnotes see p. 569.

TABLE B 11 (concl.)

c   By Organization of Practice

(1933 SAMPLE)

INCOME CLASSES (dollars)	INDIVIDUAL PRACTITIONERS				FIRM MEMBERS			
	1929	1930	1931	1932	1929	1930	1931	1932
Under −2,000[5]	6	6.9	15.5	21.4	8	4	21	20.3
−2,000 to −1,000[5]	3	8.2	4.6	21.7		7		2.7
−1,000 to 0[5]	5	9.9	24.9	21.9		3		17
0								
1 to 500	6	12	20	29		2	4	10
500 to 1,000	7	7	7	17		4	5	10
1,000 to 1,500	8	6	15	22	4	2	3	4
1,500 to 2,000	10	13	24	18	2	5	5	15
2,000 to 2,500	11	12	8	17	2	8	11	12
2,500 to 3,000	14	13	9	7	16	2	9	6
3,000 to 3,500	11	7	16	18	2	5	14	10
3,500 to 4,000	10	12	12	8	5	2	8	21
4,000 to 5,000	21	24	15	16	15	27	9	14
5,000 to 6,000	12	18	20	10	12	17	14	17
6,000 to 7,000	16	13	20	6	7	22	4	2
7,000 to 8,000	20	17	7	10	4	6	11	4
8,000 to 9,000	18	18	7	4	21	9	18	8
9,000 to 10,000	7	12	11	5	11	4	8	2
10,000 to 12,000	20	14	7	4	15	13	7	3
12,000 to 14,000	9	6	7	3	11	7	17	2
14,000 to 16,000	9	10	7	2	14	24	15	15
16,000 to 18,000	10	10	4		5	2	7	4
18,000 to 20,000	10	5	1	2	5		6	5
20,000 to 25,000	8	4		2	4	17	7	2
25,000 to 30,000	3	2	2	1	11		4	
30,000 to 40,000	6	3	2	2	15	11		
40,000 to 50,000	1	2	1		8	2		
50,000 and over	2	3	2		11	8		
No. of engineers covered	263	268	269	268	208	213	207	206
A.M. (dollars)	8,535	7,472	4,943	2;483	16,019	13,264	7,114	3,940

Measures computed from the distributions.

Absolute (dollars)

Q_3	10,650	9,384	6,411	3,955	18,800	14,896	12,500	5,735
Md	6,414	5,125	3,190	1,524	9,545	6,841	6,125	3,300
Q_1	2,769	2,000	570	0	4,867	4,343	2,653	575
I.D.	7,881	7,384	5,841	3,955	13,933	10,553	9,847	5,160
S.D.	10,363	10,724	9,391	6,139	17,580	21,615	8,455	6,835

Relative

R.I.D.	1.228	1.440	1.830	2.596	1.460	1.543	1.608	1.564
V^1	1.214	1.435	1.900	2.472	1.120	1.636	1.239	1.759

For footnotes see p. 569.

TABLE B 12

Average Coefficient of Variation and Relative Interquartile Difference

a By Region

AVERAGE COEFFICIENT OF VARIATION

	PHYSICIANS				DENTISTS			LAWYERS	CERTIFIED PUBLIC ACCOUNTANTS				CONSULTING ENGINEERS
	1933 sample	1935 sample	1937 sample	All samples [13]	1933 sample	1935 sample	Both samples [13]	1935 sample	1933 sample	1935 sample	1937 sample	All samples [13]	1933 sample
New England	.969	1.194	.854	1.002	.684	.565	.633	1.164	.682	.663	.547	.636	1.984
Middle Atlantic	.960	.950	.901	.940	.888	.993	.933	1.160	.830	.877	.866	.855	1.545
E. N. Central	1.077	1.630	.761	1.148	.712	.703	.708	1.254	.846	.897	.695	.816	1.320
W. N. Central	1.341	1.003	.822	1.084	.666	.608	.641	1.056	.507	.690	.750	.635	1.426
S. Atlantic	1.178	1.283	.909	1.129	.804	.945	.864	1.038	.929	.592	.593	.729	} .952
E. S. Central	1.443	1.449	1.051	1.327	.602	.590	.597	1.446	.467	.621	.589	.550	
W. S. Central	.972	.834	.853	.895	1.062	.621	.873	1.539	.683	.716	.567	.658	1.050
Mountain	.738	1.629	.913	1.058	.560	.709	.624	1.595	.732	.629	.671	.683	1.382
Pacific	1.515	.906	.871	1.139	.694	.782	.732	1.402	.542	.633	.510	.560	1.100
U.S.	1.206	1.264	.883	1.126	.813	.831	.821	1.297	.830	.832	.748	.806	1.638

AVERAGE RELATIVE INTERQUARTILE DIFFERENCE

	PHYSICIANS				DENTISTS			LAWYERS	CERTIFIED PUBLIC ACCOUNTANTS				CONSULTING ENGINEERS
	1933 sample	1935 sample	1937 sample	All samples [13]	1933 sample	1935 sample	Both samples [13]	1935 sample	1933 sample	1935 sample	1937 sample	All samples [13]	1933 sample
New England	1.266	1.040	1.112	1.152	.907	.790	.857	1.784	.841	.821	.988	.879	2.551
Middle Atlantic	1.133	1.218	1.031	1.128	.832	.905	.863	1.511	1.071	.878	.746	.916	1.749
E. N. Central	1.128	1.099	.853	1.037	.797	.836	.814	1.395	.834	.861	.813	.836	1.344
W. N. Central	1.272	1.189	1.071	1.187	.802	.806	.804	1.407	.812	.810	.836	.819	1.775
S. Atlantic	1.308	1.230	1.326	1.290	.815	.819	.817	1.457	.646	.720	.774	.707	} 1.191
E. S. Central	1.416	1.355	1.174	1.328	.804	.770	.789	1.492	.680	.875	.622	.721	
W. S. Central	1.351	1.231	1.005	1.211	.597	.618	.606	1.394	.752	1.026	.759	.836	1.856
Mountain	1.044	1.422	.979	1.138	.719	.650	.689	1.279	.750	.846	.925	.831	1.462
Pacific	1.210	.925	1.067	1.082	.774	.830	.798	1.263	.646	.625	.552	.612	1.838
U.S.	1.250	1.164	1.027	1.158	.817	.842	.828	1.430	.850	.829	.758	.819	1.717

For footnotes see p. 569.

TABLE B 12 (concl.)

b By Size of Community

AVERAGE COEFFICIENT OF VARIATION

SIZE OF COMMUNITY	PHYSICIANS			DENTISTS			LAWYERS	CERTIFIED PUBLIC ACCOUNTANTS				CONSULTING ENGINEERS
	1933 sample	1935 sample	Both samples[13]	1933 sample	1935 sample	Both samples[13]	1935 sample	1933 sample	1935 sample	1937 sample	All samples[13]	1933 sample
1,500,000 and over	{1.170	{1.485	{1.305	{.959	{1.060	{1.002	1.272	.832	.891	.849	.855	1.398
500,000 - 1,500,000							1.160	.646	.674	.715	.675	1.318
250,000 - 500,000	{1.381	{1.006	{1.220	{.738	{.744	{.741	1.380	.904	.820	.596	.787	1.505
100,000 - 250,000							1.015	.775	.685	.674	.718	1.008
50,000 - 100,000	.872	1.177	1.003	.762	.773	.767	{1.265	{.582	{.747	{.586	{.633	{.995
25,000 - 50,000	.944	1.019	.976	.612	.692	.646						
10,000 - 25,000	.878	1.117	.980	.564	.605	.581	1.302					6.207
5,000 - 10,000	{.956	{.942	{.950	{.544	{.498	{.534	{.913	{.733	{.666	{.694	{.701	{1.536
2,500 - 5,000												
Under 2,500	1.135	.847	1.012	.612	.556	.588	.794					
U.S.	1.206	1.264	1.231	.813	.831	.821	1.297	.830	.832	.748	.806	1.638

AVERAGE RELATIVE INTERQUARTILE DIFFERENCE

SIZE OF COMMUNITY	PHYSICIANS			DENTISTS			LAWYERS	CERTIFIED PUBLIC ACCOUNTANTS				CONSULTING ENGINEERS
	1933 sample	1935 sample	Both samples[13]	1933 sample	1935 sample	Both samples[13]	1935 sample	1933 sample	1935 sample	1937 sample	All samples[13]	1933 sample
1,500,000 and over	{1.269	{1.205	{1.242	{.936	{1.013	{.969	1.497	1.002	.945	.781	.927	1.764
500,000 - 1,500,000							1.233	.674	.746	.752	.719	1.504
250,000 - 500,000	{1.224	{1.085	{1.165	{.796	{.870	{.827	1.718	.864	.789	.782	.816	1.605
100,000 - 250,000							1.699	.708	.693	.720	.707	1.322
50,000 - 100,000	1.187	1.175	1.182	.764	.892	.819	{1.534	{.802	{.738	{.739	{.764	{1.183
25,000 - 50,000	1.084	1.275	1.166	.850	.775	.818						
10,000 - 25,000	1.264	1.047	1.161	.701	.763	.728	1.446					2.708
5,000 - 10,000	{1.055	{.989	{1.027	{.712	{.657	{.689	{1.139	{.605	{.776	{.836	{.726	{3.180
2,500 - 5,000												
Under 2,500	1.312	1.243	1.282	.745	.809	.772	1.057					
U.S.	1.250	1.164	1.214	.817	.842	.828	1.430	.850	.829	.768	.819	1.717

For footnotes see p.569.

FOOTNOTES TO APPENDIX B TABLES:

[1] In computing the coefficient of variation, we used the arithmetic mean computed from the frequency distribution (where total income was estimated by multiplying the midpoint of each income class by the frequency in the class and summing over all classes).

[2] Includes some returns for which location of practice is unknown.

[3] Data for dentists have not been adjusted for the restriction of the samples to American Dental Association members.

[4] Before any weighting or adjusting.

[5] The distribution in the negative income classes was obtained by raising the number of known losses by the ratio of total losses to known losses. This was done separately for each region, each size of community class, and the United States. For this reason, the sum of the regions and size of community classes does not equal the number for the United States in the negative income classes.

[6] The frequency distributions for the 1933 medical and dental samples do not incorporate final revision (see Explanatory Note).

[7] Arithmetic means for all regions, all size of community classes, and the United States incorporate final revisions and are, therefore, not based on the number of individuals shown in the table.

[8] Measures for the United States incorporate final revisions.

[9] All data from the 1937 medical sample have been weighted to correct for the nonrandomness of the sample among the states.

[10] The data from the 1935 legal sample have been adjusted for the firm member and size of community biases.

[11] The averages from the 1937 legal sample are weighted averages of the averages for each state, and have been adjusted for the size of community bias.

[12] All data from the accountancy samples are adjusted for the firm member bias.

[13] The average for all samples is a weighted average of the averages for each sample, the weights being the number of years covered by each sample.

This form used also for Physicians 1932-34, and for Lawyers 1932-34.

UNITED STATES DEPARTMENT OF COMMERCE

Division of Economic Research

Dentists

	1932	1933	1934
Gross income	_____	_____	_____
Net income	_____	_____	_____
Number of professional employees	_____	_____	_____
Number of other employees	_____	_____	_____
Salaries and wages paid professional employees	_____	_____	_____
Salaries and wages paid other employees	_____	_____	_____

UNITED STATES DEPARTMENT OF COMMERCE

Confidential Data for Use Only in Preparing Estimates
of the National Income by Direction of
United States Senate Resolution 220.

MEDICAL PROFESSION

Dollars

Gross receipts from practice: 1929   ....

1930   ....

1931   ....

1932   ....

Net Income (gross receipts less
expenses of practice): 1929   ....

1930   ....

1931   ....

1932   ....

Kindly fill out the above, giving your closest estimates where
actual figures are not available, and return in the enclosed
envelope which requires no postage.

UNITED STATES DEPARTMENT OF COMMERCE
Bureau of Foreign and Domestic Commerce
Division of Economic Research

To Physicians and Surgeons:

If received by a practitioner who is a salaried employee of a private firm or public institution, please disregard our request. We desire information only from the independent medical profession. No signature is desired.

I. Give the name of the city and state where the major part of your practice occurs. City_____ State_____

II. Check the population of the above city:
(1) Less than 1,000 _____ (2) 1,000 – 9,999 _____ (3) 10,000 – 99,999 _____ (4) 100,000 and over_____

III. Indicate the type of practice in which you are engaged:
General practice _____
Specialized practice (such as surgery, neurology, obstetrics, etc.) _____
Special interest with General Practice (such as pediatrics, surgery, gynecology, etc.) _____

IV. State the number of years you have practiced medicine._____

While we shall appreciate as complete data as you can furnish, we are particularly interested in the years 1929, and 1934 to 1936, inclusive. Where data are not provided indicate in space "None" or "Information not given".

Items	1929	1930	1931	1932	1933	1934	1935	1936
1. Gross Income from independent professional medical service, excluding fixed salaries from firms or public institutions and income from investments or other sources.								
2. Net Income, which is gross income less expenses incidental to your professional practice. These expenses include neither living expenses nor income taxes.								
3. Average Monthly Number of all employees (nurses, secretaries, etc.)								
4. Total Salaries paid to all employees.								

Confidential Data for Use Only in Preparing Estimates of the National
Income by Direction of United States Senate Resolution 220.

PUBLIC ACCOUNTANTS

	1929	1930	1931	1932
1. Is the business individual or partnership?		....	....	
2. Total number of offices operated		....	....	
3. Total number of offices included in this report (all if possible)		....	....	
4. Number of partners or firm members:	....	....	....	....
5. Number of employees, full time: (average for the year) part time:	....	....	....	....
6. Gross annual receipts:	....	....	....	....
7. Salaries and wages paid , full time: (excluding compensation of firm members) part time:	....	....	....	....
8. Net income (gross receipts less operating expenses):	....	....	....	....
9. Withdrawals by firm members (include salaries if on salary basis):	....	....	....	....

Kindly fill out the above giving your closest estimates where actual figures are not available,
and return in the enclosed envelope, which requires no postage.

UNITED STATES DEPARTMENT OF COMMERCE

Bureau of Foreign and Domestic Commerce

Division of Economic Research

Public Accountants

(Practicing on Own Account and Members of Public Accounting Firms)

NOTE: If received by a firm member please enter data below for the entire
firm and enter for Item 1 the number of members of the firm. One
return from entire firm is preferred to individual returns from
each firm member or for each branch office.

	1932	1933	1934
1. Number of firm members (if practicing on own account, answer "one")			
2. Gross income from independent practice of profession			
3. Net income (gross income less all expenses incurred in professional practice, before payment of Federal income taxes)			
4. Total cash withdrawals by the individual or by all members of the firm submitting questionnaires			
5. Number of accountants (other than firm members) employed (average monthly)			
6. Number of other employees (average monthly)			
7. Total salaries, wages, commissions, bonuses, etc., paid to accountants (other than firm members) employed			
8. Total salaries, wages, commissions, bonuses, etc., paid to other employees			

UNITED STATES DEPARTMENT OF COMMERCE
Bureau of Foreign and Domestic Commerce
Division of Economic Research.

To Public Accountants:

If this questionnaire is received by a public accountant who is a salaried employee of an accounting firm, please hand it to the employer; if received by a public accountant who is a salaried employee of a non-accounting firm or public institution, please disregard our request, since this questionnaire is designed to obtain information for independent professional service, and should be filled in only by accounting firms and independent practitioners. We desire only one return for each office. We do not ask for your signature.

Items	1929	1934	1935	1936
1. Number of firm members (If independent practitioner, answer "one").				
2. Gross income of firm from professional practice (If independent practitioner, exclude salaries from firms or public institutions; but in both cases exclude income from investments and other sources).				
3. Net income (Gross income less expenses incidental to your professional practice only, as rents and salaries. Such expenses should not include your living expenses nor your income taxes, state or Federal).				
4. Total cash withdrawals by the individual or by all members of the firm.				
5. Average monthly number of accountants employed other than firm members.				
6. Total salaries, commissions, bonuses, etc. paid to accountants included in item No. 5.				
7. Average monthly number of other employees, such as secretaries and other non-professional assistants.				
8. Total salaries paid each year to all employees included in item No. 7.				

Indicate the city and state in which your office is located _____

#2451

_____ (City)   _____ (State)

Confidential Data for Use Only in Preparing Estimates of the National Income by
Direction of United States Senate Resolution 220.

ENGINEERING PROFESSION

	1929	1930	1931	1932
1. Branch of engineering:	....	....		
2. Is the firm individual or partnership?	....			
3. Number of partners or firm members:	....	....	....	....
4. Number of employees, full time: (average for the year) part time:	....	....	....	....
5. Gross annual receipts:	....	....	....	....
6. Salaries and wages paid, full time: (excluding compensation of firm members) part time:	....	....	....	....
7. If incorporated:				
a. Net income less taxes:	....	....	....	....
b. Dividends paid:	....	....	....	....
8. If unincorporated:				
a. Net income (gross receipts less operat- ing expenses):	....	....	....	....
b. Withdrawals by firm members (include salaries if on salary basis)	....	....	....	....

Kindly fill out the above giving your closest estimates where actual figures are not available, and
return in the enclosed envelope, which requires no postage.

DEPARTMENT OF COMMERCE
Bureau of Foreign and Domestic Commerce
Division of Economic Research

To Attorneys at Law:

Instructions - If this questionnaire is received by an attorney who is a salaried employee of a legal firm, please hand it to your employer since there should be only one return for an entire firm for the first seven questions. For the last five questions (number 8-12) each firm member and each salaried attorney of the firm should make separate returns. If we have not enclosed sufficient copies of questions (8-12) we shall be pleased to send additional ones on request or attorneys may write letters giving the complete information in the order stated. Individual practitioners should answer all 12 questions. Attorneys employed by non-legal firms or public institutions should answer only questions 8-12, inclusive.

Where data are not provided, please indicate whether it means "None" or "Information not available." This distinction is important for statistical purposes. The information asked will be held in STRICT CONFIDENCE. To assure complete anonymity, please do not state the name of your firm or of firm members and give no signature.

Questions	1929	1932	1933	1934	1935	1936
1. Number of members in law firm (If practicing alone answer "one".).						
2. Gross income of individual practitioner or of firm from legal practice, including retainers (If practicing alone exclude salaries whether from part-time positions from firms or public institutions; but in all cases exclude income from investments and other sources.).						
3. Net income (Gross income less current expenses applicable to legal practice only. Do not deduct capital outlays, income taxes, or personal expenses.).						
4. Average monthly number of professional employees (Lawyers on salary).						
5. Total salaries paid to all employees included in question No. 4.						
6. Average monthly number of other employees (Secretaries, etc.)						
7. Total salaries paid to all other employees included in question No. 6.						

(questions 8-12, inclusive, are to be answered by individual attorneys)

Name of the city and state where the major part of your practice occurs. City _____ State _____

8. Educational Qualifications:

   A. Non-legal and pre-legal education -

   (Circle year completed)

   High School 1 2 3 4

	Graduated Yes or no	Degrees	Name of Institution
College 1 2 3 4	x	x	x
Graduate 1 2 3			

   B. Legal education -

   Studied law in office (Yes or no) _____ Studied law in school (Yes or no) _____

   If in a law school, name of institution _____ Number of years _____

   Day School _____ Night School _____ Have you a law degree? (Yes or no) _____

   C. General -

   Were you in the upper quarter of your class in college? (Yes or no) _____ In law school? (Yes or no) _____

   Number of times bar examination taken in State _____ (Name) where admitted to practice _____ (number)

9. Number of years engaged in legal practice as of December 31, 1936: Total _____ As salaried employee of legal firm _____ Of non-legal firm _____ As individual practitioner _____ Firm member _____

10. Nature of principal legal practice as of 1936:

    Domestic Relations _____ Criminal _____ General Corporate Work _____ Probate _____ Negligence _____

    Public Utility _____ Banking _____ Real Estate _____ Public Office (Specify) _____

    Other (Specify) _____ General _____

11. Net Income (Defined as in question number 3) or salary:

    From practice as individual or with legal firm in 1929 _____ 1933 _____ 1936 _____

    If with non-legal firm, salary in 1929 _____ 1933 _____ 1936 _____

12. Are you actively engaged in remunerative activities other than practice of law? (Yes or no) _____

    A. If so, state nature of such activities: Banking and finance _____ Insurance _____ Real Estate _____

    General Mercantile _____ Industrial _____ Other (Specify) _____

    B. Net income from 12A exclusive of inheritance and rents, interest and dividends on investments:

    1929 _____ 1933 _____ 1936 _____

REFERENCES ARE TO TABLE NUMBERS

	PHYSICIANS (1)	DENTISTS (2)	LAWYERS (3)	CERTIFIED PUBLIC ACCOUNTANTS (4)	CONSULTING ENGINEERS (5)	ALL PERSONS, EARNERS, OR NON-RELIEF FAMILIES (6)
ADMISSIONS TO						
Profession	2					
Professional schools			3			
ARITHMETIC MEAN						
U. S.						
Final estimates						
Avg. for period	11, B3	11, B5	B8	11, B10		
Standardized with respect to						
Region	7, 11, 16, 17, 18, 29	7, 11, 16, 17, 18, 29	16, 17, 18	7, 11, 16, 17, 18		
Size of community	18	18	18	18	18	
Original estimates						
Avg. for period	17, 29	17, 29	17	17	17	
By type of practice	10, B1, B2	10, B4	10, B6, B7	10, B9	10, B11	8, 17, 18
Standardized with respect to						
Region	36, 37, 43				16, 17, 18	7
Size of community					18	
Indices						
By organization or type of practice	64	64	64	64	64	
By size of community	36, 37, B1c	36	47, B6c	47, B9c	47, B11c	64
Avg. for period	84					
By years in practice	43					
Indices	33, 34		68	68	68	
Standardized with respect to size of community	67					
of community	44					
By regions						
Final estimates						
Avg. for period	B3	B5	B8	B10		
Standardized with respect to size of community	18, 29	18, 29	18	18	18	
Original estimates						
Avg. for period	29	29				
By size of community	B1a, B2	B 4a	B6a, B7	B9a	B11a	18
Avg. for period	25					
Percentage change	66	66	66	66		66

TABULAR INDEX (Cont.)

	PHYSICIANS (1)	DENTISTS (2)	LAWYERS (3)	CERTIFIED PUBLIC ACCOUNTANTS (4)	CONSULTING ENGINEERS (5)	ALL PERSONS, EARNERS, OR NON-RELIEF FAMILIES (6)
By size of community classes						
Final estimates	B 3	B 5	B 8	B 10		
Avg. for period	16, 17	16, 17	16, 17	16, 17	17	
Original estimates	B1b, B 2	B4b	B6b, B 7	B 11b		
Avg. for period				16, 17		
By regions	25					
By type of practice	34					
Avg. for period	43					
By years in practice	34					
Percentage change	65	65	65	65		
By years in practice	32	32	32			
By size of community	34					
By type of practice	33, 34					
COEFFICIENT OF VARIATION						
U. S.	13, 39, B 1	13, B 4	13, 49, B 6	13, 49, B 9	13, 49, B 11	
Avg. for period	B 12	B 12	B 12	B 12	B 12	
Standardized with respect to						
Region	22	22	22	22	22	22
Size of community	21	21	21	21	21	21
By organization or type of practice	39, B 1c	40	49, B 6c	49, B 9c	49, B 11c	22
By regions	B 1a	B 4a	B 6a	B 9a	B 11a	
Avg. for period	22, B 12a	22, B 12a	22, B 12a	22, B 12a	22, B 12a	
By size of community classes	B 1b	B 4b	B 6b	B9b	B 11b	21
Avg. for period	21, B 12b	21, B 12b	21, B 12b	21, B 12b	21, B 12b	
CORRELATION ANALYSIS						
Analysis of variance ratio	59	59	59	59		
Constants of regression equations	60	60	60	60	60	
Correlation coefficients	56	56	56	56	56	
Correlation table		55				
Rank difference correlation coefficients	20	20	20	20		20

DISTRIBUTION OF INCOME					
U. S.	B1a	B4a	B6a	B9a	B11a
By organization or type of practice	B1c	B4a	B6c	B9c	B11c
By regions	B1a		B6a	B9a	B11a
By scholastic rating			31		
By size of community classes	B1b	B4b	B6b	B9b	B11b
DISTRIBUTION OF PRACTITIONERS					
By organization or type of practice	41, 42		50	50	50
By age, by size of community	35				
By regions	41		50	50	50
By size of community	41, 42		50	50	50
By years in practice	45				
By years in practice	33				
INTERQUARTILE DIFFERENCE					
U. S.	13, 39, B1	13, B4	13, 49, B6	13, 49, B9	13, 49, B11
By organization or type of practice	39, B1c	40	49, B6c	49, B9c	49, B11c
By regions	B1a	B4a	B6a	B9a	B11a
By size of community classes	B1b	B4b	B6b	B9b	B11b
MEDIAN					
U. S.	10, 12, 38, B1	10, 12, B4	10, 12, 48, B6	10, 12, 48, B9	10, 12, 48, B11 8
By organization or type of practice	38, B1c	40	48, B6c	43, B9c	48, B11c
By regions	B1a	B4a	B6a	B9a	B11a
By size of community classes	B1b	B4b	B6b	B9b	B11b
By type of school attended			30		
By years in practice	32	32	32		
METHOD OF SELECTING SAMPLES					
U. S.	4	4	4	4	4
NUMBER OF PERSONS					
U. S.					
Covered by					
Correlation analysis	56	56	56	56	56
Samples	4, 10, B1, B2	4, 10, B4	4, 10, B6, B7	4, 10, B9	4, 10, B11
In profession	1	1	1	1	1
By organization or type of practice	37, B1c		46, B6c	46, B9c	46, B11c
By size of community	34, 43		53		
By years in practice	33, 34				

TABULAR INDEX *(Cont.)*

	PHYSICIANS (1)	DENTISTS (2)	LAWYERS (3)	CERTIFIED PUBLIC ACCOUNTANTS (4)	CONSULTING ENGINEERS (5)	ALL PERSONS, EARNERS, OR NON-RELIEF FAMILIES (6)
By regions	B1a, B2		B6a, B7	B9a	B11a	
By size of community classes	25	B4a				
By size of community classes	B1b, B2	B4b	B6b, B7	B9b	B11b	
By regions	25					
By type of practice	34, 43, B1c					
By years in practice	34					
By years in practice	33		53			
By organization or type of practice	34					
By size of community						
QUARTILES						
U. S.	12, 38, B1	12, B4	12, 48, B6	12, 48, B9	12, 48, B11	
By organization or type of practice	38, B1c	40	48, B6c	48, B9c	48, B11c	
By regions	B1a	B4a	B6a	B9a	B11a	
By size of community classes	B1b	B4b	B6b	B9b	B11b	
RATIO OF QUARTILES						
U. S.	13	13	13	13	13	
By organization or type of practice	39		49	49	49	
RELATIVE INTERQUARTILE DIFFERENCE						
U. S.	13, 39, B1	13, B4	13, 49, B6	13, 49, B9	13, 49, B11	
Avg. for period	B12	B12	B12	B12	B12	
Standardized with respect to						
Region	22	22	22	22	22	22
Size of community	21	21	21	21	21	21
By organization or type of practice	39, B1c	40	49, B6c	49, B9c	49, B11c	
By regions	B1a	B4a	B6a	B9a	B11a	
Avg. for period	22, B12a	22, B12a	22, B12a	22, B12a	22, B12a	
By size of community classes	B1b	B4b	B6b	B9b	B11b	
Avg. for period	21, B12b	21, B12b	21, B12b	21, B12b	21, B12b	
STANDARD DEVIATION						
U. S.	13, 39, B1	13, B4	13, 49, B6	13, 49, B9	13, 49, B11	
By organization or type of practice	39, B1c	40	49, B6c	49, B9c	49, B11c	
By regions	B1a	B4a	B6a	B9a	B11a	
By size of community classes	B1b	B4b	B6b	B9b	B11b	

Author Index

Adams, B. L., 36
Arant, H. W., 36

Baker, K. L., 41
Bevan, A. D., 12
Bierring, W. L., 12
Byrnes, T. W., 41

Capen, S. P., 13
Carson, Daniel, 68, 366
Clark, C. E., 34
Clark, H. F., 86, 145, 146, 149, 150, 151, 412

Davis, H. T., 67
Dodd, P. A., 164, 472, 473
Douglas, W. O., 34
Dunbar, C. E., Jr., 34

Eden, T., 346
Edwards, A. M., 3, 82

Fisher, A. G. B., 91
Fisher, R. A., 339, 350
Flexner, Abraham, 9
Fraser, Andrew, Jr., 45, 486, 487
Friedman, Milton, 115, 223, 227, 452

Garrison, L. K., 31, 38, 60, 237, 241, 483, 484
Gibrat, R., 67
Gies, W. J., 9, 21, 24

Harno, A. J., 34
Harriss, C. L., 131
Hinrichs, A. F., 486
Horack, H. C., 34
Hotelling, Harold, 331

Isaacs, Marvin, 40

King, W. I., 67, 79
Kinnane, C. H., 35
Kirkwood, M. R., 35

Knauth, O. W., 67, 79
Kneeland, Hildegarde, 73
Knibbs, G. H., 78
Kuznets, Simon, 3, 68, 76, 366

Lasken, Herman, 168, 418
Leland, R. G., 8, 11, 144, 145, 162, 231, 232, 257, 259, 263, 267, 270, 271, 273, 274, 275, 420, 422, 424, 449, 453, 455, 475
Leven, Maurice, 5, 21, 122, 138, 140, 146, 147, 186, 228, 241, 246, 264, 265, 267, 269, 299, 416, 417, 420, 442, 443, 461, 462, 463, 466, 469, 473
Lewis, S. R., 23
Lorenz, M. O., 73
Lyon, E. P., 12

Macaulay, F. R., 66, 67, 79
Marshall, Alfred, 89, 90, 97, 129
Martin, J. L., 162, 191, 381
Mill, J. S., 92
Miller, J. A., 12
Mitchell, Wesley C., 67, 79, 141
Molitor, F. A., 44
Moore, G. H., 349
Myers, B. D., 15

Nathan, R. R., 162, 191, 381
Nissley, W. W., 42
Noyes, C. R., 181

Pareto, Vilfredo, 66
Pearson, E. S., 346
Penrose, E. F., 164, 472, 473
Phillips, O. J., 35
Pinkham, C. B., 12, 18

Reed, A. Z., 31, 33, 34, 36
Rogers, J. G., 32, 35
Rypins, Harold, 12, 18

Secrist, Howard, 331
Shafroth, Will, 38

Shea, F. M., 37
Slifer, Walter, 47
Smith, Adam, 83, 129
Smith, Y. B., 35

Teiser, Sidney, 35
Thomas, R. P., 6, 26, 164, 168, 449, 453, 483
Timmons, G. D., 23

Wallbank, S. T., 35
Wallis, W. A., 349

Walsh, J. R., 84, 85, 86, 87, 90, 91, 92
Walters, Raymond, 12
Weiskotten, H. G., 264, 278
Wickser, P. J., 35
Wilbur, R. L., 9, 12
Wormser, I. M., 35

Yates, F., 339, 346
Yntema, D. B., 66

Zappfe, F. C., 14

Subject Index

Accountancy
  Examination, percentage passing, 41
  Salaried practice predominant, 296
Accountants
  Admitted to practice, 42
  As salaried employees, 120, 262, 295-7
  Distinction between certified and noncertified, 40
  Distribution by organization of practice, 39
  Function of, 39-40
  Number of, 119
    Adjusted for overrepresentation of firm members, 56
    Reporting income, 281
  Percentage of
    In firms, 260
    In salaried positions, 39
  Training requirements, 40-1, 42
  see also Tabular index
Accountants, firm members
  Coefficient of variation, 289
  Income of
    By size of community, 293
    Compared with individual practitioners, 282
    Temporal change in, 389-90
  Number reporting income, adjusted for bias, 281
  Percentage of, 281, 282
Accountants, income of
  Adjusted for overrepresentation of firm members, 56, 435-8
  Level, 99-100, 102-3
  Regional differences, 225
  Size of community differences, 225
  Variability, 111-5, 116-8, 139-40, 141
  see also Income, temporal change in; Tabular index
Accountants, individual practitioners
  Coefficient of variation, 289
  Income of
    By size of community, 282, 293
    Temporal change in, 389

Admissions, see Tabular index
Age at death
  Nonprofessional workers, 149
  Professional workers, 149
Analysis of variance ratio
  Affect of nonnormality on, 346-9
  Affect of unequal variance on, 341-6
  Test of linearity of regression, 338-9
Arithmetic mean
  Use in supply curve, 157
  see also Tabular index
Australia, distribution of income in, 78

Bar examination, percentage passing, 37-9
Biases in samples
  Distribution of firm incomes, 107, 289
  Inclusion of salaried employees, 52, 414-5
  Misinterpretation by respondents, 53, 445-6
  Nonrandomness by states
    Lawyers, 55, 419, 21
    Physicians, 53, 419-21
  Overrepresentation
    Firm members, 55-6, 430-8
    Prominent practitioners, 56, 429-30
    Specialists, 54, 429-30
  Possible sources of, 50, 411-2
  Refusal ratio, 439-45
  Selection of usable questionnaires, 446-8
  Trend in income, 51-2
  Underrepresentation
    Dentists, nonmembers, 54, 415-9
    Engineers with low incomes, 57
    Lawyers in large communities, 55, 425-9
    Physicians in small communities, 53, 421-5

California dentists, income of, 475-7
California lawyers, percentage firm members, 294
California physicians, income of, 472-5
   By type of practice, 246, 264-5
   By years in practice, 246
Certified public accountants
   Number, 119
   see Accountants
Citizenship required for professional practice
   Dentistry, 23
   Medicine, 18, 19
Clark's estimates
   Discounted value of earnings, 86
   Present value of earnings, 87
Coefficient of correlation, *see* Correlation coefficient
Coefficient of variation
   Corrected for bias in firm incomes, 289
   Defined, 66
   Regional differences in
      Compared with size of community differences, 215-9
      Relation to income, 322-5
   Size of community differences in
      Compared with regional differences, 215-9
      Compared with relative interquartile difference, 213-9
      Professions, 206-7, 212
      Public, 206, 212
   see also Tabular index
Committee on Costs of Medical Care
   Income of dentists, 467-72
   Income of physicians, 228, 264-5, 461-7
Competition, effect on income, 138-9, 256
Complete specialists
   Compared with general practitioners, 269
   Concentration of
      In large communities, 268
      In young age groups, 276-7
   In California, 475
   Income of
      Average, 264
      By size of community, 273

Compared with general practitioners, 274, 279
   Compared with partial specialists, 264, 274, 279
   Standardized with respect to years in practice and size of community, 277
   Percentage of, 263
      By size of community, 269-71
      By years in practice, 271, 276
      In California, 267
   Regional differences in income eliminated, 273-4
   Size of community differences in income eliminated, 273-6
   Variability of income, 267-8
   see also Physicians, by type of practice
Consulting engineers
   Functions, 43-4
   Number, 119
   see Engineers
Consumer, type of
   As determinant of proportion in salaried practice, 3-4, 295
   Effect on stability of professional income, 304
   In small communities, 292
   Served by
      Business professions, 261-2
      Curative professions, 260
Correction factor applied to dental incomes
   Alternative ratios, 153, 418
   Selection of, 415-9
Correlation analysis, *see* Tabular index
Correlation coefficient
   Compared with partial correlation coefficient, 308-9
   Consecutive and nonconsecutive years, 307-8
   Measure of stability of relative income status, 301-9
   Professions compared, 303
   Statistical significance, 303-4
   Unweighted and weighted, 318
Costs
   Dental training, 143-4
   Medical training, 143-5
   Professional training, 84-7, 91-2, 149

Demand
  Dentistry, 164-72
  Medicine, 161-3
  Professional services, 132-4, 155-73
Dental course, length of, 22, 23
Dental schools
  Admissions to, 22
  Number, 22
Dental students, number of, 24
Dental training
  Development in, 21
  Length of, effect on income, 125-6
  Requirements for licensure, 23
Dentistry
  Group practice of, 261
  Length of working life in, 143
Dentists
  By type of practice
    Distribution, 21, 146, 263
    Incomes compared, 264
  Length of working life, 146
  Members of A.D.A.
    Percentage by regions, 228
    Percentage of all dentists, 54, 415-7
  Number of, in relation to physicians, 29-30, 133, 234-5
  Percentage general practitioners, 146
  Restriction of samples to members of A.D.A.
    Correction of mean income, 54-5, 103, 153, 416-8
    Effect on frequency distribution, 418-9
    Effect on median, 106-7
    Effect on quartiles, 106-7
  Salaried, 262
    Percentage of, 120, 260
  see also Tabular index
Dentists and physicians compared, 29-30, 111-2, 118-37, 142-8, 154, 229-35
Dentists, income of
  Adjusted to include nonmembers of A.D.A., 54-5, 103, 416-8
  Affected by geographic location, 123
  Affected by years in practice, 123
  Average for last three years of practice, 146
  By year of graduation, 122
  By years in practice, 240
  In California, 475-7
  In Minnesota, 481-3
  In relation to physicians, 111-2, 118-37, 142-8, 154, 229-35
  Level of, 99-100, 102, 103
  Median, 111
  Members of A.D.A. compared with nonmembers, 54, 415-7
  Present value of, 143, 145
  Regional differences in, 232, 233-4
  Reliability of data tested, 467-72, 475-7, 481-3
  Variability, 111-5, 116-8, 139, 140
  see also Income, temporal change in; Tabular index
Distribution of income, see Tabular index
Distribution of practitioners, see Tabular index

Earnings, discounted value of, see Clark's estimates
Earnings, present value of, see Walsh's estimates
Engineering, salaried practice in, 296
Engineers
  As salaried employees, 262
  Number of, 57, 119
  Percentage in firms, 260
  Training received, 44-5
  see also Tabular index
Engineers, firm members
  Coefficient of variation, 289
  Income of, 283, 294
    Temporal change, 389-90
Engineers, income of
  Affected by fluctuations in construction, 368
  Level of, 102, 103
  Regional differences, 225
  Reliability of data tested, 486-8
  Size of community differences, 225
  Variability, 111-5, 116-8, 139-40, 141
  see also Income, temporal change in; Tabular index
Engineers, individual practitioners
  Coefficient of variation, 289
  Income of, 283, 294
    Temporal change in, 389-90
Equilibrium difference, 126, 131, 132-5
  Measured by supply and demand curves, 159-60
Equipment
  Cost of, 145
  Sharing of, 261

Family income
  Compared with individual income, 76-8
  see also National Resources Committee estimates
Final estimates, 103
  see also Tabular index
Firm members
  Concentration in large communities, 280
  Distribution
    By region, 290
    By size of community, 290
  Income of, 282, 290-1
  Percentage of, 281-2
    By years in practice, 294
    Decrease in, 282
  Regional differences, 290-1
  Relative income status, 280-1
  Size of community differences, 290-1
  Specialization among, 279-81
  Variability of income, 289
  see also Accountants, firm members; Engineers, firm members; Lawyers, firm members
First quartile, 66
  see also Tabular index
Foreign schools, requirements for medical graduates, 18
Foreign medical students, see Medical Students, foreign

Gainfully occupied, income of, 368
General practitioners
  Compared with complete specialists, 269
  Income of
    Average, 264
    By size of community, 273
    Compared with complete specialists, 274, 279
    Compared with partial specialists, 264, 274, 279
    Standardized, 277
  Percentage of, 263
    By size of community, 269-71
    By years in practice, 276
  Regional differences in income, 273-4
  Size of community differences in income, 273-6
  Variability of income, 267-8

see also Physicians, by type of practice
Group practice of medicine, 261

Health insurance, 261
Hospitalization, 261

Income, components of, 327, 328, 352, 353
Income, distribution of, see Distribution of income
Income, temporal change in
  By organization of practice, 387-90
  By region, 379-84
  By size of community, 373-9
  By type of practice, 384-6
  Contrasted with demand, 368
  Determinants of, 365
  Pattern of, 365-8
  Professions and all gainfully occupied compared, 368
  Professions compared, 368-9
Independent practice
  Compared with salaried practice, 3, 296
  Number in, 3
Individual practitioners
  Income in small communities, 290-1
  Regional differences, 290-1
  Size of community differences, 290-1
  Variability of income, 289
  see also Accountants, individual practitioners; Engineers, individual practitioners; Lawyers, individual practitioners
Interest rate in computing present values, 147, 151
Internship required, 10
  Foreign students, 18
Interquartile difference
  Defined, 66
  see also Tabular index

Law
  Course, length of, 33
  Limitations to admission to practice, 35-7
  Schools, number of, 32, 35
  Students, number of, 35
Lawyers
  As salaried employees, 262
  Distribution by organization of practice, 31

Lawyers, *Continued*
  Number of, 34
    Adjusted for biases, 55, 56
    Percentage in firms, 260
    Training requirements, 31
    see also Tabular index
Lawyers, firm members and individual practitioners compared
  Coefficient of variation, 289
  Income, 282-3
    By size of community, 293-4
    Temporal change in, 387-90
Lawyers, income of
  Adjusted for
    Nonrandomness, 55, 419-21
    Overrepresentation of firm members, 56, 430-35
    Underrepresentation of large communities, 55, 425-9
  Affected by
    Extent of education, 236
    Law school grades, 237
    Type of school attended, 236
  By years in practice, 243, 294-5
  In New York County, 484-6
  In Wisconsin, 483-4
  Level of, 99-100, 102-3
  Regional differences, 225
  Reliability of data tested, 483-6
  Variability of, 111-5, 116-8
  see also Income, temporal change in; Tabular index
Length of training, 4, 10-11, 22-3, 34, 40-1, 44, 83, 149
  Effect on choice of profession, 83, 125-7
Length of working life, 149-50
Level of income, relative position of professions, 99-100
Limitation of entry, medical schools, 11-5, 135-7
Logarithmic normal curve, 67
Lorenz curve, 72-3

Mean income
  Professions compared, 99
  see also Tabular index
Median
  Defined, 66
  Professions compared, 100
  see also Tabular index
Medical course, length of, 9

Medical schools
  Applications to, 14
  Limitation of entry into, 11-5, 135-7
  Number of, 9
  Requirements for admission to, 9
  Requirements for degree, 10
Medical license, examination for
  Percentage failing, 19-20
  Requirements for admission to, 17-8
Medical students
  Foreign, requirements imposed on, 18-20
  Number of, 9
  Number studying abroad, 17
  Premedical training, 10-11
Medical training
  Length of, 10-11
    Effect on income, 125-6
  Required for license, 10
Medicine, group practice of, 261
Michigan physicians, 479-80
Minnesota dentists, 481-3
Mobility in the professions, 175-8, 188-9, 196-7

National Resources Committee estimates
  Average income, 69
  Compared with
    D.O.C. samples, 76
    NBER estimates, 78-80
  Family and individual incomes compared, 76-8
  Groups covered, 68
  Income differences among communities, 81, 183-9
  Shortcomings in, 69-71, 75-6, 80, 81
  Variability of income, 71-2
  see also Nonrelief families
Net income from independent practice, defined, 50
New York County lawyers, 239, 241, 484-6
Nonpecuniary factors affecting choice of profession, 130-2
Nonrelief families
  Distribution by size of community, 183
  Income of, compared with professions, 68-80, 183-9
  see also Tabular index
Number in independent practice, 3, 4
  see also Tabular index

Organization of practice, *see* Lawyers, Accountants, and Engineers, firm members and individual practitioners; Tabular index

Pareto Law, 66-7
Partial correlation coefficient
 Compared with correlation coefficient, 308-9
 Professions compared, 308
Partial specialists
 Income of
  Average, 264
  By size of community, 273
  Compared with complete specialists, 264, 274, 279
  Compared with general practitioners, 264, 274, 279
  Standardized, 277
  Percentage of, 263, 276
  Regional and size of community differences in income eliminated, 273-6
  Variability of income, 267-8
  see also Physicians, by type of practice
Per capita, *see* Public; Tabular index
Permanent component
 Defined, 325
 Discussed and measured, 326-38
Physicians
 Age, by size of community, 256-8
 As salaried employees, 262
 Competition in small communities, 256
 Concentration in large communities, 256-8
 Length of working life, 146
 Number of
  Adjusted for nonrandomness, 53-4, 419-21
  In relation to dentists, 29-30, 133, 234-5
  In relation to total population, 11
 Percentage in salaried practice, 120, 260
 Training requirements, *see* Medical training
 Young, 256-9
 see also Tabular index
Physicians and dentists compared, 29-30, 111-2, 118-37, 142-8, 154, 229-35

Physicians, by type of practice
 By years in practice, 276-8
 In California, 472-5
 Income of, 264
  Affected by size of community, 274
  By size of community, 247-55
  By years in practice, 245, 246-55
  Committee on Costs of Medical Care, 264-5
  In California, 246, 264-5
  Standardized, 277
  Temporal change, 384-6
 Percentage distribution, 8, 263, 475
 see also Complete specialists; General practitioners; Partial specialists; Tabular index
Physicians, by years in practice
 By type of practice, 276-8
 Complete specialists, by size of community, 271
 Distribution, 123, 243
 Income, 240, 277
 see also Tabular index
Physicians, income of
 Adjusted for nonrandomness of samples, 53-4, 419-21
 Affected by
  Geographic location, 123
  Training, 278-9
  Years in practice, 123
 By size of community, 273
 By type of practice, 262-79
 By years in practice, 237-60
 In California, 246, 264-5, 472-5
 In Michigan, 479-80
 In relation to dentists, 111-2, 118-37, 142-8, 154, 229-35
 In Wisconsin, 478-9
 In Utah, 480-1
 Level of, 99-100, 102-3
 'Life cycle,' 246
 Median, 111
 Regional differences, 223-4, 233
  Committee on Costs of Medical Care, 228
 Relation between gross and net, 267
 Reliability of date tested, 461-7, 472-5, 477-81
 Size of community differences, 187-8, 223-4, 259-60
 Variability of, 111-5, 116-8, 139, 140
 see also Income, Temporal change in; Tabular index

Population shift, effect on medical income, 259
Professional career, development of, 237-40
Professional income
Compared with nonprofessional, 67-8, 71-5, 81, 82, 83-4, 87-8, 93-4, 180-9, 197-9
Compensation for added expense, 83
Nonpecuniary factors affecting, 88
Present value, 149
Regional differences, 188-99, 232
Size of community differences, 180-9
see also income entries for various professions
Professional training
Cost of, 84-7, 91-2, 149
Investment in, 89-90
Length of, 83
Professional workers, number of, 82
Professions
Choice of, 92-3, 95-7
Definition of, 3
Entry into, limited, 88-9, 97-9
Number in, 46
Training requirements, 4
Public, income of
Compared with professions, 183-99
Regional differences, 189-99
Size of community differences, 183-9
see also National Resources Committee estimates

Quartiles, see First quartile; Third quartile; Tabular index
Quasi-permanent factor
Defined, 352, 353
Interpreted, 355-64

Ratio of quartiles, see Tabular index
Regional differences in income
Dentists, 232
Physicians, 232
Physicians and dentists compared, 234
Ranks used in measuring, 222
see also Tabular index
Regions
Income by, see Tabular index
Size of community composition, 229
States included, 179
Regression analysis, 309-33
see also Analysis of variance

Relative interquartile difference
Compared with coefficient of variation, 213-9
Regional differences, 215, 218
Size of community differences, 212-3, 213-9
see also Tabular index
Reliability of data tested, 448-88
Samples compared with one another, 455-61
Samples compared with other studies, 461-88
Dentists, 467-72, 475-7, 481-3
Engineers, 486-8
Lawyers, 483-6
Physicians, 461-7, 472-5, 477-81
Samples compared with universe, 448-55

Salaried practice
As step toward independent practice, 296
Compared with independent practice, 3, 296
Predominant in accountancy and engineering, 296
Variability of income, 297-8
Samples
Biases in, see Biases in samples
Collection of, 47, 50, 411-2; see also Tabular index
Coverage of, 47
Information obtained from, 49-50
Reliability of, 57-62
Services rendered
Affecting type of specialization, 260-2
By physicians and dentists, 261
Volume of, 368
Size of community classes, 179
Regional composition, 229
Income by, see Tabular index
Size of community differences in income
Physicians, 273
Ranks used in measuring, 222
see also Tabular index
Sliding scale, 138
Specialists, certification of, 279
Specialists, complete, see Complete specialists
Specialists, partial, see Partial specialists

Specialization, development of, 260, 263-4
Stability of relative income status, see Correlation coefficient
Standard deviation, 66, 319-22; see also Tabular index
Standard error of difference between medical and dental incomes, 152
Standardized averages, 229-32
　Ineffective as precise measures, 233
　Physicians by type of practice, 273-6, 277
　see also Tabular index
Supply
　Dentistry, 164-72
　Medicine, 161-3
　Professional services, 155-73

Third quartile, 66
　see also Tabular index
Training
　Cost of, 84-7, 91-2, 143-5, 149
　Effect on physicians' incomes, 278-9
　Requirements, 4, 10
Transitory component
　Defined, 325
　Discussed and measured, 326-38
　Fallacy in application, 331-2
　In linear regressions, 332-3
　In nonlinear regressions, 334-5
　Interpretation of, 326-7
　Measurement of, 327-31
　Professions compared, 332-8
Type of practice, see Physicians by type of practice; Dentists by type of practice

Utah physicians, 480-1

Variability, absolute, 66
Variability of income
　Accountants and engineers compared, 139-40, 141
　Annual, 105-15
　Effect on choice of profession, 127-30
　For long periods, 115-8
　Medicine and dentistry compared, 139, 140
　Professions
　　Compared with public, 80, 203
　　Regional differences, 203
　　Relative position, 111
　　Size of community differences, 203
　Public, 203
　Regression analysis, 319-25
　Relation to income level, 372
　Temporal change in, 369-71, 372
　see also Coefficient of variation; Interquartile difference; Ratio of quartiles; Relative interquartile difference; Standard deviation

Walsh's estimates
　Cost of training, 84-7
　Present value of earnings, 84-7
　Procedure compared with NBER, 86-7
　Shortcomings in, 86-7
Weights used for standardized averages, 229-32
Wisconsin lawyers, 239, 241, 483-4
Wisconsin physicians, 478-9

Years in practice, effect on income level, 309

Some National Bureau Publications

PROSPECTIVE AND RECENT BOOKS

Personal Income during Business Cycles   (in press)
Daniel Creamer

Mortgage Lending Experience in Agriculture   (in press)
Lawrence A. Jones and David Durand

Long-Range Economic Projection: Studies in Income and Wealth, Volume Sixteen   (in press)
Conference on Research in Income and Wealth

Short-Term Economic Forecasting: Studies in Income and Wealth, Volume Seventeen   (in press)
Conference on Research in Income and Wealth

Minimum Price Fixing in the Bituminous Coal Industry   (in press)
Waldo Fisher and Charles M. James

Business Concentration and Price Policy   (in press)
Universities-National Bureau Committee for Economic Research

The Frontiers of Economic Knowledge (1954)   410 pp., $5.00
Arthur F. Burns

Regularization of Business Investment (1954)   512 pp., 8.00
Universities-National Bureau Commitee for Economic Research

Shares of Upper Income Groups in Income and Savings (1953)   768 pp., 9.00
Simon Kuznets

The Volume of Corporate Bond Financing since 1900 (1953)   464 pp., 7.50
W. Braddock Hickman

Wesley Clair Mitchell: The Economic Scientist (1952)   398 pp., 4.00
Arthur F. Burns (ed.)

A Study of Moneyflows in the United States (1952)   620 pp., 7.50
Morris A. Copeland

The Trend of Government Activity in the United States since 1900 (1952)   288 pp., 4.00
Solomon Fabricant

Federal Grants and the Business Cycle (1952)   136 pp., 2.00
James A. Maxwell

Commercial Bank Activities in Urban Mortgage Financing (1952)   152 pp., 2.50
Carl F. Behrens

Studies in Income and Wealth, Volume Fifteen (1952)   240 pp., 3.50
Conference on Research in Income and Wealth
Eight papers on size distribution of income

Conference on Research in Business Finance (1952)   360 pp., 5.00
Universities-National Bureau Commitee for Economic Research

ALL OCCASIONAL PAPERS IN PRINT AND IN PRESS

3 *Finished Commodities since 1879: Output and Its Composition* (1941)   .25
William H. Shaw

5 *Railway Freight Traffic in Prosperity and Depression* (1942) **$ .25**
Thor Hultgren

10 *The Effect of War on Business Financing: Manufacturing and Trade,
World War I* (1943) .50
Charles H. Schmidt and Ralph A. Young

11 *The Effect of War on Currency and Deposits* (1945) .35
Charles R. Whittlesey

12 *Prices in a War Economy: Some Aspects of the Present Price Structure
of the United States* (1943) .50
Frederick C. Mills

13 *Railroad Travel and the State of Business* (1943) .35
Thor Hultgren

14 *The Labor Force in Wartime America* (1944) .50
Clarence D. Long

15 *Railway Traffic Expansion and Use of Resources in World War II* (1944) .35
Thor Hultgren

17 *National Product, War and Prewar* (1944) .50
Simon Kuznets

18 *Production of Industrial Materials in World Wars I and II* (1944) .50
Geoffrey H. Moore

19 *Canada's Financial System in War* (1944) .50
Benjamin H. Higgins

20 *Nazi War Financing and Banking* (1944) .50
Otto Nathan

22 *Bank Liquidity and the War* (1945) .50
Charles R. Whittlesey

23 *Labor Savings in American Industry, 1899-1939* (1945) .50
Solomon Fabricant

24 *Domestic Servants in the United States, 1900-1940* (1946) .50
George J. Stigler

25 *Recent Developments in Dominion-Provincial Fiscal Relations
in Canada* (1948) .50
J. A. Maxwell

27 *The Structure of Postwar Prices* (1948) .75
Frederick C. Mills

28 *Lombard Street in War and Reconstruction* (1949) 1.00
Benjamin H. Higgins

29 *The Rising Trend of Government Employment* (1949) .50
Solomon Fabricant

30 *Costs and Returns on Farm Mortgage Lending by Life Insurance
Companies, 1945-1947* (1949) 1.00
R. J. Saulnier

31 *Statistical Indicators of Cyclical Revivals and Recessions* (1950) 1.50
Geoffrey H. Moore

32 *Cyclical Diversities in the Fortunes of Industrial Corporations* (1950) .50
Thor Hultgren

33 *Employment and Compensation in Education* (1950) 1.00
George J. Stigler

34 *Behavior of Wage Rates during Business Cycles* (1950) $1.00
   Daniel Creamer

35 *Shares of Upper Income Groups in Income and Savings* (1950) 1.00
   Simon Kuznets

36 *The Labor Force in War and Transition: Four Countries* (1952) 1.00
   Clarence D. Long

37 *Trends and Cycles in Corporate Bond Financing* (1952) .75
   W. Braddock Hickman

38 *Productivity and Economic Progress* (1952) .75
   Frederick C. Mills

39 *The Role of Federal Credit Aids in Private Residential
   Construction* (1953) 1.00
   Leo Grebler

40 *Transport and the State of Trade in Britain* (1953) 1.50
   Thor Hultgren

41 *Capital and Output Trends in Manufacturing Industries,
   1880-1948* (1954) 1.50
   Daniel Creamer

42 *The Share of Financial Intermediaries in National Wealth and
   National Assets, 1900-1949* (1954) 1.50
   Raymond W. Goldsmith

43 *Trends and Cycles in Capital Formation by United States
   Railroads, 1870-1950* (in press)
   Melville J. Ulmer

44 *The Growth of Physical Capital in Agriculture, 1870-1950* (in press)
   Alvin S. Tostlebe

45 *Capital and Output Trends in Mining Industries, 1870-1948* (in press)
   Israel Borenstein

ALL TECHNICAL PAPERS IN PRINT

3 *Basic Yields of Corporate Bonds, 1900-1942* (1942) .50
   David Durand

4 *Currency Held by the Public, the Banks, and the Treasury, Monthly,
   December 1917-December 1944* (1947) .75
   Anna Jacobson Schwartz and Elma Oliver

5 *Concerning a New Federal Financial Statement* (1947) 1.00
   Morris A. Copeland

7 *Factors Affecting the Demand for Consumer Instalment Sales Credit*
   (1952) 1.50
   Avram Kisselgoff

8 *A Study of Aggregate Consumption Functions* (1953) 1.50
   Robert Ferber

9 *The Volume of Residential Construction, 1889-1950* (1954) 1.50
   David M. Blank

10 *Factors Influencing Consumption: An Experimental Analysis of
   Shoe Buying* (in press)
   Ruth P. Mack

How to Obtain
National Bureau Publications

The National Bureau of Economic Research is a nonprofit membership corporation organized to make impartial studies in economic science.

Its books are published and distributed (since April 1, 1953) by Princeton University Press; its *Occasional Papers* and *Technical Papers* are published and distributed by the National Bureau itself.

Publications may be obtained either on contributing subscriptions or by purchase.

A contributor of $25 or more a year is entitled to receive a complimentary copy of each current publication — *books, Occasional Papers, Technical Papers,* and the *Annual Report* — in advance of release to the public and, in addition, is entitled to a one-third discount on all National Bureau publications purchased.

An associate contributor of $10 a year receives a complimentary copy of each *Occasional Paper, Technical Paper,* and the *Annual Report,* and is entitled to a one-third discount on all publications purchased. Only the following are eligible to become associates; teachers, students, and libraries in recognized educational institutions; members of scientific societies or of private nonprofit research agencies.

A contributor of $4 receives the next five *Occasional Papers* (or, if desired, any *Technical Paper* issued during this period may be substituted) and the *Annual Report.*

Contributions to the National Bureau are deductible in calculating federal income taxes.

NON-CONTRIBUTORS should send orders for *books* to:

Princeton University Press
Princeton, New Jersey

NON-CONTRIBUTORS should send orders for *Papers* and requests for the *Annual Report* directly to:

CONTRIBUTORS should send all orders for *books* and *Papers,* and requests for the *Annual Report* directly to:

NATIONAL BUREAU OF ECONOMIC RESEARCH, INC.
261 Madison Avenue　　　　　　　　　　　New York 16, N. Y.